Germany and the Germans

GERMANY AND THE GERMANS

An Anatomy of Society Today

by

John Ardagh

Consultant and Research Assistant:
Katharina Schmitz

1817

HARPER & ROW, PUBLISHERS, New York
Cambridge, Philadelphia, San Francisco, Washington
London, Mexico City, São Paulo, Singapore, Sydney

FIRST U.S. EDITION

Library of Congress Cataloging-in-Publication Data

Ardagh, John, 1928–
  Germany and the Germans.

  Includes index.
  1. Germany (West)—Social conditions. 2. Germany (East)—Social conditions. 3. Germany—Civilization—20th century. I. Title.
HN445.5.A73   1987   943.087   87-45264
ISBN 0-06-015839-5

87 88 89 90 91 HC 10 9 8 7 6 5 4 3 2 1

To my son Nicholas

CONTENTS

1 **Introduction** 1
Preface: why a francophile turns to Germany 1
A post-war historical survey: ruins to riches 8

2 **The regional patchwork, an ancient legacy** 23
A diversity of dominant cities: life today in Munich,
Stuttgart, Frankfurt, Bonn, Cologne, Düsseldorf,
Hamburg and Bremen 30
Buoyant Berlin, the survivor that came in from the cold 49
The *Bund* and the *Länder*: how and why federalism works 65
Benevolent technocrats in the *Rathaus* 70
North v. South: Bavarian boom and rustbelt Ruhr 74

3 **The 'economic miracle' and its after-strains** 83
Industrial splendour – but can it meet the high-tech
challenge? 86
A paradise of labour harmony – but what of the waning
work-ethic? 101
Death of the beloved forests: is car exhaust to blame? 116
The ignored rural world and its grumbling peasantry 127

4 **Daily life: a modernised society re-examines its
traditions** 145
The social snobberies of a semi-classless nation 146
Women, sex and children: a few crusades yet to be won 161
A spick and span suburbia where the shops shut early 174

Contents

From *Wurst* and dumplings to fancy French and food fads 180
Assidous tourists and crazy Cologne carnivalers 187
The spa romance – by courtesy of a lavish health insurance
   system 197
Schools: educating the mind, but not so much the
   character 204
The never-ending university malaise 212
Catholics and Protestants: a new amity, but new internal
   conflicts 226

5 **Turks and other 'guests': a painful path towards
   acceptance** 237

6 **Arts and intellectuals: lively activity, but low
   creativity** 257
The novel: waiting for successors to Böll and Grass 258
The State's role as Maecenas: taking culture out of the
   'temples' 265
Theatre: morally serious, wilfully provocative 272
Fassbinder, Herzog and Reitz's *Heimat*: triumphs for the
   Cinderella of German arts 287
Tame television and barbarous *Bild* 308

7 **Daily life under German-style communism** 319
Behind the drab façades, an economic mini-miracle 320
Jobs and security for all: the rewards and restraints of
   collectivism 328
Privacy and a quiet life in the 'niche society' 338
Dilemmas for the Church, wooed but wary 342
The watchful grip of the one-Party State 348
Brecht to Biermann: dealing with the intellectual
   dissidents 358
Travel to the West: harshest of the curbs on freedom 366
Inter-German relations: the reality of détente, the mirage
   of reunification 378

8 **Conclusion: how stable a democracy?** 389
Digesting the legacies of Nazism 389
Political strengths and community weaknesses 403

Contents

The Greens and their values: fundamental change, or just another youth protest?   421

Germany and the world: how crucial is national identity?   447

ACKNOWLEDGEMENTS   461

BIBLIOGRAPHY   465

INDEX   469

Germany and the Germans

1

INTRODUCTION

Preface: why a francophile turns to Germany

Like my books on France, this one on Germany is primarily a study of society and of regional, economic and cultural affairs: it is not about party politics or foreign policy. Nor is it a history of post-war Germany so much as a portrait of this complicated nation as it is today in the later 1980s.

This certainly does not mean that I have ignored the major 'German' themes that still today make Germany something of a special case in Europe. The legacy of Nazism and of wartime defeat; the two Germanies and their co-existence; the wary search for a new national identity, in a land where nationalism's 80-year record before 1945 had been so catastrophic; the federal structure and the lack of a proper capital city; the waning of authoritarianism and the forging of a genuine democracy; the clash of generations, values and life-styles, possibly sharper in Germany than elsewhere; the advantages and drawbacks of the Germans' famous thoroughness and perfectionism; the old streak of insecurity and anxiety, assuaged by economic success yet also revived by a new anxious world climate – these are *Leitmotive* running through the book or examined more closely in its final chapters. But I have also tried to look at Germany not just as some peculiar problem child but as a normal modern society, with many of the same pleasures and problems as the rest of us. Forty-plus years after the war's end, that ought now to be possible.

Primarily this is a book about the Federal Republic, and in it I use the words 'Germany' and 'Germans' to mean 'West Germany' and 'West Germans'. It does however include one long chapter on life in the Democratic Republic (which I visited twice) and on its relations with West Germany. But the book is *not* a comparative study of the two Germanies.

Why should a French specialist of thirty years' standing have now turned to Germany? I am often asked the question, and it is easy to answer. It seems entirely natural that a francophile Englishman with 'European' convictions should want to extend his range to the third main pillar of the European Community and thus to learn more about this Europe that we belong to and believe in. I have always liked and admired the Germans, too, and been fascinated by Germany, and for many years I had wanted to explore it more fully one day. The field research for my book about provincial Europe, *A Tale of Five Cities* (1979), had given me a foretaste: this included an 85-page chapter on Stuttgart, a city that I grew fond of. Today, if I have to choose between the two countries, of course I still prefer France and the French to a Germany where I frequently miss the Gallic lightness and sharpness. But for an Englishman to have a bigamous liaison with both seems to me quite proper.

I researched and wrote the book between April 1984 and November 1986. Then there were Federal elections in January 1987, but these made no difference at all to all that I had written. The Christian Democrats were returned to office with much the same majority as before and they continued to govern in coalition with their junior partners, the Free Democrats, with Helmut Kohl remaining as Chancellor. The only difference was that the Christian Democrats did slightly less well than before, and the Free Democrats slightly better. On the Left, the Socialist Party (SPD) under Johannes Rau lost some ground and scored one of their worst performances since the war, whereas the Greens did very well, increasing their overall share of the vote from 5.6 to 8.4 per cent. However, politics is not the main concern of this book. Moreover, there still exists a broad degree of consensus between the main German parties (Greens excepted), save on some nuclear and defence issues. It is true that after Chernobyl the SPD voted to phase out nuclear power stations within 10 years, if returned to power, and also to seek the removal of US missiles from German soil. But it seemed uncertain that these plans would be applied in practice.

I must intrude a brief personal note that is highly relevant to the book. I began the research as an outsider, with hundreds of excellent contacts and some German friends, but no inside connection. Then in Stuttgart in November 1984 I met Katharina (Katinka) Schmitz who was working for the Baden-Württemberg State Tourist Board. She was born in Berlin in 1951, was brought up in Munich and studied at Göttingen and Tübingen universities and had been living for eight years in Stuttgart. We became engaged, and for nearly all the time since I met her she has worked with me full-time on the book, as co-researcher, consultant, typist, guide to 'the awful German language' (Mark Twain's phrase) and – above all – interpreter of the subtleties and contradictions of her fellow-citizens and their make-up. She has provided me with a perspective that I could never have achieved on my own. As a result, through Katinka and her friends and family, I have become as emotionally involved in Germany as in France, despite the far briefer acquaintance.

I lived in Germany for ten months in 1984–5, part of the time in Stuttgart with Katinka but most of it on tour with her by car to the other main West German cities and to the GDR. For this field research we spent several weeks each in Munich, Frankfurt, Bonn, Hamburg and Berlin, with shorter visits to Cologne, Düsseldorf, the Ruhr, Bremen and many smaller towns and rural areas. In France too I have always tried to concentrate on the provinces rather than Paris: but in Germany this is ten times more imperative, for Bonn is a tedious little place and nearly all the interest is in big real cities. So I have got to know those fearsome *Autobahnen* all too intimately, and in my sleep I could retrace every curve of those giddy gradients in the Schwäbische Jura or the hills south of Kassel, with the BMW 700s flashing arrogantly by. Apart from this hazard, I find Germany a very pleasant and easy country to travel and work in – cosy little hotels, good simple food always well served, attractive scenery (at least in the south), relative absence of urban traffic jams, efficient public services, telephone kiosks that have seldom been vandalised. Everywhere I felt very much at home; even the average industrial city, though outwardly no beauty with its anonymous concrete blocks and officious ringways, is very civilised in its way and far less drab than in Britain. Some foreigners get irritated by German tidiness and efficiency: for the visiting reporter they do carry advantages.

This today is a very open society, and using the normal techniques of the journalist I found it easy to see the people I wanted and obtain the information I needed. If I have nonetheless found Germany a harder country to write about vividly than France, I do not think this is really because my background knowledge goes less deep, nor because the Germans are a more complex and baffling people. Rather it is that Germany is a less lively place, at least on the surface, without the same Latin sense of show. The Germans are more methodical but less innovative than the French: there is endless talk, and even some violence, but constructive reforms and changes take place in so muted and legalistic a way that it is much harder to spotlight them than in France with its penchant for pioneering and confrontation. Above all, the number of really colourful or outspoken personalities in public life is amazingly small – and I am thinking not just of politicians but of the leaders of industry, the trade unions, the farming lobbies, local government or education, or indeed autonomous figures who have risen from the rank-and-file to champion some cause. The French love an eccentric show-off who has wit and originality, and they will rally to him; the Germans are more wary. In politics, a

Franz-Josef Strauss is rare; and in other fields the flamboyant stars tend to be not in positions of formal responsibility but lone outsiders, often in the arts (Werner Herzog and the late Josef Beuys have been prime examples). Those who become the elected heads of organisations or even of private pressure-groups may well possess drive, ability and real qualities of leadership: but they also tend to conform to a standard that is sedate, reassuring, and not too startling. One explanation could be the prudent desire to avoid any new Nazi-style personality cult (before Hitler's day, showy individualism was much more readily accepted). After the excesses of the past, the understandable search for consensus has militated against those who do not easily suit it; and, in this still rather conventional and careerist society, those who abide by the norms are the most trusted. Flamboyance is suspect, and so even is elitism. Today the shaggy and outspoken Greens may be challenging this pattern – but they too have their own conformities, among themselves.

If the Germans are seldom colourful, they are nearly always helpful, hospitable, efficient in carrying out what they have promised, and ready to talk. That they lack a sense of humour is one foreign myth that needs exploding – if indeed it still exists. Among friends they are lively, gossipy and amusing, especially Berliners and Rhinelanders. But to be frivolous about serious or important subjects, in the British or French manner, still makes them strangely uneasy and usually they are incapable of it. This is a trait that goes back deep into their past and seems to be related to an old idealism and love of absolutes, but there may be a more topical explanation for it too: because their democratic values and institutions are still so recent, and because in a way they still feel insecure about them, so they are not able to be flippant about things that a Briton can take for granted. Around a dinner-table, there can be plenty of animated jokey conversation on personal matters and then, if someone mentions a 'serious' topic, the tone changes abruptly and lengthy debate ensues. And, once the Germans get their teeth into a subject of this kind, they like to worry at it for hours.

This seriousness can sometimes be tiresome, but it has its appealing side. Younger Germans in particular – apart from a stubbornly bigoted minority – I have found to be more than averagely thoughtful, concerned, gentle, modest, and internationally-minded. The Germans may still be a shade too earnest, but they are less pompous than they used to be. And their old tendency towards arrogance and lofty superiority, once associated with the Prussian upper classes, took such punishment from wartime defeat and Nazi shame that today it is very little present, at least in their dealings with foreigners, on whom they are still generally keen to make a favourable impression. I encountered very little arrogance, noticeably less than in Paris – the only exceptions being possibly the haughty executives of some of the big industrial firms, who are so successful and confident that presumably they can afford not to worry what foreigners think.

There may still be other aggressive and domineering instincts lurking somewhere beneath the surface of this polite and placid new Germany – or that is certainly the impression one gains from observing the German behind his steering-wheel. I repeat that my least happy image of modern Germany is the Wagnerian spectacle of those imperious *Autobahnen* that sweep remorselessly through the rolling fields and forests, their lanes packed with neat-suited executives in their powerful Mercedes, Audis and BMWs. There is no speed limit, so if you dare to stay in the fast lane at a mere 140 kph, they nose up behind you, lights flashing angrily, and then race ahead at maybe 250 kph as you meekly move aside. It is the most unnerving driving that I know in Europe: I'd rather be on a precipitous potholed track on a Greek mountain, any day. 'German male drivers are the most aggressive in Europe,' a leading woman psychologist, Carmen Lakashus, suggested to me in Frankfurt, 'and this feeling of power behind a wheel, this desire to dominate in a fast car, is stronger than elsewhere. It's not new. It goes far back into history and has been developed over many generations, this inherited internalised frustration of the German. Jung would have called it a basic national characteristic.'

For centuries the Germans have been regarded as an unstable and unpredictable people, even by some of their own greatest thinkers. 'The Germans,' said Goethe, 'make everything difficult, both for themselves and for everyone else,' while Nietzsche wrote, in *Beyond Good and Evil* (1886), 'The German soul has corridors and interconnecting corridors in it, there are caves, hiding-places, dungeons in it; its disorder possesses much of the fascinating and mysterious; the German is acquainted with the hidden paths to chaos . . .' Foreigners were equally perplexed, especially the neighbouring French who had reason to be suspicious: de Gaulle, who fought the Germans in the First World War, has an extraordinary passage about them in his *Vers l'Armée de Métier* (1934): 'A bundle of strong and troubled instincts, born artists without taste, technicians who are still feudal, fathers of families who are warriors, oppressors who want to be loved, separatists who are strictly obedient, knights bearing garlands who vomit beer . . . a sublime green ocean where the net hoists a tangle of monsters and treasures.'

And today, in the new democratic Germany, so reasonable and well ordered, what does the net hoist up? The contrast between the Germans' passion for orderliness and their tendency towards romanticism, irrationality and extremism has long puzzled observers of this nation, and the two elements would seem to be inter-related: the Germans, being aware of these 'troubled instincts', feel a special need to impose order and discipline on their society, but this in turn has built up frustrations leading to just the kind of outbursts that it is designed to prevent. And the Germans seem to be one thing one day, another the next – as the late Luigi Barzini suggested in his book *The Impossible Europeans* (Weidenfeld and Nicolson, 1983), where in a brilliant chapter headed 'The Mutable Germans' he argued that their society has various diverse facets which would come to the fore one by one under differing circumstances. He noted that before 1860 the patchwork of German states seemed to be a peaceful Arcadia, full of picturesque old towns and earnest, moral, tenderly sentimental people. Then the new united Germany under Bismarck emerged as militaristic, aggressive, even cruel, and this led to the 1914–18 war. The ensuing Weimar period, said Barzini, was a bizarre interlude filled with confusion, civil strife, moral decay and freakish exhibitionism, but then all returned to tidy orthodoxy after the Nazis' arrival. Nazism later produced the most barbarous of excesses behind its façade of *Ordnung*: but after the catharsis of defeat in 1945 the Germans swung to the other extreme, turning their heels on heel-clicking and embracing the new ideal of democracy. Soon they settled into a very sane, peaceful, bourgeois mould which Barzini found 'Swiss-like' and felt to be no new invention but something that had always been hibernating in the German soul. However, the sceptical Milanese wondered whether the youth malaise and anxieties of the 1970s and '80s – leading to fringe terrorism and to the wilder fantasies of certain Greens and Leftists – might not be heralding yet another mutation. Is the German, he asked, still 'acquainted with the hidden paths to chaos'?

Certainly the Germans would seem to have changed radically since their Nazi aberration of 1933–45. But how deep does the change go, and are there still some danger signs? In very many ways the picture since the war has been extremely positive. The Germans have developed a new and open society that is far less class-divided than it used to be, or than Britain and France still remain; here labour relations have blossomed in remarkable harmony, and democratic reasonableness has put down firm roots, helped by the stability afforded by economic success. If it has proved to be rather a conformist society, this in a sense has been an unconscious result of the attempt to tame the wild streak that led to Nazism by putting the premium on decent dull codes of conduct, practical rather than idealistic. It has also proved to be a very legalistic society, festooned with a million petty rules and regulations and obsessed by the need to abide by them. This is by no means a new German trait, but the law-making has intensified since the war, and this too may in a sense have been a price paid for the new stability: the post-war Germans seem to have felt instinctively that the necessary way to safeguard a fledging democracy is to hedge it about with laws that direct the citizens on how to behave in it, and thus prevent a return to past excesses.

It is true however that the trait of automatic obedience has begun to weaken in recent years, and this is one of a number of significant new changes now emerging. Under the impact of the ideas of 1968, society has started to become a little more socially informal, less deferential to authority, and perhaps more tolerant. A new generation has arrived with new values, and although some of the wilder ideas of the Greens may be altogether too fanciful, even dangerous, there is undeniably a sympathetic side to many of the new trends – not only the concern for nature and quality of life, but the renewed interest in tradition. The links with the better side of the German heritage were smashed by the Nazi experience which after the war led to a blanket rejection of the entire past, in the bid for a clean new start. This was understandable, but in the longer term it could be harmful. Today, enough time has gone by for there to be a cautious return to tradition. It can be seen in the new vogues for restoring ancient houses, rather than tearing down everything old, as happened in the 1950s. Young people, as in other Western countries, have been turning towards private values and feelings, alike to spiritual and to hedonistic satis-factions. They want to get more fun out of life, and they reject the work-for-work's sake ethic of their elders. This is in some ways attrac-tive, but it may create problems. The Germans, especially those over 40, are still very attached to their high standard of living so effortfully built up since the war. And this could be threatened if they now work less hard – in an age of rising world competition and high unem-ployment. Like so many of us, the Germans want it both ways – leisure *and* affluence – and the clash of priorities could lead to social tensions. Already there are signs of it.

There are some other trends that have begun to worry the worria-ble Germans. The birth-rate is now the world's lowest, which may be due in part to mere selfishness but also to a general lack of faith in the future. There seems also to have been recently a decline of confidence in the country's political leaders and even in its institutions, notably among younger people: this may well have been aggravated by the corruption scandals of the mid-1980s and it has led some older commentators to ask whether democracy is as firmly anchored in hearts and minds as had been supposed. Patriotic feeling and the sense of national identity are still noticeably weaker than among the young of other Western countries: this is hardly surprising, in view of Germany's past, and it might even be considered positive – except that it does not seem to be compensated by a strong faith in any other level of community. As an antidote to nationalism, post-war German generations turned readily to an idealistic belief in Europe: this still endures, but it has been given something of a dusty answer by the bureaucracy of Brussels and the wrangling of the politicians. And so, in an age of nuclear anxiety where Germany occupies an exposed front-line position, many people have been turning to neutralism, coupled quite often with a virulent anti-Americanism.

These are some of the question-marks over the West Germany of the later 1980s. But they should not obscure the fact that the overall post-war record, for a nation that lay so morally and physically shattered in 1945, has been astonishingly successful not only in economic but in democratic and human terms. A brief post-war history will now help to sketch in this background.

A post-war historical survey: ruins to riches

In the spring and early summer of 1945, after the final surrender, the cities of Germany lay in ruins. They were pervaded by a strange dazed silence and full of the stench of death, for thousands of bodies lay beneath the piles of rubble that took months to shift. More than three million homes had been destroyed. Motor ambulances were so few that the sick and the dead had often to be carried by cart and stretcher. Many districts were without drinkable water. And the Allied occupation forces authorised only the meagrest of rations – not so much out of vindictiveness as because Germany's transport and distribution systems were crippled, and there was a world food shortage too. While the British and American troops had a daily ration of some 4,000 calories, for German civilians it was only 700 and often less – well below the minimum needed for good health. Main meals tended to consist of just potatoes and cabbage or a little bread, with two tiny slices of meat once a week. Many workers were thus too weak and under-nourished to be able to do their jobs properly; thousands of people died each week from malnutrition and some others committed suicide. The Germans were literally stunned by the scale of the defeat and desolation. Some of them raged in silent fury at the Allied bombings: but they also awoke as from a trance to face the enormity of their national guilt in permitting Nazism to happen.

This was the famous *Stunde Null*, or Zero Hour, when Germany was at its bleakest point since the end of the Thirty Years' War. And it left the Germans with no other choice but slowly and painfully to make an entirely new start. If their history in the 40 years since then has been mainly such a success story, alike politically and economically, most experts are agreed that one of the principal reasons is precisely this: the sheer magnitude both of the Nazi crime and of the military defeat necessitated a radical break with the past and a total rethink of German values and society, in a way that had never happened after 1918. And, after their initial period of paralysed exhaustion and despair, the Germans found the will and the energy to respond to this challenge.

Long before the war ended, the Allies had begun to address them-selves to the task of deciding what to do with a defeated Germany. Stalin, Churchill and Roosevelt all toyed at first with the idea of breaking up the former Reich into four or five separate self-governing states, so that Germany could never again become a major power in Europe: Roosevelt even proposed this at the Teheran Conference of November 1943. But the plan was soon dropped in favour of a par-tition between the Allies, for a period of military occupation during which the Germans would be 're-democratized'. The borders of these military zones were then decided on at a conference in London 1944. The Americans allowed the British to take the industrialised north-west, including the Ruhr, while allocating themselves the more rural southern regions, including Bavaria, Württemberg and Hessen, and the port of Bremen in the north; the French were later given two strips close to their own borders, comprising the Saarland, Baden and parts of the Rhineland and Palatinate. The Russians took the east-central part of Germany for their zone, which is now the GDR. As for the areas further east, at the Potsdam Conference of August 1945 the Western Allies agreed 'in principle' that the northern part of East Prussia including Königsberg should come under Soviet administra-tion and later be annexed by Russia (as has since happened). They also accepted that 'pending a peace settlement' Poland should administer southern East Prussia as well as a huge slice of territory comprising Silesia and most of Pomerania, as far west as the Oder and Neisse rivers: Poland soon afterwards annexed these areas *de facto* and expelled their former German populations (see pp. 13–14). As a result, the area today made up of the two German states covers only 75 per cent of the Germany of 1937. As for Berlin, the Lon-don Conference of 1944 decided that the former capital should form an island inside the Russian zone, also to be divided into four zones administered by the four Allied Powers.

The Allies had next to decide what to do with the German people, alike the guilty and the less guilty. At the Nuremberg trials of 1945–6, seven Nazi leaders were given lengthy prison sentences and 12 others were condemned to death by hanging. All these sentences were carried out, save that Göring succeeded in taking his own life just before he was executed, and Martin Bormann, tried in absentia, had escaped to South America and was never found. A harder task than punishing the leaders however was the wider one of dealing with the lesser Nazis and trying to work out who had been truly criminal and who had simply obeyed orders or been seduced by propaganda. After 1945 the Western Allies embarked on a general policy of 'de-Nazification':[1] but this was carried out clumsily and failed to achieve its true purpose. Many really guilty people were never convicted: many others, such as *Wehrmacht* officers or local officials who while outwardly doing their duty had made efforts to limit Nazi injustices, were nonetheless penalised. This led to anger and cynicism among Germans and it left a sour taste. But another kind of denazification, also known as 're-democratisation', bore much better results. This was the policy of re-educating the Germans in a free way of life after the years of tyranny. In the Western zones, the Allies rapidly found local personalities with good anti-Nazi records to appoint as mayors of cities – notably, Konrad Adenauer in Cologne – while others were selected to run radio stations and newspapers under Allied supervision. The trade unions and former political parties were helped back onto their feet; the most nazified schoolteachers were dismissed, but others were retrained in democracy. Everywhere freedom of speech was encouraged, even the right to criticise the occupying forces. This enlightened policy was on the whole carried out sensibly, and it laid the foundation of the new Germany of today.

The next question was what to do with the shattered German economy. With millions near to starvation, it was a heavy liability for the Allies in 1945. So the issue was how to restore it quickly to some kind of working order, without allowing German industry to escape unpunished or to regain its dominance too easily. Here Western views differed sharply as to what should be done. During the latter part of the war the US Treasury Secretary, Henry Morgenthau, had argued for a very tough treatment of Germany after its defeat: he wanted not only forced labour and the mass execution of war criminals, but a 'pastoralisation' of the country, with its larger industries closed down or placed under foreign control. For a while both Churchill and Roosevelt looked sympathetically on these ideas, and in September 1944 they even signed a joint memorandum for 'converting Germany into a country primarily agricultural and pastoral'. But other influential voices argued that the Morgenthau plan would be counter-productive: 'Such methods do not prevent war, they breed it', said Henry Stimson. And finally, after wavering, Churchill and Roosevelt threw their weight behind a more moderate policy, closer to the precept that Churchill later quoted in his memoirs, 'In Victory, magnanimity'. It is true that the Western Allies did enforce some reparations during the first post-war years: but

[1] For the legacy today of the Nazi period, see pp. 389–403.

these were modest compared with those of the post-1919 period, or with the Russians' exactions in their zone (see p. 326). The more far-sighted Western leaders were aware of the views expressed by Maynard Keynes and others in the 1930s, that the economic severity of the Versailles Treaty had been directly responsible for the rise of Nazism. In all, only about 5 per cent of German industrial plant was dismantled between 1945 and 1949, and then Adenauer, newly elected Chancellor, managed to persuade the Allies to discontinue the policy.

Before long, Krupp, Thyssen and other industrial barons who had worked for Hitler were back in business. The rapidity of this rehabilitation caused some dismay in the West, and today it seems undeniable that as individuals these men were treated too leniently. Yet in a wider sense it is also clear that the Western Allies showed wisdom and foresight in helping Germany's economy to revive rapidly, so that it could play its part in building the new Europe. When the European Recovery Programme (Marshall Aid) was launched by a generous United States in 1948, West Germany was allowed to benefit from it under the same conditions as the countries that had fought against her. And over the next five years she made dynamic and resourceful use of this aid.

Even more crucial than Marshall Aid in making the recovery possible was West Germany's famous currency reform of June 1948. Until that date, with Hitler's discredited old Reichsmark still the only legal tender, the economy had been limping along on a barter and black market basis, and inflation was high. A repetition of the terrifying currency collapses of the 1920s seemed on the cards. Then early in 1948 a Bavarian professor of economics, one Ludwig Erhard, was appointed economic director for the Western zones, and with Allied backing he changed the currency. Overnight on June 20 the Reichsmark was abolished and a new Deutsche Mark introduced. As a nominal concession, each citizen was allowed to exchange 60 old Marks for new ones on a one-to-one basis: but for all their other assets people were given only one DM for 10 old Marks, and later the rate was reduced to 1 to 15. Of course reactions were mixed. People were dismayed to see their savings virtually obliterated: but they also found that their modest sums of new money had real purchasing power at last. So the black market vanished, as did the hoarding of stocks, and the shops suddenly became full of things to buy. This was achieved not by currency reform alone, for Erhard also set about dismantling the tight system of wage and price controls, food rationing and trade restrictions, that had survived from the Nazi period. It was a gamble, but it paid off. The lifting of controls initially set prices rising fast: but soon they settled down, and before long the West German inflation rate had fallen to well below British and French levels, and it stayed there.

Erhard has been described, not inaccurately, as 'the father of the Economic Miracle'. Thanks to his bold policies the economy suddenly took wing, and it soon acquired a momentum that was to carry it through the years ahead. Factory production changed to a higher gear, as did the construction industry: 'Everywhere the noise of new buildings going up replaced the deathly silence of the ruins,' reported one observer. So in the period after 1948 the Germans energetically set about rebuilding their devastated cities and providing new homes for the homeless and for the refugees pouring in from the East. In a few towns, such as Nuremberg, picturesque old streets were meticulously restored to their original state: but in most cases a modern town centre was implanted in place of the cleared-away ruins. Sometimes the new architecture was pleasant, as at Hanover, but more often the style was heavy and graceless. At least however the basic needs of housing were fulfilled quite rapidly.

The currency reform was quickly extended to West Berlin, where it angered the Russians who feared that it could pose a threat to the economy of their own zone. By now the two halves of Germany were growing steadily apart, for the Russians from the outset in 1945 had begun to impose their own Communist system in their zone, in breach of the Potsdam Agreement which had stipulated that Germany during the occupation period should be treated as one economic entity. On June 24, 1948, the Russians began to blockade Berlin by sealing off all land traffic leading to the West. In its timing this move was a retort to the currency reform; but it also had a more ambitious objective, for Stalin by now was determined to take control of the Western sectors of the city and thus end this 'nuisance' of a hostile enclave within his territory. But he had reckoned without the firmness of the Allied response and the courage of West Berliners in withstanding the siege throughout a long cold winter. The US and British Air forces immediately began their great airlift, and over the next ten months they made some 200,000 flights, bringing 1.5 million tons of supplies to the beleaguered city. Finally in April 1949 Stalin admitted defeat and lifted the blockade.

Long before this episode, the Western Allies had come to realise that there was little hope for reaching agreement with the Russians on a united Germany, and so they began to lay their own plans for introducing normal political life into their zones. They started at the regional level, in 1947, by sanctioning elections for local parliaments in the 11 *Länder*[1] of Western Germany. Then in the spring of 1948 they gave the signal for the setting up of a separate West German state, by

[1] For the *Länder*, their numbers and their role, see pp. 25–7.

proposing that the *Länder* should elect a constituent assembly to draft a federal constitution. The assembly duly began work in September, and within seven months it had completed and approved a lengthy document that was entitled not 'Constitution' but 'Basic Law' (*Grundgesetz*) so as to emphasize its 'provisional' character – for Germans still believed that their country before long would be reunited. (Today, 40 years later, this same *Grundgesetz* is still the constitution and is still officially 'provisional'.) In August 1949 the West Germans went to the polls to elect the lower house (*Bundestag*) of their new federal parliament, and in September the Bundestag by a narrow majority chose Konrad Adenauer, the Christian Democrat leader, then aged 73, as the new Republic's first Chancellor. Though full sovereignty was not restored until six years later, West Germany was now well on the way to becoming an independent state after four and a half years of occupation. At the same time, Moscow encouraged the East Germans to match these moves. In May 1949 a 'People's Congress' in East Berlin approved its own constitution, and in October the German Democratic Republic was formally proclaimed. The division of Germany was now complete.

The early 1950s were the first heady years of West Germany's 'Economic Miracle'. Already by 1950 its GNP had climbed back to the pre-war level, and then in 1950–64 it trebled in real money terms. Income per capita almost doubled between 1950 and 1955, as families equipped themselves with TV sets, new clothes and furniture, and the streets filled up with Volkswagen 'Beetles'. Though loosely described as a 'miracle', this sudden recovery was in fact the result of a happy combination of several identifiable factors (see also pp. 83–4). As well as the Erhard reforms, these included the incentive for renewal after so total a defeat, and the German flair for disciplined hard work and thoroughness. The outbreak of the Korean War in 1950 brought a mass of orders for machinery and other equipment. And, not least, the millions of refugees from the east helped to provide the labour force that industrial expansion needed.

This exodus of Germans from the eastern territories invaded by the Soviet Army took place amid terrible suffering. Overall it was the greatest migratory movement of modern times, and there were several distinct waves of it. First, at the 1945 Potsdam Conference the West had agreed to the Russian demand for the 'transfer' into Germany of the German populations of Hungary, Poland and Czechoslovakia: this involved some 3.5 million people, mostly from the Sudetenland in Bohemia. But, even before this, as the Red Army advanced some 4 million Germans had already fled from their homelands in East Prussia, Silesia and other regions of Germany itself. Then, after the Russians' arrival, most of the remaining 4.5 million Germans were expelled by force from the areas east of the Oder and Neisse rivers that were to be seized from Germany. Figures vary, but about 2 million are believed to have come from Silesia and 1.4 million from East Prussia. All in all, in 1944–6 about 8 million Germans were on the move westward, many of them on foot, straggling along weary and underfed, clutching a few precious belongings. Over a million are estimated to have died en route. The world at large tended to feel, understandably, that this suffering even of the innocent was a part of the just price that Germany must pay for Nazism. And this view was even shared by some of the more open-minded of the refugees themselves – for example my own wife's mother's family who lost their stately home and their big farm in Silesia. But many other Germans felt that the evictions were a gross injustice – and some of them still feel that today: little groups of exiles, notably Silesians, have formed *Heimatverbände* (homeland associations) that campaign for the recovery of their own particular lost territory – sometimes to the embarrassment of the Federal Government.

Some of the refugees stayed in the zone that was later to become the GDR. But most moved on to the West, where they were joined later by other waves of migrants escaping from Communism in the GDR, a total that had reached over 3.5 million by the time of the building of the Berlin Wall in 1961. So, altogether, some 13 to 14 million Germans from the east settled in West Germany during the years after the war – and their ultimate integration, not easily achieved, was an amazing saga. Initially, as the cities were so ruined, the vast majority of the newcomers were directed to rural areas where some were billetted on the inhabitants and others were placed in former barracks or hastily constructed huts. So numerous were they that the population of rural Bavaria rose by 30 per cent and that of Schleswig-Holstein by 60 per cent; and, despite the war casualties, the area that is now West Germany saw its overall numbers increase by 20 per cent. This influx was not at all well accepted by the local people: far from welcoming the refugees as fellow Germans in distress, they tended to look on them as tiresome intruders come to crowd their living space and aggravate their food shortages. In Bavaria, newcomers from Silesia were often insultingly dubbed '*Polacken*' – a bitter irony for those who had just been expelled from their homes by the Poles! Of the many people I myself have met who came from the east in those days, nearly all have tales to tell of how at first they were cold-shouldered and insulted. Often they were asked angrily, 'What are you doing here? – why don't you go back home?' – for most Germans in those days still had little idea of the horrors in the east caused first by the Nazis and then by the vengeful Russian troops. What is more, most of the refugees were from towns (many were skilled workers or professional people), yet they were planted down amid simple country folk and quite often were set to work as farm labourers. Inevitably this led to conflicts, especially as the German regions in those days still had little knowledge of each other (see pp. 24–5), so that to a Schleswig peasant a teacher or technician from Breslau was an alien breed. Housing was so short that anyone with a room to spare was ordered to lend it to a refugee family, and this too caused ill-feeling. And a further problem was that, once the economic recovery began, the new jobs were not in the rural areas where the refugees had been sent. So after 1949 the German authorities started a reset-tlement programme that led to about a million people being transfer-red to the rebuilt towns.

Gradually the newcomers became accepted and integrated. 'For us,' said an East Prussian I met in a small town near Stuttgart, 'it took about fifteen years before these stuffy Swabians began to accept us. That's why today I have such sympathy for the Turkish immigrant workers.' From the start, the Allied and then the German authorities gave the refugees the same rights as other German citizens. Then, in 1952, an 'equalisation of burdens law' (*Lastenausgleichgesetz*) was enacted, whereby those Germans who had been able to preserve all or most of their property through the war were obliged to cede a portion of it to those who could prove that they had lost everything or almost everything. Beneficiaries from this compensation fund included not only the expellees from the east but those who had suf-fered war damage or had emigrated to escape the Nazis in the 1930s; and contributors to the fund had to pay one half of the value of their 1948–9 assets, in instalments over 30 years. By 1982, 121 billion DM had been redistributed.

This was just one aspect of the official campaign to help the refugees to resettle: it took time, but ultimately it was successful. As for the refugees themselves, many of them displayed the kind of tenacity and adaptability that is so often the hallmark of destitute immigrants in a new land; and today one finds them everywhere in the Federal Republic, in positions of affluence and influence, happily integrated. Maybe I shall be suspected of personal bias, seeing that my wife's mother came from Silesia and her father from Dresden: but even before I met Katinka I had been very forcibly impressed by the fact that an amazingly high percentage of the most cultivated, liberal-minded, intelligent and generally sympathetic Germans I met on my travels around the country had come from the eastern areas, above all Silesia, Thuringia and Pomerania. Was it, I wondered, that those easterly lands with their Slav influences had bred the best Germans (it used to be said in Weimar days that the best Berliners were all from Breslau)? Or was it that hardship and the pioneer spirit had brought out the best in them, making them seem less provincial than most Germans, just because they had been uprooted? Maybe a little of both, I decided. At any rate, the immigrants might not have been integrated for many decades, were it not for the 'economic miracle': nor could that 'miracle' have succeeded so triumphantly without their contribution.

This post-war economic resurgance was matched by political recovery too, as West Germany's new democratic institutions found their strength and proved their worth in the period after the 1949 elections. This too was a remarkable success story – especially in the context of the weakness of democratic tradition in Germany in the 19th and early 20th centuries. Whereas the Weimar Republic of the 1920s had proved feeble and unstable and so fell an easy victim to Nazism, the post-1949 Bonn regime turned out to be made of far sterner stuff. This contrast has been much analysed by political scientists, and some of the reasons for it I have already mentioned. One was the more positive and sensible treatment by the Western victors after 1945; another, the far more horrific defeat leading to a more radical new start. When they awoke from the paralysing trance of the Nazi period, responsible Germans were so appalled at what had been allowed to happen that they took special pains to build a more effective democratic framework and to keep it running smoothly (see pp. 403–5).

Another reason for the greater success of the Bonn regime was that this time the Germans had the good fortune to find a strong *and* wise leader (albeit an elderly father-figure) to guide them through the difficult post-war years. Konrad Adenauer, who had been mayor of Cologne from 1917 to 1933, was a *Führer* of a somewhat novel kind for Germany. He provided the firm, patriarchal leadership that Germans tend to like: but he showed that this could be combined with democratic government, shorn of much of the old authoritarianism – 'he was the first German statesman,' the American historian Gordon Craig has written, 'who was able to overcome the unconscious tendency of his countrymen to believe that leaders could only be taken seriously when they wore uniforms.'[1]

Along with Jean Monnet, Paul-Henri Spaak and Alcide de Gasperi, Adenauer was also one of the first post-war leaders to champion the new ideal of European unity, for he believed strongly that the best way to prevent a possible recrudescence of German nationalism was for Germany to find a new identity within a new kind of European framework. He preached this Europeanism to the German people, and won a strongly favourable response. First, in 1951, Germany joined with France, Italy and the Benelux countries in setting up the

---

[1] *The Germans*, p. 44 (Putnam's, New York, 1982; Penguin Books, London, 1984).

European Coal and Steel Community. This helped the German coal and steel industries to find their feet again; more important, it was to prove a valuable dress rehearsal for the Common Market. Adenauer, next, was one of the most fervent advocates of the proposed European Defence Community which would have created a supra-national European Army; when this EDC project was torpedoed by the French Parliament in 1954, the Chancellor was deeply disappoin-ted, but he quickly accepted the Anglo-American suggestion that the best alternative was for Germany to join the North Atlantic Treaty Organisation which had been set up in 1949. So in 1955 the Federal Republic duly became a member of NATO; at the same time it won its full sovereignty and – in the face of understandable opposition from many Germans of all kinds, not only pacifists – it set about creating a new army, the *Bundeswehr*, as well as navy and air force. West Ger-many was now fully integrated into the Western camp as a firm and loyal ally. Then in 1957, with the signing of the Treaty of Rome, it became a founder member of the European Economic Community.[1] After de Gaulle returned to power in 1958, he and Adenauer formed a remarkable approchement, and this led in 1962 to the signing of the Franco–German Treaty of Friendship. It was the Chancellor's crowning achievement. After three Franco–German wars in the pre-ceding hundred years, the hatchet was finally buried and this Paris–Bonn entente was henceforth to be the central pivot of the EEC and the foremost guarantor of stability and unity in Western Europe.

At home, Adenauer retained his popularity throughout most of the 1950s, and the federal elections of 1953 and 1957 brought growing majorities for his Christian Democratic Union in partnership with its Bavarian sister-party, the Christian Social Union. But by the end of the 1950s the ageing leader had grown steadily more autocratic, and this led to mounting criticism within his own ranks. He finally retired in 1963, to be replaced by Ludwig Erhard who then proved a some-what ineffectual Chancellor: despite his colossal economic reputa-tion, ironically enough it was under his rule that the booming German economy ran into its first mild recession, in 1965–6. This and other factors led to a certain malaise and to demands for a change of government: so, late in 1966, the Social Democratic Party (*Sozialde-mokratische Partei Deutschlands*) agreed to enter into a 'grand coalition' with the CDU/CSU under the chancellorship of the conservative Kurt-Georg Kiesinger, and this lasted until the elections of 1969. The

[1] The official name of this organisation today is the European Community (EC): it has dropped the word 'Economic' because it considers itself just as much political. However, for clarity's sake, in this book I am using the more familiar and more easily identifiable initials, EEC.

coalition was possible because the SPD had shifted centrewards since the 1950s. Under its first post-war leader, Kurt Schumacher, it had adopted a radical left-wing stance as a working-class party favouring nationalisation of industry. But this failed to find much favour with a German electorate then in a conservative, materialistic mood, and the SPD fared rather badly in the elections of the 1949–57 period. So, at a crucial congress in 1959 in the Bonn suburb of Bad Godesberg, the party decided to shed its Marxist dogmas and to assume a clearly social-democratic colouring, in favour of the mixed economy. For this and other reasons, the 1960s and 1970s were a time of considerable consensus in German parliamentary politics. Two extremist parties, the neo-Nazi *Sozialistische Reichspartei* and the Communist Party, had been outlawed respectively in 1952 and 1956 on constitutional grounds; and although another extreme-right movement, the *National-aldemokratische Partei* (NPD), made sudden progress in some *Land* elections in the mid-1960s, bringing fears of a rise of neo-Nazism, it soon fell back and lost all its seats. The mass of German voters in those years showed little desire to experiment with new ideas or policies: they were too preoccupied with extending their new-won affluence, in a society that had become noticeably conformist and even complacent – or so it appeared. And yet, outside party politics, in 1967–8 an entirely new kind of challenge appeared quite suddenly. It came from the left-wing students, teachers and others, who began forcefully to question the whole basis of society and even the validity of parliamentary democracy. The university uprisings of that time were to make a strong impact on the German mood and on German politics over the years ahead.

With Willi Brandt as foreign minister and Karl Schiller as an economics minister, the SPD made a favourable showing in the 1966–9 coalition; and then in the elections of 1969 it did so well that it was able to form a left-of-centre government in alliance with the small 'liberal' centre party, the *Freie Demokratische Partei* (FDP). Brandt, a charismatic idealist who had won renown as a sturdy mayor of Berlin during its crisis years of 1958–61, now became the first SPD chancellor and his first priority was foreign affairs. Believing that it was high time that West Germany normalised its relations with the Soviet bloc (and undeterred by the Russian invasion of Czechoslovakia the year before), he launched his famous *Ostpolitik*, a policy of detente with the East. He opened direct talks with Moscow and Warsaw, and in 1970 became the first West German leader to pay an official visit to the GDR. The result was a treaty with the Soviet Union, and then another with Poland, whereby the Federal Republic agreed to recognise the controversial new Polish and East German frontiers, while not ruling out the possibility of German reunification later on. Brandt was angrily accused of a 'sell-out' by the German Right: but the majority of German opinion appeared to be behind him. His efforts paved the way for a new four-power Agreement on Berlin in 1971, whereby the Russians made the concession of finally accepting the validity of West Berlin and the right of the Western Powers to protect it. And in 1972 a treaty between the two Germanies set the stage for a period of discreet rapprochement. Brandt was awarded the Nobel Peace Prize in 1971. His *Ostpolitik* helped to reduce the tensions of the Cold War and to further East–West détente in Europe as a whole.

With his domestic reforms, however, Brandt was less successful. He was a good democratic chancellor, who developed an open style of government based on team-work rather than autocratic command: but he was also too trusting and incautious – and this finally led to his downfall, when in 1974 it was discovered that a senior official in his office, Günter Guillaume, was an East German spy. Brandt accepted responsibility and resigned. His successor as SPD chancellor was Helmut Schmidt, a hard-headed pragmatic Hamburger on the right wing of his party, who proved a better manager than Brandt and overall the best chancellor since Adenauer. He dealt effectively with the extreme-Left terrorist wave of the mid-1970s, led by the Baader-Meinhof gang. But after the first oil crisis of 1974 he had to face a worsening world economic situation that put strains on Germany's own economy: 1979–82 were bad years, with very low growth, rising unemployment, and inflation at an unusually high level for Germany. The 'miracle' seemed to be finally at an end. The unions became restive, and it was not certain whether Germany's envied pattern of harmonious post-war labour relations would survive. Finally in November 1982 the SPD/FDP coalition collapsed and the CDU/CSU returned to power, this time under Helmut Kohl who had been the CDU's leader since 1973. In March 1983 the CDU/CSU won a snap election and proceeded to govern in coalition with the FDP, which had switched alliances.

Chancellor Kohl from Mainz, a huge burly man with an affable manner, did not prove a very exciting or scintillating leader. But behind the scenes he was an excellent party organiser who inspired loyalty, and he had dogged qualities of prudence and unflappability that the German public seemed to find reassuring. After an awkward start, he managed to bring the economy back onto a firm footing; and despite various mistakes and *gaffes*, and more than a whiff of corruption in high places, he and his party remained rather popular – at a time when Germany seemed to be entering a new period, with a new range of problems. Unemployment, very low in the post-war decades, had now climbed high, as in other Western countries. The debate in 1983 over the implantation on German soil of new American nuclear missiles served to divide the nation sharply and threatened to destroy the party consensus on defence issues. And in the early 1980s the Greens emerged as a new force in party politics, flag-bearers of a new ecology-minded generation that questioned the entire ethos of Germany's hard-working and materialistic post-war society. The alarming sickness of the Germans' beloved forests, and the belief that motor-cars were the main cause, became a symbolic issue in this new troubled Germany. I shall return to these themes in later chapters. But next we shall look at one of the most distinctive features of modern Germany: its federal structure.

DENMARK

BALTIC SEA

NORTH SEA

Kiel

SCHLESWIG –
HOLSTEIN

○ Rostock

Hamburg

Elbe

GERMAN

POLAND

Bremen ○

LOWER SAXONY

WEST
BERLIN

EAST
BERLIN

HOLLAND

● Hanover

DEMOCRATIC

FEDERAL

NORTH-RHINE

WESTPHALIA

Rhine

Leipzig ○

Elbe

Dresden ○

Düsseldorf ○

■ BONN

REPUBLIC

REPUBLIC

BELGIUM

Cologne ○

HESSE

OF

CZECHOSLOVAKIA

Wiesbaden ○ Frankfurt ○

GERMANY

RHINELAND-
PALATINATE

● Mainz

SAARLAND

● Saarbrücken

○ Nuremberg

BADEN-

BAVARIA

FRANCE

● Stuttgart

WÜRTTEMBERG

Rhine

● Munich

AUSTRIA

SWITZERLAND

■ National capitals
● *Land* capitals
○ Other major cities
▬ · ▬ · ▬ · International boundary
▬ ▬ ▬ Federal State boundary

0   50   100
└─────┴─────┴─────┘ miles
     50   100   150
        km

[22]

2

THE REGIONAL PATCHWORK, AN ANCIENT LEGACY

Germany, it is often said, is very diverse, not so much an integrated nation as a patchwork of different *Länder* and of local identities and loyalties. But this can be overstated. Germany's political history as a united country may be no more than 120 years old: but in terms of temperament and life-style, of culture and geography, I am not at all sure that the diversity is any greater than, say, in Britain, France or Italy – is a Hamburger really any more different from a Bavarian than a Scot or Geordie from a Londoner, a Norman from a Provencal, or a Torinese from a Sicilian? It is simply that in Germany the differences tend to be more apparent, or to have more expression, because of political factors – the decentralised federal system of government, and the lack of any single big capital city to provide a focus.

Since 1945 Germany has been divided into two, politically and ideologically, between East and West. But, culturally and geographically, the older and truer division is between north and south. Within a very complicated framework, generalisation is hazardous: but in a few sentences one could summarise by saying that south Germany is hilly and wooded, gentle and picturesque, close in spirit to Austria and very much a part of Central Europe, a land of vineyards and half-timbered houses, baroque churches and old castles on hilltops, while the north is a more austere territory of windy plains and harsh winters, turned towards Scandinavia and to Britain and the open sea. The people of the south, notably the Bavarians, also the Rhinelanders to the west, tend to be Catholic; they have a reputation for extrovert jollity and *Gemütlichkeit*, they drink beer heavily, also wine, and sing noisily in their taverns, swaying together, arms linked. This is the Germany of the tourist brochures. In the north, the people are mostly Protestant, more stolid and reserved but also possibly more reliable and, in the big cities, more liberal and sophisticated. Compare, for example, the difference in temperament between Bavaria's Franz-Josef Strauss and Hamburg's Helmut Schmidt.

Look more closely, however, and you see that these broad north-versus-south stereotypes can be misleading, for the true pattern is more complex. In the north, for instance, radical Bremen with its open maritime spirit is a world away from its hinterland in conservative lower Saxony. And the two main peoples of the south, Bavarians and Swabians, longtime rivals, form a clear contrast – Bavarians jovial and mostly Catholic, fun-loving but with touches of brashness and even cruelty, Swabians more kindly and gentle, but slow and solemn, marked by a puritanical Protestantism that is generally untypical of the south. Germany, in short, remains a patchwork, where local patriotism and the sense of belonging are often focussed on some quite small, distinct area – such as the Hohenlohe in northern Württemberg, or the Emsland along the Dutch border, or the Hunsrück district east of the Moselle, so lovingly detailed in Reitz's aptly-titled film *Heimat*.

In many such areas, indeed throughout Germany, local and regional dialects survive more actively in daily use than is usual in Europe today. In Bavaria, the dialect of the south is quite different from that of the north, Franconia; some cities, notably Berlin and Cologne, retain their own dialects which a visitor from a village even twenty miles away may find hard to follow; and the *Plattdeutsch* of Friesia by the North Sea is more than just a dialect but a distinct language with its own literature. Today all German children in school are taught the official standard language, *Hochdeutsch*, and they can understand it on radio and television. But in many areas, even in cities, local people still use their dialect for daily speech, and in rural areas they often understand it better than *Hochdeutsch*. Politicians need to take account of this. Strauss makes his official speeches in *Hochdeutsch*, but in a strong Bavarian accent of which he is proud; when he gets down among his rural electorate he is careful, and glad, to talk to them in dialect. And Lothar Späth does likewise in Swabia.

The variations between dialects are great: for example, 'We have seen it' is *'Wir haben es angesehen'* in *Hochdeutsch*, *'Mir hams ogschaut'* in Bavarian, *'Mr hannet gesäh'* in Swabian, and *'Wir haben's angekiekt'* in Berlin. Small wonder that a German visiting another region may find it hard to follow a conversation in a pub or train – and this helps to explain why some Germans still think of distant parts of their country as alien. Or that is how southerners think of northerners, more than vice versa. North Germans nowadays visit the south so often for their holidays that they have come to accept Bavarians or Swabians as at least vaguely familiar and picturesque, however 'different': but for many a southerner the north remains an unknown world, dour and unwelcoming, peopled by taciturn dullards. A Stuttgart charlady, returning from her son's wedding to a girl in Schleswig, spoke to me as if her daughter-in-law were a Mexican or Australian.

This kind of mutual ignorance used to be far stronger in the old days. But in post-war times it has modified considerably, as shifts of population and other factors – television, modern travel and consumerism – have brought cities and regions closer together and more aware of each other. Perhaps it is just because the different parts of the republic now have more frequent contact with each other that they are now more aware of their differences and continue to cherish the regional stereotypes so fondly, endlessly making music-hall jokes about parsimonious Swabians, thigh-slapping Bavarians, stiff-upper-lipped Hamburgers and the like.

First in the early post-war years came the mass influx of German refugees from the east. As we have seen, they had difficulties at first but are now more or less integrated, and they have brought an enriching new diversity to West German cities: Stuttgart alone has 80,000 Silesians or children of Silesians, and is thus far less homogeneously Swabian than in pre-war days. In addition, the boom years of the 1950s and '60s created a new mobility among West Germans, as new jobs multiplied and engineers, executives and other professional people (but workers more rarely) moved readily across the country in pursuit of well-paid careers, especially to the south where economic growth has been fastest. Today amid high unemployment this movement has slowed right down, but it has left decisive change: Germany's cities are far more varied in their German populations than before the war, and on top of this four million immigrants have arrived from Mediterranean countries. Add again the influence of the networked TV news programmes, the uniformity of modern consumer trends, and the fact that most of the shattered city centres were rebuilt in much the same modern style – all these factors have made German cities grow to resemble each other more and more. Something important has been lost in the process: but at the same time they have each become more internally variegated, and much more open to the outside world. It is indeed remarkable that each *has* managed to retain so much individuality. This is due in part to the degree of autonomy that German cities enjoy under the decentralised system of government.

Federalism is a natural outcome of German history and tradition. Until the unification of 1866–71, Germany was made up of some 30 kingdoms, duchies and free cities, varying in size from tiny fiefs to the empires of Prussia and Bavaria. Even Bismarck did not remove the local rulers, though he did bring them all under the Prussian umbrella: they survived until 1919, when the Weimar Republic instituted a kind of federal system not so very different from today's. Then the Nazi regime greatly strengthened central government at the expense of *Länder*: but this served to discredit centralism in 1945 and was a major argument then for moving back to an even stronger federalism. Also the victorious Allies felt that a decentralised Germany of medium-sized units would be less powerful and aggressive. In the event, federalism has proved a source of strength and harmony more than a weakness, and on the whole the system works well, as we shall see.

The German Länder:

Land (German name in brackets)	area (sq. km.)	population	capital
Baden-Württemberg	35,751	9,200,000	Stuttgart
Bavaria (Bayern)	70,553	11,000,000	Munich
Bremen	404	677,000	Bremen
Hamburg	755	1,640,000	Hamburg
Hessen	21,115	5,600,000	Wiesbaden
Lower Saxony (Niedersachsen)	47,447	7,200,000	Hanover
North-Rhine-Westphalia (Nordrhein-Westfalen)	34,062	17,000,000	Düsseldorf
Rhineland-Palatinate (Rheinland-Pfalz)	19,848	3,600,000	Mainz
Saarland	2,571	1,100,000	Saarbrücken
Schleswig-Holstein	15,721	2,600,000	Kiel
West Berlin	480	1,960,000	West Berlin

There are ten *Länder* (excluding West Berlin which juridically is not a part of the Federal Republic) and they vary greatly in size and population. Their borders have remained unchanged since 1945, save that in 1951 three smallish *Länder* merged to form Baden-Württemberg. Some *Länder* – notably Bavaria, also Hamburg and Bremen – correspond to historic boundaries and have a genuine historical identity. But others are more hybrid, pieced together from small ancient duchies or bits of the Prussian empire – for example, Hessen, Rhineland-Palatinate and North-Rhine-Westphalia. It is thus inevitable that popular sentiments of *Land* identity and patriotism should vary greatly. They are weak in the more artificial *Länder*, where the stronger attachment is often to a city (e.g. Cologne) or to a former royal domain (Badeners feel that they belong to Baden and they resent Württemberg). But the sentiments are strong in Hamburg and Bremen – and uniquely strong in Bavaria, still vividly conscious of its proud past as a kingdom until 1918, and the only part of West Germany that still feels itself to be a separate 'nation', rather as Scotland does. This is a matter of cultural identity more than political fact, for juridically Bavaria today is no more autonomous than any other *Land*. But it considers itself different. 'I feel Bavarian first, European second and German third,' one Münchner told me, while a senior Bavarian official said, 'Yes, we have had to give up our formal sovereignty since Bismarck's day, but we are still in many ways masters of our own destiny.' Perhaps this is why so very few Bavarians, unlike the Scots, nourish dreams of separatism: they know that they are better off within the Federal Republic. And visiting Scots (Munich is twinned with Edinburgh) often envy Bavarians their degree of practical autonomy.

The federal system leaves the *Land* governments in charge of many matters, notably education, culture, justice, and some aspects of economic policy. This decentralisation has advantages. It creates a fertile spirit of competition between the *Länder*, and it brings decision-making closer to the people – certainly an asset in an age when complex bureaucracy, the world over, has been tending to make government more remote and impersonal. Germany's system is frequently admired and envied, and several of her European partners – Italy, Spain, and now even France – have been taking steps in her direction by devolving some power to their regions. But federalism can have drawbacks too; and one, in the case of Germany, is that the country has no proper capital. Not that federalism itself is to blame for this, for a decentralised structure need by no means be incompatible with central rule on a loose rein from a major metropolis – indeed this was roughly the pattern in Germany itself before 1933, even if Berlin for historical reasons never exercised the same dominant role as London or Paris. It is true that today, in other federal countries, the capital is very rarely the main town – and, in Australia, Canberra has some of the same inadequacies as Bonn. But Washington and Delhi, though smaller respectively than New York or Bombay, are nonetheless big cities of great importance. Upstart Bonn, Germany's 19th town in size, has fewer inhabitants (288,000) than Bielefeld or Gelsenkirchen.

When it formally became the federal capital in 1949, Beethoven's birthplace was a modest university town on the Rhine. Why was it chosen? In those days most politicians believed – or paid lip-service to the belief – that Germany before long would be reunified and Berlin would resume its rightful role. So a purely provisional site was needed in the meantime. Bonn had the advantages of being (a) fairly obscure, without pretensions to any permanent role as capital, and (b) quite central, neither in north nor south Germany. Frankfurt, also central, was seriously considered too, and had many advocates; but it was rejected as being too large and powerful, and too bound up with German history. Hamburg and Munich were excluded for the same reasons, plus another one too: south Germans would never accept being governed from the far north, nor north Germans from Bavaria's capital. What is more, Bonn was warmly favoured by Chancellor Adenauer, who was CDU deputy for the town and a native of nearby Cologne. This ageing leader wanted to stay near his *Heimat* – and his voice proved decisive. Since then, *c'est le provisoire qui dure* . . . Bonn has steadily acquired a large number of solid and expensive government buildings, so that a move to another town would now be costly and not so practicable. Yet as a capital city it still wears a vaguely unreal and makeshift air: this is because neither politicians nor public have yet come to believe in it completely as the nation's *Hauptstadt*, even if rationally they have ceased to expect a return to Berlin.

Some efforts have at least been made to spread a few federal institutions around the country, rather than group them all in Bonn. Thus the important Constitutional Court is in Karlsruhe, the Federal Bank in Frankfurt and the main employment office in Nuremberg. But Parliament, the ministries and embassies are all in Bonn. Here in this boring little town with its enervating climate (*das Bundesdorf*, federal village, it is called), politicians and bureaucrats, journalists and diplomats, co-habit in an unreal world. It helps to explain why Federal politicians, despite their media limelight, are so often criticised for being out of touch with the public. 'Bonn is the kiss of death,' said one writer. It is a great pity: Frankfurt, brash and ugly but dynamic and cultured and a true metropolis, would have made a much better capital, far more capable of providing Germany with the national focus that it now lacks. Adenauer's choice was wrong, as many people now realise.

Outside the narrow world of federal politics, Bonn plays little part in the social and cultural life of Germany, and it seldom comes up in conversation. By contrast, the seven or eight major German cities and their rival merits or defects are an inexhaustible topic of lively discussion at dinner parties and other gatherings, and many professional people spend much of their time travelling between one and another; or they live first in one for a few years, then another. 'I was born in Berlin, then moved with my parents to Munich where I went to school, then after university at Heidelberg I worked for five years on the *Stuttgarter Zeitung* and am now with *Der Spiegel* in Hamburg,' is the not untypical itinerary of an acquaintance of mine.

The main cities:
Population, 1985, in 000s' NB: these are the populations of the municipality in each case; that of the conurbation is often much larger.

West Berlin	1,960	Düsseldorf	569
Hamburg	1,640	Stuttgart	555
Munich (München)	1,297	Bremen	550
Cologne (Köln)	1,008	Hanover (Hannover)	550
Essen	650	Duisburg	548
Frankfurt	625	Nuremberg (Nürnberg)	480
Dortmund	600	Bochum	409

The four largest German cities put together, including their suburbs, would be considerably smaller than greater London or greater Paris. Germany is unusual in Europe, having no one dominating metropolis but several rival cities of roughly equal importance. Berlin, Hamburg, and Munich are the leaders, but Frankfurt comes not far behind, then Cologne, Düsseldorf, Stuttgart, Bremen and Hanover (the Ruhr cities, though large in population, have less influence). Many activities that in Britain or France are centred on the capital are in Germany divided out among various towns, each with its own *forte*. Thus the head offices of the big banks are in Frankfurt; the employers' federation is in Cologne, the trade union federation in Düsseldorf, the film industry in Munich and Berlin; the big weekly magazines, like *Stern* and *Spiegel*, and *Die Zeit* are edited in Hamburg, the second national TV network is run from Mainz, the principal art dealers are in Cologne, the publishing industry is in half-a-dozen cities, the Goethe Institut (equivalent of the British Council) operates from Munich, capital also for the fashion and high society worlds; the main consumer defence body is in Berlin, while the leading opinion survey institute is in a village on the shores of Lake Constance . . . and so on. This dispersion has some advantages. Towns are in healthy rivalry, especially for cultural life; and the larger cities, many of them *Land* capitals, have rather more autonomy and self-confidence than their British or French equivalents such as Manchester or Lille, and can exert more influence on national life. But, as there is no one city that sets a standard and provides a magnet and focus, may not the result be to make all Germany a little provincial? This theme will be explored in later chapters (see pp. 263 and 267). First, a voyage of discovery round the main towns, from south to north – starting with Munich, which likes to call itself *'Weltstadt mit Herz'* (a world city with warmth and a soul) but is also dubbed *'das Millionendorf'* (the village of more than a million people).

A diversity of dominant cities: life today in Munich, Stuttgart, Frankfurt, Bonn, Cologne, Düsseldorf, Hamburg and Bremen

The image of an elegant baroque capital, and the boozy beer-drinking thigh-slapping image, are both of them accurate but only parts of the total reality. Munich is the most smart and stylish of big German cities, the most hedonistic and culture-packed, outwardly the most opulent, and the most exuberant, self-confident and self-congratulatory. Despite Bavarians' relaxed and affable humour, daily business life has a fast, nervous tempo that sometimes reminds me of Paris. Indeed this the most Paris-like of German cities.

All this, plus the fact that in many cultural and social ways it is a trend-setter, has led Munich to be dubbed by the media 'Germany's secret capital'. The phrase does not bear much close scrutiny. Certainly Munich is not accepted as a capital by other parts of Germany; nor is Germany 'secretly' governed from Munich – Frankfurt, if anywhere, has more power. And yet Munich more than other cities still retains something of the atmosphere of a capital – not of all Germany but of the most assertive of its *Länder*. The spirit of the Wittelsbachs, who ruled here from 1180 to 1918, first as dukes, then as monarchs, is still very much alive. They have bequeathed numerous buildings of regal grandiosity, such as the massive Residenz palace, the Schloss Nymphenburg and the ugly but imposing Parliament that towers on its hill above the river Isar. And Bavarians are sharply aware of this royal legacy and happy to flaunt it. Everywhere the city flies the blue-and-white chequered flag of *Freistaat Bayern*, the 'Free State' of Bavaria; and the head of the Wittelsbach family today, the Duke of Bavaria, is still addressed as 'your Royal Highness' (see p. 150). Bavarians have a fondness for father-figures – it helps to explain the popularity of the emperor-like Franz-Josef Strauss.

The city has expanded greatly since the war, to reach a population of 1.3 million, and has benefited as much as any from the 'economic miracle'. It was not formerly a very industrial place. But after the war Siemens and some other big companies moved their headquarters here from Berlin; BMW is here too, and MBB, the aerospace firm, and these and other giants have created a spin-off effect, so that Munich now is an expanding centre of electronics and other advanced industries. People of all kinds have flocked in – farm emigrants from depopulating rural Bavaria, and refugees from the lost eastern parts of Germany and elsewhere in eastern Europe – so that most inhabitants of Munich today were not born in the city and 20 per cent are not German. This is also the favoured destination of the newly mobile West German middle classes, and according to opinion polls it is the city that most Germans would prefer to live in if they left their own.

People are attracted not only by its own qualities but by the weekend delights of the nearby Alps and lakes and the easy access to Austria and Italy – but less so by the climate, often marred by the *Föhn*, a dry, sultry headache-inducing wind from the mountains.

The suburbs sprawl for many miles: but the *Innenstadt*, the older inner city bound by a ring-road, is very compact, less than a mile across, and this gives Munich a strong sense of cohesion. Here is one of the world's great opera houses, and one of Europe's grandest hotels, the Vier Jahreszeiten. All is sleek and cosmopolitan: and Munich lies securely on the top international circuit for visiting celebrities of all kinds. But if it nonetheless misses the true metropolitan stature of say, London or Paris, is this because of its smaller size, or its lack of any major political or financial role, or because many of its true original Bavarian inhabitants are still just a little provincial, not quite in tune with its new *Weltstadt* vocation? By no means are they always pleased and flattered by its new popularity and diversity: many of them complain of its being 'de-Bavarianised', and they resent the 'stiff new Prussian influences'. Beneath all the glamour and diversity, this old hard-core Munich still has more than a touch of parochialism about it – as I noted in 1984 on a visit to *München Leuchtet* ('Munich is shining' – a variation on Thomas Mann's famous phrase 'Munich was shining'), a satirical play-cum-revue that for many months packed out one of the main theatres. Lovingly self-indulgent, it was a succession of in-jokes and jibes about local politicians, and cosy little send-ups of Munich habits, folklore and myths about itself – and it brought ecstatic applause.

The Bavarians, Münchners especially, are certain they are the best and they constantly say so – they have the best beer, the best music and the best football team, Bayern München. Always grumbling but warm-hearted, rough-tongued but sentimental and great lovers of folksy kitsch, they cultivate a breezy *Gemütlichkeit* that is less sweet and refined than the Austrian brand. Above all, they are great fun-lovers and hedonists, in contrast to most Germans who, Rhinelanders apart, are not so adept at enjoying themselves. To laugh a lot, to be seen in public to be having fun, to relish your beer, women and song – for this you score high marks in Bavaria.

This rollicking city also has style and stylishness – or rather several styles, for Munich today has many diverse faces. There is rough style of a kind in the traditional popular culture of beer-and-Lederhosen which is not just laid on for tourists but belongs vibrantly to local life. Gladly the Münchners go in big family parties to the annual *Oktoberfest;* and in summer they spread their picnics on the tables in the beer-gardens, where babies squall, students debate, lovers fondle and foaming two-litre tankards are downed – a Teutonic scene. Then in winter they make for the beer-cellars where thighs are slapped and brass-bands deafen, and the high-piled sausages are as vast, pink and coarse as the faces of the citizens roaring out the choruses, arms linked, swaying together – '*In München steht ein Hofbräuhaus, Eins, Zwei, Gsuffa. . . .*' But this unsophisticated image is only one of the city's faces. It is true that in the streets you still see plenty of veterans in patterned Lederhosen, with hairy knees and feathered green hats – but today in the city centre they are outnumbered by svelte girls from the pages of *Vogue,* for in recent years Munich has asserted itself as the German capital of fashion, high society and *Schick* (see page 156). Here is Germany's Hollywood, also its Mayfair and Madison Avenue, with boutiques in the Maximilianstrasse as smart as any in Paris – and who says the Germans are not smart when they try? Here is the showy world of the *Lodenmantelschickeria,* the smart set of aristocrats, industrialists, film and fashion people, for whom the height of *Schick* is to wear Bavarian *Tracht* (green *Loden* capes and jackets, for men and women) redesigned in stylish cuts by top fashion houses such as Dior. In Munich society, you do best to flaunt your wealth and status, and you are outcast if you do not dress modishly.

A third contrasting face, the bohemian one, is to be found in the Schwabing district, which in the early part of the century was a distinguished centre of European intellectual life – Brecht and Mann, Klee and Kandinsky, Trotsky and Spengler all lived there. Today Schwabing's glory has faded and Munich's true avant-garde has left it to create a new focus in the humbler district of Haidhausen across the Isar. But Schwabing still houses scores of little fringe theatres, art cinemas and arty pubs. The Leopoldstrasse, its main avenue leading up from the university, can be magical on a warm summer night in its own gaudy way-milling youthful crowds, art students hawking their work, and terrace-cafés, unusual for Germany. Just to the east is the Englischer Garten, created by an American, Count Rumford, in 1793, and claiming to be Europe's largest city park, four miles long. Here in summer youth besports itself in the style of the beaches of St-Tropez: this is tolerated (except when girls step naked out of the park into city trams), for Munich itself is today as easy-going as its Catholic rural hinterland is still strait-laced.

Bavaria is often regarded as 'reactionary'. But the heartland of Strauss's right-wing CSU support is in rural areas and smaller towns, while the capital itself since Wittelsbach has enjoyed a liberal tradition. True, it has known periods of extremism: there was the insurrectionary 'Red' commune of 1918–19, and then in the 1920s Hitler made Munich the headquarters of his Nazi movement and staged his abortive *Putsch* there in 1923. But since the war the city with its new mixed population has been politically moderate, ruled most of the time by the SPD. Since 1984 an SPD mayor with no overall majority has run the Rathaus in tacit coalition with the CSU, on a broad consensus policy disturbed only by the vocal Green minority. There is a degree of endemic corruption, and the occasional flare-up when the CSU finds the cultural programme too permissive: for instance, in 1985, to mark the 175th *Oktoberfest*, the City Museum, well known for its provocative Leftist policy, staged a highly critical exhibition, 'The Bavarian National Drunken Frenzy'. The CSU, enraged at this 'affront to national dignity and our cherished traditions', organised a boycott. Such incidents lend local politics a theatrical Latin flavour, agreeably un-German. Another point of controversy has been the council's decision to hire its own police force to patrol the Metro, in a bid to combat crime. These sinister pistol-bearing figures in black leather, dubbed *Schwarze Sheriffe*, may indeed have deterred some muggers: but local radicals and leftists have found them 'fascistic', reviving bitter memories of Munich's guilty past.

There are still various visible traces of this Nazi past. Hitler had some hideous buildings erected in the city, and those that survived the bombing have been allowed to stand as grim memorials. Thus his *Haus der Kunst*, built to enshrine Nazi principles of art, is still in use as a modern art museum, and its swastika patterns are still there on the porch. The gloomy limestone building that now houses the Music School was built by Hitler as his Munich headquarters: here he reviewed parades from its balcony, and here in 1938 Chamberlain signed away the Sudetenland. But, apart from this, Munich has obliterated the Nazi period. Badly bombed in 71 air-raids, many central streets were then hurriedly rebuilt in a somewhat graceless style. But luckily the vast majority of the many fine baroque buildings were spared the bombing, or have since been carefully restored, so that the city still keeps something of its special harmony of lovely façades glowing gold in the sunset. And it is all sparklingly clean and tidy, remarkably so even by German standards.

Post-war planning has mostly been intelligent, avoiding the highrise rash that disfigures Frankfurt and some other cities. Munich allows no downtown skyscrapers. The ugly Arabella/Sheraton towers, built in the 1960s and now much regretted, at least stand two miles out; the strange four-cylinder BMW building, and the nearby 900-foot Olympic Tower, are further out still. Here the 1972 Olympic Games have left the city with the useful legacy of a mammoth sports and leisure complex, adorned with its 18-acre curly roof of acrylic glass, looking like some giant fish-net hung out to dry. All in all the Games were a boon for Munich. They gave it the incentive to build a much-needed modern infrastructure that includes ring motorways and a gleaming super-efficient Metro. The modern public transport system, integrating Metro, suburban trains, buses and trams, is one of the best in Europe, about as good as Hamburg's. Parts of the inner city are now a pedestrian zone where broad shopping malls converge on the Marienplatz beside the Rathaus, still the hub of Munich life and all-year-round quite an impromptu carnival scene – one spring Saturday, for instance, young out-of-work musicians playing a classical harp-and-oboe duet while Leftist demonstrators brandished anti-Strauss placards. In December the square is given over to the astonishing *Christkindlmarkt*, a huge bizarre bazaar of every kind of Bavarian Christmas kitsch such as marzipan Wise Men and Virgin-and-Child candles. Such is the magic of Munich.

Stuttgart, capital of Baden-Württemberg, has a quaint south German charm of a somewhat different kind. Its best single feature is its physical setting, much the prettiest of any big German city. The others are all on wide plains, but central Stuttgart lies in a hollow, cradled by forested hills; the tidy terraced suburbs rise steeply on either side, and one vineyard slopes up from the main station. This nest-like frame, leafy and bucolic, lends a quality of gentleness to this modern industrial city, home of Bosch and Daimler-Benz. It also makes Stuttgart seem smaller than it is, for its industrial areas sprawl unseen in other valleys. And it gives a feeling of intimacy that chimes in well with the local character of these cosy Swabians, lovers of the twee, for whom even a big mansion is not '*Haus*' but '*Häusle*' (wee house). A godfearing and, even more, an untidiness-fearing race. The second worst sin is to be seen weeding your garden on the sabbath. The worst sin is not to weed it ever.

Swabian piety and provincialism may irritate, yet this remains my favourite German city – or, at least, I know it far better than the others, and *tout comprendre*. . . . The contrast with Munich is striking – not only the setting, but the atmosphere, more cosy and relaxed; and the people, gentler, kindlier and much less show-off than the Bavarians. These slow Swabians with their big moon faces may be somewhat ponderous and unsophisticated, but they are as solid and dependable as the Mercedes they produce: and they have a pawky sense of humour, typified by Stuttgart's famous mayor, Manfred Rommel, who said when I asked him if pietism was still strong in Swabia, 'Local Protestants used to feel that if they laughed, the Lord would be worried. Today they think better of Him and realise that He too has a sense of humour.'

Stuttgart is the main town of Swabia, which covers a sizeable chunk of south-west Germany from the Black Forest to Augsburg, including most of Württemberg. Once a duchy, Swabia today is not a political unit of any kind: but its people retain a sharp identity, and they tend to be mocked by other Germans for their odd-sounding sing-song accent and ungainly provincial ways. Introduced in the 16th century, the Protestant ethic used to be so strong that dance-halls were forbidden in some areas, and people seen doing house-work on a Sunday might be reported to the police. Today this severity has declined under modern influences, such as the influx of thousands of outsiders, notably Catholics from Silesia. Stuttgart has thus become less Swabian and more tolerant: but in many ways the local character persists. Even more than most Germans, the Swabians are ultra-house-proud, nervous if a cup is left unwashed or a shelf undusted. More than most Germans they have also held on to the old hard-work ethic, which enabled them to build up their famous preci-sion industries with such thoroughness. 'Schaffe, schaffe, Häusle baue' ('work, work and build your little house') is their notorious motto. Fortunes are to be made but not seen, for unlike Bavaria this is a society where to display your wealth is considered bad taste – one millionaire factory-owner kept his big Mercedes at home, used it only for weekend motoring and drove to his office each day in a little Volkswagen because he did not want to show off to his workers. So this is the status-symbol society turned on its head, where money is saved or reinvested and thrift sometimes reaches comic proportions: it is told that the late Robert Bosch, founder-owner of Stuttgart's great electrical firm, would go around his factory picking up stray paperclips and complaining, 'Look how you waste my money!'

There is some fascination in the recurrent contrast between Swa-bians' temperament and life-style and the busy modern surface of their successful and cosmopolitan city, the wealthiest in the EEC. As the capital of the third largest Land, it enjoys quite a political role; it has world-class industries, not only Bosch and Daimler-Benz but Por-sche, Standard Electric Lorenz and German IBM; it has a ballet com-pany of international renown, forty consulates (mostly honorary), restaurants from a score of nations and daily jet flights to the main European centres. Though less metropolitan than Munich, it is all in all quite a place, proud of its world links and happy with its slogan, 'Partner der Welt'. And yet, it is just a big village – thanks to local char-acter, and geography. Within its sprawling borders it produces more wine than any other German commune, and excellent it is too, light and fruity. There are vineyards everywhere, some just a grape's-throw from the main Mercedes factory, where rows of vines climb neatly Swabian-style over the crests of knobbly hills, like newly-combed hair. Many factory workers still own plots of land and are part-time farmers or vine-growers; in some of the city's suburbs you can still find small unmodernised farms, archaically pastoral. Whereas sleek Munich is sharply different from its rural hinterland, in Stuttgart city and country merge into one and there is little difference in spirit between rural Swabia and its bucolic capital.

It is true that parts of the rebuilt downtown area are the usual modern concrete-and-neon jungle of assertive office-blocks, banks and car showrooms. But through-traffic at least has been kept away from the central area, which is now mostly a pedestrian zone around the wide Schlossplatz – here you can walk for almost a mile through the heart of the city and hardly see a car. There is more sense of open space than in central Munich, and the scene is pleasant and relaxed, with open-air cafés, strolling students, modern sculpture and other splashes of colour. Ducks and swans glide on the Schlossgarten lake, in front of the opera house where John Cranko built the ballet company into one of Europe's finest. Nearby is the palatial Neues Schloss where the kings of Württemberg reigned, just across a noisy main road from the Staatsgalerie museum so controversially redesigned by James Stirling. The small and beautiful Schillerplatz, restored after the bombing, glows gently at night under the floodlights, and just beyond is the unbecoming new Rathaus where Rommel, son of the Desert Fox, rules so benignly – 'I became a general quicker than my father', he told me, 'and I fight better wars in a better cause.' Stuttgart's elected 'general' is on the liberal wing of the CDU, governing in easy coalition with the SPD. Ever since the war, there has been a stronger spirit of consensus here in politics than in any other major German city, and virtually no corruption as far as is known. That is one of Swabia's many virtues. Out in the suburbs, the Mercedes factories symbolize another Swabian merit: innovation and application in industry. Beside the spa centre in Bad Canstatt you can see the modest shed where in 1883 Gottlieb Daimler, a local engineer, invented the world's first moving vehicle to use an internal combustion engine. And today Stuttgart, along with the Munich area, is one of Germany's two main centres of high-technology. As much as ever, it makes its money from industry – just as Frankfurt's industry is the making of money.

The city of Frankfurt on the river Main began to be a thriving money market in the 16th century. Then in the 19th it became a major world banking centre, thanks to Rothschild and other financiers, many of them Jewish. Most of the Jews today alas are gone: but the banking remains. This is Germany's commercial capital, site of its main Stock Exchange and of the headquarters of most leading German banks and many insurance and advertising firms. Much of this activity takes place inside one or other of the score or so downtown skyscrapers that have won Frankfurt the nickname of 'Mainhattan' and have made it unique in a Europe where no other city has so many tall office tower-blocks so close together in the centre (the new cluster at La Défense, in Paris, is out on the periphery). Individually these skyscrapers may not be so lovely: but their harmonious grouping is impressive, and some of them are admired by fans of this kind of modern structure – for example, the new 24-storey Deutsche Bank building with its smooth and gleaming blue-grey façade of glass and steel. But the earlier post-war rebuilding was done hurriedly in a very graceless style, as witness the hideous main shopping mall, the Zeil. And the town's general reputation for mercenary brashness has given it a bad name around the world: it is considered soulless, characterless, too materialistic, too Americanised, especially by older people who remember the pre-war Frankfurt with one of the largest and finest mediaeval centres in Europe. But this adverse image is not entirely deserved. Frankfurt may be no beauty: but it has improved greatly in the past 20 years and today is one of Germany's most lively and exciting cities, teeming with new ideas, new ventures and conflicts, and it has a more active and varied cultural life than any other except Munich and Berlin. It may lack the chic and grace of Munich: but it is pleasingly international and has a real metropolitan flavour quite out of scale with its mere 600,000 population. People who come there to live and work are generally surprised to find it so sympathetic – 'It's a very open, modern society,' said one cultivated banker from Berlin, 'much less cliquey than places like Hamburg and Munich. If you arrive from outside, knowing no one, you are rapidly accepted on your merits. People are competitive, even ruthlessly so, but they are also hospitable and open-minded. Yes, it *is* rather American.'

The presence of so much high-level commerce makes Frankfurt a rich city, able to spend lavishly on the arts. And the presence of so many well-to-do bankers and businessmen, by no means all philistines, helps to provide large audiences for 'established' culture. Until 1977 the city was SPD-run: then, like Stuttgart, it acquired a mayor on the liberal wing of the CDU, Walter Wallmann, and he poured money into culture, into new parks, piazzas and other amenities, and into restoring parts of the mediaeval centre around the Römer – all with the additional aim of giving a face-lift to Frankfurt's sorry image. And he was fairly successful. The opera is excellent; so are the attractive and original new museums along the river. The Goethe Haus, where the poet was born and lived for many years, and the cathedral where from 1562 to 1808 the Holy Roman emperors were elected and crowned, both serve to make Frankfurt central to German tradition and history. And today it still plays an important role in German intellectual life. Two of Germany's three most influential dailies are published here – the conservative *Frankfurter Allgemeine Zeitung*, strong on the arts as well as on economics and politics, and the radical *Frankfurter Rundschau*. Several leading publishing houses moved here from Leipzig after the war; here too is the celebrated Book Fair, which alas is such a frenetic hurly-burly that it tends to give visiting British and American publishers a jaundiced and distorted view of the city.

The huge and famous university, with 45,000 students, has won a post-war reputation for Leftism, especially in its philosophy and sociology departments. And this brings us to one of the most blatant features of modern Frankfurt: its noisy political polarisation. Can the reason be that so much successful capitalism, some of it with an ugly face, has served to provide the Left with a target for its opposition and has led to a sharpening of its knives? Certainly left-wing protest since the war has been stronger than anywhere else except West Berlin. The student riots of the late 1960s even began four years sooner in Frankfurt than elsewhere, and since then the discontent has rumbled on, taken up by Greens, anarchists and others. It has led to running battles between demonstrators and police, culminating in the great saga of the campaign against the extension of Frankfurt international airport, Germany's largest (see pp. 426–7).

But the Left in Frankfurt is not simply concerned with agitation. New ideas flourish here too. Danny Cohn-Bendit has been running a Marxist bookshop here. The city has a small Schwabing-like bohemian quarter, across the river in Sachsenhausen, full of jolly pubs. And the 'alternative' cultural and social scene of little fringe theatres, art centres and communes is livelier than in other towns except Berlin. Some of the fringe drama groups are made up of immigrant workers, notably Italians. Frankfurt has proportionately a larger *Gastarbeiter* population, 22 per cent of the total, than any other German city – and this adds colourfully to its diversity, but also to its problems. Drug-trafficking and other crime are at a higher level here than elsewhere. Near the main station is a sizeable red-light district, smaller than Hamburg's St-Pauli but sleazier and more sinister, operated mainly by Greeks, Turks and south Italians. So, warts and all, this is quite a metropolis. It makes Stuttgart, a city of the same size, seem dozily provincial in comparison. It was a great missed opportunity not to make Frankfurt the federal capital.

That role has fallen to Bonn, which still retains its earlier roles too – that of quiet residential centre for well-to-do retired people from nearby Cologne and the Ruhr, and of sedate university town with an old campus right next to the Altstadt. Just to the south, on what used to be open meadowland beside the Rhine, the government quarter has now been tacked on – a series of anonymous modern buildings in side-avenues, all very neat and not at all grandiose, but distinctly suburban in flavour. Compared with the majestic Palace of Westminster or Assemblée Nationale, the Bundestag building could pass for the office of an insurance company in Wimbledon. A mile or so further south is Bad Godesberg, formerly a fashionable spa town, now annexed by Bonn and the home of many embassies and senior diplomats' residences: the British Ambassador has an especially splendid old mansion by the river. Godesberg with its broad leafy avenues has a certain passé charm in a Cheltenham-like way. Some ministries are here, others are in central Bonn or lie scattered out in new suburbs, so that the city today is rather a sprawl. And beside it there flows the broad Rhine, between green hills on either side, crowned by the ruined castles of Godesberg and Drachenfels. It is a pretty setting, and there are pleasant river-walks where you can admire the barges and pleasure-boats. But the climate is dreadful. Humid and enervating, it causes lethargy, liverishness and bad circulation: not the best recipe for dynamic government.

Bonn's essentially provincial atmosphere is still much the same as evoked in *A Small Town in Germany* by John Le Carré who served as a diplomat here. There are four distinct societies – the old residential Bonn, the university milieu, the government people, and the diplomats – and they rarely intermingle except the last two. The formal and stuffy *Regierungsviertel*, though today the best-known aspect of Bonn, is not the only one fortunately; once you get away from it into the older districts, you could be in any friendly and unpretentious Rhineland town, given over to wine-drinking and jolly jokery. The centre of town, quite badly bombed, has been rebuilt in the usual antiseptic style, now a pedestrian zone of narrow streets converging on a market-square where tourists and teenagers loll in open-air cafés and concerts play in summer. Students sit on the grass in the park beside the yellowish main university building, and strains of music float out from the dignified mansions in the old bourgeois streets. It is all quite charming.

But the politicians, bureaucrats and diplomats live and work apart in their own milieu, in an atmosphere described as one of 'hectic boredom'. The senior civil servants have usually been seconded for a few years from their *Land*, so they do not put down roots, and they tend to return to their home town at the weekends, leaving 'official' Bonn deserted and lifeless. As a capital it seems neither purely provisional (which might be more acceptable), nor really permanent either. The Government is not blind to this problem and has tried to make Bonn more cheerful and homelike by lavishing money on the opera and ballet, on art exhibitions and theatre – one June evening in the market square we saw a delightful free show by a *Commedia dell' Arte* troupe from Venice. But despite such efforts Bonn remains artificial, cut off from the authentic life of the country. Foreign journalists posted there often complain how hard they find it to get to grips with the 'real' Germany.

I am scarcely more enthusiastic about the other main Rhineland cities. The two leading ones, Cologne and Düsseldorf, are in intense rivalry with each other, part in jest, part in earnest. Cologne is the

Rhineland's cultural capital, Düsseldorf its commercial capital and the political one too, for the government of North-Rhine-Westphalia is there. The cities are very different in style – 'Cologne,' said one local observer, 'is more open and friendly; rich and poor jostle and chat together in a jolly, democratic way. Düsseldorf is more uptight, status-conscious and *nouveau riche*, and the social classes keep apart.' That was my own impression too.

Central Cologne was exceptionally badly bombed, then rebuilt in a casual jumble of styles. The traffic-jams are worse than in most big German cities; and a few ungainly high-rise blocks have been allowed to mar the view of the cathedral from some angles. The city's overall appearance is not attractive. Yet scattered here and there one finds a number of individually fine buildings, such as the well-restored Romanesque churches, and some pleasant surprises and contrasts, such as Roman remains cheek-by-jowl with graceful new glass-and-steel structures, or modern sculptures and gargoyles in old cobbled streets – notably in the restored ancient quarter by the Rathaus. Above this pot-pourri there soars the cathedral, merciful survivor of the worst of the bombing. Visible for miles across the Rhine plain, its twin black spires dwarf the rest of the city and look magical at night, floodlit in a soft silvery light.

The cathedral is the symbol and badge of local identity for the inhabitants, the Kölner, whose city patriotism is as vibrant as any in Germany. A Münchner, though proud of Munich, considers himself foremost a Bavarian: but the Kölner's loyalty is to Cologne far more than to the Rhineland. Phlegmatic Hamburgers may cherish as strong an attachment to their city: but they do not express it in the same extrovert emotional way as the Kölner, with their endless whimsical joking and songfulness. I was reminded of Italy, of the way that Bolognese or Neapolitans sing and joke about their cities. Indeed, Cologne's city-state mentality seems essentially Italian – hardly surprising, maybe, seeing that this was the Romans' leading colony in what is now Germany, and many traces of their imprint have survived, not only in the Roman ruins but, so it is claimed, in the local people themselves, with their dark looks and lively, Latin-like, rather un-German temperament. More than most other Rhinelanders, the Kölner are lively, gregarious, talkative, fond of their wine and beer, and more than a little vulgar. Their boisterous whimsy finds its fullest expression at Carnival-time (see p. 195). But it goes on all the year too, especially in the big *Kneipe* (pubs) where the locals drink their mild *Kölsch* beer in slim tall cylindrical glasses and are served by the famous Cologne beer-waiters, known as *Köbes*, whose jokey tradition it is to insult and provoke their customers (if a man in a group of three orders three beers, the *Köbes* may reply, 'Three beers, that's very kind – but what will *you* drink'?). It is a quirky cliquey society, much given to in-jokes told in the strange Kölsch dialect that an outsider can hardly follow; many of the stock jokes centre round the city's two mythical comic characters, little rotund Tünnes and tall bowler-hatted Schäl. Some visitors may find it all somewhat tedious; but it is good-natured. And this is a pleasantly informal, somewhat bohemian town, brimming with culture – some excellent museums, the best German TV station for plays and films, and scores of art galleries, for this is the leading German city for art-dealers.

Düsseldorf too is a thriving centre of the art trade, more commercially orientated than Cologne. Here everything breathes money. It is the commercial capital of the nearby Ruhr, and its two tallest skyscrapers house the head offices of two of the main Ruhr steel firms, Thyssen and Mannesmann. This is also, after Frankfurt, the leading centre of international banking and finance in Germany with over two thousand foreign firms including 400 from Japan. The Japanese have made this their main trading centre in Europe, and the resident Japanese colony, 6,000, is the largest outside Japan. This wealthy city has a *per capita* income 25 per cent above the German average, and is said to contain more millionaires and big jewellers than any other. In smart society here, more than anywhere else in Germany, you are judged by your money and how well you display it. This can be observed in the Königsallee, known locally as the 'Kö', a fashionable boulevard where luxury cafés and boutiques face onto a central canal. Here some of the ladies are very chic indeed, but in a brittle, hard-faced, almost frightening style, lacking the gentler grace of Munich. The rest of Düsseldorf is mostly dull and ordinary, save for some parkland walks by the Rhine and a few lively Soho-like streets in the Altstadt with cheap outdoor restaurants. All in all, this is my least favourite of big German cities, and I am not alone in this opinion.

Hamburg, by contrast, is a town warmly liked and admired by almost all those who know it. It may possess some of the drawbacks of a northern climate; but it has an extraordinary spaciousness and serenity, a comfortable, confident red-brick quality, at once mercantile and truly cultured. It is Germany's opposite pole from Munich in the far south, its rival (along with Berlin) as leading metropolis. Whereas baroque and showy Munich recalls Austria, even Italy, Hamburg in looks and ambience has something of an English feel, unhurried and gentlemanly. Unlike Bavarians, its citizens seldom burst into song in public; they are heirs to a great liberal and seafaring tradition. Unlike Munich, capital once of a kingdom and now a large *Land*, Hamburg has always been a self-contained city-state and so it remains: it never ruled over its own hinterland, and so when the modern federal structure was created it was allowed to be a smallish *Land* on its own, covering just 748 square kilometres. In the 13th century it joined the

Hanseatic League of north European trading cities and later became a 'Free and Hanseatic City', a title it still uses. For centuries it was run by its wealthy merchant families who made it immensely influential, the most prosperous of big German towns. Today, its mighty port is in trouble, some of its older industries such as shipbuilding are in decline, and as an economic pace-setter it has been losing out to south Germany. But it still retains much manifest wealth. Bred of its long trading tradition, it still has an open, outward-looking, world-embracing spirit. It is still a most graceful and civilised place.

Water is its element – the huge port, the wide river Elbe, the Alster lake, and the canals. Hamburg holds the world record for bridges – 2,195 of them, compared with London's 850, Venice's 400. No other town in Europe encloses so large a lake right in its centre as the lovely Alster, almost two miles long, the shimmering focus of the city's life. Long-legged Nordic types with capes and scarves go striding along its shore-paths with their bounding, barking dogs, while sails glide against a backdrop of waterside weeping-willows, stately mercantile villas, and the line of spires that are Hamburg's sober skyline. In summer people sit in open-air cafés by the water. In a hard winter, the lake freezes over so firm that cars drive across it: one January in 1985, stalls selling hot *Glühwein* were set up on the ice and 4,000 people flocked there for a party, despite police warnings of disaster.

Hamburg has a tidy symmetrical shape. Its downtown business and shopping area lies neatly between the Alster and the port, bounded by a ring-road that follows the line of the old city walls, while residential and factory districts spread out spaciously beyond. One curious paradox is that, while overall it is a handsome, even beautiful town, it contains hardly any individual buildings of real distinction, either old or new. And this is not just due to the wartime bombing. Long before that, the merchants who built and ruled the city were rather philistine and took little trouble to endow it with fine art treasures, palaces and churches, as did the Wittelsbachs in Munich. They created opulent villas for their own use, but were less concerned with civic splendour. Then in 1842 a great fire destroyed most of the mediaeval nucleus of narrow streets with half-timbered houses, and after this the city was rebuilt on the spacious pattern it still has today. The lavish and pompous Rathaus was erected in 1897 in neo-Renaissance style, its vast interiors and heavy leather furnishings a symbol of the wealth and pride of the city at that time. In 1943, Air Marshal Harris's fire-raids wiped out much of the port and the working-class and factory districts east of the main station: but – a curious if unintended social discrimination – they left almost unscathed the smart bourgeois areas around the Alster and the stately green-roofed buildings that line the smaller Binnenalster in the heart of town.

Post-war reconstruction was better planned and executed than in most German towns devastated on this scale. 'The bombs killed 52,000 civilians, but in one sense were a blessing in disguise,' I was told by the city planning officer, Professor Egbert Kossak, 'for they enabled us to rebuild with much less congestion. Previously, many poorer areas housed 200 to 300 people per acre: now it is 40 to 60 people, and fewer still in the better districts. We have one of the lowest densities of any big European city.' Spacious already, the city has now become even more so. Broad avenues and through-roads have been laid out, where traffic moves easily with an almost total absence of jams. The downtown business area, rebuilt mostly in local red-brick style, is not especially beautiful but lacks the ugly concrete assertiveness of so many German cities. And there are no tall skyscrapers in the centre to mar the graceful skyline of spires. A 25-storey hotel, built in 1968, is at least well away from the inner city where restrictions are now quite strict: 'In 1984 the Springer group wanted to put up an 18-storey block,' said Kossak, 'but we beat them down to nine floors.' In residential areas, one finds streets of brick houses with distinctive Jugendstil wrought-iron balconies, and the odd zany splash of colour from a big modern pop-art mural on a blind wall. Many rebuilt streets still keep their strange ancient names – Ole Hoop, Hopfensack, Dammtordamm.

Today the city is culturally very much alive and has one of the world's finest opera companies, managed by the great Rolf Liebermann (see p. 282). Hamburg is also known as 'Germany's media capital', but this is something of a simplification, for it has no daily paper of the class of those in Frankfurt and Munich. But the TV news programmes are edited here, and so are most of Germany's leading weekly magazines. One of these, *Die Zeit*, typifies the liberal political tradition of this city of free-thinkers that never warmed to Nazism (pro-Hitler rallies were always less enthusiastic here than in other German towns). The merchant class, mainly conservative, has in modern times played little part in governing the city, which has a large working-class population and back in the 1870s was a cradle of German Socialism. Since 1945 this home town of Helmut Schmidt (he was once a senator) has been ruled without a break by the SPD (save in 1953–7). Its governing body is called the Senate, and as it is both a city and a *Land*, the head of the Senate is both Lord Mayor *and* Prime Minister – today, Klaus von Donyani, a pragmatic moderate very much in the Schmidt mould.

The fact of being also a *Land* gives Hamburg a little more autonomy than most German cities – and it is very well governed, with excellent social services, housing and public transport. But the disadvantage is that it is financially unsupported by its hinterland in adjoining Lower Saxony and Schleswig-Holstein, whose citizens can enjoy its cultural and other amenities but pay no taxes to it. What is more, many industrial firms and well-to-do families have been moving outside its borders into the adjacent *Länder* where land prices and other costs tend to be lower. Hamburg's own population has dropped since 1963 from 1,847,000 to 1,640,000, but that of the conurbation has risen to some 2.5 million. This population drift has now finally been halted, so it is claimed, and some younger families are moving back into renovated and subsidised housing in the city centre. But the exodus of industry continues, and this leads to a serious loss of tax revenue. Hamburg is in financial difficulty, and is beset by a series of handicaps, not all of them its own fault. Not only does it suffer from modern German industry's general preference for settling in the south, but its own traditional industries happen to be those most vulnerable to today's trends. Blohm und Voss, leading Hamburg shipbuilders, have been obliged to shed about a third of their former 6,500-strong workforce in the past few years, and they survive only by diversifying into new fields, including the building of tanks for the German army.

A guided boat-trip round the huge port, one of the tourist highlights of the city, is a fascinating but somewhat saddening experience. The visitor is dutifully shown the ultra-modern container terminals and dry docks, the 40 miles of quays, the new 2½-mile-long suspension bridge, and the protection walls built against a recurrence of the 1962 floods that claimed 350 lives. But the port, like many in the world today, is having a tough time. Since 1945 it has lost much of its former natural hinterland to the east, now in the GDR and Poland, which are increasingly using their own ports in the Baltic. It is true that Hamburg has managed to forge privileged links with China, which has made this its main trade base in Europe (there are Chinese boats everywhere): but this is not enough. Hamburg has to struggle to compete with Rotterdam and Antwerp to the west, better situated for the Atlantic trade, and it suffers from EEC tariff regulations that favour road transport to Rotterdam. Today in terms of tonnage handled it is only the fourth port of Europe, below Antwerp and Le Havre, far below Rotterdam. Even so, its traffic has been increasing, from 35 million tons in 1967 to 53 millions in 1984, and this enables many merchants and shipowners to remain very rich: but it does not help the employment situation in the docks. This is because Hamburg, in order to compete with other ports, has built very modern terminals that can load or unload very fast, using few dockers, and this speed suits the big container ships, for harbour dues are high (some 100,000 DM for a 50,000-ton vessel to remain berthed for two days). One union leader said ruefully: 'Twenty years ago the port was busy all night and all weekend with big gangs of dockers working overtime. Now the work is done so fast by just a few men and the port deserted at weekends. No wonder so many dockers are out of work.'

This situation worries the local SPD rulers, in a city where unemployment in 1985 was 12.5 per cent, well above the federal average. Hamburg today is making strenuous efforts to attract new industries, with some success: MBB, the Munich-based aerospace firm, for example, has expanded its local plant where it makes the fuselage for Airbus. But for years after the war Hamburg lived too easily on its reputation, and for this Donyani blames the merchants: 'For so many centuries,' he told me, 'they had success coming out of their ears: they looked down arrogantly on those "peasants" in Munich and didn't feel they needed to compete. Even a mere twenty years ago the city was actually turning down new investment proposals, one of them from Volkswagen, because it felt it did not need them. This absurd attitude is now changing but it takes time.' There are still plenty of rich merchant families around. Like the gentlemen of the City of London, they have a cautious, traditional way of doing things, and they find it undignified to have to use dynamic tactics to go out and 'sell' their city. This mentality is now on the wane. But merchants and SPD city rulers still cooperate too little: it is symbolic that the Rathaus and the Stock Exchange stand back-to-back, facing in opposite directions.

Despite these difficulties, there is still a great deal of wealth in Hamburg, and it can be seen in the streets, where really smart people are almost as numerous as in Munich. Many of the shop-windows too are dazzling, especially in the five big new shopping-arcades near the Binnenalster, among the most stylish and opulent in Europe. All were built since 1979 and are doing quite well despite the mild recession. Hanseviertel and Galleria are the most strikingly beautiful, with domed glass-and-steel roofs. Their specialised boutiques sell things you do not really need, like rare teas, Tiffany lamps, and clothes and toys for cats and dogs, and their window-displays are the height of colourful arty originality – a jeweller's bedecked with broken eggshells, that sort of thing.

The Hamburgers themselves, less flamboyant than their shops, do not flaunt their wealth like the people of Munich or Düsseldorf. Yet in their own way they have great style. Some are the northern blond type, tall and lean, and they stride the streets in a lordly way; sometimes the men wear those blue Hamburg sailor's caps beloved of Helmut Schmidt. Yet there is very little true *Schickeria* or gossip-column café-society. People prefer to entertain discreetly in their own homes. They are affable and helpful to visitors, but they do not make friends easily and their inner social circles are hard to penetrate. There is less easy informality than in British society today – yet the breezy tolerance and understatement of Hamburg has a decidedly

[45]

English feel, and it is well known as the most 'English' of German cities, alike in its looks, habits and mentalities. It remains proud of the close historic trade links: 'When it rains in London, Hamburgers put up their umbrellas,' the saying goes. Repeatedly it reminded me of London – a richer, cleaner, tidier London. And more modern too, even though, paradoxically, the strong English influences and affinities relate mainly to the old pre-war England of claret-drinking, beamed pubs, blue blazers and bespoke tailors. Tall brick Victorian-era mansions, set amid lawns and tall trees, recall London. And out in the straggling suburbs there are echoes of old England, even rural England: beyond Altona, within the city borders you find leafy lanes, old timbered farmsteads, country houses with neat gardens, and you might be in mid-Surrey.

The Elbe is now so polluted that little fresh fish is caught locally. But the famous fish-market on the quayside at St-Pauli survives, and gives a lovely idea of the old traditional Hamburg. It is held every Sunday from 5 to 10 a.m., when it must close promptly under an old bye-law forbidding it to compete with church services. Even on a cold winter morning this huge market is lively and crowded with buyers and sellers of all sorts – a brave sight at break of day, with the seagulls flying and the dinghies bouncing on the choppy water. It is now mainly a food-cum-flea market selling anything from rabbits to pot-plants. But some fish is still sold too – notably by the ebullient 'Eely Dieter' whose loud fast-patter sales line in eels draws the crowds. There are comic Dutch traders too, in clogs and high black hats, and a fruitmonger whose successful sales technique is to pelt his audience with bananas. Late revellers from the nearby night-spots of the Reeperbahn descend on the market in the early hours, blearily sozzled or otherwise sated. Often they make for the big popular Fischer-haus restaurant which does a special early Sunday trade: here, one crisp dawn, in the company of accordionists, tipsy sailors and necking couples in evening dress, I enjoyed a hearty breakfast of beer, soused herring and Hamburg's remarkable eel-plum-and-vegetable soup.

Up the hill is St-Pauli proper and its garish and sleazy main street, the Reeperbahn. This is a curious story. St-Pauli used to be an old fishing-village and working-class district. Then in the later 19th century, when Hamburg's transatlantic passenger trade boomed, a large entertainment district grew up here, most of it quite respectable, to cater for the people waiting often several days for their sailings: there were many theatres, smart restaurants and terrace-cafés with live orchestras, and a few brothels too of the discreet, luxurious kind. In the side-alleys were the sailors' pubs and whorehouses. But times have changed. The liners are gone; even the sailors are few, for they have little time for amusements now that their ships turn round so fast in port. St-Pauli has slipped steadily down-market into the abyss of the sex-and-voyeurism industry, catering mainly for provincial businessmen and foreign tourists. It is true that some vestiges of the older Reeperbahn remain. For example, Café Keese, incongruous amid the sex-parlours – a big, plushy, very decorous dance-hall for genteel pick-ups, mostly middle-aged. But the Star Club in the Grosse Freiheit street, where the still unknown Beatles performed in the early '60s, is today a burnt-out ruin. Nearby are the erotic cabarets, where the live sex act comes in every shape, style and colour; also the brothels of the Herbertstrasse, where the girls display their wares by sitting in wide ground-floor windows in a lurid pink glow. Some worthy Hamburgers are vexed that the city's popular image around the world should have come to be identified with the Reeperbahn. But they make no moves to have its excesses curbed. Hamburg, after all, stands for tolerance.

Germany's other great North Sea port, Bremen, on the river Weser, has no St-Pauli and no Alster; but otherwise it has much in common with its larger rival and neighbour. Like Hamburg it is a Hanseatic free city, very old and very proud, and therefore is likewise allowed to be a *Land* on its own (forming an enclave within Lower Saxony and comprising also the port of Bremerhaven, down on the coast). Like Hamburg, it is a town of seafarers and prosperous merchants, and as at Hamburg the port and shipyards are today in difficulty. Like Hamburg, it has a liberal spirit and strong English connections (there are three daily flights to London). But in some ways the looks and ambience of Bremen are less English than Dutch or Flemish, and this is noticeable especially in the architecture of the tall gabled town houses, and the weather-beaten looks of the men that stride the cob-bled streets – you almost expect them to be wearing clogs.

While Hamburg is somewhat sedate and serious, Bremen has a cheeky quirkiness, a folklorish quality, that I found most appealing. This finds expression in the two curious statues that stand outside the lovely old Gothic Rathaus in the main square – the one, dating from 1404, is a giant 30-foot figure of the knight Roland; the other, entirely modern, is a bronze pyramid of a cock standing on a cat standing on a dog standing on a donkey, and it represents the famous Street Musi-cians of Bremen from the story by the brothers Grimm. Across the square, I was surprised to find a young man in top hat and tails, sweeping rubbish and confetti from the steps of the cathedral, while a group of other young people stood by laughing and throwing down more rubbish: I was told this is an old Bremen custom, whereby a man still unwed by his 30th birthday must perform this ritual, and then marry the first pretty girl who kisses him. Typical Bremen. In another corner of the square, a chorus of men in nautical dress were singing sea-shanties. Then I explored the adjacent Böttcher-strasse, a delightful red-brick shopping arcade built in the 1920s in *art nouveau* style, lined with highly original boutiques selling hand-made toys and assorted ornaments of eccentric but clever design. The Ratskeller under the Rathaus, by tradition, sells no beer but only German wine: it has charming little cubicles for private parties, dating from 1600 – and even in today's age the tradition is still observed that a cubicle's door must be left open if a man and a woman are alone in it.

Not that Bremen today is at all puritan or diehard. It has even acquired the reputation of being one of the most avant-garde and 'Red' of German cities, thanks largely to its new and progressive university (see p. 214). Applied to the city as a whole this Leftist reputation is somewhat unjustified, for its own Socialist leaders, who have controlled the council without a break since 1945, are on the moderate wing of the SPD and pride themselves on having better relations with Bremen's conservative merchants than is the case in Hamburg. 'My council and my merchants run my city in a spirit of great solidarity,' I was told by the extraordinary Hans Koschnick, governing mayor and prime minister from 1967 to 1985 – a large, expansive man, eloquent and flamboyant, demagogic but extremely amiable. He had the kind of self-satirising tongue-in-cheek mock arrogance that is very much commoner in France (he even reminded me of the 'emperor' Paul Bocuse) than in a Germany where most politicians are so boringly decorous. Bremen quirkiness, once more.

'My university has now settled down peacefully,' Koschnick went on, 'and my GDP is still high. But my shipyards have been forced to contract, and my unemployment level has risen to 14 per cent. Some 20 per cent of industrial jobs here used to be in shipbuilding: now it's 8 per cent.' There are other problems too: fisheries have slumped badly, and the port, which formerly grew rich on cotton and coffee imports, is in the same kind of trouble as at Hamburg. The local shipyards, like others in Europe, have been suffering from Japanese and South Korean competition: for many years they also made the mistake of continuing to build large container vessels and tankers for a saturated market, rather than switch in time to more specialised ships. One local firm, AG Weser, closed in 1983. Bremer Vulkan, the largest of all German shipyards, ran into grave trouble about the same time and was forced to shed a third of its workforce. The Thyssen-Bornemisza group, its main owners, lost some 75 million DM in the process and grew so disillusioned with shipbuilding that they sold out 40 per cent of their share, which has now been acquired by the City of Bremen itself. BV is diversifying, and at last seems to be doing better. The German shipbuilding industry as a whole is still the world's third largest, and after a hard period of rationalisation it is now holding its own, but only with the help of large subsidies. As for Bremen itself, it is making an effort to attract new modern replacement industries, in fields such as aerospace and electronics, and with sporadic success. Koschnick himself resigned in June 1985, to move on to politics in Bonn, having sworn to me a month previously: 'I want to stay here in my Rathaus. I'd rather be first in Bremen than fourth or fifth in Bonn. Or rather, I'm second in Bremen – my wife is stronger.'

So ends this tour of the main German cities. It excludes Hanover, the only big German town I have never visited. It also excludes the Ruhr cities – but see pages 77–82. And it excludes Berlin – but that comes next.

Buoyant Berlin, the survivor that came in from the cold

A Berlin senator said to me: 'Many foreigners, especially Americans, think of this as a tight, claustrophobic place, hemmed in behind a high wall, and beyond that nothing but Russians with guns. It's not really like that.' He is right. The first impression one has on touring West Berlin is one of space. It is a spread-out city, and within its wide borders one-third of the area is water and greenery, with big forests and lakes where in summer Berliners go bathing and sailing.

Of course Berlin's situation remains highly unusual. Isolated 120 miles inside East German territory, it depends heavily on financial support from Bonn and is still formally under Allied military rule. But access to and fro along the corridors to the West is today easy, apart from some queueing at checkpoints. As for the Wall that divides the city, West Berliners have grown so used to it that they hardly notice it. Their daily life is normal. Berlin may be somewhat messy and unbeautiful, with much run-down tatty housing, but it teems with vitality, and for many people – myself included – it is the most exciting of German cities. It still retains something of its old capital-city spirit, quick, mercurial, unconventional, and today its society is rather more informal, less conformist and materialistic, than over in the Federal Republic – one reason why so many young people are attracted to come and live in a town that has become the leading German centre of the artistic avant-garde and the 'alternative' scene, a place of cultural innovation, of social mix, sometimes of violence. 'Berlin,' they say, 'lets it all hang out.'

Despite its isolation, it is an integral part of the life of West Germany and plays a major cultural role. It is prosperous too: the glitter and bustle along the Kurfürstendamm, its main avenue, provide some evidence for the fact that living standards are as high as in West Germany itself. In 1958, during one of the city's many crises,

EAST BERLIN

Spree

Wedding

Unter den Linden

Brandenburg Gate

Charlottenburg

Spree

Kurfürstendamm

Kreuzberg

Neukölln

FRENCH SECTOR

BRITISH SECTOR

AMERICAN SECTOR

Havel

Havel

Potsdam

Boundary of Berlin, East and West
East/West Berlin frontier
The Wall
Western military zone boundaries

miles
10

km
15

10

5

5

0

Khrushchev predicted, 'West Berlin will fall into our hands like a rotten apple'. But the apple is still rosy and firm. The economy has even taken an upturn recently. Against all the odds, thanks to Western firmness in times of crisis and to the spirit of its own citizens, Berlin has survived.

The years after the war were extremely difficult ones. In 1945 Berlin was given a special status and placed under the joint authority of the four Allied Powers, each with its own military sector. But it soon became clear that the aim of the Russians was to gain political control of the whole city. After the failure of their blockade in 1948–9, their pressure continued intermittently during the 1950s, and in 1958 Khrushchev issued an ultimatum for the Western Powers to leave the city. The West stood firm, and his threats of a new blockade were never carried out. Instead, in 1961, the Wall was built that sealed the city in two (see p. 368). Not only were East Berliners now denied access to the West, but West Berliners were no longer able to visit friends and relatives in the East, and many families were severed for years. So the 1960s were a sad and lonely time for West Berlin, when it needed all the morale-boosting it could get – it was in this spirit that President Kennedy in June 1963 proclaimed from the balcony of the Rathaus: 'All free men, wherever they may live, are citizens of Berlin. And therefore, as a free man, I take pride in the words, *"Ich bin ein Berliner"*.'

When Willy Brandt began to develop his *Ostpolitik* in the late 1960s, a period of détente emerged. In 1971 the three Western powers succeeded in persuading the Soviet Union to sign a treaty with them that did not alter Berlin's basic legal status but did greatly alleviate its general situation, for the Russians now formally acknowledged the rights of the Western Powers in the city and agreed to accept its close ties with the Federal Republic; travel between Berlin and the West was to be simplified and safeguarded, and West Berliners were again to be allowed to visit the GDR and East Berlin. This agreement has held good ever since then, and by considerably strengthening Berliners' feelings of security it has proved something of a turning point. Companies have become readier to invest in the city, and individuals more willing to settle there. Even so, Berlin remains an anomaly, caught in the time-warp of 1945s conquest and occupation, the most vivid physical symbol of the world's division into two ideological blocs.

One obvious aspect of this is the role of the Western Allied forces. There are some 14,000 of them, each in their own sector: 7,000 Americans in the south, 3,000 French to the north – and 4,000 British in the central sector, using as their headquarters the Nazis' pompous old Sporthalle in Spandau, still decked out with Hitlerian nude strength-through-joy sculptures. A neat cricket-ground separates it from the 1936 Olympic stadium. Legally the Allies are still in Berlin as 'occupiers' under the 1944–5 agreements: in practice, their main role today is to protect the city, which under those agreements can have no defence force of its own. The protection is mainly psychological, for no one doubts that the surrounding Warsaw Pact forces could mop up the city in a few hours, if they chose. But that would start a war. And, as a reminder to the Russians, the Allies scrupulously show their presence: they hold a big annual parade in the Tiergarten, near the Wall, and they go on regular armed patrols in the eastern sector, as they have a right to do, and as the Russians also do in the west – 'Silly games, you might say,' said one British officer, 'but vitally important.' The Allies of course leave the running of the city to its elected government and mayor, and mostly they avoid flaunting their occupying status. But they carefully preserve the protocol of their rights: the American commander, for example, officially plays host to State visitors in his sector, and it is he and not the Berlin police who signs orders banning demonstrations.

The Bonn Government pays in full the cost of the Allied forces (some 1.3 billion DM a year) and it whole-heartedly supports their protective presence, as do both main parties in Berlin, CDU and SPD, as well as the vast majority of Berliners, especially older ones who remember with gratitude the 1948–9 airlift. However, a younger generation has grown up with no such memories, and many of them vocally resent the Allies. The Alternative List group in the Senate, which includes the Greens, wants West Berlin to be neutralised and demilitarised – 'It's an old-style military colony, worse than India under the Raj,' one Green lawyer told me. Probably only 10 to 15 per cent of Berliners hold views of this kind. But a great many others, while glad of the Allies' presence, nonetheless feel that they do some-times exercise their rights too high-handedly. This has become quite an issue in the past few years. Once recently, when the US Army decided to build housing for its personnel in an environmentally pro-tected rural area, opponents of the scheme found they had no legal basis for taking their case to a Berlin court. Much the same happened in 1984 when the British Army began to build a new firing-range in the quiet woodland suburb of Gatow. Local residents found out that the noise levels might be up to five times the federal legal limit. Alarmed, and unable to appeal to any local court, they took their case to the High Court in London, where they sued the Ministry of Defence, but without success. General Gordon-Lennox, the British Commander in Berlin, pleaded: 'I am the rightful successor of Doe-nitz, the last Chancellor of the Third Reich, and I can do what I like.' Berliners were not impressed with his tact.

It is true that the Allies do enjoy huge reserve powers. Of the 6,000 or so military rules that were imposed when Berlin was conquered in 1945, few have been formally revoked. The Allies can still, if they wish, censor Berliners' mail, tap their telephones, or jail anyone who criticises them (one left-wing paper was fined for printing 'Reagan go home' stickers). Firearms are not permitted, nor even knives. The death penalty is still in force (as it is not in the Federal Republic). Once, when I was dining with a mild Berlin housewife (a CDU supporter), she went into her kitchen and returned with a carving-knife: 'For owning this, I could be shot at dawn.' No court would impose such harshness . . . but even so: though the numerous draconian laws are today very rarely enforced, their continuing existence irritates many otherwise moderate Berliners who do not like to be reminded that they are still 'occupied'. Sensitive to this resentment, the Allies have gradually been lifting some of the rules, including one that allowed the death penalty for children. Clearly they need to be highly discreet about their special powers, in this age of détente and normalisation. Nonetheless, they argue that for them to alter their legal position in Berlin too blatantly would provide the Russians with an alibi for causing difficulties – and avoidance of this is still the West's main concern.

This also explains why West Berlin has never been made fully part of the Federal Republic. An official in Bonn summed this up for me: 'The Russians and East Germans have cheated, by integrating East Berlin totally into the GDR and making it the capital. This contrary to the 1944–5 agreements, which are still in force and lay down that all Berlin is a single unit. But if the Russians cheat, that is no reason why we should do so too. Berlin is still vulnerable, so we should avoid any provocation. Also, we need to remain in the stronger legal position, against the day when we might want to negotiate a reunification of Germany with Berlin as a capital.' In the meantime, West Berlin has no sovereignty and legally belongs to no one. It has a peculiar role in Bonn, for the deputies it sends to the Bundestag are not directly elected but mandated by the Berlin Parliament, and they cannot take part in votes in either the Bundestag or the Bundesrat. Berlin citizens cannot appeal to the Karlsruhe Court, they have special passports, and they are not called up for military service. Lufthansa and the other West German airlines do not fly to Berlin, which is served exclusively by the Allied airlines such as Pan Am: this is because the Allies want to retain their rights under the 1945 and 1971 agreements such as that of being guarantors of the air corridors to the city.

These limitations have little effect on daily life; and in all other respects, economically and culturally, Berlin is fully a part of West Germany. It is the home of over 60 federal institutions, and even the President of the Republic has an official residence there. It is governed as a city-*Land* in much the same way as Hamburg, with a

Parliament that elects a Senate, and a governing mayor who is on a par with the prime ministers of the other *Länder*. The SPD was the ruling party until 1981 (Brandt was mayor in 1957–66) and since then it has been the CDU. Government generally works smoothly, save that it has sometimes been marred by corruption scandals involving alleged attempts by property developers to bribe senators and officials: in 1986 this led to the resignation of three CDU senators. Observers also note that Berliners' latent insecurity, bred of hard times, still tends to show itself in their dislike of politicians who 'desert' them. Richard von Weizsäcker, not himself a Berliner, became CDU mayor in 1981 and promised that he would always devote himself to the city. He proved a very good mayor. But he did spend rather a lot of his time travelling; and when in 1981 he opted to stand for the Federal Presidency, and was elected Berliners, instead of feeling proud of this great honour for their mayor, complained that he had betrayed them. His successor, Eberhard Diepgen, also CDU, was elected on the slogan, *'Einer von uns'* ('one of us' – he *is* a Berliner).

The sense of insecurity in the post-war decades was fuelled by fears that, even if the Russians left it alone, this city cut off from its natural hinterland could not continue to survive economically. Just after the war several major firms, notably Siemens and AEG, moved their headquarters to West Germany, leaving behind only their manufacturing plant, or parts of it. German companies were reluctant to invest in Berlin, so the city failed to share fully in the *Wirtschaftswunder*. It came to depend heavily on subsidies from Bonn, as it still does today. 'Without these,' I was told by Günter Rexrodt, Senator for the Economy, 'I think Berlin would have collapsed in the 'fifties or 'sixties. Before the war, more than half of its revenue came from its functions as capital. Now it has to rely largely on industry – in fact it is still the leading industrial town in Germany, in terms of jobs.' Today over 52 per cent of the city's budget, or 13.5 billion DM in 1985, comes from subsidies and other aid from the Federal Government, paid for by the West German taxpayer. Among the various incentives to industry, manufacturers can benefit from a 'turnover bonus' of up to 10 per cent, while a new investor can write off 75 per cent of his initial overheads.

For some years these inducements had no great effect. But matters began to improve after the 1971 agreement with Russia, which gave renewed confidence in Berlin's future alike to its own citizens and to outside investors. Today the industrial decline seems to have been averted and new firms are moving in. Whereas in the 1960s the number of industrial enterprise dropped by a third, in 1981–5 some 2,000 new firms were set up, 200 of them in high-technology, and in 1984 more manufacturing jobs were created than lost; for the first time for many years, Nixdorf, the successful computer firm, was in 1985 building a new plant, to provide 6,000 jobs; Siemens, still the city's largest industrial employer (20,000 staff), was also planning an expansion. In 1984 Berlin's growth rate (2.9 per cent) was ahead of that of West Germany as a whole (2.6 per cent).

The strategy today is to develop Berlin as a centre of high-technology, suitable for the kind of modern firm that does not depend on bulky transport of heavy goods, where the city is so obviously handicapped. This policy was begun in the Helmut Schmidt era, and more recently was enthusiastically promoted by mayor von Weizsäcker. It is today bearing some fruit – witness the new investments. Amid much publicity, a Centre of Innovation and New Enterprises has been set up in a huge old red-brick AEG factory building near the Wall, in Wedding: known by its cryptic initials, BIG, the aim of this ambitious project is precisely to help and encourage small entrepreneurs working in such fields as robotics and to promote close R&D collaboration, of a kind still uncommon in Germany, between these little firms and scientists and professors at Berlin's universities (see p. 98). 'Berlin', one local scientist told me, 'is well suited as a centre of high-technology and innovation. We have a strong tradition of this, dating back to the *Gründerzeit*, the "foundation period" of industrial boom in the late 19th century. The only drawback is the Allied ban on all military output and research in Berlin, and this could be a problem, because so much high-tech has possible military applications.'

So Berlin today is exploiting its brains in order to survive: grey matter has always been a major asset of this capital city. Its mood is now more optimistic than at any time since the war. But the demographic situation, though improved, remains preoccupying. In the post-war decades there was a steady emigration of people, especially the more youthful and ambitious, who felt understandably that long-term prospects were brighter over in the Federal Republic. The city's human resources were draining away. Its population, 2.1 million in 1949, was then swollen artificially by the refugees from the GDR, and had risen to 2.3 million by the time the Wall was built: but it has since fallen steadily, to 1,964,000 in 1985.[1] The net emigration has now slowed down: but Berlin's population is not being replenished by arrivals from its rural hinterland, as is usual in big cities: and more Berliners die each year than are born, as the German birth-rate is so low. The age-pyramid is significant: the over-65-year-olds account for 23 per cent of the population, against a federal average of 15 per cent,

---

[1] East Berlin's population is 1,160,000. The whole city before the war had 4,300,000 people.

while for the under-15-year-olds the comparative figures are exactly the reverse.

The Federal Government has been seeking to remedy this situation, through inducements for people of working age to stay or settle. Personal income tax is 30 per cent lower than in the Republic; and an 8 per cent bonus on all wages has served to push Berliners' incomes to a level 4 per cent above the federal average. So this is anything but a poor city (unemployment, 10.5 per cent in 1985, is only slightly above average). The effect of these inducements is hard to judge: possibly they have not done so much to reduce the population drift as the generally improved climate since 1971, plus the fact that the absence of military service has enticed some 20,000 young draft-dodgers into the city from the Federal Republic. All in all, some 15,000 more people are still leaving the city each year than arrive to live in it; and, if the total population is now holding steady, it is thanks to the very high birth-rate among the Turkish immigrant community of 118,000. However, matters may now at last be improving, as ordinary middle-class families become more prepared to settle or return. A well-placed civil servant suggested to me in 1985: 'Five years ago, when I took up this job here and moved with my family from the Ruhr, our friends there thought we were crazy to sell our house and buy one here in Berlin. But at last more people like us are doing just this, and are buying property. They no longer feel it is such a risk.'

Apart from one or two scattered buildings such as the Reichstag and Charlottenburg Palace, there is little left physically in West Berlin that suggests a great capital city. The old heart of the city, the former government and business district around the Unter den Linden, is over beyond the Wall. In the west, the main focus now is the Kurfürstendamm, a broad avenue of cafés and hotels, shops and cinemas, which was previously the 'West End' entertainment area, well away from the true centre. This Ku'damm (as Berliners call it) and the streets around it are still today the main amusement and shopping district, offering the brash but intriguing spectacle of neon-lit signs, pop-art street decorations and pleasure-bent motley crowds. The grace and dignity of a capital, or of a town like Munich, are markedly absent. And yet, there is something in the air, something hard to define, that still sets Berlin apart . . . You notice it at once, coming from Munich or Hamburg, cities more handsome but somehow less metropolitan. Berlin still stays open very late, more so than most North European towns: at 2 a.m. the Ku'damm is thick with crowds and cars, its cafés and eateries full. And all day long the people in the main boulevards are a strange mixture, relatively few of them in normal city dress – coxcomb punks and camera-clutching tourists, bohemian students and trendy mannequins, and wizened old bourgeois ladies in flowery hats.

Talk to native Berliners, and you find they still preserve something of that sharp, sardonic, restless big-capital-city quality that gives them, temperamentally, more in common with a Parisian or New Yorker than, say, with a Hamburger. Gordon Craig in *The Germans* has summed it up historically: 'Berliners tended to be energetic ebullient, colourful in their speech, quick at repartee . . . and in time of trouble courageous. They gave the impression of being in perpetual motion.' Visitors are often impressed by Berliners' facility with words, their sense of irony, and their quickness of response. In a theatre, they laugh at the jokes more rapidly than in other cities; and I even have the impression, though I have never checked, that the traffic-lights change more frequently than elsewhere, perhaps because Berlin pedestrians would never accept to wait patiently for green like most other Germans! As for their droll sense of humour, this is noticeable in the nicknames they have given to many of their post-war buildings. Thus the lopsided Kongresshalle in the Tiergarten is known as 'the Pregnant Oyster', or else as 'Jimmy Carter's Grin' because of its façade like an open mouth. The Philharmonic Hall with its tent-like roof is dubbed 'Zirkus Karajani' (Sarassani is the best-known German touring circus). And Berlin's most famous landmark, the gaunt Memorial Church at the top of the Ku'damm, preserved as a ruin, is 'the gaping Tooth', while the new church buildings beside it are 'the Powder-Box' and 'the Lipstick Tube'.

Berlin has little of a *Schickeria* set. New arrivals soon discover that the upper ranks of society are remarkably fluid, informal and uncompartmentalised. 'If I go to a big party,' said one businessman, 'I can expect to find not only my own colleagues but actresses, Allied officers, avant-garde sculptors, CDU politicians . . . That's common in London but much less so in Germany.' Perhaps one explanation is that Berlin for so long has been a melting-pot with a tradition of assimilating all sorts; or else that Berliners, despite their differing views and the usual Left/Right tensions, still feel an underlying sense of solidarity, born of the hard siege years. When I told one CDU senator that I was going to visit the hippy leader of an 'alternative' commune, the UFA-Fabrik, he said, 'Ah yes, my good friend Yupi – do give him my regards.' Though the alternative scene is strongest in the Kreuzberg district (see below), it seeps out across the rest of the city too, so that in many areas you see as many bohemian-looking people as smart ones (and also rather a large number of sad, broken-looking older ones, shuffling along, survivors of the 1940s nightmares). Values in Berlin are less materialistic than in the Federal Republic. There is a pleasantly unconventional ambience, noticeable especially in the many arty *Kneipe*; some of the best are in the Savignyplatz area north of the Ku'damm, for example, Zillemarkt and Dicke Wirtin.

Culture thrives, generously subsidised by Bonn and the city Senate whose objectives are in part to help Berlin's trade by means of promoting its image: the big new summer arts festival was expressly the brainchild of the Senator for the Economy. 'Our aim,' I was told at the Rathaus, 'is for Berlin to remain the cultural capital of the German-speaking world.' Whether it quite manages to fill this role is not certain, for Munich too is important in a different style – and what about Vienna? But culture at the higher level is certainly impressive. The Berlin Philharmonic under von Karajan is one of the world's finest orchestras; the Schaubühne during the years of Peter Stein's direction has been one of Europe's most brilliant theatre companies (see p. 276); and all the year there are festivals, seminars, international meetings of scholars. A group of museums in the suburb of Dahlem houses the distinguished art treasures of the Prussian Cultural Foundation, the heritage of the Prussian kings. During the war the Nazis removed these collections from Berlin and scattered them around Germany where they were confiscated by the Americans and Russians. In the 1950s these two Powers agreed each to give back its own share of this loot to 'its' Germans. So some of the treasures are now in East Berlin, while the rest, the major part, was inherited by the Federal Republic. A strong lobby in Bonn wanted this divided up between the *Länder*. But the view prevailed that it should all go back to Berlin, in line with the policy of helping the beleaguered city. At a time when Berlin's future looked so precarious, this was a courageous decision.

Only a tiny proportion of the cultural subsidies goes to helping the alternative, avant-garde and pop scenes. It is hard to generalise about a world so diffuse and kaleidoscopic, but probably it is fair to say that this scene, though livelier and more creative than in other German cities, is much less rich and varied than in New York or maybe London. But Berlin is Europe's rock capital, with over 200 rock groups, some of them officially funded. There are countless little way-out art galleries, a few struggling fringe theatres, innumerable 'happenings' of all sorts, and an extraordinary modern art centre in Kreuzberg, the Haus Bethanien, housed in a gigantic neo-Castilian ex-hospital near the Wall.

Berlin also remains Germany's gay capital, a role it has held since the last century (except under the Nazis, who persecuted homosexuals). A leading figure in this world is the film-maker who calls himself Rosa von Praunheim (see p. 297): he has depicted it vividly in his film about American gays and transvestites in Berlin, *City of Lost Souls*. I met him when he was preparing a festival to raise money for Berlin's estimated 15,000 AIDS victims: 'Yes, the gay scene has developed a lot in the past ten years or so, though it's still far smaller and duller than in New York where I used to live. But I don't care much for the social round of Berlin's sub-culture, I prefer a quiet life.

As in Munich, there's a lot of false glamour here – a phoney anti-elegant punk glamour, just as Munich has a phoney elegant glamour. Young people come to Berlin from other cities, seeking something they don't really find.'

There are reckoned to be well over 100,000 people attached to Berlin's various contrasting sub-cultures, living on the margins of 'normal' society – dedicated idealists trying to build an alternative economy around small cooperatives and communes; bohemian artists and intellectuals; punks, drop-outs, drug-addicts and other ne'er-do-wells. The majority have come to Berlin from elsewhere. Some have been drawn by its tradition as a city of permissiveness and experiment, or by the 'glamour' von Praunheim spoke of, or by the chance to avoid military service, or by the good prospects (at least recently) of finding very cheap or derelict housing near the Wall. Together these factors have had a multiplier effect, drawing others in turn, especially to Kreuzberg which the 'alternative' scene has made its citadel. This is a sizeable district of central Berlin, adjacent to the Wall, full of old tenement blocks and other mixed turn-of-the-century housing, much of it today extremely run-down. In the 1960s Turkish immigrant workers settled here in large numbers with their families, and they now make up 25 per cent of the population. The 'alternatives' co-exist easily with the Turks (see p. 245).

An abandoned factory, known as Mehringhof, has been taken over by a network of some 30 small cooperatives of all kinds and is dubbed 'the Alternative Rathaus'. It has vegetarian stores, a bicycle shop, a sort-of theatre, a sort-of publishing house, a kindergarten run by parents. This is one focal point of an excitingly varied Kreuzberg scene that is rich in romantic squalor and quirky self-expression. Provocation graffiti abound – 'Raus mit dem Schweine-Schwanz System' (away with the swinish penis system) scrawled by feminists at the entrance to an old ballroom offering tango and swing sessions; slogans in support of Nicaragua and extreme-Left terrorists daubed on the doorways of fancy new blocks of expensive flats beside a tree-lined canal (not all of Kreuzberg is a slum). Blackened bomb-scarred buildings stand next to bright pop-art façades newly painted by squatters. Turkish women in scarves squat on the steps of a neo-Byzantine church. Nearby, sinister black-jacketed punks hang out around the Kottbusser Tor, while drugged weirdies and drop-outs of the saddest kind haunt the night-bars of the Oranienstrasse.

In the late 1970s the presence of a great deal of empty tenement housing enticed squatters to descend in force on Kreuzberg and some other areas.[1] When the police began to evict them, their cause was

---

[1] For a fuller picture of Berlin's alternative scene and the squatters, see pp. 437–41.

backed by various violent extremist groups who arrived from as far afield as Holland and Switzerland. There were riots and pitched battles and militant window-smashing, car-upturning raids on the Ku'damm area. All this gave the city very bad publicity, just when it was trying so hard to attract new business. Finally in 1981–2 the crisis was resolved: the squatters were removed, or legalised and allowed to stay, and the fanatics departed. Calm and confidence returned: this was a major reason for the brighter economic mood and the surge of new investment after 1983. On my own visits to Berlin in 1985, I was surprised to find political tensions very much milder than I had been led to expect by the city's reputation. 'We may not care much for the *Alternative*,' said one CDU politician, 'but, so long as they do not behave violently, we recognise that they add spice and colour to the city's life and thus are good for tourism.' In parliament, relations are sometimes so relaxed that CDU deputies have been known to tease their Alternative List colleagues by putting flowers on their desks.

Physically as well as socially, Berlin is something of a jumble. Of course it has its share of well-to-do residential districts with big villas set in gardens, such as Dahlem and Grunewald.[1] But much of the rest of the city looks rather tatty. This is not so surprising, for it was worse bombed than any others except Dresden and maybe Cologne, and was then rebuilt under exceptionally difficult conditions, since most of the heavy construction material had to be specially imported from the West. Not only were costs therefore high, but money was short, for few private developers felt inclined to invest in Berlin in those anxious days. Much of the earlier post-war building has a cheap and tawdry air – as compared, say, with Frankfurt, where it is just as ugly but at least looks solid. And Berlin still suffers as well as from an earlier legacy of bad housing. As a big city it is relatively young: in 1871 its population was only 900,000, but there followed a period of hectic expansion, with numbers more than doubling to reach 1.9 million by 1890. Peasant families poured in to provide a workforce for the new industries, and were housed by none-too-scrupulous authorities in huge apartment blocks, hurriedly built with minimal sanitation and plumbing, in poorer districts such as Wedding, Kreuzberg and Neu-kölln. The teeming life of these tenements, where children played in the dark, dank inner courtyards, has been poignantly portrayed by

---

[1] These are west of the centre. In Berlin in the old days, as in London and Paris, the smarter residential suburbs were developed to the west, not the east, so as to escape the soot and smoke from industry carried by the prevailing westerly winds. For the well-to-do, this has accidentally brought another blessing, now that the city is divided; it has preserved their freedom.

Heinrich Zille in his satirical sketches of the 1900–14 period. Strangely enough, much of this housing survived the bombing. And since then, for various economic and legal reasons, little of it has been renovated or replaced: many blocks have absentee landlords, including Jews who left for America in the 1930s, while other owners, whether public or private, have been deterred from making improvements by the heavily controlled rents. The slums may provide useful shelter for Turks, squatters and others, but they are a disgrace for the biggest city of a wealthy country where housing standards are elsewhere so high. However the city rulers are now at last making widespread improvements. The Hansa Quarter on the edge of the Tiergarten was created back in the 1950s as a pilot venture in modern-style housing, much admired by architectural critics at the time. It has now been followed by other new estates and by the overdue renovation of tenements. Gradually Berlin is emerging from the scars not just of war but of post-war.

At least, by a kind of paradox, this walled-in city enjoys spaciousness, for its 19th-century expansion followed a generous grid pattern of broad streets and avenues: in this respect it is truly a city of northern Europe, in contrast to Munich, the Rhineland or any congested Mediterranean town. And the loss of over a quarter of its pre-1939 population has had the incidental advantage of providing even greater elbow-room. Moreover, the 1945 division of the city fortunately preserved its existing wide external boundaries. Go today to the western outskirts, around Spandau, Gatow, and Wannsee, and you find not only great forests and lakes but pastoral woodlands and gentle landscapes with meadows and cottages – you might almost be in Constable's Suffolk. Of all West German registered pleasure-boats, no less than half are moored in Berlin. And in the tiny village of Lubars, on the northern edge, I visited a quaint old pub amidst farmland – a scene unchanged in this century, save for the Wall and its stern watchtowers at the far end of the field.

Berliners themselves may have grown used to the Wall, but it haunts the consciousness of a visitor to the city. It remains Europe's most powerful visual symbol of the post-war ideological struggle and the sufferings this has caused. Also, because large areas adjacent to it on both sides have deliberately never been rebuilt, the Wall provides one of the sharpest reminders of Germany's war-time devastation which in the Federal Republic itself has by now been everywhere tidied out of sight. One of the strangest and most disturbing parts of West Berlin is the stretch close to the Wall between the Tiergarten and Check Point Charlie, on the western edge of Kreuzberg. This used to be the very core of the busy city: the Potsdamer Platz, now an empty zone dissected by the Wall, was the equivalent of Piccadilly Circus. Today this whole area on the west side is a strange lunar landscape, some of it pure wasteland, partially covered by shacks, rubbish dumps and parking lots. Here and there a few old buildings survive as ruins, such as the grim blackened façade of the former Anhalter railway terminus. In contrast, one sector close to the Potsdamer Platz *has* been properly replanned and endowed with major cultural buildings; here are the National Library and Philharmonic Hall (1963), both designed by Sharoun, and the National Gallery (1968), the work of Mies van der Rohe. But eastwards there stretches a messy jumble, enlivened here and there by giant brightly-coloured pop-art murals on blind walls. The skyscraper of the Axel Springer newspaper group towers defiantly above the Wall as a beacon of 'freedom' (see p. 316); nearby, a rather different message is conveyed by a notice on a patch of waste ground: 'Here were the former torture chambers of the Gestapo.' There are several reasons why this whole area has been left unrenovated for so long; Berliners, it was felt, would not want to live or work so close to the Wall; hopes lingered of a reunified city that could be jointly replanned with the East; and in some cases the bombed spaces belonged to Jewish families who had long departed but might yet want to stake a claim. Today, however, the city is finally planning a large-scale renewal. New city law courts are to be built here, and a museum of history as well as offices, exhibition centres, schools and even flats – 'No one wants to live near the Wall if the area is an ugly mess,' one senator told me, 'but if it is made lively and attractive, then people will no longer object. Of this we are certain.'

Though horrifying in all that it stands for, the Wall is nothing special to look at. Only 12 feet high, made of whitish concrete topped not with barbed wire but with a concrete bulge that affords no grip, it curves and zig-zags for 75 miles across and around the city, following the old ward boundaries. In Kreuzberg, unknown artists have cheekily daubed it with psychodelic frescoes, and everywhere along the Western side it is inscribed with graffiti in various languages, political, comic or erotic – 'Fighting for German unity is like fucking for virginity' (written in English) is one of my favourites. 'What are you gawping at, haven't you seen a wall before?' is another, and, 'Darling, we love each other – why worry about the Wall?' In central Berlin the Wall has become a major tourist attraction. From observation platforms you can peer over into the East and see daily life going on – same people, same language, same buildings, same city, yet a totally alien world, just 100 metres away.

Here and there, little crosses stand as sad memorials to those shot dead while trying to escape. At the Bernauerstrasse in Wedding, the 1945 demarcation line was drawn down the middle of the street. When in August 1961 militiamen began to build the Wall here, they bricked up the ground-floor doors and windows of the houses on the east side, but a few people managed to jump to freedom from upper floors. Some died in the process, including Olga Segler, aged 80, whose cross now stands there. From this point the Wall winds along to the old Reichstag whose mighty grey hulk stands just on the Western side: it is still used for some Bund ceremonies. Next, where the Wall curves round the Brandenburger Tor in East Berlin, its concrete blocks have been specially thickened and strengthened to prevent any East German or Soviet tanks from trying to make a dash to the West during the military parades that are held here.

Next to Checkpoint Charlie, in Kreuzberg, there is a fascinating little privately-run museum devoted to the history of post-war Berlin to the Wall and the various escapes and attempted escapes. It includes souvenirs and documents relating to getaways by tunnelling, by balloon, by diving-machine, and in tiny cars or in suitcases fitted together. The most extraordinary story is of a young man in West Berlin whom the building of the Wall had separated from his wife, an East Berliner. She was not allowed to join him. But in West Berlin he managed to find a girl who looked very similar; so he courted her and persuaded her to come with him to the East on a day trip. Here he seized her identity papers, and then hurried round to his wife and easily brought her with him to the West. The poor robbed girl went to the East German police, but she could not prove her identity, and they refused to believe her story. She spent two months in jail and was released only with the help of Western Press publicity. The young man was then put on trial in West Berlin and given seven months in prison for 'damaging human freedom'. But he had won his wife back, the other girl too was free, so all lived happily. Was his venture morally justified? Perhaps it was.

That was in the hard days of the 1960s when contacts between the two halves of the city were not at all easy. Since 1971 the restrictions have been lightened and West Berliners can now easily obtain permits to visit East Berlin or the rest of the GDR for up to 30 days a year (see p. 368). Like other visitors from the West, they have to exchange a minimum of 25 DM per day, and this falls heavily on those who still have close relatives in East Berlin (an estimated 250,000) and would like to visit them frequently.

As for official exchanges, despite the close contacts nowadays between the East and West German Governments, at the local level there are very few ceremonial or personal relations between the ruling bodies of the two cities: the Mayor of the West does not go to the East's parties, nor vice versa. This is inevitable, given the odd legal status of the city. However, discreet regular contacts do of necessity take place on some technical matters, such as water supplies, sewage and industrial effluent; and in 1985–6 a joint working party was quietly consulting on how to avoid clashes in the programmes for the city's 750th anniversary in 1987, which the two Berlins were due to celebrate quite separately.

In most material matters except for basic access, West Berlin manages to avoid dependence on the East: but this has not proved so easy in the case of rail transport. Berlin's complex U-Bahn (metro) system was sliced in two when the city was divided; but today there is still one Western U-Bahn line that transits under East Berlin, passing through ghost stations on its way from Kreuzberg to Wedding via the Friedrichstrasse, the East's main entry point by rail. A more serious problem was posed by the above-ground suburban railway network, the S-Bahn; and the wrangles over this have typified the legal absurdities of Berlin's situation. As the S-Bahn belonged not to the city (like the U-Bahn) but to the former German State Railways, the Reichsbahn, the Allies after the war did not allow West Berlin to take over its 110 miles of track in the West. Instead the entire network continued to be operated by the GDR, which had inherited the parts of the Reichsbahn in Eastern Germany. But this was hardly very practical. And after 1961, to give vent to their fury about the building of the Wall, the citizens of West Berlin began a spontaneous boycott of the S-Bahn. They were encouraged in this by the city authorities, who laid special parallel bus lines to reduce the inconvenience that their gesture was causing them. So the GDR lost most of its revenue from the S-Bahn in the West, whose stations and track became more and more decrepit. The GDR was anxious to sell; and West Berlin, after some hesitations, finally became ready to buy. But the protocol-conscious Western Allies objected that the sale would not be entirely legal; and the Soviet Union for its part did not like the idea of its ally giving up this possibly useful little foothold in the West. Finally West Berlin managed to overcome these objections, and after long negotiations it acquired its share of the S-Bahn in 1983. Some of the old *art nouveau* stations, much dilapidated, are now gradually being restored to their original 19th-century splendour, and closed lines are being reopened.

And so West Berlin survives – by ingenuity, patience and persistence. 'Of course its situation is absurd,' said a senior British diplomat, 'and everyone keeps saying, "this can't last". But why *shouldn't* it last? Who has an interest in changing the status quo? It suits even the Russians in a way.' Indeed so. The crowds on the Ku'damm, or in Kreuzberg, or by the Havel lakes in summer, do not look as if they are living on borrowed time or on the edge of a precipice. And, of the many Berliners I met in 1985, a very large number said to me, in so many words: 'Despite all its difficulties, this city is now more happy, calm, stable and confident than at any time since 1945 – or indeed 1914.'

The Bund *and the* Länder: *how and why federalism works*

In the large and elegant spa town of Wiesbaden, capital of Hessen, the *Land* government and parliament today inhabit the sumptuous former palace of the Dukes of Nassau, all gilt chandeliers and painted ceiling. Here one day in 1985 I attended a session of the *Landtag* (parliament). Amid repeated heckling, CDU and Green orators were engaged in sharp debate about a local nuclear power station; then CDU and SPD crossed swords over the *Land*'s policy on primary schools. Some CDU deputies were quietly reading *Bild Zeitung*; a young Green left her seat to go and flirt gently with an elderly SPD man; behind the Speaker's platform stretched a big tapestry of the ancient Lion of Hessen. All was lively and informal. The *Landtag*'s Americanised young PRO told me that so popular are its debates with the public that seats in the visitors' gallery need to be booked months ahead; I saw several parties of schoolchildren there, and a contingent of *Bundeswehr* conscripts.

The scene may have changed since Nassau days – and so have Hessen's boundaries, for the modern *Land* is composed of several former autonomous states of the old German Confederation, one of them the dukedom of Nassau. But in a town such as Wiesbaden it is easy to see how very much today's federal system is the inheritor of an age-old German tradition. Federalism comes naturally to the Germans, who find it perfectly normal to elect one parliament in Bonn and another in their *Land*; and, although the Constitution sets precise limits on a Land's autonomy, its government is nonetheless a potent reality to its citizens, and is headed by a *Ministerpräsident* (prime minister) who is always a local figure of some power. Some of these men play a major role simultaneously both in their *Land* and in Bonn, though they do not hold ministerial office in both at once. Franz-Josef Strauss, a senior minister in Bonn in the 1960s, is now Prime Minister of Bavaria: but as chairman of the CSU he continues to wield great influence in federal politics. Some other prime ministers prefer to devote themselves mainly to their land, yet they always have some voice in Bonn too through their membership of the *Bundesrat* (see below). In Baden-Württemberg, Lothar Späth has had a brilliant career, becoming Prime Minister in 1978 at the age of 41; and, although by 1986 he was being tipped as a possible future CDU Chancellor, he had never sought to become first a federal minister, but had chosen to identify himself with his *Land*. Indeed it is sometimes argued that too much of the best talent tends to stay in the *Länder*, and the quality of Bonn politics suffers accordingly.

Each *Land* has its own sizeable office in Bonn, the *Vertretung* (representation), which acts as a kind of embassy and is headed by a man with the rank of *Land* minister: here it defends its interests by

[65]

lobbying the Federal Government and trying to influence its policies. At Baden-Württemberg's *Vertretung*, which has a staff of 40, I was told: 'Before 1918, the German dukes and kings each sent a representative to the court of the Emperor in Berlin: our office there was the *Vertretung der Könige von Württemberg*. And that system continues. Federal Canada has a somewhat similar one, but not the United States.' Bonn, on the other hand, has no representative offices in the *Länder*, nothing at all resembling the *préfectures* in France. In Bonn, each *Vertretung* entertains lavishly, rather like an embassy, and vies with the others to stage the best parties or hold the finest concerts. Bavaria's 'embassy', close to the *Bundestag*, has a big beer-cellar in its basement where Bavarian-style parties are held nearly every night – I attended one, to mark some anniversary, and found it packed with people in local costume, swaying to and fro with their foaming tankards as a brass band played. It could have been the Hofbräuhaus. 'We're on foreign soil here,' said one beefy typist, 'so we have to show the flag.' Scots, I felt, might be envious: might it not be nice to have some wee bagpipe-filled corner of Scotland in the heart of Westminster?

Who calls the tune, the Federal Government (*Bund*) or the *Länder*? The share-out of responsibilities between them is a complex business. Under the Constitution, the *Länder* have competence in all matters except those that it has expressly assigned to the *Bund*, and these include, principally, foreign affairs, defence, currency, post and telecommunications, and railways. The *Länder* in turn have almost exclusive responsibility for cultural affairs, education, radio and television, police, environment, and local government and planning. Then there exists a third sector, the so-called 'concurrent tasks', where the Constitution allows the *Bund* a prior right to legislate, leaving the *Länder* to do so where it has not taken up its option: this field includes civil and criminal law, labour law, road traffic, and a number of economic matters. In practice the *Bund* nearly always does exercise its right, so a *Land*'s effective legislative role is limited. However, the *Länder* in many cases have the task of administrating federal laws within their borders, and a Land is often able to take its own decisions within the broad framework of a *Bund* law. Thus, for example, the *Bund* lays down the overall policy regarding nuclear power, but a *Land* has the right to ban or authorise any nuclear plant on its territory.

Bund and *Länder* derive their incomes from taxes divided between them under a complex set of rules. In a word, personal income tax and corporation tax are shared out fifty-fifty, while the proceeds of turnover taxes go two-thirds to the *Bund* and one-third to the *Länder*. Some tax revenue is passed on to the cities and other local authorities, who also levy their own taxes (see below). All tax legislation is formulated by the *Bund* and applies uniformly throughout the country, so as to avoid imbalances in the tax burden. What is more, since some *Länder* are richer than others and therefore derive more from local taxes, there is an Equalisation Law (*Finanzausgleichgesetz*) that enforces a redistribution whereby no *Land* ends up with a net tax revenue more than 5 per cent above or below the federal average. As the table below shows, Hamburg and Bremen are the wealthiest of the *Länder*, followed by Berlin: this may seem curious, in view of their economic difficulties, described earlier, but it must be remembered that these three are city *Länder* without hinterlands, whereas in rural areas the standard of living is lower. Thus Bavaria, despite its new industrial boom, is still below average in wealth. Under the equalisation scheme, Hamburg, Bremen, Baden-Württemberg and Hessen all contribute to the pool, while the six other *Länder* are all recipients (Berlin is not included, because of its special subsidies). And it is not surprising that the *Länder* are constantly bickering about this share-out, some complaining that they have to pay too much, others that they do not receive enough: in January 1986 the Federal Constitutional Court heard formal pleas from no less than six of them.

Economic performance of the Länder

	Gross domestic product per capita, 1984 (in DM):	Real economic growth (in percentage), 1970–84:
Hamburg	45,500	27.9
Bremen	33,800	26.7
West Berlin	29,300	27.7
Hessen	26,500	38.5
Baden-Württemberg	26,100	38.2
North-Rhine-Westphalia	24,800	29.5
Bavaria	24,000	40.5
Rhineland-Palatinate	23,000	42.9
Saarland	22,600	46.2
Lower Saxony	21,900	40.9
Schleswig-Holstein	21,200	44.1

The Equalisation Law is just one example of federal control over the *Länder*. In many other matters, too, the *Bund* over the past 30 years has subtly increased its powers (the Constitution has been amended 34 times in this direction) and this is not too popular with the *Länder*.

Some of the changes however have been made purely in the interests of greater fairness and efficient standardisation. For example, until ten years ago police uniforms were grey in Bavaria, green in Hessen – and dark blue in Hamburg (as in Britain) which is what firemen wear elsewhere in Germany. So visitors to Hamburg from other regions often thought its policemen were firemen – very confusing! So the *Bund* stepped in with a new law, and now all German police wear green coats with khaki trousers. Similarly the *Bund* has standardised civil servants' salary scales and pension rights, so as to remove discrepancies that disadvantaged employees in some *Länder*. The *Bund* has also made efforts to induce the *Länder* to harmonise their systems of education – a field where they are sovereign – but this has not proved particularly successful (see p. 204).

More significant has been the recent tendency of the *Bund* to increase, or try to increase, its general control of the economy – a centralising trend common to many other advanced countries. The *Bund* has allocated generous new funds to the *Länder* for such matters as research and technology, but with the condition that it retains a say in how this money is spent. While glad of the hand-outs, the *Länder* resent the various encroachments on their autonomy: but they are not powerless to defend themselves. For example, in 1984 they succeeded in getting a federal law adopted that bans the *Bund* from interfering in a *Land*'s policy for building and running hospitals. Previously this was a joint responsibility, since much of the money for health services comes from the *Bund*. But now each *Land* receives a lump sum from Bonn and is free to spend it as it wishes. 'This has been quite a victory for us,' Lothar Späth told me; 'it is the first example for years of the tide of power moving back towards the *Länder*.'

The *Länder* are regularly able to influence federal policy through the *Bundesrat*[1], the Upper House of parliament, which is entirely composed of their delegates. As this chamber has the power to block federal legislation in certain cases, the *Länder* can use it as a weapon. Voting in the *Bundesrat*, as in the *Bundestag*, very often goes on party lines – but not always. Sometimes the *Länder* perceive that they have common interests which override party considerations, and one finds surprising coalitions. Thus the four northern *Länder* – Hamburg and Bremen, both SPD, and Lower Saxony and Schleswig-Holstein, firmly CDU – will vote jointly against measures which they feel are harmful to north Germany.

[1] By the end of 1986, Bavaria, Baden-Württemberg, Rhineland-Palatinate, Lower Saxony and Schleswig-Holstein were controlled basically by the CDU, and the other *Länder* by the SPD, alone or in coalition.

Inevitably the Federal Government tends to enjoy easiest relations with *Länder* of its own political colour, while with others there may be frictions: one SPD Minister in North-Rhine-Westphalia complained to me, 'This Kohl Government has Thatcherite policies against public spending, and as we cannot fix our own level of taxation, this makes it hard for us to apply measures to reduce unemployment, as we would like.' But it is rare that Bonn goes so far as openly to victimise a *Land* in opposition hands – the Constitution anyway would make this very difficult – and in general a spirit of fair play and cooperation prevails. Never has any *Land* staged an open revolt against Bonn, nor even been as unduly obstructive as it might have the power to be. What is more, in no *Land* is there any separatist movement worth taking seriously, of the kinds found to some degree in Brittany, Scotland or the Spanish Basque provinces.

The federal system indeed works well, and its basic structure is very rarely questioned by Germans in the way that the French, for instance, ceaselessly criticise their own contrasting heritage of centralisation. The *Land*/Bonn power struggles that I have described do not really amount to much more than normal rivalry of interest and they are not destructive. The system is popular with the public and has been getting more so: according to surveys made regularly by the Allensbach Institute, Germany's best-known opinion poll body, the proportion of people wanting to see *Land* governments abolished and all main decisions taken in Bonn has fallen steadily from 49 per cent cent in 1952 to 9 per cent in 1980.

The system is popular because it helps to keep government in closer touch with the governed, over a whole range of human welfare matters – education for example – where it is felt that local politicians and bureaucrats will have better understanding of local needs than grey men in far-off Bonn. Federalism has also probably been an advantage to Germany's economic development, for the *Länder* do possess a degree of autonomy in economic planning and subsidies, and this helps local initiative and encourages flexibility – as Lothar Späth explained to me in the case of agriculture: 'I am able to concentrate on helping the small family farms here in this *Land*, which need a different support system from the bigger ones in the north. Of course we are limited by EEC rules, but I do have some freedom of action. Our federal system is in this sense more human.'

In some other respects however the system can sometimes prove a handicap. Elections for the *Bundestag* do not coincide with those for the various *Land* parliaments, nor do these coincide with each other, so that each year there are usually two or three of them. A federal government of any colour therefore has to be careful that its actions do not harm the chances of the party of that same colour in a forthcoming *Land* election. This can be inhibiting to policy-making in Bonn and can sometimes delay the taking of necessary action. And in those fields where the *Länder* hold the responsibility – for example, television (see p. 308) and education (see p. 204) – effective reform or other action can likewise be impeded, for the *Länder* need to coordinate their measures and this, for obvious political reasons, they frequently fail to do. So federalism has its drawbacks. But few doubt that overall it has helped to contribute to Germany's post-war record of good government.

Benevolent technocrats in the Rathaus

Decentralisation does not stop at *Land* level but goes on down to cities, towns and smaller communes, all of which enjoy rather more autonomy than is usual in most other European countries. The city of Stuttgart has 15,000 full-time municipal employees and an annual budget (in 1984) of 2,993 million DM: it is responsible for its own gas and electricity supplies, for the three largest hospitals, and for many welfare services and cultural activities, and must also pay for much school building. Even a semi-rural commune of 3,000 people will be in charge of its own planning, roads and building policy, and might have a budget of 5 million DM or more.

This German civic tradition can in one sense be traced back to the privileges of the Free Towns of the Middle Ages. In another sense it is quite new, for the municipal system was reconstituted just after the war: when the Allies set out to rebuild democracy, each occupying Power saw fit to impose its own model – and this has remained. The Americans, in the south, set up something close to their own pattern: full-time, fully-salaried professional mayors. The British in the north installed a system rather more similar to their own: the mayor is part-time and has another profession that brings in most of his income, while the main executive work is done by a salaried town clerk. It is thus not easy to generalise about German local government.

In north Germany, the mayor is very often a local businessman, lawyer or teacher. But, although he is not full-time, he is very much more than a mere figurehead chosen annually to preside at banquets and open flower-shows, as in Britain. He may well spend twenty hours or more each week on his mayoral duties, and has much serious policy-making work to do. In an average north German town, local affairs are highly politicised, yet they are run on a coalition basis that makes for a remarkable degree of consensus. If the majority part in the town council is CDU, then it will elect a CDU mayor, but his two deputies may well be from the other parties, FDP and SPD. And the *Oberstadtdirektor* (town clerk) and other senior salaried officials appointed by the council also have declared political affiliations.

These posts are shared out between the parties according to their local strengths, and it could even be that the town clerk is of a different political colour from the mayor. This *de facto* coalition system owes nothing to the British model and is not a statutory obligation but very often a gentleman's agreement, worked out pragmatically as the most efficient and democratic way of doing things. In Göttingen, a former mayor told me: 'In the old pre-war Prussian days, officials and councillors tended to be autocratic and very conservative, and there was little real debate. This then made it easier for the Nazis to gain control of local affairs. We feel that our new multi-party coalition system, more open and politically honest, provides checks against such abuses. Of course there are tough debates in the council on many issues: but then comes the vote, where the majority party usually wins, and the officials have to apply the policy whether it suits their views or not.'

In a south German city, the chief mayor (*Oberbürgermeister*) is more of a boss figure. He too is usually a party man: but, highly paid, he doubles up the roles of political leader and chief executive, and can devote his full energies to his job. Moreover, he is directly elected by popular mandate, initially for eight years, with options for renewal. It is a system that puts a strong mayor in a hugely powerful position. He is assisted by five *Bürgermeister*, full-time salaried specialists who are chosen by the city council. This council is sovereign, on budgetary matters and for major new projects: but the mayor, by law, is alone responsible for day-to-day administration, where he cannot be interfered with. In practice it is the mayor who initiates many projects. The council has the right to overrule him, and sometimes does so. But the councillors, unpaid and busy with their own professions, generally defer to the mayor and his salaried deputies with their technical abilities. So a city tends to be run by benevolent technocratic oligarchs who see themselves as business managers, more concerned with getting things done than with wheeler-dealer politics.

This tradition of highly professional city management can sometimes lead to a certain high-handed paternalism – or so it is alleged by some younger critics, Green and others. But it carries undoubted advantages. As mayors and deputy mayors draw handsome salaries and do valuable jobs, the career tends to attract men (or women) of high calibre and qualifications, and senior civic officialdom thus carries higher prestige than, for instance, in Britain. Mayors, often men with a legal background, see themselves as forming a clear-cut profession. Some belong to no party but present themselves to the electorate on their managerial record, as if applying to be head of some big firm; in this spirit they will sometimes seek to move on from one town to a larger one, in search of better pay or prospects. In Konstanz by the Swiss border, Dr Eickmayer comes from Münster in the north: he stood on a non-party ticket and was elected mayor in face of SPD and CDU candidates, both local men, because the citizens knew about him and trusted him. It is a state of affairs that often makes for consensus – in Stuttgart, Mayor Rommel gets on as easily with SPD councillors as with his CDU colleagues – but today it is being contested by Greens newly arrived in councils, who want to shake up the cosy ententes between the older parties (see pp. 432–3).

In smaller towns and rural areas, alike in south and north Germany, the mayor is a part-timer assisted by paid officials. In the industrial townlet of Unterföhring (pop. 2,500), on the edge of the Munich conurbation, the mayor, SPD, is a salesman for an oil company: he told me that he is frequently in conflict with the larger district (*Kreis*) to which the town belongs, for its right-wing CSU-run council manages to block his schemes for low-cost 'social' housing. In Dörpen, a big village of 2,500 souls in Lower Saxony, near the Dutch border, the CDU mayor is a prosperous farmer: he said that his father was mayor before him, and he took on the job 'for idealistic civic reasons'. In the 1970s, the communes (*Gemeinde*) in rural areas were regrouped into larger units, rather as in Britain in the same period, and for the same reasons of administrative efficiency. There are now some 8,500 communes, against 24,200 before, and few have less than 2,500 inhabitants. All communes, except for the larger towns, are grouped into districts, with an average population of 170,000, in most areas there are thus four levels of government: *Gemeinde, Kreis, Land* and *Bund*. It is costly and bureaucratic, but it works quite smoothly, and few people are in favour of modifying the structure any further.

The financing of local government has recently become a problem. During the boom years German cities were able to spend lavishly on new projects and even today they are still quite wealthy by British standards. But the money that a city can raise from local taxes is not intended to be adequate for all its needs, and for many of its main activities it either receives further grants from *Land* or *Bund* or it operates in partnership with them. Thus a *Land* helps pay for school building and shares the running costs of opera houses; *Land* and *Bund* pay substantially for new hospitals and bear most of the cost of major new road and traffic schemes. This involves a good deal of joint decision-taking, and of course there are frictions. In particular, Mrs Thatcher's views on the need to cut public spending have been shared to quite an extent by the Kohl Government, which has reduced its level of grants to cities and has tried to induce them to make their own economies. Even if no SPD-led councils have responded with open revolt in quite the Liverpool manner, they have nonetheless grown resentful, for cities have been obliged to cut back their budgets or resort to large bank loans. Nearly all big towns are heavily in debt.

Matters have frequently been aggravated by the tendency of a city's sources of revenue to move out into the nearby towns – as in the case of Hamburg. Well-to-do ratepayers desert the city to build new homes in the suburbs where there is more space and land prices are lower. Industry moves too, for much the same reasons – and this is an economic blow, for a German city's major source of revenue is from the *Gewerbesteuer*, a tax on local industry and business. Towns thus vie with each other to attract new firms. And it is the larger, densely-packed ones that are losing out. In some, notably Cologne, Hanover and Karlsruhe, the *Land* government has enacted laws to force the suburbs to merge with the city into a new larger unit, and the problem is thus solved. But elsewhere this has proved politically impossible.

One such case is Stuttgart. So much of its territory is hilly forest that virtually all available building land has long been used up, and land prices are the highest in Germany: up to 15,000 DM per square metre in central office areas, compared with 1,200 DM or so in a good residential district, and a mere 400 DM outside the town. So house-loving Stuttgarters have been moving out in their thousands: since 1962 the city's own population has fallen from 643,000 to 560,000, while that of the four surrounding *Kreise* has risen by 300,000 to reach 1.9 million. Industry has followed suit: in the past thirty years more than 300 firms left the town to resettle nearby, including the world head office of the mighty Bosch. Several of the towns around Stuttgart have thus grown richer *per capita* than the city itself, and have been able to build themselves luxurious new civic centres, swimming pools and so on. Sindelfingen, home of the largest Daimler-Benz factory, is said to be the richest town in Germany. And Stuttgarters have grown resentful. 'The system penalises us,' says Rommel; 'people from these places freely make use of our own central amenities – opera, museums, hospitals and so on – but the towns refuse to help pay for these directly. They guard their independence jealously and have grown too big and powerful for the *Land* to be able to impose a merger, as it did at Karlsruhe some years ago. Meanwhile Stuttgart is rotting away. I have had to reduce the funding for housing, sports centres, and new town-planning schemes.'

In the early years after the war, the replanning and rebuilding of towns was seldom done very imaginatively. The urgent need was to give shelter to millions still virtually homeless, and then to get the economy moving again. Blocks of flats were thrown up all over the place, and city centres were decked out with ungainly new office buildings. The imperatives of the *Wirtschaftswunder* came before aesthetics. Only a few cities – Hamburg, Munich and Hanover are examples – made any concerted efforts to plan more harmoniously. Many of the others developed into visually characterless places, barely distinguishable one from the other.

Then in the early 1970s there emerged a gradual change of mood. As environmental needs came to the forefront, so the call went out for 'a more humane city', more agreeable to live in. Since then, the centres of many towns have been improved quite remarkably. Shopping streets have been closed to traffic, and pedestrian zones laid out, with flowering shrubs, modern sculpture and outdoor cafés – on a more lavish scale than in most parts of Europe. Handsome old townhouses are no longer being recklessly torn down to make room for more practical modern ones; instead they are now being restored where feasible, even if this adds to costs. My own view is that in the earlier post-war years the Germans were understandably so obsessed with obliterating their terrible past that they tended to abolish many good things along with the bad, in their eagerness to make a clean start. And so they even added to the Allied bombers' toll by pulling down perfectly respectable older houses, undamaged but unpopular simply because they were not new (see p. 175). But this period has ended: 19th-century downtown blocks are now in some cases being refurbished and modernised, so that their inhabitants, often quite poor and elderly people, can stay there rather than be rehoused in some unfamiliar suburb. And, now that the centres of big towns have been made more attractive, many younger middle-class people have been rediscovering the charms of living centrally, in a smallish flat, rather than emulating their parents' migration to big homes with gardens on the periphery. The trend may be of some comfort to Rommel. But today his main concern is how to catch for Stuttgart as much as possible of that lucrative new high-tech industry that is flowing into Baden-Württemberg and Bavaria.

North v. South: Bavarian boom and rustbelt Ruhr

The so-called 'Nord-Süd Gefälle', the 'descent to the south' of so much modern industry, has become a major talking-point in Germany in recent years. As the older declining industries happen to be in the north, and for a whole range of reasons the newer go-ahead ones tend to prefer to settle elsewhere, the image has developed of a Germany split between 'sunbelt south and rustbelt north', as Rupert Cornwell of the *Financial Times* has put it, adding with a touch of poetic licence: 'The southern states are exemplified by Baden-Württemberg and Bavaria which seem to consist of little else than glossy new aerospace and robotics plants nestling in pretty countryside, promoted by evocative slogans such as "come and work where others go on holiday". Meanwhile, the north carries the now familiar images of closed shipyards, steelworks and oil refineries enveloped in a suitable wintry setting.'[1]

Der Spiegel in its cover-story of January 7, 1985, 'The Great Trek to the South', pointed out that unemployment in the five northern *Länder* is 20 per cent above the federal average, and in the southern ones 20 per cent below it. Other statistics tell much the same tale. As the table on page 67 shows, the economic growth rate has been much lower in the northern industrialised *Länder* than in the southern ones, where most of the new companies have settled. Unemployment in 1985 was 14 per cent in Bremen and in the Ruhr, and a mere 5.6 per cent in Baden-Württemberg and 7.6 per cent in Bavaria, and inevitably this has led to a drift of population – some 17,000 people, mostly young ones, left the Ruhr in 1984 to seek jobs in the south. So the Germans have been worrying over the prospect of a growing imbalance in their economic geography, with possibly serious social and political consequences. As so often in Germany, the whole issue has been exaggerated by the media and may not be as bad as it seems. Look closely and we see that Baden-Württemberg's growth has begun to slow down after its great strides in the 1970s; Hamburg and Bremen, though in difficulty, are still very rich, and the main problems is that of the decline of the old coal and steel-based industries of the Ruhr. Germany is still far from developing a north-south drift on the same scale as in Britain or, in a different way, in Italy. Hers is still a well-balanced economy, geographically, with a fairly even spread around the country not only of industry but of other activities, commercial and cultural. In fact, the *Nord-Süd Gefälle* has helped to make this so. In the old days, the imbalance was greater, to the advantage of the north.

Baden-Württemberg has possessed successful medium-sized machinery firms since the 19th century. But the heavy industry was all further north – the shipyards by the sea; some iron and steel in the Saar, which had ore as well as coal: and massive iron smelting and steel works in the Ruhr, where there was iron ore and plentiful coal as well as excellent transport outlets along the Rhine. Bavaria, without raw materials or such good communications, remained agricultural. But today the mines are wearing thin, steel and shipping are in crisis – and the new high-technology industries do not depend on heavy raw materials to the same extent, nor on the same kind of bulk transport, so they can settle where they like.

They tend to choose the south for a variety of reasons. Climate, scenery and life-style certainly play a part: it is easier to woo engineers or executives to come to work near Munich than in Duisburg.

[1] *Financial Times*, June 18, 1985.

Wage costs are substantially lower in the south; and the farms have long been smaller and more backward, so their modernisation has produced a steady flow of local labour; moreover, peasants generally adapt more easily to modern factory work than coal-miners do. In Baden-Württemberg, the Swabian appetite for hard work has provided another strong attraction for new investors; and the region's existing machine-tool and precision industries are better suited for conversion to the new technologies than are the cumbersome old Ruhr firms or the North Sea shipyards. For moving into micro-circuits, cuckoo-clocks provide a better background of expertise than iron girders.

Other enticements are educational, even political. The south for historical reasons has a far better infrastructure of traditional universities, such as Heidelberg and Tübingen, and it has now supplemented these with a large number of new research centres and scientific colleges, highly valuable to modern industry. In the north, there is no university older than Göttingen (1773): strange as it may seem, the rich merchants of old Hamburg and Bremen did not feel the need to educate their sons but put them straight into trade, and those who wanted a higher education went south. In the Ruhr, moreover, it was the deliberate policy of the industrial barons such as Krupp, backed up by Bismarck and the Kaisers, to prevent the founding of universities, for they feared that these would foster a radical intellectual leadership that might stir the workers into revolt! – 'This is a region for work, not for thought,' said Kaiser Wilhelm. Today things have changed, for the Ruhr has five new universities, and like Hamburg and other northern towns it is making efforts to develop scientific institutes – but rather late in the day, in face of the very dynamic policies of Späth and Strauss. Lastly, while the northern industrial *Länder* are SPD-ruled, the two big southern ones are in conservative hands – and this, for many would-be investors, is an attraction. 'Why should I go to the Ruhr, where the unions are so strong, in league with the SPD in every local council?' said the manager of one big electronics group; 'Bavaria is not only less unionised, but its leaders have a better understanding of a modern firm's needs.' Even if that last point is not really true, capitalists tend to think that way.

In Bavaria, Strauss has for years been attracting investors with his free-market, profit-orientated philosophy. Today this *Land* claims to have the largest concentration of micro-electronics factories in Europe, employing some 200,000 people, a figure that has been growing by 20,000 a year. The trail was blazed by Siemens which switched its headquarters from Berlin to Munich after the war and now employs 100,000 people (a third of its total world-wide staff) in its 25 factories and research centres scattered around Bavaria, many of them in 'high-tech' sectors. Other international firms have moved in, including Motorola, Texas Instruments and Hitachi; scores of smaller German ones have sprung up too, so today the old farming plains around Munich, and north towards Nuremberg, contain a whole web of burgeoning little Silicon Valleys.

Baden-Württemberg's rise has been less spectacular, for it was already industrialised and so has not started virtually from scratch. But today IBM has its main European plant there, with 30,000 workers, while other electronic titans are also active in the Stuttgart area, including Bosch and Standard Electric Lorenz. This *Musterländle* ('model little *Land*'), as Swabians like to call it, is intelligently exploiting its older industrial skills in the precision field – and this today is very much the policy of prime minister Späth, who has staked his reputation on a drive to make Baden-Württemberg into a power-house of the new technologies. He believes that industry will go where the research is done, and so he has set up an agency which is master-minding the creation of 30 research institutes and ten new 'science parks'. He has cajoled local firms into financing institutes for data-processing, micro-electronics and molecular biology, including one at Stuttgart University costing 13 million DM. Apostle of an un-usual kind of close association between universities and industry, he has even encouraged professors to leave their jobs and set up their own small firms (an amazing departure for Germany), where they take charge of the technical side and leave finance and production to hired managers. Späth urges young people to become engineers rather than unemployed teachers – and has stressed the point by closing three teacher training colleges.

Impressed by this research-orientated model, the northern *Länder* have belatedly begun to imitate it. Berlin, as we have seen, has launched its own high-technology programme, while North-Rhine-Westphalia too is promoting twelve new research institutes, and Bremen has had some modest success with new aerospace and elec-tronics ventures. But where does the funding come from? Berlin of course gets special aid from Bonn, while large federal subsidies are also given on a sector-by-sector basis to whole industries in difficulty, notably coal, steel and ship-building. But, apart from this, regional aid and planning exist only on a small scale in Germany, as compared with France. Each *Land* is left to compete on its own. And that is not so easy for North-Rhine-Westphalia and its problem region, the Ruhr.

The *Ruhrgebiet* (Ruhr district), named after a river that flows into the Rhine at Duisburg, comprises a dozen or so industrial towns with a total population of 5.4 million, in an area 55 miles wide by 40 deep. Duisburg, Essen, Bochum and Dortmund are the main ones. Today the Ruhr is not nearly as grimy and polluted as it once was, and it even contains a surprising amount of woodland and parkland. But it is still Europe's leading industrial area, producing 62 per cent of the EEC's bituminous coal and 21 per cent of its crude steel.

Until about 1850 it was rural farmland. Then its industrial development took place very rapidly, over a period of some years, and was based on the fortunate presence of coal and ore in the same area, right by the Rhine. Steel mills and engineering works were built, mainly by family firms such as Krupp and Thyssen that grew rapidly into gigantic and famous enterprises. The area soon became the stronghold of the German armaments industry, and so it continued to prosper during the First World War and again in the Nazi period. Despite heavy Allied bombing, its industrial capacity was still 80 per cent intact in 1945, but was then somewhat reduced by the Allies' dismantlement policy. This ended in 1949, so the Ruhr was able to play a central role in the 'economic miracle' of the 1950s and it became richer than ever.

By about 1960 however the first danger signs were appearing. The more easily exploitable mines were beginning to wear thin, and Ruhr coal soon found it harder to compete with cheaper sources of energy such as imported oil and gas. The first pit closure was in 1957, followed by others in steady succession over the next 25 years. Of 152 former pits, only 27 are active today; Essen, once the foremost coalmining town of Europe, saw its very last pit close in 1986, and today this city of Krupp has more white-collar workers than manual ones. With modern techniques, productivity in the mines has increased hugely, so that since the 1950s coal output has fallen by less than half, from some 120 to 61 million tons a year. But in order to remain competitive the mines have to stage massive staff reductions: over 250,000 jobs have been lost, and only 119,000 miners are still at work today. The early retirements, retraining schemes and other palliatives were generously funded and were worked out in close consultation with the generally cooperative miners' union (see p. 105): as a result, there was not a single strike. But the financial cost has been great, and is born partly by the Federal Government, which in 1969 obliged the various private mine-owners (no mines are nationalised) to merge into a big consortium, Ruhrkohle, that now receives subsidies of over 1 billion DM a year. Its major problem today is that the mines near the surface, mostly in the Ruhr valley area to the south, are now virtually used up, and it has become necessary to dig for the coal further north, around the Emscher valley, where the seams lie deeper and are therefore more expensive to exploit. This explains why Ruhr coal, once so cheap, is today undercut by imported coal; and why Germany, unlike some other countries, did not find it worthwhile to increase its coal production again after the sharp oil price rises of the 1970s.

The coal cutbacks of the 1960s at least took place during a period of general economic boom, when it was possible to find replacement jobs for many miners. Most of the other big Ruhr industries – notably chemicals and machinery – were expanding during this period, and Opel opened a larger car plant in Bochum. But the steel crisis since 1975 has come at a much harder time. Germany's steel industry is much the largest in Europe and the most efficient, and over half of it is located in or near the Ruhr where Thyssen is much the largest firm, followed by Krupp and Hoesch (all are in private hands, like the coal-mines). The industry was doing well until the mid-1970s, when along with the rest of Europe it began to be hit hard by world over-production and Japanese competition. In line with EEC policy direct-ives, it has now trimmed its capacity, cut back production, and moved over from ordinary steel to a higher quality product which is more saleable. But the German steelmakers resentfully complain that the British and Italian industries in particular, less efficient but more highly subsidised, are competing against them unfairly with their artificially cheaper steel. The Federal Government has been trying to persuade Thyssen, Krupp and some other firms to merge into two big groups, as a way of rationalising further and cutting costs. The mer-ger talks failed in 1985. Even so, a fair amount of streamlining has already taken place: German steel today employs less than 230,000 people, against 420,000 in 1960. And these cuts have fallen heavily on the Ruhr steelworkers who can no longer so easily find other jobs when made redundant. Once again, there has been a remarkable absence of strikes – thanks to harmonious labour relations and to Ger-many's generous and successful 'social net' of welfare benefits. The Duisburg mills may be crumbling and unemployment be high: yet the Ruhr as a whole still wears a remarkable aura of prosperity.

I half expected a black and noisy inferno, and was pleasantly sur-prised to find that many parts of the Ruhr today are green and pasto-ral, especially to the south of Essen and Bochum, where the mines were closed in the 1960s. Here with true Germanic neatness the old coalpits and railtracks have been grassed over, the pitheads removed and the slagheaps planted with trees; and the river Ruhr again mean-ders through quiet woods and meadows, past the neat suburbs of the new commercial middle class. It is almost idyllic. Further north and west, on a line roughly from Duisburg to Recklinghausen, the scene becomes grimier, for here there is still a good deal of heavy industrial activity – and no steel foundry can be expected to look as tidy as Herr Späth's new micro-chip factories. Though pollution has been much reduced, the river Emscher still swirls black and thick. Here the disused coalworks have not all been tidied away: but one pitwheel in the centre of Bottrop has been preserved as a kind of modern sculpture, and near Dortmund a fine old *art nouveau* colliery is being turned into a museum. Here and there between the pits, the old mansions of rural landlords survive incongruously from an earlier era, blackened by a century of non-rural soot. And, everywhere, the giant satanic mills . . . So much higgledy-piggledy industrial desolation carries, I find, a certain poetic beauty and awesome fascination. Many of the iron- and steelworks are still active, belching their smoke and flames, dirty, maybe, but heartening tokens of life. Others are closed and silent, reminders of yesterday's hard toil and today's leisured anxiety.

The Ruhr towns themselves, away from the industrial zones, are remarkably spruce and civilised places. They grew so rich in their heyday that they were able to create splendid municipal parks and fine opera houses, and today this heritage actively survives and has even been extended: Bochum is the home of one of the very best theatre companies in Germany. Housing, too, is impressive. As the industrial revolution came later to the Ruhr than to Britain, it was possible to avoid some of the British mistakes: when Krupp and others built cheap housing for their battalions of new workers, they did not imitate the cramped and squalid back-to-back dwellings that can still be found in some north of England town, but instead they established settlements that were well-spaced and comfortable by the standards of those days. Many of these workers' *Kolonien* still exist, especially in the western parts of Essen, near Krupp's old main factory: they have been modernised, and are cosily lived in by today's well-paid workers. Often one sees a Mercedes parked outside old miners' cottages. Working-class life-styles may have been changing since the war (see p. 146): but the Ruhr, rather like industrial Yorkshire or Tyneside, remains a warm, friendly community with strong local loyalties and a greater sense of neighbourliness and caring solidarity than is usual in urban Germany. Despite unemployment, it is also a pleasanter place to live in than twenty years ago, if only because private firms and local authorities have spent huge sums on curbing industrial pollution – in response to Brandt's famous appeal in 1965, 'Let us have blue skies over the Ruhr'. Inevitably, some factories still emit smells. But smog and soot no longer cast such a pall.

Old Alfred Krupp (1801–87) founder of the Krupp empire and foremost creator of the Ruhr, was the kind of patriarchal paternalist who combined genuine benevolence with clever self-interest. Scared of the nascent trade unions, he believed that, if he treated his employees well, they would be less likely to revolt. So, as well as good housing, he provided crèches, old people's homes, and better welfare services than were usual in those days, and he tried to induce his 16,000 workers to feel that they were part of one big caring family. But he was also tough with workers striking for more pay – the grim strike rallies of those days, and the dour life of mine and mill, are vividly evoked in the photographs and souvenirs at the Folkwang museum of Ruhr history, in Essen. Krupp lived grandly, and for himself and his large family he built the extraordinary Villa Hügel, a vast neo-Renaissance monstrosity on a hill above the Ruhr valley: today it too is a museum, filled with revealing portraits of the Krupp dynasty across the years, down to their time of pro-Nazi collaboration. The family firm survived the ensuing Allied reprisals, but under poor management it later fell into a decline, and finally in 1968 it was turned into a public shareholding company. The Krupp family, defeated not by the war but by peace, today own very few shares.

After sailing triumphantly through two lost wars and other disasters, the Ruhr became so convinced of its own invincibility that its leaders failed for a long time to react to the dangers when the coal and steel crises began. They simply could not believe that the Ruhr's industrial might was seriously threatened, or that these were any more than passing setbacks. Employers and unions were united in a conservative desire to preserve the status quo: they were afraid of having to cope with new technologies, and so for a long time they failed to adapt their production or encourage new investment. This has made the situation today worse than it need have been. But, better late than never, attitudes have finally changed. Mannesmann, formerly one of the major steel producers, diversified massively into machinery and equipment during the 1970s and today produces little steel. This is also one of several older local firms that have preferred to put their recent investment not in the Ruhr but in south Germany. Disturbed by this trend, the *Land* and municipal authorities are now trying hard to woo new investors from outside, but in today's economic climate it is not easy. A number of smaller firms have arrived, but there has been no major new investment since Opel set up its car plant in Bochum in 1962. It is not hard to see why new industry fights shy of the Ruhr. As mentioned earlier, ex-miners and ex-steelworkers do not adapt easily, or are not thought to adapt easily, to the very different work of a modern factory. The Ruhr also suffers from its old image of an ugly, polluted area in the grip of strong trade unions. But this is unfair, for not only has pollution declined but the unions are rather moderate.

The local coal and steel firms benefit from the federal subsidies for those industries: but apart from this the Ruhr does not get nearly as much general regional aid for new investment as it thinks it should. Quite largely this is because centrally-planned regional development has long been something of a Cinderella in this decentralised free-market Germany. Not until 1965 was a Regional Planning Act passed, setting up a joint committee of the Federal Government and the *Länder* that meets annually to allocate subsidies to areas in need. Under this scheme, grants totalling up to 15 per cent of investment costs can now be obtained for new projects in parts of the Ruhr affected by steel closures. But this does not go far. The joint committee has less than 1 billion DM a year to spend overall, and the political haggling between Bonn and the *Länder* sometimes prevents the money from going where it is most needed. North-Rhine-Westphalia's specific complaint is that the fund was first conceived mainly to assist under-developed areas which had inadequate infrastructure, and this remains its raison d'être; the Ruhr, with an excellent modern transport network but other problems, is not properly catered for. However, the Ruhr's plight today should not be exaggerated. Several other parts of Europe have similar problems with their older declining industries, and in this respect the Ruhr is not faring as badly as Tyneside or Clydeside, Lorraine or south Belgium. It still holds strong reserves of infrastructure and expertise, and it could yet stage a come-back against the south. This powerful spirit of competition between the *Länder*, as the rulers in Stuttgart, Düsseldorf or Bremen vie with each other dynamically to attract new investment, certainly outweighs the disadvantages of the lack of centrally-directed regional planning. And it helps to account for the striking success record of post-war German industry.

3

THE 'ECONOMIC MIRACLE' AND ITS AFTER-STRAINS

Much has been written about the success of West Germany in pulling itself up from the ruins of war to build the free world's third most powerful economy, founded above all on high-quality goods. During the golden years of the so-called 'miracle', in the 1950s and '60s, its growth rate was the fastest in Europe (averaging 8 per cent a year in the '50s) and purchasing power more than trebled. Since then the growth has slowed, as in many countries, and some weaknesses in the German economy have become more evident, raising doubts as to how effectively it can meet the challenge of the new high-technology age. But the basic strengths are still considerable: and the record is remarkable for a nation with few natural resources of its own and relatively little inherited wealth. Manufacturing output is 60 per cent greater than in Britain (for a comparable population) and the standard of living 30 per cent higher. The economy has gained added confidence from a stable currency, with much the lowest inflation rate in the EEC (in 1975–83 it averaged 5.1 per cent, against 18.5 per cent in Britain, 16.0 per cent in France, 10.6 per cent in the United States). And exports amount to as much as 30 per cent of GNP, for German companies have been assiduous in exploiting the appetites of foreign markets for their finely made products – this applies not only to the giants that are household names, such as Bayer, Bosch and BMW, but also, for example, to some specialised family firm in a Swabian valley, turning out the world's best punching-machines or liquid level indicators.

The reasons for the economic success are not hard to enumerate. In the early post-war years, the Germans were powerfully motivated by the desire to rebuild their nation through sustained effort. And they did not have to start entirely from scratch, for, despite bomb damage to many factories, industrial plant was basically intact to a surprising degree, and able to be repaired. In 1945, much less than half of German industry was in ruins; many smaller firms in out-of-the-way places were unscathed. Then came the era of Allied dismantling, but in the Western zones this reduced plant only by 5 per cent; and, like the bombing, it was something of a blessing in disguise, for it obliged firms to reorganise with modern equipment. Germany also emerged from defeat with a pool of skilled labour and a background of expertise which the Nazi war effort had encouraged, while the refugees from the east brought the added talent and manpower that were invaluable for industry's take-off. The Germans then made energetic use of Marshall Aid and of the markets soon opened to them by the Americans. Later, from 1958 onwards, the creation of the Common Market gave a further huge impetus to West Germany's export trade: in the brief period 1958–62 its sales to the rest of the Six almost trebled, and by 1984 some 47.7 per cent of its total exports were going to other EEC countries. Lastly, throughout the post-war period the Germans have known stable government, and despite the alternations of power they have benefited from a degree of continuity in economic policies, for in this field the divergences between the main parties are less great than in France or Britain.

These factors have all played their part – and so has the positive climate of labour relations. The Allies after the war laid the foundations of a sensible trade union structure, and of a legally enforced system of consultation between unions and employers – and this has led to a stronger spirit of consensus than exists in many countries. Unions have tended to collaborate with management rather than fight it. This has favoured wage restraint, which in turn has helped keep down inflation. It has resulted also in a very low strike level and in great advances in productivity, for seldom do unions oppose technological change. This remains broadly the pattern today, despite greater union restiveness due to rising unemployment.

But the single most important explanation of Germany's post-war economic success may be a simple human one, hard to prove or quantify. This is the fact that Germans at all levels, from shop-floor workers to managers, just happen to be very disciplined, thorough and realistic. Their perfectionism may sometimes be a draw-back, but on the whole it has brought great economic dividends – and it still does so even today when a younger generation has become less work-obsessed. The Germans do not work such long hours as some others – their weekly rate is well below Japan's – but when they *are* at work they tend to work hard and methodically (at least in industry – less so in public offices). And that is true at all levels. On the shopfloor, an extensive and efficient apprenticeship scheme has produced a work-force that is far better skilled and motivated than Britain's; and managers and owners, though tending to be too cautious and routine-minded, possess a technical flair and a detailed concern for the quality of their product that have played no small part in the triumphs of the export drive.

During the past ten years or so, the economic picture has become slightly less rosy, for Germany's industrial strength has not bought her any immunity from the new world conditions; and like other Western countries she has been experiencing periods of mild recession, due in part to the growth of Far Eastern competition and to the oil price increases of the 1970s. The most worrying trend has been the rise in unemployment, which hit Germany later than most Western countries but was then sharper: from a modest 3.3 per cent in 1983, the level rose to some 9 per cent in 1986 (over 2 million people), though this remains some way below the EEC average. The economic slow-down was at its worst during the final years of the Schmidt government, 1979–82, a period marked by some spectacular crashes of big firms, such as AEG-Telefunken, and by the dreaded emergence of 'stagflation': 1981 and 1982 were years of nil growth, while in 1981 inflation reached 6.8 per cent, a high figure for Germany and one that brought troubling reminders of the old German nightmares. There was even talk of the economy 'beginning to go down the drain'. The Germans had grown so used to steady growth that they could not easily adjust to the new climate; they began to panic at signs of recession, fearing worse to come, and they found little solace in the fact that many other Western countries were faring worse still. In the familiar German manner, they over-reacted.

Then in 1983 the election of a CDU-led Government under Helmut Kohl brought a renewal of business confidence, and it happened to coincide with an American-led up-swing in the Western economy as a whole. The public mood changed rapidly. According to opinion polls taken every December by the Allensbach institute, putting the question, 'Do you look on the New Year with hope or anxiety?', the proportion feeling hopeful had fallen to 32 per cent in 1981 (except for 1973, the lowest score since 1950), but by December 1984 it had risen to 55 per cent. The entire economy had become more buoyant again, registering annual growth rates of 2.5 per cent in 1984 and 1985, and over 3 per cent in 1986, while in 1985 the trade surplus soared to a record 73 billion DM. There was talk of a 'new economic miracle'.

These short- and medium-term ups and downs should perhaps be viewed in a broader perspective. The underlying message is that West Germany's economy still displays great power and resilience, but that a number of factors today are causing some disquiet even to the most detached and non-over-reacting observers. The Germans have shown themselves supreme at the great traditional industries of the past decades, such as cars and machinery: but do they possess the flexibility for making the jump into an era of new-style industries where the Japanese and Americans are so far ahead? Are their banking traditions, and their capital market structures, ideally suited for making the required investments? Are managers and entrepreneurs showing the necessary spirit of risk-taking and adaptability? All these questions are in the air today. At the same time, a younger generation has been querying the work-ethic and materialistic appetite of its elders and wants a different life-style – and many captains of industry are concerned that this trend may reduce productivity and so render Germany less competitive, just when international competition is becoming fiercer. Can the Germans have it both ways?

Industrial splendour – but can it meet the high-tech challenge?

West Germany is run on the principles of a mixed economy, with a very strong social welfare element but only a small amount of direct public ownership of industry and a fairly modest degree of government interventionism. This philosophy is broadly subscribed to by the main parties, though with nuances: the SPD puts a greater accent on social spending, on 'the social market economy', while the CDU especially since 1983 has stressed 'the free market economy', with cuts in public spending and reduced intervention.

Despite the existence of a Stability and Growth Act (1967) which sets out the rather obvious goals of expansion and price stability, there is not in practice very much forward economic planning at a federal level, as compared with France and its five-year Plans. Nor, as we have seen, does Bonn play any sizeable role in regional development. Nonetheless, federal governments have accepted the necessity of shoring up certain sectors with large public funds: Bonn gives a great deal of money to agriculture, and in recent years it has stepped up its subsidies to the declining industries, mainly coal, steel and shipbuilding, also textiles. The total aid had reached 27 billion DM by 1983. The Kohl Government has been opposed doctrinally to such spending and would like to reduce it, but has not found it politically easy to do so. At least the level of direct government subsidy to industry remains lower in West Germany than in many countries: 1.8 per cent of GNP, against 2.4 per cent in Britain and 2.8 per cent in France.

The role of public ownership in Germany is a complex matter. In the financial field, the governments of the *Länder* each own big banks and are able to utilise these for their local economic policies. But nationwide the main commercial banks such as the Deutsche Bank are all in private hands. Thus the federal government has little direct control over the financing of the private sector – in contrast with France, where since the war most banking has been in State hands. However, the railways and the postal and telecommunications services are federally owned. The government also holds large industrial assets, in some 80 companies, but in a rather peculiar way: it does not own big firms outright, as is the case in France and Britain, but it does part-own quite a number – in many instances (one example being the Salzgitter steel corporation) these holdings are legacies inherited from the Third Reich. Seeing that even SPD governments have shown little desire to increase this kind of ownership, nationalisation has never proved the same kind of stormy issue in Germany as it has in Britain or indeed in France. The Kohl Government, sharing Mrs Thatcher's philosophy, has even been privatising – but not very rapidly. It came to power with a list of proposals for removing or reducing its holdings, including its 20 per cent share of Volkswagen (to be achieved by 1990), and it made a quick start by selling a third of its stake in the huge Veba energy conglomerate. But its plan to slim down its control of Lufthansa, from 80 per cent to 51 per cent, ran into opposition from Franz-Josef Strauss who feared that in semi-private hands the airline might become less inclined to favour the German aircraft industry with its orders – and notably MBB, co-builder of Airbus, which is based in Munich. Strauss, as so often, got his way. It was an illustration of the influence that a *Land* can have over Bonn, and of the tendency of *Land*/Bonn disputes to end up tamely by reinforcing the status quo. But the Kohl Government did have successes on other fronts. It managed to reduce public-sector borrowing and public spending, and to bring inflation down to below 2.0 per cent in 1985, its lowest level for 15 years, and then to zero per cent in 1986, helped by the fall in oil prices. Industry was grateful to Kohl on the whole, and it backed his efforts to reduce the role of the state and encourage private initiative.

German economic strength depends above all on industry, which plays a larger role than in other advanced countries: according to OECD, manufacturing industry (excluding energy, mining and building) represents 31.8 per cent of GDP, compared with 30.5 per cent in Japan, 25.3 per cent in France, 21.1 per cent in the United States, and 21.0 per cent in Britain. German industrialists, even many of the small ones, are unusually export-minded. Helped by the low level of strikes, they are scrupulous about meeting delivery dates; and they employ talented salesmen who speak foreign languages and try to come to terms with foreign habits and cultures. All this presents an object lesson to the British. And it helps to explain why Germany has nearly always produced a large external trade surplus. This in turn helps to account for the Deutschmark's strength.

The very big firms like Siemens and Daimler-Benz may have led the way: but much of the success has been due also to smaller or medium-sized concerns, many of them still family-owned and -run. This can be observed especially in an area such as Swabia, around Stuttgart, whose industrial rise has been an exceptional saga. In the mid-19th century this was still no more than a poor agricultural region of small farms, much of it stony and unfertile, and often there were famines. Many farmers emigrated; but others turned to clock- and watch-making as the best way of topping up their incomes and avoiding starvation. They mysteriously possessed some innate flair for precision work and innovation – and this has grown. Here Gottlieb Daimler, a local engineer, invented the automobile in the mid-1880s. Others in Stuttgart created the electric drill, and even the telephone (at the same time as Bell), while Messerschmitt, a pioneer of the aircraft industry, was a Swabian too. Little specialist firms of many kinds grew up, in textiles, woodwork, watchmaking, machine-tools and other branches of precision machinery. Each patiently developed its own pool of skilled labour: and this diversification, plus the stress on quality rather than size, has helped Swabia through the periods of recession. Bosch and Daimler-Benz may have grown into giants; but most others have preferred to stay in the smaller-scale league and to base their success on intelligent specialisation: one thriving family concern exports its liquid level indicators around the world, yet has a staff of no more than 200.

The typical Swabian factory is still likely to be owned and actively run by a self-made man, or the son of one. He may earn 300,000 DM a year, but he lives very simply, probably works a 70-hour week, knows exactly how to turn a lathe or adjust an engine, and will readily go to the shop-floor and discuss technical details with his workers. He has a close and benevolent contact with them, usually knowing them all by name: and he is anxious to avoid his firm becoming too large for his personal supervision and thus less efficient. His manner tends to be genial but uncouth; for all his creative intelligence, he can rarely express himself eloquently; and he has a blithe disregard for showy public relations, believing that sheer quality will win through – as usually it does. One such rough diamond is Hugo Kunze, whose factory in industrial Stuttgart-Feuerbach, a stone's throw from Bosch and Porsche, is one of the world's most successful producers of stirring, kneading and shredding machines. He explained to me in his song-song Swabian drawl: 'My father, who was an engineer, founded this firm in 1929 and invented ice-cream-making machines. After the war he sold them to the US Army. Now, we've expanded into kneading machines for dough, and we make the world's best. I too am an engineer, and I'm continually inventing new machines and product. That's how we stay ahead. Some 56 per cent of our product goes for export, much of it to Arab countries. My staff is only 130, and I have not expanded for 15 years: if we grew too big, we'd become vulnerable.' He showed me round his tidy, highly computerised factory. His manner with his staff struck me as a mixture of diffident shyness and quiet authoritarianism.

Appropriately, Stuttgart today is the home of two of Germany's three most prestigious producers of luxury cars and of Europe's leading manufacturer of electronic car components. The automobile industry remains the brightest jewel in the crown of the German economy, the premier showcase of its talents of precision engineering and of its concern for quality and reliability. It is much the largest car industry in Europe, with 4 million vehicles produced in 1985; and, with over 60 per cent of its output sold abroad, it is Germany's leading exporter. What is more, it has recently fared much better than its main Western competitors in adjusting to a period of saturation of mass markets and of growing Japanese competition: while the American, British, French and Italian car industries have all been laying off workers in large numbers, the German industry actually increased its workforce from 740,000 in 1974 to 800,000 in 1984, despite a growth in automation.

The principal explanation is that Germany specialises in the kind of expensive high-performance car – very fast and comfortable, full of the latest gadgets – that the Japanese do not yet make, and it therefore has a surer market than for the ordinary family vehicle. Opel and Volkswagen may have many foreign peers, but BMW, Porsche and Daimler-Benz have few. And all around the globe there is a definable and steadily growing minority clientele for this kind of up-market automobile – whether it be companies buying stately Mercedes for their executives, or jet-setters wanting a snappy Porsche for private use. These cars, and BMWs too, have durability and a high resale value, and so they are often seen as a sound investment. They also appeal, as one BMW official suggested to me, 'to people who want a car as a kind of toy or status-symbol, as a life-style concept rather than mere transport equipment. They may not use all the gadgets, but they like them to be there. And they like to know that their car *could* do 250 kph if it tried even if their country's speed limits prevent them in practice from driving at more than a hundred and twenty! Silly, but there it is.' So why has Germany come to concentrate on this luxury market? – the same official went on: 'Partly it is a matter of tradition: Daimler was making cars for kings and presidents before 1914. Partly it derives from German skills in precision engineering. And partly it's because wage costs in this country are so high that we need to make a product with a big sales value. And if we produce such fast cars, well, remember that 40 per cent of our buyers are Germans, and this is the one country in the world with no speed limits on main roads. We at BMW regard the *Autobahn* network as one non-stop test track.' A point that a visitor like myself, in a mere Renault 20, soon discovers to his peril.

Consistently the most successful of the German automobile firms, and the one with the strongest mystique, is Daimler-Benz, maker of

Mercedes. Its origins have acquired the quality of legend. In the mid-1880s, while Daimler was inventing the petrol engine in his garden shed at Stuttgart, by a coincidence Karl Benz was pioneering his own engines at Mannheim, 80 miles away. The two men later associated, though their firms did not fully merge until 1960. In the second war, they were making aircraft for the Nazis. Today no members of the Daimler or Benz families are directly involved in the firm, which is owned by the Deutsche Bank (28 per cent), the Kuwait Government, and various holding companies and small shareholders (the Flick group sold its shares in 1986). So who on earth was Mercedes? Answer: when in 1899 Daimler built a new car, his leading salesman, Emil Jellinek, named it after his daughter, Mercedes. Today, all the firm's vehicles bear this name.

Besides its overseas factories, Daimler-Benz today employs some 155,000 workers in Germany, mostly in the Stuttgart area and at a big new plant in Bremen. It is the world's leading producer of heavy trucks, but is better known for its solidly-built saloon cars, probably now the most esteemed in the world in their class: recent clients include the Pope. Rolls-Royces may be even grander, but their output is much smaller. After the outbreak of the first energy crisis, Daimler-Benz was the only car firm in the world to increase its sales in 1974, and it since has expanded steadily, with demand nearly always exceeding supply: in 1985 its output of cars rose well above 500,000, half of them going for export. The management put this progress down to the fact that motorists now seek a durable car that will last at least ten years. But Daimler-Benz has also moved with the times by extending its range into smaller luxury cars, such as the compact new 190 whose sporty elegance marks a break with the firm's previous rather staid image and is presenting BMW with a tough challenge. The firm's record is certainly awe-inspiring – and the directors and publicity staff never miss a chance to rub it in. Their sublime arrogance takes a lot of beating: to be conducted round the Stuttgart plant by a PR man is like being shown Buckingham Palace by the Queen's lady-in-waiting. Other firms are regarded as non-existent: when I asked an executive what he thought of the latest Audi model, he claimed not to have heard of it, and after I was seen driving away in my muddy, scratched Renault 20, I was not invited again. This kind of smooth conceit is untypical of Swabia, but then few of the directors or senior staff today are Swabians. It should be added that in its own lofty way the firm is an excellent employer, offering its staff an extensive range of welfare and profit-sharing schemes (see p. 101).

Porsche, also a Stuttgart firm, was founded in 1931 by an Austrian professor, Ferdinand Porsche, and is still largely in the hands of the family. Its bullet-like sports cars, with the look of racing-cars, are especially popular in the United States where Porsche now sells 50 per cent of its select output of some 50,000 vehicles a year. Its appeal is very different from that of Daimler-Benz, as I was assured by the firm's current chairman, Peter Schutz, a Berlin-born American: 'In a word, our surveys show that people buy a Mercedes to look ten or twenty years older, and a Porsche to look ten or twenty years younger. Mercedes appeals to the rising young executive in a neat suit, who wants to show that he has status, that he has "arrived" (even if he has not). Porsches are for those who definitely have arrived and are not trying to prove anything except how young and fit they are. Our average client is a slim, relaxed man in his fifties, in a jersey or anorak, maybe a film-director or champion golfer with a young blonde on the seat beside him.' Good sales talk, and maybe not too wide of the mark.

The appeal of BMW probably lies somewhere between those two. The Bayerische Motoren Werke, of Munich, began life in the First World War as a maker of aircraft engines, then moved into producing motorcycles, and then into sports and racing cars. These played a dominant role in European motor rallies and races, in the 1930s and again after the second war. But by the late 1950s the firm was facing bankruptcy, for it had over-extended its range. It was taken over by the wealthy Quandt family, who are still the main shareholders, and they hugely restored its fortunes: since 1970, annual output has risen from 160,000 cars to some 450,000, 60 per cent of them exported. BMW's head office in northern Munich is an extraordinary modern building, in the shape of four tall cylinders. Some cars are made here, and others at a large factory in the small Bavarian town of Dingolfing, where many workers are ex-peasants or part-time farmers (see p. 134). A new plant at Regensburg, due to open late in 1986, will employ staff of a similar kind, and will enable production to rise to 550,000 cars a year – demand tends to exceed supply, as at Daimler-Benz. Sixty per cent of output consists of the medium-sized 3-series cars, which outwardly may look no more exciting than a family Ford or Fiat but inside are packed with wizardry, allowing for remarkable speed and road-holding. The range extends to the luxurious 7-series, selling for up to 70,000 DM and rivalling the larger Mercedes. A BMW is more fun to drive than a Mercedes, more flexible and responsive, and it has a stronger appeal to the kind of people who are really interested in cars.

The market for smaller models and ordinary family cars is represented in Germany by two American-owned firms (Ford, with a plant in Cologne, and Opel, part of General Motors) and of course by the mighty Volkswagen, which like Daimler-Benz is something of a modern German legend. Its gigantic factory at Wolfsburg in Lower Saxony, a few miles from the GDR border, was founded by Hitler in 1938 to produce the 'people's car'. After the war it was commandeered by the British, and there was some talk of transferring the works to Britain by way of reparations. But British car makers considered that its main product, the famous 'Beetle', was too ugly and noisy to be worthwhile, so the factory stayed where it was. Soon VW was allowed to resume its own production, under a very dynamic manager, Heinz Nordhoff, who set about catering for the rocketing demand for cheap cars as the German economy got on the move. So VW expanded phenomenally, playing no small part in the *Wirtschaftswunder* of the 1950s. Being one of the State-owned legacies of the Third Reich, it remained fully nationalised until 1961: then the Government sold off 60 per cent of it to a million and a half small shareholders, keeping half of the rest while the *Land* retained the other half.

In the days before many people could afford Mercedes, the ungainly but robust little Beetle not only dominated the German market but spread across Europe and into America, becoming the world's most popular car, by far. But Nordhoff made the mistake of failing to develop any other model, and as buyers' wallets fattened and their tastes in cars widened, so VW's sales began to slip in the later 1960s. It went through a difficult period, which was not resolved until the development of the Golf and other new models in the 1970s. Today, thanks in part to robots, it is again doing well (and the faithful old Beetle, its global sales now beyond the 20 million mark, is still being produced in Mexico, by the VW subsidiary there). Of the group's eight factories in Germany, much the largest is the original one at Wolfsburg, which today employs 63,000 people in a town of 130,000, built for and by Volkswagen – a true 'company town'. Here, ahead of any other car firm in the world, Volkswagen in the early 1970s began to develop industrial robots, and it put them into mass operation in 1980. These strange orange creatures swirl and twist their limbs in precise balletic movements, like birds of prey, as they assemble wheels and engines, brakes and batteries, onto Golfs and Jettas moving along the assembly lines. Officials explain that 25 per cent of the final assembly on Golfs is now automised and robotised, leading to a saving of a thousand jobs, yet there have been no redundancies: as modern cars with their multiple gadgets grow ever more complex, they require more overall work, so the same labour force is needed. The unions have therefore not opposed automation.

Volkswagen also owns Audi, a smaller firm making larger, smarter cars, such as the sporty Quattro and the sleek 100. Recently Audi has done well by moving up-market as a high-performance challenger to BMW and Mercedes, and in 1984 it was the third largest European importer into the United States in the luxury category, behind Volvo and Mercedes but ahead of BMW. The Volkswagen group as a whole continues to have its ups and downs, making losses in 1982–3 but then a profit in 1984. Its success still centres around the Golf, the most popular small car in Europe (674,000 of them sold in 1984). And in 1985, when most of the other European giants were reporting losses, VW remained in the black, actually nosing ahead of Fiat and Ford to become Europe's largest group in terms of numbers of cars sold, with 12.9 per cent of the total market.

So the German car industry would appear to be better placed than any other in Europe for coping with the uncertain times ahead. It cannot produce cars as cheaply as the Japanese, but it still has the edge over Japan in modernisation and applied technology – not only VW's robots, but the range of electronic equipment being developed by Bosch, including anti-skid and fuel-injection systems. Indeed, the visual array of electronic devices on and around the dashboards of some new Bosch-fitted BMW models gives the driver, in the words of one motoring writer, 'the sense of being an airline pilot in a cockpit'. However, Germany's car makers do have some anxieties. They have yet to come to grips with the impending new European regulations on the installation of catalytic converters to reduce exhaust emissions (see p. 125). And they face the problems of European over-capacity and growing market saturation, and of the Japanese challenge. All Europe is in the same boat here: Germany, though more strongly placed than most, is by no means exempt. At present Japanese imports do not amount to more than about 10 per cent of the German market: but this leaves unsolved the threat of Japanese inroads into Germany's own export fields elsewhere. So the less upmarket firms, Volkswagen, Opel and Ford, could begin to suffer. All in all, German technical process will need to be backed up by very skilful sales strategy.

A quick look at other leading traditional industries reveals some similar strengths. The aircraft industry made a very slow recovery after the war, partly because of the Allied ban on German development of sophisticated armaments. But today it has built itself a secure niche in European aerospace, albeit in a secondary role to the French. The biggest firm, Messerschmitt-Bölkow-Blohm, has been formed from a merger of various Bavarian and Hamburg interests and no longer has much connection with the Messerschmitt family. It has its headquarters outside Munich and big factories there and in Hamburg and Bremen, which devote themselves above all to doing the fuselage work for the European Airbus, in which it has a 38.5 per cent stake. It makes the Transall military transport aircraft in partnership with Aérospatiale of France, and it builds the Tornado combat fighter together with the British and Italians. It also makes helicopters and missiles, and it shares in the French-led European space programme for the Ariane rockets. MBB with its 36,000 employees is a well-run and successful firm, mainly private but with some *Land* involvement, too. It has been faring better than its smaller competitor, Dornier, of Friedrichshafen on Lake Constance, which has been racked by family feuds since the death in 1969 of old Claude Dornier, the founder.

The chemical industry is also a post-war success story. In the 1930s, the chemical group IG Farben was by far the largest of all German firms. In a bid to prevent it from becoming again so powerful, the Western Allies then split it into three parts: Bayer, of Leverkusen; BASF, at Ludwigshafen: and Höchst, near Frankfurt. Today all three have grown bigger than the old IG Farben: after ICI, they are the leading chemical firms in Europe and they export more than half of their product. As for the textile industry, like some others in Europe it went through a serious crisis in the 1960s and was often regarded as a dead duck: but, after shedding three-quarters of its workforce and installing modern machinery, it has since made a remarkable comeback and now exports nearly 40 per cent of its output.

The picture in these traditional industries may seem fairly bright, as it is throughout the mechanical engineering field. But many other sectors are less well placed. It is thus not easy to give any balanced assessment – and today there are plenty of Jeremiahs who predict that German industry as a whole may soon run into trouble unless it can succeed in making certain major adjustments. The OECD, in its 1984 report on the West German economy, identified three main problems: the need to shift to higher technology products; the difficulties in raising risk capital; and the low profitability of industrial firms. Certainly it is true that even in periods of rapid expansion German companies have generally tended to show only modest profits. Managers lay the blame in large part on the high wage levels and very high social charges, whereby on top of its basic wage-bill a firm must pay out a further 80 per cent on social security and various fringe benefits. They complain also about the heavy taxation in Germany, which reaches 70 per cent on the major part of a company's profits – and in 1986 the Government was dragging its feet over carrying out its promises to reduce this burden. Yet such a step is much needed, for although in the boom years the level of industrial investment in Germany was around 25 per cent of net profit, ahead of the rest of Western Europe, it has since fallen back to about 21 per cent – and this is affecting the ability of firms to modernise their equipment and so face up to the new challenges from the United States and Japan.

There is little doubt that the over-riding problem facing German industry today is the dual one of (a) coping with Japanese competition in nearly every sector, old and new alike, and (b) adapting to the new technologies. Already in a number of traditional fields that used to be among their specialities – cameras, motor-cycles, clocks and watches – the Germans have lost ground heavily to Japan and other Far Eastern producers. Now the Japanese are starting to make inroads into the German machine-tool market, too, and are threatening the optics industry. But it is over the technologies of the future, especially micro-electronics, that the main battle is now being fought. Here for some time the Germans were curiously slow to wake up to the challenge – 'Maybe we had it too easy in the boom years,' suggests one computer expert today, 'and we basked too complacently in our progress in the classic industries.' The Germans are indeed bestirring themselves at last: but like the British and French they find that others, Japanese and Americans, have moved well ahead. In the 1970s the Government poured money into trying to develop a world-class national computer industry: but this failed, and today the German computer market is dominated by the Americans, notably IBM, with Nixdorf as the only successful home-grown independent. More recently the German consumer electronics industry has run into heavy trouble, and two of its household names have moved into foreign hands in order to survive: Grundig has passed under the control of Philips, and AEG has sold Telefunken to Thomson of France – a victory for European integration, but not for German pride. It is true that, as consumers, Germany's offices and factories are equipping themselves fast with the new micro-chip equipment (Germany is Europe's foremost user of semiconductors, just ahead of Britain). But, as manufacturers, German firms' share of world high-technology markets fell from 26 per cent in 1972 to 17 per cent in 1983, as the Japanese surged ahead.

Some critics lay the blame on German firms' reluctance to take risks and to innovate. Others suggest that the true causes may lie deeper, in German education, culture and basic attitudes. The Germans may have industrial flair, but their education system remains stubbornly conservative: far fewer schools than in Britain have yet begun to acquire computers or make children literate in how to use them. And, for all the Germans' affluence and modernism, remarkably few individuals have yet bought personal mini-computers; one sees fewer high-street 'chip shops' than in Britain. Maybe this relates to the rise of a less materialistic younger generation, and to the influence of the Greens and of their campaign against industrial growth and the allegedly dehumanising effects of modern technology – according to one much-quoted set of opinion polls, the number of Germans regarding technology as a 'blessing' dropped from 72 per cent in 1966 to a mere 30 per cent in 1981. Maybe such figures should not be taken too literally: but the trend has worried the Kohl Government, whose Foreign Minister, Hans-Dietrich Genscher, caused quite a national stir in December 1983 when he stated dramatically: 'Whoever visits Japan finds a country in which state and society face the future full with vigour. Whoever visits the United States finds . . . a vision of a high-technology society opening up undreamed-of possibilities. Whoever returns home is struck by the whining cultural pessimism in Germany. Green ideologists and those who think like them preach fear of life, fear of technology and fear of the future.'

It was around this time, in a mood bordering on panic, that the Government decided to take stronger action. In March 1984 it approved a programme for allocating 2.9 billion DM over the next four years to the promotion of research and development in the high-technology industries, notably in data-processing and micro-electronics – a remarkable sum for a government doctrinally committed to non-intervention and lower spending. And in 1985 Kohl readily lent his backing to France's new Eureka project for European joint ventures in advanced fields. These new Government moves have gone to support those already being made by Baden-Württemberg and other *Länder* to promote the new technologies. So it all adds up to quite a buzz of new activity, although sometimes the complaint is voiced that the federal system makes it hard for Bonn and the *Länder* to coordinate the research projects adequately.

A number of individual firms are now making greater efforts to meet the new challenges. While Bosch is progressing with electronic car equipment, the dynamic Nixdorf has been expanding fast in data-processing and telecommunications. Inevitably, much will depend on the results achieved by the greatest colossus of all, Siemens, which employs a staff of 30,000 on research and development and devotes 3.5 billion DM a year to it – an effort without equal in Europe. Since 1984 Siemens has joined with Philips of Holland in launching a 2.2 billion DM five-year 'Megaproject' for leapfrogging into the next generation of micro-chip technology. It all sounds impressive. And it indicates that, after their slow start, German and other European firms have now truly girded their loins. The Germans still have plenty of energy and flair; and, if they choose to apply these qualities, they may yet be able to make the Japanese tremble.

But German industry still carries some handicaps too – and one of these, much talked about, is the paucity of venture capital for starting new businesses. This hardly matters for a big established firm like Siemens, which can easily find the money it needs. But it does make life harder for the smaller entrepreneur, whose contribution is also heeded in this age of micro-technology. The reasons for this situation lie in the somewhat unusual nature of banking, in a Germany where the banks play so powerful a role in industry. In the continental manner, German banks are of the full-service kind, covering a wide range of operations, including acting as stockbroker and investor. Many of the larger banks are regional ones in public hands operated by the *Länder*: but, nationwide, the scene is dominated by three big private commercial bodies, Deutsche Bank, Dresdner Bank and Commerzbank. In the 19th century, private banks of this kind played an important part in financing the new industries, and thus they acquired part ownership of them. This tradition continued in the darker days of the 1920s, when banks injected capital into many firms in order to shore them up; then again after 1945 the banks provided much of the finance for the great industrial revival. Deutsche Bank in particular did well from this by investing astutely, and under its legendary former chairman, Dr Hermann Abs, it built itself a considerable empire. Today in terms of assets it is only the fourteenth largest bank in the world, and the seventh in Europe: but from its gleaming new 24-storey headquarters in Frankfurt it controls many of the levers of Germany industry, and is part-owner of many leading firms, including Bayer, Bosch, Siemens and Volkswagen.

Deutsch Bank however has become a byword for caution, investing only in enterprises with sound credentials and an existing record of success. Other big banks are scarcely less prudent – and so the saying goes, 'In Germany you can easily obtain credits, so long as you don't need them.' So to whom is the smaller, newer firm to turn? Risk capital is hard to find, for reasons that may be in part connected with Germany's past. One private financier suggested to me that rich family trusts which had twice seen their fortunes eroded by inflation, in the 1920s and 1940s, were still hesitant to provide backing for uncertain projects. It is also true that most risk financing used to be done by Jewish bankers, who then left after 1933; and, though Oppenheim and Warburg since returned, most others including the venerable Rothschild have not. Since the war, some German entrepreneurs have tended to seek their venture capital in London or New York, where the market for it is more highly developed. But this is not always convenient. At last, in the past five years or so, the Germans have taken stock of the problem and some banks have begun to make venture capital more available: by 1985 some 30 funding outfits for it had been set up, with a total of 700 million DM for investment. So the finance itself is now more forthcoming: but the banks have yet to develop a tradition of being able to provide a small firm with back-up advice on how to make best use of it.

Another potential industrial handicap, much discussed nowadays, is that the Germans have ceased to be in the forefront of innovation science. This is not for want of effort; their spending on R&D has been consistently high, averaging some 2.5 per cent of GNP in the past fifteen years, half of it financed by industry. But the Germans have won few Nobel prizes since the war: they seem to have become more successful at adapting other people's inventions than producing their own – a change since Daimler's day. Various reasons have been adduced for this. One, as in banking, is the loss of Jewish talent since the 1930s. Another, the trend in school education towards egalitarianism and non-specialisation (see p. 207): this, so it is alleged, may well have brought social and cultural advantages but it handicaps the bright up-and-coming science student. A third factor, perhaps the most important, is the climate of rigidity and orthodoxy in a great many academic research institutes, as was stressed to me by one expert British observer of the German scientific scene: 'The absurdly elevated status of German professors makes them almost godlike in their students' eyes. So it may be more than his career is worth for a young researcher to question the opinion of his professor who may well be in his seventies – with a few honourable exceptions, German research tends to be dictated by a cadre of rather elderly men. And the traditional jealousy between professors leads to a narrow tribalism where cross-fertilisation and the multi-disciplinary approach cannot easily flourish. All this leads to a situation where mediocre "safety-at-all-costs" research may be the order of the day.' Strong words.

If the German industrial record nonetheless remains so positive – and who are the British to be critical of *that*? – in part this is because firms do so much applied research of their own. But they do need the universities too – and research collaboration between the two is still less highly developed than in Britain, let alone the United States. Companies grant large contracts to universities for specific jobs: but rarer are the cases of academic scientists leaving their ivory towers to take part in the 'real world' of industry or to help smaller firms. This is something that Lothar Späth has been trying to change in Baden-Württemberg, as we have seen, and so has the new innovation centre in Berlin, BIG, whose coordinator, Hans Fiedler, told me: 'One of our member firms developed a new machine, but it was too noisy. So I found them a professor who had worked in this field, and I took him along to the company. After five hours at the drawing-board with them, he discovered a solution. That's our day-to-day work: to be brokers between small firms and the university. It sounds obvious, doesn't it? – but it's quite a novelty in Germany.'

German managements today are certainly taking research seriously. They are usually excellent too at the technical side of production, and at personnel relations: but their broader commercial and financial expertise is more often open to question. And this brings us to another of today's major talking-points: are German firms too cautious? Here, as in scientific research, it can be a matter of generation. The older breed of family owners and managers, who performed so brilliantly in the post-war decades, are now growing tired and conservative, wary of adapting to new techniques, and in many cases they have made the mistake of holding on too long, rather than finding a successor. Go to an average chamber of commerce meeting, and it is noticeable how many heads of firms are greybeards. And yet, the Germans are a people who still depend very much on dynamic individual leadership, as opposed to group work. Many of the family bosses have allowed their firms to become too big, therefore bureaucratised and hierarchical, so that the younger middle management may feel frustrated and unable to put its ideas across. Older Germans are not good at delegating responsibility to subordinates: so if for example a senior man is away, his junior will be wary of taking decisions and will let papers pile up on his desk. It all adds up, in many firms, to a certain inflexibility and a spirit of over-prudence. Younger executives may be more open and group-minded: but they are also less industrious and dynamic. There are fewer successful young whizz-kids around in German than in French industry, even though for other reasons French industrial perform-ance is less good.

This may add up to a harsh picture. German managers do have many qualities too, which should equally be stressed. They are adept at handling their staff firmly but kindly, and they tend to have a stronger social ethic than British or American ones, believing that only a happy firm can be a profitable one. They are perfectionist almost to the point of neurosis, but this does carry advantages. It makes them punctilious over delivering goods on time, and over checking and re-checking the tiniest technical details to ensure that no flawed product goes through – no wonder German cars have so fine a record of reliability. But managers, like other Germans, also have a mania for security. They feel the urgent need to reduce uncertainties, to prepare careful safety margins and fall-back posi-tions, and to do all they can to avoid crisis, for they are not very good at handling these. So long as they are working to a set routine they do fine: but, if something unexpected happens, they are not so good at improvising. As an example, I was quoted the case of strikes: if a few key workers strike in a factory, French and British managers show much more initiative in swiftly altering work schedules so as to keep the plant going, whereas Germans will simply close it down (but then, it could be argued that the British and French have had rather more practice at coping with strikes!).

One especially negative aspect of this caution is that few younger executives in Germany are prepared to risk leaving the security of a larger firm to set up on their own. It is true that this pattern is just beginning to change, now that mammoth organisations have become less popular with younger recruits who feel that 'small is beautiful'; the old pioneering spirit of enterprise and risk-taking, that used to be common in Germany in the time of Krupp or Daimler, is starting to be seen again in the micro-technology field. But it is still much rarer than in France or the United States. One deterrent factor could be the lack of venture capital: or the typically German fear of the stigma of failure, in a nation that does not readily condone weakness; or even the softening effects of affluence and the Welfare State. All these are cited as reasons. And another explanation certainly is that German colleges and universities provide very little training in business administration and entrepreneurship.

Traditionally Germany has no business schools, either public or private, of the kind so dominant in America and recently copied in Britain, France and elsewhere. Nor is there any equivalent of the French elitist Grandes Ecoles that turn out top engineers and administrators. All the training is done in the ordinary universities, which increasingly have become similar to each other and non-specialised (see p. 219). It is true that a number of Germans go to attend INSEAD (in France), or Harvard, or other foreign graduate business schools: but, when they return to Germany, they tend to go into management consultancy rather than industry. This lack of elitist education has sometimes worried Germans, especially those on the Right, and in 1967 Chancellor Kiesinger tried to set up a German version of France's prestigious Ecole Nationale d'Administration. His cabinet approved, but the project was then vetoed by a committee of civil servants. After all, education is a *Land* matter, and if a college of this kind were put in one *Land*, then the others would want them too and chaos would ensure – or so the argument ran.

So how do companies select their future senior staff? Answer: direct from the universities. The recruiting officer of a big firm will make it his duty to keep in touch with a few key professors in certain universities, who are doing specialist work of interest to the firm, and he will ask them to recommend their best students. He may know that Professor X at Heidelberg is the best for precision engineering, or Professor Y at Aachen, and so he will go head-hunting there, in rivalry with other firms. It is an *ad hoc* kind of elitism in a way, on an old-boy basis, not especially democratic. Moreover, the bright young stars thus recruited tend to have had an engineering or other technical education, rather than one in the skills of management. The bigger firms then conduct their own in-service training of graduate staff, in a range of skills including finance and administration, and this they do extremely well: Siemens in particular has a high reputation. Its senior recruiting officer, Peter Thust, explained to me: 'In the United States, management is a separate profession in itself. Here, it is not. In Germany, a manager will have the technical background of whatever his firm deals with: thus, in a bank, a manager will probably have studied economies at college; and here, at Siemens, engineering. Our sales manager is an engineer, our R&D manager a physicist; on our main board of eleven directors, only two are non-technical. This has many advantages, for it means that directors understand a firm's product. We're quite happy with the present university system, and anyway we have no means of changing it. We do not need business schools.'

Others are less sure. They argue that the system may suit a giant like Siemens which has the means to do its own training, but that it is failing to supply the wider industrial world, especially smaller firms and new ventures, with a new business breed that has the required entrepreneurial flair and modern managerial skills. Germany here is falling behind its competitors. A young man trained by Siemens to be a cog in their big machine, who then leaves to strike out on his own, may feel a little inadequate. A further argument, which I heard from several German INSEAD alumni, is that the growth of student numbers and the decline in university standards have made business schools far more necessary than they used to be. It was this thinking that in 1984 led a group of industrialists to found Germany's first private university for business administration, in Koblenz. Financed by industry and the payment of fees, it is unashamedly elitist – and it marks a totally new departure for Germany.

Daimler-Benz is a firm quite as traditionalist as Siemens. But there I was given a different slant on the problem, by the sales director of its Untertürkheim factory, Hans-Wolfgang Hirschbrunn: 'The universities are just not giving us the highly-qualified people that we need. Germany today is as weak at university education as it is strong on the training of shopfloor apprentices. On the other hand, my shopfloor and office staff here work very well and I have excellent relations with the works council. The ongoing success of German industry derives more than anything from its good labour relations.'

A paradise of labour harmony – but what of the waning work-ethic?

Over brandy and cigars in their comfortable oak-panelled office, I discussed German labour affairs one day with a group of smartly-dressed trade union executives in Stuttgart. One of them had a doctorate in economics; another was on the supervisory board of Robert Bosch; nearly all spoke perfect English. They could have been company directors in a board-room. One of them said: 'It is true that relations have become a little more conflictual nowadays, owing to lower growth and higher unemployment. But basically we still believe that it is by cooperating with management, rather than fighting it, that we stand the best chance of securing better pay and working conditions – and the results prove it. What is more, as we see it our moral obligation is not just to our own members or other workers, but to German society as a whole, where we must play an active role in upholding democracy and the rule of law. So, if you like, we're part of the establishment and proud of it. We're certainly not revolutionaries: we do not want to overthrow capitalism but to reform it from inside, in a more "social" direction, within the social market economy. We have moved beyond the class-war phase where so many French and British unionists are still bogged down; and we believe that workers have an interest in helping their firms to remain profitable. Not that we have illusions about German employers. Some of them, it is true, in being generous to their staff and cooperative with the unions are genuinely sincere and even idealistic. But others behave well because they have no other choice: you see, they are bound hand and foot by a powerful set of labour laws, among the world's best.'

That seemed to me an eloquent summary of the various interrelating factors that underly Germany's envied industrial harmony. This can even be traced back to the 19th century, for the industrial revolution arrived later than in Britain, so workers did not have to struggle for so long to achieve tolerable conditions. Bismarck in the 1870s, in an effort to avoid class conflict, was ahead of the rest of Europe in promoting welfare legislation and in sanctioning factory councils. This did not prevent all confrontation: but it did help to imbue German workers with some sense of cooperation and involvement in their firms. However by the early 1930s, though strong in overall membership (6.5 million), German unions lay fragmented in some 200 separate bodies, divided on religious and ideological lines, Catholic and Protestant, Communist, Socialist and so on – and this was to prove a fatal weakness, for it made them incapable of forming a united front against the Nazis, who thus found it easier to get their hands on German industry and to abolish the unions and imprison many of their leaders.

The survivors emerged from the war with a carefully thought-out resolve to build a stronger and more unified union structure, better able to stand as a bulwark of democracy. Some of them had fled to Britain, where TUC colleagues gave them friendly support. And so it was, after 1945, that Vic Feather and other British union leaders actively helped the Germans to set up the kind of sensible, logical framework that they would dearly have liked to see installed on the chaotic British labour scene, too! This was one of the manifold ways in which Germany by being able to make a clean start, actually benefited from losing the war.

The system thus created still exists today, and it is exemplary. While Britain has some 400 unions, often at loggerheads, the German federation, DGB, comprises just seventeen; and they are organised in such a way that, within one factory, all the manual and technical staff tend to belong to the same union, whereas in Britain there may be a dozen or more, split up on craft lines. Thus, for example, if you work for Bosch you are in the metalworkers' union, whether you are employed as mechanic, electrician or computer programmer. So there are no demarcation disputes. Nor is the German labour movement divided politically, as in France or Italy where the big national unions pursue their destructive rivalries within each firm. Moreover, the closed shop is illegal, and so are political strikes. This rational structure lends strength to the unions, and it greatly simplifies collective bargaining and other dealings with employers. It is certainly one of the main elements making for harmony on the German labour scene.

The 17 unions federated into the *Deutscher Gewerkschaftsbund* (DGB) have a total membership of some 7.6 million; the biggest of them, IG Metall, for the metalworkers, claims to be the free world's largest trade union, with 2.5 million members. There are also three other unions outside the DGB, including one for salaried staffs, and another for civil servants, who are not allowed to strike and therefore under DGB rules cannot qualify to make up a union. With rising unemployment, overall union membership has been tending to fall slightly, but less so than in most Western countries: it still stands at some 38 per cent of all employees. The figure is as much as 85 or 90 per cent in the steel and mining industries, but only 28 per cent in banking and commerce. All in all, the DGB with its headquarters in Düsseldorf is a rich and powerful organisation, and it is not ashamed to try its hand at capitalism in order to add to its resources: it owns a number of commercial enterprises with a total staff of 100,000 including one of Germany's largest banks (useful for funding strikes, when needed), the second largest insurance company, a travel agency, and shops and printing firms, and until 1986 owned the mammoth house-building firm, *Neue Heimat* (see p. 406). The DGB also stages arts festivals and has its own economic institute.

Probably the biggest single reason for the success of German labour relations is that they are governed by a strong legal framework – and in Germany you can never get very far without a good law behind you. In the first place, important federal laws provide for employee delegates to share in the process of decision-making in larger firms, while others oblige managements to consult with their staff, and seek their approval on a whole range of matters, through the works councils. Other laws lay down the rules for job security, working conditions, welfare and fringe benefits, collective wage bargaining, and so on. Of course this kind of machinery exists in other countries too: but in Germany it is particularly extensive and precise, and is strongly weighted in favour of the employee, sometimes in a manner that is almost comic (in the civil service in Baden-Württemberg, there is a rule that the head of an office *must* send a bouquet of flowers to a member of staff who has been away sick for six weeks). This battery of legislation more or less forces a German firm to be a good employer and to take labour relations in a positive spirit: benevolent paternalism is possible, but not union-bashing. And, as the Germans are a cooperative and law-abiding people, both sides in the labour partnership tend to desire actively to work together, so as to make the laws work fairly and fully.

What is more, strikes in Germany are illegal except under certain conditions. Under the labour laws, each annual wage agreement becomes a kind of 'peace treaty': unions are committed to refraining from wildcat or other strikes while the agreement is in force, and when it expires at the end of a year they can strike only in pursuit of a genuine grievance, after all means of arbitration have been exhausted. Remarkably, these restrictions were not imposed on the unions against their will by a right-wing government, but were actually elaborated by the DGB itself as guidelines for strike action, back in 1949. The DGB laid down that a strike should be called only as a last resort and not without the backing of a union's national headquarters, and only if a secret ballot of members concerned had thrown up a 75 per cent majority in favour of it: in Baden-Württemberg in 1982, a planned strike by the public employees' union was called off because the vote for it was only 74.3 per cent! In defiance of the DGB, the left-wing printers' union in 1983 changed its rules to allow its executive to call a strike without a ballot, but it is the only one to have done so.

These laws and guidelines are generally observed, and this goes a long way to explain the low strike level in Germany which in 1983, for example, involved only 94,000 workers and led to the loss of 41,000 working days, compared with 1,484,000 days lost in France, 3,754,000 in Britain, 13,312,000 in Italy and 17,461,000 in the United States. It is true that matters have been changing a little recently, with the rise of a more militant breed of union leader: but even IG Metall's strategic seven-week strike in the south-west in 1984, something of a new departure in Germany, was voted for with some reluctance by the rank and file. Being not only law-abiding but by nature work-motivated, German employees tend to have the gut-feeling that a strike is a sign of failure, an irritating symptom of disorder, a break in the decent business of getting on with the job – not always the British attitude: Scargill's year-long miners' strike in 1984–5 would, in Germany, have been not only illegal but psychologically impossible. Not however that all is totally serene within factories – as we can see by looking next at collective bargaining, worker participation and the works councils.

The collective bargaining is conducted on a regional and sector-by-sector basis: in every *Land* the employers' association of each branch of industry meets annually with its union counterpart to thrash out a deal on rates of pay, hours of work, holidays and other conditions. The agreement is then legally binding. As a result, governments have never found it necessary to impose a wage or price freeze, or to create a legal minimum wage as there is in France. Unions have generally concentrated on the battle for better conditions, while on wages they have shown restraint. Maybe this derives from the deep-rooted German fear of inflation, in a land still haunted by the trauma of the 1920s.

Worker participation in management (*Mitbestimmung*) began soon after the war in the coal, iron and steel sectors; it was an initiative of the victorious British, who chose it as a way of punishing the private owners of these firms for the support they had given to Hitler. The system then spread to the US zone; it became federal law, and is still in force today. Each coal and steel firm has a supervisory board (*Aufsichtsrat*), half of whose members are appointed by management and the other half elected by the staff. The board then chooses a neutral chairman from outside the firm, and he has the decisive vote. This system has generally worked smoothly and is appreciated both by owners and unions. The board of management retains the last word on policy matters, but it does pay attention to the *Aufsichtsrat*, which can use its influence quite powerfully. And this partnership is often cited to explain the absence of serious conflict during the periods of major lay-offs in coal and steel, when the unions were able to use the *Aufsichtsrat* and the works council to negotiate a 'social plan' of phased redundancies, high pensions and retraining schemes, generously funded by Bonn.

Since 1952, all limited and joint stock companies in Germany with a staff of over 500 have had supervisory boards with one-third worker representation. Then in 1976 a controversial law was passed, bringing this quota of staff delegates up to 50 per cent in all firms with a personnel of more than 2,000. But their position is not as strong as in the coal and steel industries, for their numbers must include the senior employee of the firm, and he tends to side with management; and, instead of a neutral chairman, the board is chaired by a shareholder who has an extra casting vote. This weights the *Aufsichtsrat* towards the owners – and the unions are none too pleased. Nor are employers either so happy with this *Mitbestimmung*. They opposed its introduction in 1976, and especially they object to the clause whereby it is the *Aufsichtsrat* that elects the company's own board of directors. However, many managers do find virtues in the system: 'It has proved a useful instrument for controlling the workforce and has helped to create a social consensus,' said a senior Daimler-Benz executive. But unions do not see it that way. At the Blohm & Voss shipyards in Hamburg, a militant IG Metall official told me: 'As members of the *Aufsichtsrat* we can exercise a personal influence: but management can always get a majority and we cannot block its decisions. Our economic influence is zero.' The DGB view is that *Mitbestimmung* in these firms may be better than nothing, for it at least allows the staff to give their views, but it is no real co-determination. The unions would like to see the coal and steel system applied more widely, but they see little hope of this. In the meantime, the real influence of unions and workers within a firm is exercised much less through these boards than through the works councils. These are highly prized by the unions, and along with collective bargaining they are much the most significant feature of German labour relations.

In every enterprise employing five people or more, the management must agree to the setting up of a works council (*Beitriebsrat*) if the staff ask for it – and this they nearly always do, except in very tiny firms. Many a smallish company may contain no union members at all, but will still have a *Betriebsrat*. The council is elected by the staff in secret ballot, from independent and/or union-sponsored candidates. It has an office on the premises, and in a firm of any size its senior members will work full-time on their council duties while still being fully salaried by the company. The council enjoys considerable scope, with a consultative voice in economic matters and real powers of co-determination in welfare, personnel and working life. In the economic field, the law says that every three months the management must inform the council of its investment projects and financial plans and must seek its views, though it need not act on them. Over a whole range of matters that affect the daily life of the staff, including safety regulations, the installation and use of new equipment, the canteen, working hours and holiday schedules, management must seek the approval of the council making changes. The council can object, if it can argue that the measures contravene a law or wage agreement or would disadvantage employees. If no solution is found, then the matter is sent to be decided by a labour court (these generally favour the employees).

In the vast majority of firms, these procedures tend in practice to work quite smoothly – and the unions and employers alike speak much more warmly of the works council system than of the *Aufsichtsrat*. However, there have recently been growing frictions over such matters as dismissals, flexible working time, and the introduction of new technologies. These last had up till now been accepted fairly easily by unions and workers (as in the case of the robots at Volkswagen) and most employers had smoothed the way by carefully phasing the redundancies caused by automation. However, with productivity still rising steadily, some unions have grown more restive in the past two or three years. There have been cases of works councils taking employers to court over their right to introduce

Computer Aided Design or electronic devices for controlling work rhythms.

The issue of recruitment and dismissals has been causing worse tensions. A works council has the right to be consulted about all new appointments, even to read the candidates' applications: the management makes the final choice, but must state its reasons. If it wants to make the lay-offs on economic grounds, then it must also give reasons: but usually it will get its way, if it can present a strong case. It may however have more difficulty if it wants to dismiss an individual for incompetence or indiscipline, or even to transfer someone to another department. Here the council can insist on full-scale negotiations, which may drag on for weeks: at one Stuttgart factory, the personnel director told me, 'We had a woman clerk who became hysterical and disruptive, but it was hard to get the *Betriebsrat* to agree to our sacking her. By law, we do have the last word in such a case. But we have to weigh this against the need to keep on good terms with the works council and our staff. Naturally, the *Betriebsrat* sees itself as the defender of labour, and on principal it is against sackings of any kind. If we dismiss someone against the council's wishes, then we usually find ourselves taken to court.'

Relations between management and councils are variable in nature, usually smoothest in the older family-run paternalist firms and not easy in larger ones where a militant union is strong. There are no shop-stewards in Germany, and a union is not institutionally represented inside the firm as it is in Britain, so it must exert its influence via the works council. And this today can cause problems. At Bosch, a group with an excellent record of benevolent staff policies, the personnel manager nonetheless expressed anxieties to me: 'Formally the unions deal with firms collectively, not individually, through the annual bargaining system. They would like to make more impact inside firms, but they can do this only through their members on the works councils. So, in the Bosch group, our works councils are becoming more politicised, owing to the presence of little handfuls of youngish IG Metall militants. They go off on trade union courses in the firm's time, and they come back breathing their dogma – so *we* are paying for them to be indoctrinated against us! With the councils as a whole our relations are excellent: it is just a few troublemakers here and there that provoke us.' I heard the same story in some other firms: 'The works council is starting to throw its weight around too much, even rebuking the managing director for parking his car in the wrong place,' or, 'The council took down the photo of our revered Founder from the wall in their office, and put up one of the union leader instead.' Such are the problems caused by the rise of a new breed of union activist ready to exploit the tensions caused today by unemployment.

The economic difficulties of the past ten years have shown that German unions are more concerned about unemployment than wage stagnation. The three years 1981–3 actually saw an overall drop of 3.5 per cent in real earnings (according to union estimates): but there was very little unrest, and unions repeatedly put their signatures to annual wage increases below the rate of inflation. This could be seen as a triumph for the collective bargaining system. It may also have been related to the fact that the Social Democrats were in power until October 1982 – and, although the DGB has no organic link with the SPD (unlike the TUC with the Labour Party), nonetheless there is much in the way of close informal links and sympathy, and a general desire by unions not to make things too difficult for an SPD government. But after the CDU came to power the picture changed. Not only did the unions dislike the Kohl regime as such, but they saw that its Thatcherite policies were unlikely to do much for employment. Kohl, it is true, produced some extra money for job creation schemes: but he refused any reflation that might stem the rise of unemployment, which reached a peak of 10.6 per cent in the icy January of 1985 and averaged 9.3 per cent (some 2.3 million people) over the year as a whole. And so, as in other countries, how to deal with this problem has become a major political issue. Kohl and his Labour Minister, Norbert Blüm, have favoured early retirement and have provided special funding for it. This palliative is also popular with a number of the unions, led by those in heavy manual sectors – construction, mining, railways – where workers soon get physically worn out. But others have preferred to go along with the EEC Commission's proposals for shorter working hours, even though Germans for long have been working fewer hours than in most advanced countries.

The campaign for a 35-hour week was taken up in earnest by IG Metall in 1984. This union had just acquired new and more dynamic leaders, who were anxious to rally their rank-and-file and to refute criticism that it was being too cosily chummy with employers. So they decided to make a test case of the issue, and they produced figures to support their claim that a phased reduction from 40 to 35 hours could yield 1.4 million extra jobs within two years. The employers retorted that this was dangerous nonsense: if, as the unions demanded, there were no cuts in pay, then costs might rise by up to 16 per cent, leading to a serious drop in German competitiveness – 'Yes, the 35-hour week would create more jobs – in the Far East,' read the car-stickers. Most independent economic analysts leaned towards the employers' view, and so did the Kohl Government, very vocally: whereas federal governments since the war has usually taken care to keep neutral in labour disputes, this time Kohl rather tactlessly put his weight behind the metal industry bosses – and this further inflamed IG

Metall, who began to see their projected strike as a political challenge to Bonn. It was an unusual departure in post-war German labour relations. 'This is an issue that could well decide a new balance of power within European society!' proclaimed Franz Steinkühler, the aggressive and acid-tongued new deputy leader of IG Metall (he is also on the *Aufsichtsrat* of Daimler-Benz).

Since the employers refused to negotiate, the union felt that it had a legal case for industrial action. As is common in Germany, rather than stage an expensive nationwide strike it preferred to select regional target areas – in this case, the wealthy automotive industries of Baden-Württemberg and Hessen, where the employees were highly-paid and secure in their jobs, and thus were prepared to risk and to fund a long-drawn-out stoppage. Here the much-publicised strike began in May: 60,000 workers were called out, the employers replied with lock-outs, and soon 300,000 were idle, some of them as far afield as Wolfsburg and Munich, where VW and BMW factories were forced to close too because of lack of spare parts from Bosch and others in the south-west. The world's Press screamed their banner headlines: 'Is this the end of Germany's vaunted labour consensus? – is Scargillism finally on the march in *Wirtschaftswunderland?*' In fact, it was not. For all Herr Steinkühler's sharp words, the strike was conducted in a fairly gentlemanly way by both sides, without violence. Most workers took part out of union loyalty rather than real enthusiasm: reporters found them apathetic, and one opinion poll indicated that only 31 per cent of IG Metall members were in favour of a 35-hour week. After dragging on for seven weeks, the strike finally ended in a negotiated compromise, on the basis of a 38½-hour week, without cuts in pay, for all workers in Germany's metal industries. Neither side seemed to have won, the union least of all, though it put a brave face on things, claiming that this was but a first step. The employers had made concessions, but were glad that the 1½-hour cut was to be applied flexibly so that in some factories, for example, key skilled workers could remain on 40 hours, while less important manual ones could go down to 37. Above all, by re-organising and taking up slack, employers found it necessary to take on no more than 70,000 or so extra staff. It was quite a blow for the IG Metall thesis.

Germany today expects to have to go on living with high unemployment until about 1990, when demographic factors should start to provide relief. At present, owing to a fairly high birth-rate in the late 1960s, the potential labour force is still growing by some 200,000 a year. And, in view of this, an annual GNP growth rate of at least 3 per cent would be needed to prevent the jobless total from escalating further, bearing in mind that productivity too is likely to rise by some 2 per cent a year. However, in the early 1970s the contraceptive pill suddenly spread widely in Germany, leading to a sharp decline in the birth-rate: as a result, the number of 16-year-olds will have fallen from around 1 million in the early 1980s to 630,000 in 1990. Germany's slumping population, in other respects quite worrying (see p. 171), is here at least a kind of blessing. 'And that is one reason why we are so much opposed to the 35-hour week, for it would soon lead us again to a shortage of workers,' I was told at the German employers' federation in Cologne; 'we prefer early retirement, flexible hours and job-sharing schemes – all of them much less costly to operate and easier to rescind when the time comes.'

In the meantime, various short-term solutions are being tried out. Some firms offer reduced hours in the years before retirement, with little loss of pay; or half-time work at half-pay for ex-apprentices, which amounts to job-sharing; or fluctuating hours in line with demand for product; or extra holidays on part-time pay. In this leisure-conscious age, such schemes are often popular with younger employees, who appreciate the extra freedom. But they are resisted by some unions, such as IG Metall, who find that the flexibility makes it harder for them to maintain a unified control over their members or to negotiate coherently with employers. In a large number of firms, however, staff have readily gone along with plans for early retirement, supported by a federal scheme that enables a worker to leave at 58 on three-quarters salary, part of it paid by the Government. The federal employment agency has also given pump-priming money to cities and *Länder* for local job creations of a minor nature, such as tidying public parks – better than nothing. More important, in 1985 the Government pushed through a bill making it much easier for firms to hire staff on short-term contracts of up to 18 months: previously many employers were reluctant to take on more than the bare minimum they needed, because of the difficulties with dismissals, so the new law was expected to lead to a surge of new jobs. Unemployment did in fact fall back to an average 9 per cent for 1986, from 9.3 per cent the year before.

On all this the unions remain sceptical. They have been angry, too, at Chancellor Kohl's welfare spending cuts, which have not spared unemployment benefits. In Germany these are scaled according to previous earnings, rather than being paid at flat rates as in more egalitarian Britain; and in 1984 they were brought down from 68 to 63 per cent of previous pay, for people without children, and for the first year without a job. Even so, the benefits remain fairly generous by most Western standards, and they are remarkably easy to obtain, if you try. The story is told of Peter Milz, a contractor at Siegburg, near Bonn, who fired a lady employee in order to give a job to a girl apprentice. The dismissed woman drew over 15,000 DM in benefits in one year, before it was discovered that she was Herr Milz's wife and the apprentice was his daughter. What is more, Milz was a CDU member of the *Bundestag*. His party made him promise to pay back his wife's indemnities – but he found that he couldn't. All had been entirely legal, and the state employment office refused his money. He had to give it to charity.

The question widely discussed today is how far Germany's vaunted labour harmony can survive, in this new period of job insecurity, declining work-ethic and disruptive technological innovation. Certainly the old values are being challenged for times have changed. In the early post-war years, union leaders easily found common cause with employers in their mutual desire to forge a democratic society and rebuild the country by sustained hard work: but today's new leaders, now taking over the reins as the old ones retire, no longer have such priorities. Many of them were students in the 1968 period. Very few are Greens; in fact they show a contempt for the Greens' 'alternative economy' ideas. But they have radical ideas and are much less ready than their elders to come to terms with capitalism. And this worries some employers, as the owner of one family firm in Bavaria told me: 'The old union leaders had come up from the shopfloor, they were close to the workers and understood realities. The new ones are university theorists, trying to impose dogmatic solutions.' But from a 38-year-old union chief in Stuttgart I heard the view: 'Our generation is certainly more dynamic and alert than the old one: we bargain more toughly, for we have to, in today's hard times. But very few of us are Marxist. We do *not* want to overthrow the system.' It may be hard to generalise about so fluid a situation: but the overall picture would seem to be that the new union leaders remain quite moderate by most British or French standards. Some unions may have moved leftwards, but they are still open to realistic compromise: the printers' union for example has become rather militant, but after a rearguard fight against planned redundancies it did finally accept the new computer technologies – as has not exactly happened in Fleet Street.

Above all, the legal framework still holds strong, adhered to by both sides and enabling most disputes to find an acceptable solution. And it is generally agreed that the 1984 strikes, for all the angry words at the time, did little to alter the basic labour cohesion. Younger union activists in some firms may be adopting more aggressive tactics; but workers as a whole remain cooperative, industrious, and not anti-capitalist. In the older family firm of the Swabian type, they still respond happily to benevolent paternalism – the kind of firm where the boss may take his foreman to a pub lunch on a Sunday to discuss his financial policies, or where a working family may feel proud to have served the same employer for three or four generations. If less so than thirty years ago, German employees still display quite a degree of company loyalty – and this may be one of the fruits of the excellent apprenticeship system.

Germany is recognised as the leader of Europe in youth vocational training. Its apprenticeships go back centuries, to the guilds of the middle ages, and today the system is highly extensive and elaborate: arguably it is one of the most impressive features of modern Germany, bringing massive advantages both to the economy as a whole and to the young individuals concerned. The rules for the scheme are laid down by the *Bund*, but it is operated and largely paid for by the firms themselves, great and small – and nearly every German employer, from Siemens down to the village butcher, will at one time or another have taken on an *'Azubi'* (*Auszubildende* – trainee). Apprenticeship places are thus provided each year for the vast majority of school leavers: in 1984, no less than 705,000 youngsters took them up.

The *Azubi* is given a contract for a two- or three-year course, on a 'dual training' basis, whereby he or she spends roughly three and a half days of the week in a firm, learning a particular job, and one and a half days at a *Berufsschule* (state-run vocational centre), continuing general education and acquiring a variety of skills. Formal training is offered in over 400 different vocations, among the most popular being car mechanic, bank clerk and hairdresser. The apprentice receives a small wage from the firm, some 600 to 700 DM a month, which is usually topped up by parental support. If he went straight from school into unskilled work, he might start at 1,500 to 2,000 DM: on the other hand, once qualified, he can soon be earning over 2,500 DM, so the apprenticeship is a good investment.

Some 60 per cent of apprentices then get salaried jobs in the same firm: the figure would be higher, if employers could provide more posts. Others have to look elsewhere for work, which of course has become harder to find: even so, about nine out of 10 apprentices do find jobs somewhere. This goes to explain the low level of youth unemployment in Germany, only 7.7 per cent in the 16-to-20 age group, the lowest figure in the EEC: of all those out of work in Germany in 1984, 23.8 per cent were under 25 in age, which may sound a lot, but it compared with over 38 per cent in both Britain and France. So it is not surprising that the apprenticeship scheme is widely popular both with young people and with the unions. As well as school leavers of 16, an increasing number of places are now being taken up by those who stay on to get their *Abitur* at 19 or 20 but then feel that a trainee qualification offers better prospects than a university pass degree (see p. 216). With demand in this way outstripping supply, the Kohl Government in 1983–4 managed to coax more firms into offering places, with the result that all but about 40,000 applicants a year now find them. However, one growing problem is that especially in rural areas it may be far from easy for a youngster to secure an outlet in the kind of trade that interests him: cases are reported, for instance, of farmers' sons wanting to train as factory mechanics but being obliged to settle for *Azubi* posts in the local bakery or butcher's shop, in their anxiety to avoid the dole. This is frequent, and it has brought the apprenticeship system under some criticism.

In other respects, by heightening the skills of the workforce the scheme has been of immense benefit to German industry and is one of the main factors behind its post-war success. Leaving aside higher education, nearly 70 per cent of Germans are occupationally qualified, compared with only 30 per cent in Britain. And according to one recent international survey,[1] the higher standard of technical expertise among shopfloor workers is the principal reason for Germany's much greater level of productivity. A study of several firms making simple metal products such as coil springs found that German output per employee is 50 per cent higher than in Britain. The secret lies with the apprentice system, especially in the big firms with their extensive training workshops.

Robert Bosch, the very archetype of a kindly paternalistic Swabian firm, has retained its original philanthropic spirit even though it has now expanded into a worldwide group, and it has a good personnel record too. It created its own apprenticeship scheme in 1913. At its main factory in Stuttgart, I talked to the head of training, Horst Bohne: 'I myself began as an *Azubi* here, aged seventeen. Later I went to a technical college and became an engineer. One member of the Bosch board of directors is an ex-apprentice, as are several of the supervisory board. Today we have thirty applicants for every place we can offer, we take on 950 a year, and 80 per cent of them then stay with us – a very high record.' I visited the workshop, where a group of lively Swabian girls were doing metal-work; boys in neat blue overalls, several of them Greek and Turkish immigrants, were working at micro-processors or making useful implements such as torches or electric drills. Later I went to a local *Berufsschule* (these are not run by the firms, but are part of the *Land* education system). Here, intent-looking teenagers were being taught a range of skills, from beauty treatment and tiling bathrooms to engine assembly and using word-processors. Those doing machinery in their firms study carpentry at the *Berufsschule*, or vice versa.

Bohne said: 'The dual system provides the ideal transition from school to work life for the less academically-minded youngster. Our apprentices appear to be grateful to us for training them, so they develop a loyalty to the firm and become more motivated.' Though not all employers are as enlightened as Bosch, I heard Bohne's view echoed by a secondary-school teacher in a working-class district of Karlsruhe: 'Kids who at fifteen were bored, rebellious and awkward

[1] Quoted in the *Financial Times*, February 22, 1985.

in school seem to change completely when they become apprentices. I meet them a year later, and they are polite, enthusiastic and self-confident.' So does this mean that they still feel the incentive to work hard, as their parents' generation did?

There has been much public debate recently about the alleged decline of the work ethic, in this nation that traditionally has not only been industrious by temperament but has also believed religiously in hard work as a primary virtue. Are the old attitudes changing, as the socio-logists claim? According to Allensbach surveys, in 1962 only 33 per cent of Germans would admit to preferring leisure to work time, but this figure has risen to 48 per cent by 1979; and when an international enquiry in 1983 asked for comments on the statement, 'I often give more to my job than is demanded of me, it's so important to me that I sacrifice a lot to it,' only 43 per cent of the Germans agreed, compared with 68 per cent Americans and 66 per cent of the supposedly lazy British. It might be naive to interpret such findings too literally: but they do correspond to a shift that is noted by employers, teachers and anyone who talks to young people. Work used to be an end in itself: now it is smart to find it less so. Many observers see this as a healthy trend, a sign that the all-work-and-no-play Germans are at last learn-ing to relax and enjoy life. But for others it is a symptom of the decline of the old moral values and a threat to the economy. And so the Ger-mans have been thrown into a frenzy of self-analysis and self-doubt on the issue. Are we, they ask, swinging from workaholism to the other extreme? A 'Nein!' yelled a *Bild Zeitung* headline in 1983, *'Wir sind NICHT faul!'* (significantly, *'faul'* means not only 'lazy' but also 'foul, rotten, putrid', whereas 'lazy' in English is less pejorative). And so the debate goes on. Certainly attitudes to work have become more relaxed, less moralistic: but does this mean that those Germans with jobs are actually working less hard in practice?

The issue has to be seen in a post-war perspective. After the war the Germans worked demoniacally hard, not only in order to rebuild their country and find a new prosperity, but also as a kind of instinctive act of expiation for the evil of the war and of Nazism, and a means of regaining dignity and respect among nations. Then this motivation gradually waned. Already the rising generation of the late 1960s was beginning to question the work ethic, and this mood was to spread during the 1970s as older people, exhausted by the earning of their wealth, wanted more time to enjoy it, while younger ones grew up with less materialistic attitudes. These trends pre-dated the arri-val of the Greens. They also had little to do with the rise in unem-ployment, which did not make its impact until the early 1980s. In fact, unemployment has if anything produced a swing back towards hard work, for people today find that they can no longer take a job for granted and they are more prepared to be dedicated about work when they find it.

So the Germans are becoming less neurotically workaholic, more normal and more like other nations. They have discovered the leisure ethic, but without really losing the work ethic. As one manager put it, 'After the war we made superhuman efforts. Now we have slowed down, but not become lazy.' And because the Germans still tend to work thoroughly and methodically, with care and concentration, they can get through a great deal of effective work without having to devote as much time to it as those who loll about on the job, with endless tea-breaks, like the British. After the Belgians, German employees have the shortest working year in the West: in 1986, it was an annual 1,708 hours, compared with 1,763 in France, 1,778 in Britain, 1,912 in the United States, 2,166 in Japan. Most German employers grant five to six weeks' paid leave: this, with public holidays added, means that the German in 1984 had an average of 39 days' holiday a year, against 34 in France, 33 in Britain, only 23 in the United States.

The work ethic today varies with class and age-group, and tends to survive most powerfully among middle-aged people in the middle classes, where often it is a matter of pride and social status, of keeping up with the Müllers. To lose your job, even if it is not your own fault, is a matter of dishonour, to be hidden if possible from the neighbours. And so there are stories of jobless clerks and executives who continue to leave the house each day in their office clothes, and return in the evening. Sometimes the ex-breadwinner will even seek to hide his shame from his own family – and his kids on their way back from school may be startled to come across *Vati* not at his desk but feeding the pigeons in the park.

Such behaviour is much less likely among working-class people, who have always shown more solidarity and less petty amour-propre in face of common problems such as unemployment. Nor in the middle-class would it be found so often amongst the young. This generation is not so much lazy and work-shy as more critical and demanding than its elders in its attitude to work: 'My father,' said an engineer of 30, 'would never admit that he doesn't enjoy his job. If mine doesn't satisfy me, I say so. Yet in practice I work almost as hard as he does. If he found that he couldn't spare the time for a holiday, he'd feel proud of that: but I and my friends, we take pride just as much in finding better ways of spending our leisure.' So the accent today is on trying to avoid jobs that are boring, rather than on merely looking for higher pay. In Allensbach surveys, when people wanting to change their job were asked their reasons for doing so, those answering 'Because I want a more interesting one' rose from 26 to 44 per cent between 1953 and 1979, while the replies 'In order to earn more money' fell from 27 to 22 per cent. The advent of automation and modern technology has left some young employees with a sense of bewilderment in face of new impersonal work routines, and this may help to explain another Allensbach finding: in answer to the question 'Do you feel free in your job?', 49 per cent said "yes" in 1973, but only 36 per cent ten years later. Either the work has been growing less attractive: or, more probably, expectations of job satisfaction have been rising. So this new generation rejects work for work's sake and demands better quality of work. This is in line with their drive for better quality of life, better environment and less pollution.

Death of the beloved forests: is car exhaust to blame?

The debate on environmental pollution has in recent years centred on the highly emotional issue of car exhaust and its suspected responsibility for the terrible sickness affecting Germany's forests. The debate has also embraced the future of nuclear power stations, especially since the accident at Chernobyl in the Ukraine in April 1986. Therefore we should look first at Germany's overall energy situation.

West Germany is a country with substantial reserves of coal and lignite, some natural gas, but very little oil, and it has to rely on imports for over half of its total energy needs, against an EEC average (in 1984) of 40.6 per cent. Imports of cheap oil rose fast during the heady years of industrial growth: but the pattern changed after 1973 when oil became much dearer, and since then the aim has been to reduce dependence on it, through energy conservation measures and some switching to other fuels. This has been fairly successful. Between 1973 and 1984 the role of imports fell from 55.7 to 50.6 per cent, largely because oil purchases were reduced from 145 to 103 million tons; in the same period, energy-saving enabled overall consumption to be cut by some 6 per cent. Today Britain is by far the major supplier of oil to Germany, with Nigeria and Libya second and third, and relatively little coming from the Middle East. Germany produces a modest 4 million tons a year of its own oil, mostly in Lower Saxony: but the reserves are not believed to be great, and it has been unlucky in its own segment of the North Sea. Germany does much refining of imported crude oil, but unlike Britain, France and Holland it does not possess any big international oil companies operating abroad.

Hard coal, the main domestic energy asset, is seen as a crucial national resource. Therefore, although the industry is no longer so economically viable (as we have seen in the Ruhr), the Government helps the private companies to maintain it in working order, so that it could be expanded again in an emergency if imported energy supplies were to be cut off. Despite the wearing thin of many seams, output has been cut back only gently since 1973, from 103 to 84 million tons a year. Extractable hard coal reserves are still enormous, estimated at some 25,000 million tons. In addition, West Germany is the world's third largest producer of lignite (brown coal) after the Soviet Union and the GDR, and this is still being mined profitably (some 130 million tons a year), although it does cause some pollution. As for natural gas, Germany's own reserves cover about one-third of its needs, and the rest it imports mainly from Holland and the Soviet Union. In the early 1980s the gas companies joined with other European interests in promoting the construction of a huge new pipeline from Russia that has since led to a big increase in gas supplies from that source. Some voices on the Right had joined with the Americans in opposing the project on strategic grounds: but the Schmidt Government decided that there was little risk of becoming too dependent on energy imports from Russia, so long as the general trade balance remained favourable. Moreover, for Bonn to have intervened to prevent the gas companies from sharing in the scheme would have been an unprecedented step requiring special legislation, for Germany is the only EEC country where energy strategy is not dictated by the Government (save in the case of coal) but is left to the free play of the market. The main gas, electricity and nuclear companies are in private hands (with *Land* involvement too in some cases).

The Federal Government has however been providing incentives for energy conservation. It has spent over 4 billion DM since 1973 on subsidies to house occupants to introduce double-glazing or other insulation, and this has led to a reduction of 30 per cent in the use of domestic heating oil, while industry by moving over to other forms of energy has cut its fuel oil consumption by 60 per cent. However, Germany has made less progress than many other countries in developing the 'new' energies – biomass, photovoltaic and geothermal power, or indeed solar heating for which hot sunlight *is* rather lacking. Nor does Germany possess many possibilities for hydraulic power, so its electricity comes mainly from conventional and nuclear sources. The share-out of primary energy sources since 1963 and the planned previsions for the year 2000 (with the rate of nuclear expansion scheduled under the Kohl Government before the Chernobyl accident) are as follows:

Total energy used (millions of tons of coal equivalent):	1963 249	1973 379	1983 358	1985 380	2000 (projected) 369
shares (in percentages):					
Coal	51	22	21.4	20.4	22
Lignite	13	8.7	10.5	9.3	10
Oil	32.4	55.2	43.5	41.5	33
Gas	0.8	10.2	15.5	15.5	17
Nuclear	0	1.0	5.9	10.6	16
Other	2.8	2.9	3.2	2.7	2

After a fairly slow start, Germany has been pressing ahead with nuclear energy. By early 1986 there were 16 nuclear power plants in operation, providing 31 per cent of the nation's electricity, a higher figure than in Britain, though less than in France. While Kraftwerk Union, a Siemens subsidiary, has been selling nuclear stations abroad, the Germans have also been preparing their own fast-breeder reactor and taking part in France's Super-Phénix project. Even before Chernobyl all this nuclear development was running into a good deal of opposition, as in other countries – and more so than in most owing to the influence of the Greens and Germans' special sensitivity over the environment, as well as to fears that even a civil programme might have military applications. Just as war guilt has lent a special strength to the Peace Movement in Germany (see p. 449), so the hatred of nuclear arms has spilled over into a general mistrust of anything nuclear. The Greens have found some popular sympathy for their complaints that German-made plutonium, if exported, could be used elsewhere for bombs, and this would flatly contravene the Allies' interdiction on German nuclear weapons.

It is hardly surprising that the Chernobyl disaster should have caused a greater furore in Germany than almost anywhere else in western Europe. As levels of radio-activity rose, for some weeks a great deal of farm produce was banned from sale and destroyed on Government orders, and the farmers angrily demanded compensation. Greens and others redoubled their anti-nuclear demonstrations all over the country. At a congress in Hanover on May 18, three weeks after Chernobyl, the Green party demanded the immediate closure of all nuclear plants and voted to withdraw from its coalition with the ruling SPD in Hessen if the Social Democrats would not agree to the closure of the nuclear plants in that *Land* by the end of the year. Partly in response to this, the SPD at its annual conference in August voted to phase out all nuclear power stations within ten years, should it be returned to power in 1987. But the Kohl

Government's reaction was to declare that for its part the nuclear pro-gramme would go ahead. Aware that this stance might cost the CDU many votes, Kohl tried to allay public fears by pointing out that the Chernobyl plant would never have been licensed in West Germany, where safety standards were far higher than in the Soviet Union. He also specially created a new Ministry of the Environment to look after nuclear and other matters, headed by the popular and persuasive Walter Wallmann, mayor of Frankfurt. It was an astute pre-election move.

For some years, since long before Chernobyl, one main issue as in other countries has been that of nuclear waste. The Greens and other 'anti-nukes' have succeeded in alerting public opinion, or large parts of it, and in arousing local opposition to new ventures, so that a fami-liar scenario has often been repeated. A power plant project would be announced, at first the local population might take it calmly, but then Green activists would arrive and explain the dangers, there would be demonstrations, and maybe the local council would take fright and get the project postponed. The final decision to licence a new plant lies with the *Land* government. But first the scheme must run the gauntlet of an archi-complex process of court appeals and hearings on the safety and waste disposal issues, and by skilfully exploiting this it has been possible to slow down a number of projects by years. Political factors play a part too. As the SPD has always been more divided and uneasy about nuclear energy than the CDU, most of the plants have been built in CDU-run *Länder*.

The best-known and longest-drawn-out case has been that of the Brockdorf plant, in CDU-run Schleswig-Holstein, not far from SPD-run Hamburg. The decision to build it was taken in 1973. Then in 1976, when construction started, 30,000 demonstrators clashed one day with the police and many people were hurt. Opponents of the scheme managed to get work on it halted under a court ruling. Then a crisis broke out in Hamburg, which was to be the main client: the Senate, split on the project, kept changing its mind and finally voted against using it, whereupon the city's electricity company, private and commercial, threatened to take it to court. Building work began again in 1982 and was finally completed in 1986, when the Senate and the company agreed on a compromise. There have been similar if less spectacular disputes in other places – for example, over a new plant in Bavaria to be used by Munich. In Baden-Württemberg, the unortho-dox and strong-minded Lothar Späth showed remarkable political courage for a CDU leader by actually siding with the environmenta-lists – partly out of genuine conviction and partly in order to outflank the Greens, very strong in his *Land*. Announcing that energy needs had been over-estimated, in 1984 he clamped an indefinite post-ponement order on a projected nuclear plant at Whyl, on the Rhine near Freiburg, which had been much besieged by both German and French sit-ins. And so the nuclear tussle will certainly go on.

The nuclear debate is just one aspect of a nationwide obsession with environmental problems that immediately strikes any visitor to Germany. It has developed momentously over the past decade or so, and embraces everything from sulphuric factory fumes to non-returnable milk-bottles. Health hazards, over-use of resources, soil pollution, noise, aesthetic damage to the landscape, threats to flora and fauna – all such ills are argued about and worried over end-lessly, and campaigned against not only by Germans but by govern-ments and local councils of every political shade. Go on a duck-shoot with a party of bland businessmen and they may well spend the time fretting about soil erosion or tree sickness. And once, when I went to dinner with friends in Munich, my middle-aged hostess, certainly no Green, said to me without a trace of irony, 'Don't eat the skins on those potatoes. They might have been planted near a motorway.'

The Germans recycle 42 per cent of waste paper and reprocess 70 per cent of old tyres; according to one estimate, they spend 6.7 per cent of GNP on environmental schemes. But why this greater con-cern than in any other European country? Possibly it is related to the German passion for order and tidiness, or to their sense of claustro-phobia that comes from being cooped up in a fairly small, thickly populated and highly industrialised country where space is precious. And certainly the environmental craze is being pursued with typical German obsessiveness: once they discover a cause, then they go for it twice as hard as anyone else. Might there not be a lurking subcon-scious element of guilt about the past, too? – like Lady Macbeth's 'Will these hands ne'er be clean?'

The Greens loudly led the way into the campaign in the later 1970s, abusively haranguing chemical firms to reduce their toxic pol-lution, or local councils to suspend some motorway project or improve their garbage system – 'It's a real religious war, this,' said one industrialist, 'like in the middle ages.' The Greens struck a chord of wide popular feeling; and, though some of their ideas may have been far-fetched, others did alert the established parties to some real dangers. And so the Greens have successfully made a clean environ-ment into the new piety to which all parties must subscribe. Every German politician is now at least a little bit green, and actively so: at every level, *Bund, Land* and local council, authorities have been pour-ing money into helping the environment (Bonn earmarked 1.7 billion DM for it in 1984) with a mix of motives, part sincere, part electoralist. Friedrich Zimmermann, Kohl's Interior minister, has proclaimed, 'After peace, environmental protection is the most important task of our time.'

Some German reactions may appear hysterical and out of proportion. But their practical efforts to deal with the problems are often impressive. West of Cologne, I went to look at the open-cast lignite mining that has been going on there for many decades on a huge scale. Whole areas must be cleared, and in some cases villages and townlets destroyed, before the giant holes can be dug in the ground, many kilometres long and up to 370 metres deep. The farmers and villagers are handsomely compensated, and few of the locals seem to object very much, even in this ecological age, for the Rhinelanders are realistic people and they know that the mines bring thousands of jobs. And the private mining company, Rheinbraun, is obliged by the *Land* to respect the environment as far as possible. The hills of loose earth dug out from each hole are neatly planted with trees; and, when a mine is exhausted, it is given back to nature and to human pleasure. One string of old mines has been turned into a vast recreation zone, with forty new lakes amid woodlands, where the Kölner now have better scope for fishing, surfing, sailing and swimming than the city's vicinity ever offered them before.

Later I visited the Ruhr soon after its smog alert of January 1985, during a cold, foggy spell. The Ruhr, battling with its grimy image, is the only area of Germany to have instituted this kind of alert system, and this was the first time it was used. A grade-three 'maximum alert' was sounded, leading to a 24-hour closure of all factories and ban on all private cars, while doctors advised people to stay indoors. Whether all this was strictly necessary is uncertain. The local CDU accused the SPD-led *Land* Government of over-reacting, while the Greens charged it with not doing enough.

Industrial pollution, leading to smog and worse ills, is now one of the major environmental issues. The chemical companies have come under pressure to reduce their poisonous fumes and other harmful waste matter. In 1984 a campaign by environmentalists in Hamburg led to a court ruling that obliged one local family firm, Böhringer, to close down its pesticide plant after lethal dioxin had been found on a rubbish dump. This was the first court case of its kind in Germany. Hopefully it was an isolated incident, for the chemical industry spends some 10 per cent of its total investment on fighting pollution and is subject to some of the world's strictest safety regulations that, so it claims, would make impossible in Germany any tragedy such as those at Soveso in Italy or Bhopal in India.

Sulphurous emissions from coal and oil-fired power plants present a much wider problem, and one that is international in nature because of prevailing winds. It is reckoned that West Germany 'exports' some 637,000 tons of these emissions a year, and 'imports' another 762,000, much of it from East Germany. For obvious reasons it is hard to negotiate a solution: but meanwhile the Federal Republic is trying hard to put its own house in order. In 1976 the Schmidt Government imposed some fairly strict measures on the power stations, and these were further strengthened by a law passed as soon as Kohl came to power in 1983. So, in marked contrast to Britain, Germany's power industry now has the toughest clean air standards in the world, along with Japan's: and in order to meet them the electricity firms are currently having to spend between 10 and 15 billion DM on reducing sulphur emissions at the older coal-burning power plants, while a new station may well have to spend over 20 per cent of its capital costs on meeting the requirements. As a result, sulphur dioxide emission is expected to have been reduced by half between 1984 and 1988. The power industry has reluctantly accepted the necessity for these measures, and is passing on much of the cost to the public. But the issue can also lead to the dilemma of cleaner air versus more jobs. In 1984 a much-publicised row blew up over the decision of the Lower Saxony Government to allow a new coal-fired plant at Buschhaus to start operation three years before its sulphur scrubbers had been installed. The decision was legal. With an eye on the next *Land* elections, the CDU was all too aware that the plant would create over 1,000 jobs.

In Stuttgart, I found Lothar Späth in characteristically philosophic mood about pollution: 'After the war we spent our money on non-environmental goodies like cars and TV sets. Now it is the turn of environment. We are a rich enough society to be able to spend far more on it than we do – and people accept this. So we shall have dearer electricity – and why not? Industry will go along with this, so long as there are laws that force it to do so.' Not only does Späth's capital city produce Germany's fastest and therefore most pollutant cars, but his wooded *Land*, comprising all the Black Forest, bears the heaviest toll of Germany's tragically dying trees. He is truly in the hot seat.

'*O Wald, O Waldeseinsamkeit, wie gleichst du dem deutschen Gemüt,*' wrote the poet Julius Hammer in 1851 ('O forest, O solitude of the forest, how similar thou art to the German soul'). Germany's woodlands have always lain close to the heart of the German psyche, a constant theme of popular songs and nursery tales, and of opera and literature from Wagner and Goethe to Brecht and the Brothers Grimm. Much of this feeling is purely romantic and cerebral, the fancy of wan city-dwellers who could hardly tell an oak from a beech (see below). But much of it too is real and practical. Germany's forests, covering 30 per cent of its territory, are an important national resource and they play a big part in modern leisure and tourism. With rucksacks and strong shoes, and maybe in lederhosen too, parties of Germans young and old go hiking and camping in the wide woodlands, where you never see a 'Keep Out' sign, for by law even privately-owned forests are freely open to all.

So the tree epidemic has upset Germans badly. Some reactions may have been too hysterical: but the overall mood of panic is understandable, for this *Waldsterben* is a true catastrophe – it is distressing indeed to walk along the heights of the Black Forest, called 'black' because of the velvety opaque panorama of its pines, and to see the trees today with their thinning crowns, yellowing needles and peeling bark. According to the experts, the growth-rings show that the inner sickness began 20 to 30 years ago: but it was not really noticed until about 1980. Then the first cries of alarm by a few sylvan Cassandras were dismissed as nonsense. But in 1982–3 the disease began to spread fast and the nation suddenly woke up to the peril – maybe too late. In 1982 an official report had declared that only 8 per cent of all trees were afflicted: but a year later the figure was put at 34 per cent, and by the end of 1985 the federal Ministry of Agriculture was saying that every second tree was dead or sick, while among some types of conifer the ravage was much greater still. The disease had first attacked firs and spruce, and then spread to deciduous trees such as oak and beech. It is not a pretty sight. In the case of firs, first the needles turn yellow and start to drop off, then the branches droop wearily, pus weeps down the bark, roots begin to warp and shrink, insects colonise the trunks, and fresh twigs sprout bizarrely as the tree seems to be trying to compensate for its starvation. It is not merely sentimental to feel that the tree is somehow in pain, crying out for help like an animal.

But how can they be helped? By 1984 the campaign for action had become a national crusade, uniting all classes and parties, linking dreamy Greens with hard-nosed businessman who value their Sunday rambles, and city workers with the potent lobby of the timber industry. Edward Steen in the *Sunday Telegraph* (May 12, 1985) wrote of the trees: 'They stab at the national conscience, images of unthinking industrial progress, an economic miracle that has lost its magic. The trees provide both a post-war guilt complex (neurotic luxury of the prosperous) and a national cause.' One opinion poll late in 1983 found the Germans more concerned about their forests than about the topical issue of whether to accept Pershing-2 and Cruise missiles in Germany. Some critics felt that this was a little excessive: but there were many excellent reasons for the alarm. Scientists pointed out that a decline of forests could upset Germany's entire ecological balance, leading to soil erosion, death of wildlife and severe damage to agriculture. By 1984–5 the tourist industry in the south was reporting a serious fall-off in business, for many of its regular clients no longer fancied a holiday amid sick trees. And timber and related industries, on whom 800,000 jobs depend, were claiming to be losing over 1 billion DM a year, with the danger of this rising tenfold.

As the precise causes of the epidemic were far from certain, no one was quite clear what should be done. Some forest-owners tried the expensive palliative of spraying the trees with lime. More important, a vast diversified research effort began, with some 200 different programmes, many identical: the Baden-Württemberg Government was soon spending 20 million DM a year on research. And so a cacophony of bickering scientists came up with many scores of rival theories. Some thought that a plant virus might be responsible; others laid the blame on drought. The fact that there had been at least four previous forest epidemics, over the past 200 years, seemed to lend some credence to the 'climatic' or 'virus' theories. But this time the disease was on a far worse scale than before. Moreover, it was noted that the trees in the GDR and Czechoslovakia were now suffering just as badly as West German ones, whereas France, Britain and Scandinavia, with their very different prevailing winds, were hardly affected at all. This lent strong support to the view of the majority of German tree experts that the ailment was caused by 'acid rain', which forms when sulphur dioxide from factories or power plants, or nitrogen oxide from vehicle exhaust, mixes with moisture and oxygen to form sulphuric or nitric acid in the atmosphere. This can be carried by the wind a very long way, thus explaining why the trees worst affected are often on high ground and not at all close to any industrial area or motorway. What is more, experts have found that the growth-rings on many trees started to narrow in the late 1950s and 1960s: this is when the disease probably began, just at the time of the first big post-war boom in industry and car-driving.

This view today is received wisdom, and has been endorsed by Federal Government reports. It is pooh-poohed in some quarters, especially by the British who do not like to be told accusingly that the westerly winds have been blowing their own nasty acids away from healthy British forests and onto German ones. But Bonn, under pressure from the Greens and others, and needing to do something urgently, decided to act on the 'acid rain' theory. This was one of the main reasons for the new controls imposed on power stations. And it led in 1984–5 to the almighty furore over catalytic converters for cars.

Even before this issue arose, technical improvements to reduce exhaust emissions had already been in progress for about 15 years throughout the world's motor industry, and with some success, for they had cut nitrogen oxide discharge by up to 50 per cent on some models. However, when the forest panic spread, the newly-elected Kohl Government decided that more drastic action was needed, for political reasons: and so in 1983 it suddenly set the very early target date of January 1986 for the obligatory fitting of a catalytic converter onto every new car sold. This gadget, which goes underneath the car, removes most but not all of the noxious element from carbon monoxide and nitrogen oxide; but it costs about 1,500 DM, and it requires lead-free petrol. The German car industry at first moaned a little but fairly soon it accepted the need for converters and rallied to the Government in a disciplined way. As it had already been fitting converters onto its cars exported to Japan and the United States (where the gadgets had been in force for some time), it had no lack of expertise or equipment. And the German motoring public, anxious about the trees, also demurred very little.

But Germany's EEC partners were furious. Jacques Calvet, chairman of Peugeot, claimed that a 'bunch of hysterics' in Bonn was putting Europe's motor industry in peril. The EEC governments, supporting their car firms, did not want Bonn to go it alone with the new controls, for this would sabotage their own imports to Germany (they even talked of 'an underhand act of disguised protectionism'): but nor were they keen to join in the scheme themselves, for they had no forest problem at home and no public pressure, and their car industries were most unwilling to start installing converters. In particular they argued that, as the cost of a converter is the same for any size of vehicle, the measure would unfairly prejudice the sales of smaller and cheaper cars, such as Fiats and Renaults, that make up a much larger part of French and Italian than of German output. The British went further than this, claiming that the catalytic converter was a cumbersome and outmoded piece of technology that would soon be superseded by the much cheaper and simpler system that *they* were working on, the 'lean burn engine': but the Germans retorted that it could not be in mass production before the early 1990s, and this would be too late. In this angry war of words, British officials complained that the Germans were 'pressing on with an expensive ride down a blind alley'.

Finally in March 1985 a compromise was reached in Brussels that amounted to a greater climb-down by the other EEC countries than by Germany. Bonn merely agreed to delay its timetable, so that the others could catch up; but they rallied basically to the German thesis, by deciding on a new European exhaust emission standard that would be at least as stringent as that of the United States. In practice it was agreed to make converters compulsory for different engine sizes at different dates, starting with the largest. For new cars in this high-speed range, including most Mercedes and larger BMWs, the measure will come into force in 1990; for medium-sized saloons, in 1991; and for smaller cars, in 1993. It is supposed that this will help protect the small-car market and give time for the cheaper lean-burn engine to become available.

To the anger of the Greens, the Government had already backed down from its original 1986 date in order to help make an EEC compromise possible. However, in 1985 it did introduce a series of tax incentives, to encourage motorists to move ahead of the legal deadlines by voluntarily buying new converter-fitted cars right away, or getting their existing ones adapted. The virtuous would benefit from a reduced motor tax; others would have to pay extra. But the response was not as good as hoped: in 1985 only some 12 per cent of car buyers gave proof of their love of trees by acquiring a model with converter. One deterrent factor may have been the shortage of service stations with lead-free petrol. Munich had set an example in 1983 by installing three experimentally: but by 1985 it still had only 15 or so, and other cities had fewer still, while not all motorway stations sold *bleifreies Benzin*. Motorists were also uncertain whether they would be able to find it when touring abroad: France and Italy, despite the importance to them of the German tourist trade, seemed in no hurry to urge their petrol companies to make lead-free fuel available, and by 1986 few motorway stations were yet selling it. Such are the travails of a not-yet-united Europe.

Meanwhile in Germany it was being pointed out that surely there existed another method, far more cheap and simple, and above all more rapid, of securing results from reduced exhaust levels – and that was to impose a speed limit. Germany is the only country in Europe without one, at least on motorways. The Greens produced scientific surveys to show that a limit of 100 kph on the *Autobahnen* would in a flash cut nitric oxide emissions by 18 per cent: the car-makers retorted that, according to their own tests, the saving would be only 3 per cent. And so a debate rich in passion developed, for if most Germans love their trees, a potent minority of them love their fast cars even more. The average German driver is highly disciplined and prudent in town, keeping carefully to the traffic-lanes, and braking at lights even when there is no pedestrian in sight: but behind a wheel on an open *Autobahn*, where there are no speed laws to hold him back, he becomes a creature possessed, especially if he is in a fast car, tearing down the outside lane, lights flashing, at 200 kph or more. Psychologists can put this down to a pent-up masculine aggression that finds little other outlet in today's peaceful, orderly republic; or else to German competitiveness; or to the German tendency to obey laws by the letter rather than apply common sense. Whatever the reasons, the practice can be unnerving for a visiting foreign motorist. In 1974, after the first oil crisis, attempts were made to impose speed limits so as to save fuel: but they were soon dropped, under pressure from an angry motorists' lobby which coined the slogan, *'Freie Fahrt für freie Bürger'* (roughly, 'a free people should have free right of way'). And this battle-cry is again being used today, for the Germans still seem to regard unlimited speed as a constitutional right, an article of faith.

Caught in what one writer called 'an emotional clash between speed freaks and tree lovers', the Kohl Government hesitated, especially since the opinion polls were conflicting. Some of these indicated that most motorists were opposed to any *Autobahn* speed limits; others, that a majority of citizens might favour them, if it could be proved that this would help the trees. Finally in March 1985 the Government did embark on a nine-month experiment on the Hamburg–Bremen and Nuremberg–Ingolstadt motorways: speed was limited to 100 kph, with fines of up to 400 DM, and special test cars patrolled the routes at varying speeds, fast and slow, checking and comparing emission levels. For Germany, this was quite a bold move. But, when I myself travelled those roads in the summer of 1985, few drivers seemed to be keeping to the limit, nor did I, and none of us was stopped by the police as far as I saw. A blow for my own theory that the law-abiding Germans would instinctively obey limits if told to do so?

Curiously this whole debate about speed has centred on the issue of air pollution, and damage to trees, with very little even said about the role that fast driving may play in Germany's high-road accident rate. This has led some unkind critics to suggest that the Germans seem to care more about trees than people. But the real issue is more complex. First, through the introduction of compulsory seat-belts, better-built cars, and various other safety measures, it had been possible to reduce the annual toll of road deaths from 19,000 in 1970 to some 11,500 in 1985 – but that is still alarmingly high. Secondly, and more to the point, Germany's 7,000 km of motorways are among its safest roads, for they carry 25 per cent of traffic but account for only 6 per cent of fatal accidents. This lends some support to the arguments of the car industry and the motoring clubs, that Germany's fast cars are still very safe when driven at high speeds, that German fast drivers are not the maniacs they may appear but are skilled and responsible, and that a speed limit would probably reduce the accident rate hardly at all. Deaths are caused mainly by less experienced drivers on country roads. So the car-makers, while accepting converters, remain firmly opposed to other restrictions on the high-speed performance of their prized products. But it may take many years to discover whether converters can really do anything to save the dying trees.

The ignored rural world and its grumbling peasantry

It is rare for a rural problem such as forestry to become a major national issue in Germany, for in this urbanised and industry-focussed society the world of farming usually gets overlooked. Most city-dwellers have only a hazy idea of what modern country life is really like, and this was certainly one reason for the extraordinary impact of *Heimat*, Edgar Reitz's celebrated 16-hour film portrait of a village near Koblenz, which burst upon German cinema and TV viewers in 1984 like the revelation of an unknown world. This ignorance is curious in a way, for German farmers historically have never constituted a society apart to the same degree as the French peasantry. Today most of them live in neat modern villas, they have much the same leisure interests and home equipment as city folk, and many do office or factory jobs at the same time. They are not isolated from the community, however misunderstood they may sometimes feel.

This is one of a number of paradoxes in the world of German farming today, where the gulf between rich and poor is at least as great as in France. The wheat barons of the north drive around in Mercedes and take holidays in the Caribbean; many Bavarian dairy farmers struggle to make a living with a herd of ten cows and 20 acres – 'the Cinderellas of the economic miracle', they have been called. These smallholders are not as violent as the French in pursuit of their grievances: they do not block the roads with their tractors, nor set fire to lorryloads of imported produce. But in their way they have now become just as recalcitrant, and they have won a bad reputation in EEC circles for being backward, inefficient, and unwilling to pull their weight in the campaign to reduce surpluses. Much small-scale farming in Germany is, to be sure, curiously inefficient for so modern a nation. And yet, viewed from another angle, German agriculture shows an impressive record of post-war modernisation. Paradoxes, indeed.

The Federal Republic today comprises only 40 per cent of the farming land of pre-1945 Germany. The rest, including all the great livestock- and grain-producing estates of Prussia, lies in the territories lost to Communist rule. So after the war a cramped West Germany faced an urgent challenge – that of developing its agriculture to meet the needs of a hungry people, including the millions of refugees – Governments and farmers made concerted efforts, and the success was considerable – as the figures show. Productivity has risen seven-fold since 1950. Thanks to huge increases mostly in the production of meat, dairy products, wheat, sugarbeet and wine, Germany on balance now meets over 85 per cent of its own needs in food and drink. The rest it buys from abroad – and it is the world's second largest food importer, after Japan (mainly of fruit and vegetables, feed grains, eggs and fish products). But, more surprisingly for so thickly populated a country, Germany has also become the world's fourth leading exporter of food and drink, after the United States, France and

Holland. Its principal sales are in meat and meat products, and dairy produce including cheese. All this points to an extensive two-way trade, two-thirds of it being with the rest of the EEC. As in other countries, the progress has been achieved through intensive modernisation, much of it in the form of mechanisation. The ox-drawn plough is almost everywhere a thing of the past. It is not uncommon today to find big grain farms with only two or three hired labourers where there used to be 30 or 40: the total of paid workers has dropped to a mere 100,000 or so. Millions of people have moved off the land, and the decline in agriculture's share of the active population, from 20 per cent in 1950 to just 5 per cent today, has been almost as striking as in France: it is still falling today, though more slowly, and may level off at about 4.5 per cent. As farmers move away or retire, their properties are usually sold to neighbours, so that farms have become larger: their overall number fell from 1,600,000 in 1950 to 740,000 in 1985.

These have been familiar trends in much of Western Europe. It would be wrong however to deduce that Germany today is a land of highly effective medium-sized or large farms, like Britain. The pattern of rationalisation has been extremely uneven, with big regional variations. In a word, the north is rich and the south rather poor. The farms of the northern plains, in Schleswig-Holstein, Lower Saxony and Westphalia, are many of them large and prosperous, and so are some in Bavaria: but southern farms have always been on average much smaller than those in the north, and so they remain. As a result, the average size of a German farm is a mere 40 acres, compared with 65 in France, 173 in Britain. France is often regarded, wrongly, as a patchwork of tiny holdings: but the image better fits Germany, whose farms are on average the smallest of any non-Mediterranean country of the EEC. And the problem lies especially with the dairy farms, which account for over half the total: the average herd in Germany is 15 cows – and only 12 or 13 in the south – compared with 60 in Britain.

There are clear historical reasons for this state of affairs. The most important is the equal inheritance law that was introduced under Napoleon into most areas of what are now Baden-Württemberg, Hessen and Rhineland-Palatinate, and some parts of Bavaria. Here a farmer's land was divided between all his sons on his death, and this led to growing parcellisation. Today, though the system still has some legal force, it is seldom applied as such, for under modern conditions it is rare that more than one son will want to inherit land, so the division of property is usually done on a cash basis. But the law has left a heavy mark on farm structures. In the north, and in much of Bavaria, primogeniture has always been the rule: hence the greater size of farms there. And, if so many Bavarian holdings are small, it is more often due to the terrain.

A second major historical factor is that since the mid-19th century German agriculture has been cosseted by protectionism, with strong tariff barriers and prices fixed fairly high. This was the policy of Bismarck and then of Weimar, and it was intensified by the Nazis who gave generous subsidies to farmers (and thus derived much of their support from rural areas). So, right up until recent times, farmers could survive with smallish properties and they had little incentive to enlarge them. Equally, the smallholders failed to develop a dynamic sense of marketing. The protectionist policy was somewhat modified after 1945, but it has since been taken over by the EEC within a wider European context.

During Germany's boom years of the 1950s and '60s, small farmers were carried along by the general national progress and most of them easily became more prosperous. Then the arrival of the EEC's Common Agriculture Policy (CAP) helped the dairy producers in particular by opening up new export outlets to Italy. But, since the mid-1970s, the tide has turned against them. Costs of fuel and fertiliser have been rising much faster than prices, so that farm incomes have been falling. And now, since the early 1980s, the CAP's expensive pile-up of surpluses has reached the point where all EEC farmers are being asked to make sacrifices, notably through quotas for milk production and cuts in cereals prices. German farmers, being on balance the smallest and least efficient in these fields, feel themselves to be hit the hardest and have been squealing the loudest. They have a powerful political lobby which repeatedly has put pressure on Bonn to resist the CAP reforms (see below). So Germany, as the British at least tend to see it, has become the 'arch defender' of the CAP's major abuses and a main obstacle to improvement. It is a strange reversal from the early days of the Community when it was the Germans who feared that France's backward peasant farming would be the EEC's principal handicap.

Federal and *Land* governments have certainly made great efforts since the war to rationalise farming structures. Small farmers have been encouraged to organise themselves into cooperatives, for marketing and for the sharing of modern equipment; and they have been given subsidies to help them regroup scattered parcels of land into more viable units. This has borne results. Most farms now are well-equipped, within their means; and the old polyculture has given way to greater specialisation. Even quite small farms can often be profitable if they specialise in particular products, such as fruit, or poultry. But at the same time governments have always backed the smallish family farm as the basic unit. And their earlier post-war policy of encouraging farms to merge, and so increase in size, has now been modified at a time of rising urban unemployment, for other jobs are no longer available for those who leave the land. Social needs are thus being put ahead of economic efficiency. Hence also the continued official support for part-time farming.

One of the most unusual and controversial features of German agriculture is that 40 per cent of all farms, and the majority of really small ones, are worked on a part-time basis by people who have other jobs too. They account for 13 per cent of total farm area, and 10 to 12 per cent of all produce. This kind of dual activity has obvious advantages for those who do it: but it is criticised by many modern-minded experts for creating a 'black' economy and other distortions. It dates from the 19th century, when many small farmers were so poor that they clutched eagerly at the new work outlets offered by the factories springing up in nearby towns. Especially was this so in Swabia, with its small-scale precision industries in semi-rural settings; but even in the Ruhr a number of coal-miners and steelworkers have always been part-time farmers too. And the practice persists, especially in the south where many a Daimler-Benz welder will hurry home to tend his vines, or a Siemens worker to milk his cows. Generally the factory or office job provides by far the greater part of such a family's income: but the smallholding is kept on, maybe as a kind of hobby, or for sentimental reasons, or as a useful extra source of revenue or a prudent insurance against unemployment. Usually the wife does most of the work, and the husband helps out in his free time.

Industrial Stuttgart sprawls out widely, with dozens of village-like suburbs and hundreds of little farms within its borders. One of those I visited, at Plieningen near the airport, was quite extraordinary. Its friendly and hospitable owner worked as a clerk in a nearby milk control office, but still kept his ten dairy cows and a few acres for feed. His parlour, where we drank *Obstler*, was quite spruce: but the cowshed behind was positively mediaeval, with one sick cow, piles of stinking straw, peasanty little wife and cretinous brother, and no hint of modernisation. This, in Europe's richest city. 'We've owned this farm for many generations,' said my host, 'and I just can't bear to give it up, for farming is still in my blood – even though it brings in little money and involves a lot of hard work and getting up at 5.30 a.m. But my son, who's an electrician, sees no future in it, so when I retire in ten years or so, we'll probably sell it.' He spoke of Stuttgart, '*Die Grosstadt*', as if it were another civilisation. I felt I was witnessing the end of an era, the twilight of a certain way of life. Like this one, many part-time farms today mark a transitional phase and are run by families who are on their way out of agriculture: often the sons have wives who refuse to do the work. However there is now a small but growing counter-trend, *into* agriculture, led by young ecologists and others with city jobs who buy a small farm as a weekend or holiday activity. Teachers or civil servants sometimes do this. So part-time farming, though it may wane, is not likely to die out fast.

Various arguments are advanced in favour of it. Perhaps the most valid is that it has served the social purpose of maintaining closer links between town and country, and this may be one reason why the German peasantry has felt less isolated than in France. In some areas, part-time farming may also be helping to save the countryside from over-depopulation. Also, so it is suggested, it adds a certain flexibility to employment, for a factory can more easily put workers onto shorter hours when times are hard, and a smallholder conversely is less vulnerable to the usual ups-and-downs of farming. But the counter-argument, advanced cogently by many economists, is that part-time farming acts as a drag on the efficiency and modernisation of agriculture; as one agronomist said to me: 'These part-timers don't take the job seriously, they run their holdings in an amateurish and unproductive way. They undercut the professionals. And, above all, they are simply adding to the EEC's surpluses. At the taxpayer's expense, they draw subsidies that they do not really need, and they make life harder for the full-timers who do need them. It's a black economy.' And the full-time farmers themselves feel resentful of the others, for the same reasons. So the European Commission is opposed to part-time farming and has been trying to get it reduced, in all member countries. But, in Germany, federal and *Land* governments – especially the more conservative ones – continue to support it. After all, it helps to bolster many farmers' incomes and thus to contain their grievances. And it serves a political purpose too: factory workers are much less likely to be militant left-wing unionists if they also own little farms and have roots in the soil. This could well be one of the reasons for the harmony of labour relations in an area such as Swabia.

In the more remote rural areas the picture is entirely different, for here the scope for finding alternative jobs is far less great than near a town; small farmers have no other source of income, and if their soil is poor they face bleak prospects today, in a time of rising costs and EEC production squeezes. Their expectations have risen since the war, they want some degree of modern comforts, and quite rightly they are not prepared to accept the drudgery and simple poverty that their parents and grandparents endured.

One such area is the northern strip of Bavaria along the GDR border, between Coburg and Hof. Here the division of Germany has separated farmers from some of their traditional markets: but this is not the main cause of their problems today, nor is the psychological impact of the border's proximity, which is something they have grown quite used to (see p. 366). The real trouble is the terrain. This windy, hilly Franconian plateau with its thin soil and bitter winters has long been known as the 'Bavarian Siberia' – and the allusion is purely physical, not political. Farmers have been drifting away to the towns and some land is now derelict, for buyers are hard to find. One small village I visited, Neuengrün, looked neat and prosperous in the usual German manner, with newish white-and-grey houses in a tidy circle round a wide grassy square, and pastures and grainfields rolling to far horizons: but the farmers I talked to were universally pessimistic. The Grebners, for example, farm 125 acres, with 45 head of cattle, quite a lot for south Germany; and they live in a modern house with colour TV, washing machine, and a new garden patio with smart white benches – all rather different from the rural squalor one still so often finds in, say, the French Massif Central. But Frau Grebner seemed sad and depressed, a handsome woman of about 40, old before her time: 'Farming used to be a pleasant way of life round here, but now it's *kaputt*. The soil is too stony for cereals: we get only 3 tons of barley per hectare, against 5 or 6 in a good area. Dairy farming's okay, but now the CAP milk quotas have hit our income – so what's the use of the expensive investments we made ten years ago, on a new cowshed and milking equipment? It's a waste. Our three sons are going to factory jobs elsewhere and they don't want the farm. We'd like to sell it, but we can't find a buyer.'

I heard the same lament at other nearby villages – '*kaputt!*' But were things any better in earlier days? At one upland farm close to the GDR border, I met a white-haired, rosy-cheeked peasant lady of 76, Frau Kraus, who showed me the family's neat house built in 1960 and its big barn full of modern machinery: 'In pre-war days we had no running water, electricity or tractors. Often we worked an 80-hour week, and in winter we'd get up at five to break the ice in the pails for washing, before we milked the cows. Today the family works less hard and has more comforts, but we've 20,000 DM of debts still to pay off on our investments. But why shouldn't we enjoy some of the same advantages of modern life as city people? Times have changed. I've never been farther than Bamberg in my life, 80 kilometres away: but my son is now in New Guinea. If we were prepared to live and drudge as in the old days, maybe this farm would still be viable. But we're not. Brewer's barley, wheat, potatoes, a few milk cows and bullocks – this kind of mixed farming doesn't seem to make sense any more. . . .'

Maybe the answer is that poorer districts of this kind should not be used for agriculture any more. After all, the surplus-ridden EEC hardly needs their produce. But what other future might they find? Nearly all ecologists and rural experts agree that it would be wrong to let them depopulate to the point of becoming a wasteland. Some of the more attractive areas, with lakes, woods or hills, could well be turned into nature parks or tourist and recreation centres, as has been happening in many places around the Eifel, the Black Forest and the lower Alps: here farmers could stay in their villages and derive income from looking after tourists, or else become salaried 'guardians of nature' (a concept pioneered in France). But the north Bavarian plateaux, though plentifully forested, are too dull and desolate to appeal to many holidaymakers. They thin soil may not be suited for grain crops or dairy pastures, but it might still find a future in large-scale sheep farming, of the kind so common in similar upland areas of France: but the problem first would be to convert the German consumer to the habit of eating lamb and mutton, and the farmer to the techniques of sheepbreeding.[1]

So for these lonelier rural areas there remains the possible solution of bringing the mountain to Mohammed, that is, not of expecting the farmer to migrate to the town, but of bringing modern industrial jobs to the countryside. This already has been taking place on quite a large scale, more so in Germany than in most countries. Everywhere in small towns and even in villages one finds little factories of all kinds. Some of them are traditional and relate to soil deposits or other local conditions, such as the pottery firms of northern Bavaria (e.g. Rosenthal at Selb) or the clockmakers of the Black Forest. But others are fairly new products of the 'economic miracle' years. Many have been created by ex-farmers themselves or by other local people – witness the fictional but credible example of the clever young peasant in Reitz's *Heimat* who in the 1950s founded a successful optics factory in the desolate Hunsrück. In other cases, big well-known companies have developed new plant in or near the countryside as the best way of finding the labour they need. The star case is that of BMW which in 1966 took over a small ailing independent car-making firm in the little town of Dingolfing, 100 kilometres north-east of Munich, and has since built it up into the largest of all its factories, with 16,000 employees. Nearly all of them live in the villages and farms around, and every morning a fleet of several hundred BMW buses brings them in to work from a radius up to 100 kilometres. 'Most firms find, as we do,' one BMW executive told me, 'that country people of this kind make better skilled mechanical workers than, say, ex-miners or ex-dockers do. Many still keep their little farms, and this gives them a sense of freedom and dignity – of not being slaves to factory work.' Such operations are the basis of the success of part-time farming in

[1] The British eat 50 times as much sheepmeat as the Germans, and produce 23 times as much of it, while the Germans produce and eat three times as much pork and pig products as the British. One explanation given to me is that German farms, being so small, are better suited to breeding pigs, which require less space than sheep.

Germany, which will thus survive for a long time. The problem of rural unemployment and rural emigration is thus less acute than, say, in France. But, in today's economic climate, it is not easy to find new little firms for the lonelier areas where farming is doomed to decline further. The plateaux of northern Bavaria have no easy solution for their plight.

Here, as in many other areas, rising costs above all are blamed for the fact that a small farm can no longer be made viable. In a fertile spot near Stuttgart, one smallholder in his seventies, producing cabbages for *Sauerkraut* and wheat, told me: 'D'you know, in the 1930s fifty kilos of wheat would buy me two pairs of shoes: now they buy just half a shoe. Yes, productivity's gone up too, but not that much. It is costs, of fuel and so on, that are the problem. Fifteen hectares used to be enough round here for a decent living: now you need twice as many. And that dreadful Common Market is making matters worse.' Of course, farmers the world over are notorious for grousing endlessly and exaggerating their woes. Their present dilemma may be to quite an extent their own fault. But the mad logic of Community economics does give the smaller ones some cause to be upset.

The mechanism of the CAP is highly complex. Briefly summarised, it consists of a Community levy on agriculture imports into member countries from outside the EEC, redistributed to farmers in the form of price supports and export subsidies (the supports cover, essentially, sugar, beef and pigmeat, dairy products, most cereals, table wines, some fruit and vegetables). This protectionist system aims to encourage EEC self-sufficiency, and certainly it has done so. But it has proved expensive for national budgets, since the supports and subsidies have been allowed far to exceed the size of levy, thus leading to heavy annual deficits. This is because the EEC, yielding to pressure from various farming lobbies, originally fixed the prices for most products around the level of the highest then obtaining and not the average. For instance, as wheat was cheapest in France and dearest in Germany, it was the German price that was chosen for the CAP. This has simply encouraged farmers to overproduce in many sectors, knowing that their surpluses would be bought anyway and then sometimes dumped on world markets. The 'butter mountains' of the 1970s and '80s, with the cheap sale of surplus butter to Russia, caused a scandal; by 1986 the EEC also had gigantic surplus stocks of beef, cereals, wine and some other products, and the CAP was eating up about 75 per cent of the EEC's budget. Political horse-trading too has falsified the price policies – for example, with Paris yielding to Bonn's demands for high wheat prices in return for favours elsewhere. What is more, as the subsidies are paid on quantity of produce, inevitably the system benefits most the big farmers who need it least,

[135]

and this is the major injustice of the CAP. Alike in Germany as in France, the large farms of the north with their high productivity have done handsomely, while smallholders gain relatively little: clearly the CAP's unified price system is unfairly suited to a Europe where farming is so diversified. The cost of the supports falls heavily on the EEC taxpayer: but British opinion is wrong to suppose, as it often does, that 'it's all the fault of the French'. Rich British farmers, too, have benefited excessively; and German farmers' lobbies have been as much to blame as any for the insistence on high prices.

Germans farmers' attitudes to the EEC are highly ambivalent. The CAP so dominates their working lives that they have become the most Europe-conscious of all Germans: for them, the Common Market is no distant abstraction but a daily reality. The more senior or export-minded ones are constantly travelling to meetings in Brussels, or going on sales or study tours to other EEC countries; and even a humble stay-at-home smallholder will discourse knowledgeably about British cattle-breeding techniques or the impact of Danish barley prices. But how far they approve of the EEC is another matter. Most of them still express a general faith in the European ideal: but they have grown sceptical as to whether the CAP as such is a benefit to them. This is a recent development. Most German farmers were initially wary of the CAP, which they feared would mainly help the French: but then during its first decade or so of operation, roughly until the mid-1970s, they were surprised to find it much more advantageous than they had expected. It served to boost their exports and in particular to provide huge new Italian outlets for Bavarian milk and dairy products, thus belatedly compensating for the loss since 1945 of the East European markets on which Bavarian dairy farmers had once depended.

German farm incomes were rising on average by about 7 per cent a year in real terms until 1975; then, with a few ups-and-downs, they began to fall, by a total of some 15 per cent between 1975 and 1983, and faster still in the freak year of 1984. Various factors were responsible for the change of fortune, one of them being American export policies and the vicissitudes of the dollar. But partly to blame also was the CAP with its new policies of tighter pricing and campaigns against surpluses – or at least the German farmers felt it was to blame. Not that all of these farmers are unreasonable. Most have not been blind to the CAP's injustices and wastages, and have been prepared to help in making sacrifices, especially the prosperous ones in the north. But they feel that the cuts are being unfairly applied – and, much worse, that governments over the years have misled them. One farmer expressed to me a very widely felt sentiment: 'For many years, up until recently, governments in Bonn and officials in Brussels encouraged us to produce more and more, to modernise and invest, promising that the CAP would always foot the bill. Josef Ertl[1] in particular did this. So we've invested expensively in new equipment, we've piled up big debts on the loans for it – and now, all of a sudden, we're told to cut production and accept lower prices. The politicians have been plainly irresponsible. We've been duped. Nay, swindled.' German farmers, like others, may be in many ways pig-headed: they should have seen the writing on the wall much sooner, and have cooperated earlier with CAP reform plans. Nonetheless one cannot avoid a certain sympathy for their feelings of having been led up the garden path.

Of the various CAP economy measures introduced in 1984–5, the quotas for milk production especially annoyed the German farmers. All agreed in theory that dairy surpluses must be reduced: but Brussels had left each member government free to adopt its own system of quotas, and the one chosen by Bonn was universally condemned on the farms. The small dairy producers claimed that *they* were being penalised, since they could least afford the cutbacks; the big ones retorted that, no, *they* were the ones to suffer most, as the system was unfairly exonerating the little men. 'What's more,' said one producer, quoting a common view, 'we Germans are being penalised by our own honesty. The Italians and French aren't applying their quotas properly, they let their farmers cheat. We, being German, stick to the rules – and we pay for it.' There's the European spirit for you. As for cereals, when in 1985 Brussels decided on a 3.5 per cent cut in prices, the German farm lobby showed its strength by successfully pressuring Bonn into blocking the measure. So, for the first time in EEC history, Germany used its veto in the Council of Ministers ('to defend a vital national interest') – and on this occasion it stood alone. Later, it is true, a compromise was reached.

The farm lobby also gave proof of its power during the crisis in 1984–5 over the dismantling of the 'monetary compensatory amounts' (MCAs). These were a complex set of subsidies designed to shelter farmers from exchange-rate movements and in particular to protect Germans from being undercut by EEC competitors with a weaker currency than the Deutschmark. After much horse-trading with Paris, Bonn finally agreed to a phasing out of the MCAs. But the farmers, fearing for their incomes, caused a gigantic outcry – so much so that Kohl had to persuade other EEC leaders to let him breach Community fair-trading rules and grant them extensive tax concessions in compensation. This was just one instance of the clout that German farmers wield in politics – in Brussels, Bonn, and Munich

[1] A Bavarian, member of the FDP, and Federal Minister of Agriculture, 1969–83. The most influential figure in post-war German farming.

too. Ignaz Kiechle, Ertl's successor as Federal Minister, is also a Bavarian, but CSU, not FDP. In 1983–5 he tried loyally to help the rest of the EEC to reduce costs and surpluses. But this won him the wrath of Bavarian farmers (90 per cent of them CSU voters): they turned for support to Strauss, and not in vain, for the 'emperor' of Bavaria, knowing the importance of their vote, waged a campaign against his CSU colleague and won some concessions. It caused quite a rumpus. In short, Germany's farmers may be down to 5 per cent of the population, but they seem able to wield much more than 5 per cent of the political influence.

Not all the pressures however come from southern smallholders: the big landowners of the north hold even more of the power on the main farmers' union. This is the 'other face' of German agriculture, and its farms are rather different from those I have described so far. They are run not by *Bauern* (peasants) but by *Landwirten* (educated yeoman farmers), or in some cases by aristocrats or gentlemen farmers; and they do very well. An elder son is usually keen to stay on the land and to take over when his father retires; if a farm is to be sold, there is no shortage of applicants to buy it. On the flat plain of the Ems, near the Dutch border, an area where farming used to be very poor, I visited one medium-sized cattle-breeder, mayor of his village, a tall, rather cocky man with an assertive handshake: 'I've kept my farm to its same modest 125 acres, but by careful breed selection and intensive cultivation I've become quite rich. My parents never took a holiday: but now my wife and I go annually to Tenerife. Agriculture round here has completed its modernisation, it's as efficient as can be.' Heavy vulgar repro furniture in the big modern lounge; two Mercedes in the drive; a manicured lawn the like of which I've never seen on any French farm.

Up in Schleswig-Holstein, I visited big grain and livestock farms of the kind one sees in eastern England and the Paris basin. One was quite bizarre. It lay beside the North Sea coast, on a *Koog* (polder) reclaimed from the sea in the 1920s and protected by a high dyke; on the seaward side was newer reclaimed land where, to my surprise, sheep were grazing. A strong chill wind blew incessantly (it was May). The owners, a charming and sophisticated young couple, Peter Rabe and his wife, he a graduate of Kiel university, lived in a strange mansion, rather elegant, with a huge Hollywood-style stairway curving down into the big parlour: I half expected Liz Taylor to appear at the top, in a ball-gown and a tantrum. The house, like all others on the polder, had a flat green tin roof. Rabe explained, as we drove in his Mercedes along the top of the dyke: 'When my father created this *Koog*, in 1926, it was terribly poor and isolated, with no mains water, so the flat roofs were put there to collect rainwater. Today we breed sheep and export the meat to the French who –

unlike the silly Germans – know how to appreciate its delicious *pré salé* taste that comes from these sea-meadows. We grow cereals, too, on this rich soil. And we have pigs – or we did, but our big new piggery burned down in the night last winter and the 200 pigs suffocated in their sleep. We found just their charred carcasses.' The odd sense of drama thickened as he went on: 'We love it here, my wife and I, we work 70 hours a week in summer but don't miss city pleasure or social life. But the Friesland peasants on the *Koog* seem not so happy. They're a weird lot, these Frieslanders, laconic, almost speechless, and mental retardment is rife. It's lonely round here, and the cold wind whines constantly through the long dark winters, fraying nerves and causing depressions. The *Koog* has a high rate of alcoholism, incest, divorce and suicide.' Peter Rabe's elderly, crippled father told me that he lived on his own. Was he widowed, I asked? 'No, my wife went away.' Maybe she couldn't stand *Koog* life. Definitely Ibsen territory, I felt.

Not far away, near Flensburg, I went to see a stud farm that collects sperm from bulls for artificial insemination. The earnest young geneticist in charge explained to me that this is international big business: he travels to America in search of the right breeds. The key to the operation is a wooden 'phantom cow', looking rather like a 'horse' in a gym. This somehow excites the bull, who mounts it and ejaculates into a rubber vagina, manned by a technician. The other bulls, standing by, who have probably never seen a real cow since they left their mother's side, get contagiously excited too and start to mount each other. Beate Uhse's sex domain (see p. 169) is just a few miles away. Pure coincidence, I was assured.

The post-war changes in German rural society, and more especially in city-dwellers' attitudes to it, are rather curious and reveal a good deal about modern Germany. As in other Western countries, the agricultural revolution has greatly reduced the old poverty and changed farmers' life-styles, but at some cost to warm traditional values – as Edgar Reitz showed in *Heimat*. Reitz himself was born in 1932 in the little town of Morbach on the Hunsrück plateau, between the Rhine and Moselle valleys, then an isolated and poor region of peasant mixed farming. At the age of 20 he left for Munich where he later directed a number of feature films: but he always cherished the idea of one day returning to make a film study of his own *Heimat* (homeland). This he finally achieved in 1980–84, when he spent a total of some three years in the small village of Woppenroth, east of Morbach, researching, scripting and then filming his masterpiece, made initially as an 11-part television series.[1] It was a labour of love,

---

[1] For more details of Reitz and *Heimat*, see pages 298–305.

an intensely personal work. It details the changing fortunes of three families, related by marriage, from 1919 to 1982 – from the old days of poverty, through war and Nazism to the 'economic miracle' years and beyond, when the eldest son of the Simon family becomes a prosperous local factory owner. It shows how, after the war, its fictional Hunsrück village of 'Schabbach' (based on Woppenroth and some other places around) changed gradually from a narrow, enclosed peasant community into a kind of semi-urban suburb in the middle of nowhere; and how the old caring solidarity bred of hard times gave place to a new ambitious acquisitive society, far more mobile and open to the world, but in danger of losing its roots.

Reitz, a gentle, thoughtful person, most impressive to meet, talked to me about *Heimat* and the Hunsrück in his office in Munich's Schwabing in 1985: 'I made the film in order to tell people in the cities what village life is like. When I was a boy, in a place like Woppenroth there were 50 farmers, and now there are four. People were so poor that each winter it was doubtful whether all the members of a family would survive. But then in the 1950s people for the first time could get good jobs, buy cars and travel. Most of the young ones left; farmers sold their land, and the four that remain now live quite well. Some villagers rent flats to tourists, or they commute daily to jobs as far off as Mainz. Some elderly people come to the Hunsrück to retire. But its tradition is dead: today's industrial agriculture has nothing to do with the traditional farming life. There's still a kind of village solidarity, it's true, and old people feel less isolated than in the cities. But the relationship of people to their village has changed. They live with the thought, "We don't know how long we shall stay here, or whether it will be a worthwhile place for our children" – so they invest the minimum in it, both materially and emotionally. They're no longer interested in making the place look attractive, so it isn't. As they've no long-term view, they accept any old eyesores and the pulling down of nice old houses.' These were sad words. Reitz did however agree with me that the human warmth and solidarity of those days hardly justified the poverty and hardship: they were in fact a reaction against it.

In some other part of Germany, matters are not so different. On the dull Ems plain, near Holland, I stayed in a once-poor village that had also become semi-urbanised, with several small factories: it had far less character than the Hunsrück, and was curiously lacking in any sense of tradition. When the peasants became prosperous after the war, their first reaction was to knock down their handsome brick farm-houses and build new, ugly, almost identical villas; even the church, dating from the 1860s, was torn down because it was judged too old, and a new one put up. The villagers, it seems, had wanted to obliterate the traces not only of their poverty but of Germany's recent tragic past as a whole: so all tradition, good or bad, was banished. Only in the past five years had they begun to found an association for local history and even to plan a museum: but much of the damage had by then been done. Today many German villages, with their modern houses, well-stocked shops, maybe banks too, and other tokens of affluence, have come to resemble miniature townlets; only in a few areas, mainly in the south, does one still find really picturesque old places with half-timbered cottages and flower-filled balconies. And, whereas country people used to dress distinctively, today they look just the same as city folk. They play tennis, go to local discos, and of course watch TV, the great leveller. So many little factories and offices have set up in rural areas that a great many villagers have been able to embrace modern life without shifting their habitat – an advantage, socially, in many years. Emigration to the towns has therefore been much less extensive than in France: on the other hand, French villages have remained much more village-like, and so indeed have many in Britain, where the tear-it-all-down-and-modernise craze has been far less rife than in Germany. Fortunately, in the past few years German country people have become less insensitive: they are now taking far more trouble to restore old buildings and generally to cultivate their past (see p. 176). But in many cases it is too late. No one would want to deny them their new prosperity: but it could have been achieved less destructively.

While the villages have become submerged by urban values, the reverse trend – the seeking out of the countryside and of rural values by people from the cities – is much less pronounced than in some other modern countries. It is true that the Germans claim to love their forests and like to hike in the hills, while the Greens profess an ecological concern for nature. But in some ways this is all very superficial and even unrealistic. Middle-class town-dwellers very seldom choose to go and *live* in the countryside, or really get to know country people, as they do much more frequently in France or Britain. And this has always been the case in Germany, where city people have either ignored the country or used it merely as a romantic backdrop for their own feelings – witness so much of classic German literature. German poetry, even more than English, is full of the love and longing for nature: trees, rivers and meadows are personified, almost mystically. But this is rarely accompanied by any sense of a tough daily local life; poets visit nature to explore their own souls and to discuss philosophy. The German novel, equally, has seldom treated themes of rural life. Theodor Storm wrote about Schleswig, while Fontane set some of his books among the gentlefolk of the Prussian estates; but there have been few equivalents of, say Hardy or Giono, local writers identifying themselves with the peasant pleasures and hardships of their homelands.

[141]

Those who did try, in their way, to elevate rural and agriculture values were the Nazis. They promoted the nationalistic ideals of *Heimat* and of *'Blut und Boden'* (blood and soil), and within this context the farmer and his wife, true blond Germanic types honestly tilling the land, were given pride of place; farmers were granted special financial help, and were encouraged to feel that as guarantors of national self-sufficiency in food – and as guardians of honest Aryan virtues – they had an important role in the Nazi scheme of things. But after the war this reputation simply rebounded against them, and in the public mind the average farmer came to be seen, rightly or wrongly, as a clumsy peasant, old-fashioned, primitive and politically reactionary. This image may have been frequently unfair: but it carried some credibility, seeing that in the 1960s the extreme-Right NPD won its highest level of support in rural Schleswig-Holstein and in northern Bavaria. And, of the many thousands of young people who migrated from the rural milieu in the post-war years, some of them who later became writers of journalists gave highly critical portraits of its narrowness and intolerance, rather than sympathetic ones of its warmth and poverty. Kroetz's savage little plays about Bavarian peasant life (see p. 274), or films like Fleischmann's *Hunting Scenes in Upper Bavaria*, were hardly calculated to dispel urban prejudices against country life.

Today the reality of that life may have changed, but its reputation does so more slowly. This may help to explain why relatively so few middle-class Germans – writers or artists, retired people, or commuters near to a town – will choose to make their home in a village. Another reason is more or less the reverse: they know that the villages are no longer picturesque but dull and pseudo-urban, so for a pleasant social life they would do better to stay in town: 'My dear, one just *can't* live in Unterwaldheim, there'd be *no one* to talk to!' In Suffolk and the Cotswolds, in Provence and the Dordogne, and in many other parts of Britain and France, you find countless villages colonised by sophisticated people from the cities who have a full social life there: and they are not present merely as tourists or outsiders, for in a great many cases they integrate into village life and play an active role. It is the multiplier effect, which in Germany has hardly begun. My wife has a close English friend who, after early retirement from his job as an Army officer in Singapore, chose to settle in a small Wiltshire village where he and his wife ran the local shop and rapidly made many friends of all sorts; that, says Katinka, would be inconceivable in Germany. Of course it is true that many well-to-do Germans today have secondary homes in the country for holidays or weekends, especially in scenic spots in the south: but they go there for rest and seldom take much interest in the village life around them. The Germans may claim that they do not want it that way: according to Allensbach polls, the number of people saying that, if they could choose freely, they would ideally like to live 'in the country' has risen from 25 per cent in 1950 to 35 per cent in 1980, while the numbers of those opting for 'a large city' have declined in that period from 27 to 14 per cent. But how many of them think of 'country' as anything other than the old poets' world of sylvan glades and burbling streams? In practice, as several farmers told me, the city commuters and weekenders in their villages have tended to lodge complaints, German-style, against the smell of manure and even the crowing of cocks and mooing of cows in the early morning. Farms offend against the profound Teutonic need for silence.

It is true that in recent years quite a number of young Greens or other ecologists, full of good intentions, have come from the towns to settle in the countryside. Some have tried their hand at organic farming, or at nature preservation schemes (see p. 441). But in many cases they have simply irritated the local farmers, who do not like being lectured by city amateurs on how to sow their crops or plant their hedges. 'Some of these Greens are sensible and have done their homework,' said one Schleswig wheatgrower, 'and they understand about things like soil erosion. But others are dotty dogmatic idealists. They tell us to go back to primitive farming with hand-tools, and they just don't realise that we'd starve that way. And they seem to think that every bird or insect they come across is a tragically endangered species.' On the whole the movement has not been a success – as Reitz suggested to me: 'A lot of these "alternatives" and ecologists went with romantic ideas of the countryside and then they all came back. They found that the reality was more tough and humdrum than they thought, and they were disappointed. So they left, because it's more convenient to live in a town.'

So the villages today are caught in something of a vicious circle – once ignored and despised for being remote and primitive, now disdained as being too ordinary and predictable. And many small farmers seem likely to continue as the poor relations of the *Wirtschaftswunder* society.

4

DAILY LIFE: A MODERNISED SOCIETY RE-EXAMINES ITS TRADITIONS

The tidy and affluent new Germany appears in many ways as a very modern and rational society where the old tensions have been eased and individuals can live in considerable freedom. The centuries-old hatreds and prejudices between Catholics and Protestants have waned away and the two faiths now co-exist in amity. Class barriers have been dismantled far more radically than in Britain, France or many other parts of Western Europe and a new-rich semi-classless society has been emerging. Women have stepped out of their old *Kinder, Kirche, Küche* role into a broad emancipation, and along with this has come a high degree of sexual permissiveness, including the legalising of abortion. The old authoritarian spirit in school education has also greatly diminished.

These changes would seem to be mainly for the better. But do they imply that valued tradition has been thrown out of the window too? The Germans have a particular difficulty with their national traditions, because of the way that the Nazis exploited and debauched so many of them. Therefore after the war many of them reacted by turning their backs on their whole past and embracing modernism perhaps a little too crudely and thoughtlessly; architecture, such of it as had survived the bombing, was a notable casualty. Today there are signs that this trend is ending. Germans are warily turning back to their past, and this can be seen in their new concern for restoring old houses rather than pulling them down, and in their growing love for the old local festivals and carnivals. But there are some other traditions, or rooted modes of behaviour, that perhaps still need to be modified but are proving more resistant to change. Women, for example, though they now have an easier time in social life, are still largely excluded from politics. The stiffness and formality of a great deal of social contact, and the unneighbourliness of the Germans, still strike an Anglo-Saxon as curiously inhibiting – though there are signs of an easing-up under the impact of a new generation. The old traditions of liberal university education have still not been adapted to the very different needs of a mass age. And, though the two Churches may now be at peace with each other, a new war between radicals and diehards has broken out within Protestant ranks, suggesting that Germany's old tensions may have not so much disappeared as shifted their ground to emerge in a new form. These are some of the paradoxes to be explored in this very diverse chapter.

The social snobberies of a semi-classless society

Germany today is much less of a class-divided society than it was in former times. One reason is that the war and the Nazi period destroyed much of the old order and removed many long-standing privileges, both economic and social. The war and then the 1948 currency reform knocked the bottom out of many acquired fortunes, forcing people to make a clean start. What is more, so many families have had something from the Nazi past to keep quiet about that since the war an upper-class structure based on family elitism has largely disappeared: people are wary of looking too deeply into each other's families or of asserting their own. So they depend more on themselves and their contacts than on their pedigree. After the war, the new Germany made a fresh start with an ethos of democratic equality enshrined in the Constitution. Of course this has since been modified in practice by consumer affluence and the uneven sharing of newly acquired wealth: even so, Germany today is a land of fluidity and freedom of opportunity, rather than of inherited privilege. It is something of a *nouveau riche* society, closer in some ways to the United States than to the old European order; less class-obsessed than Britain, less class-divided than France.

Factory workers, major beneficiaries of the 'economic miracle' in the boom years, have been adopting bourgeois life-styles and losing much of their class identity and former resentment of the middle classes. In Germany there was never so strong a working-class culture and tradition as in Britain, where the industrial revolution had come earlier and hit the workers more harshly; the Ruhr developed later along gentler and more paternalistic lines (see page 80), while some of the oldest and toughest German working-class areas such as the Silesian coal-mines are now in the lost eastern territories. Today West Germany has extremely little in the way of specifically working-class life and leisure pursuits; what there was has largely vanished. In the Ruhr, the miners used to get so tired from physical work that they found it relaxing to breed rabbits and racing-pigeons; today their work is automated, they sit cooped up in metal cabins all day, so they prefer to play tennis and squash like the bourgeoisie. And, as most of the dirty menial jobs in Germany are now done by immigrant labour, the German workers have upgraded themselves. They earn higher wages than the majority of office and shop employees; they are as well housed as the lower middle classes, they go to the same restaurants and places of amusement, and they dress and look so much the same that you can hardly tell them apart – especially the young ones. All this is more markedly so than in Britain or France.

The class struggle, still a motif of strong sections of the Left in those two countries, has almost disappeared from Germany's political vocabulary; it is not used by the SPD, and only seldom by the unions. Of course more workers vote SPD than CDU/CSU: but few working-class bastions remain, and there is not much class bitterness, and no basic class rift in society as there is in Britain. The battle between conservatism and radicalism is fought less on class than on generation lines. And, if a gulf exists in Germany today – as indeed it does – between the haves and the have-nots, this is due mainly to rising unemployment. It is the gulf that separates those with steady jobs from those who fail to find them and so become marginalised. Or in some cases they drop out deliberately and marginalise themselves. For those in regular employment, the inequalities of income are lower than in many Western countries (leaving aside the fringe of wealthy people who have done well in business or the arts, or in some key professions such as law or medicine).

The table below, prepared by Inbucon management consultants, London, gives average annual net salaries (in £ sterling) in 1986. The figures in brackets show the differentials of net pay.

	Germany	Britain	France	Italy
Managing director	38,600 (4.5)	23,900 (3.6)	43,800 (7.3)	28,000 (4.5)
Middle management	21,030 (2.5)	12,440 (1.9)	27,800 (4.6)	18,200 (3.0)
Skilled worker	13,800 (1.6)	10,750 (1.6)	20,200 (3.4)	10,140 (1.7)
Unskilled worker	8,440 (1)	6,650 (1)	5,900 (1)	6.140 (1)

In other words, German workers are much better off than others; top managers earn more in Germany than in Britain or Italy but less than in France; differentials in Germany are the same as in Italy, higher than in Britain but much lower than in France.

Of course, social differences and class distinctions do still exist in Germany, resulting partly from education. Most children first attend the same kind of state primary schools: but then at eleven they are streamed, either into grammar-schools (*Gymnasien*) which prepare for university, or into junior secondary schools (see pp. 205–6). In theory opportunities are equal – and certainly the number of working-class youngsters entering *Gymnasien* has greatly increased. But many working-class families still feel inhibited about sending their children, however bright, into this more cultured milieu; one reason is that they find it hard to help them with their homework (an essential task of the German parent). So they tend to prefer schools that will lead straight to jobs or apprenticeship. Hence only about 15 per cent of university students are from working-class homes.

These divisions continue to affect life-styles, values and interests in later life. In Frankfurt, I heard an interesting view from a psychologist, Carmen Lakashus: 'The classes may have moved together, and except for the top ten per cent of the middle-class their income levels may be fairly similar: in clothes, cars and modern equipment, there's little difference. And yet you can still recognise the working-class by its vocabulary, gestures, and above all its tastes. Workers clutter their homes with all kinds of heavy, ugly furniture; middle-class houses are more sparely equipped with light furniture. One class spends its money on Schnaps, the other on books. The middle classes wear casual clothes for leisure, even for parties; workers and farmers, when they've finished their messy jobs, want to put on smarter clothes afterwards, even to go shopping. Middle-class people like to be outdoors whenever possible, even if it's just to sit and read or chat in their gardens and patios; it hardly occurs to workers to go outdoors, except for organised sport. On excursions and on holiday, middle-class people like to be alone, to find empty forests and beaches; workers are ill-at-ease except in a crowd of their own kind. When abroad, the bourgeois make for the museums and cathedrals, and they like to explore local life and local food; the workers want a big hotel where they can stay around the bar and pool and hear German spoken.' This clever analysis I thought a little too schematic and I can think of plenty of exceptions, especially as regards clothing (surely the bourgeoisie too likes to dress up for parties? – see below). But Frau Lakashus summed up acutely: 'The biggest difference of all is that bourgeois are far more aware of these differences than workers. The new-rich working class thinks that affluence has made it just the same as the old bourgeoisie: but the latter, at least the more cultivated ones, are all too aware of the gulf of taste dividing them from the uncouth workers.'

It follows that the classes do not entertain each other much in their homes. However there is plenty of free-and-easy mixing in the context of *Vereine* (associations), sports clubs and other get togethers, especially in smaller towns and villages. And, amid today's upward social mobility, quite a number of skilled workers do in fact acquire the culture and tastes of the bourgeoisie – for example, taking their children to the theatre and opera, or playing Bach at home on their expensive hi-fi. A journalist in Stuttgart, aristocratic by origin, told me: 'Our new house in the suburbs was put up by a local building worker in his spare time. When he'd finished, we invited him and his wife to dinner as our first guests. They chatted easily and confidently, about their holidays in Greece and Paris, and the football and TV that interested us both. A generation ago, they'd have been far less at ease.' This may not be very typical: but it is becoming less and less *un*typical, in a land where workers are much less chip-on-shoulder and aggressive than in Britain. Nor can a person's class background be assessed by his accent as easily as in Britain. Swabians' range of vocabulary may vary with their class and education, but they all talk Swabian in much the same voice – in a Germany where regional differences have always been as pronounced as class ones. And, above all, the younger generations are remarkably un-class-conscious. Children of all kinds become friends at school, with little concern for what their fathers' professions or incomes are. So a doctor's son may bring a bricklayer's son home to play – and the parents, too, will mind far less than once they might have done. These trends are bound to influence the future.

I have written so far about the middle and working classes without mentioning the stratifications within the middle class that play so crucial a role in British and French social snobberies. In Germany, these differences are less clear and less important. Today Germany has no real 'Establishment', of the kind traditionally fostered in Britain by the public schools and Oxford and Cambridge, or in France by the Grandes Ecoles and a few top Paris lycées. One explanation is that the old German power establishments, formed by the aristocracy, the army and a small caste of senior administrators, were dismantled by the ending of the monarchies and by defeat in two wars and the Nazi catastrophes. Also, in a federal country with no true capital, power today is inevitably dispersed. A third factor is that, unlike Britain and France or indeed the United States, Germany has no elitist pinnacles in her education system. The sprawling universities today are all roughly equal in calibre; the *Gymnasien* too are much on a par, while the handful of small private boarding schools have little influence.

It could even be argued that the prevailing ethos in German public life today is lower-middle-class, or *nouveau riche* middle-middle class. And a great many political leaders have come from such backgrounds. That rough diamond Franz-Josef Strauss, intellectually brilliant, was the son of a butcher; Helmut Kohl's father worked in a local finance office; Lothar Späth, who never went to university, was the son of a bank employee. This relatively open and egalitarian state of affairs has much to be said for it. And yet, there are quite a few Germans today who look a little enviously at the elitism of Britain and

France that can produce leaders of a more patrician stamp; they lament the lack of class and style in public life, the prevailing mediocrity, provincialism and *Kleinbürgerlichkeit*. When a leader from a different mould does come along, he is often welcomed. One of the reasons for the huge current popularity of Richard von Weizsäcker – certainly the most admired federal president since the war – is that with his patrician background he does possess those rare old-fashioned qualities of dignity, breeding and cultured thoughtfulness.

It is thus significant, if at first sight paradoxical, that in this new semi-classless society the one class that does survive most distinctively is the old aristocracy. Today it has no formal status: but it still uses its titles, and it is quite widely respected and not solely out of snobbery. Aristocrats as a whole were less contaminated by Nazism than the business and professional classes; most of them served quietly in the armed forces during the war, they provided the leadership of the July 20 plot against Hitler, and so they emerged with some honour left. Today they tend to behave discreetly, even usefully, and are seen as a link with tradition. The aristocracy no longer exerts power as a class: but many individuals are in positions of public influence.

The most striking example is the heir to the Wittelsbach dynasty in Munich, the Duke of Bavaria, who is still treated with ceremony there as a kind of unofficial head of state. In all Europe, this must certainly be the dethroned monarchy still enjoying the best privileges and honours in its homeland – and there are good reasons for it. Having ruled so benignly across the centuries, the Wittelsbachs were expropriated in a very gentle manner after Ludwig III's abdication in 1918: their principal castles and art treasures passed to the Bavarian state, but they were allowed to keep a fair amount of property and sources of revenue, as well as the right to throw parties in Schloss Nymphenburg and to reside in a wing of it for part of the year. Later they resisted Hitler rather bravely. One Wittelsbach ran an anti-Nazi paper in Munich in the 1930s, some others were put in concentration camps, including Ludwig III's son, the Duke. This helps to explain the family's prestige today. The present Duke, Ludwig's grandson, is now over 80 and has moved into retirement in his *Schloss* at Berg on the Starnbergersee. But his son, Prinz Franz, an art-collector well known internationally, represents him on formal occasions and plays an ubiquitous role in Bavarian life: he is on cordial terms with Strauss and is invited to all sorts of official social functions where he is solemnly addressed as 'your Royal Highness'. The family have a free box at the opera, where they are seen regularly. Foreign consuls call on them to pay respects. Their parties at Nymphenburg are the highlights of Munich's glittering social season.

There is more to this veneration than Munich society snobbery: the family is widely popular with ordinary Bavarians too, because of its record. And most important, in this very special *Land* with its exceptional heritage and sense of identity, the Wittelsbachs are seen as the emblem and guarantors of that tradition, helping Bavaria to remain its proud self. In no other *Land* would this be possible to the same degree: The Duke of Württemberg, though also courted for his royal lineage, plays a lesser role. And the Wittelsbachs take their duties very seriously, believing that they still have a moral obligation to serve Bavaria as best they can. Just as there is no Bavarian separatist movement, so there is absolutely no local demand to restore the monarchy: both are seen as unrealistic aims. And yet, many Bavarians still look nostalgically at their royal past, and even secretly envy the British and others for their reigning sovereigns. There are some dissident voices in SPD and Green circles, but they are seldom very vocal. When the Pope came to Munich in 1980, he was greeted at the station by Strauss, the Archbishop and the Duke. An SPD woman deputy then asked in the *Landtag*, 'Why was Herr von Bayern at the station too?' The Speaker demanded that she refer to him by his real legal name, 'Herzog von Bayern'. She refused. So he ruled her question out of order.

Germany's 50,000 or so other aristocrats are hardly in this same pampered class, not even the Kaiser's family, the Hohenzollerns. However, a fair sprinkling of noble families still retain their landed wealth and their great castles set so romantically on hilltops, mainly in the south. The Fürst von Thurn und Taxis in northern Bavaria, one of the richest, is said to own 250,000 acres. A great many other aristocrats, including nearly all the Prussian barons, arrived as refugees from the east after 1945, abandoning their fortunes and their local servitors, and with nothing left but their breeding, their social contacts and their name. But most have shown great resilience and powers of adaption. Like most other titled people today, they have moved quietly into business or other jobs, and they live ordinary bourgeois lives. You find them everywhere, in banks, running shops or art galleries, even in Ministries: sometimes they still use their titles, sometimes they drop the prefix but not the 'von'. Marion Gräfin von Dönhoff, co-editor of *Die Zeit*, is one of the best known. In the south, some of the less wealthy noblemen have converted their castles into hotels in order to keep them going. Though integrated into society, many aristocrats tend to stick together in their own social circles, calling each other by peculiar nicknames such as 'Mopsi', 'Putzi' or 'Pong'. Each year they stage exclusive 'nobility balls' evoking past grandeurs. Some of the richer ones hold boar-hunts on their estates.

However, German aristocrats seldom resemble the familiar English or Scottish stereotypes of the barbarian backwoods peer or debs' dopey delight. More usually they are cultured, urbane and serious-minded – the kind of German that an older generation of foreigners most admires (one thinks of the officer portrayed by von Stroheim in Renoir's *La Grande Illusion*). Some do charity work, many retain a real sense of public service. The dapper young Rupert Graf Strachwitz, manager of the Wittelsbach estates, gave me a democratic beery lunch in the public garden-café at Nymphenburg: after telling me that his forebears had been Silesian landowners, he went on, 'My family feels that it owes something to society for the privileges and position that we've enjoyed for so long. So we want to serve. That's why my father became a diplomat. We also feel that Germany today has a need for this kind of benevolent aristocratic tradition, which is not at all incompatible with a modern democracy.' But of course there is more to it than this. In a society with so strong a respect for titles, the nobility are appreciated for the magic of their names as well as for their real virtues: and many a big company or public institute is only too eager to put a lord on its board. Mainrad Prince von Hohenzollern, of the Swabian and not the Prussian branch of the family, who lives during the week in a smallish flat in Stuttgart, told me of his voluntary work for cancer research and other charities: 'I'm besieged by requests to serve in this way. I do it gladly, for I feel that my family still bears a duty to Germany and to Europe, and if my name can help to promote this or that worthy cause, that's fine.'

Aristocrats may consort together, but they are seldom aloof or cliquey; most are accessible, easy, democratic. It is true that the nobility in former days had some reputation for arrogant feudalism: but this related mainly to the great landed barons of Prussia – the ones who today are exiled and dispersed. In the south, by contrast, with its mass of tiny principalities and baronies, the rural aristocracy was always much closer to the people, benignly paternalistic, and respected. And they, by some divine justice of the division of Germany, are not the ones who have been thrown out. They are typified by the Hohenlohe of northern Württemberg, a sprawling tribal family who still own a dozen or so castles in the lovely rolling Hohenlohe farming countryside. One of these, on a low hilltop, visible far across the plain, is the compact brown *Schloss* of Friedrich Fürst zu Hohenlohe-Waldenburg, a tall, mild, civilised man in his fifties. He and his pretty wife gave me tea and sticky cakes in their modern sitting-room: 'During the war, this castle was occupied by the *Wehrmacht* and we lived in the outhouses. Later we renovated it. Today, if I'm liked and trusted by the villagers, as I think I am, it's above all because they see me as a hard-working professional man doing a serious job. I went to forestry school, and now I farm my 5,000 acres, mostly forest, and run a farm machinery business. Yes, I have landed wealth: but my income is no more than that of an average company director. I keep out of politics, but I work for Catholic charities. I chat to the villagers in pubs and generally try to be as un-seigneurial as possible, while my sister has a full-time salaried job as probation officer for ex-criminals in Munich. A lot of people round here try to suck up to me, that's inevitable, but no one attacks me for being an aristocrat. In France, where we have good friends with châteaux in Burgundy, the landed aristocracy tends to be far more feudal. They spend much of their time away in Paris and keep aloof from village life. We here in Germany have much more of the common touch, and that's why I believe we shall survive.'

He explained that he took the title of '*Fürst*' (prince) after his father died; but, owing to the peculiar juridical status of noble titles today, he could not accede automatically as in the old days – 'I had to persuade my friendly local *Landrat*[1] to sign papers allowing me to call myself "Fürst", and I paid him a fee.' The rules are bizarre and somewhat hypocritical. Whereas in Austria noble titles have been abolished, in Germany they can still be used, but they are a legal part of the surname and are supposed to be unalterable – you cannot succeed to a higher rank. In former days, the elder son of a *Herzog* (duke) or *Fürst* took over the title on his father's death: but since 1918 the offspring must remain '*Prinz*' or '*Prinzessin*' (oddly, a fairly low rank in Germany), so the higher titles will gradually die out. Hohenlohe got round this by changing his name by deed poll and paying maybe 3,000 DM: but it was a bit of a legal fiddle, and was possible only because the *Landrat* was fond of the family and respected its tradition. In Lower Saxony, in a similar case, a *Prinz* appealed to a court to be allowed to upgrade himself, but was refused. Nor is it easy to get rid of your title: there you are all your life with '*Prinz*' or '*Baron*' on your identity card or other papers. And the same applies lower down the scale, where all the children of a *Graf* (count), *Baron* or *Freiherr* inherit those names. So the titles will proliferate and devalue: this was precisely the aim of the democratic legislators of 1918. Even so, it seems probable that the aristocracy will long continue to flourish and be honoured – in a Germany today eager to renew contact with the less tainted aspects of its old traditions.

If a *Graf* is revered for his title, so in a different way is a *Herr Professor*, an *Oberkirchenrat*, an *Oberregierungspräsident*, or even a simple *Herr Doktor*. This abiding German fondness for titles may at first sight seem strange in this somewhat *nouveau riche* society with its lower-middle-class ethos. But probably there is a logical connection: just because they are slightly disorientated by the new class fluidity, so the German cling to the outward forms of the old hierarchies, and to

---

[1] The head of administration in a *Landkreis*, see page 72.

their need for categorising people which bring the security of *Ordnung*.[1] Though it may be changing with the younger generation, this remains a rather formal society, preferring formal modes of address and judging by appearances. And so anyone with a university doctorate (and there are plenty of them everywhere) will exploit the respect he can win from using his title 'Dr' – many people are even quite touchy about it, and will take offence if addressed as plain 'Herr' on an envelope or in conversation. What is more, a wife and indeed a widow takes her husband's title and expects to be called say, 'Frau Professor'. I know one woman, who years after her husband's death, is still addressed by all and sundry as *'Frau Justizrat'* (Mrs Legal Administrator).

It is true that younger people are showing less concern for titles. Many students no longer call their teachers 'Herr Professor' but just 'Herr X'; and some radio and TV interviewers dare to drop the 'Herr Doktor', unimaginable even 20 years ago. But the more deferential ranks of society – junior officials, shop assistants, domestic servants – still seem to be overawed by titles and by people judged 'important'. A Swabian friend told me, 'I get better service in the shops now that I've got my doctorate,' while an English businessman's wife in Stuttgart said of her charlady: 'This good working-class *Putzfrau* is always fuming against the *Gastarbeiter*, but she adores the rich and famous. When I told her that my husband was a partner in his firm, her eyes glowed with joy: *"Ihr Mann ist Direktor! Wunderbar! Ich habe nur prominente Leute!"* ("I work only for prominent people").' Once on the *Autobahn* near Stuttgart I was stopped for speeding, and when the policeman found my driving licence had expired he threatened to arrest me. 'Can I ring the British consul-general?' I asked, and added forcefully, *'Er ist mein Freund'* (which happened to be true). He quickly handed back my papers and shooed me on.

It is thus no surprise that, in some big German cities, rich businessmen vie with each other to acquire honorary consulships from small Third World countries. Sometimes they even buy them, for 50,000 DM or more – a cynical arrangement that suits both sides. The title of *'Herr Konsul'*, however empty in itself and however footling the work that the post demands, provides a ready passport to a new world of social prestige. And so in some *Land* capitals there exists a fantasy diplomatic life – in Munich, Düsseldorf and Stuttgart, though not in serious Hamburg which looks down on such follies. Of the 41 consuls in Stuttgart, only five are foreign career diplomats; the rest are local Germans with 'honorary' status. Some of these, including

---

[1] For the German respect for authority, and how far it is waning, see pp. 412–3.

the man who represents Britain,[1] have a serious and worthwhile job to do. Others work for countries as tiny and remote as Haiti and Chad, which have virtually no contact with Baden-Württemberg, and I would guess that a third or more have bought their titles. A businessman never admits to having done this, yet he will probably feel that the large sum has been well spent. He gets no diplomatic immunity, but has perks of other kinds. He may be a small garage owner, or a maker of underwear, so the status of 'consul' lifts him out of his narrow rut onto the social Olympus. He gets invited *ex officio* to the *Land* President's annual party; he can throw a posh party himself on his country's national day. The 'CC' plaque on his car helps him with the police – needless to say. And his wife too enjoys her kudos as *'Frau Konsul'*. There is a touch of the absurd about two minor Swabian tycoons solemnly calling each other, *'Ja, Herr Konsul'*, *'Nein, Herr Konsul'* – but that's Germany. Of one of these wealthy local worthies representing a small banana republic, a colleague said, 'Being a consul does actually help his business – he goes to a score of diplomatic parties a year, and these bring new contacts. He adores putting the national emblem on his firm's gate.' The consul of another tiny state told me that he had barely heard of it before his appointment, nor were there any citizens of it living locally, yet he threw a consular party each year for 200 guests in a leading hotel. Rich Germans of this kind have no doctorates and no other title, and they feel inadequate. So they create this fantasy world. It is like Genet's *Le Balcon*, where people parade as something they are not. Everyone knows the titles are void of meaning, yet they still pay extravagant respect to them. No one tries to call society's bluff.

In the 1960s and '70s this craving for consulships was cunningly exploited by the notorious Hans Hermann Weyer of Munich, playboy, ladykiller, braggart and practical joker, one of post-war Germany's most flamboyant characters. He set up a brokerage to put rich Germans in touch with small far-off countries, taking a fat cut on each deal; and in his heyday he claimed that about one-third of Germany's 300 honorary consulships had been arranged by him. The vendor nations were contravening the Vienna Convention of 1963, which forbade the sale of these posts, and so Bonn tried its best to stamp out the traffic. But it was not easy, for Weyer did his work in secrecy. He also sold aristocratic titles, honorary degrees, and even professorships, so that thanks, say, to the University of Tegucigalpa, some Bavarian grocer who had left school at 15 could flaunt his academic distinction (but this was too unsubtle and usually got found out).

---

[1] Amid universal outcry, the official British consulate-general in Stuttgart was closed down for economy reasons in 1985, and replaced by an honorary consul.

Weyer himself was Bolivian consul in Munich: he called himself '*der schöne Konsul*', he grew very rich and lived in a grand jet-setting style. The Gatsbyesque parties at his villa on the Starnbergersee were frequented by princesses and millionaires from Munich's high society, who thought it a great lark to share his weird fantasy and accepted him as an amusing joker in their snobby pack. His trade may have been odious, but at least he treated it as one big giggle: 'I like turning values upside down and poking fun at society,' he told me when I visited him; 'it gives me a nice sense of power, and of the absurd, when mighty magnates come fawning humbly to beg titles from me. My father was a close friend of Hermann Göring. Ever since the time when, as a small boy, I saw those rows of medals shining on his chest, I've never looked back.'[1] Weyer was later charged with tax fraud. So he left Germany for Paraguay, one of his client countries, where today he is still sometimes featured by German magazines, living it up by his pool, with champagne, gorgeous girls, and a big grin on his face.

Munich is the one city with a genuine café-society on any scale. This is the trendy world of media stars, fashion designers, sons and daughters of rich industrialists, and exiled or local nobility such as 'Prinz Poldi', younger brother of Prince Franz of Bavaria. They throw parties in their homes, or on big rafts on the Isar with Dixie bands, and they congregate in such haunts as the Käfer café restaurant or St-Emmeransmühle beer-garden. To be accepted in this set, you need to have a name and some money, and above all to dress very well and be stylishly self-confident. You can wear either the latest fashions or elegantly-styled Bavarian *Tracht* – for this milieu fully merits its nickname of the '*Lodenmantelschickeria*' (see page 32). Its studied Bavarian folksiness is part of the cult, and its parochialism is partly deliberate. A leading Munich beauty surgeon said to me: 'My wife takes these cocktail parties seriously and likes to meet the "right" people and appear in the gossip-columns. I go just for a bit of amusing distraction after a hard day's work. Compared to Paris or London, where the smart set is far more diverse and international, here it really is very provincial.' The daily doings of the *Schickeria* are chronicled in the '*Leute*' column of the Munich boulevard paper, *Abendzeitung*, which reports who was wearing what and where. 'Gräfin X, in *Loden* with a Cardin leather collar, was sitting in Käfer with her poodle when along came Baron Y in his new Savile Row suit. She said "hello"; he said "hello" and passed on' (an actual item) is roughly the intellectual level. Some society ladies telephone the

---

[1] See my article on Weyer in the *Telegraph Magazine*, June 7, 1974.

Abendzeitung to tell what parties they are going to and ask that a photographer be sent; some even pay to be written about.

In more ordinary middle-class circles, in Munich and in other cities, social life is less pretentious than this; but by Anglo-Saxon standards it is still rather stiff and conformist (except between close friends and family). Peter Frei, a radio journalist now back in Germany after spending some years in London, observed to me: 'Suddenly all the parties seem to be serving slices of kiwi-fruit, or an expensive variety of smoked meat, or whatever the latest trend may be. Some society hostess will have set the fad, then it's publicised by big-selling magazines such as *Bunte Illustrierte*; and the new-rich lower middle classes slavishly take it up. The same is true for clothes, both for men and women. Even the intelligentsia here I find to be markedly more competitive, snobbish and conformist than their equivalents that I knew in Britain. This is a symptom of our German provincialism, of being a series of big villages. At parties, people are also extremely conscious of each other's positions. When you meet someone new, he will first ask what you do, not so much out of polite interest as to try to size up your importance in your job so as to see whether you are worth talking to.'

At the opera in Munich, bejewelled elderly women in chic black dresses, with modish touches of pink in their hair, can be seen parading up and down in the intervals, their hawk-eyes fixed on their rivals' attire. But this old-style conventionality is today giving way in certain circles to a new individualism, equally mannered – as Carmen Lakashus explained: 'The same person has cheap rag-like clothes *and* elegant expensive ones, and she wants to wear both – and so long as it's individualistic and doesn't look plain, that's fine. People try *not* to look just like each other: that's new, and it's running through all ages and classes.' In Schwabing I saw a girl with a very smart hair-do, in stained dungarees torn to shreds – frightfully chic. But, whereas in Britain casualness is widespread and purely casual, in Germany it is calculated for effect. You can dress any old how, but you'll be summed up for it; in Britain, people often just don't notice. And this varies from city to city. In Munich, anything goes, but in the Stuttgart bourgeoisie conventions are more old-fashioned: one francophile lady there told me that in Lyon she had found some excitingly modernistic ear-rings – 'I was longing to buy them, but I knew that I could never wear them here, as I might anywhere in France. People would have been genuinely shocked, and I'd never have lived it down.' And the wife of an English businessman in Stuttgart said: 'We get invited to parties because of my husband's position and I must dress smartly but inconspicuously. The ideal is to be "*dezent*" (discreet). My conversation, too, must not stand out. If I were to break these rules, I would be bitched at behind my back. Everyone, too, has the same kind of smart car, usually a Mercedes, and you are classified by the size of your car as well as by your job status. Even these Swabians, though they think it bad taste to show off their wealth in public, still judge each other by it in private.' In the more ostentatious towns, Munich or Düsseldorf, wealth is lavishly flaunted – but this must be done with style and assurance, not any old how.

This may seem a severe picture. But I should add that Germany is also a scrupulously polite society, in its formal way. People may flare into sudden rudeness if you inadvertently offend them, or break a rule: but mostly they are courtesy itself, even the young shaggy ones. *'Auf Wiedersehen'* is said on every conceivable occasion, even when total strangers have done no more than share a lift for two floors in a public office; similarly, if you silently share a table with a stranger in a pub, he wishes you *'Guten Appetit'*, and then *'Wiedersehen'* when he leaves. But social occasions are still marked by a good deal of stiffness and ceremony. English friends told me of a Stuttgart dinner-party in the home of a rich lawyer: 'There were lots of servants and our hostess seemed tense, anxious that all should be just so. We went into dinner in pairs on each other's arms. Later the men made formal speeches with toasts – yet this was only a private party for ten.' This admittedly is an extreme, untypical example. Even so, the Germans' idea of a party is often to sit round in a neat circle of ten or twelve, and to have just one conversation going, dominated by two or three people: they are less used to the Anglo-American fluid stand-up style. However, matters have been easing recently among some of the younger generation. Some Greens and *Alternative* have even gone to opposite extremes of informality: but they too have their own social codes and categories (see pp. 442–3).

It is true also that in very small towns and villages, where the community is tighter, among all classes there is much more casual matiness and relaxed informal interchange than in the cities: but this may in turn lead to intolerance, jealousy and intrigue. The stiff formality is at its most severe in the bourgeois districts of cities, and one of its most obvious aspects is the lack of easy chumminess between neighbours. Fear of neighbours is an old German tradition: 'See what your neighbour is like, before you build your house: if he's a scoundrel, you'll be building yourself a tomb,' wrote Friedrich Rückert in 1837. Today the commonest attitude to neighbours is that with just a very few you make close friends, and with all the others you have as little contact as possible: the in-between casual acquaintanceship so normal in Britain or America is unpopular since it might lead to loss of privacy, if the Müllers next door were continually popping round uninvited. This has also something to do with habitual German reserve about making new friends. People may ask a neighbour for strictly practical help on minor matters, such as leaving keys or taking in a parcel, but that's about all. If the neighbour does something really absolutely frightful, like playing the violin after 10 p.m., or failing to sweep the snow from his share of the pavement, then lawyers' letters may be quick to ensue (see page 410). And as the German, paradoxically, not only relishes his own privacy but is also keen to mind his neighbour's business for him, life-styles may get criticised even if they are causing no active harm at all. One girl I know who worked late, and then slept till noon with the curtains drawn, had neighbours shouting at her, 'Only lazy people work at night!' Oddity of behaviour offends against the desire of the German soul for social tidiness. Once again, however, an improvement can be detected amongst younger people. Allensbach surveys of all Germany (not just of middle-class urban areas) report that the number of people inviting neighbours to their home increased from 14 to 35 per cent between 1953 and 1979.

Just as striking as unneighbourliness is the gulf in Germany between office and private life. The pattern here is much the same as in France, of which I wrote in *France in the 1980s*, 'Except at senior executive level, office colleagues do not often try to meet each other socially, and casual friendship is rare between staff of differing grades. Thus the social ambience of the traditional French office is less chummy and relaxed than in Britain.' In Germany, there may be more chumminess, but the unwritten convention remains that office colleagues are one thing, social friends are quite another; junior staff may share a friendly lunch-break for years, without it occurring to any of them to meet at the weekend. This is not so in factories, where workers play football and then drink beer together: but office life is austerely asocial. And this can make life lonely for anyone who arrives to work in a new town without existing friends. I think of poor Katharina Blum, in Böll's novel, going for long car-drives on her own, because she had so few friends. And the head of an office in Hamburg told me that, when a seemingly cheerful clerical assistant suddenly killed herself, not a person in the firm knew anything at all about her life, or had had any social contact with her, although she had been there for three years.

A major aspect of this reserve is the German non-use of Christian names. This frequently startles a British or American visitor – and it can reach comic proportions. Young typists sharing an office, of the same age and background and on cordial terms, will go on calling each other '*Fräulein*': business colleagues will remain on '*Herr*' terms. An American woman journalist, working for a US Army paper in Stuttgart, told me that she once wrote a story about a senior German official and, following American practice, needed to include his Christian name. So she rang his secretary to ask for it. 'Sorry. I don't know.' 'Oh, have you only just started to work for him?' 'No, I've been here four years. But he signs his letters with his initials. I've never heard him use his first name.' This kind of thing happens all the time. It is true that in the media and fashion worlds there is more informality: but even the open-minded *Die Zeit* remains surprisingly stiff, or so I was told by one journalist there who said that for his first five years on the paper he had remained '*Herr*' to all his colleagues. The art in Germany is to know at what point you can start saying 'Hans' without being snubbed. Generally, between males, it is wisest to leave the older or more senior man to make the first move; between a man and a woman, leave it to the woman.

Maybe the British and Americans have debased the Christian name coinage into virtual meaninglessness. But in Germany this whole situation – including the barrier between '*du*' and '*Sie*' – seems to me to perpetuate an artificial barrier between friendship and acquaintanceship, making passage from one to the other an edgy and embarrassing business, and adding to the general uptightness of public social life. In France, where the use of Christian names has increased far more than in Germany, it is common today to call someone 'Jacques' or 'Françoise' while remaining on '*vous*' terms: I have a score of French friends in that category. But in Germany it is much more usual for the moves to Christian-name terms, and to '*du*' from the formal '*Sie*', to go together. In the middle classes, the more intimate address is still largely restricted to family and close friends. But it is far commoner between workers, and in SPD party circles it is a ritual tradition (a junior party worker can call Brandt, '*du, Willy*'). For many years it has also been universal among students, and since 1968 it has been gaining ground between Greens and other younger radicals. So a thaw is in progress which may eventually permeate the upper age groups. And anyway, what's in a name? I am on warmer terms with some Germans who still call me 'Herr Ardagh' than with many Britons who call me 'John' at first sight.

It would indeed be wrong to infer from the formality that Germans are cold with each other. The positive side of their relationships is that they are very warm and caring between true friends – more than the British. Friendship for them is an emotional business. After a due period of time, when trust has taken root, a man will suggest to his new friend that they move to '*du*' and to '*Hans*': they will then drink on it and embrace, in a kind of ritual. And the friendship is for life. The Germans draw a far sharper distinction than the British between true friends and the rest; they take great trouble with their friends, keeping in touch, sending cards and presents on their birthdays, and enquiring after their problems; they depend more than the British on possessing a circle of good friends whom they see regularly. But one crucial question remains: do the Germans need these friends so much, just because their society is somewhat stiff and uncaring, and sometimes hostile? – or, conversely, do they benefit so much from their friendships, and from the smooth organisation of public life, that they have less need for the more open and pally Anglo-Saxon style of society? Maybe, the answer is, a little bit of both – but quite a lot of the former, I do suspect. And this may not be the best of situations. It could be said that the complicated Germans have two very distinct sides to their nature. On the one hand, they are powerfully drawn to the rich interior life, to the world of emotion, idealism, privacy, depth and sensitivity – and friendship belongs to this. On the other, they are very practical and ambitious, admirers of efficiency, order and authority. The two do not easily fit together – and the result is a certain hiatus in German social life. Is a younger generation, with different values, working towards a better synthesis? – a theme to be explored towards the end of this book.

Women, sex and children: a few crusades yet to be won

'The image of the German *Frau* has changed. Because women today have a far better diet than in former days, and do more sport and gymnastics, so we are now much slimmer. And that makes it easier to be more elegant too. This in turn has helped German fashion to advance on the European scene. For example, my own firm today sells widely in Italy and holds successful shows in Milan – something unthinkable till quite recently. What! – Italians buying German clothes?'

The fashion designer Jil Sander, herself extremely slim and pretty, was talking to me in her cool white Hamburg studio – and I readily agreed with her. Personally I have always found German women much more attractive than French ones, and in their own way just as chic and glamorous. Socially and psychologically too, no less than physically, there is today something entirely out-of-date about one's old picture of the typical *Hausfrau* (if indeed it were ever true), buxom and a bit frumpish, forever baking cakes and breeding flaxen-haired children. Following upon the *Wirtschaftswunder*, the late 1950s and early '60s was the era of the so-called *Fräuleinwunder*, with the emergence of a seemingly new breed of young women, more prosperous and self-confident, more slender and well-dressed, more set on full emancipation. German women today may still tend to be ultra-house-proud and tidiness-prone, but then so are German men, so this is not a sex characteristic. In most other respects, women have freed themselves from the heavier constraints of the old *Kinder, Kirche, Küche* ideal, once so widely preached – and accepted – as the female role. As in other Western countries, they have moved quite a way since the war towards legal equality and social and sexual freedom, in a country that now is as permissive as most and that legalised abortion in 1974. Women have edged away, too, from the desire for motherhood – indeed, rather too much so, in the eyes of those who are now so alarmed about the declining population of this nation with the world's lowest birth-rate.

This is not a Latin country, and even in Catholic Bavaria there are few fathers who feel it a point of honour to protect a daughter's virginity, as many still do in parts of France and Italy. Teenage girls are free to do much as they please. And, in social life, women of all ages and classes mix easily and equally with men. Sometimes, it is true, men prefer to gather on their own round a *Stammtisch* in a pub: but on the whole Germans enjoy the company of women, and in this respect there is less *machismo* than in the clublands of upper-class London or working-class Tyneside, let alone in southern Italy. Why, then, do most German women feel that they still lack real equality? – why has the recent fight for equal rights been fiercer than in most other European countries? It may be something to do with the perfectionism of a nation where demands and expectations are always pitched high. But, more to the point, there does still exist a very potent *machismo*, not in social or private life but in politics and the professions, where men have fought to keep their hold on the senior positions. This is today's great problem – and it has a long history.

In 19th-century Germany, women in middle-class society were subordinated even more harshly than in Victorian England – as was shown so movingly in the novels of Theodor Fontane, whose masterpiece *Effi Briest* (1895) tells of a young wife abandoned by husband, parents and friends after a brief and transient affair with another man. Finally she wastes and dies. Flaubert's Emma, Ibsen's Nora and Hardy's Tess were never treated quite so inhumanely. After this, determined campaigning by women's rights leaders did achieve some progress – but later than in Britain. Not till the 1914–18 war were women admitted to the Universities. They won the vote in 1918, and under Weimar they at last began to make their way in the professions and to gain a little more emancipation and social life. But then the Nazi period set the clock back. Hitler's idealisation of home and family at first appealed strongly to women's conservatism, and they provided a large part of his popular vote in 1930 and 1933. But then in the interests of baby-breeding he ousted women en masse from the professions and the universities and sent them back home – to *Küche* and *Kinder* if not *Kirche*. Abortion was made a capital offence. However, as the war wore on, with so many men away fighting, the Nazis were obliged to modify this women-at-the-hearth policy: they came back into jobs such as teaching, and in some sectors such as farming and small business it was they who virtually kept the country going. Then after 1945, when so many millions of men came home morally or physically broken, or had been killed, the women of Germany emerged strongly placed to play an important role in the post-war renewal. From a feminist viewpoint, this was perhaps the one bonus from this tragic time.

But the struggle was by no means ended. The Constitution of 1949 stated, 'Men and women have equal rights': but the juridical implementation of this broad ideal did not happen over night. Only in 1957 did a new law grant equality to women in marriage property rights. And up until 1977 the Civil Code contained an astonishing clause that gave the wife sole responsibility for the household and permitted her to take a job only if her husband agreed and if it were compatible with her domestic duties! This was abolished by the 1977 Marriage Law which declared that such matters should be settled by joint agreement. It also removed the guilt factor in divorce cases, which had often prevented a wife found 'guilty' from obtaining her fair share of alimony – this was in line with similar reforms in other countries at that time. So today a woman does at last have virtual equality, in the private sphere. But in employment, and in public life in general, women still feel badly discriminated against – not in law, but in practice, by a male-dominated society that battles harder than in most modern countries to retain its entrenched positions in the professions. And it still feels superior. When in 1972 the first woman newscaster appeared on television, one leading TV presenter, Karl-Heinz Köpke, commented, 'The news has to be read with detachment: women are too emotional,' and another, Werner Höfer, added, 'Of course I was thinking about her bosom, so I didn't listen properly.' In 1985, the film director Margarethe von Trotta, a moderate feminist, gave me her view on this: 'Men are very self-protective, they don't like talented women coming up to rival them. If I'd been a man, I'd probably have made my first film ten years sooner. In my generation, women were not trusted by society, so they did not trust themselves. But this is now changing.'

In politics, women are markedly fewer in top positions than in Britain or France, let alone the United States. Whereas 10 per cent of members of parliament were women in 1919, by 1980 the figure in the *Bundestag* was down to 7 per cent. It climbed back to some 9.8 per cent in 1983, thanks largely to the Greens. The main reason for the low figure is not that women are unpolitical but that the local party associations selecting the candidates are heavily male-dominated and they put women low down on the lists. It requires great effort for women to break through this, as they have managed to do in one or two towns that now have all-female local councils – a real sex war! As it is also men who draw up governments, it is little surprise that post-war cabinets in Bonn and in the *Länder* have each contained no more

[163]

than one or two 'token' women, usually in ministries such as family affairs and health. And yet, all the evidence suggests that the political awareness of women has greatly increased and they no longer vote the way their husbands tell them. The SPD leadership at least has responded to this and since 1983 has put a number of women into shadow cabinet posts. The arrival of the Greens in politics has also made some difference, notably when in 1984 a Junta of six women assured control of their party in the Bundestag (see p. 430): but this may have been counter-productive, for Green ladies can seem rather extreme and may not be the best ambassadresses for their sex. Nor is it certain whether male attitudes as a whole are evolving. According to Allensbach polls, the number of men 'pleased to see a woman active in politics' rose steeply from 27 per cent in 1965 to 62 per cent in 1976, but then dropped back to 56 per cent in 1984. All in all, it may be a long time yet before a woman becomes even a *Land* prime minister.

In the professions, the situation is not much better. The proportion of women university students has risen since 1957 from 22 to 40 per cent: but women still account for only 5 per cent of full professors, 5 per cent of lawyers, 3.4 per cent of senior civil servants. The percentage of female doctors has quadrupled since 1933, to reach 20 per cent; in 1985 there were four women ambassadors; and the Protestant Churches now admit women as priests (which is more than can be said for the Church of England). But there are no women in the armed forces except as medical assistants. And even in the media, though women can do well in freelance jobs, they still find it hard to secure promotion in staff executive positions, simply because men bar the way: Marion von Dönhoff is a rare exception. The same applies in the trade unions, where Monika Wulf-Mathies broke new ground in 1982 by being elected head of the large Transport and Public Services Union, the first woman in such a post. In banking, business and industry, it is reckoned that only 2 per cent of all top positions are held by women. Here male chauvinism is especially strong, and a woman can rarely succeed in climbing up through the hierarchy. When she does sit at a chairperson's desk, nearly always it is either because she has inherited from a husband or father or – quite often – because she has had the courage to start her own business. This frequently pays off – as in Jil Sander's case ('Starting my own firm I saw as my only hope, if I were to get my ideas across'), or that of the redoubtable Professor Elisabeth Noelle-Neumann, head of the Allensbach public opinion institute whose surveys I have been quoting.

At the more ordinary job level, women today account for 37.4 per cent of the total workforce, slightly less than in Britain or France. By law, they get equal pay for equal work, but in practice men are often paid more, under the pretext that they are expected to do the heavier chores or work at night when needed: men's gross hourly wages in industry in 1982 averaged 15.59 DM, against 11.32 DM for women. Women can appeal to the courts over this or other discrimination, but the legislation is vague and there are no sanctions: Germany lacks a proper Sex Discrimination Act, as exists in Britain and America. When a job is vacant, the employer will frequently prefer a man, who after all is not going to get pregnant and then take the statutory six months' paid maternity leave. Girls also find it harder than boys to secure apprenticeships, and some two-thirds of today's youth unemployed are female. Recently, with rising unemployment, this whole situation has tended to get worse, or at least is perceived as having done so: according to Allensbach, the number of people thinking that women have equal professional opportunities has declined since 1967 from 40 to 17 per cent. Furthermore, the Kohl Government since 1983 has been accused by women's rights leaders of trying to 'push married women back into the home' with the dual aim of easing pressure on the labour market and of stimulating the birth-rate. The Government has denied any such thing. However, right-wing politicians rarely manage to conceal their old-fashioned sexist image. In the 1983 election campaign, Kohl crassly wooed the female vote with the phrase, 'Our pretty women are one of Germany's natural resources'. Feminists and others hooted with indignation.

A strongly militant feminist movement developed in Germany in the late 1960s and early '70s, much as it had done in the United States. It at least had the merit of dragging the problem of sex discrimination into the limelight and forcing a public debate. But the movement rapidly displayed a humourless stridency and fanaticism, of a kind not uncommon in German radical politics, and before long it had fragmented into numerous rival factions, divided over aims and tactics. Some feminists allied their cause to the violent extremist Left,[1] believing that only in a revolutionary new world could women gain equality. Others, far from fighting for equal rights within society, staged a retreat into their own all-female circles, breathing lewd slogans of hatred against all males, and preaching lesbianism as their ideal. Some opened bookshops and cafés from which men were barred. Such extremism probably did little good to the female cause, for it gave feminism a bad name and alienated the sympathy of most ordinary German women. However, since those heady days matters have now quietened down. The more fanatical viragoes are isolated,

---

[1] In German post-war politics, many of the most extreme radicals have tended to be women, without being primarily feminist. This is true of some Green leaders today, as it was of Ulrike Meinhof, Gudrun Ensslin and others in the terrorist movements of the 1970s

and others have mellowed. Angelika Sirtl, a pragmatic 'moderate' feminist on the woman's magazine *Brigitte* in Hamburg, gave me the picture as she saw it in 1985: 'Fifteen years ago you could tell a feminist from her looks and dress, all greyish and no make-up. But now they've discovered that feminism need not exclude femininity, and that you can enjoy looking pretty and sexy and well-dressed, to please yourself as well as men. Those old arch-feminists may have been too aggressive, and some still are: but we all learned a lot from them. And a society needs fighters. Even some staunch conservative CSU women leaders have publicly declared their gratitude to the feminists for what they have achieved.' Yet there remains a divergence in the women's movement, between those seeking fuller equality within the present social system, and those like the 'fundamentalist' Greens who want society itself to be changed first.

Many of the more militant feminists today concentrate their efforts on trying to help other women who, as they see it, are 'victims' of a *macho* society. In particular they set up and run *Frauenhäuser*, which are refuge hostels for women battered or otherwise maltreated by their menfolk. Inspired by the English model, these homes today exist in over 100 German towns; most are run as private initiatives, but some are municipally funded too. Hamburg has four, one of them for St-Pauli prostitutes who are trying to leave their profession but are terrorised by their pimps. The addresses of the homes are kept strictly secret, for there has been more than one case of an angry pimp or husband turning up with a gun, and women have been shot dead. I was not myself allowed to visit a *Frauenhaus*, naturally: but the social workers at one of them consented to meet me in a Hamburg café, where they brought with them two desperately pathetic inmates. Both had been raped – one by her father, repeatedly, as a teenager. Both struck me as badly in need of medical help. But the severe-faced social workers said: 'These are normal, healthy women. They are simply the victims of men, and of a sick society. On principle, we allow no doctors or psychiatrists to visit the homes.' Their argument is that women in this situation tend to be frightened of the welfare authorities: they have too often suffered from the clumsy, officious attempts of doctors and others to get them back into society ('We'll help you to make a new start with your husband') and they just want to be left alone. But for adopting this stance the *Frauenhäuser* have been much criticised. In some towns it has cost them their municipal financing.

As in other countries, the past 30 years have seen great changes in attitudes to sexual morality and in man/woman relations. Marriage is in decline. The annual total of weddings reached a peak of 530,000 in 1962, but by 1978 had fallen to 328,000, while according to Allensbach surveys the proportion of people considering marriage 'a necessary institution, not out-of-date' fell from 89 to 64 per cent between 1949 and 1985. The practice of living together unmarried, once so frowned on, is now judged acceptable by 80 per cent of Germans, according to another poll; and some 40 per cent of couples in the 18 to 35 age-group live in just this way. But often they retain two separate flats, out of prudence, seeing that relationships tend to be more fragile than property leases. Today the vast majority of young couples live together for a while before getting married and often they leave the wedding until the girl is about to have a child. Divorce now terminates about one marriage in three, as in Britain. Women especially are now more demanding of their partner; marriages have become more honest, so that a couple who are basically incompatible will split up rather than make each other's lives a misery: and the laws have been eased, so that divorce by mutual consent is now quite easy after a year's separation. All these are reasons for the rise in the rate of divorce, which no longer carries any social stigma.

There has been a general rise in tolerance, too. Even 20 years ago, an unmarried mother had a hard time of it in society: today she is easily accepted, except maybe in some rural areas. And she has proper legal status; a child born out of wedlock, too, enjoys the same welfare and inheritance rights as any other. There are reckoned to be about 500,000 women who live on their own with their children and have never married; some young feminists prefer this style, using a man simply to sire their child. Homosexuality too has become more readily tolerated, both by law and by opinion; as in Britain, it is now legally permitted between consenting adults in private, while Allensbach surveys indicate that numbers of women thinking homosexuality a 'vice' dropped from 48 to 20 per cent between 1963 and 1976. A gay English teacher who has lived in Germany for 20 years told me: 'In my university circles there is absolutely no problem, though of course in schools a master has to be very careful. I'd say that, in private and social life, homosexuals are as free here as in Britain. The only difference is that here it's more hidden behind a façade of decency. You don't get all those camp jokes on television. But that's partly due to the prudishness of German TV.' A homosexual in a senior official position may still be in difficulty, especially in the armed forces – as was shown in 1984 by Defence Minister Wörner's onslaught on General Kiessling, suspected of frequenting gay bars in Cologne. But it turned out that this scandal had less to do with the general's alleged mores than with political factors – and anyway the public did not seem especially shocked.

In general, if a German politician has an 'unorthodox' private life (homosexuality, mistresses, prostitutes, multiple divorces, or whatever), he may not emerge quite as unscathed as in France, but he is less likely to have his career damaged or destroyed by it than in hypocritical Britain. There has been no post-war German equivalent of the Profumo or Thorpe affairs. Maybe a minister who behaved as caddishly as Cecil Parkinson would likewise have been pressured into resigning. But a politician who more innocuously shows himself to be one for the girls may even win a certain kudos for it, as in France – and oddly enough this seems especially so in Catholic Bavaria. There is a true story that Franz-Josef Strauss, on a visit to New York some years ago, lost his wallet and passport when on a spree with whores; and another story, less authentic, that on the same trip he slept with Marilyn Monroe. Both tales gleefully went the rounds of the Bavarian beerhalls, and Strauss's popularity ratings went shooting up. *'Das sieht unserem Franz-Josef ähnlich, dem alten Bazi!'* ('That's typical of the old devil').

The 1960s and early 1970s saw a sharp rise in promiscuity among young people. Allensbach again has revealing statistics: the percentage of single girls claiming to have lost their virginity before the age of 19 went up from 31 to 73 per cent between 1963 and 1978! Since then, as in other countries, there has been a swing back, not to chastity, but towards seriousness, fidelity and the steady teenage couple. Carmen Lakashus (see p. 148) said to me, 'Sex in the 'sixties was very much a body thing, but now it's more emotional and romantic. The young can have sex whenever they want, so they no longer have to prove it. It's now a full rich sexuality, much more than for the 'sixties generation.' But I am less sure myself about the romantic aspect. The Germans may have the reputation of being a romantic people, as regards nature, poetry, music, Wagnerian heroes and all that. But the younger ones today seem practical and down-to-earth in relationships – especially the men, who are definitely *not* Latin lovers full of erotic charm. 'All these shaggy types, they're so gentle and kind and serious,' said one pretty German girl I know, 'but they're far more ready to ask your views on nuclear missiles or the next *Land* election than to hold your hand and say how lovely your eyes are.' Among this generation there has been a marked decline in the old gallantries; many young people think that opening a door for a woman is just silly. Yet there are plenty of girls who regret the change. Their scope for using their charm is more limited. The climate of gentle flirtatiousness, of pleasurable sexual tension, that still infuses social life in France or Italy, is much less present in Germany, which has probably become even less romantic than Britain or America.

After the arrival of the pill, the 1960s were the breakthrough era in popular sex education. Oswalt Kolle scored a wide success with his sex-instruction books and films such as *Deine Frau, das unbekannte Wesen* ('Your Wife, the Unknown Being'), all very explicit, serious and helpful. This was followed by the age of liberation of pornography, linked to the extraordinary phenomenon of Beate Uhse and her commercial empire of sex shops and hard-porno movies. This Godmother of German sex – and grandmother of nine children – is Germany's supreme example of a businesswoman who started her own firm and then fought her way to supremacy in her chosen field. She began, like Kolle, as a sex adviser, but has ended up somewhat differently. I went to see her one day in her smart head office at Flensburg, by the Danish border – a slim, wiry, rather manic little lady in her sixties, grimacing, gesticulating, very quirky and appealing. I had supposed that she based herself on Flensburg because it is the nearest German town to sexy Copenhagen, but she gave me the true reason: 'I am from East Prussia. I was a transport pilot in the Luftwaffe during the war, in Berlin, and just before the Russians arrived I managed to take a small plane and escape with my baby son to Schleswig-Holstein. I had lost my husband and parents in the war, and I've stayed here ever since. I found that the wives on the local farms were fearfully ignorant and worried about sex, so I decided to try to help them. As my mother had been a doctor, I had some background. I began to print and distribute leaflets explaining the Knaus-Ogino method, and steadily this developed into a large mail-order business, selling sex-advice pamphlets and contraceptives. Of course I had to face plenty of opposition in those days, and some lawsuits, but I won through – and today the climate has changed right round and has vindicated me. I am convinced that I did a lot of good. I helped to make the Germans less repressed. Repression led to Nazism.'

So successful was Frau Uhse that later she moved into a wider and more contestable field, marketing sexual aids and stimulants of all sorts, and producing and selling her own hard-porn magazines and films. She opened her first high-street sex shop in 1962, and now has 30 of them all over Germany, patronised in part by couples wanting to improve their sex lives but also, inevitably, by the lonely mackintosh brigade. In the hygienic ambience of a superior chemist's shop, they offer vibrators, erection creams, and much else. The 14 Beate Uhse Blue Movie cinemas show the films, few of them exactly educational, that her firm produces or sponsors. 'I don't pretend to be Jesus Christ, I'm a normal businesswoman,' she told me; 'since 1975 pornography has in most respects been legal in Germany – and I'm simply catering to a market as the law allows me to. Germany today is one of the most liberal countries in this field. And the Germans are a very sexually liberated people – more than the Americans, who are somewhat inhibited except for some groups in California.'

After a canteen lunch she showed me round her new open-plan headquarters, all as neat and antiseptic as a doctor's surgery. The demure-looking staff, in white medical jackets, were packaging plastic penises. It was the birthday of one girl clerk, who proudly showed me her gift from Beate: a small ivory penis as a brooch. Frau Uhse then pointed to the big photo of herself with Willy Brandt and the mayor of Flensburg at a local party – 'As the model employer of an expanding industry, I'm very popular here. At the golf club, I'm the colourful bird they love.' Back in Hamburg, however, I found women's leaders more sceptical. Eva Rühmkorf, head of the Senate's Office for Equal Rights for Women, said: 'Beate Uhse began usefully. Now she's merely serving the interests of men who want to use women as sex objects.' The majority of Germans, men as well as women, would probably agree with this. However, Germany is a free country; and no one is compelled to enter a sex-shop or porn cinema (the street advertising of such films anyway has to be discreet). It would seem to me that it is better to permit pornography than to suppress it into more devious channels.

Rather more important, the new liberal era has led also to the legalising of abortion. The reform was enacted in 1974, about the same time as in Britain and France; and, though opposed by the Catholic Church, it was supported by a large part of the Catholic laity, who knew the anguish that women had suffered. The richer ones used to go to private doctors in Holland, while the poor resorted to back-street abortionists (*Engelmacher* – angel-makers) who often did the job badly. But now abortion is free on the health service during the first three months of pregnancy, so long as the woman can convince a panel of doctors and social workers that she has a case. She must satisfy at least one of four conditions: that the child would be handicapped or deformed; that her own life would be in danger; that she was a rape victim; or, the case most commonly and controversially used, that she would be 'socially' unsuited to having a child, e.g. if she is out of work, or has no husband or parental support, or is in a depressive state.

This complex legislation still confronts women with all kinds of obstacles and is being applied varyingly from *Land* to *Land*. In most parts of north Germany, abortion is now fairly easy to obtain. But, in the rural Catholic areas of the south, not only do the medical panels tend to be stricter, but a great many doctors and hospitals refuse on conscience grounds to perform the operation. So a woman must look for another doctor in another town, and for the less educated or resourceful ones this is quite a stiff challenge. In one small Catholic town in Württemberg, I was told by a local doctor, herself Catholic but in favour of the reform: 'The Catholic villages round here are incredibly conservative, and the pressures of the social environment weigh heavily on any woman thinking of an abortion. Seldom does she have the courage to go through with it, for she'd be putting herself outside her social context and would feel guilty.'

The old-style Catholics in Germany have not given up the fight, and have been trying to get the reform repealed. In 1983 an extraordinary article by a priest appeared in a Catholic paper in Munster, *Kirche und Leben*: 'The Nazi extermination of the Jews was a horrible crime, but I'm not sure it was the cruellest ever. The Nazis at least had an ideology, but abortion is cold-hearted egoism. And the Nazis attacked adults who could defend themselves, not the innocent unborn.' The Church itself would hardly back such a view. But through its allies in the CDU and CSU it has been putting pressure on the Government. In 1984, 76 deputies tabled a bill for the removal of the 'socially unsuitable for motherhood' clause that accounts for the vast majority of abortions. The Government shelved the project. But there was, and is, quite a strong feeling within its ranks that abortion should again be made more difficult – in part, because of Germany's very low birth-rate.

After reaching a peak of 62.1 million in 1973, the population of West Germany has been falling and by 1986 was a bare 61 million. The drop would have been greater, were it not for the immigrant workers, who breed much more abundantly than Germans. The West Germans' own birthrate has been the lowest in the world since 1974: six people are born for every seven who die, and there are now 1.3 children per marriage, on average, whereas 2.2 would be needed to keep the population at its present level. The reasons for this strange and disturbing decline are multiple and complex and have been endlessly analysed. It is frequently supposed that one major cause is the so-called 'cultural pessimism' of many younger Germans – their lack of faith in the future, their fear of nuclear war, of unemployment or ecological disaster, or their general reluctance to bring children into a world that has lost its sure values. Such feeling may well play some part, at least among Greens and other young radicals. But the wider reasons for the decline are probably more practical: notably, the difficulties of combining a job with motherhood, in an age when so many women either actively desire to pursue a career or else do not want to reduce their living standards, or both. Paid maternity leave and family allowances are today fairly generous (see below): but these inducements to child-bearing are seldom decisive. Other factors weigh as much as the financial ones – for example, couples with children have more trouble in finding a flat. And as one woman journalist suggested to me, 'The whole structure of everyday life in Germany is weighted against the working mother.' Children come back from school at 1 p.m. expecting to be fed; the little ones too must be collected from kindergarten well before most office jobs end; the shops close at 6.30 p.m.; and most German husbands are still reluctant to help with the chores. So a mother needs some ingenuity, and endless hard effort, to keep both a home and a job going. What is more, many young professional couples prefer to remain childless rather than sacrifice their nice life-style of theatres, late-night parties and foreign holidays. These tend to be bourgeois people spoilt by affluence: at the other end of the scale are the Greens and radicals, more generous-hearted and unselfish, maybe, but pessimistic about the future. Both these two important contrasting categories are reluctant to rush into parenthood. And so, if the Germans today tend to be *either* more materially ambitious than most nations, *or* more gloomy and apprehensive, this could go some way to explain their low birthrate.

Of course it can be argued: in an over-populated world, and in a densely-populated country such as West Germany, does a slightly declining population really matter? This is a complicated issue, much debated alike for its economic, psychological and even military ramifications (see p. 449). Most of the experts do believe that a low birthrate is related to national decadence. Be that as it may, the Kohl Government after 1983 grew worried, partly for practical reasons, fearing that the armed forces would increasingly lack manpower and the rising proportions of retired people would put a strain on social security budgets. So in 1984–5 Bonn launched a new programme of incentives. This included the setting up of a 'Mother and Child Foundation', offering financial aid to young hard-up mothers-to-be who might otherwise have turned to abortion. Maternity benefits were also improved: by law, an employer must now keep a working mother's job open for up to a year, and her leave during this time is subsidised partly by the state. Monthly child allowances run at 50 DM for the first child, 100 DM for the second, 220 DM for each one thereafter. Calling for a target of '200,000 extra babies a year', Chancellor Kohl in 1984 appealed to German patriotism: 'We must change this back into a child-loving country.' But his tone hardly pleased those feminists who habitually resent any move to 'push women back into the home.' So this problem of the birth-rate is not an easy one. Probably it will not be solved by cash incentives but only by change of attitude. One sociologist, Uli Schmetzer, has suggested that German thoroughness might finally tip the scales: 'Just as German women went over to the pill more thoroughly than others, so, if they could but be convinced that baby-making is fun, they might again set themselves to it wholeheartedly.'

Matters might also improve if society as a whole could become more tolerant and understanding of children – or so is often argued, by Germans who will readily admit that there is some truth in the nation's long-standing reputation for *Kinderfeindlichkeit* (hostility to children). This goes back into history and includes a failure to comprehend a child's imaginative world: were the Grimms' fairy tales and the *Struwelpeter* stories not only violent and cruel but too symbolic to relate properly to children? And, today, child abuse is well above the European average. According to the German Children's Aid Society, some 30,000 children were maltreated in 1984 and over 100 committed suicide, most of them as a result of parental brutality or neglect. These may be extreme examples, and it would be wrong to get the problem out of proportion. In this family-minded country, the vast majority of parents are in fact loving and kind to their children. Probably they do treat them with rather more discipline and authority than is common today in the West; but this has been getting less so, and anyway might it not basically be more caring than the opposite American tendency of so many parents to let their children run amok?

As so often in Germany, this problem of *Kinderfeindlichkeit* lies much less with private than with public attitudes. Society does not like children in public places because they are noisy and restless, they make a mess, they tread on the flowers or put finger-marks on tidy new paint – in short, because they behave like children. If a small child cries in a restaurant, or even in a supermarket, people make an angry fuss. Whereas Latins drool over their neighbours' children, Germans are constantly lodging complaints about their noise – and so it is little surprise that many young families find it hard to rent flats and much resort to buying houses at a cost they can barely afford. Today there are plenty of toyshops and clothes boutiques for children, but few town councils bother to provide adequate playgrounds for them. Yet politicians often warn against the hostility, and the public itself seems to be aware of it: when in 1978 Allensbach asked, 'Do you agree that the Germans are not fond of children?', almost as many (42 per cent) said 'yes' as 'no' (46 per cent).

The most hopeful sign is that the younger generation is behaving differently. Many young parents are exemplary, especially Greens, often organising voluntary crèches to help working mothers. Most remarkable of all is the new attitude of German fathers, who used to leave the minding of small children to their wives but now take an eager and active part. Everywhere you see young men wheeling prams, or clutching babies in shops; they would certainly breast-feed too, if they could! Emotionally they are far closer to their children than before, and even officialdom is recognising this: in divorce cases, the number of fathers being granted custody of the children has doubled in ten years. Since January 1986, a new law has decreed that the 12 months' subsidised vacation after childbirth can be taken by the father rather than the mother, if it is the wife who wants to continue working – and employers are obliged to agree. This paternity leave is already quite popular, and many young couples are accepting that it is the wife who should remain the breadwinner. When I asked the young leader of the Greens in Munich what his job had been before he entered the city council, he said proudly, '*Haus-mann*'. Might not this trend in the long run provide some solution, alike to the problem of *Kinderfeindlichkeit* and to that of women's equality in the professions?

A spick and span suburbia where the shops shut early

The post-war rehousing of the Germans was one of the more striking aspects of the 'economic miracle'. In 1945, in the area that is now West Germany, more than 8 million people were homeless. But soon the authorities embarked on a subsidised crash programme to make good the losses, and with typical German energy this went racing ahead: in the 1950s, Germany was completing new dwellings at a rate of over 500,000 a year, more than in Britain and far more than in France. Today over 70 per cent of German homes were built since the war. Not all this new housing is beautiful, by any means: but it is better equipped and more sturdily constructed than the European average, and the Germans are now certainly the best-housed people in Europe after the Scandinavians. Quality has been improving steadily: the average floor space of homes built today (100 square metres) is twice what it was in 1952, and for some years now all new dwellings have been provided with bathrooms and central heating. Nearly all the old slum areas have been cleared away. Today the average worker and his family live in a comfortable, well-lit rented flat, or quite often in a house that they own.

It is claimed officially that the housing shortage ended in 1974, when for the first time available dwellings exceeded private households in number (23.2 million). But this neat statistic does not alter the fact that, even today, not everyone is well housed – as is clear from the many stories of immigrant workers or young Germans moving into derelict tenements. Good cheapish flats for younger families are still in inadequate supply, partly because of the steep rise in land prices in cities. In Germany, subsidised 'social' housing for lower-income groups is built mostly by semi-public agencies and cooperatives, and the rents are controlled by the *Länder*. But in recent years land prices have reached such a high level, and the required quality of housing has risen so high too, that most agencies have begun to find it too expensive to build in central city areas. So since 1965 the Federal Government has operated a system of rent-topping grants paid direct to poorer tenants on a means-test basis: some 1.8 million families benefit. But this has not in itself solved the shortage of suitable cheaper 'social' housing inside cities. Today the monthly rent including heating for a 3-room 80-square-metre city flat is around 800 DM, or about 20 per cent of an average worker's earnings.

Middle-class people generally prefer to own rather than rent, and for them the problem of land and building costs has become quite acute. Land prices per square metre may be only 200 to 300 DM in a residential part of Bremen or Hanover, but they rise to 800 to 1,200 DM or more in Stuttgart, Germany's most expensive city, where a five-room flat may cost up to 1 million DM and a family house in a good area 1.5 million or more. And, as building societies usually require a minimum 30 to 40 per cent down-payment for a mortgage, the vast majority of young couples must first spend some years in rented accommodation unless their parents can provide a substantial amount of capital. But rents too are very high, and in the private sector they are not controlled. My wife when I first met her was living in a pleasant one-room studio flat in central Stuttgart for 300 DM a month (unfurnished) and her widowed mother was paying 450 DM for a good two-room flat in a pleasant suburb of Munich, but both had secured bargains: over 1,000 DM a month for a 3-room unfurnished flat in Stuttgart is nearer the norm. These prices may seem low by the extortionate standards of *furnished* accommodation in London: but London families, if not eligible for council housing, will generally buy property, and house prices are a good deal lower than in Germany and mortgage terms more generous. When they can afford it, the Germans too will usually prefer to buy: some 40 per cent of them are owner-occupiers. Especially in Swabia the ideal is still *schaffe, schaffe, Häusle baue* (work work and build your little house: see page 35), and many a Swabian father starts putting money into a savings bank for his son at birth, so that by the time he is 30 the young man may have enough credit to meet the mortgage conditions. And preferably it must be a real '*Häusle*' in its own garden, not a semi-detached or a flat. Look down on any townlet around Stuttgart, and you see an undulating sea of little red roofs. But this is not the dreary ribbon-development of Britain, for each house is separately conceived; nor is it the anarchy of the pre-war Paris suburbs, for individualism is tightly checked and you must build to harmonise with your neighbours.

Most spruce little German houses of this kind were either built fairly recently or have been newly modernised, inside and out. Older dwellings of character are far less common than in Britain or France. Not only were many of them destroyed by bombing, but Germans in the post-war decades actually tended to *prefer* modern surroundings. After the war they wanted, as I have said, to make a clean start, rejecting anything that reminded them of the awful past – and this led to some travesties of taste. Much perfectly pleasant old-fashioned housing that had survived the bombing was torn down hurriedly and thoughtlessly, when it could have been kept and modernised. Villagers pulled down their nice old farmhouses and built stereotyped new ones, more comfortable, with central heating; often they covered over half-timbered façades with fancy new walls of aluminium or plastic, considered more chic and practical – Edgar Reitz's film *Heimat* (see p. 298) gives a sharp picture of a local contractor cleverly exploiting this craze. And much the same happened in the towns. All became new and suburban; the only visible link with tradition was provided by the little painted ceramic gnomes, fawns and other animals that were – and are – still used by workers and petit-bourgeois to adorn their gardens and allotments (kitsch dies hard). However, since the mid-1970s there has been a radical change in attitudes. The traumas of war have been digested; the new ecological era has brought a new concern for the past and for traditional values. So the old is back in favour. Half-timbered houses – such of them as survive – are now being carefully restored rather than pulled down or disguised; and people are again looking for old homes of character. But there are not many of these left. In the wake of the Allied bombers, the ravages of peacetime bad taste have taken another heavy toll.

The living-rooms of the professional classes are nearly always smart and well-decorated, with each expensive object neatly in its place and none of the casual untidiness or unkemptness that one often finds in equivalent homes in Britain. This is evidence alike of the higher German living standards and of the Germans' passion for order and neatness. And there is even more to it than this – as Anthony Sampson astutely observed in his book *The New Europeans*:[1] 'The special relationship of a German family to their house or flat is unmistakable. A visitor is shown around the house as soon as he comes in; the objects, furniture and gadgets are laid out as if in a contemporary shop-window. . . . The completed stage leaves little room for development or disruption, and it helps to give that frozen look to German homes. There are no old sofas, junk or messy corners: and in this formal stage, people move uneasily, and the objects seem to acquire a power of their own.' I share that impression – and I would say that it goes for all social classes. Though less than formerly, many working-class families still retain the custom of '*kalte Pracht*' (cold splendour), a front parlour used only on special occasions and normally kept unheated, its formal furniture covered in dustsheets. In middle-class homes, even a lived-in sitting-room often has an oddly unlived-in feel, its books all within glass-front cupboards lest they attract dust. Once I visited an extreme example of this, a Munich home where the television set was hidden inside a Bavarian chest,

[1] Hodder & Stoughton, London, 1968, p. 224.

and the books too were invisible behind cupboard doors; the furniture was heavy repro and the atmosphere funereal. But the average home, though as tidy as this, is rarely so gloomy. Twenty years ago the middle-class vogue was for modern Scandinavian furniture; today, in line with the new eco-nostalgic trend, German-style repro is preferred – or real antiques if they can be found or afforded.

Today, however, there has been yet another U-turn of home living styles – among some people. Young Greens and others will frequently flaunt their contempt for bourgeois values by deliberately making their living-rooms and kitchens as messy and cluttered as possible. I have visited the homes of teachers and writers where the chairs and sofas were covered with books and papers, cupboard doors were hanging open, dirty boots were strewn on old newspaper in the parlour, and the dirty plates and half-eaten food on the dining-table was making some ideological statement. Who says the Germans do not still fly to extremes?

When it comes to the possession of consumer durables, even Greens have their homes equipped with fridges and dish-washers, and maybe video-recorders too. In this prosperous Germany, 18 per cent of families now have more than one car, and even the three-car family is not unusual. West Germans tend to have more of the various modern appliances than other European nations, as the table below shows (source: EEC. Year: 1984):

Percentage of homes equipped with:	Germany	Britain	France	Italy
Passenger car	61	58	67	66
Refrigerator	96	92	95	93
Deep-freeze	56	28	25	25
Dishwasher	15	3	13	14
Washing machine	81	76	73	80
TV set, colour or b. & w.	108	96	93	100
(figures include homes with more than one set)				
Telephone	90	67	53	54

Patterns of spending have been changing in much the same ways as in other Western countries. Expenditure on food and drink has continued to rise in real money terms, but not nearly as fast as in other sectors such as travel, homes and leisure. As a percentage of the average family budget, food, drink and tobacco declined from 41 to 26 per cent between 1964 and 1983, while housing rose in the same period from 11 to 17 per cent, and transport and telephones from 9 to 16 per cent. Consumer attitudes have been changing, too. In the first years after the war, when money was still tight, consumers were very price-conscious, always looking for bargains. Then, from about the mid-1950s, they paid more attention to quality: they wanted goods to be expensively made, and in the shops the dearer lines would often sell out more quickly than the cheap ones. This remains so today, save that a new 'quality of life' trend has also appeared, as ecology-minded people look for healthier food and more 'environment-friendly' leisure equipment.

Large shopping-centres and hypermarkets have sprung up on the edge of towns, pushing out of business many small traditional shops such as dairies and groceries. However, in the past few years this trend towards bigger stores has been halted, as a result of opposition not so much from the small traders' lobby as from civic activists who have pointed to the human hardships that the trend can cause. A hypermarket may be ideal for those with a car; but closure of small local shops has been hard on sick or elderly people who may now have to make a long walk to find basic essentials like bread or milk. So in 1977 the Schmidt Government produced a law allowing communes to refuse licences for new hypermarkets of over 1,500 sq. metres selling space (these are unpopular with ecologists too). But this has not led to any great increase in the numbers of little general stores. Their places have been taken by new specialist shops and boutiques, selling fancy foods, unusual clothes and the like.

Under one of Germany's most controversial laws, virtually all shops of any kind must close at 6.30 p.m. sharp on weekdays, all day on Sunday, and on Saturday by 2 p.m. (it is 6 p.m. on the first Saturday of each month). This today is one of the tightest laws of its kind, in a Europe that on the whole has been relaxing the rules for shopping hours – and it surprises and annoys many visitors to Germany. It is also much debated and criticised by the Germans themselves; but efforts to get it reformed have not made much progress. This *Laden-schlussgesetz* (Shop Closure Law) was passed in 1956 under joint pressure from the unions and retailers. The unions, notably the *Gewerkschaft Handel, Banken und Versicherungen* that covers shop assistants, wanted to prevent staff from being exploited by long hours; the retail associations wanted to protect the little local shops (*Tante Emma Läden* – Auntie Emma shops – they are nicknamed) from too much competition from the rising new supermarkets. The legislators also had the motive of protecting small shopkeepers from themselves, in a nation then in the throes of manic workaholism. So this law was well-intentioned – but silly. It was much contested at the time, by Erhardt and others, and has remained unpopular, for it causes massive inconvenience to millions, including trade union members. A working mother has to hurry out of the office to fit in some rapid shopping; buying aspirins in the evening for a headache is not easy; impromptu weekend dinner-parties are unfeasible; and so on. No wonder that Germany leads the world in automat selling-machines and in the mail-order business.

Just a few exceptions are allowed. Bakeries can trade on Sundays from 11 a.m. to 3 p.m. Chemists stay open at weekends on a rota basis. Florists – oh, compassionate lawgivers! – can trade then too if they are within 300 metres of a cemetery or hospital. And shops in the foyers of airports or main railway stations can stay open till late and at weekends 'in the interests of bona fide travellers'. You are supposed to be able to produce a travel ticket, if asked, but checks of this kind are rare: the Feinkost grocery at Stuttgart station, mercifully only eight minutes' walk from our flat, several times saved us from near-starvation. However, in other ways the law does tend to be rigidly applied, German-style. A petrol station can sell a can of beer at night to a motorist as 'journey necessity', but not to a local resident. I heard a tale of a man who walked into one service station in Hamburg at 6.45 p.m. and asked for a crate of beer; the kindly attendant, taking a chance, handed him one – whereupon the visitor whipped out his police card and booked him for a fine! A great many little local shops do gently break the law by allowing regular customers to knock on the back door at night for some item of grocery: but they have to be careful, and will not sell to a stranger. The ambience of subterfuge recalls America under Prohibition!

Britain too has had its disputes over Sunday trading. But, though attempts to repeal the law failed in 1986, it is still more honoured in the breach than in the observance and many big food stores defiantly remain open. The trouble with the Germans is that, if they have a law, they tend to keep it. And this one has proved hard to reform, even though opinion polls have stressed its unpopularity. Recently a few bold efforts have been made, often with municipal support, to circumvent it and show up its idiocy. Notably, in Stuttgart, 27 small stores of all kinds in a new underground arcade beside the station stayed open till 10 p.m. on weekdays, under a concerted experiment that lasted ten years, from 1976 to 1986. In fact it was the police who first proposed the idea, in a bid to combat mugging and theft in the area: and this brought results. Mayor Rommel enthusiastically lent his weight to the scheme, which according to one poll found favour with 96 per cent of Stuttgarters. The shops in the arcade, too, were pleased, for it increased their turnover by 25 per cent; and it created 100 part-time jobs. But the German Retailers' Association fought it tooth and nail as a 'dangerous precedent'; and finally they won a protracted court battle, on the grounds that the shops were not merely selling necessities to rail travellers – as indeed they were not. So the scheme appeared doomed to failure, like others before it. In Bremen in 1985, the small shops in one street had staged their own revolt, staying open till 11 p.m.: they were fined twice, then threatened with prison sentences, so they stopped. However, in 1986, the Kohl Government finally agreed to a modest modification of the law, that would allow shops in the vicinity of airports and main railway stations to remain open in towns of over 200,000 people. This amendment was due to come before the Bundestag in July, and if passed it would legalise the Stuttgart venture.

But any wider change in the law would seem to remain out of the question, for there is still an unholy alliance of unions' and retailers' interests in favour of the status quo. The unions remain opposed on principle to any reform that would run counter to their present campaign for a shorter working week – even though their argument here is very weak, for shop assistants' hours could easily be staggered and no one expects them to work longer. 'The real truth,' said one observer, 'is that the unions see this law as one of their last remaining bastions. They dare not to give in.' And the retail lobby still wants to protect its smaller and weaker members from further competition and higher overheads. But this too could be regulated. In 1984 the Green party put forward a sensible compromise proposal, whereby the law should still apply to larger stores, but smaller family-run ones should be allowed to stay open later and at weekends if they wished, so long as the owners were themselves working. The SPD and unions rejected the idea – because it came from the Greens. And the Kohl Government, with many other problems on its plate, was wary of any reform that would antagonise the unions. So the Germans remain saddled with a law that few members of the public want. It is a typical German example of a well-meaning piece of legislation that in practice does more harm than good.

From **Wurst** *and dumplings to fancy French and food fads*

The Germans are often seen as being almost as barbaric as the British in matters gastronomic. Their cuisine, with its sauerkraut and dumplings, its fat pink *Wurst* and steaming knuckles of pork, is regarded as wholesome and tasty maybe, but coarse and monotonous. But is this image an accurate one? Of course it is true that German cooking lacks the exceptional variety and finesse of the French, or even the Italians; just as the French are less musical than the Germans, so the Germans do not imbibe gastronomy with their mothers' milk as the French still do. They do not possess the same heritage. As in Britain, the industrial revolution separated the new urban population from the old peasant tradition of inventive cooking (never very strong, anyway, compared with France), with the result that regions such as Hessen, Rhine/Ruhr and Lower Saxony are today almost as denuded of good local specialities as the British provinces.

And yet, over the country as a whole, there is much more variety and subtlety to be found than may at first be apparent. Germany produces some 200 different kinds of bread, and almost as many sorts of *Wurst*. In Baden, with its long French affinities, people have a real concern for good eating; and to some degree the same is true of Württemberg and the Moselle valley, of Franconia and some other parts of Bavaria – in fact, wherever wine is produced except, strangely, for the Rhineland. In pubs and restaurants, cooking tends to be excellent in its own way when it sticks to the simple traditional dishes; when it tries to experiment with more sophisticated ideas, or to copy French styles, then it is usually phoney and tasteless, as is so often the case in big hotels and smarter restaurants. But if a visitor learns how to avoid these pitfalls, he can find remarkable value-for-money in pleasant, inexpensive *Gaststätten* nearly everywhere, even in the north. And, even if the cooking is somewhat bland and predictable, at least the helpings are generous and the service and the presentation uniformly excellent, in line with the usual German efficiency and attention to detail. I have had dull meals in their country, but very few really bad ones, sloppily cooked or served, of the kind all too common in Britain.

It is true that one meets plenty of people with absolutely no feeling for food. Kindly hosts have sometimes taken me to nice-looking restaurants where their conversation has shone but they have passed no comment on what we have eaten: not out of stinginess, I am sure, they have maybe proposed taking a dull set menu of unseasoned cream-of-vegetable soup, a slice of beef with cabbage, a tasteless custard flan and one glass of white wine. But such barbarism is growing less common. Among much of the middle class, the past 30 years have seen quite an upsurge of interest in gastronomy, prompted by foreign holidays, by the presence of so many restaurants run by foreign immigrants, and by the new prosperity. Food is 'in'.

For centuries the Germans were famous for their hefty appetites – and their waistlines proved the point. The fat-faced, beer-bellied Bavarian, two-litre tankard in hand before a plate piled high with *Wurst* or dumplings, was a stock cartoon character and not far from reality. In pre-war days, poverty often dictated diets, and potatoes, bread and cakes were staple items of nutrition. In the 1950s, this pattern changed dramatically, as sheer greed steadily replaced subsistence eating: The *Wirtschaftswunder* period was equally that of the notorious '*Fresswelle*' ('wave of guzzling'), when a new-rich nation reacted against the deprivations of wartime by tucking in more avidly than ever before – and this time to a far richer diet. This continued until about the early 1970s, when alarming medical statistics appeared suggesting that 10 million Germans were overweight, including 25 per cent of children (spas began to offer cures for fat children). As *Time-Life*'s book *Germany* has commented wittily, 'The news that the Germans' new-won prosperity was indirectly harming them was just the sort of bloomy paradox that their social history had taught them to appreciate.'[1] So, reacting to the warnings with their usual thoroughness, they began to move over to healthier foods and physical fitness campaigns.

These changes in diet have some parallels in other countries too, but are especially remarkable in Germany. Before the war, the Germans consumed nearly three times as many potatoes as the British, per capita: now they eat 13 per cent less. Before the war, they ate less fruit than the British; now they eat well over twice as much. Between 1953 and 1980, annual per capita consumption of potatoes dropped from 163 to 86 kilos; of cereal products and rice, from 96 to 69 kilos. In the same period, consumption of vegetables rose from 46 to 73 kilos, and of fruit from 69 to 109 kilos. Meat-eating went up from 63 to 88 kilos per head between 1961 and 1982.[2] This is not to say that Bavarians do not still enjoy their flour dumplings, or Swabians their *Spätzle* noodles, or Germans anywhere their thick slices of brown bread with ham, *Wurst* or cheese. They are still the world's heaviest beer-drinkers, too, after the Belgians. And at least among the older generation there are still plenty of bulky, beefy figures around to bear this out. But young women, as I mentioned earlier, are far slimmer than their mothers and grandmothers were at the same age; they are eating fewer of those sticky *Torte* with cream. And many Greens and younger people have gone over to a diet that is low on starch, high on organically-grown rice and vegetables, and quite often vegetarian.

Unlike the French, the Germans do not stick rigidly to two big meals a day at set times. They prefer various little snacks at odd hours, often including a *zweites Frühstück* taken in the office at 10 or 11 a.m., a cake for tea, or a late-night nibble. But, rather like the French (see my *France in the 1980s*, p. 409), their food habits have been tending to polarise. Day-to-day eating has become more perfunctory, with greater use of convenience foods and less real home cooking; on the other hand, as in France, and more so than in Britain, there has been a striking increase of interest in really good food for the once-or-

[1] p. 128 (Amsterdam, 1984).

[2] Sources: EEC and West German Food Ministry.

twice-a-week occasion, whether it be restaurant dining-out or the dinner-party at home. For ordinary daily home eating, lunch is still the main meal of the day for most families; this is when the kids come back from school, and they need something hot. Today it may well be something easy from a tin or packet, though quite often it is still a home-cooked stew or *Schnitzel*, or a local meat dish with dumplings and sauerkraut. And father at work will have a hot meal in the canteen or pub. In the evening, the traditional meal all over Germany is *Abendbrot* – as its name suggests, a cold supper of bread with sliced meats, cheese and pickles, maybe some salad and fruit, and perhaps preceded by a warm soup. In working-class families, this is often taken at 5.30 or 6.0 p.m., when father is back from work; in the middle-classes, it is more usually at 7.0 p.m. or so. *Abendbrot* goes well with TV-watching and is still popular. But in some bourgeois circles it is being replaced by a hot cooked meal.

In the home, the new interest in gastronomy is reserved for the special occasion, which might be a family reunion or a little dinner-party for friends. Here cooking has become a modish hobby, and often it is the husband who is at the stove, trying out new recipes and using quality ingredients. Food magazines proliferate, and in the 1970s one 'Dr Oetker' cookbook was the biggest seller of any title except the Bible. Hosts will sometimes produce an 'exotic' dish discovered on a foreign holiday, such as *paella* or *moussaka* (the *Gastarbeiter* stalls in downtown covered markets are much patronised by Germans who come to buy fresh herbs and spices, peppers, black olives, feta cheese). Or they will offer a *fondue bourguignonne* or in summer a barbecue. Or they might attempt one of the old German peasant recipes now being adapted by the food writers for use with more expensive ingredients. But many couples still prefer to offer their guests an *Abendbrot*. This can sometimes be quite lavish and sophisticated; a Daimler-Benz executive's wife piled high the meat-platter with smoked salmon and rare Finnish reindeer meat; in the Ruhr, I was given a delicious supper of fruit soup, local Westphalian ham and dandelion salad with mustard dressing. But just as often this cold dinner-party fare can be rather basic – especially in Swabia, where despite their interesting local cuisine the people have an all-too-justified reputation for mean frugality. One Swabian lady who had spent some years in France told me she found this shaming: 'A company director and his wife asked my husband and me to dinner. They gave us cold meat and cheese, and sardines left in their tin. I retaliated by inviting them to a slap-up four-course French meal, which the husband devoured greedily while his wife commented sourly, "*Liebling*, you're never as hungry as that at home".'

For dining-out, the major trend over the past 25 years has been for 'exotic' foreign restaurants, ranging from the genuine simple ethnic to the pretentious pseudo-French. In the upper *Schickeria* bracket, *nouvelle cuisine* has inevitably caught on, with its usual attendance of minuscule helpings, astronomic prices, and segments of vegetable arranged artistically on the plate like Oriental flower-decorations. French chefs in France often cook brilliantly in the *nouvelle* manner: but German chefs manage far less well with this alien imported style, and the results can be embarrassing – in one smart place, I failed to appreciate duck with rhubarb, though the glossy diners around me seemed to be enjoying it. It is true that *Michelin* in 1986 awarded its top three-star rating to three restaurants in Germany, all more-or-less *nouvelle cuisine*, two in Munich, one in Cologne. But Paul Bocuse has been less impressed: 'The Germans are superb at making Mercedes. But they didn't invent cooking, even though some of them think they did.'

Social climbers may be eager to be seen dining at Aubergine or Tantris in Munich; but ordinary middle-class Germans will settle modestly for the much cheaper but tasty cuisine of Italy, Spain, Greece, Yugoslavia and Turkey. These happen to be the countries providing almost all the *Gastarbeiter* (see pp. 237–56), who in their thousands have set up restaurants on German soil, as have the Chinese too. Variety is seldom matched by quality, but at least the choice is there; and in many city centres the foreign restaurants easily outnumber indigenous ones, just as in Britain. In Hamburg the range extends to West African, Argentinian, Indian, Japanese, Portuguese, Swedish, Syrian, Thai and Tunisian. The latest vogue is for multiple eateries, where cuisines co-habit: a German may open a big pub, say, and lease out the catering, with a trattoria in one room, a Greek taverna in another, a Chinese take-away in a third. Many of the simpler immigrant-run places serve mainly their own nationals, but other visitors are welcome too – so you can eat *donerkebabs* among Turks in Berlin's Kreuzberg, or squeeze between parties of Spaniards to enjoy *zarzuela*, or join Bosnian factory-workers with their *djuveč* or *čevapčiči*. Other restaurants cater for a mainly German clientele of diners-out, but with variable results, for the food is often Germanised to suit a local taste which alas still prefers its own mushy salads to a true *horiatiki*. Nor do I personally find it appetising to read a Greek menu in German: who fancies *moussaka* when it is called *Exotisches Gericht mit geschnetzelten Schweinsfiletspitzen überbacken*?

Seduced by this foreign invasion, the Germans during the 1960s and '70s had been tending to spurn their own national restaurants, especially in the central and northern *Länder* which have little gastronomic tradition. But today there is a move back. The true German *Gaststätte* has become fashionable again, sometimes in a new and trendy style, with candlelight maybe, and pretty waitresses in *Tracht* – and in a northern city such as Hanover or Düsseldorf, an 'Altes

Nürnberg' or 'Sieben Schwaben' restaurant migrated from the south appears almost as exotic and 'ethnic' as one from Naples or the Piraeus! In a less contrived genre than this, too, all over Germany solid traditional eating-houses keep up reliable standards of German cooking – places like big *Ratskeller* to be found in the basement of many a town hall, or the wood-panelled *Stube* where locals gather to drink or play cards as well as to eat. Here it is possible to find inexpensive regional dishes which, if not very refined, are at least interesting – even in the north. Hamburg has its remarkable eel-plum-and-vegetable soup, its various ways with fresh herring, and also *Labaskaus*, a sailors' dish eaten at sea, which is a mush of pickled corned beef, herring, potato, beetroot and fried egg – a taste acquired only slowly, I felt. In Berlin, surprisingly, you still find old rustic dishes such as *Hoppelpoppel*, a kind of *omelette paysanne* with potato and ham. Frankfurt, though one of the least culinary-minded of German cities, is proud of its green-herb sauce with pork chops or beef. And in the south the variety is considerable. Bavarians still go for hearty dishes such as suckling pig, roast knuckle of pork and spicy Nuremberg sausages, while in Swabia the cuisine is more subtle. Just as Bologna is the world capital of *pasta*, so Stuttgart calls itself *Spätzlemetropol*, homeland of those crinkly flour noodles that accompany so many Swabian meat dishes and are delicious when properly *handgemacht*. Also ubiquitous in this region is *Maultaschen* ('mouth-pockets'), a kind of spinach-filled ravioli eaten usually in soup. I was told of one Stuttgart firm that exports both *Maultaschen* and *Spätzle* to France, of all places.

One particularly convenient feature of German taverns, pubs and restaurants is that almost all of them will serve you either a full meal, or just a snack or a drink, as you wish. Most pubs and wine-taverns provide a number of hot dishes; and only a very smart and fashionable restaurant will refuse a customer who wants just an hors d'oeuvre and a beer. This is common in central Europe, and it is related to the fact that the vast majority of the pleasanter German restaurants are accessible middle-price places, clean and efficient; the lower end of the market is not nearly as squalid as in class-divided Britain. Go to some local beauty spot, beside a lake or a river, or on a panoramic hilltop: in France, you will probably find a luxury restaurant, and in Britain either that or the other extreme, a cheap and squalid 'caff' for trippers, but in Germany it is much more likely to be something between the two – a comfortable democratic *Stube* with an outdoor terrace, where you can admire the view and eat a heavy meal or just a snack, in assorted company that might range from directors to dustmen, from genteel old dears in flower-hats to rough types with motorbikes. A professor and his *Putzfrau* use the same haunts. It is one of the most positive aspects of the new semi-classlessness of German society.

This democracy is equally evident in the beer-gardens, wine-taverns and *Kneipen* – but less so in the big Munich beer-cellars, which are mainly the preserve of workers and tourists, and have too high a decibel level for professors or flower-hatted oldies. Cologne has lively, quirky *Kneipen* where all classes rub shoulders (see p. 40), so does Berlin. In Munich, some of the beer-gardens are frequented by the *Schickeria*, but not exclusively so, and prices are the same as elsewhere; at others, such as the vast Chinesische Turm in the Englische Garten you see people of every kind, who come to flirt or debate, to listen to the brass bands, to enjoy elaborate picnics which they bring in hampers and spread out on the trestle tables.

In and around Stuttgart, the winter months are the season of the delightful *Besenwirtschaften* (broom-pubs): by old custom, vinegrowers in the area put a broom outside their houses in November, to signify that their new wine is ready, and until March or so they are permitted to use their premises as an impromptu pub, selling this vintage and no other drink. The practice has become somewhat commercialised, and many of the 150 or so *Besenwirtschaften* today seem little different from a normal tavern: but in some smaller ones you really do sit in rough farm buildings, in a matey ambience, drinking giant glasses of sweetish half-fermented wine at well below pub prices. At the Zaiss wine-farm in Untertürkheim, less than a mile from Daimler-Benz, we shared a table one Sunday afternoon with a boisterous quartet of artisans and their wives; at the table behind us, a well-dressed party from the Stuttgart *Schickeria* (such as it is) were celebrating a birthday.

German drinking habits have been changing since the war, owing to various factors that include rising affluence, concern for health, and stricter driving laws. Wine consumption has trebled, from an annual 7 litres per head in 1960 to some 21 litres today: but the French and Italian both drink four times as much, and Germany's wine production is only one-seventh of France's. Wine in Germany is not taxed, and in the shops it is cheap, with a bottle of simple table wine costing less than orange juice: you can buy some German *ordinaires* for 3 to 4 DM a litre in supermarkets. So why is wine consumption not greater? One explanation is that mark-ups in pubs and restaurants are very high. Also, the Germans tend to drink wine less heavily during a meal than the French, though they do go on sipping it afterwards. Their style of light and fruity white wines, Rieslings and Sylvaners, lends itself to this. So do the pale and sweetish reds of the Ahr and Neckar which I came to enjoy (the French think them barbarous).

Consumption of beer remains static at around 145 litres per head per year. Just ahead of the Belgians, the Germans are the world's leading beer drinkers in terms of per capita consumption – and they also drink it noisily and assertively. Dortmund is the world's second leading brewery town, and Munich the third: first, believe it or not, comes Milwaukee. Consumption of soft drinks has been increasing steadily, as might be expected, especially among young people (mineral water sales have more than trebled since 1972), while hard liquor drinking has declined slightly. Gin and Scotch whisky, drunk in moderation, are the smart drinks to offer guests in bourgeois homes. But by far the most popular alcoholic spirit in Germany is still Schnaps in its various forms, especially with the working-classes, and among farmers who brew it themselves on a large scale. It is the principal cause of alcoholism. If the drinking of this and other fire-waters is now pursued less recklessly, it is quite largely because the drink-and-drive rules have been tightened. Any motorist whose breathalyser test reveals more than 0.8 per cent of alcohol in the blood is likely to be found guilty and will lose his licence for a longish period. The laws are strictly applied and – with occasional exceptions[1] – the Germans take care to respect them. At social functions, I found that those planning to drive home were noticeably more abstemious than in Britain.

Assiduous tourists and crazy Cologne carnivalers

The Germans today are the world's greatest tourists – or so it would seem, if the statistics are any guide. Like the French, they have made the annual departure on holiday into a major obsession, to be looked forward to all the year and talked about incessantly. This restlessness is not new – after all, the German word *Wanderlust* has passed into the English language – but it has much increased with the new affluence. It may also mark a reaction against new urban tensions, and certainly it is a facet of the decline of the old German work-ethic and the rise of a new leisure ethic (see pp. 114–6).

All employees now have a legal right to at least three weeks' paid holiday a year, rising to five or even six weeks as they grow older. The proportion of all Germans taking an annual holiday away from home climbed from 24 per cent in 1954 to 56 per cent in 1985. This figure is slightly below those for the British (59 per cent) and the French (57 per cent), but it does not include the millions of spa-cure visitors, many of whom are really taking a disguised holiday (see p. 201). Of those who stay at home, many are elderly people, especially widows, while others include the chronically sick and handicapped, the really poor, the unemployed, and a great many farmers. Also some quite well-to-

---

[1] E.g. the Wiesheu affair in Bavaria in 1984–5, see pp. 417–8.

do people today prefer to save up for a more expensive foreign trip every two or three years: 'This year,' the saying goes, 'we're taking our holiday *nicht auf dem Balkan sondern auf unserem Balkon*' (not in the Balkans but on our own balcony).

Among those Germans who do leave home on holiday, the most striking feature is that they travel to foreign countries in greater numbers than any other nation. The proportion of holidays spent abroad has risen from 15 per cent in 1954 to 66 per cent today, and this is the world record, eclipsing Britain's 39 per cent and Holland's 50 per cent. Since 1976, Germany has overtaken the United States (with four times the population) in its annual total of citizens travelling abroad as tourists. The Germans go above all to neighbouring Austria and to the Mediterranean, where Italy and Spain are the favoured venues, followed by France, Yugoslavia and Greece. Germans account for 70 per cent of all foreign tourists in Austria, and 43 per cent in Italy.

The reasons for this annual migration are not hard to identify, the main one being climatic and geographical. Germany is a smallish and rather densely populated industrial country, with a short coastline and other nations on every side: and this induces a slight feeling, if not of claustrophobia, at least of being hemmed in. There are some pleasant tourist areas in Germany, but little spectacular scenery; the climate is central European and the beaches all northerly. So no wonder the Germans look to the sunny south. There may also be an element of desiring an annual escape from a land of unhappy memories that is still rather disciplined and conformist. And another factor is that holidays have now become a kind of status-symbol, like dressing elegantly or owing a smart car, at least in the bourgeoisie and the new-rich working-classes. Neighbours and new acquaintances will categorise you by the kind of holiday you take. To stay in Germany is to be thought very provincial (unless maybe you go to the island of Sylt, see below). To go each year to the same little house in Tuscany or Sweden is to be judged sympathetic, individual, but maybe boring. If you go to the Bahamas, or on a Kenya safari, you are interesting, but pretentious.

Two distinct trends in foreign holidays have been developing: the gregarious, typified by the Mediterranean package tour, and the individual and adventurous. Most Germans may be sheepish in their holiday habits. But by contrast a growing minority are much more spontaneous, non-conformist and enterprising, ready to seek out remote or far-flung corners on their own. They include not just the rich who jet off to Nepal or Yucatan, but all kinds of student types or young ecologists who will camp and hitch-hike or drive old jeeps up mountain tracks. These are the new German globe-trotters, more numerous than in any other European nation, and you find them everywhere – exploring the upper reaches of the Nile, following the reindeer tracks of Lapps near the Arctic Circle, or camping beside a lonely Greek mountain temple to watch the dawn break. They are serious, civilised and curious, anxious to come to terms with foreign cultures.

In between this and the other extreme, there are still a fair number of older, more conventional culture-tourists, the kind who dutifully go around Burgos cathedral, Baedeker in hand. But the great majority of Germans go abroad to relax, to sunbathe, and to have fun, and they show little curiosity about the country they are visiting. This is partly a matter of social class (see p. 148). These gregarious people, many of them working-class, prefer to stay in big groups – and preferably German groups, not so much out of national feeling as because they want to feel secure and understood, and to carry a familiar environment with them to a strange land. So the package-tour, in a hotel geared to German needs, suits them ideally. Or even if they travel on their own, in a car with a caravan, they will still make for the camping-sites where they can find plenty of other 'D' plates. In the big resorts along the Mediterranean, led by Rimini, Benidorm and Palma, a whole mass industry has grown up to cater for the German package-tourist: here you find whole streets full of cheap restaurants with menus in German, offering *Bratwurst, Eisbein* and other such comforting dishes; and bars and *Stuben* run by Willi und Heidi, providing *Echte deutsche Stimmung* for the cohorts of other Willis and Heidis from Würzburg or Wuppertal.

These are the holidaymakers who in the 1950s and '60s began to give Germans abroad so bad a reputation. They came to be seen as *more* rude, nude, lewd and crude than any others, and noisier too, with their boisterous singing in the streets at night and their brash disregard for local habits and susceptibilities. The very same Germans who at home were so mild and orderly seemed, once on foreign soil, to become creatures possessed. Maybe it was a normal holiday reaction against so much discipline; or, as one social analyst in Munich suggested to me: 'The German abroad believes that with his package-tour fee he has also bought himself the right to behave as he likes; and if the Latins or Greeks are untidy, loud and disorganised, why shouldn't he be so too? Being released from the laws and regulations and neighbours' intolerances that keep him so orderly at home, he feels himself to be on holiday from social responsibility. So he runs wild.' But German politicians and opinion-makers became worried at this national image: one writer, Gerhard Nebel, described southern beaches as 'an inferno of brown-baked, probably drunken, entangled flesh, fat buttocks and floppy breasts'. And for a few years the Federal Government even issued 'Golden Rules' for good behaviour with all new passports. Those leaflets included the advice: 'Don't deny the fact that your parentage is German, but see to it that the foreigner is pleased and surprised by it. If you are of the foolish opinion that everything outside Germany is worse, stay at home.' Whether or not these pompous admonitions had any effect, the situation does seem to have improved since the 1970s. Ordinary Germans have become more used to the unsettling novelty of foreign venues and have grown more at ease there. Whether or not foreign holidays of this kind really reduce chauvinism and promote mutual understanding remains a moot point. But if Greeks, Spaniards and other southern *Gastarbeiter* are today finding social acceptance more easily in Germany than 20 years ago (see p. 240), it may be partly because so many Germans have now visited their homelands and seen that they are not simply barbarians.

Middle-class Germans of the more conventional kind, if they go farther afield in a group, or on one of the club-holidays now so popular, will always expect good German comforts. Hence the success of the Frankfurt-based Club Robinson, which operates 20 quite luxurious club-hotels around the Mediterranean and as far afield as Brazil and Sri Lanka, catering for an 85 per cent German and Austrian clientèle. Johann-Friedrich Engel, the lawyer who runs this somewhat uninspired organisation, told me that it is *not* a copy of the Club Méditerranée, even if it has taken over a few of Le Club's best-known features such as bead-necklaces for money and shared dining-tables of eight. Club Robinson lacks the inventive flair and zany nonchalance of the wonderful and unique French club (see my *France in the 1980s*, pp. 426–37): it is more sedate, for that is what the guests expect, and more conformist and cliquey. At Club Med, everyone mixes freely at the tables of eight and a solitary newcomer is made welcome; at Robinson, a group appropriates a table and spurns strangers. The Germans do frequent the Club Méditerranée itself, in some numbers, where according to my own experience they keep a discreetly low profile, probably overawed by those exuberant Gallic types. The main complaint against them is that, sedulously *sportif*, they get up earlier than the French and others and monopolise all the best windsurfers, tennis-courts and other equipment.

Unlike the French, the Germans since the war have not innovated and pioneered with new holiday formulae. One invention of a sort however is the so-called 'coffin-bus', devised by a Bavarian firm, Rotel Tours. These giant touring caravans are trailers affixed to trucks, and they sleep 50 people, slotted in like sardines with just a few free inches above their heads. They have communal cooking and washing facilities aboard, and they tour as far as India or Morocco, taking German tinned food with them. Bar hitch-hiking, it is much the cheapest way of visiting these distant lands; and the tours are popular even with octogenarians, who find the cramped conditions quite cosy and chummy in their way. There has been a fair boom in other types of organised adventure travel too, for those who want unusual forms of travel to exotic destinations without having to fend for themselves. Firms offer jeep treks to the Sahara; safaris in Kenya; sleighing in Lapland; romantic trots round Ireland in gipsy caravans; or, a speciality for the jaded businessman, in-depth visits to the sex-haunts of Bangkok that may yield the added bonus of finding a Thai wife to bring back home. One sociologist assured me: 'The monotony and lack of challenge in German daily life make all these outlets popular.' Especially the last.

A holiday inside Germany earns less prestige, save at one or two of the Bavarian alpine resorts in winter, or on Sylt in summer. This flat island off the north-west coast, near Denmark, has become a showy rendez-vous for the *Schickeria* of fashion and the media, politics and business, from all over Germany. Playboy sons of tycoons come in Porsches with blonde starlets. Alas, I never managed to get to Sylt myself; but Anthony Sampson did, in the late '60s, and I doubt it has changed much since his visit, save to become flashier: 'A railway embankment carries trainloads of bright white Mercedes on to the island, where they distribute themselves according to income. In the richest village, Kampen, there are rows of almost identical new cottages, each with neat red brick, steep thatched roof, half-round windows, and a romantic name. In the front gardens are nautical objects – anchors, ship's lights or old bollards – and inside are ship-pictures, facetious notices, miniature bars. Social life, as in a ski-resort, is governed by a daily timetable of bars, tea-places and night-clubs. Couples in two-tone sweaters, with little white wellington boots and perfectly pressed trousers, sit up on bar stools sipping whiskies or walk systematically along the dunes. There is a mild air of naughti-ness; husbands flirt elaborately with each other's wives, and on hot summer days the island is famous for nudist beaches . . . The dream is self-conscious and regulated; and everyone can see what everyone else is up to.'[1]

More ordinary folk go to the other north coast beaches and islands; or they hike in the Black Forest or the Alpine foothills; or they bathe and boat at the Bodensee or other lakes. The resorts of hilly south Germany are crammed with elderly keep-fit walkers, firm or frail, and here tourism blends with the spa-cure trade. Though most Ger-mans may just want to relax and enjoy life, a sizeable minority also seek a holiday that does you good; hence the development of active and creative holidays. You can go on summer courses in villages to learn handicrafts or painting, harp-playing or calligraphy. Or you can

[1] *The New Europeans*, pp. 234–5.

stay on a farm: many farmers have converted their outhouses or disused cottages into holiday villas for tourists, who if they wish can lend a hand at the milking or haymaking, or can learn how to make cheese or keep bees. The vogue for these farm holidays is growing, but it is less pronounced than in France where rural traditions are much stronger.

Or of course you can go on a sporting holiday – as many do. Outdoor exercise has become something of a cult, and energetic sports with a keep-fit rationale have increased in popularity: a near-static game like *boules* or cricket would be less likely to interest the Germans. Today one citizen in three belongs to a sports club: the football federation has 4.5 million members, followed by gymnastics (3.1 million) and tennis (1.5 million). Once the preserve of the upper classes, tennis-playing has now spread widely, and it was given an added boost in 1985 when Boris Becker, the 17-year-old wonder from Leimen, near Heidelberg, became the first German ever to win the men's singles at Wimbledon. But, if the Germans love their sporting heroes, even more they love their peace and quiet, and one tennis hazard is that the ping and pong of balls in residential areas can provoke that most frightening of German phenomena, the wrath of intolerant neighbours. Some tennis-clubs have even been sued for breaking the peace: in Berlin, one resident sued a club of which he was himself a member! So it may be safer to play an indoor game like squash, today popular even with the Ruhr miners. Some 65 per cent of Germans go swimming, while 14 per cent make for the ski-slopes, mainly in the Alps. Horse-riding has come into vogue too – so much so that horses are again being bred in some numbers. In the 1950s, during the period of rapid farm mechanisation, the equine population was starting to decline: but now it is back to above its pre-1939 level.

In the 1960s and '70s, federal, *Land* and local governments poured large sums into providing new leisure amenities, so that today nearly every little town has its public swimming-pool and sports centre. There is still rather little organised sport in state schools: but children and young people find plenty of scope for it in their leisure time. They are not pressured into sports training as they are in the GDR, and this is one reason why West Germany's achievement in international competitions has not been as spectacular as that of the East (see p. 334). Nonetheless the Federal Republic has done well. When the Olympic Games were held on its own home ground, in Munich in 1972, it came fourth in the medal table, with 13 golds, and then again fourth at Montreal in 1976, with ten golds. It did not compete at Moscow in 1980; then at Los Angeles in 1984, when the Russians and East Germans were not competing, it came third, with 17 golds. West Germany has also shone at football, and its team's record over the past 20 years has been the best of any West European country: it won the World Cup (also in Munich) in 1974, and it reached the final at Wembley in 1966 (defeated by England), in Madrid in 1982 (defeated by Italy) and again in Mexico in 1986 (defeated by Argentina). Football is by far the most popular competitive sport in Germany, alike for spectators and participants, and the star players such as Franz Beckenbauer have become major national idols. Idolatry has also engulfed champion boxers and athletes: and it reached a high tide of frenzy when the media turned the floodlights on young Becker after his Wimbledon victory, causing the moralistic *Die Zeit* to ask worriedly whether the Germans were not in danger of rediscovering a Führer-style cult of personality. This of course is nonsense. In any country, sport provides a focus for national feeling, sometimes hysterical and excessive but at least better than making war; and in Germany today it offers a fairly harmless channel for the tentative rediscovery of a national spirit and a sense of identity. At least German football fans abroad do not go lethally berserk.

As with sport, so Germany's innumerable festivals and pageants, religious and secular, and its rich life of traditional clubs and associations, are also playing some role in helping to heal the psychological wounds of the Nazi period – not so much by promoting national feeling as through a strengthening of local patriotism and a reaffirming of old innocent traditions not soured by politics. Especially this is noticeable in the pre-Lenten carnivals. But first a word about the *Vereine* (clubs and associations), which play so important a role in local social life and in many cases have deep historical roots. Germany has 14,500 choral societies, with over 1.5 million members, as well as clubs for every kind of hobby such as rabbit-breeding or pigeon-racing. Everywhere in small towns and rural areas you find *Schützenvereine* (rifle clubs), often centuries old, each with its own banners, badges, uniforms, and ceremonial meetings that preserve something of the atmosphere of a medieval guild. As the *Time-Life* book on Germany puts it, 'There is no doubt that members spend more time lifting their beer-glasses than their rifles' – but they do manage to hold an annual shooting tournament too. In Bavaria, each town and village has its *Trachtenverein*, devoted to the wearing of local traditional costumes: its annual festival is often held in a big beer-tent where the Catholic Church plays a key part: there is beer drinking, then a religious service in the same tent, then more beer, and folk-dancing.

The German fondness for keeping up the old family customs and rituals shows itself at the time of the major Christian festivals. The warmly emotional family Christmas has long been a German forte,[1] and today the Germans still make much more fuss of Christmas than

---

[1] A 1978 Allensbach survey that put the question, 'What in life is most sacred to you?' found that 'Christmas in the family' came top of all the answers, ahead even of such things as 'Being able to live in a free society'.

the British or French – even if a commercial spirit is sometimes more apparent than a truly religious one. Various little ceremonies mark the Christmas period, starting with the Advent Wreath of decorated fir branches that bears four red or gold candles, one of them lit for each Sunday of Advent. Most families still place this wreath in their homes every Advent, and a great many offices, shops and hotels display one too. Then at Christmas itself, whether or not a family has children, it is much more likely than in Britain to deck out its home with holly, tinsel, stars and candles, a Christmas tree and maybe a crib: the big outdoor *Christkindlmarkt* (Christmas-present market), held in the squares of many towns, give an idea of the vast range of kitschy trinkets on sale for the occasion. Then during the year there are other rituals too, some purely secular. If you build a house, when the roof is put on you must be sure to hold a *Richtfest* (roof-topping ceremony), which means a party for friends, neighbours and above all the building workers, and the affixing of a little tree to the summit.

The main public festivals tend to centre round wine-making and the brewing of beer. More than enough has already been written by others about the world's greatest beer festival, Munich's *Oktoberfest*, which dates from 1810 and is held every year in tents on the Theresien meadow at the foot of a 60-foot statue of the goddess Bavaria. During its 16 days, locals and tourists consume some 40 spit-roast oxen and 500,000 barbecued chickens, and they down 4.5 million litres of beer, brought to them by the famous beer-hall waitresses trained to carry up to eight litre tankards at a time. Even Münchner who feign to scorn the *Oktoberfest* nonetheless go along as a matter of ritual. And many adore it. I knew one modest landlady who would save up for it each year, then go on her own every single day, make chums at the trestle-tables, and come home roaring drunk each night.

Some other towns have their own more muted versions of this kind of festival. Staid Stuttgart puts on its Volksfest, also local in origin, founded in 1840 by the King of Württemberg as a kind of harvest festival. Here the prudent Swabians keep their end up against Munich by consuming a respectable 1.5 million litres of local beer and 300,000 chickens; they sing the usual German songs swaying to-and-fro with arms linked, they visit the scores of garish side-shows, and spend more money on fun than they would dare to do in the rest of the year. But they have had to sink their pride and borrow from the Bavarians the accoutrements of jollity and folksiness, for lack of suitable ones of their own. The men, from Mayor Rommel downwards, wear pointed green Bavarian hats with feathers and grey Bavarian tunics; the waitresses are in Bavarian dirndls and high-busted white puffy bodices; the musicians of the beer-tent orchestras, clad of course in lederhosen, are mostly imported from Bavaria for the occasion.

*   *   *

German organised merriment finds its keenest expression in the big pre-Lenten carnivals, known as *Karneval* in the Rhineland, *Fastnacht* or *Fasnet* in south-west Germany, and *Fasching* in Bavaria. These carnivals are believed to have originated as pre-Christian pagan fertility rites, heralding the return of spring. Later they became more or less Christianised, in the sense that the Church sanctioned them as safety-valves of naughtiness before the serious business of Lent. Today they are pagan again – that is, rather commercialised, though the spirit of fun is very real. They are confined mainly to the Catholic parts of Germany. In the Rhine area, the main carnivals are at Mainz, Aachen, Bonn, Düsseldorf – and of course Cologne, the biggest and zaniest.

'He's got the loveliest legs in Cologne, hasn't he?' said the Socialist Lord Mayor, presenting to the crowds *'Seine Tollität'* (His Craziness) the Carnival Prince of 1985, Karl-Josef Kappes, a grinning, rather camp figure in red-white-and-gold doublet-and-hose, in real life a choirmaster. Beside him on the podium stood the two other 'Stars' who rule the city during *Karneval* – the Peasant (Reiner Toller, owner of a refuse-collecting firm) in a tall white hat with peacock plumes; and the Virgin (Fritz Voss, car varnisher), a 66-year-old in blond plaits. The Carnival Virgin has always been a man – save for a while under the Nazis, who hated transvestism.

The 'Three Stars' are elected each October from among the members of Cologne's 105 historic carnival associations. Mostly they are small businessmen – and competition to be a Star is intense, for the honour and publicity are considered good for trade, even though a Star must devote ten full weeks to his duties and dig deep into his own pocket; he pays for his costume, for the tons of toffees he hurls at the crowd during the Rose-Monday parade, and for gifts for the mayor: the Stars of 1985 gave him three grizzly bears from East Germany for the city zoo, as the Karneval theme of the year was 'Going to the Zoo'.

The city council itself also spends some million DM on *Karneval* – to the growing fury of some intellectuals who call it a waste of public funds in a time of high unemployment (14 per cent locally) and say the money should go to job creation schemes. But their outcry makes little impact, for Kölner in their mass, young and old, still adore their carnival and treat its zany jollity with true Germanic seriousness and thoroughness. 'Whoever is not foolish at *Karneval* is foolish for the rest of the year,' is a local saying. The carnival's two elements fuse together: there is the official organised *Karneval* of parades and ceremonies, very much a local Establishment affair; and also the big popular booze-up-love-in-and-laugh-in, a true mass-participation event, closer in spirit to Notting Hill than to over-commercialised Nice. It is a pre-Lent explosion of street-parties and pub-parties, of affable crowds in mad costumes and painted clown-faces. Even the dogs wear carnival cloaks and hats.

The Kölner's intense self-loving city-patriotism (see p. 40), the equal of any in Italy, finds its supreme expression in *Karneval*. And so does their peculiar spirit of jokey whimsy. This goes on all the year: but as Lent approaches it reaches fever-pitch, as the local radio blares out non-stop the *Karneval* songs in Cologne dialect that every citizen knows – for example, '*Mer losse d'r Dom en Kölle*' (i.e., 'let's leave the Cathedral in Cologne and not exchange it for the Eiffel Tower or the Pentagon'). So much of the fun-making is in local dialect, with local in-references, that a visitor to 'Kölle' is bound to miss much of the point – and be spared a thousand bad puns.

The fun starts on the Elfte Elfte Elfte Elfte, i.e. 11.11 a.m. on November 11. It continues in lower key for three months, to reach its climax in the *Tolle Tage* ('Crazy Days') before Lent. Thursday is *Weiberfastnacht* or women's day, when the fair sex, long excluded from *Karneval* in the 19th-century, take control and exact revenge by cutting off the tie of any male within reach (very Freudian?). Then on Sunday there is a big informal procession by school and suburban groups (in 1985 it included various topical anti-Kohl, anti-Flick and ecological floats); and on Monday comes the main procession with a million lining the route. There is much pelting with cheap horrid toffees, bought in bulk in East Germany (and singing of toffee songs); pirouetting by the acrobatic Mariechen (sort of majorettes); and comic uniforms. The Prince's royal bodyguard, in early 19th-century soldiers' uniforms, symbolise Cologne's anti-militarist tradition by sticking flowers in their rifle-barrels and carefully disobeying orders, e.g. turning left when ordered right. These anti-Prussian antics date from 1823 when the modern *Karneval* was created: Germany's more recent history gives them an added ironic twist today.

The entire carnival seemed to me revealing of present-day Germans' ambivalent attitudes to wearing uniforms. At the big parades and costume-balls there were citizens in every kind of attire – Attila-the-Hun groups in hairy hides and horned helmets; charming pierrots and harlequins; people dressed as animals, or as fruit; clowns clad in coloured woolly balls; a few Turks and sheikhs, even a British policeman – but not a single 20th-century German uniform. The Germans still adore dressing up en masse, but they remain wary – thank God! – of putting on anything modern and military.

The best carnival parties are private. But the big costume-balls are open to the public and not too costly. We went to one in the Gürzenich, a vast Renaissance civic building holding some 5,000 people, with five live orchestras in different halls. It was all very good-humoured and traditional, relatively tasteful and undrunken, with less rowdy vulgarity than you often find at such an event in Britain. It seemed to me a harmless outlet for the German passion for songful togetherness, and a safety-valve antidote to hard work and *Ordnung* during the rest of the year. All those neat, serious bank-clerks go wild in motley for a few days, then on Ash Wednesday are back at their desks, bleary-eyed but neat and serious again. 'Love me for Three Crazy Days' is one old carnival song – and is it not true that adultery during *Karneval* has never been grounds for divorce?

It is much the same in other Catholic areas with other carnival traditions. In Munich, *Fasching* is presided over not by three middle-aged tradesmen but by a good-looking younger couple, *'Prinz'* and *'Prinzessin'*, chosen usually from the wealthy bourgeoisie. Munich's carnival is more stylish and sophisticated, less rowdy and facetious than Cologne's, and less overwhelmingly unavoidable: you can even stay quietly at home, or walk out in ordinary clothes, without being thought quite stupidly sane. At Elzach in the Black Forest, masked fools dressed in red with large decorated hats run through the town beating people with blown-up hog's bladders. At nearby Rottweil, rival groups of fools jump through the town's Black Gate at 8 a.m. At Wolfach, fools stroll around in nightgowns and night-caps; at Überlingen on the Bodensee they crack long whips.

The entire razzle-dazzle of *Karneval/Fastnacht/Fasching* is a ritual today sedulously and lovingly kept up, more than ever, by this anxious nation seeking its identity and concerned to restore its broken links with past tradition. These traditions are variegated and local, rather than national, and they have little to do with 'Germany' as such, so this makes carnival rather different from, say, the Quatorze Juillet or even Guy Fawkes' night. One advantage of it, surely, is that in its very mindlessness and silliness it has not been tainted by politics, nationalism or ideology. So it has survived intact the national nightmare. After all, the Nazis never approved of it: first they banned it for a while, then censored it.

The spa romance – by courtesy of a lavish health insurance system

Germany's social security system is one of the oldest of its kind in the world and has long been one of the most progressive too. It was founded by Bismarck, in 1881, to meet the needs of workers at a time of rapid industrialisation; and since then it has been developed steadily, especially in the years after 1945. Today it looks impressive. It is lavishly funded by obligatory contributions – too lavishly, some right-wing critics argue, though this does enable hospitals and surgeries to be very well equipped and staffed. The medical services thus work far better than under the penny-pinching British system. The prosperous Germans get excellent free health care – but indirectly it costs them a lot.

Health insurance is compulsory for all employed and self-employed people and their dependents. Under this system, you must belong to one of a range of statutory but semi-autonomous insurance agencies (*Krankenkassen*), or in some cases you can opt for a private one. By law each employee gives his agency 5.9 per cent of his income, and his employer adds a similar amount. The system is socially fairer than in Britain, for contributions are related to earnings; the poor pay less, but they get the same service. A patient is treated entirely free of charge (save that he pays 2 DM per prescription), and the doctor or hospital then invoices the agency, under a fixed scale of charges. So in Germany there is national insurance but not really a national health service, for the doctors – and many hospitals – function free of any central control. Their position is more like that of a private garage which is paid direct by an insurance firm for car repairs after an accident. It does involve a great deal of form-filling.

Some 53 per cent of hospitals are run by the cities and *Länder*, while 12 per cent are private and 35 per cent belong to the Churches (see p. 229) and other non-profit making bodies. They charge the agencies per diem for each insured patient's stay, under an agreed scale that varies according to their level of equipment and averages 300 to 400 DM per day. So the hospitals have an incentive to advise convalescents to stay on as long as possible – so unlike the situation in Britain, where the overcrowded and under-funded hospitals will often bundle a patient back home before he is really well. Until the early 1970s, some German hospitals too were over-filled and often there were waiting-lists for operations. But this has since been remedied by a handsome increase in federal grants. Today the satisfactory record of German hospitals has been borne out by an Allensbach poll that found 47 per cent of its respondents regarding them as 'good', while only 7 per cent felt them to be 'poor'.

General practitioners, dentists, and other doctors not on hospital staffs work as an entirely free profession, like lawyers or architects. A patient can choose his GP freely, so the doctors are in open competition for custom and the bad ones simply go out of business. Doctors charge the agencies for each consultation, including the use of their surgery equipment and supply of medicines, and occasionally this has led to abuses: a team of young GPs in the Ruhr were recently prosecuted for sending fake invoices to the agencies, and this led two of them to commit suicide. But mostly the system is honestly applied; and so generous is the permitted scale of fees that a good doctor can always earn a lot of money, especially a surgeon or other specialist. These '*Götter in Weiss*' (gods in white) are among the wealthiest members of the post-war German plutocracy.

Medicine has therefore become a very popular profession. It has begun to attract young careerists greedy for money, the kind who might otherwise go into business or banking, rather than old-style hippocratic idealists with a true sense of vocation – and this trend dismays many older doctors. Students flocked into the medical faculties during the boom years; and Germany has now one of the world's highest doctor/population ratios, 2.4 per 1,000 people, compared with 1.7 in Britain and 1.8 in the United States (but 3.6 in Italy). It is true that German doctors are still too few in some remoter rural areas, where Turkish, Indian or other Asian GPs often make up the numbers; but, in the cities, doctors crowd thickly and Munich is said to have the world's highest density of paediatricians. This increase in competition has alarmed the profession, and in the late 1960s was one of the main factors that led it to induce the Government to set up a *numerus clausus* for entry to medical faculties.[1] This has since helped to slow the flood of recruits; but it did nothing to assuage the growing public feeling that doctors were *too* well paid. Then in the early 1980s a campaign by the media cast a spotlight on the huge incomes being amassed by surgeons and other specialists, who for relatively little work were able to charge the insurance agencies extravagant sums for the use of their modern equipment. Under this pressure, the medical profession finally agreed to accept some cutbacks in their scale of consultancy fees. Even so, they still do very nicely.

As in some other European countries, the social security system as a whole has recently come under growing criticism, for being too expensive and comprehensive. The Germans, more than most, have since the war built up their Welfare State into a vast protective blanket that anti-Socialists now feel has become too costly a luxury as well as a threat to the spirit of individual self-reliance. Until recently, overall spending on social security was rising much faster than national revenue: whereas in 1960 it had amounted to only 16 per cent of GNP, by 1982 the figure had risen to 32 per cent. About one-third of this sum now goes on health and the rest on other benefits, mainly old-age pensions, which are unusually generous. The health legislation guarantees an employee six weeks' sick leave a year on full pay; after this, he or she can claim sickness benefits from health insurance for up to 78 weeks. The Germans readily make use of these and other advantages. According to one estimate, the number of pills prescribed by doctors has risen ninefold since 1968.

In line with its overall drive to limit public spending, the Government has made a few modest cuts in welfare budgets since 1982.

[1] Pressure on laboratory space was the other factor: see page 216.

Unemployment benefits have been reduced and the rate of pension increases slowed – but only very gently. Though the Kohl Government has been ideologically in favour of budgetary economies, the CDU and CSU both have a strong tradition of social action, espoused by influential party pressure-groups, and this has deterred Kohl and his monetarist hawks from taking any drastic steps to dismantle the Welfare state. Nonetheless, a body of opinion on the right of those parties has been arguing, with some indignation, first that the high social charges are an obstacle to German industry's international competitiveness, and secondly that too much cosseting by welfare services (notably under Social Democrats in the 1970s) has been tending to make the Germans grow soft, over-dependent, and less ready to take risks or work hard. This lobby points to the ease with which anyone with the slightest physical handicap or sickness record can get himself registered as 'disabled' and thus receive special benefits. It is a familiar debate: is it good for people to be molly-coddled by the State in this way, as happens so blatantly under Communism in the GDR?

That humorist, Manfred Rommel, Lord Mayor of Stuttgart, gave me his own account of how he personally had dealt with the over-cosseting of one special section of society: tramps. 'In the early 1980s, this city was the German capital of tramps. We attracted them from all over the country because of our positive welfare policy: we believed that the tramp problem would not be solved by neglecting them, so we gave them money each day, and free meals and flats. Stuttgart became a tramps' paradise. We hoped that other towns would follow our noble example: but all they did was export their tramps to us. Police in other *Länder* even dumped them on us. We had up to 3,000 at a time, and our lovely Schlossgarten was full of them – not a pretty sight. When the EEC Heads of Government held their summit here at the Neues Schloss in 1983, I was so afraid of the bad impression the tramps would cause, that I had them taken in buses 30 kilometres out of the city – and they had to walk back. Later, I finally decided to clamp down on the tramps. But this brought me into conflict with my left-wing social workers, who were trying to motivate them politically. They tried to get them to demonstrate against me, but the poor creatures were mostly too drunk too cooperate. The following winter, we transferred the tramps from flats to wooden huts and we reduced the quality of their free meals. They were so angry at this that many of them left the city; word then soon got around the tramp world that Stuttgart had ceased to be utopia, so others stopped coming. Today we have fewer tramps, but we still try to re-socialise those that remain. Many of them are young drop-outs who can't stand the competition of jobs – tragic cases.'

*　　　*　　　*

The recent cuts in public health spending have fallen especially on the German passion for spa-going, thus spelling trouble for scores of resorts. The Germans are the world's most inveterate spa-cure addicts. It is an old tradition, dating back long before the days when Goethe took the waters at Marienbad in Bohemia; and, whereas in those times it was the privilege of an elite, today the practice has spread down to all classes. By 1981, over six million Germans a year were attending spas, many of them on social security; and they accounted for more than half of the domestic tourist trade. It has all become very big business. The hilly parts of central and southern Germany are fertile in mineral waters and allegedly therapeutic mud; and here over 200 resorts are officially designated as health spas, ranging from regal Baden-Baden to obscure villages. Nearly all of them add the prefix *'Bad'* to their name. Here *eine Kur* is taken by people of all kinds, most of them middle-aged or elderly, who come in search of rejuvenation, or the relief of some ailment, or just for a free rest and holiday in the *Kurort* (spa). These *Kurgäste* (they are never called patients) are put under the care of a *Kurarzt* (doctor) who prescribes their *Kurtherapie* and *Kurdiät*; they take walks in the neatly landscaped *Kurpark*, and in the evenings maybe they attend a *Kurkonzert* arranged by the *Kurverwaltung* (spa authorities) or even go dancing in the *Kurhaus* and perhaps enjoy a *Kurschatten* (spa romance).

Why is the spa habit so widespread in Germany? Maybe it is related to the new perfectionist keep-fit vogue, an antidote to post-war heavy eating; or to the fact that so many spas lie amid pleasant holiday scenery, such as the Black Forest, and not on a dullish plain like Vichy or Cheltenham. But the massive post-war growth of spa-going has above all been stimulated by an indulgent health insurance system; and Germany's new semi-classless society has readily seized this chance to behave like the monarchs of old. Until 1982, when the cuts began, it was all so easy. You went to your local GP, complaining, say, of rheumatism, or catarrh, or bad circulation, and he would send a recommendation to your insurance agency, whose own doctor would then inspect you and authorise the cure: the agency would then select the date and the place. Cures were granted very readily, often on the scantest medical evidence, so that many people were in effect getting a free holiday of three or four weeks – and employers were not always too pleased. There were frequent abuses. I heard of a Munich postman, always healthy and sport-loving, whose status as civil servant entitled him to a free cure every two years, once he was past fifty. And he took it. But his wife, a hard-working charlady, had no such rights and was not allowed to accompany him. She died of cancer.

The mounting deficits of the insurance agencies led to pressure on Bonn to take action; and the Schmidt Government, though itself very welfare-minded, finally did so in 1982. Under the law it enacted, subsidised cures are now allowed only every three years, except for the really ill, and *Kurgäste* must themselves contribute 10 DM a day. Doctors are now stricter about proposing cures. As a result, trade has slumped badly in the more down-market spas that depend mainly on paid-for clients. Bad Soden, a big popular place near Frankfurt where 95 per cent of the beds were in agency hands, lost over half of its guests in 1982–3. Some spas have tried to compensate by jazzing up their image, in a bad to attract other kinds of visitors too: they have laid on discos and pop concerts and distributed sexy posters, 'Come to fun-packed Bad Mergentheim'. This has not worked too well, for a younger clientèle would rather have fun on an Italian beach than in a sodden Bad Soden still noticeably geriatric. Some spas today have had to reduce their facilities and lay off staff; others still manage to do well, by appealing to the congress trade, or by persuading their regular clients to fork out of their own pockets. In this they seem to have succeeded for, after its initial 1982–83 slump, by 1984 the annual total of *Kurgäste* was again over the 6 million mark, even if they were now staying on average only 13.9 days instead of 15.5. The Germans still believe that a spa cure is something they cannot forego.

But what is the real value of the treatment? The war-weary Roman legions were the first to use it, and they found it soothing. Today, most British and American doctors pour scorn on the myth of a spa's healing waters, and claim that you can get the same benefit by staying at home in a warm bath. I have met plenty of German doctors who share this view, though they put it in better perspective – as did one GP I talked to in Bonn: 'In the old days, the waters were certainly valuable in the treatment of many diseases, through bathing, drinking and inhaling. But modern drugs have rendered this completely out of date, in the case of kidney ailments, arthritis and many other complaints, even rheumatism. So why use the spas? Well, the installations are there: and most people *believe* that the treatment does them good, so probably it does. The value is 90 per cent psychological. The spas are like health farms. But the exercise in warm water probably *is* of some use.' The spa doctors themselves are naturally more enthusiastic. They praise in particular the new Japanese ice-shock treatment, and the taking of baths in hot mud made of powdered volcanic stone.

A *Kurgast* usually takes his cure very seriously and will sedulously obey the spa doctor's instructions on exactly how many glasses of local mineral water to drink per day, or how many kilometres of exercise to take. If he is on social security, he will be assigned to a hotel, or more probably to a sanatorium, most of which are owned or rented by the insurance agencies. In the older sanatoria, he or she may well have to share a room with a stranger of the same sex. The new ones have single rooms – and quite luxurious these places are too, with sun-lounges, swimming-pools, thick carpets, and none of the tawdry institutional ambience of an English public hospital. At a sanatorium in Badenweiler, I met a rheumatic sexagenarian nun who showed me her lovely room with telephone, separate bathroom and panoramic balcony, and she was paying merely her 10 DM a day. The cost to the agency, including treatment and medical charges, is generally some 1,200 to 1,500 DM a week.

The routine is quite strict. Up at 6 a.m., exercise and massage, then an hour's walk, then treatment at the baths, then after lunch a two-hour rest in bed, then more treatment, then maybe a stroll into town for shopping or coffee. This is where trouble can begin, for many a *Kurgast*'s disciplined obedience breaks down at the sight of creamy cakes or a jolly beer-parlour – and nearly all cures include a strict diet with *no* alcohol. Especially is this a problem in spas frequented by bibulous factory workers. Often a spa doctor has to write to a wayward guest, 'If you're caught at it again, you'll be sent home', and to remind him of a federal law that protects the agencies against any such abuse of their largesse. In the evenings, the scope for sinfulness is less great, since most sanatoria oblige their guests to be back home and in bed by 10 or 10.30 p.m. So most spas tend to be dull places at night; they put on a few concerts and film shows, but most attempts to start up night-clubs soon fail. Not that this worries many of the *Kurgäste*, whose average age is about 60. These veterans do however go in for a certain amount of late-flowering romance. One important rule of cures is that you must not bring your spouse with you, not so much for economic reasons as because a complete break with home surroundings is part of the treatment: a *Kurgast*'s ailment is often diagnosed as psychosomatic, induced by family tensions. So here are all these delightful not-so-young people from modest backgrounds, separated from their beloveds perhaps for the first time in decades. The *Kurschatten* (spa romance) is as common a German phenomenon as the shipboard flirtation used to be on Cunard liners. The divorce lawyers are familiar with it.

At the grander spas, most of the *Kurgäste* are private. Of Baden-Baden's 200,000 annual overnight visitors, two-thirds come for congresses or ordinary holidays and only a third for cures, and of these less than 30 per cent are paid for by social security. So this queen of health resorts has not been much affected by the cutbacks. Inevitably it has declined from its 19th-century heyday as the summer capital of Europe's aristocracy, when hotel beds totalled 15,000: today their number has dwindled to 4,000, and the grand old Hotel Kaiserhof has become a supermarket. But Baden-Baden still boasts a smart summer season, with Ascot-like racing events and concerts in the garden of the stately colonnaded *Kurhaus*. Yet all this is not private enterprise:

as in the case of most German spas, the *Kurhaus* and the thermal establishments belong to the *Land*, which in 1985 built an expensive new Baths of Caracalla, circular in shape, with wide panoramic windows. Next door, in the cavernous marble halls of the old Friedrichsbad, *Kurgäste* and others come to enjoy the spa's unique speciality, an elaborate sauna-cum-Turkish-bath ritual, men and women in the nude together: it is known as the 'Roman-Irish bath', apparently because Roman colonists from Ireland in the time of Caracalla invented this technique of alternating hot-air and warm-water treatments.

Schools: educating the mind, but not so much the character

In this section and the next we shall examine education in Germany, first schools and then universities. A nation with an exceptional tradition of scholarship has been having great difficulty, more than most others in western Europe, in adapting its distinguished system to the needs of today. The primary and secondary schools, after some difficulties, are now working fairly smoothly. But for more than 20 years now the universities have been in a state of crisis and malaise, sometimes erupting into violence as in the post-1967 period, but more often – as today – characterised by apathy and mediocrity. Of all the main areas of life in Germany today, this is the one that strikes me as being the least efficient and least self-confident.

It is not easy to generalise about school education in Germany for the situation varies considerably from *Land* to *Land*. The *Länder* do coordinate their policies to the extent that everywhere you find the same types of school and examination: but, since they are virtually sovereign in this field, they display wide differences in curriculum, length of study cycles, styles of teaching, and even pedagogic philosophy. Whereas Bavaria in particular remains traditionalist, with fairly rigorous academic standards, some of the *Länder* in SPD hands, notably Bremen and Hessen, have gone over to the modern free-and-easy self-expressionist approach, much less academic. And these variations can be disconcerting for families moving from one *Land* to another. Hence in some border areas you will find cases, for example, of academically-minded parents in Frankfurt (Hessen) sending their children to day-school in Aschaffenburg (Bavaria), 25 miles away. Or a father who has strong views on education may choose his job accordingly: in Hessen, a CDU politician furious about local policy said to me, 'Why do the two southern *Länder* attract new industry so much more easily than we do? One reason, without any doubt, is that their schools have much higher standards, and senior staff are therefore readier to settle there.'

There are however many factors common to all *Länder* in a Germany where 95 per cent of children attend state as opposed to private schools. Everywhere they go first to a primary *Grundschule* from the age of six to ten or eleven, and are then divided into three streams on the basis of their monthly school marks and of teacher assessment and teacher/parent discussion. The brighter or more academic ones go to a *Gymnasium* (grammar school) that prepares for university entrance. The middle range go to a *Realschule*: this provides a general education till sixteen and often leads the way to a vocational college or apprenticeship (see page 112). And the least academically-gifted (about 40 per cent of the total) attend a *Hauptschule* until fifteen, where they receive a rather more practical preparation for apprenticeships or for the job market.

The strength of this system is that children are more carefully trained according to their aptitudes than in most countries: a comparative survey published in London in 1983 found that, whereas Britain is probably better than Germany at educating its elite, at the *Realschule* and *Hauptschule* levels German kids are some two years ahead of their British equivalents in such key subjects as maths and science – with ensuing advantages for the economy.[1] But, within Germany, the system has run into a good deal of criticism for its alleged divisiveness and social unfairness. According to this view, the streaming at an early age marks off an academic minority, mostly middle class, from the others: also it harms late developers, for a transfer from *Realschule* to *Gymnasium*, though possible in theory, is not easy in practice. It is a problem familiar to many countries. And so in the 1960s pressures grew for the introduction of comprehensives (*Gesamtschulen*). The Brandt Government produced enabling legislation for them in 1969, and left it to the *Länder* to introduce them at their discretion. The more left-wing ones rapidly began to do so; but the others found all sorts of pretexts for delaying the scheme, under pressure from middle-class parents as well as from teachers who feared a drop in academic standards if *Gymnasien* and junior schools were merged. Even the SPD too began to have qualms, when it realised that many well-to-do parents might simply switch their children to private schools, and this would accentuate privilege rather than reduce it (precisely as has happened in Britain, with Labour's merger of many grammar schools into comprehensives). And so by the mid-1980s the *Gesamtschule* venture had ground to a halt. Berlin had 25 of them, but Bavaria only one. In most *Länder*, they were still seen as merely experimental; virtually all *Gymnasien* had

---

[1] *Schooling Standards in Britain and Germany*, by S. J. Prais and Karin Wagner (National Institute of Economic and Social Research).

survived unchanged, so *Gesamtschulen* were little more than *Haupts-chulen* under another name. It was a victory for conservatism, or – as others might see it – for the realistic view that children are not equal and cannot be treated as such.

In some other respects, however, German schools have changed quite strikingly over the past 20 years. In the old pre-war days they were ruled by a rigid discipline, inspired, as one writer put it, 'not by Goethe or Socrates, but by the Prussian petty officer'. A class would rise and stand to attention as its teacher entered the room. This authoritarianism was easily exploited by the Nazis to their advantage, and so after the war it was modified. Then, as in other countries, the post-1968 reform era brought further liberalisation. The older generation of more autocratic teachers gradually retired, to be replaced by younger ones with a more informal and humane approach: and in many *Länder* they were officially directed to apply the new pedagogic principles of self-expression and group work, in place of the former heavy emphasis on learning by rote and writing long essays. And so, amid a certain amount of cheerful chaos, these changes were steadily applied. Classes became more casual, often more unruly too; it was no longer enough for teachers just to lecture the class, they now had to get the youngsters to think for themselves, and sometimes the pupils now called them by their first names. In some *Länder*, parents began to be allowed to sit in on classes if they wished. These reforms may have been for the better on the whole: but they have also brought some drawbacks. The new stress on oral rather than written expression, while it may have had little impact on maths, science or crafts, has led to quite a dramatic decline in spelling, grammar and handwriting, especially in schools other than *Gymnasien* – and many employers as well as teachers have been lamenting this. In 1984 the head of training at Daimler-Benz said that, while he was pleased with his apprentices' practical flair, 'their writing skills have reached a deplorably low level'. In some *Länder*, moves are now afoot to redress this situation, for example by re-introducing the learning of poetry by rote in primary schools.

The fall in standards does seem to be confined to the mastery of the German language (absurdly over-complicated anyway), and it has not affected wider aspects of education. On the whole, German children are still taught a remarkably full range of subject matter, and more rigorously than in most countries. Most schools, even primary ones, still hold regular little class exams and written tests every few weeks, and the marks are posted up in public. This creates a spirit of intense competitiveness and in the eyes of some radicals it can lead to nasty tensions, or worse: 'The kids,' said one mother-of-four in Bavaria, 'live under the tyranny of these marks, and of what their parents will think if they do badly. Sometimes a child gets beaten up by his father, and he may even run away from home. Hence the high level of teen-age suicides in Germany.' These may be extreme cases. It is true that ordinary German schools, with their stress on academic achievement, are still rather inept at dealing with the backward or problem child: Bavaria in particular has been slow to come to terms with dyslexia, which the authorities there still regard as a sign of low intelligence or psychological disturbance, which it is not. But, in general, German schools today are much more relaxed, humane and friendly places than they used to be.

At *Gymnasium* level, one undoubted strength of the German system is that it still lays rather more emphasis on a good general education, as opposed to early specialisation, than is the case in many countries such as the United States. A pupil is required to prepare quite a range of subjects for the *Abitur*, the major examination taken usually at 19 that is the essential passport to university. It is true that the regulations have been modified repeatedly over the past 20 years, in different ways in different *Länder* and amid much controversy. Especially in the more 'progressive' *Länder*, the *Abitur* has been made much easier, under pressure from politicians who have wanted more young people to be given the chance to go to university: the proportion of all German teenagers obtaining the *Abitur* has risen since the 1950s from 5 to 25 per cent, with consequent university overcrowding, as we shall see. Today the *Abitur*, though still on the whole a more rigorous test than its English A-level equivalent, has certainly become easier than the French *baccalauréat*; even in strict Bavaria the average *Gymnasium* now allows pupils to drop Latin at the age of 17 if they wish. Of course this has produced a stream of complaints of falling standards, from university rectors and others – and as a result the pendulum recently has been swinging back a little. In Baden-Württemberg, the most rigorous *Land* after Bavaria, it is still possible to take sport as a 'main' subject, but only if it is balanced with something more academic such as maths or history for the other main one. In a word, Germany's educationalists have been little more successful than others in trying to decide how far the old academic grind is still important for today's age.

Despite this confusion, almost all British parents who come to live in Germany and put their children into its state schools are impressed by the quality and seriousness of the teaching and the high level of pupil motivation – at least in the *Gymnasien*. Modern languages in particular are taught very thoroughly, and the youngsters throw themselves eagerly into learning them well. And one group of English sixth-formers on an exchange visit were amazed to find that their German counterparts knew more about British history and institutions than they did themselves. The syllabus, in most subjects, has become less theoretical and old-fashioned than it was 20 years ago, and is now better geared to the modern world and modern needs. All in all, and despite the new problems I have described, German classroom teaching seems to represent a happy medium between British laxness and French encyclopaedic academicism. But what of school life outside the classroom? Here, alas, a British or American visitor is far less likely to be impressed.

The traditional German view of school education, as in many Continental countries, is that its function is to train the mind rather than to indulge in character-building or to promote civic responsibility or the full use of leisure. These matters are seen as the role of parents, or maybe of the churches or of youth bodies such as scouts or guides. Hence, by Anglo-American standards, German state schools appear utilitarian places, lacking in any warm sense of community. For one thing, a school is alive only in the morning. Almost all the classroom work is done intensively between 8 a.m. and 1 p.m.; some schools do have a few afternoon classes, or they stay open then for voluntary club or cultural activities, but mostly the kids clear off home for lunch and then devote the time to their own pursuits, including at least two or three hours of homework. So, at a time when English schools are buzzing with valuable non-academic activity, German ones are largely deserted. Since about 1970, some attempts have been made to change this by promoting *Ganztagsschulen* (all-day schools), but this has been done less for educative reasons than to keep children out of mischief when both parents have full-time jobs. The experiment has not got far. Teachers and pupils resent losing some of their free time, while parents tend to complain, 'Our children are being taken from us!' Despite official efforts, these 'all-day schools' still account for no more than 3 per cent of all pupils.

Many schools do have clubs for photography, chess and suchlike, as well as choirs, orchestras and drama groups, and sometimes the results are impressive: the pupils of one *Gymnasium* near Stuttgart have used a local theatre to give public performances of plays by Wilde and Albee in the original English. Activities of this kind have intended to increase since the war: but they are hampered by the lack of suitable premises in schools, and they depend upon the enthusiasm of individual teachers prepared to give up their free time: official *Land* policy offers them little encouragement. As for sport, individual skills such as gymnastics and athletics are taught in school hours as part of the curriculum: but team sports hardly figure at all, and few schools have their own playing-fields or swimming-pool. Those who want to play football, or swim, do so voluntarily in their home context by joining a local club or sports centre. Homework permitting, many children do in fact enjoy quite an intense and varied leisure life, centred around their families and peer groups – and in defence of the

German system it can be argued that it is good for a child to remain part of adult life and the real world rather than be to cooped up within the artificial milieu of a school. Even so, it is surely an opportunity missed if an education system fails to make use of schools to develop a sense of loyalty, responsibility and teamwork. (If Britain in this century has had a better democratic tradition than Germany, is it not vaguely something to do with the Thomas Arnold tradition?)

As in France and Italy too, German state schools provide very little practical training in leadership or civics. Of course there are classroom lessons where the pupils are taught about the Constitution and the legal system, and how the *Bund* and *Länder* operate: but they are given little chance to rehearse democracy in practice. There is nothing to parallel the American system where a school becomes a parliament-in-embryo, nor the British one where senior pupils are in charge of discipline. This is left to the teachers: for an eighteen-year-old boy or girl to boss around junior ones would not only be illegal in Germany, but parents would never stand for it. Each class formally elects its own delegates, who can go to the staff with complaints and suggestions: and since the 1968 period each school has a kind of assembly where pupil, staff and parent representatives meet on an equal basis to discuss minor practical non-pedagogic matters such as whether smoking should be allowed in the corridors – but this is marginal. There are not even any school debating societies where political muscles can be flexed. And this whole system comes under some criticism from the Germans themselves: one liberal-minded *Gymnasium* headmaster, whose wife is English, said to me, 'Maybe school prefects in Britain have too *much* power, and this can lead to abuses. But your system does provide youngsters with real experience in taking responsibility for their community, and this we fail to do. As a result, though they are meticulously law-abiding, the Germans tend to be lacking in spontaneous concern for others, and in a sense of civic initiative.'

The focus of a pupil's loyalty is much more his classmates than the school as a whole. A class will organise weekend outings together and maybe go on visits abroad too, and they will often develop an intense camaraderie. Groups of ex-pupils will keep in touch, so that sometimes you come across silver-haired oldies banqueting round a *Stammtisch* in a pub to celebrate the 50th anniversary of their taking the *Abitur* together. But few of them ever return nostalgically to the old Alma Mater itself, which seldom stages alumni reunions. The reasons for this lack of community are in part logistic: many distinguished *Gymnasien* do not even have a big hall for concerts or speech days, and so the school never meets as one body. The *Land* usually refuses to pay for such an 'extra', and schools lack their own budgets for it.

In all fairness I should add that the atmosphere in all the state schools I visited was perfectly friendly and cheerful; the staff seemed kindly, and I was assured by both sides that teacher/parent cooperation was good. But the buildings were usually drab, and they lacked amenities such as good libraries for the pupils' use. This wealthy nation, whose public hospitals, sports centres, opera houses and suchlike are usually so magnificent, has never thought to devote a similar largesse to its schools. Moreover, many *Gymnasien* doubled or trebled in size during the years of the boom in *Abitur* applicants, and some even had to turn their libraries into classrooms. Today the declining birthrate may have begun to reduce overcrowding: but state budgets have tightened at the same time.

Lastly, one other major contributing factor to the somewhat soulless nature of German state schools is that they are rigidly run on bureaucratic lines by the *Land* ministries of education. The head of a school has far less autonomy than in Britain. He (or she) cannot select his own staff, but has them foisted on him by the ministry; and, as teachers enjoy civil service status and security, it is difficult for a head to get rid of a bad one. A school must also comply with rigid and uniform *Land* regulations about punishments and marking systems, which have legal force and cannot be modified. 'If a parent thinks that I have punished his child too severely, or given him too low marks, then quite probably he will sue me: the Germans adore lawsuits,' said one headmaster; 'I merely pass the file on to the ministry to be sorted out.'

Dissatisfaction with state schools has driven a growing minority of families, mainly middle-class ones, to seek refuge in the private sector which is still small in Germany (5 per cent) but getting less so. Especially they move to the Waldorf (Rudolf Steiner) schools, which originated in Germany and have since expanded steadily (except during the Nazi period, when they were banned). Steiner was an Austrian scientist and humanist, founder of the anthroposophical movement (see page 441), who set up his first school in 1919 in Stuttgart, and there it still stands and flourishes. His schools have had a worldwide influence: there are 200 around the globe, 80 of them in Germany itself. In so far as they have no prefects and few afternoon activities, these *Waldorfschulen* (as the Germans call them) are in some respects closer to *Gymnasien* than to the British system: but in many other ways they mark quite a break with German tradition, for they try to care for the creative personality in a warm, attractive environment, and they put the emphasis less on academic work than on culture, handicrafts and group activities. Boys and girls alike all learn knitting and metalwork, as well as ceramics and carpentry; much classroom time is given over to music-playing, singing and drama, including the staging of plays, a compulsory subject. There is no streaming: an age-group stays together, moving up the school as one class, with the same teacher all the time who becomes a kind of foster-parent, getting to know each pupil very closely. Another original feature is that there are no printed schoolbooks, for these are thought to result in parrot-learning: instead, children are expected to devise their own textbooks, based on research done in groups on their own initiative. It follows that academic standards tend to be lower than at a *Gymnasium:* but they have been improving recently under pressure from parents who want more than culture and joyous liberation for their young. Only the brightest 30 per cent of pupils are encouraged to sit for the *Abitur*, and they tend to do quite well at it. One lecturer at Stuttgart university was enthusiastic about them: 'Students who have come from *Waldorfschulen*,' he told me, 'may arrive with less knowledge than the others, but they have been taught to think for themselves much more. So in the end they are the better ones at university, where a student has to learn to work on his own.'

One *Waldorfschule* teacher, a large motherly lady in her fifties, very proudly showed me around the *maison mère*, a group of handsome pink buildings on the crest of one of Stuttgart's hills. I admired the décor and architecture, all intriguingly asymmetrical, with no right-angles – 'Yes,' said my guide, 'that was Steiner's idea, to make buildings gentle and irregular, just like people. After all, our heads aren't right-angled, are they?' Inside, all was wood-panelling, sloping ceilings, pretty pastel colours in varied shades – delightfully unlike usual school classrooms. One class that I visited was doing sculpture, another was playing the flute; tots of seven were making carnival costumes; an *Abitur* class had put flowers on the teacher's desk for her birthday. There was even a big school hall where all 800 pupils can attend concerts. As at other *Waldorfschulen* in Germany, the intake is mainly middle-class: but the fees, paid on a sliding scale according to means, are fairly modest, since city and *Land* both contribute sizeable subsidies. Many German intellectuals and professional people admire the *Waldorfschulen* and send their children there: recent parents have included Helmut Kohl and the late Joseph Beuys, the artist. In later life the pupils tend to do well in artistic professions, but less well in more formal careers. Nearly always they are happy at school and retain an affection for it: alumni associations flourish.

The other private schools are mostly run by the Churches. Some of the older ones have quite a sense of tradition and community; often they have remained single-sex, whereas almost all state schools are now mixed. There are also 18 *Landerziehungsheime*, private non-confessional boarding schools in rural settings, modelled partly on English public schools: the best-known is Salem, near Lake Constance, founded by the late Kurt Hahn who went on to create Gordonstoun in Scotland. Charging about 2,000 DM a month, these schools are patronised by senior German diplomats and businessmen posted abroad, or by well-to-do parents of children who do not fit into the austere *Gymnasium* world. I visited one, Schöndorf, set in parkland beside the Ammersee, west of Munich, and I found it pleasantly relaxed and convivial in spirit, but not very academic. It puts an accent on handicrafts, music and drama as well as on sport; as at English boarding schools, the boys and girls live under the supervision of housemasters and housemistresses. Alumni links are strong, and many ex-pupils look back nostalgically on the school as a kind of surrogate family. Clearly these *Landerziehungsheime* have much to commend them, but they are too few in number, and too elitist, to have any great influence on German education as a whole. They are for a privileged minority – as German universities used to be, but most definitely are no longer.

The never-ending university malaise

It is a far cry from the green calm of the old Philosophers' Walk, above the river Neckar at Heidelberg, to the overcrowded lecture-halls of some hideous new utility campus such as Bochum or Dortmund – from the old ideal of secluded scholarship to the clamour and discontent of the modern student broiler-houses. In Germany, as much as anywhere else in Europe, changing economic needs and the explosion in student numbers have been forcing the universities to adapt to a new role and to seek a new identity. But in trying to reconcile the requirements of mass and elite education they have not been too successful; and the resulting confusion and decline in standards have been causing some anxiety to politicians, employers and others. 'In our efficient modern Germany,' one CDU leader said to me, 'the universities shine out as *in*efficient. Why do we consistently fail to solve this problem?'

In the 19th-century, German universities were noble centres of pure scholarship and research, devoted to the principles developed by Wilhelm von Humboldt who founded the University of Berlin in 1809. Students were a privileged and pampered few, sitting at the feet of great professors endowed with lofty public prestige. This charmed era continued until the 1930s, when it was shattered by the universities' generally craven subservience to Hitler, as a result of which some 4,000 teachers were ejected from their posts in the denazification era. The universities did manage to recover from this shame: but then they signally failed to march with the times in the new, more egalitarian Germany. Hierarchies remained rigid and routines crustily old-fashioned; the senior professors arrogantly ruled the roost, drawing fat salaries, dictating every detail of the duties of their assistants, and rejecting all calls for change. Some rectors still insisted on being called officially by the old title of '*Ihre Magnifizenz*'. The few attempts at reform – notably at the new Free University of Berlin, where in 1949 students were allowed to elect their own delegates to the Senate – proved short-lived.

During the 1960s, as the students' numbers steadily increased, so did their dissatisfaction with the status quo – and this discontent was shared by many of the junior teachers. It paved the way for the great student uprisings (see p. 423) that began in Berlin in 1967 and the next year spread to France and elsewhere. The Leftist leaders of this rebellion were cleverly exploiting the general malaise, even if relatively few students shared their more radical political objectives: the ills of the university were for them just one aspect of the rottenness of a whole society that must be abolished. Their revolt hardly succeeded in these broader revolutionary aims: but it did manage to break the university mould and in the long run to usher in a new order. In the early stage, the years after 1967 were marked by constant left-wing agitation and disruption in many universities, notably Berlin, Frankfurt and Marburg: Maoist and other groups, in fierce rivalry, roamed the faculties breaking up lectures, sometimes locking professors into their rooms or scuffling with the police, while student boycotts led to many seminars and courses being cancelled, especially in the social sciences. The agitators hardly spoke for the average student, and in the short term their disruption did a good deal of harm: but it did impel the Federal and *Land* governments into attempting some reforms that were aimed at answering the widespread desire for more democracy and less professorial autocracy.

The results have been most uneven. At first, some of the more left-wing *Länder* introduced *Drittelparität*, a bold innovation whereby the university senate and faculty boards were each to be made up in three equal parts of professors, junior teachers and assistants, and students – and so in 1969 the Free University of Berlin elected a sociology assistant as its president. This was exciting stuff for radicals: but it did lead to a good deal of muddle, squabbling and inept decision-taking, as professors were outvoted by their inexperienced and sometimes vindictive juniors. The pendulum had swung too far to the other extreme. So in 1976 the *Bund* stepped in with an outline law[1]

---

[1] Higher education is primarily the responsibility of the *Länder*, which provide the money and decide how it should be spent, and are supposed to coordinate their policies. However, since 1969 the *Bund* has increased its own powers of coordination: it shares the financing of universities, and no *Land* can found a new one without *Bund* permission.

that abolished *Drittelparität* and called on the *Länder* to apply a more moderate and coherent system. Though the *Länder* have not reacted uniformly, the overall situation today in senates and other university bodies is that the professors have an absolute majority but other categories are by law quite strongly represented too. Thus, in the senate at Tübingen, professors have 21 seats, junior teachers seven, other staff (including cleaning ladies) seven, and students seven: as the other groups never agree, the professors can usually secure the decisions they want. Nearly everywhere, professors have now reasserted their control after the post-1967 crisis period, but in a more discreet style than before. In the more conservative faculties such as law and medicine, they may still try to be authoritarian: but mostly they have learned their lesson and are now more open-minded and easy-going towards students and junior staff. And as the older generations retire, this becomes more so. After the wasted years of muddle and incoherence, it could be said that a reasonable balance has finally been struck.

One instructive example is the University of Bremen. This was founded by the SPD-led *Land* government in 1971, as a new-style democratic venture, and it rapidly filled up with left-wing teachers and students, many of them refugees from Göttingen where radical rebellion had collapsed in ruins. With its young president in jeans and everyone on chummy *'du'* terms, Bremen soon won the reputation of being the most 'Red' of German universities and the one with the lowest academic standards: its graduates generally found it hard to get good jobs. But today it seems to have settled down and become more moderate, without having entirely abandoned its earlier ideals – as one of its sociology professors told me: 'We've managed to hold on to many of our innovations, some of them still unusual in Germany. For example, inter-disciplinary studies; a credit system in place of some exams, very popular with students; and organic links with local trade unions. We've even retained *Drittelparität*, in defiance of the federal law.'

This issue of democratisation is no longer the main problem facing the universities. It has been partially solved, or at least has become dormant, and has now been far outstripped in urgency by the more intractable problem of massive-scale student entry: this has led to overcrowding, under-funding, a bad student/teacher ratio, harrassed staff and lonely, ill-supervised students, and a general apathy and lowering of standards, with adverse effects even on research and scholarship at the upper level. It has completely overwhelmed the old Humboldtian ideal of serene academic dedication and has led to the asking of all sorts of fundamental questions, such as 'What is the purpose of a university?' or 'Should everyone have the right to higher education, or should the number of graduates be limited to the nation's requirements, as happens in the GDR?'

During the years of full employment, more and more young people came to feel that a degree was worth having, and so the student numbers in higher education rose steadily, from 200,000 in 1959 to some 1.3 million by 1985. The growth was hard to control, for it is a strong tradition, even written into the Constitution, that the *Abitur* gives automatic right to university entry; moreover, universities are forbidden by law to do their own selection on merit, as they can in Britain and the United States. Until ten or so years ago, the growth in numbers was actually encouraged by governments (except in medicine) – first for political and social reasons, since the SPD in particular felt that it was desirable for the humbler ranks of society to have fuller access to higher education; and secondly for practical reasons, for in those days it was argued that a country's economic strength was related to its number of well-educated graduates, notably in the sciences. So public money was poured into the expansion of higher education: between 1959 and 1979, 20 new universities were built as well as numerous polytechnics, and academic staff increased from 19,000 to 78,000.

But the extra funding has not kept pace with rising student numbers, especially in the past few years of budget restrictions. The major expansion of infrastructure in the 1960s was planned to cater for an expected student total of 750,000: so it has now become completely inadequate. What is more, ever since the *Abitur* has been made easier, a large number of less academically gifted people have been entering university, including – so it is widely argued – many who are just not suited for it. And this situation is made worse by the liberal German system, splendid in the old days but less realistic today, that allows a student (except in some disciplines) to study whatever he likes at university, irrespective of his *Abitur* specialisation: there are frequent cases of people taking, say, German and history as their main *Abitur* subjects and then switching to chemistry or physics. Hence many students arrive ill-prepared for their university work and are then inadequately taught owing to the pressure of numbers. Many find that they just cannot cope, and so they drop out after a year or two. Others struggle on, and achieve a low-grade degree.

In earlier days, these weaker students could generally expect to find some suitable job. But the recent rapid rise in unemployment has led to a tripling since 1979 of the number of young graduates without work: teachers and would-be teachers are the worst affected. Many are obliged to take jobs well below their qualifications. One professor told me that his best recent student was now a taxi-driver, while at a famous museum in Berlin I found that the young man hanging up the coats in the cloakroom has just graduated from an art college – it was the nearest he could get to his beloved subject! And so, politicians constantly issue the warning that Germany is creating an overqualified academic proletariat that could prove more dangerously explosive than in the 1967 period. However, the new youth generation itself is now more aware that a university education may not be so useful, and an increasing number of them now look elsewhere after the *Abitur*, often to apprenticeships. The number of *Abiturienten* going straight on to higher education, which used to be 90 per cent, has dropped down to 60 per cent since the early 1980s; I met one senior professor's daughter, with an excellent school record, who was training to be a hairdresser, unimaginable 20 years ago. The government, in an about-turn of attitude, is now pleased with this trend, which has just begun to have an effect on student numbers: in 1985 the volume of new university entrants actually fell, for the first time since the war. And yet, the overall student population has continued to rise, simply because people have been taking longer to complete their studies.

One especially striking aspect of the liberalism of the German tradition is that you can go on studying for as long as you like. Only in a few subjects, such as law and medicine, are degree courses of fixed duration, generally five or six years; in the others, they are unlimited, and if you fail your final exams, you are allowed to take them one more time, though it must be within two years. This generous system possibly made sense in the old privileged days, when 'the eternal student', cultured, dilettante and fun-loving, was a figure of some respect: but today it is a major reason for the unwieldy size of the student population, and it also means that a great many German graduates enter their careers in their late twenties, with some of their best years behind them. What is more, fear of unemployment has today been tempting many students to postpone the evil day as long as possible, often by eking out a living with part-time jobs when their grants have expired: since the 1960s, the average length of study has risen from 11 to 13 semesters, and I met one man who was in his 54th! Despite the poor study conditions, many young people still enjoy the relative freedom and leisure of student life, and they find that the official status of 'student' brings with it many perks which they are reluctant to lose – very cheap meals in university canteens, cheap health insurance, cheap theatre and train tickets, and so on.

In the past few years, the authorities have finally been making some attempts to contain student numbers by introducing a *numerus clausus* system in certain subjects. This first began to be applied in medicine in the late 1960s – partly because there were insufficient laboratories for coping with the growing flood of students into a popular profession (see page 199) – and it has since spread into related disciplines such as pharmacy, dentistry, psychology and bio-chemistry. The selection is not done by individual universities, but by a central computer in Dortmund which sifts candidates on the basis of their *Abitur* marks and other factors, and then distributes them as it pleases with typical computer caprice: the system is detested by students for its arbitrary impersonality, and by professors for its hideous complexity – 'I try not to understand it, as I fear for my sanity,' said one dean of admissions. The computer has had some effect on numbers, though many would-be medicos find ways of sneaking in through the back gate, either as 'mature' late entrants, or else by qualifying first at some foreign university with an easy open-door policy, such as Bologna. More recently, some university departments in other subjects have been empowered to start up their own *numerus clausus* (for example, political science in Freiburg), but on a first-come-first-served basis and not one of merit, for this is still banned by law as being anti-egalitarian. All in all, selective entry is so alien to German practice that it is still viewed warily by many professors as at best a necessary evil. And the student unions are flatly opposed to it.

Despite the signs that numbers may soon begin to fall, the vast majority of senior university teachers are in favour of sterner action, as much with a view to raising academic standards as to reducing overcrowding. Alike in private and in public, they have been proposing a number of related solutions. Most would like to see the *Abitur* made harder again, and/or limits imposed more widely on length of studies. Many suggest a weeding-out exam at the end of the first year; or (as in France) the division of the standard master's degree course into two short cycles, with a diploma exam after two years that would provide at least some qualification for weaker students, who could leave at that stage. Plenty of professors, especially those on the Right, want universities to be allowed to do their own selection, preferably on merit. And many would favour the introduction of tuition fees, arguing that this might deter quite a proportion of the less serious students from middle-class families, while it could actually help working-class ones, if it were based on a means test and coupled with higher grants.

These various measures would all seem to make sense, and many have long been common practice in countries such as Britain or the United States. But in Germany they would run up against all kinds of vested interests and rooted habits. In particular, the eleven *Länder* are so split between Left and Right on so many issues that they would never easily agree to coordinated action. Constitutionally speaking, a *Land* could probably get away with carrying through some of these reforms unilaterally: but it would cause such a political storm that in practice it might prove impossible. Meanwhile, a cloud of gloom hangs over the world of German professors. Nearly all of them complain that they are bogged down in administrative chores and have too little time for research. It is true that in many ways they are still quite a privileged class, very well paid and more highly respected by society than almost any other profession (in a Germany still so title-conscious, the magic word 'Herr Professor' can cast a spell of deference over any social gathering). Yet they are probably justified in their grouse that they are being asked to do the impossible in trying to combine scholarships with preparing a lumpen student mass for the labour market.

Another steady lament concerns the universities' lack of autonomy and the interference by *Land* bureaucrats. By law, German universities are subject to their local education ministry, which allocates their budget and decides how it should be spent – 'If I want a new word-processor,' said one teacher, 'it has to be approved by the *Landtag*'s finance committee, and that can take months.' Ministry permission is also needed for the creation of a new chair, and for changes in the curriculum, especially if money is involved. A university elects its own president (rector) and can choose its own junior teaching staff, but all new appointments of professors are decided by the Minister, on the basis of a short-list drawn up by the Senate: generally he accepts its own preference, but he need not do so. Of course this whole situation leads to running feuds between *Land* and university authorities, with the latter complaining that 'the bureaucrats do not understand our problems', and rectors being obliged to devote much of their time to political lobbying. In this struggle, the civil servants have the whip hand, for in true Germanic style they rule the universities through a vast and complex battery of formal regulations – 'Look,' said the head of administration at Tübingen University, showing me the set of fifteen fat green lawbooks behind his desk, '*this* is what we're up against!' And financial 'meddling' by the ministries has even tended to get worse recently, as universities' needs have grown more complicated while budgets have got tighter. Professors have sometimes been refused funds for travelling to seminars abroad, while the august president of Munich University had his official car's logbook scrutinised to see whether he was illicitly using it for private purposes. An Oxford don would throw up his hands in amazement and horror; even in centralised France the universities nowadays at least receive their budgets in a lump sum to spend partly as they choose. But the Germans still sweat it out under a tighter tutelage.

This all seems a far cry from the old historical image of Heidelberg, say, or Göttingen, as noble self-governing centres of learning. But times have changed – and recent decades in particular have seen a deliberate government policy of levelling down of all universities towards a dull uniformity, in the sacred name of fairness of opportunity. It is true that Germany has never possessed an elitist superstructure in quite the manner of Oxbridge, the Ivy League or the *Grandes Ecoles*: even in the good old days, German universities were bound by a certain concept of equality, enabling a student to move freely from one to another and spend a year or two in each, in pursuit of a degree. But the universities then were relatively few in number, and students likewise. The system did also enable great professors to take root in a particular place, endowing it with a reputation in their field – as Göttingen for maths and science, and Tübingen for philosophy and theology. Today there are some 40 full universities (as well as seven technical and seven 'comprehensive' ones), all bound by much the same regulations, all with very similar systems of admission, study methods and per capita budget allocations. And they fall into three main types: the ancient classic universities in medium-sized towns (Heidelberg, Tübingen, Freiburg, Göttingen, Münster, Marburg); those in very big cities, founded mostly in the 19th centuries (Berlin, Munich, Hamburg, Frankfurt, etc.); and the score or so of post-war ones, some of them pleasant smallish campuses on the edge of historic towns (e.g. Konstanz, Regensburg), others large new concrete eyesores (e.g. Düsseldorf, Dortmund).

Of course they still look and feel very different from each other. Heidelberg, founded in 1386, with its romantic old student taverns and its lovely buildings in the heart of the medieval town below the great red castle, seems to inhabit another world from, say, Bochum, largest and ugliest of the new utility campuses of the Ruhr. But look more closely and you find much the same students facing much the same problems and conditions, the only major distinction being that Heidelberg is still able to attract a more distinguished kind of senior professor, simply because he will find it a pleasanter place to live in. In the same way, a few universities do still manage – if less than in the old days – to outshine the others in some particular field, owing to the presence of a few star professors. Thus, for example, Cologne is noted for economics, Aachen for engineering, and Tübingen still for theology (with Hans Küng) as well as for medicine. But that is about as far as dissimilarity goes. As a university cannot select on merit, and as the vast majority of German students go to the one nearest to their home, it follows inevitably that the average quality of students varies very little and that almost all universities have today become equally provincial – even the most world-famous. It is all rather sad.

After 1969, this trend was deliberately accentuated by the SPD-led governments of Brandt and Schmidt, with the aim of giving all students equal chances as far as possible, and of making degrees more directly comparable. Their policies put pressure on the *Länder* in this direction. But the result – in the eyes of most university leaders and all right-wing politicians – has been a levelling down towards a general mediocrity. Lavish research funds are now spread so evenly that there are few concentrations of specialised excellence any more, with consequent dangers for German economic progress, especially in high technology – and this state of affairs is often blamed for Germany's very poor recent showing in the Nobel prize-lists, as compared with pre-1933 days when it was gaining more such awards than any other nation.[1]

In 1984 the president of the Technical University of Munich, Professor Wolfgang Wild, issued a stern warning: 'The intellectual sparks which glitter in the stimulating atmospheres of Harvard and MIT, Tokyo or Kyoto, Oxford or Cambridge, are extinguished here in the ashes of prevailing mediocrity. Researchers, able to achieve the extraordinary when working at a top-class university abroad, achieve only the ordinary on their return to German universities.' This recurrent Cassandry-cry of 'mediocrity' has been voiced also in 1983 by the Foreign Minister, Hans-Dietrich Genscher, in a boldly-worded speech (see also p. 95) that was to make a distinct impact: he claimed that the equalisation process of the past decade had severely damaged the universities, with disastrous results for research, for academic excellence, and for training the top scientists needed for Germany to make up lost ground in high-technology.

Urged on by Genscher and others, the Kohl Government in 1983 began to do just a little to redress the balance. Genscher argued eloquently that the only way to bring any rapid results was to loosen the state monopoly in higher education and sanction the setting up of private fee-paying universities, elitist in nature, which could train specialists in certain fields. And today this has begun to happen, on a modest scale. In 1983 a small university, mainly for medicine, opened at Witten in the Ruhr; another followed in 1984 at Koblenz, for training business managers (see p. 101). Both are financed by industry, and from students' fees, and they have made a good start. The trend seems likely to develop and has been warmly welcomed in many circles, even by the liberal *Die Zeit* whose co-editor is Helmut Schmidt. But this radical break with German tradition has also aroused much criticism and scepticism: Schmidt's SPD colleague Willy Brandt called Genscher's ideas 'an attack on the democratic and social foundations of the German Constitution'. Other critics have wondered whether it is indeed possible to create a truly superior university from scratch in the space of a few years, short of quite excessive funding. And some have even argued, not very convinc-

---

[1] This may have been a factor: but a far more important one was surely the emigration of the best scientists, especially Jewish, after 1933.

ingly, that past elitism in German society led to Nazism and must not be encouraged again in any form. Nonetheless, there will probably be more private ventures of this kind. Possibly they will help the economy a little: but they hardly solve the problem of what to do with the swollen graduate-producing factories.

Tübingen, just like Heidelberg, is a charming old town on the Neckar in Baden-Württemberg. Untouched by wartime bombing, its 15th-century gabled houses stand terraced on the steep slope above the river, all prettily painted in pastel shades of pink, blue and ochre. Here is the Protestant *Stift* where Hölderlin shared lodgings with Hegel and Schelling, and the old tower-house by the river where the poet lived in later life. The university today has spread out everywhere, even into the courts of the great 11th-century Schloss on the hilltop; and in termtime the streets are filled with idling or scurrying students, so that Tübingen certainly has the feel of a university city, with 29,000 students and staff amid a total population of 75,000 – 'we have a town on our campus,' the local saying goes. But what is there of live tradition or true university life? A few student pubs and cafés; some venerable old bookshops; the literary and intellectual activity of a few select cliques, centering around brilliant figures such as Küng or the writer and critic Walter Jens; and on warm days the lively impromptu forum of the Holzmarkt where buskers perform and Greens and Leftists argue and harangue. In summer on the river, there are even student rowing-races, and girls lazing in punts, as pretty as any on the Cherwell. But of stirring ritual, or collegiate or club life, or sheer zany youthful fun, there is not much sign. No Commem balls, no dons at high tables, no Union Society debates, no degree ceremonies in full regalia. Might it not be said that Tübingen is as inferior to Oxford as Austin Rover is to Daimler-Benz?

One tradition that does still just about survive – though at Tübingen as elsewhere it has fallen mightily into disrepute – is that of the student fraternities (*Verbindungen*), many of them still addicted to the archaic pastime of sabre-duelling. These are all-male residential clubs of a sort, whose members live, study and drink beer together in handsome, crumbling old houses. In the old days, most higher-class students belonged to these bodies, which were supposed to inculcate a respect for tradition and hierarchy and a sense of honour. Today they are somewhat out of favour; but a number still exist, mainly in the older universities where sometimes you see their little cohorts parading through the streets in their bright sashes and funny caps, singing lustily. At Tübingen they hold a big annual torchlight procession where they regularly clash with left-wing students. Today not all *Verbindungen* practise duelling; but the more purist and conservative ones still do, and it endows them with an even more reactionary image than is really justified. One wintry night, a young professor took me along to a seedy Victorian mansion in a Tübingen residential street, whispering as we entered, 'Look out for the bloodstains on the cellar floor'. We didn't in fact see any – but the inmates did put on a duelling display for us, wearing eye-shields but bare-headed. The president, a law student, explained that it was compulsory for every member to duel in a tournament twice a year – 'Today many student members would like duelling to be dropped, or at least made voluntary,' he said, 'but our rules are fixed by our alumni association, and the old boys insist nostalgically on keeping up the tradition. They feel that the younger generation should not have things easier than they did. And besides,' he added lamely, 'duelling teaches physical courage and self-control, and surely that is good, isn't it? If your head is cut, you mustn't flinch.' Afterwards we drank beer in the refectory where three girl-friend visitors (innovation!) had come for dancing. I was shown the yellowing photos of past members on the walls, the collection of uniforms, sabres and other cabalistic souvenirs, and I was told of their parties and their punt, and their difficulty in recruiting new members – the club once numbered 60, but now it was down to 15, seven of them living in. The place reeked with tradition, but oh so sad and moribund. My host explained that this *Verbindung*, like others of its kind, was not directly political or right-wing – 'It's just that we uphold conservative values.' He also pointed out that it was no longer socially elitist. That was clear. One of the inmates was the son of a Stuttgart baker.

The *Verbindungen*'s fortunes reached a nadir during the post-1967 period of Leftist upsurge, when they hardly dared show their faces in public. Now they have revived just a little, in line maybe with the general ideological recovery of the Right in Europe during the 1980s. Some students join them out of sheer loneliness; others because they think it will help them later to get jobs, seeing that the old-boy networks are dedicated to mutual self-help among members and many of these *alte Herren* (alumni) are now in influential positions. Some of the non-duelling *Verbindungen* have cultural and sporting activities and are quite sensible and up-to-date: but these are only a minority. Overall *Verbindung* membership even in Tübingen is now down to a mere 2.5 per cent of all students (most are in law or medicine faculties). In a university system that has no collegiate life other than dull student hostels, these fraternities are surely in principle a splendid concept – and it is sad that it has proved impossible to adapt and modernise them.

Neither the social nor the working life of the average student is any paradise. There has never been any organised tutorial system in the Oxbridge sense, and now the rise in numbers has made direct contact with senior teachers even more remote, so that the nearest a student will often get to his professor is at seminars, which in popular subjects may well be groups of 30 to 40. It is true that links with junior teachers are closer, and many professors do hold *Sprechstunde* ('consulting hours') where students can come individually to seek their advice – but many are too shy or confused to make use of this, or so the professors allege. The fault may be on both sides. Certainly nearly all students complain of a lack of guidance and supervision in their work and a sense of intellectual isolation – and it takes some ingenuity to get round this barrier, as one girl I met at Göttingen had managed to do. She was a keen linguist: but, rather than opt for the hurly-burly of the French and English departments, she chose Slavonic languages, and in Serbo-Croat found herself the *only* student in her year. So she and her professor held their 'seminars' together in a café – and she got a first-class degree. But such *ad hoc* tutorials are quite exceptional.

When teachers and students do make personal contact, relations are generally much more friendly and easy-going than in pre-1968 days: professors have become more relaxed and human, and many junior lecturers do now make efforts to get to know at least a few students personally. But there is virtually no sherry-with-the-dons social life of the British kind – and one reason is that teachers do not have this kind of chummy activity with each other. Even today, hierarchic dignity is still such that a full professor will seldom hobnob socially with a junior one. Faculties have little informal contact with each other, and even within a faculty there is rarely any kind of friendly social club. It is all a long way from the cosy Oxbridge college world where a history don's best friend may be a teacher of physics. At one modern German university, I met a British lecturer who said of his colleagues: 'If they rarely entertain each other, and if I certainly don't want to entertain *them*, it's because they're all such bores – *Fachidioten*, narrowly obsessed by their own little subjects and incapable of talking about anything else. An expert on 19th-century literature knows nothing of the 18th century, and vice versa. They lack all curiosity, and they can't cope with me at all, because I enjoy, and talk about, pop music, jazz and Rossini. This is how they've been trained – force-fed and blinkered. It's the system that makes them like this.' And of course this rubs off on students and adds to their loneliness and confusion. If one of them has a personal problem, he (or she) has no 'moral tutor' in *loco parentis* to whom he can turn – only the university welfare department, which may perhaps send him to a psychiatrist. 'The trouble with our German system,' said one sympathetic teacher, 'is that it has always assumed that students are mature adults who do not need looking after. But now the rising suicide rate has been forcing us to change.' Most professors remark that they find their students docile, passive, reticent, and doggedly studious. One positive sign is that they seem to be showing a renewed interest in their subjects for its own sake, and not merely as a means of getting a degree – or so several teachers told me. My British acquaintance again: 'I've been here twenty years and I've seen three distinct waves. The restless post-'68 generation were contemptuous of their studies, or affected to be. Then in the '70s the students were cramming-minded, anxious to get good grades and not very concerned with the subject. But today's vintage seem to have swung back to a greater interest. Maybe, paradoxically, it's because they're so despondent about job prospects that they feel they might at least enjoy academic study while it lasts. Ten years ago, when I laid on a seminar on modern English poetry that was outside the syllabus and not "useful", I had no takers; this year, I have twenty.'

Since the mid-1970s, political activism has died right down and the campuses have returned to a sullen calm, apart from the occasional flare-up in Frankfurt or Berlin where the Left has always been strong. Elsewhere, the few surviving extremist groups appear completely isolated, while the mass of students concentrate on their work, on private life and values, or on ecological causes which they pursue outside the university. 'It's all rather dull and disappointing,' said one professor in Göttingen: 'I think I really preferred the old restless, troublesome days, when the students in lectures asked difficult and interesting questions. Now they're so tame.' The students do not even wax militant over matters that effect their own position. For instance, in 1983 the Federal Government presented a bill to replace the usual grants with a system of loans, to be repaid later over 20 years when the graduates had started their careers (the motives for the scheme were partly Hayekian and money-saving, and partly to deter the less serious entrants and thus reduce numbers). The students of course were opposed, and they did manage to stage a few feeble demonstrations – but not enough to prevent the law from being passed, and applied. Yet, in Britain at the same period a similar move by the Thatcher Government collapsed under student hostility!

German students have also been showing curiously little concern to make use of their new role in university co-management, through their representation on the Senate and faculty boards. In elections for these bodies, their voting turnout rarely exceeds 10 to 20 per cent, and, as most *Lander* have a quorum system, this means that they cannot take up all their seats. In Baden-Württemberg there is no quorum, but student delegates have been boycotting Senates because, as one militant girl told me in Tübingen, 'the Senate does not even listen to our views, and we feel we have absolutely no influence. If we present motions on the kind of external political issues that interest us, such as Israeli aggression, we get ruled out of court. And there's no point in raising university issues, since everything is decided by the *Land*, not the Senate.' The more radical students, usually still the ones who get elected, are also angry that since 1976 the federal student union organisation, ASTA, has been barred from political activity as such and confined to social and welfare activities. Its leaders have retaliated by refusing to cooperate with the authorities. So at this level there is a kind of cold war, even though informal and personal relations remain quite friendly.

Apart from the activities of church associations and the occasional student orchestra or drama group, there is not much organised cultural or club activity in universities. One possible exception is Heidelberg, which does have a degree of Anglo-Saxon-style animation – but maybe that is due precisely to its strong leavening of American students! Elsewhere the pattern is much as described to me by one teacher at Tübingen: 'Students today look on the university just as a facility for getting a degree, and not as a community where they can have fun and find personal enrichment. They lead their active lives outside its framework.' For some of them this is a positive choice. They do not want to be cooped up in what they see as an artificial academic ghetto, cut off from the rest of society and its problems; so they may prefer for example to join local youth or arts centres, or citizen initiative groups, where they can mix with 'real' people like workers or immigrants. It is in many ways laudable. But in the eyes of an Oxford man like myself it does leave a depressing vacuum at the heart of what should be a rich university experience.

In the big cities such as Munich or Hamburg, most students are local and live at home; they keep to little circles of friends they have known since childhood and do not readily make new ones through the university. Only Berlin remains, as it always has been, a melting-pot attracting young people from all over Germany and abroad, and there the scene is more vibrant. In big cities, it is easy for students to be part of a real metropolitan world if they choose: but at the older universities in smaller towns they have less scope – as one professor at Göttingen remarked to me: 'Today they come mostly from petit-bourgeois families in the towns around; during the week they stick with a little group of pals of their own kind, they go home every weekend and have no real university life. Students in the old days had much more sense of fun.' The old tradition of migrating from one university to another has declined – partly because of economic reasons, partly because the *numerus clausus* computer tends to allocate people near to their home, and also because today's ordinary mass-student often fears being lost and lonely if he were to move to a strange part of Germany where he would know no one. So the universities have become more local. At Tübingen, the proportion of students coming from its Baden-Württemberg catchment area has increased from 40 to 80 per cent since 1965, with 15 per cent from the rest of Germany and 5 per cent foreigners – and one professor remarked sadly, 'Most of them today are so unadventurous, so narrow in their horizons. Tübingen used to be the focus for some of Europe's greatest scholars. Today it's provincial.'

Repeatedly in Germany I have been struck by the contrasts between the dispirited, antiquated ambience of the universities and the dynamism and confidence not only of economic life but of so much of local government and the public services. Not only is the malaise doing some practical harm to the German economy (as Genscher and others have warned), but in the long run it might be damaging to the morale of society as a whole, as generations of graduates are soured by their university experiences. Possibly this danger can be exaggerated, for young people the world over habitually show astonishing resilience, and most of them seem able to surmount the handicaps of a poor education – as France and Italy have shown in recent decades. In those two thriving countries, the educational crisis is if anything worse than in Germany: but all that this proves is that western Europe as a whole has not yet worked out what the purpose of its universities should be in today's world. In Germany, serious reforms will have to come: but as one paediatric professor remarked, 'As we've seen with the crisis in the medical schools, the reforms always limp along piecemeal about ten years or more behind the needs.' Maybe the much-praised German federal system is in this respect a handicap, for the *Länder* never find it easy to achieve a common policy and the *Bund* has only limited powers of imposing its own; on the other hand, centralised France has hardly fared any better with the problems. Clearly some more effective means of controlling student numbers will have to be found. And probably the best hope of halting the decline in standards will lie with the spread of the new small private universities. These, if they became numerous enough, could break the sterile monopoly of the *Länder* in higher education and bring in at last a real spirit of competition and feeling for excellence. After all, the healthy competition between Catholic and Protestant churches has worked wonders for the liveliness of Christianity in Germany today – as we shall now see.

Catholics and Protestants: a new amity, but new internal conflicts

On the face of it, West Germany appears to have been slowly becoming de-Christianised, like so much of the Western world: since 1950, regular church attendance has declined from some 55 to 33 per cent among the Catholic population, and from 20 to less than 10 per cent among Protestants. But such figures hardly give the full picture, at a time when many people have come to practise their religion outside the framework of church buildings. What I find more remarkable is that the Catholic and Protestant Churches do still play so lively and vital a role in the life of Germany, certainly more than in either Britain or France, or many other countries. But how far this is for strictly moral and spiritual reasons, rather than more secular ones, remains to be examined.

The overriding secular factor is that the Churches in Germany are very rich. They derive enormous incomes from voluntary taxes levied on over 90 per cent of Germans, and they devote much of this money to running a vast array of schools, hospitals, charities and other welfare bodies. This gives them a much stronger base in society, and a bigger voice in public affairs, than they might have if they were poor like the Catholic Church in France. Of course they have a spiritual role too. And they exert a curious influence in German politics, ranging from the conservative to the radical. On the more conservative side, this can be seen for instance in the links between the Catholic Church and the ruling CSU party in Bavaria. At the other end of the spectrum, the powerful progressive element among Protestants has actively promoted a number of radical causes – priests in cassocks can often be seen at CND rallies.

Have the Churches become *too* concerned with secular issues? The question is often asked. And this is just one of many subjects of lively debate and conflict that spill out into a wider public discussion, in the Press and on television: what the Churches think and do is often front-page news. Among a people as serious and self-questioning as the Germans, maybe it is not surprising that the moral issues raised by the Churches should find so wide an echo, or that young people should be turning back to religion in some form. I noticed this at the Protestants' Kirchentag in Düsseldorf in 1985, a vast biennial five-day rally that drew some 200,000 people from all over Germany, most of them young, to sing and pray together, and to debate *Angst*, the bomb, and other issues. I have been impressed also by the vitality of oecumenical links today in parishes throughout Germany: the long-lasting rift provoked by Luther's Reformation seems to have healed at last, and the two confessions are now living together in an active harmony that extends even to their neat numerical balance, for Germany today has almost exactly as many Protestants (26.5 million) as Catholics (26.7 million).

The prestige of the Churches today may seem surprising in view of their dubious role during the Nazi period; but in fact that débâcle enabled them afterwards to renovate their image. In the 1920s, and earlier, both Churches had been profoundly conservative and deferential to established power, and this hardly fitted them for the task of opposing Nazism. The Catholics' Centre Party even helped to vote Hitler to power in the Reichstag in 1933, and then stood helpless when he signed his Concordat with the Vatican. As for the Protestants, whose tradition of support for the State stemmed direct from Luther's day, they at first did nothing to counter the new regime. Then the Nazis made efforts to win control of the Protestant Churches and to unite them in a new German Christian movement, liberated from its Jewish origins: but this encountered such opposition from a number of brave pastors, led by the young Martin Niemöller, that Hitler soon dropped the scheme. After this, however, none of the official Church organisations, Protestant or Catholic, showed any boldness in speaking out against the persecution of the Jews, the shackles on the Press, the political imprisonments, or other Nazi evils.

It was left to a few courageous individuals to salvage what they could of the Churches' honour. Some priests and pastors went into underground resistance, or they took the courageous step of denouncing the regime from their pulpits, and paid for it with their lives or by imprisonment – like Pastor Niemöller, who was in a concentration camp from 1938 to 1945, and Dietrich Bonhoeffer who died in one. This movement was wide enough for the Churches after 1945, hurriedly purged of their 'collaborationist' bishops, to re-emerge with some credibility as bodies that were not totally tainted with Nazism, and to plan a new start. Many Christian leaders publicly expressed their genuine guilt at not having resisted more actively. And, in that anguished *Stunde Null* period of hardship and desolation, millions of Germans turned back to Christianity as the sole meaning in life: the churches (such as were still standing, amid the ruins) were packed every Sunday. The Churches now began to plot a new course that would make them less passively subservient to the state and more able to influence it independently and to play their part in building a new Germany. It was in this spirit that both Churches joined to support the creation of the Christian Democratic Union, which then became the ruling party of Germany, under Adenauer, a convinced Catholic. Catholics have always wielded more influence than Protestants within the CDU, and even more so in the Bavarian CSU. The SPD on the other hand (while formally a lay party) is much closer to Protestantism. Helmut Schmidt for example is an active Lutheran. Today the Churches enjoy a rather special juridical status. They are not established within the State to the same degree as the Church of England: but they are certainly not *dis*established like the Catholic Church in France. Their rights and status are guaranteed under the Constitution and by separate concordats, and they have senior representatives in Bonn to protect their interests. The State pays towards the salaries of the clergy. In all State schools, religion is taught in separate confessional classes as part of the curriculum (though there are no religious services as in Britain). And the State universities contain faculties of theology where many future clergy are trained. It is a privileged situation, free of the petty feuding over *la laicité* that still bedevils education in France.

The major feature of this entente is the right granted by the State for the Churches to derive tax from their members. This system is rare in Europe, though it does exist in a different form in Scandinavia. In Germany, it dates from the 19th century, when the Churches were allowed this privilege in return for being dispossessed of some of their lands. Today the tax is collected by State revenue offices on behalf of the Churches. Amounting to some 5 billion DM a year for the Catholic Church and a roughly similar sum for the Protestants, it equals about 8.5 to 9 per cent of an individual's income tax and is paid alike by churchgoers and non-churchgoers. This *Kirchensteuer* makes the Churches wealthy – as is easy to observe. Senior prelates have comfortable modernised offices and drive around in large Mercedes; ordinary parish priests live rather well; the churches themselves, and the imposing new church social centres, are noticeably better maintained than in Britain or France. Even in areas that were not bombed, a remarkable proportion of German churches are new: and new ones are constantly being built.

Not that the Churches spend the tax just on their own affairs. They use a large slice of it to run kindergartens, old people's homes, centres for the handicapped, hospitals, schools, and so forth, and they see this as a part of their social duty. Their hospitals are often more popular than the *Land-* or city-run ones, for they tend to be cheaper and more efficient, since the nuns who work them are on the whole more dedicated and hard-working than medical staff in the public sector. The Churches also spend part of the *Kirchensteuer* on helping their colleagues in the GDR (see p. 343), and part of it on massive aid to the Third World (such as famine relief in Ethiopia) where the German record is much the best in Europe. At one Catholic church in a small Württemberg town, I found the vestry piled high with parcels about to be sent to Africa. 'We still feel so grateful, to the Americans in particular, for their generous aid relief to the Germans just after the war, that we now have a special obligation to help others in our turn,' I was told by the head of the Protestants' *Brot für die Welt* (Bread for the World) organisation.

Well over 90 per cent of Germans are still registered as tax-paying members of their Churches, even though most of them no longer practise their religion. To cease paying the tax, you must formally leave the Church by going to sign a declaration in the *Rathaus* – and few people are willing to take this step despite the money it would save. Probably they are held back by vague feelings of guilt, loyalty and tradition, or by the thought that they might need the Church again one day. In particular, most Germans want a Christian burial and officially a priest is not allowed to provide this for a non-member (though a few can usually be found who are prepared to bend the rules for a family they know and like). Many parents also feel that they should stay in their Church for the sake of the children – one Protestant doctor in Munich summed up a fairly general view: 'My wife and I are not churchgoers, but what right have we to deprive our kids of the benefits they may later find in the Church? It's much easier for them to opt out later, if they want, than to opt in to something they have never known. What's more, I think the Churches do a very useful job with their welfare work. Their competition keeps the public welfare bodies on their toes. If they stopped, the State would have to take the work over, and we'd be paying the same tax in another way.' Another factor, in the more devoutly church-going areas, is that to opt out can carry a social stigma. Under a new Secrecy Act, the Rathaus is legally forbidden to divulge that a member has left the Church. But an employer knows, for the tax deduction will appear on the individual's PAYE slip, and so the news can leak out. Some employers might even take reprisals: in Bavaria, where the Education Minister is a militant Catholic, there have been cases of teachers in State schools being refused promotion if they leave their Church, and this has even deterred a number of them from doing so. (Shades of trying to leave the Communist Party in the GDR?)

Even so, the steady trickle of Germans who go to sign off at the *Rathaus* has been increasing recently, to reach a level of some 170,000 a year: this is largely due to economic factors, in a time of high unemployment. A few others leave because they can no longer stomach their Church's political stance: especially this has been true of the Leftward Protestant trends, which caused the late Axel Springer, right-wing Press tycoon and devout old-style Christian, to leave the Lutherans and switch to some small free church group. Many other people, while accepting to remain members, think that the level of tax should be reduced: recent proposals to cut it by 10 per cent won a very favourable response but have not yet been applied. As for the Church leaders themselves, in the post-war years some of them expressed dislike of the *Kirchensteuer* system because they felt it made them too dependent on the State: but today such complaints are rarely heard. 'The tax enables us to play a full part in a prosperous society,' one Protestant bishop told me; 'if we had to rely on voluntary gifts, or on our revenue from landed property, we could not do our job adequately.' Catholic leaders share this view.

*   *   *

This is one of the many questions on which the Churches today see broadly eye to eye. Indeed, the growth of a tolerant oecumenicism has been one of the major success-stories of post-war German society. It is quite an achievement in a land with so tragic a history, where the Reformation and then the Thirty Years' War split the nation into two warring halves, racked by a religious bitterness and intolerance which has deeply marked the German character and from which it has only recently freed itself. Even as late as the 1950s there were still many tensions and prejudices to be found, such as a wide-spread hostility to mixed marriages, and some bizarre barriers: in some villages, separate bakeries for Catholics and Protestants; in some schools, separate bicycle-racks for pupils of the two confessions. However, a post-war virus of change was steadily at work, induced not only by the new oecumenical spirit in the world but by population shifts within Germany. Until 1945, its Catholic and Protestant areas had mostly been separate from each other, and this bred an intolerance based on prejudice and sheer ignorance: a Catholic breathing fire and damnation against Protestants, or vice versa, had very often hardly met one in his life. In pre-war days, the territory that is now West Germany was two-thirds Catholic, while most Protestants were in the east. Then, when Germany was split in two and the refugees arrived in their millions, a surprising number of Protestants opted to settle in Catholic areas (e.g. Bavaria), while many Catholics from regions such as Silesia moved into the mainly Protestant districts, such as Stuttgart. So the two populations became much more jumbled up, and each found the other to be not so bad after all. This was one factor in the new tolerance: others were the painful lessons learned from Nazism and the war, and the general desire to build a better, more democratic Germany.

Today in the 1980s, on visits to urban and rural parishes all around the country, I failed to discover much trace of tension or bigotry, save in a few corners of north Germany where the Reformed (as opposed to Lutheran) Church is still somewhat anti-papist. Elsewhere I found co-existence and even cooperation. Of course oecumenicism still has its limits: but Germany today is full of examples of partnership at local level – joint prayer and discussion meetings, joint welfare activities, the lending of churches, and even a few joint services. In many parishes, priest and pastor are close friends. And mixed marriages, once so rare and so frowned on, now account for as many as 47 per cent of all church weddings. 'It's marvellous,' said a Protestant leader in Munich, Kirchenrat Paul Rieger; 'this peaceful competition between two Churches of equal influence is extremely fruitful. It keeps both of us on our toes, and it offers the faithful a real choice' (a nice consumerist touch, I felt) 'between Catholic authority and ritual and Protestant openness and flexibility.'

This is the situation at ordinary parish level. Between the senior hierarchies, however, oecumenical relations have become a little less warm in recent years, notably since the election of Pope John Paul II. His visit in 1980, the first made to Germany by any Pope for nearly 200 years, was the occasion for some tactless public criticism of the Lutheran tradition by one or two Catholic leaders. And since then a new Catholic Archbishop in Munich has been dissuading his parish priests from consorting too closely with their Protestant colleagues. Even so, a certain amount of oecumenical work does go on discreetly at a high level. The Churches are even prepared to campaign jointly on certain issues – for instance, to protect the human rights of Muslim immigrant workers.

The two confessions have very different histories in Germany. The Reformation reduced the Catholics to a mere one-fifth of the population, and since then the predominant culture of the country has been Protestant; its great poets and philosophers have come mainly from that background. The Prussian Kaisers were Protestant, as were most of the ruling princes (but not the Wittelsbachs in Bavaria), while Catholicism was strongest among poorer people and peasants. Bismarck even tried to suppress the Catholics. So inevitably the Catholic Church has long been on the defensive in Germany, and is only now emerging from this. Today it remains much more preoccupied than the Protestant Churches with its own internal problems of doctrine, discipline and liturgy. It was heavily shaken in the 1970s by the affair of Hans Küng, the Swiss theologian at Tübingen University who wrote books questioning the infallibility of the Pope and other dogmas, and was finally dismissed from his sacred offices by the Vatican. At the same time, the Church in Germany as elsewhere has been struggling to come to terms with changing attitudes to abortion (see p. 170) and to the celibacy of priests. The maintenance of the celibacy rule has contributed to the steady decline in recruitment to the clergy, with the result that the average age of priests is now over 55, and in many dioceses one priest has to look after two or three churches. This crisis is less serious than in France, but it is growing. Many priests who wanted to marry have now abandoned holy orders, while others have been permitted to resolve their private problems in an elegantly hypocritical manner – at Tübingen University, I was told that eight of the ten priests teaching at the faculty of theology co-habit openly with their common-law wives, and they are accepted in society as couples; the Church turns a blind eye. But, if they were to commit the monstrosity of legalising their liaison, they would have to give up their priesthood and their jobs. It is a charmingly Alice-through-the-looking-glass inversion of society's traditional attitude to married versus non-married couples. Of course, in a Bavarian village a priest would not be able to behave so brazenly: but Tübingen is more sophisticated.

In many Catholic parishes, tensions over moral issues today frequently exist between older traditionalist Christians and younger ones who are more critical of the Church's official teaching and more politically and socially involved. Yet the Church as a whole remains unified and disciplined and the level of attendance at Mass is fairly high, ranging from some 15 per cent in the big cities to 60 per cent or more in parts of Bavaria. In these smaller towns and villages, the Church is still the dominant local force, and regular appearance at Mass is necessary for social acceptance. Many rural parishes are still deeply conservative, but newer suburban one less so – in the Munich commuter suburb of Baldham, I found a big bright modern church animated by a young priest who conducted his Sunday morning service in a breezy get-together style, using a mike to chat up members of the congregation like a compère in a TV talk-show.

In contrast to the Catholics, the Protestants have a low level of church-going (about 9 per cent, falling to 5 per cent in the cities) but far fewer problems of recruitment of clergy: there are twice as many good candidates as posts to be filled. Another important difference is that the Protestant Churches are a loose federation of semi-autonomous regional bodies where secular leaders play as influential a role as ecclesiastical ones. This federation, the *Evangelische Kirche in Deutschland* (EKD), is an alliance of 17 *Land* churches, of three main kinds: seven Lutheran (strongest in the south and around Hanover); two Reformed (in the north-west); and eight United (in Berlin and the Rhine regions), formed of mergers between Reformed and Lutheran groups. These Churches are heirs to two traditions, Lutheran and Pietist. Just as Lutheranism began as a revolt against the corruption and worldliness of Rome, so the Pietist movement first developed in the later 17th century as a reaction to the Lutheran Churches which by then had become deeply conservative and wedded to the established political order. The Pietists, whose influence is still alive today in parts of north Germany and Swabia, laid their emphasis on the individual's spiritual life, on prayer and moral renewal, and on parish welfare activity, without any regard for politics. It was in many ways an austere and puritanical faith – but not without its inner warmth. Even today, the Germans' concern for the interior life of feeling and for the close emotional bonds of family and friendship, the value they set on celebrating birthdays and feast days and on giving little presents as tokens of affection, to a degree that some foreigners may find sentimental – all this can be related to the Pietist tradition.

It is possible also to trace some link between these earlier German anti-materialist reform movements, Lutheran and Pietist, and today's post-war radical Leftist trends among Protestants – but only in the wider sense of 'protestantism', for today's Christian protesters

[233]

are not exactly Lutheran in spirit. Since the war, a number of Protestant leaders and their followers have consistently sought to influence politics in a Leftist direction – with greater or lesser success. Pastor Niemöller in the 1950s argued in vain against German rearmament and entry into NATO. But then in the 1960s the Protestant Churches did play a crucial role in preparing the ground for Brandt's *Ostpolitik*, by urging reconciliation with Poland and a gentler attitude to the GDR. A few Church leaders also supported the student Left during the 1968 period, and even spoke up for justice for the Baader-Meinhof terrorists.

More recently, the peace movement (see p. 449) has become the major focus of attention. While the Catholic Church still officially tolerates the nuclear deterrent as the lesser of evils, the EKD has taken no formal stance on the matter, for its members are deeply divided. Many priests and lay readers, and some bishops too, have spoken out publicly against American missile bases in Germany, and in a few cases priests in cassocks have scuffled with the police at peace rallies. Some pastors urge the young men in their parish not to do their military service with the *Bundeswehr*; and many radical Protestants argue that it is the moral duty of the Church to remain neutral in the East/West ideological struggle, for Communism with its stress on brotherhood is just as near to Christianity as Western capitalism.

Needless to say, all of this has led to mighty arguments within the Church, and some bitterness. Older conservative Protestants have sometimes walked out of church services when radical pastors, involving the Sermon on the Mount, have preached against the bomb from the pulpit. And, in Hamburg, the middle-of-the-road Bishop Krusche explained to me his dilemma: 'Some of my young clergy preach that it is a Christian's duty to refuse to serve with the *Bundeswehr*. I say to them, no, you can give private advice of this kind, as a friend, but you should not involve the Church as such. It's the same with priests who go in their cassocks to peace demos. We say to them: go along if you like, but not in a cassock, for that gives the public the false impression that the Church officially is against the bomb. A lot of priests disobey us on this – but what can we do? Unlike the Catholics, the Protestant Churches today are so decentralised and liberal that anyone can do what he likes.' Down in Pietist Swabia, I heard a very different slant on this issue from Erhard Eppler, a former chairman of the EKD, former SPD minister in Bonn, and the best-known lay Protestant leader in the peace movement: 'The split in our Church today is very severe. Old-style Pietism is rising up again, in a new ultra-conservative guise. These Pietists seem to be just as concerned as in the old days to steer Christianity away from politics and secular issues – and so they denounce the peace movement. But, for us, Christianity and disarmament are inseparable. It's a fundamental divergence.'

It is an ironical situation. The old pre-war conflicts *between* Catholics and Protestants have now been replaced by others almost as sharp *within* each of the Churches – Catholics against Catholics over abortion, Protestants against Protestants over the bomb, and so on.

Some idea of the mood of liberal German Protestantism today can be gained from a visit to the famous *Evangelische Kirchentag*, a five-day event held every two years. This is not an official synod but a big popular rally of 200,000 or so people, organised mainly by lay leaders, and in its sheer size it is unique among Protestant gatherings in Europe: the pilgrimages to Taizé, in Burgundy, may be more fervent, but they are much smaller. I attended the 1985 *Kirchentag* held in June in the decidedly uncharismatic setting of the Düsseldorf trade exhibition centre. Its vast halls, normally full of tidy short-haired salesmen parading the latest consumer products, were this time given over to untidy long-haired radicals in charge of stalls denouncing consumerism, or promoting such causes as homosexuals' rights, help for battered wives or support for Nicaragua. There was hardly a cassock or dog-collar in sight; the priests were in mufti, and the only 'uniform' was the purple scarf of the peace movement, worn by most of the younger pilgrims. The scarves were all over town too, as the rally spilled out unofficially into the heart of this fearful city of Mammon, whose piazzas and terraces in the shadow of the big banks were filled incongruously with little groups of hymn-singers, meditators, mimes and buskers.

Each day at the *Kirchentag* one could choose from scores of bible meetings, prayer meetings, concerts, cabarets, hymn-singing sessions and talk-ins. Yet it was all curiously low-key and earnest, rather than animated, lacking either the pageant of Catholic ritual or the emotional revivalist fervour that would surely mark any such rally in the United States. A group of swaying white-robed nuns, chanting their love for Jesus, struck a rare note of true spiritual joy. By contrast, much the biggest attendances were for the lengthy talk-in sessions on serious lay topics, some of them addressed by senior politicians including President von Weizsäcker and Johannes Rau of the SPD. Here young people in their thousands sat uncomfortably on the floor for up to three hours, to hear debates on unemployment, disarmament, Third World aid, East–West relations, and so on. After one session, on 'Why are the Germans so full of *Angst*?', we were split up into little groups of eight to discuss with strangers our own private *Angst* problems, and then our *rapporteurs* spoke from the floor. One girl announced solemnly, 'What gives me *Angst* is worrying about whether or not I ought to feel *Angst*.' No one laughed. To an outsider, the session seemed close to a self-parody of the German talent for being unblinkingly serious.

The radical bias and secular preoccupations of the *Kirchentag* have so annoyed the more conservative Protestants than in 1985 they staged a boycott and held their own rival assembly in Stuttgart, dedicated to what they saw as the true spiritual values. So this is one of today's major talking-points: is radical involvement compatible with true religious faith? – is there not a danger, amid all the discussions on nuclear missiles and unemployment, ecology and the position of homosexuals, that real devotional questions and the love of God might be overlooked? Many, such as Eppler, believe that the two go hand-in-hand: but many others, and not only the diehard Pietists, are worried that young Christians' concern with secular rather than spiritual matters may be going too far. Probably this is a question that only the individual conscience can answer. Some not very religious people may be using the Church as a forum for social attention: others, as they parade their anti-nuke placards, may be genuinely fired by the mystical love of Christ. Who can tell? Certainly it would be wrong to deduce that religious interest as a whole is declining in Germany: after a trough in the 1950s and 1960s, all the signs point to a modest revival in the past few years, alike among Catholics and Protestants. The churches may have been emptying for their formal services of worship, but the faithful have been turning to other forms of religious expression – not only to secular activism, but to all kinds of informal prayer meetings, Bible readings, charismatic groups and the like; 'The best Christians today are often not churchgoers,' said one Protestant leader. When Allensbach surveys have put the question 'Do you think religion can provide an answer to most of the problems of our day?', the proportion answering 'yes' rose from 29 to 33 per cent between 1975 and 1980, while those thinking religion 'too outmoded and out-of-date' fell from 52 to 48 per cent. This supports the general impression of nearly all observers that the Germans today, and especially the young have been turning towards Christianity in an age of uncertainty.

5

TURKS AND OTHER 'GUESTS': A PAINFUL PATH TOWARDS ACCEPTANCE

You can see them in their hundreds at the weekends in the vast halls of the German railway termini, which they take over as informal meeting-places and endow with the ambience of some Mediterranean town square. Here shops and stalls sell them kebabs and pizzas, or their national newspapers such as *Hurriyet* and *El Pais*, while the trains coming and going from Istanbul, Athens or Naples provide nostalgic hints of home. Or you notice them in the streets of the poorer quarters, outside cafés and groceries with strange names and spicy smells – spare dark-eyed Sicilians, moustachioed Montenegrins, and dumpy Anatolian peasant women in headscarves. Including their families, these foreign workers total well over 4 million: about one-third are Turkish, with Italians, Yugoslavs, Greeks and Iberians as the next most numerous. They were invited so pressingly to Germany during the years of fast economic growth, when labour was in short supply: but, though some have now been here for decades, few have integrated into German society or have felt encouraged to do so. Today, in a time of high unemployment, they have become something of an embarrassment – especially the Turks, whose culture, life-style and religion are so different. They live in run-down housing that the Germans don't want, their children swell the classes of German schools, and they smart under the resentments they arouse. It is all quite a problem. As the liberal writer Max Frisch has put it, 'We called for a labour force but we got human beings.'

Much has been written about the plight of the immigrant workers in Europe, especially in West Germany. Sometimes the newspapers carry reports of Turks committing suicide in desperation; or the slogans aerosolled on walls, *'Türken raus!'* (Turks out), bring echoes of the *'Juden raus!'* of the 1930s. So, when I myself began to explore this subject, I feared the worst. However, after much research in the main cities and talks with Turks, Germans and others, I reached the conclusion that although of course the problem exists it has tended to be exaggerated. For there is a positive side to the picture. First, one comes across countless examples of personal friendships and good neighbourly relations, while innumerable German organisations and individuals of all kinds devote their time generously to helping the immigrants. Secondly, there is much less violence or open conflict than in a country such as Britain with a higher degree of integration; the average German's attitude is one of polite indifference, or grumbling contempt, rather than active hostility. But of course the foreigners chafe at their treatment by a society that takes their labour but does not make them feel accepted – in a Germany that, unlike the United States or the ex-colonial powers, has virtually no experience of absorbing alien cultures. And this complex problem of the *Gastarbeiter* (guest workers) – as they have long been called unofficially, with what today seems a touch of irony – has come to trouble the conscience of the more liberal Germans. Does it not cast a shadow over the new Germany's bright ideals of 'Europeanism' and 'internationalism'? – or even raise basic questions about just how kind and tolerant this new German society is?

In the first years after the war, the arrival from the east of some 14 million refugees, nearly all of them German, provided the reborn economy with the extra labour it needed. But by the later 1950s this supply had become inadequate (in 1961 there were some 500,000 unfilled job vacancies): so the Federal Government began to look abroad, to the poorer countries of southern Europe. And they poured in very readily, these Italians, Yugoslavs and others: most of them at that time were single men without their families, attracted by the opportunities to learn some skills and above all to earn far higher wages than was possible back home, and thus buy a house or land or start a business. The governments of the 'donor' countries happily supported the emigration too, for it eased their own unemployment, it brought in foreign currency, and it provided free training for workers who in modern factories picked up techniques that their homelands could never have given them. Therefore several nations, including Turkey in 1961, signed treaties allowing Germany to set up recruiting offices in their cities for use by German firms. The arrangement suited all sides. Some *Gastarbeiter* were even welcomed with bouquets at railway stations by grateful mayors; the millionth to arrive officially, a Portuguese, in 1964, was fêted as a hero by the German media and given a motorbike as a present. Those were the days . . .

Around 1970, German industry was making another leap forward, and even more immigrants were needed. But by now the Spanish and Italian economies had so far improved that the supplies from those quarters were drying up, and many Spaniards and Italians were returning home. So the Bonn Government turned to the best other source available: the Turks, already present in modest numbers. Whereas many of the south European workers were by now semi-skilled or even skilled, the Turks were most of them poor peasants from Anatolia; and they have always proved quite ready to take on the more menial jobs – in the mines, on building sites, as sweepers and refuse-collectors – that the Germans spurn. They arrived intending to remain just a few years, but most have stayed on far longer – 'finding German money sweeter than Turkish honey' (as one Turk said to me), and often deterred by the acrid taste of that honey in a Turkey of high unemployment, great poverty and political severity. And yet, like most other *Gastarbeiter*, they have not really put down roots in Germany. All foreign workers legally employed are entitled to the same pay as Germans; they have full welfare and social rights and most employers treat them fairly. But hardly any have even applied for German citizenship. They retain their ties with home and their dream of returning to live there one day, and so in Germany they remain in a kind of limbo between two cultures. There is little of an American-style 'melting-pot'.

Ever since the first signs of world recession at the end of 1973, the Government has imposed a virtual ban on new recruitment from outside the EEC. But this has had a paradoxical effect. Knowing that they might lose their work permits if they left Germany for more than three months, many hitherto itinerant *Gastarbeiter* simply decided to settle there and to get their wives and children to join them; the Turks in particular, so family-minded, were also unhappy at remaining as single men in an alien Christian culture so far from home. So the Turkish families have blossomed and bred: despite the ban, the overall Turkish population rose from 1,028,000 in 1974 to 1,581,000 in 1982. Other figures are equally striking: whereas the ban did succeed in reducing the numbers of active foreign workers from 2.6 million in 1973 to 1.9 million a decade later, the overall foreign population continued to rise in this period, from 4.0 to 4.6 million (it has since been dropping slightly, to about 4.3 million in 1985). Family dependents today account for 60 per cent of the total, whereas in the 1960s some 90 per cent of the workers were single men – living in the sad dormitories of cramped hostels and chasing German girls (or at least, the Italians did; the Turks, whatever their other 'faults' in German eyes, are much less lecherous). Today (1985 figures) the Turks number 1,425,000, while the other main communities are the Yugoslavs (600,000), Italians (545,000), Greeks (287,000), Spanish (158,000) and Portuguese (83,000), with some 200,000 others also in the *Gastarbeiter* category (such as the Moroccan in Fassbinder's *Fear Eats the Soul*, or redundant Glasgow shipyard workers). Today the general German view, alike governmental and popular, is that there are too many of these foreigners for the good either of society or of the economy. And so, with unemployment rising, resentment has been growing – ironically, just at a time when integration, especially of the non-Turks, has finally been making some progress.

One day, in the little Swabian town of Horb, I enjoyed a lunch of taramasalata and moussaka, washed down with retsina, in a big, stylish restaurant adorned with blown-up photographs of Greece, owned and run by a dapper and self-confident 35-year-old born in Salonika. His wife did the cooking, helped out by young *Gastarbeiter* from Izmir, Sarajevo and Liverpool. He said: 'Ninety per cent of my guests are German. I have no problems here, I've always got on well with the Germans and I learned good German here at school. Life is far easier for me than it was for my father when he arrived here from Greece as a manual worker, 25 years ago, speaking no German. Yes, we Greeks *are* integrating slowly, and we're far better liked than those illiterate Turks, who don't bother to pick up the language or even to learn the rules of living here. But I still want to live in Greece again one day. It's still my home.' This, with its touch of Hellenic turkophobia thrown in, is a not untypical experience. The Greeks, Yugoslavs and others are still rather socially separate, but they have finally won a certain acceptance and respect. A great many Germans go on holiday to their countries and to Spain and Italy: thus they discover at first hand that these are civilised European societies, they often acquire a smattering of the language too (especially Italian), and they enjoy the cuisine and folklore.

Quite a few of the immigrants are middle-class educated people, or they have moved into that category (like the Greek in Horb), and quite often they open shops, restaurants (see p. 184) or other businesses. They have added greatly to Germany's cultural variety. At Hechingen, a small town not far from Horb, a colony of Italians arrived in the 1950s and soon took over the local sheep and cattle trade that used to be in Jewish hands: they made money, and as well as running the best boutiques and eating-places in town they have now acquired and beautifully restored a number of lovely old half-timbered houses damaged in the war. All in all, a triumphant neo-colonisation in the footsteps of their Roman forebears who settled in the area 2,000 years previously.

Of all these nationalities, Yugoslavs tend to be the best liked, and are much appreciated by employers for their intelligence, politeness and hard work. Spaniards are popular too; but there is still some prejudice against south Italians, thought of as feckless and noisy. In one suburb, the Germans complained so much of *bambini* shouting in the playground that the police arrived with decibel measures. Working-class *Gastarbeiter* are seldom invited socially into German homes, and for their leisure they still stick to their own communities – as witness the Greek pub I visited in a poor quarter of Stuttgart, all bouzouki music and sirtaki-dancing, where old peasant grannies in black sat along one wall and I was the only non-Greek present. In this as in other suburbs, the Greeks have their own shops and cafés, bakeries and laundries. For their welfare problems, throughout Germany the Greeks are helped by a German Protestant organisation, federally subsidised, while Caritas, an international Catholic welfare body, takes care of the Spanish and Italians. Ever since the inception of the EEC's free labour market, the Italians have been at liberty to live and seek work in Germany much as they please: but this has not led to any flood, for the reasons I gave earlier. The Greeks, who joined the EEC in 1980, have since then been acquiring a similar freedom during a seven-year transitional period; and since January 1986 the same has begun to be true of Spaniards and Portuguese too. Again, no flood is expected. So these nationalities are not regarded as posing any great threat – and when a German today says, 'I hate *Gastarbeiter*', he usually means, 'I hate Turks'. Some 80 per cent of all Turks in EEC countries are in Germany.

If they were all from the Istanbul middle classes, there would be much less of a problem. But they have tended to come from rural Anatolia, often illiterate; and in so many ways they are so 'different' that inevitably the mutual culture shock has been far greater than in the case of the European immigrants. Reacting with blind prejudice rather than trying to understand, many ordinary Germans fear and despise the Turks for their 'alien' Muslim religion, their seclusion of their womenfolk, their teeming kids, their 'dirt' and 'noise', their garlicky breath and cooking smells (not necessarily worse than those of Greeks or Sicilians) and the more bizarre of their household practices. I heard tales of sheep and goats kept tethered on tenement landings; and in one extreme case a peasant family horrified their Berlin landlord by taking three sheep up to their flat, slaughtering them in the living-room for a festival and then stuffing the remains down the toilet. Usually it is the newly-arrived ones who have behaved like this: after a while they learn to 'adapt', so today such incidents are much more rare.

It is not easy to draw a fair and balanced picture, for much of Turkish peasant custom and behaviour (concerning more serious matters than sheep-ritual) does seem genuinely shocking to the very same European liberals who plead for kinder treatment of Turks – just as it does to radical modern Turks themselves, such as the film-maker Yilmar Güney who died in exile in France 1985: his masterpiece *Yol* gave a terrifying portrait of the feudal cruelty of a rural society where a man can torture his adulterous wife to death. In a less harsh form, such patriarchal severity can sometimes manifest itself in Germany too, where a kindly German teacher may well be horrified when a Turkish boy appears in class, pulls up his shirt to display the weals and bruises on his back, and says, 'Look what my father did to me. He was angry that you gave me such low marks – so it's *your* fault!' One German told me that he came across a Turk beating up his ten-year-old son in a park. When he tried to intercede, the Turk took the boy up to his flat nearby, opened the window and went on beating him in full view, calling out, 'You can't stop me exercising my parental duty in my own home!' Many Turks will indeed claim that this paternal discipline is a wise and just system: they point to the solidarity and security of Turkish family life, where the very old are warmly cared for, and they compare this with 'heartless' European society with its drugs, promiscuity, broken homes, dangerous freedom for young girls, and grannies left lonely in old people's homes . . . it all leaves German liberals in quite a dilemma. On the one hand, they plead with their fellow-citizens to show more sympathy and humanity towards the Turks in their midst. On the other, they hope fervently that Turkey's own society will evolve and modernise, and that German education and standards (for all their shortcomings) may have some beneficial influence on Turks living here.

Like the Blacks in Britain and America, the Turks in Germany have grouped themselves into some of the seedier parts of inner cities. These get dubbed 'ghettoes' by the media: but the term is hardly accurate, for generally the population remains mixed, including a few poorer Germans – even though most Germans do move out when Turks begin to settle in force in a tenement. Here they do their best to recreate their home ambience. They run shops selling Turkish books and video-cassettes, as well as Turkish rugs, strong dark coffee, lentils and spices; oriental music strains out from café doorways in the dark, slummy streets. The Turks cling to Islam and traditional ways, often converting upper shop-floors into little *ad hoc* mosques which serve also as Koranic schools for their numerous children (their high birth-rate, three times the German average, is one cause of German alarm). By law the kids must also attend German state schools all morning, boys and girls together in class (oh, Allah!) – and so they are caught in quite a culture conflict, often speaking neither language well. Hence they tend to be under-achievers at school, and few go on to *Gymnasium*. When they do secure apprenticeships, they usually do well at them: but their youth unemployment rate is far above the average and this leads to frustration and delinquency – as with young Blacks in Britain. Certainly the *Land* education authorities have been making efforts to help the children, including the training and paying for hundreds of Turks to be teachers in state schools (320 in Berlin alone), so that some classes are held in both languages. But this has not worked out easily, owing to the great differences between the Turkish and German school systems. In most areas, the Turkish pupils go into the ordinary German classes, where in some cases they account for well over half the numbers. This tends to slow down the others – and it can lead to tensions with German parents, even though between the children themselves there are seldom conflicts. At a *Hauptschule* in Karlsruhe, a most sympathetic German Jewish woman teacher told me: 'The Turks in my class very seldom get bullied or teased. The boys are high-spirited, naughty, charming – and not keen on work. The girls are terribly pretty, very intelligent, but quiet and shy: the only problem is that the German kids don't like sitting next to them because, to be honest, they do smell. The fourteen-year-olds explain to me: "We're not allowed to bath more than once a week, the Koran says it's immodest for girls to be naked." A pity – it's just the kind of silly thing that makes these silly cleanliness-obsessed German parents so racist.'

But I must again stress that many Germans of all kinds do make great efforts to help the Turks and other immigrants. Not only do the Churches run welfare centres and kindergartens, but in 1984 they successfully campaigned to kill a callous project by Kohl's hard-line Interior Minister, Friedrich Zimmermann, that would have reduced from 16 to six the maximum age at which children remaining abroad should be allowed to join their *Gastarbeiter* parents in Germany. The *Bund* and *Land* governments and city councils, though certainly they could do much more (see below), at least have social affairs departments staffed by well-meaning liberals who wield sizeable budgets and generally do their bit – as witness the city-funded local street festival I found one Sunday in Munich, where a troupe of Turkish youths and blonde local *Mädchen* gave a display of folk-dancing.

Individuals are active too: in Bavaria alone, there are some 30 German volunteer organisations who help Turkish children with their homework. The unions, in defiance of the racist element in their rank-and-file, also have a good record: *Gastarbeiter* make up 10 per cent of DGB membership, and a few have even been elected to factory works' councils. As for employers, most of the larger firms at least treat their immigrants well and will seldom dismiss a Turk if he is a good worker.[1] Some companies have even made efforts to come to

---

[1] However, a different picture was given by the investigative journalist Günther Walraff, who in 1983–5 spent two and a half years disguised as a Turkish worker and took all kinds of menial jobs in order to find out how bad the experience could be. The resulting book *Ganz unten* ('Right at the bottom') sold over 1.7 million copies. Wallraff alleged that some leading firms, including Thyssen, exploited illegal immigrants as virtual slave labour. Much of his reporting may have been genuine, even useful: but it was widely claimed that he had faked many incidents in order to strengthen his story.

terms with the Turks' religious customs: a Turkish leader in Berlin told me that he had persuaded Siemens and some other firms to instal little Islamic prayer-rooms in their factories, as well as to provide special canteens serving Oriental food. As for the old Koranic rule that even a man must not be seen washing naked, for some years this caused problems in the big communal shower-rooms of the mines and steelworks, for the Turks demanded separate cubicles, but were refused. Finally, a senior 'liberal' mullah came from Istanbul and explained to the workers (who in Germany tend to be under the sway of reactionary mullahs) that the new modernised Koran had lifted the ban on male nudity. So all ended happily.

Robert Bosch is a marvellous firm with a long philanthropic tradition and a first-class personnel record (see page 113) and its *Stiftung* (charity foundation) has been running projects for teenage children of *Gastarbeiter* in Munich, Berlin, and its home town of Stuttgart. Here, in a large and gloomy old working-class housing-estate behind the main station, I talked to Bosch's team of young German social workers, some of whom had specially learned Turkish. The flats, mostly built in the 1920s without indoor plumbing, are used by the *Bundesbahn* and the Post Office to house their own workers and families, German and foreign: Turkish bronze ornaments and bright carpets were decorating many balconies. I was told that relations between Turks and Germans on the estate were satisfactory, for there is a certain worker solidarity; but each national group tends to keep on its own, socially. At one street corner, a group of Italian men were earnestly discussing football or politics, just as in any Italian town. 'But,' said my guide, 'it's through the kindergarten and the youth club that we're hoping that the next generation will start to integrate' – indeed, in the club, Italian and Spanish girls (but of course not Turks) were flirting with Yugoslav boys, and then two Turks of 14 and a Neapolitan came in from playing football together. One of the Turks, moustachioed and looking at least 17, said he wanted to be a doctor and to go back to Turkey, 'because it rains too much here.' They giggled, and laughed off my question about whether they felt there was prejudice against Turks in Germany – 'Oh well, yes, what do you expect? – we don't take it too seriously.' I was then taken to the Bosch centre, to meet some Turkish girls, and was told by the social workers: 'Their parents won't allow them here at all, and very few Turks let their daughters aged 13 or more go swimming with boys. The girls have to stay at home, helping mother.' In a room with Güney film posters on the walls, three Turkish girls of 14, lively, precocious, enchanting, all with good German, were allowed to talk to me (my greyish hair presumably put me outside the taboo age-group). One of them said her father worked on night-shift cleaning trains: 'My parents are left-wing and not very religious, so they let me go out. I've been in Stuttgart since I was six, and I feel as much German as Turkish. I want to spend my life here, for women have so much more freedom, and I'd be glad to marry a German.' Another girl, alas less untypical, said, 'My father would never let me marry a German, it's against Islam. Yes, Turkey is still my home and I want to go back one day.'

In Stuttgart, and in Munich or the Ruhr, nearly all the Turks are in more-or-less working-class jobs; likewise in Frankfurt, where tensions are much the worst and 22 per cent of the population are *Gastarbeiter*. Berlin is the one German city where the Turks, like the coloured minorities in London or New York, have their own educated elite, playing some part in local intellectual life. Here you find Turkish writers and lawyers, and exhibitions by Turkish artists, while the number of Turkish university students is far higher than elsewhere. This city with its 115,000 Turks (the biggest Turkish town outside Turkey) also has much the best municipal record of trying to help them: this was due quite largely to Richard von Weizsäcker, now Federal President, who as CDU governing mayor in 1981 poured funds and staff into a new *Land* welfare centre for immigrants, and also plastered the city with propaganda posters of happy young Turks and Germans, hand-in-hand together.

This was not the picture ten or fifteen years ago, after the Turks and their sheep had first settled en masse in the slums of the Kreuzberg district, near the Wall, and the startled Germans had reacted angrily. This was the 'Kreuzghetto' of the tabloid headlines, where rival gangs of youths were reported to be assaulting each other nightly. But today this image of Kreuzberg is out-of-date. All has become fairly amicable. First, the Turks are now numerous enough (35,000, or 25 per cent) to feel reasonably secure and at home, in a 'town' of their own of some two square miles (though by no means a ghetto). Secondly, Kreuzberg since the mid-'70s has become a true Greenwich Village, filling up with middle-class Greens, Leftish intellectuals and the kind of radical-*Schickeria* who, unlike working-class Germans, actually think it smart to live in a racially-mixed area, where they can have Turks as neighbours and get friendly with them. Kreuzberg is 'in'. During the squatter period, young radicals eagerly helped Turkish families to settle in empty buildings; and nowadays the local Turks seem to be almost outnumbered by the sociologists, media Lefties and assorted do-gooders who have come to scrutinise them like some rare wild-life species. True, this idyll is sometimes shattered by the *Schlägerbanden*, gangs of young neo-Nazi skinheads, usually out-of-work, who bash up Turks – and the young Turks bash back. But such incidents are far rarer than they used to be. By contrast, in some tenements the Turks have finally become friends with their poor and elderly German neighbours, the original inhabitants, and mutual help has developed: the Turks haul up coal and wood for the oldies, who in turn do baby-sitting when the Turkish wives are at work.

I visited the city-funded Turkish social centre in Adalbertstrasse, right by the Wall. It is run by and for Turks. More Güney posters on the walls, and portraits of Ataturk. There was folk-dancing, an engagement party, and a more emancipated atmosphere than in Stuttgart. Here I met Emine Altiok, a dazzling young woman from Adana who had studied at Berlin University and was now with the state *Rundfunk*, making radio programmes for local Turks: 'I'm second generation. I came here as a small girl with my father, who makes furniture. I'm married to a Turk, who is culturally "integrated", so he doesn't try to dominate me: I'd never stand for that. Most second-generation Turkish marriages split up, however, simply because the women have become emancipated in Germany, they earn their own living and won't accept the usual role of a Turkish wife.' Turning to the general position of Turks in Germany, she went on: 'In every way, things were far tougher for my father's generation: they had language problems, and the Germans were more xenophobic in those days. For us it's easier, but we have a new problem of identity. Are we Turkish or German? We cherish our own culture and religion, but we see positive things in European society especially for women. Many women who go back to Turkey just can't cope any more with the restrictions, at least not in the provinces – it's easier in Istanbul or Ankara. We, who plan to stay in Germany, intend to work out a middle way between Turkish female subservience and German excess of liberty. A Turkish *kleine Unterschied* (*petite différence*)?

It is ironical that just when Turkish/German personal contacts seemed to be improving, and the Turks were at last starting to feel more at home, so now the rise in unemployment has increased German prejudice against them. Generalisation is not easy: but broadly the pattern seems to be that, on the one hand, friendliness and neighbourly good-will have increased among those who know each other personally, but at the same time there has been a growth in indiscriminate ill-feeling towards foreign workers as a whole – 'Kemal next door, he's a good chap – but what of all the other Turks?' – is a common German attitude. And, since *Gastarbeiter* are supposed to be stealing jobs from Germans, the facile equation can be made, 'Two million foreign workers = two million German unemployed, so send them all home!' Sensible people realise that this is nonsense, for most out-of-work Germans are not seeking the same jobs as Turks, too often relegated to the most menial chores. And if they *were* sent home, who could be found to do this kind of work? In Düsseldorf, the SPD-led city council commissioned a study which showed that, if the 36,000 immigrant workers departed, rubbish disposal services and public transport might well collapse, and hospitals and the building industries would be seriously short of labour.

Even so, by 1982 the opinion polls were indicating that over 80 per cent of Germans thought that there were far too many foreign workers. Moreover the Turks themselves were the worst victims of unemployment: by 1983, 16.7 per cent of them were out of work, twice the federal average, and this put a burden on the social security budget. So the Kohl Government decided to take action. Large-scale forced repatriation was not an option – for political and humanitarian reasons, and also because Turkish workers do possess some rights of access to Germany under Turkey's EEC association agreement of 1963. But for a few months in 1983–4 Bonn did try out an incentive scheme for voluntary departure, whereby any *Gastarbeiter* on short-time work or made redundant through plant closure could obtain a grant of 10,500 DM (plus 1,500 DM for each child) and a refund of his pension contributions, so long as he and all his family left promptly. It was not exactly a generous offer, but it did have some success: about 80,000 wage-earners applied for the money, and in all some 300,000 immigrants left, 80 per cent of them Turkish. Hence the fall in overall numbers since 1983. But for most Turks the choice was a painful one: it was quite a wrench to leave a Germany where they were paid well and had begun to settle, and to return to their backward homeland with its 25 per cent unemployment. No longer at ease in either culture, many Turks find it very hard to readjust if they go back home. Hence, the vast majority remain in Germany.

The English sociologist and immigration expert Stephen Castles, who lives and works in Frankfurt, has analysed the subject from a Marxist viewpoint in his interesting book, *Here for Good: Western Europe's Ethnic Minorities* (Pluto Press, London, 1984). He told me: 'History shows that labour immigrations always lead to permanent settlement, unless forcibly prevented – look at the Asians and West Indians in Britain, or the Polish miners in France. German governments have failed to understand this, so they have applied only *ad hoc* short-term solutions to the problem and have not accepted that many families will remain and finally integrate. Holland, Sweden, and even France have far more intelligent policies. Today the Germans have at last woken up to the real issues, so there's quite a political debate in progress.' Mr Castles may well be proved right. But neither the Germans nor the Turks have yet fully faced up to what permanent settlement would involve. Would it lead to integration? – or assimilation? – or either? Integration means that immigrants adapt to German standards and are accepted into German society, while retaining their own culture and, probably, citizenship; assimilation means a much fuller process of Germanisation, which very few Turks wish for. But, in the longer term, is integration possible without assimilation? And is Germany ready yet for a multi-cultural society?

Though the Turks in Germany would certainly like to feel more secure and better accepted, most of them remain wary of integration. Here they are under powerful pressure from fundamentalist Islamic forces which, strangely enough, are stronger in Germany than in Turkey itself, and are also linked with the Turkish extreme-Right political movement, the Grey Wolves. These groups exert considerable influence over a bewildered peasant population in a strange land: they preach that integration into this 'infidel' society is wicked, and that Turks should not adopt 'decadent' European habits such as alcohol or freedom between the sexes. The mullahs in Koranic schools sometimes tell their pupils not to believe what they are taught in German classes. Here I quote a leading article in *The Times* of September 5, 1983, about the North Africans in France as well as Turks in Germany: 'In both countries, fundamentalist Islamic groups, suppressed by their home governments, are exploiting the relatively free and plural nature of West European society, as well as the alienation and disorientation felt by many of the immigrants, to try to impose on the immigrant communities a totalitarian and intolerant world view, with the result that the most well-meaning attempts by the French and Germans to assimilate, emancipate or simply educate the immigrants sometimes encounter a discouragingly hostile response.' Hence, for example, the difficulty in persuading Turkish parents to permit their teenage daughters any leisure life outside the home. And the few families who dare to step out of line and Germanise are often rejected by their own people – 'There's a growing dichotomy,' I was told by Carla Baran, a psychologist from Istanbul who works for the official Bavarian welfare service for Turks, in Munich; 'some families are growing more liberal, others more traditional. And it can be the same inside families: I get visits from girls of 14 who've run away from home, or attempted suicide, because they can't stand their parent's strictness. These tensions are worse here than back in Turkey, because of the German influence and the fears of Germanising. It's a tough situation: but I think integrating is bound to come within another generation or so. The fanatics will lose in the end.'

Within Muslim circles in Germany, as in the Islamic world at large, there is quite an ideological conflict. Moderate Turkish Muslims are disturbed that fundamentalism (in Iran and elsewhere) should be spreading so harsh and archaic an image of their religion, thus fuelling German prejudices. One day, in the 'red light' district of Frankfurt near the station, I explored the Turkish Bazaar, a large complex of shops and cafés, and here I called unannounced on the little makeshift mosque upstairs, where a charming, soft-mannered acolyte plied me with mint tea: 'If the Germans bothered to learn more about Islam, there would be fewer tensions here. We see Mary and Jesus as holy, and we are taught a lot about them – but what do Christians ever bother to find out about Mohammed and the Koran? Ours is a very kind and gentle religion at heart, and its paternalist tradition is humane. My father is 82, and I still obey his very word. That's good. But the Germans have destroyed family life, so their young people are adrift, they commit suicide, they have a hunger in the soul.' When I cautiously asked him about the video-cassettes in the shop downstairs, with their lurid covers of Turkish mediaeval warriors butchering Christian crusaders, he said, 'Yes, we regret them, of course, but we can't stop them. The fundamentalists encourage them.' These cheap imported video films, Turkish equivalent of Westerns, depict the crusaders pillaging and raping, and the Turks exacting revenge – and Turkish children sit at home by their TV sets, cheering as the hated Christians are tortured and decapitated. It is the usual problem of video-nasty violence – but especially nasty in a social context where young Turks and Germans are supposed to be learning to love one another. The reactionary mullahs bear some of the responsibility. Fortunately, the right-wing army-backed government in Turkey, whatever its faults, is anti-fundamentalist, and with the active support of Bonn it has been sending some modern-minded mullahs to Germany (like the one who persuaded miners to accept communal showers) to preach a more moderate version of Islam. So the struggle for and against integration goes on.

'Integration' is the current catchword – but what does it really involve? The German authorities claim that it is official policy for *Gastarbeiter* to integrate into German society: but the Turks say, 'This is hypocritical. If they were sincere, they would make it easier for us to stay. They do not give us enough security of residence.' Here the legal position is that a foreigner is first given a short-term permit; after a few years he can acquire a permanent one, as well as an indefinite residence permit. He does not lose his work permit if he loses his job; but if he commits a crime he is likely to forfeit his rights of residence and be expelled. A German also by law has preference over a foreigner for filling a job vacancy. German officials claim that today some 85 per cent of foreign workers have unlimited work permits, and that in the present employment climate it would not be politically feasible to grant them fuller rights. And yet, many Turks claim that they still feel insecure. One factor may be that anyone with a dark face is vulnerable to the frequent random identity checks by the police who are trying to hunt down the large number of illegal immigrants.

Another issue is citizenship. Many German politicians, especially in the CDU, argue that if the *Gastarbeiter* really want to stay they should take German nationality, for this would help them to inte-

[249]

grate, it would also ease tensions and solve the problem of residence rights. So this is official policy: but the Germans do not make it so easy to acquire citizenship. As in many countries, there are various hurdles on the way: you must have been in Germany for ten years and have had a secure job and residence and no criminal record; you must pay a fee of about 2,000 DM per head; above all you must pass a stiff language test that may even include speaking the local dialect, such as Bavarian. These are not insuperable obstacles, and most applicants do manage to gain citizenship if they try. However, the real problem is that Germany is more strictly opposed than most European countries to the granting of dual nationality, whereas Turkey is more easy-going. Many Turks would take German citizenship if they could keep their own: but for emotional as well as practical reasons they are most reluctant to make this break with their homeland. And the same is true of other *Gastarbeiter* too. As a result very few apply, and Germany has one of the lowest levels of naturalisation of any Western country: of resident foreigners only 0.3 per cent a year become German citizens, compared with 2.0 per cent in Britain, 1.2 per cent in France, and 5.2 per cent in Sweden. Since the war, only 100,000 immigrants have become naturalised. In France, a child born to foreign parents living there can automatically take French nationality at 18 if he wishes, but not so in Germany, and a recent opinion poll suggests that any such measure would be very unpopular with Germans. These attitudes do not exactly encourage integration. The problem was emphasized to me vividly by a gentle Turk of 25 in Munich who had studied at Mainz University and was now driving a bus: 'I get on well with the Germans and I like living here. My main problems are legal and political, for neither government makes things easy. I feel that I now belong to both cultures and I'd like to be able to move freely between the two countries. But Germany won't grant me citizenship unless I give up my Turkish passport, and Turkey won't let me take that step legally unless I first do my military service – and I hate the thought of 22 tough months in the Army under that harsh regime. So I can't even visit Turkey till I'm 32, when I would no longer be liable for service. But it's hard to find a job here as a non-EEC foreigner. I have no legal security, yet I love Germany.'

One step forward, so it is suggested, would be to allow *Gastarbeiter* to vote in municipal elections, as they now can in Sweden and Holland. This might give them a greater feeling of involvement in Germany, as well as encourage local politicians to take more account of their interests. The Churches have campaigned for the proposal, which is backed also by the Greens and most of the SPD. But the Kohl Government has said no (could it be that local CDU leaders are fearful of how most *Gastarbeiter* might vote?). In general, the CDU's local record on helping *Gastarbeiter* is patchy to say the least. In Berlin it has done well: but elsewhere many CDU-led councils have appeared reluctant to spend too much money on helping immigrants, for they fear this would lose votes. So they leave most of the work to the Churches and other bodies. In Frankfurt and some other cities where latent racism is high, CDU leaders in local election campaigns have even demagogically accused the foreigners of aggravating unemployment. This, says the Left, simply fuels xenophobia. 'And it's stupid of Bonn,' added one Marxist I met, 'to ban the Turks' own political parties from activity in Germany, for this throws Turks back on their religion, reactionary and nationalist, and so makes integration even harder.'

And yet, only a further massive rise in unemployment would make it politically possible for any German government to send the Turks home. So, if they are going to stay, what is the solution for them? They want better security, kinder acceptance by the German people, and the possibility to keep their own culture. For this to be possible, each side will have to take a few steps towards the other, and Islamic and German popular attitudes will both need to be modified. In the United States, many immigrant groups have retained their own culture and customs while at the same time becoming Americans both legally and psychologically. So it can be done: but in Europe it is much more difficult, if the immigrants want to retain their own citizenship. Moreover, the Germans have never been a major colonising people like the British, French and Dutch, and so have little experience of coming to terms with non-European races and religions. Though their conscience today is still troubled by the Nazi purge of the Jews, they cannot cope with alien cultures. 'Germany,' said Stephen Castles, 'is becoming *de facto* a multi-cultural society. But the trend still frightens people here.'

In human and cultural terms, no less than economic ones, the immigrants are surely a great asset for Germany, for they add vitality and variety to local life, just like the ethnic minorities in Britain or France. But this potential is sadly under-used. Occasionally a civic hall or theatre will offer a stage to some Latin or Balkan dance troupe; a Turkish rock group won fame in Berlin; and a Sicilian fringe theatre company based in Frankfurt tours all Germany (see page 280). But it is not so often that *Gastarbeiter* arts and folklore are given chances of this kind to emerge from their ghettoes onto the wider German scene. And yet, matters have been steadily improving; and the more liberal of the immigrants' own leaders are relatively optimistic that social integration will in the long run become easier, as a new generation grows up, both Turkish and German, that has sat together on the same school benches and is more open-minded than its elders. With some exceptions, young Germans are markedly less racist than their elders. So the problems of the *Gastarbeiter* may well ease with time.

Even today, it is less acute than that of young Blacks in Britain.

Lastly, I heard a charming note of objectivity from a Japanese girl at the Trumpf factory in Stuttgart, secretary/interpreter of the sales manager. When I asked her whether there were many Turkish or other foreign workers in the firm, she replied with a smile, 'I wouldn't know. You all look the same to me, you Westerners.'

One special test of radical attitudes has been provided by the recent influx of refugees demanding political asylum, most of them from Third World countries. Anxious to make amends for the Nazis' treatment of the Jews, the Federal Republic today has Europe's most liberal legislation on this matter: the Constitution itself declares that no one arriving on German soil and claiming asylum can be turned away without a fair investigation. And many people have made use of this. Germany has thus taken generous quotas of Boat People as well as many fugitives from Communist Europe and from right-wing regimes such as Chile and Iran – and indeed Turkey. But since 1981 the numbers seeking asylum have risen so rapidly that the Germans have grown alarmed. And officials have become convinced that many of the would-be refugees are not political but 'economic': enticed by tales of the good life in Germany and its generous social security, they flood in from very poor countries, using asylum as a dodge. Many of them fly first to East Berlin on Aeroflot or Interflug (GDR) flights, much cheaper than those of Western airlines. There they can cross easily into West Berlin, which operates no frontier checks on anyone at the zonal border (see page 372). Next they go by train to West Germany where they *do* face controls – but they simply ask for asylum. In the early 1980s, Tamils from Sri Lanka were the most numerous group. Of course, as the world knows, Tamils have genuinely been suffering persecution at home: but the Federal authorities felt certain that most of the migrants had been lured by 'fantasy' stories, put about by the airlines and other traders, of Germany as a land of easy money. Many stayed in Berlin, often taking to drug-trafficking or other crime. Bonn also grew suspicious that the GDR and the Soviet Union might be fostering the inflow deliberately in order to create political trouble. So in 1985 Bonn opened talks with the East German Government on the matter, and finally in return for a promise of commercial loans (the usual German–German barter in human beings: see page 377) it did persuade it to limit the illegal Tamil entries. Their flow slowed down: but their places were simply taken by Iranians, Indians, Ghanaians and others, over whom there was no agreement with the GDR, and during 1986 the problem grew graver than ever. In the first six months, 42,000 foreigners applied for political asylum, compared with 74,000 in the whole of 1985.

While his case is being heard, which may take up to three years, the refugee is put in a camp or hostel at public expense, and is not allowed to work. The hearings are rigorous: only about 30 per cent are finally granted asylum. The rest are sent back home – including almost all the Indians and Ghanaians, who are regarded as the worst cheats. If there is any doubt on an individual case, then a German official is supposed to travel with the expellee, to make sure he comes to no harm: but this precaution does not seem to be fool-proof, for there have been reports of Tamils arrested at Colombo airport as they stepped off the plane. This is one aspect of official handling of the problem that is criticised by German radicals. But they reserve their sharpest indignation for the conditions in the refugee camps, which are run by the *Länder*. At one camp in Tübingen, a former French Army barracks, independent witnesses in 1985 found 500 asylum-seekers cooped up in premises intended for 250: they had 'appalling' sanitation and were forbidden to do their own national cooking. Some went on hunger strike. Most were middle-class, university-educated people. Many German radicals believed that the CDU-led government of Baden-Württemberg, and Bavaria's too, were deliberately creating harsh conditions in the camps so that the word would get around and thus deter future asylum-seekers. Politicians tacitly admitted this. When I asked Lothar Späth about the Tübingen camp, he said, 'Yes, of course the people are poorly housed: but they'd be worse off in their own country, wouldn't they? We have the world's best liberal laws to protect genuine refugees. But if we let in the mass of phoney ones, and then devote big sums to giving them a life of ease, sooner or later there'd be a German popular backlash against *all* refugees. So I have to be severe, to protect our liberal laws.' No doubt Späth had read the opinion polls, showing that 71 per cent of Germans thought the authorities 'too generous' towards refugees, while only 4 per cent found them 'too mean'. So well-meaning politicians like Späth are clearly in a dilemma. On the one hand, they are under popular pressure to be tougher with the flood of entrants (and in August 1986 Bonn did finally introduce some modest restrictions, including transit visas). On the other, they are saddled with this liberal legislation that Germany, because of its black past, could not make more stringent without causing an outcry at home and abroad. Most German leaders, except for a handful on the hard Right, genuinely wish to remain liberal in these matters, and to educate the public towards more tolerant attitudes. They do not always have quite the courage of their convictions.

Having absorbed some 14 million fellow-German refugees from the east after the war, the Germans since then have not been especially generous in granting refuge to others. In 1953–83, only 86,000 foreigners were given permanent asylum, fewer than in Britain; and today only one resident in 617 is a refugee from abroad, compared with one in 231 in the United States, one in 333 in France, one in 384 in Britain. Moreover, in 1983, without altering the asylum laws as such, the Government did tighten the rules on visa entry, and the penalties for illegal immigration, after a mounting wave of abuses, notably drug-trafficking. Many escaped criminals or heroin-pedlars had been arriving from Third World countries, posing as fugitives from political persecution – so the clamp-down was justified. The Left however continues to allege that some refugees do not get a fair hearing – and it may have some case, for errors do occur. Seven Sri Lankans and Pakistanis once committed suicide together, when they learned they were to be expelled. And so, notoriously, did a young left-wing Turk, Kemal Altun, in Berlin in 1983. The Turkish Government was demanding his extradition for some alleged crimes. At first he was granted asylum, but then Bonn insisted on further hearings; and, after Interior Minister Zimmermann returned from a visit to Ankara, he demanded Altun's 'immediate' extradition 'in the interests of good cooperation with Turkey'. At this, Altun threw himself from the sixth-floor window of the courtroom that was trying him. It was all too obvious that Zimmermann had traded him for Turkish promises to try to reduce the *Gastarbeiter* flow. There was an outcry, and the Minister's resignation was called for. Of course he refused.

The question 'Just how xenophobic are the Germans?' is not an easy one to answer. Certainly horror-stories can be quoted by the score, but these may not give a fair picture. First we must distinguish between xenophobia, i.e. dislike of all foreigners, and racism, which is more selective. The Germans today are one of the least chauvinistic of major Western countries: they positively fawn over Scandinavians, Britons or even French . . . But, when it comes to darker-skinned or more alien folk, matters are different: probably the Germans *are* on average more racist than the British, or even the French, but they are well behind the Swiss, European champions in this field. In Germany, there is little actual violence towards immigrants, as we have seen. Neo-Nazi thugs try to whip up hatred, and some have been jailed for it: but these tiny extremist groups have little popular following (see page 396), and their slogans (e.g. 'We finished off the Jews: Turks, it's your turn next'), though nauseating, are not representative. The average German may not warm towards *Gastarbeiter*, but he shows little residue of the old Aryan super-race mentality of the Nazi creed: it is significant that the Allensbach polls, though recording plenty of xenophobia in other respects, found only 8 per cent of respondents saying 'yes', and 69 per cent saying 'no', to the crucial question, 'Are German children more intelligent than those of foreign workers?'

Guilt over the Holocaust may have exorcised this kind of feeling:

and yet, the old prejudices that bred anti-semitism do linger on, in a milder form. Ordinary people may no longer feel racially superior: but they do want the *Gastarbeiter* to keep their distance and leave them alone. They dislike having them as neighbours: Turks, Blacks and others with dark faces usually have difficulty in finding lodgings. In this neighbour-prying country often this is more a matter of 'What will the Müllers next door think?' than of personal prejudice. I know a liberal couple in a rented flat in Stuttgart who befriended a Turkish family living nearby and invited them twice to their home: at this their landlady, a typical Swabian bourgeoise, said, 'Please stop that, we don't want a Turkish commune in our house! We're not racist our-selves, mind you – but you know what people round here are like, and we have to keep on good terms . . .' If this kind of vicious circle could be broken, matters might improve. It is also true that ignorance is the main barrier. Those who do get to know Turks or others, as neighbours or at work, frequently end up on friendly terms, yet remain convinced that 'their' Turks are a special case: 'We're so lucky, *we* have such a nice family next door. But all the others . . .'

When it comes to marriage, most German parents today are perfectly happy for their daughter to wed, say, a Dane or Canadian (this used not to be so). But, if a Greek or South Italian suitor turns up, there may be trouble: and this may not always be xenophobia so much as a legiti-mate parental anxiety that the girl might not be happy living in a *macho* society. The girls are wary, too. When an Allensbach poll asked, 'Would you marry a Turk?', only 4 per cent said 'yes': but even for an Italian the 'yes' was a mere 10 per cent, against 14 per cent for a Yugo-slav. Blacks scored 7 per cent. Generally, the lighter the hair and face, the milder the prejudice. But, as this poll indicates, Blacks tend to be better accepted than Turks – partly because they are far less numerous and usually better educated. What is more, many Blacks in Germany are American. I heard of a family who refused to let their younger daughter marry a Turkish worker she loved, so she tried to kill herself. The mother would not relent, saying, 'I'd rather she starved to death than married that wild rat!' I tell this horrific and (I hope) untypical story, simply because the elder daughter had already been cohabiting happily with a Black GI for two years, and had two kids by him. 'Oh, but he's an American,' said the mother. There are legal obstacles, too, in the path of foreigners who wed German girls and live with them in Germany. Until recently, marriage did not grant them right of resi-dence. However, some potent campaigning has now been done by the Frankfurt-based Association of German Women Married to Foreigners. Thanks to them, foreign husbands now have better security; and a child born to a German mother and foreign father can now acquire German nationality at birth, as was previously possible only for the child of a German father.

However, in this law-ridden country, one surprising and serious lacuna remains, the absence of effective laws against racial discrimination. Small ads for job vacancies or flats to let often stipulate, '*Nur für Deutsche*' or '*Nur Europäer*'; many pubs refuse *Gastarbeiter* and one in Frankfurt even had a notice up, '*Kein Zutritt für Hunde und Türken*' (No Entry for Dogs and Turks); some public discos in Frankfurt deny entry to coloured people (except if a white man brings a coloured girl – that's quite chic). In Britain, under the Race Relations Act, all this would simply be illegal. In Germany, to pass such a law would require huge political courage; and it might take many years, for it would involve the amendment of 40 existing laws.

In the meantime, could not the media and the authorities play a firmer role in trying to educate people away from prejudice? Weeklies such as *Die Zeit* and *Der Spiegel*, it is true, have an excellent record of anti-racist articles, while any average regional daily is usually quite free from xenophobia. But this positive side is counterbalanced by the pernicious influence of the mass-selling tabloid *Bild Zeitung* (see page 317): it is not openly racist in its editorials, but with their shrieking headlines its new stories do endlessly sensationalise the 'misdoings' of Turks and others (e.g. stories about child-beating), and this whips up popular prejudice. The public television channels give a balanced news coverage: but they provide too few background programmes about the lives and problems of *Gastarbeiter*, the nature of Islamic religion, and so on. So potent a medium could certainly be playing a stronger educative role. And, as I have already suggested, the Federal and *Land* governments could do more to lead opinion and set a positive example. As all politicians know well, the treatment of immigrants remains one of the most crucial tests of the new German democratic ethos. The *Gastarbeiter*'s very presence forces the Germans to look at themselves more closely.

6

ARTS AND INTELLECTUALS: LIVELY ACTIVITY, BUT LOW CREATIVITY

In Germany, as in many other Western countries, this seems to be the age of the performing arts rather than of individual creation. The theatres and museums, concert halls and opera houses draw large and enthusiastic audiences, and are backed by generous public subsidies on a scale unequalled in Europe. The cultural scene is refreshingly cosmopolitan, too. Many front-rank musicians and other performers come from abroad to live and work in Germany, where managers and public alike are alert to the latest influences from the outside world. It is all very open and stimulating.

But where is the new creative artist? – or the great new philosopher, in this land of *Dichter und Denker* (poets and thinkers)? The novel, since the heyday of Grass and Böll, has gone into a strange hibernation; few post-war painters or sculptors have made much impact apart from the extraordinary Joseph Beuys; the cinema blossomed unexpectedly in the 1970s, but its condition is now again precarious; *und so weiter* . . . This creative malaise, in contrast to performing vitality, is not confined to Germany: it is even more noticeable today in France, though maybe less so in Britain, and it has a number of complex causes common throughout the West. In Germany, one particular factor is that the Nazi period created a rupture with the past that cut writers and artists off from their natural traditions and left them rootless and confused, and these wounds have taken a long time to heal: the Nazis distorted German culture for their own purposes, debasing the coinage of many crucial German ideas and styles which thus could not easily be used any more. Continuity was shattered. In addition, the vast majority of worthwhile intellectuals and creative people had moved either into exile or into prison, and many of them – notably the Jews – either never returned or were exterminated. Germany's culture has been tragically impoverished by the loss of its Jews, who before the war had played so fertile a role.

Summed up in a word, German culture in the past has been

marked by two major traditions – one of quiet philosophic humanism, and the other much closer to the Gothic or baroque, full of violence and fantasy, as seen in the work of Hieronymus Bosch, the Brothers Grimm or the expressionist cinema of the 1920s. Since the war, the philosophical trend has become less abstract, and German humanism has moved closer to daily life, as is seen for example in the novels of Heinrich Böll or in Edgar Reitz's film *Heimat*. But it is the violent/fantastic tradition that has come more strongly to the fore. In an age when, in many countries, art sets out to shock or provoke, the Germans have made a speciality of it – and much of their most striking work has been in varying degrees extravagant, grotesque, frenzied, baroque, expressionist, bizarre or downright romantic. One could trace this through the *Leitmotiv* of physical foulness in the novels of Günter Grass; the *arte povera* belligerence of Beuys' conceptual sculptures; Peter Zadek's provocative stage reworkings of Shakespeare or Schiller; the violent expressionism of Pina Bausch's dance theatre; the extravagant romanticism of the films of Werner Herzog; and even in the despairing stylised brutality of the work of Fassbinder or the tender cruelties of the plays of Franz Xaver Kroetz. All these possess essentially German imaginations and are products of the German psyche, moulded also by the *Angst* of modern times.

The novel: waiting for successors to Böll and Grass

German literature since 1945 can be said to fall into three main periods. First was the time of the so-called 'literature of the ruins', when writers were painfully struggling to come to terms with their experiences of the war and of Nazism and were groping towards new values. This was followed by the left-wing political commitment of the 1960s, a period of angry disillusion with Germany's materialistic and conformist new society. Then since the early 1970s writers have been retreating again from public and social themes into their private worlds of individual feeling, nostalgia and *Innerlichkeit* (inwardness). The first two of these periods produced at least two novelists of major world rank, Heinrich Böll and Günter Grass, as well as a number of other significant writers such as the poet and critic Hans Magnus Enzensberger, the novelist Martin Walser, and the playwrights Peter Weiss and Rolf Hochhuth. The third period has been much less distinguished.

After 1945 some writers returned from exile abroad and others from the 'inner emigration' of silence imposed by Nazism. They were free again to write what they wished in their own land: but amid the numbing desolation of the *Stunde Null* they had great difficulty at first in finding the words to express their feelings and experiences, and some were tempted to share the sharp judgement of the Frankfurt philosopher Theodor Adorno, who said that to go on writing lyric poetry after Auschwitz was 'barbaric'. The Nazis with their propaganda literature had so debauched the German language and values that no words were safe any more, and this induced in writers a certain verbal paralysis. But some gradually found their outlets through a kind of dazed deadpan description of what they had witnessed – the early stories of Böll, who had served on the Russian Front, are full of war-wounded youths and war-weary veterans, the muddle and futility of battle, and the shell-shocked apathy of those who will never re-adapt to normal life.

The rebirth of German literature was given a special impulse in 1947 when two left-wing authors and ex-POWs, Hans Werner Richter and Alfred Andersch, founded the famous '*Gruppe 47*'. This was an informal association of young writers from all over Germany who began to hold meetings where they would comment on each other's work. Böll and Grass, Enzensberger and Uwe Johnson were among those who joined *Gruppe '47*, which soon was exerting a good deal of influence: it mobilised petitions fostered friendships, helped writers to find their voice again and even organised meetings abroad. It was neither a formal political movement nor politically cohesive, but most of its members were on the Left and they believed that writers should band together to play a part in shaping the new German democracy. As such, *Gruppe '47* remained a vital force for the next two decades. Many writers during this period were directly involved in political and social questions, both in their writing and in their lives – Günter Grass for example campaigned actively for the SPD – and in so doing they were making a significant break with the main tradition of German letters: though Theodor Fontane, Heinrich Mann and a few others had been exceptions, literature hitherto had generally preferred to restrict itself to philosophical, spiritual and private subjects. But writers after 1945 felt that these ivory tower attitudes had led to Nazism and should not be repeated.

Even more than Grass, the towering figure of German post-war literature was Heinrich Böll, and he remained so until his death in 1985. Son of a cabinet-maker from Cologne, he had a typical Rhinelander's sense of humour allied to a poetic eye and a sharp sense of social satire. Above all he was a humanist, defender of the underdog and critic of established society. His novels *The Clown* (1963) and *Group Portrait with Lady* (1971) both explored the theme of how a sincere and gentle outsider in society can become rejected and trampled on by the parvenue bourgeoisie. Böll publicly expressed sympathy for the student rebels of 1968 and then spoke up for a fair trial for the Baader-Meinhof terrorists and a better understanding of what had driven them to their desperate adventures. For this he was lacerated by the entire German establishment and especially the right-wing Press. He retorted with his short and brilliant polemical novel *The Lost Honour of Katharina Blum* (1974), the story of a young woman harried and destroyed by a ruthless and mendacious tabloid newspaper (similar to *Bild Zeitung*: see p. 317) because she was suspected of sheltering a terrorist. In *The Safety Net* (*Fürsorgliche Belagerung*, 1979), Böll then described the paranoia of the wealthy class in the face of a youth protest movement that it was unable to comprehend. He was a shy and retiring man whose outspokenness on such issues propelled him into a moral leadership of a kind that he had never sought; in the eyes of many liberals and radicals, he came to appear as the voice of the nation's conscience in a time of confused values. He was a practising Catholic who never ceased to criticise official Catholicism, and he was one of the earliest supporters of the Greens. In 1972 he became the first German to win the Nobel Prize for Literature since Thomas Mann in 1929.

The novels of Günter Grass dealt less often with contemporary Germany than with the war period (witness his most famous book, *The Tin Drum*, 1959): yet he too would sometimes poke a satiric finger at the insensitivity of the new-rich society around him. His dominant theme was the failure of ordinary Germans to come to terms with the Nazi past. The novelist Martin Walser also wrote satirically about the bourgeoisie, focussing on the competitive status-conscious world of Swabia and Lake Constance, where he lived. One strength of all these writers, and of some others too, was that they gave vivid and realistic portrayals of precise settings that they knew well – Walser's Bodensee, Böll's Cologne district, and the pre-war Danzig of *The Tin Drum*. The poet and essayist Hans Magnus Enzensberger, two years younger than Grass, was an even more vitriolic critic of the new society of the 'economic miracle' and in 1967–8 he sided with the student rebels and urged Marxist revolution in the streets; but later he was to become much more moderate. A number of playwrights such as Rolf Hochhuth and Peter Weiss (see p. 273) were also turning to political themes during this period.

From the late 1950s much of the best German writing was coming not from the West but from the GDR (see p. 358). Uwe Johnson, born in what is now Poland, lived in East Germany until 1959 when with some regret he moved to West Berlin in order to have the freedom to publish his novels: *Speculation about Jakob* and *The Third Book about Achim* were two honest and thoughtful critiques of GDR-style socialism, written from a left-wing viewpoint. Some others later took the same route to the West, including the poet and singer Wolf Biermann: but several good writers have chosen to remain in the GDR, where sometimes they resort to allegory or coded references in order to express their thoughts on society. The best of them is probably

Christa Wolf who is concerned mainly with private themes and has been called 'the GDR's Virginia Woolf': her best-known novel, *The Quest for Christa T.* (1968), about a sensitive young woman ill at ease amid socialist collectivism, probably had some autobiographical element. It seems that the difficulties of living under a restrictive regime, far from stifling these writers, have in some cases acted as a creative stimulus.

In West Germany, by contrast, the permissiveness and normalcy of daily life today seems to be depriving writers of inspiration. The anti-bourgeois indignation of the 1950s and '60s has played itself out; subjectivity has come back into fashion and novelists have again been dealing with the age-old subjects of love and family, childhood, nostalgia and private sensibility. These are no bad themes for literature, but in Germany today they have certainly produced no Prousts. All the critics lament a decline in the novel that is even more acute than in France – and it is hard to think of a single significant name that has emerged in the past ten or fifteen years. An exception could be much-in-vogue and possibly overrated Botho Strauss, a novelist and playwright who deals in a semi-philosophical way with the modish themes of shallowness of feeling, lack of true human communication, and general purposelessness in society today.

As in France, much of the best story-telling talent seems to have migrated into the cinema. But there may be other reasons too for the current decline of literature. In Tübingen I visited the left-wing critic Walter Jens, a doyen of German letters and one of the early members of *Gruppe '47*, and he said: 'The crisis of the novel is common to all the West. In Germany, writers today find it hard to identify with any political line, there are no dreams any more, no causes to espouse like Dubček or Allende, and in literature no *maîtres-à-penser*. The Greens and young "alternatives" are anti-literature, they prefer the visual – Wim Wenders and Werner Herzog are the kind of people they look to, so writing is not "in". A *Gruppe '47* would be inconceivable today.' And in Munich I heard a perceptive and fascinating explanation from another *Gruppe '47* veteran, Hans Magnus Enzensberger, who has mellowed a lot since his Angry Young Man days: in his airy flat in Schwabing we talked for two hours over a whole range of subjects, one day in July 1985, and of all the hundreds of conversations I had for this book, I would single out this as the most stimulating, and Enzensberger as the most interesting individual I met in modern Germany. Of the plight of the writer he said: 'Intellectuals in the 1960s felt strongly about the injustices and rigidities in German society, and we fought hard against them – with some success. We made an impact in those days. Thanks in part to the student revolt of the 1968 period, certain barriers have been broken and Germany has become a more open, tolerant and informal society, more so than ever before in its history, and an easier place to live in. But in the process the edges have been blurred and it's also become a duller place, a sort of porridge. And it's not easy to write about a porridge. So there is a price to pay for normalcy.

'Another problem for the writer,' he went on, 'is that he's too cosseted today. All these subsidies for literature and culture don't necessarily make for high creativity. If you invest a billion dollars in the car industry, you probably get some interesting new models; but that doesn't hold good for artistic creation. A young man publishes his first novel, maybe something about his childhood, the kind of book that anyone has it in him to write: this let us say has a certain success, and so he becomes "a writer" and thinks of himself as such, and he embarks on a phoney career. He gets interviewed and lionised, he wins a scholarship or little prize and maybe his home town does something for him. So he finds it easy to do lecturing, or to go round Germany giving readings of his work, which pays very well, and to do radio as well – we have eight cultural radio networks in this country, and they all pay good money, better than the BBC. So there are all sorts of fundings and semi-fundings for the writer, it's much easier than in Britain. But what is our young chap to write about next? He lacks experience of real life. So you find writers writing about writers who want to write a book – so depressing! Or you come across this tame little novel about living in the communal flat and going to the peace demo. People have such narrow horizons. Admittedly, in the past, writers would often produce great art out of solitary confined experiences – but somehow there was more intensity in those days and the writer's fight was much harder, the oppression was greater. Today it's all too easy. And there's a simple lack of talent, too – hard to explain.'

Another factor is that, rather as in France, a great gulf exists between 'literature' and mere popular entertainment. The kind of robustly readable but basically serious fiction of the John Fowles or Graham Greene type that so solidly fills the middle ground in Britain is hardly present in Germany, where the critics expect a new novel either to be avant-garde in a self-conscious 'literary' way or else to deal solemnly with philosophical or moral themes; 'Once a book is entertaining,' said one publisher, 'then it ceases to be culture.' This inhibits many a young novelist, who has to choose between being pretentiously highbrow or merely commercial. Yet at the same time the prestige of intellectuals is much *less* great than in France, and so is their impact on public life. They may, as Enzensberger remarked, have been able to play a part in changing society in the 1968 period: but their own world of verbal polemic and clashing ideas does not fascinate a wider public as it does in France where Sartre and Barthes, Foucault and the *nouveaux philosophes* have in their time been popular stars like athletes or singers. Possibly one reason is that the French enjoy novelty and exhibitionism, and they like to be startled by ideas they do not necessarily share: the German public, much less secure, more anxious and conformist, does not. So the parading on television of a view generally thought 'shocking' will not provoke hoots of out-raged delight (as in France) or tolerant smiles (as in Britain) but a solemn outcry that few network chiefs will want to risk. And German politicians, at least those on the Right, have always disliked intellec-tuals (who are nearly all somewhere on the Left or centre-Left): Ade-nauer despised them, Erhard once called them *Pinscher* (pipsqueaks), and Chancellor Kohl, who has taken pride in identifying himself with the no-nonsense man-in-the-street, has enjoyed relations of mutual hostility with them. The cultured de Gaulle would never have adopted such a stance: nor would Giscard, who once invited Sartre to the Elysée.

Another difficulty facing the intellectuals is that they suffer more than most Germans from the lack of a true capital city. Munich, Berlin, Frankfurt and some other towns each has its little milieu of writers and thinkers: but they are somewhat separate and there is no national focus of the kind provided by Paris, London or New York. This makes German intellectual life more provincial, and its impact less great, both at home and abroad. *Gruppe '47* marked an attempt to overcome this handicap, by summoning writers from all over Ger-many to its sessions: but it imposed a strain on their time and their budgets, and ultimately it failed. The influence of the literary maga-zines such as *Neue Rundschau* has also waned: today the main impact comes from the literary pages of the weekly *Die Zeit* in Hamburg, of the *Süddeutsche Zeitung*, and of the *Frankfurter Allgemeine Zeitung* whose literary editor, the renowned and feared Marcel Reich-Ranicki, remains the pope of German letters, able to make or break a new book's sales with a few strokes of his caustic pen.

Although these papers do provide some interchange of ideas, most intellectuals tend to live in narrow little circles, separated from each other not only by city but by profession: academics, journalists and creative writers do not have much communication across their self-imposed barriers. The university world in Germany is notoriously closed (see p. 223), and it is less common than in Britain or the United States, or even France, for academics to appear on TV debates or write newspaper articles (except on their own special subjects). Modern German philosophy has been highly distinguished in its way: of the older pre-war generation who survived into the 1960s and '70s, mention should be made of Karl Jaspers, Ernst Bloch and Martin Heidegger, as well as of the so-called 'Frankfurt school' led by Max Horkheimer, Theodor Adorno and the much younger Jürgen Haber-mas who is still in his fifties. But the trouble with many of these wise men is that they wrote so obscurely as to be almost unintelligible even to specialists. Honourable exception should be made of those great humanists Bloch and Jaspers, who wrote with admirable lucidity on a range of topics. But Habermas is extremely hard to comprehend, and so is Adorno, whose ideas on 'the authoritarian personality' would appear to be so interesting and pertinent. There is a story from the 1968 period that when a student said to Adorno, 'Your theory just does not equate with reality', the sage replied, 'Then we must change reality'. And this is the trouble with much German intellectual discussion: it is either extremely practical, i.e. about nuclear power or dying forests, or else it is maddeningly over-theoretical, and never the twain do meet. Philosophical writing can also seem wilfully obscure, as witness this example by Reiner Wiehl, quoted in English in *The Times Literary Supplement* of May 4, 1984 (I do not have the original German, but it probably sounds even worse): 'Particularity is no rational datum that comprises within itself or beneath itself in the mode of a highest concretion a given simplicity and universality. Also, particularity is no third independent datum of equal concretion and reality as given singularity and universality.' Quite so.

Professors cling together socially, and more than in most countries they tend to look with disdain on any outsider, such as a mere journalist who trespasses on their speciality. To me they were unfailingly courteous: but sometimes they failed to hide their astonishment that I should be writing a serious book on Germany without, like them, holding a university post. That is a normal reaction: more curious maybe is the gulf that exists between the academic world and that of creative writing. Few German novelists come from a university milieu – Böll and Grass had no higher education at all – and rarely would a professor dare to do anything so frivolous as write detective stories or children's books in his spare time (as Oxford dons have been doing since Lewis Carroll's day). That would make him lose credibility with his colleagues as a serious thinker. Creative writers in their turn tend to lead secluded lives, and sometimes they complain of feeling isolated and ignored. But this may be unfair, and is probably due more to their own social reticence than to any hostility against them: for while a writer may not enjoy the same public prestige as in France, he nonetheless tends to be better treated by publishers and reading public than in Britain, another land with a strong literary tradition. Writers are frequently invited to give public readings of their works – by bookshops, adult education institutes, literary societies and so on – and for these they can expect audiences and good fees.

The novel may be in creative decline, yet the Germans still read and buy books as much as ever, and the statistics show that they are greater book readers than either the British or the French. Television and video have not made such inroads as might have been feared, at least not with more educated people: Allensbach surveys have found that the numbers of those claiming to read a book 'at least once a week' rose from 42 to 44 per cent between 1967 and 1980. Municipal lending libraries have been improving and are far better than in France, though less impressive than in Britain: Munich's big new central library and its 27 branches report a total of some 7.5 million borrowings a year, roughly six books per head. Bookshop sales of all kinds have also held up well. Travel and practical books and light fiction are of course the most popular, but there is still a heavy demand for the classics and for serious modern books. Again according to Allensbach, the proportion of families with at least 100 bound or paperback books in their home rose from 26 to 34 per cent between 1967 and 1978 – but admittedly, as one publisher put it, 'many of these house-proud Germans buy series of handsomely-bound books as part of the furniture and maybe never read them.' For these and other reasons, the German publishing industry is still in rather good shape, though of course it complains of crisis just as in other countries. Since the war it has had to come to terms with the loss of its markets in the former eastern parts of Germany, and with the decline of the German language to the benefit of English in areas such as Scandinavia. Nonetheless it manages to produce some 60,000 titles a year, far more than France, and much more too than Britain with its infinitely wider world market. Munich, Frankfurt and Stuttgart are the main publishing centres: Bertelsmann, based on the modest town Gütersloh, is the largest publishing group in Europe. And, notoriously, Germany plays host to the world's leading annual book trade fair. Before the war this was held in Leipzig, now in the GDR, and in 1949 it moved to Frankfurt where every autumn it now attracts some 5,700 publishing houses from about 80 countries, exhibiting some 300,000 books. The general bedlam tends to horrify the average Briton or American who visits the fair only because professionally he must. But in Germany its doings are always front page news. It may be concerned more with commerce than literature: but it remains a symbol of how seriously books are still taken by a nation that has always liked to call itself *'das Land der Dichter und Denker'*.

The State's role as Maecenas: taking culture out of the 'temples'

The exceptionally generous scale of public patronage of the arts in Germany derives from a tradition dating back to the 18th-century and earlier, when each royal court, dukedom or free city would maintain its own opera house, theatre and museums. Today that responsibility has been inherited not by the Federal Government but by the individual *Länder* and city councils, and they feel a sense of duty and of local pride in keeping up the tradition. Add to this the prosperity of the Germans and their formal respect for *Kultur*, and maybe it is not so surprising that public spending on the arts should be the most lavish in the free world – per capita it is roughly four times the British level, and even higher than in France with its parallel but more centralised system of largesse. In Germany today, some 50 opera houses and 70 orchestras, over 100 theatres and nearly 1,300 museums, receive subsidy. All the opera houses and nearly all the main German theatres are publicly owned either by *Land* or city, or in some cases by the two in partnership. And some leading private theatres – such as the celebrated Schaubühne in Berlin – have become so dependent on subsidy that in practice they are similar to the public ones.

One advantage of this structure is that it provides a fairly even spread of activity around the country. Even quite a small town will often possess a good civic theatre and concert hall, while the metropolitan culture found in London or Paris is in Germany shared between several cities, and a big place like Frankfurt or Cologne will offer a much better quality and range of artistic performance than its British or French equivalents, say Manchester or Marseille. Municipal councillors, and their electors too, regard culture as an important element in their city's overall prestige and so are ready to devote large sums to it. They may even see it as a valid economic investment too, a means of attracting new industry and commerce, as the arts officer of Stuttgart suggested to me: 'Without the culture that we sponsor, this would be a boring place and many dynamic citizens would move away. Besides, we have a duty to cater for Stuttgarters' spiritual needs.'

Cities are constantly in competition with each other, to see which of them can lure the most distinguished talent and which in the eyes of the critics has the finest opera, ballet or theatre companies: as many observers have noted, it is rather like a football league. As in football, much depends on the general manager, the highly-paid *Intendant* who is hired by the authorities to run the theatres or opera houses, or sometimes the two combined. Once appointed, he is then allowed artistic freedom: but, as in football, if his teams do badly he may be the scapegoat and get the sack. And cities' rival fortunes tend to rise and fall with their *Intendanten*: Stuttgart for example in the 1960s enjoyed a golden age under Walter Erich Schäfer when its ballet was the best in Germany and its theatre and opera among the three or four best, but it has since declined. Cities tend to specialise. Summed up in a few words, the form in the mid-1980s was that Hamburg had the best ballet under John Neumeier, with Stuttgart perhaps still second; Hamburg and Munich vied for first place in classical opera, with

Frankfurt excelling in avant-garde productions thanks to Michael Gielen; the best theatre companies were at Berlin, Hamburg, Munich, and Bochum in the Ruhr; the finest symphony orchestra was still the Berlin Philharmonic under von Karajan; Cologne excelled in modern music and modern art; the best classical art museums were in Munich and Berlin, the best modern ones in Frankfurt, Stuttgart and Düsseldorf – and so on. Many critics might query these placings, but they would probably agree that Munich's forte is conventional classical culture, while Berlin holds the blue riband for the modern and experimental, with a strong international flavour.

These rivalries undoubtedly are healthy in many ways – but not in all. Leading managers and producers travel around Germany to scrutinise each other's work, as do the critics, though with a certain *parti pris* of local patriotism: when, say, the music critic of the *Süddeutsche Zeitung* goes to Hamburg to review a new Wagner production, he may be hoping fervently that he will be able to report that it is not as good as Munich's – and who can say if judgements are thus not sometimes clouded? But only a tiny proportion of the total audience travels in this way. As nearly all productions are home-produced, and as there is very little touring by national companies as in Britain or France, this means that the average culture-goer in say, Stuttgart, will see little all year except his own city's opera and theatre performances and he may thus form an exaggerated opinion of their merits. Berlin is the only city that regularly holds pan-German and international festivals with visiting companies of high quality. Elsewhere, the lack of opportunities for comparison may encourage a certain provincialism of taste and outlook – a drawback to the federal system that I referred to earlier and will return to later.

A few statistics will give some idea of the size of the sums officially devoted to culture. In Munich, *Land* and city each spends about 200 million DM a year; the town has also just built itself a big new multi-purpose arts centre, the Gasteig, at a cost of 350 millions. In Frankfurt, 11 per cent of the city's overall budget goes on the arts. Several German opera companies have much larger subsidies than Covent Garden, while the average public theatre expects to need to derive only 15 to 20 per cent of its income from box office, even though houses are often full or nearly full: this allows for more money for productions, and tickets are a little cheaper than in Britain. This scale of public spending would in Britain not only have given Mrs Thatcher a heart attack but also would soon spark off a ratepayers' revolt. In Germany it is considered normal. One reason certainly is that the citizens tend to share the council's views about prestige and local patriotism. In Dortmund, a town with a mediocre opera company and 17 per cent unemployment, there was some talk in 1986 of closing down the opera to save money: but local people, *including some of the unemployed*, retorted with protests in the streets, arguing that such a terrible step would spotlight the city's decline and thus be counter-productive. Exactly the same happened in Bremen, and in both cases the operas were saved. In many towns, to attend the opera or ballet is a way of showing loyalty to the city – yes, it *is* a bit like going to cheer one's local football team. In Stuttgart, when the great John Cranko was running the ballet under Schäfer, this company's biggest ever ovation was for its first performance after returning from a triumphal American tour – and Cranko and his dancers were a bit put out, fearing that they were being applauded less for their own merits than for having waved the local flag in New York.

Another factor that goes to explain the support for high subsidies is the traditional German veneration for culture, still very strong at least among the older middle-class generation. The average consumer of this kind tends to be more self-consciously 'cultured' than his English or even French counterpart; and he may well hold to a very Germanic concept of *Kultur* as an immutable value system that you learn to receive – like taking Communion – with a view to self-improvement. Culture is not just entertainment but a means of permanent education, both moral and spiritual. Such a person may even feel a sense of duty to himself in being able to speak about music and theatre and keeping in touch with what is offered locally. And of course, in many bourgeois circles, this ties in with a good deal of social convention and keeping-up-with-the-Müllers: people want to be seen at the right cultural events and to be able to talk about them with friends and neighbours, and much more than in Britain they like to dress up for the occasion. Most of them take out an *Abonnement* (lower-price season ticket) that commits them to seeing a certain number of shows each year. Nor is this dutifulness confined to the middle-classes: the trade unions have a system of block bookings at low rates, and these are very fully patronised (especially for the more popular classics) by an important minority of skilled workers, technicians and clerks. So, all in all, there is no lack of takers for the vast amount of officially-sponsored culture available. In Munich, for example, the distinguished Kammerspieltheater plays to 90 per cent capacity, while the opera and ballet tend to be booked out months ahead: at the start of an opera booking season, it is not uncommon for devotees to queue all night for tickets. And in Stuttgart I was told that nearly twice as many people each year go to drama, ballet and opera at the Staatstheater as to football matches in the city stadium.

It is of course the established classics – alike of music and drama – that tend to draw the biggest and most regular audiences. But there is also a somewhat different but sizeable clientèle for 'difficult' or provocative modern plays, and another for modern music. So an

Intendant can skilfully appeal to various sections of the community. In the German manner, however, whether classical or contemporary, his offerings will almost all be serious and 'cultural'. As we shall see, commercial comedies or new musicals of the *Cats* kind are seldom considered worthy of the subsidised houses and will not find their way there – until maybe they have acquired through time the status of minor classics, like *My Fair Lady* which was staged recently by the Hamburg State Opera.

This formal and often highbrow programming has in recent years come under frequent criticism from the new radical generations – Left-wingers, Greens and others – who have claimed that it is too elitist and out of touch with the taste of most ordinary people. It is not that they are demanding more commercial mass-entertainment, for this they equate with the Americanisation that they detest most of all. What they do want however is more 'participation' and spontaneity, and less of the well-intentioned official spoon-feeding by paternalists who think that they know best what is good for the public – the kind of spoon-feeding that the older German audiences have long accepted with happy docility. 'I'm opposed to this sterile "temple" culture, a feudal legacy from the royal days,' said one Stuttgart radical, Klaus Hübner, in 1973; 'we must take culture out of the museums and opera houses and into the streets. I'd like to see a big outdoor leisure zone in the city centre, with music and "happenings" and café-theatres. But the bourgeoisie are always scared that if something spontaneous occurs the police will turn up. As no doubt they would.'

So in those days all over Germany the call went out for more street festivals and suchlike. As in other countries, worthy efforts were also made to 'bring culture to the workers', to the philistine masses who enjoy *Bild* and the comic-strips and would never join the elites of the union block bookings. Several major directors led this movement, including Peter Zadek, then in charge of the famous Bochum theatre, who would put on little plays in pubs and factories and try to woo workers to his own stage with simple popular works and soup served in the interval. Experiments of this kind have borne some fruit in populist Britain: but in Germany with its different traditions they were not a great success and were abandoned. As the deputy manager of the Bochum theatre said to me, in 1985: 'We are not workers, our interests are different from theirs and it's pointless to try to reconcile them. The way to woo the working-class is through the next generation, by inviting teachers to bring school groups here so that *they* can get used to what a theatre is all about. This we do.'

Meanwhile, in the past five or ten years many cities have given some positive responses to the kind of anti-elitist challenge formulated by Hübner and others. Culture has at last been widened out and some of it made less formal. The programming of the 'temples' themselves has scarcely been altered, nor their budgets reduced: but city councils have begun to put money into street festivals and 'happenings', now much in vogue. They have also sponsored new small-scale arts centres in the suburbs where modest professional events of all kinds are held from time to time – recitals, art shows, etc. – and where amateur groups can operate too. This is routine in any Western country today: but for German official policy it marks quite a bold departure, an enlarging of the classic concept of *Kultur*. Even in these centres there is still quite a dosage of municipal spoon-feeding: but spontaneity and participation are present too, linked to the recent blossoming of 'citizens' initiative' units so much favoured by the Greens (see p. 433). Little groups will sometimes write and act their own playlets about local history and folklore – all a little too parochial and inward-looking maybe, but very much in tune with the current anti-consumerist, small-is-beautiful, love-your-local-*Heimat* trends. Councils are also giving some money to the professional 'fringe' theatre, but less than in many European countries (see below).

In their overall patronage policies since the war, most cities and *Länder* have shown themselves remarkably liberal and have often supported theatre or art that is provocatively modernistic or highly critical of society. Of course the pattern varies. Some smaller towns in right-wing hands have been reactionary. But in the big cities like Munich or Frankfurt, so much in the limelight, so intensely in rivalry, and with sizeable and demanding 'egghead' audiences, even CDU or CSU rulers have not felt it prudent to oppose the new cultural trends too openly. Councillors who admit to hating modern art will often vote public money for avant-garde exhibitions, or for buying works by Beuys and others, so that their city can keep up with its peers in this field. And in some cases a strong and liberal-minded CDU mayor has been able to override his more conservative colleagues and give backing to progressive local arts managers.

This has been the case in Frankfurt under Walter Wallmann, and also under Manfred Rommel in Stuttgart, a city that provides a good illustration of the various culture conflicts. The local Swabians with their pious and cautious temperament are not exactly the most obvious patrons of the avant-garde, and they have fought battles against both *Land* and city schemes. In 1971 the *Land* Government, wanting to do its bit for modern art, spent 50,000 DM on a reclining figure by Henry Moore, whom they knew to be a big, acceptable name. But there was an outcry, many burghers denounced as 'ill-minded' this harmless sculpture of a draped female – and for 13 years it remained hidden away behind bushes. 'Typical,' was one liberal's comment; 'these Swabian culture-snobs, they want to buy the best, then don't like it.' Finally in 1984 the Moore was reprieved and now stands very conspicuously just across the motorway, at the entrance to the no less controversial new extension to the Staatsgalerie, the town's main art museum, owned by the *Land*. Designed by Britain's James Stirling (see p. 286), this striking and unusual building also came in initially for its share of local abuse: but, when the world's architectural critics proclaimed it a masterpiece, the Swabians soon started to feel proud of it. The Moore, too, now causes hardly a murmur. So there has been a certain progress.

The theatre in Stuttgart has faced somewhat similar problems. The main civic theatre is owned by the *Land*, with city participation; and in 1963 *Generalintendant* Schäfer chose as its director the already well-known Peter Palitzsch, a Marxist and former pupil of Brecht in East Berlin. In picking such a firebrand for so prudent a town, Schäfer wanted to bring in new ideas and put Stuttgart on Germany's theatrical map. He succeeded – at a cost. Palitzsch gave a Marxist twist to Shakespeare's histories; he introduced Stuttgart to Brecht and to Brechtian methods, and he drew round him a new regular audience in beards and duffle-coats, very different from the conventional opera-goers. But increasingly he fell foul of the *Land* Government. The *Theaterbeirat*, a *Land*-cum-city advisory board, did not have the right to veto his plays directly, but they could and did put pressure on Schäfer, complaining that his productions were too Leftist *and* too erotic. Ultimately Palitzsch wearied of the feuding and moved off to Frankfurt. It was a saga typical of that politicised era. He was succeeded in 1974 by Claus Peymann, equally celebrated but less political, and for a while he did well. But he too fell out with the *Land*, especially when in 1976 he posted up in the theatre an appeal for funds to help pay the dentist's bills of Gudrun Ensslin, the terrorist leader then in prison outside the city. Lothar Späth's patience snapped and Peymann was eased out and went to Bochum. After this, radical theatre in Stuttgart went through a lean period, but finally Rommel himself came to the rescue. Werner Schretzmeier, a young left-wing producer who had been running an 'alternative' arts centre in a town nearby, was invited by Rommel to take over a disused factory in the city and turn it into a similar kind of informal multi-purpose complex, with a 300,000 DM annual subsidy. This duly started up, with a mixed fare of jazz, political cabaret, talk-ins and the like. Some councillors were indignant, but Rommel got his way. 'There are two cultures in this big city, official and alternative,' he told me, 'and it is only fair to cater for both. Schretzmeier is a political opponent of mine, yes, but one would never find a right-wing person suitable for such a venture.' In short, this city of Pietist tradition will still fight its rearguard battles and will sometimes win them, for a while. But finally it has accepted the need to march with the times.

[271]

Theatre: morally serious, wilfully provocative

Since the war, the London theatre and the German theatre have both of them frequently been described as 'the best in the world'. But so different are they that it is hard to judge their rival merits. The British theatre is much more commercial: not only are fewer companies subsidised but its attitudes and those of its public are very different from those in Germany. When Schiller in the 18th-century described theatre as a 'moral institution', its role being to instruct and not simply to entertain, he carried out this precept in his own plays, and so did others who came after him, including Büchner, Wedekind and Brecht, all of them writing dramas that were quite often didactic and political. And, since the war, Hochhuth, Weiss, Dorst and others have done likewise.

Today, theatre managers may not necessarily want plays to be directly political, but at least they expect them to be serious, to shed light on social or philosophical problems, and not to appear too frivolous – and that is what their public expects too. So, just as in the novel, there exists a far greater gulf than in Britain between this 'moral' theatre and mere commercial entertainment. The Anglo-American genre of sophisticated comedy, above all witty and amusing but also casting a satirical eye on the human condition – this hardly exists in Germany, where the commercial 'boulevard' theatre is of low prestige and generally low quality, devoting itself mostly to humdrum farce and sit-com. And this poses a problem for anyone trying to import good new British plays into Germany. Where are they to fit in? The state and civic theatres usually turn up their noses at Frayn, Ayckbourn and Neil Simon as being much too light; sometimes they will produce Pinter or Stoppard, but with a slightly guilty conscience; and even Shaffer they and the critics fail to take quite seriously. *Amadeus*, treated as such a cultural event at London's National Theatre, was performed apologetically by some of the big German companies rather in the way that an opera company will sometimes lower its sights to stage an operetta. After all, did Shaffer not treat the plight of our great and wonderful Mozart rather too . . . *flippantly?*

Because theatre has so long held this moral role in Germany and is so central to the nation's intellectual life, it was encouraged to play a part in the reforging of German democracy after 1945. By September 1944 the Nazis had closed down all theatres in Germany and Austria, and by May 1945 most of their buildings lay gutted or in ruins. The Allied occupiers then actively helped them to make a new start, and during the next decades over 100 theatres were restored or rebuilt, some quite sumptuously. In the early years, the companies eagerly set about playing the many works – by Brecht and many others – that had been banned under the Nazis and were still largely unknown to

German audiences. Then in the early 1960s the new German political playwrights arrived upon the scene, prompting the radical British critic Kenneth Tynan (amongst others) to call the modern German theatre the finest on earth. These new plays were of various kinds. Some dealt in a forceful semi-documentary style with major themes of guilt and responsibility for the war and the Holocaust – for example, Rolf Hochhuth's *The Deputy* (1963), about the failure of Pope Pius XII to condemn the Nazi crimes against the Jews; the same author's *Soldiers* (1967), which questioned Churchill's role in the war; and *The Investigation* (1965), a meditation on Auschwitz by Peter Weiss, who had lived in Sweden since 1939. A few other political plays were on post-war themes, such as Grass's *The Plebeians Rehearse the Uprising* (1966), which criticised Brecht's failure to support the East German workers' revolt in 1953. Others again took historical subjects and hinted at their contemporary relevance: among them, Weiss's *Marat/Sade* (1964), the shorter title of his masterpiece about the murder of Marat, and Tankred Dorst's *Toller* (1968), a study of the left-wing insurrection in Munich in 1919. These and other such plays were enthusiastically performed all over Germany in the 1960s and early '70s, and so were the works of the great Swiss dramatists, Max Frisch and Friedrich Dürrenmatt, and (a little later) the Austrians, Peter Handke and Thomas Bernhard. (Rather as the British will sometimes appropriate Synge or O'Casey, but even more blatantly so, German theatres and critics have a habit of annexing these German-speaking Swiss and Austrian writers and regarding them as part of German drama – a cultural *Anschluss* that seems to me questionable.)

Just as in literature, political theatre has gone largely out of fashion since the mid-1970s, yielding place to plays on more personal and reflective themes.[1] This shift has mirrored basic changes in the mood

---

[1] There has also been a decline in the excellent German tradition of political satiric cabaret, whose brilliant heyday was in pre-Nazi Berlin. It made a modest comeback in the 1950s and 1960s, but has since suffered from the impact of television, and more especially from the fact that German society has become more open and placid, so that cabaret lacks effective targets – as Heidi Zerning of the *Kommödchen* cabaret in Düsseldorf told Richard Mayne in a BBC interview in 1984: 'Twenty years ago people had the feeling that cabaret was very daring and courageous, but today it is no longer necessary to be so bold, for democratic freedom has become established.' Some cabarets do still survive – the best, along with the *Kommödchen*, are probably *Die Stachelschweine* in Berlin and the *Lach und Schiess Gesellschaft* in Munich – and they play to full houses of neatly-dressed bourgeois groups enjoying the cosy jibes about the neatly-dressed bourgeoisie. But the bite and the wrath are not there. Mild satire of this kind has now spread out into full-scale productions in the big civic theatres, and these can be very successful – as witness *München Leuchtet* (see p. 31) and a lively revue, *Unsere Republik*, devised and performed by the Bochum company. But, for true German satiric cabaret as an outlet for political frustration, one must go to the GDR (see pp. 355–6).

of the times: but in part it was also a reaction against the political tur-
moil that affected theatres in the 1968 period, when young actors and
staff sometimes tried to unseat or demote the *Intendant*, to bring in
collective leadership and fill their stages with agit-prop activity. That
phase has now long since ended: as in the universities, the old guard
has discreetly reasserted itself. Meanwhile, the new writers of the
1970s and '80s have not turned their backs on moral and social questions, but they treat them in a more oblique and philosophical manner. Plays dwell on the isolation of the individual, the pressures of
modern society, the contradictions and absurdities of life, illusion
versus reality, and the artifice of theatre itself; or they indulge in low-
life social realism.

Much the most talented and prolific member of this new wave is
the Bavarian arch-realist Franz Xaver Kroetz, whose 40 or so plays
have been translated and performed in over 30 countries. Kroetz has
at various times held jobs as lorry-driver, male-nurse and casual
labourer: he has a keen empathy with the joys and miseries – mostly
miseries – of the peasantry and working-class, and he depicts them
with a savage candour that some audiences find hard to take. Actors
swear foully, masturbate on stage, and so on. Mental retardment,
peasant primitivism, divorce, unemployment, the corroding effects
of capitalism – these are among Kroetz's themes, and his characters
indulge in incest, rape, murder and even crucifixion. Yet he is not just
seeking shock effect: he writes with great sincerity of feeling and
appears to be a genuine poetic misanthrope and pessimist, a little like
the French film-maker Maurice Pailat. *Stallerhof* is the compassionate
study of a Bavarian farm-worker's love for the mentally-defective
daughter of a brutish farmer who cruelly puts an end to the affair;
Through the Leaves, which I saw beautifully performed by Scottish
actors at London's Bush Theatre, charts the hopeless liaison between
an affectionate middle-aged woman and an emotionally-deprived
worker who can express his feelings only through abuse and rejection. More recently, Kroetz has turned away from this kind of lyrical
realism towards didactic social analysis (*Furcht und Hoffnung der BRD*)
or portentous fantasy (*Bauernsterben*), and some critics feel that he has
begun to lose his touch. *Bauernsterben*, a study of young peasants
destroyed by city life, was presented in 1985 by Munich's Kammerspieltheater, complete with pissing and copulation on stage, and was
then prosecuted for obscenity (unsuccessfully) by a Catholic
institute.

Even more fashionable today than Kroetz, though less interesting a
writer in my own view, is Botho Strauss of Berlin, whose plays deal in
various ways with lack of human communication, the yearning to
find a meaning in life, and other modish themes. In 1984 his five-hour
Der Park enjoyed a huge cult success throughout Germany, where it

was staged by as many as 20 different theatres: a free updating of *A Midsummer Night's Dream*, it showed Oberon and Titania coming to the earth in search of true feeling, but finding only selfishness and triviality. Some critics felt that with this clever-clever self-indulgent work Strauss had fallen into his own trap and was himself showing a lack of feeling.

These and other modern playwrights – including Heiner Müller of the GDR, and the Austrians and Swiss – appear from time to time in the repertory programmes. So do the German classics, and very much more frequently, with Schiller and Brecht (now a classic) in the lead, followed by Goethe, Lessing and Kleist. The subsidised theatres have a statutory duty to perform these considerable authors, who apart from Brecht are too little known in Britain. Happily, this ignorance is not reciprocated. The Germans may pooh-pooh modern British drama: but they adore Shakespeare, who in the fine 19th-century translations of Schlegel and Tieck (and sometimes in modern ones too) is much the most widely performed of *any* playwright. Shaw and Molière, Ibsen and Chekhov are popular too.

Major productions of these classics are quite often flamboyantly experimental, and this has led to heated controversy. Almost as much as in the France of Chéreau and Planchon, the German stage today has become a director's theatre: led by Peter Zadek, Peter Stein and Claus Peymann, a new kind of virtuoso director has come to the forefront, and he more than the actors or the author becomes the play's real superstar. For better or worse, he imposes his personality on the text, not necessarily changing its words but often restaging so as to alter their significance. It is a theatre of gesture, movement and elaborate lighting effects. Sometimes, in the right hands, the results are brilliant and they bring out new subtleties in the play – witness Stein's recent *Three Sisters* in Berlin – but in other cases a showy director has been over-experimental and this has shocked the older generation. 'No one has a right to object to new interpretations of old plays,' Gordon Craig wrote in *The Germans* (op. cit. p. 225); '. . . on the other hand, one is entitled to expect of new versions a decent fidelity to the author's purpose and his text, or so one would think. In the West German theatre this was not always a sound expectation. What often took place there was nothing less than an unashamed manipulation of the classics. Schiller was so often the object of this kind of treatment that one was almost persuaded that directors were revenging themselves upon their schoolmaster for having made them memorize passages from *Maria Stuart* or *Don Carlos*.'

More to the point, these gifted directors were bored with the prospect of mounting yet another loyal presentation of some play that had been done hundreds of times, and they wanted to add their own creative bit. Freed by their subsidies from the usual box-office restraints they were keen to impress the critics with their originality – and sometimes they went too far. Professor Craig instances Zadek's *Othello* at Hamburg in 1976, with Desdemona as a prostitute in a bikini; Alfred Kirchner's *The Tempest* in Berlin (1978) that made Caliban, not Prospero, the true hero; and similar liberties taken by Stein with Goethe's *Tasso* and Hansgünter Heyme with Schiller's *Wilhelm Tell*. Other examples include a *Hamlet* staged in Munich by Maximilian Schell who wrote a modern translation, to have the Prince declaiming to Ophelia, 'Go to a brothel, go!' In one *Maria Stuart* production, the queens Mary and Elizabeth appeared on roller-skates; in another, done by Heyme in Stuttgart, these two royal enemies became friends and lesbians united in a feminist cause, dancing together and combing each other's hair. Audiences would tend to walk out from such oddities – leading one Stuttgart cloakroom attendant to complain to my wife, 'It's infuriating! In the old days, once I'd taken people's coats I could settle down to a quiet three hours knitting jerseys for my grandchildren. Now I'm continually interrupted.'

It would be wrong however to give the impression that all the innovative productions by star directors have been of this kind. Many have preserved the authentic spirit of the original play while exploring it from new angles – this has been true of much of the work of the Schaubühne in Berlin which over the past 20 years has been generally regarded as the best theatre company in Germany. It was founded in the early 1960s on a collective basis by a group of ex-students, and today it is still privately run, though it receives a large subsidy from the city. It inhabited a modest theatre building in Kreuzberg until 1981, when it moved to a splendid and expensive new one on the Ku'damm: here it has much better scope for elaborate staging, though some critics feel that the move has dampened the exuberance of its spirit. Up until 1985 its presiding genius and co-manager was Peter Stein, a gentle but intense individual, who himself directed many of its finest productions – for example, Chekhov's *The Three Sisters*, ecstatically praised. I missed it myself, but I quote from Michael Ratcliffe's account in the *Observer* of March 17, 1985; 'Few non-German speakers could fail to be moved at the very start by the clamour of birdsong, the distant bells in the town and the brilliant spring sunshine flooding the deep-set windows. . . The virtuoso second act is lit almost entirely by candlelight and spoken in the low voices of evening . . . The wind rises in soft moans about the house, as though lifting it a little above the earth . . . Most graphic of all are the little gestures of arm and hand . . .' Stein had in the 1960s played his part in the let's-bring-theatre-to-the-workers movement: but by the 1980s his and the Schaubühne's concerns had become much less social than aesthetic, and he was on record as saying, 'Theatre and the politics of direct action do not mix. Theatre is an irrational, undoctrinaire medium.' In 1985, feeling that he had been with the company long enough, he left Berlin to freelance and was soon in Cardiff, directing Verdi's *Otello* for the Welsh National Opera. But he planned to remain an associate and guest director of the Schaubühne.

If Stein is unquestionably Germany's greatest director, number two is probably Peter Zadek, much more the extrovert maverick and given to making highly quotable remarks such as, 'We Germans are surely the only people on earth who enjoy a bad conscience more than a beautiful woman.' The 'we' should perhaps be qualified, for Zadek having fled Germany with his parents to avoid Hitler, then spent 25 years in London where his theatre work began: his staging there of *Le Balcon* led him into a famous row with Genet. Zadek later was one of the relatively small number of Jews who have chosen to return to Germany to pursue artistic careers, and in the 1970s he was *Intendant* of the Bochum Schauspielhaus which he built up into one of the three or four best in the country. Since 1985, also as *Intendant*, he has been reviving the fortunes of Hamburg's famous Schauspiel-haus, where his blood-and-gore *Duchess of Malfi* raised some eyebrows. 'Theatre,' he says, 'must be free from all taboos.' Hence his deliberate shock treatment of the classics – an Othello in tails with black paint running down his face, hanging the dead Desdemona nude over a clothes-line.

It is clear that this German system of highly-subsidised non-commercial theatre has both strengths and drawbacks. The free rein that it gives to innovations of the Zadek kind may lead to some excesses, but it can also stimulate a degree of creativity that would be harder to achieve in the commercial theatre. It makes for handsome productions on good modern stages, with large companies of well-paid actors used to working together. Freed from the constraints of needing to pander to the star system, they can stick to the German tradition of ensemble acting: big names are seldom invited from out-side, and the repertory cast take it in turns with parts large and small. But the other side of this coin is that the theatres with their big public budgets tend to get weighed down with bureaucracy and civil service regulations; the actors, most of them on permanent contract, cannot easily be dismissed if their work deteriorates, and this makes for a static situation that can affect quality. Even the high level of subsidy can in some ways be a handicap, as Zadek once told the BBC: 'Of course it's marvellous for someone working in the theatre, but it's also a killer – after a while you stop thinking realistically about your audience, as the play is going to run anyway.' Moreover, even though a theatre does not live under the tyranny of the box-office, there are other masters it must take account of – the politicians who supply its budget and the voters on whom they in turn depend. Indi-vidual productions cannot be interfered with, but if a manager's or producer's policy becomes too unpopular, he can face heavy pressures or even dismissal, as we have seen in Stuttgart. During a local election campaign in Berlin in 1970, the CDU charged the Schaubühne with 'subversive indoctrination' because of its production of a Brecht adaptation of Gorki's *The Mother* – whereupon, soon before polling day, the SPD-led city council cravenly reduced the theatre's subsidy. Fortunately, this kind of direct political victimisation happens only rarely.

Nonetheless, the dependence on local subsidy does tend to influence an *Intendant*'s policy in one of two contrasting ways. Either a theatre will seek to demonstrate its independence by staging productions that are artistically or politically provocative. Or else more frequently, at least in the smaller cities, it will prefer to play safe and follow the latest fashions set elsewhere. After all, it may not depend commercially on large audiences but it may still want to show its sponsors that it knows how to please the public. In their choice of new plays, these smaller theatres generally prefer to cash in quick on some modish trend coming from Munich or Berlin, rather than try out some little-known author they have found themselves: for example, Botho Strauss wrote *Der Park* under the aegis of his friend and mentor Stein, and in 1984 the Schaubühne was one of the first to stage it, whereupon 20 other theatres around Germany applied to do so too, since Strauss is so à la mode. This state of affairs was strongly criticised to me by Christof-Johannes Vitali, a Swiss cultural manager working in Frankfurt: 'New plays tend to be given these very spectacular, highly-financed productions, and then they just disappear. Every theatre today feels obliged to do the new Strauss: but I bet his agent will have trouble selling that play in five years' time. It's a feverish, unnatural situation, less healthy in my view than the one in Britain or America where a new play has a more continuing life. Plays there may need to be more accessible and amusing: but with all the varied commercial theatres they really find it easier to win an outlet.' A few established figures like Strauss and Kroetz do very well: the rest find it hard to gain recognition. It may well be that very few good new plays are being written: one manager told me that he and his staff read 150 new texts a year and only about five are at all worth considering. But it is probable that many young would-be playwrights feel deterred from writing for the theatre, not only by the lack of interest, but, as in France, by the star directors' obsession with their own *mise-en-scène* that distorts or ignores the text. Many authors prefer to write for radio or TV, where they get more money and quicker recognition. Or else, for lack of scope in the big theatres, they fall back on the 'fringe'.

This fringe – the so-called 'free theatre groups' and others – has developed later and less effectively than in many neighbouring countries and today it is not as flourishing as in Holland, Britain, Italy or even France. One reason generally given is that the authorities in those countries grant much less subsidy to the public theatres and so are readier to help the fringe, which in Germany is starved: in Munich the city council allots 22 million DM a year to its Kammerspieltheater but only about 1.5 million DM to the 30 or so fringe groups put together, and this pattern is much the same elsewhere. There are some German drama critics who argue that this is as it should be, for the quality of the fringe is mostly poor – this is true – and there is no point in wasting public money on it. Others retort – perhaps more fairly – that the fringe does at least contain latent talent, and if it were encouraged it could improve and make a real contribution which at present lies wasted.

Berlin unsurprisingly has the liveliest fringe scene in Germany, followed by Frankfurt: also Munich, which even sponsors a fringe and experimental theatre festival each July, claimed to be the leading one of its kind in Europe after Nancy's. Of the more than 40 theatres and theatre groups in Munich – a lot, for a city of that size – three are public, five or six are 'boulevard', and the rest are fringe in one way or another: only about half these groups have their own theatre and the rest are itinerant and ephemeral, using improvised premises such as rooms at the back of beer-halls. As Munich is Germany's film capital and the site of Germany's main drama academy, there are always plenty of young actors looking for work, and some of them turn to forming fringe groups, with varying success. Some of them put on modest but respectable productions of, say, Sartre or Stoppard. Others, the more radical or 'alternative' ones, prefer to write or improvise their own little plays about their own little lives and problems (being ill or out of work, going on peace demos, sharing a flat), such as the tediously wordy non-drama about unemployment that I saw in Hamburg at an improvised theatre complex in a disused factory. Other groups prefer the avant-garde: at the aptly-named little Black Box Theatre in Munich's new Gasteig complex, I attended a 'happening' devised by a local luminary of the high fantastic Alexis Sagerer, who looks as seedy as Fassbinder and is said to have been influenced by Beuys. Helped no doubt by this pedigree, he mounted a satire on the Munich composer Carl Orff that included making music with saucepans, saws and squeaky toys, against a flickering backdrop of thirty-banked-up video screens showing old films, while a girl combed five live and rather smelly pink pigs. In the intervals of nodding off, I fell to reflecting that the fringe and avant-garde in Germany, like so much else, do suffer from the lack of a big capital city that could set a standard and thus separate the sheep from the goats – or pigs. Sagerer is well-known in Munich, but not in the rest of Germany. Inevitably his shock tactics smack of provincialism.

[279]

Frankfurt has a remarkably active fringe, whose various groups often play to full audiences and include an English company that on my last visit were doing *The Mousetrap* – not quite Sagerer's style. Much the most impressive fringe venture in Frankfurt, indeed in all Germany, is the Gallustheater, operating from a very crummy hall in an industrial-cum-working-class district. In the wake of the ideas of 1968, it was founded some years ago by a handful of Leftist people, as an amateur-drama-cum-youth-and-social-centre and a 'forum for research into cultural conflict and integration'. A few years later its liveliest habitués were some Italian *Gastarbeiter* teenagers, mostly born in Sicily or Apulia, then brought up in Germany and feeling adrift between two cultures. So good was their amateur acting that the Gallus *animateurs* formed them into a semi-professional group which still flourishes today and has won quite a success. In a mix of German and Italian they improvise their own plays on the problems of immigrants' integration, and they tour Germany and other countries, including their own south Italy. It is probably the most striking single contribution that *Gastarbeiter* have made to the German cultural scene (see p. 251). 'They are young factory workers who've become real professional actors,' I was told by Brian Michaels, an English theatre producer living in Frankfurt who took the lead in creating the group. 'But,' he went on, 'the city gives us only 50,000 DM a year in subsidy, compared with 19 million for its civic theatre – disgraceful. Mayor Wallmann may have an enlightened policy towards the "official" culture, such as the opera's avant-garde productions, but he and his council are far more concerned with these prestige-winners than with the poor old fringe which most of them find too Leftist. All over Germany, there's far too great a gulf between the official theatre and the fringe, which gets pushed aside. Yet the big theatres *need* the fringe as a breeding-ground of new ideas and talent.'

Some others would disagree. One leading critic, Peter Iden of the *Frankfurter Rundschau*, told me that he felt the established theatres did a perfectly adequate job in spotting fringe talent or nurturing their own. But the more general view in Germany today is that the theatre, after some brilliant periods in the 1960s and '70s, is marking time and resting on its laurels. The structure is impressive and the potential is there. But the whole operation has grown top-heavy and lacking in new inspiration. Rather as in the university world, the big public theatres with their near-monopoly of talent could probably do with a little competition not only from the fringe but from the despised commercial sector – and here Germany may even have something to learn from Britain, where the National and the RSC may set the pace but are usefully kept on their toes by Shaftesbury Avenue. Probably, above all, the serious Germans need to be able to forget Schiller's dictum and to laugh and relax a little more in the theatre. That is why in 1985 I was cheered by seeing *Unsere Republik* at Bochum, a lively and light-hearted ensemble revue, home-produced by the company. It had serious overtones, but it also wittily poked fun at many of the foibles of post-war Germany. It was truthful yet *entertaining*. Such torch-bearers of the old flame of satiric cabaret are most welcome – but still rare.

Music in Germany today, despite the inevitable rivalries between devotees of classical and modern, is much less controversial a matter than theatre – but it is even more omnipresent and well patronised. Any visitor is at once impressed by the richness and variety of the musical life of this nation that still has music in its blood and lovingly cultivates its marvellous heritage – and this applies not only to professional performance but to amateur activity. Many people eagerly join choirs or chamber groups in their leisure time. And the attractive old tradition of family *Hausmusik*, which had been in decline during the hectic *Wirtschaftswunder* period, is now blossoming again in an age that puts more stress on quality of life and personal values. At a middle-class social evening, it is not unusual for the host and hostess and their teenage children to perform quartets for their guests. Maybe the daughter is a gifted pianist and the son plays the flute. It is endearing, and like something out of Jane Austen.

As music by its nature is less 'ideological' than the other arts, it suffered less from the Nazis' distortions of German culture – apart from Hitler's appropriation of Wagner – and so after 1945 it was more easily able to regain its position. The Germans turned to it thankfully as one of the least desecrated of their traditions, a valued link with the older past. Today there are some 70 subsidised symphony orchestras, the best still being the Berlin Philharmonic where in 1985 the great Austrian, Herbert von Karajan ('the last of the dinosaurs', he has been called), celebrated his 30th anniversary as chief conductor. Stuttgart has no less than five symphony orchestras, whereas an equivalent British city might have just one; and its main concert hall is always filled in advance with block-bookings, at least when the better-known classics are being played. But all over the country the interest in modern music is quite strong too, and in this field Germany has played an important role, attracting a number of leading composers. Pierre Boulez for some years made Germany his home base, before he was finally welcomed home by his native France; Mauricio Kagel, born in Argentina but now a German citizen, settled in Germany in the early 1960s because, he said, he found it the most stimulating country for modern music. The electronic studios of the radio station in Cologne were at that time the most advanced of their kind in the world, while the Darmstadt summer school also played a major role as a meeting-place for the post-war avant-garde. Its regular attendants included Germany's two most influential modern composers, Hans Werner Henze who lives in Italy, and Karl Heinz Stockhausen who still lives in Cologne.

The traditional of classical opera is alive and well. Some 50 subsidised houses have regular companies, and they attract varied audiences: though a Munich first night or the Wagner season in Bayreuth may be diamond-studded high-society affairs, many a simple typist or technician will happily pay 50 DM to see *Figaro* in Kiel or Karlsruhe. Hamburg's opera, which plays to 98 per cent capacity houses and gets a 62 million DM annual subsidy, is today probably Germany's best. Its prowess was built up by the great Swiss, Rolf Liebermann, who was *Intendant* in 1963–73 and then returned to the post in 1984 after a brilliant period at the Paris Opera. A tall, relaxed figure in his late seventies, he received me with warmth and charm: 'I'm here in the front row of the stalls every night – the audience expect it of me. It's like running a restaurant. My main problem here is the shortage today of really good European singers, plus the fact that my permanent ensemble of chorus and orchestra cannot be sacked and many are simply too old.' When I asked him which was today the best opera in Europe, he answered pat, 'Geneva'.

All over Germany, opera-goers tend to prefer the classical repertoire: but Liebermann, Schäfer and a few others have made serious efforts to woo them to modern or even to specially-commissioned works. 'In my view,' said Liebermann, 'an opera house only justifies its vast subsidy if it puts on at least some new works, and thus helps living composers. Why should the taxpayer give us large sums to stage *Tosca* for a moneyed minority?' This policy has borne some fruit, but not as much as was hoped. Instead, in the past ten years the emphasis has switched to new interpretations of traditional operas – sometimes experimental, though seldom as iconoclastic as in the case of drama. Patrice Chéreau's inventive productions of the *Ring* at Bayreuth marked the high point of this movement, and they delighted even German Wagnerians. In the 1980s the principal regular testing-ground of this kind of new creativity has been the Frankfurt Opera, which under the *Intendant*-ship of the conductor Michael Gielen has become 'Europe's most radical and controversial centre of music theatre', in the words of Peter Heyworth of the *Observer* (December 15, 1985). Gielen has sponsored productions that have sought to return to what the composer really had in mind and to free the work from later accretions – while also making use of some accretions of his own in the form of startling modern decor and lighting. The results have frequently split the local public, so that the opera lost part of its old audience but gained a new one. Gradually Gielen wooed many Frankfurters to his ideas: and he was consistently backed by Mayor Wallmann and his council who may not have relished this style of opera themselves but were glad of the fame and prestige that it brought the city, in a country that thrives on operatic controversy. Gielen was due to leave in 1987, but not because he was given the push.

As much as opera is a great German tradition, classical ballet is not. Dance training has always been neglected. Times however are changing and Germany since the war has finally built up several world-class ballet companies, albeit that this has been achieved mostly by hiring outside talent: some 85 per cent of dancers are foreign, and the two best ensembles have been raised to their present quality respectively by an American, John Neumeier, now in charge at Hamburg, and by a South African, the late John Cranko, who after some years as a choreographer at Covent Garden ran the wonderful Stuttgart Ballet from 1960 until his sudden death in 1973 at the age of only 47. It is ironic that Cranko should have needed to come to Germany to find the scope and recognition that had eluded him in London. He told me soon before his death: 'I've had opportunities here that I'd never have found at the Garden. We do about eighty evenings of ballet a year in this opera house, and we can stage three new programmes a year. This is a better deal than the ballet gets anywhere in Britain.' How did it happen? Schäfer, believing in Cranko, persuaded the *Landtag* to vote the money needed to build the company – 'It had to be explained to them,' I was told, 'that a dancer needs more than one pair of new shoes a month.' Cranko then set about creating a regular audience, in a town that had virtually forgotten ballet. His genius lay essentially in the reworking of classical ballets in new forms, and this suited local taste: but he also created some memorable modern pieces, such as *Poème de l'Ecstase* written for Fonteyn. He helped Marcia Haydee, his Brazilian prima ballerina, to become one of the world's great dancers, and he was able to spot young local talent and create soloists from it. He became a hero in Stuttgart even with the people with no taste for ballet. After a period under Glen Tetley, the American choreographer, the company was then taken over by Haydee herself. Still in charge today, she has retained most of Cranko's repertoire and has built up his ballet school into the foremost in Germany. Though still excellent, the company has inevitably been tending to mark time, and in most critics' view it has now been overtaken by Hamburg.

It is in the area of modern as opposed to classical dance that Germany's own home-grown talent has made its more distinctive contribution – thanks above all to the celebrated Pina Bausch and her Tanztheater in the Ruhr town of Wuppertal. It might seem an unlikely setting – but this is decentralised Germany. Bausch was born in 1940 in nearby Solingen and, after training and working in New

York with the New American Ballet and the Metropolitan Opera, she decided to return to her roots to form her own company; and here she won subsidies from city and *Land* as well as the right to use the Wuppertal opera house as her base. She draws big audiences from the Ruhr and Rhine towns, as well as frequently touring abroad. Local people were hostile at first to her strange and provocative work – it harks back in some ways to earlier German expressionism – but, typically, they soon accepted it when the world's critics acclaimed it. Yet it is not for all tastes, this highly emotional mix of mime and dance, theatre and circus, acrobatics and incantation that has been described, less than kindly, as 'a collective therapy session'. Children's games or scenes of great stillness alternate with bouts of frenzy as actors hurl themselves against walls or mime sexual couplings, while the stage is sometimes covered with turf, earth or water that impedes their movements. Bausch refuses to see her work as therapy: but dance for her certainly signifies release of feeling and expression of personality – 'I am interested,' she says, 'not in how people move but in what moves them.' Her concern, she has said, is to project the emotions that classical dance tends to cloak or stylise.

In the world of the visual arts, Germany in the first post-war decades went through a somewhat barren period as far as new creative work is concerned, with the exception of the efforts of the late and much-contested Joseph Beuys. Whereas the First World War had led to a remarkable flowering in the 1920s, with the work of Beckmann, Dix, Ernst, Grosz and many others, this was not repeated after 1945. Most of the best artists had emigrated to escape the Nazis' persecution of 'degenerate' modern art, and those who stayed or then returned did not seem inspired by the experiences of war and post-war to the same degree as the novelists and poets of that time. A few sombre works evoked the ruins and desolation, but they were not especially memorable; and the 1950s and '60s were a humdrum period when it was hard to pick out any new painter of great worth and only the Düsseldorf abstract 'Zero' group made much impact. In the past 15 or so years however the scene has become more lively and a number of new talents have emerged, most notable among them being Baselitz, Penck, Hodicke and Anselm Kiefer. Their paintings mark a certain return to figurative art and to traditional German themes and techniques. Berlin in particular has become highly effervescent, the home of a large number of young painters such as the so-called '*Junge Wilde*' (young savages), using bright, bold colours and vivid subject-matter. More artists today live in Berlin than anywhere else, but the art-dealing and exhibiting scene is concentrated primarily in Cologne, followed by Düsseldorf, Munich and Berlin, and it is very active: many Germans and visitors to Germany are prepared to spend lavishly on new works. New York may still hold the lead: but most experts would agree that the interest in modern art is far more intense and widespread in Germany today than in either London or Paris. Whether this is any indication of the quality of the work being produced is another matter.

High prices are still being paid for the 'action sculptures' of the conceptual artist Josef Beuys, who lived in Düsseldorf where for some years he was a professor of sculpture. Beuys always arouses strong feelings. Like many people, I myself am no great lover of his work, but I am intrigued and attracted by his personality and what he stood for, and I recognise that he had a far greater influence on post-war German art than anyone else. When he died in 1986, aged 64, Waldemar Januszczak wrote of him in the *Guardian* (January 25), 'He was the most radical, charismatic and evocative artist of his times', and another critic called him 'the father of the avant-garde'. But many other art-lovers have sneered at his 'creations' – as when, for example, he filled a piano with washing-powder or painted frankfurters with brown shoe polish. He adored rough materials and would make sculptures out of bits of wood and steel, old newspapers, discarded junk and refuse – and especially felt and fat. These last two were his private symbols of rebirth, for in the war he had been a bomber pilot, and when his aircraft crashed in the Crimea he was saved from death by some Tartars who wrapped him in felt and rubbed fat into his skin. To protect an old war wound, he would also always wear a felt hat. But he was not simply a pretentious poseur, nor was he 'sending up' modern art. He had a generous belief in the potential of every individual for creating art; he also liked to involve himself in public issues and was a founder member of the Greens. With his craving for absolutes, his poetic extremism and his gift for abstract ideas, many critics have seen him as a quaint, essentially Germanic artist. Whether he was also a great one, time will tell. But he certainly helped German artists to recover their identity and self-confidence after the bleak post-war years.

Ours may not be the age of the solitary creative artist, but it is certainly that of the big public museum and the large brilliantly-mounted exhibition: from Beaubourg to Guggenheim this is a world-wide trend, and in Germany the results are as striking as anywhere. Generously funded, imaginatively set out and quite often 'socially relevant', German museums are far from being the dead fusty places that the term so often evokes – and the public responds to them: it is claimed that more people visit museums and exhibitions than go to football matches. Of Germany's 1,500 or so museums, some 86 per cent are publicly subsidised, while many of the others receive funds from private foundations, churches, and commerce and industry. Somewhat later than in the United States, many leading firms such as BMW have now begun to support modern art on a big scale by giving money to museums, galleries and exhibitions, thus supplementing the funds that come traditionally from the cities and *Länder*. Thanks to this varied patronage, new museums of all kinds are being built all over the place: seven devoted to modern art were opened in 1983 alone. In Frankfurt, the council has recently created or refurbished six museums along the banks of the Main. One of these, for handicrafts and applied art, is in a lovely bright shimmering new building designed by the New York architect Richard Meier; another, a museum of local history, follows the 'culture for all' philosophy of the city's well-known socialist culture manager, Hilmar Hoffmann, and tries to relate history to the daily life of working people. The superb Folkwang Museum in Essen does the same for the industrial history of the Ruhr.

Remarkable new art museums, or major extensions to existing ones, have been opened recently in Mönchen-Gladbach and Düsseldorf, and in Stuttgart where the excitement over Stirling's new wing to the Staatsgalerie has resuscitated interest in the contents of the museum as a whole: in the extension's first year of operation, 1984–5, annual entrances went up five-fold from 210,000 to over 1,300,000. This is encouraging, for the old and new parts of the Staatsgalerie between them house the best 20th-century art collection in Germany outside Düsseldorf. Stuttgart is not otherwise so noted for the visual arts: but it benefits from a most enlightened policy of the Baden-Württemberg Government which since the 1950s has been devoting a major part of the profits of the state lottery to the acquisition of new works for the various *Land* museums. Currently this runs to 3 million DM a year, ten times the Staatsgalerie's own purchasing budget. This does of course lead to disputes over choice. When the museum wanted to buy a Beuys for 500,000 DM, the *Landtag* raised its horrified Swabian eyebrows very high: but the *Land* Minister of Culture had the last word, and he backed the idea. So there this great debris-like sculpture now sits, filling one entire hall in all its Beuysterous glory, and it is almost the first work you see as you enter across Stirling's green rubber floor and mount in his glass-walled lift. Beuys, Kroetz, Schretzmeier, Zadek, Bausch, even Achternbusch . . . there is no doubt that Germany's official patrons are on balance liberal in accepting modern culture that they do not much care for themselves. Or at least they do not want to appear to be fuddy-duddies.

Museums will from time to time stage special exhibitions of a documentary nature than can shock the older generation. In Stuttgart in 1984, one small municipal museum mounted a remarkably frank survey of life in the city under the Nazis (see p. 393). And in Munich the Stadtmuseum under its left-wing curator, Christoph Stölzl, has on several occasions angered the CSU establishment – for example, with its critical survey of the *Oktoberfest* (see p. 35). In 1984 it held a brilliant and astonishing exhibition on the theme of Bavarian attitudes to death – room after macabre room filled with coffins, skeletons, and sculptures and paintings of deathbed scenes, operations, torture, and Death visiting the dying. 'Munich,' wrote one paper, 'has broken Vienna's monopoly of the death cult.' And Stölzl himself told me: 'Our policy here is to provoke, to look critically at society, to present new values, not bourgeois ones. And Munich is so self-confident that it feels prepared to be tolerant towards its *enfants terribles*. It's a city where culture loves to be provocative. Look at me. Look at Kroetz, Achternbusch, Sagerer. Look at Fassbinder!' Indeed: let us next look at Fassbinder.

Fassbinder, Herzog and Reitz's Heimat: *triumphs for the Cinderella of German arts*

If in the past twenty years so few new novelists, playwrights or painters of any significance have emerged in Germany, one reason could be, just as in France, that much of the best new creative talent has preferred to express itself through cinema. Suddenly in the late 1960s and 1970s the moribund German film industry produced out of nowhere a wonderful flowering of highly original work by gifted young directors – Fassbinder, Herzog, Schlöndorff, Wenders and others – and this 'New German Cinema', though in no sense forming a 'movement', soon came to be recognised as one of the three most fertile developments in West European film since the war, exceeded in achievement only by the Italian Neo-Realists and the French *nouvelle vague*. Today, decline may well have set in, with Fassbinder dead so young and other directors running short of inspiration or financial backing, or preferring to work abroad: but the appearance as recently as 1984 of the best film of the lot, Reitz's masterly *Heimat*, shows that the German cinema is still perfectly capable of surprising us again.

The renaissance of the 1960s was especially remarkable in its context, seeing that Germany was, and still is, a country with very little film culture – unlike France or the United States – and its previous cinema record had been extremely patchy. There had been a distinguished period in the 1920s, with the work of Lang, Lubitsch, Murnau, von Sternberg and others: but even before the rise of Hitler many of the leading directors had succumbed to the lure of Hollywood, and then the Nazis yoked the cinema to their own propaganda machine even more thoroughly than in the case of the other arts. After the war, an effective new start proved much more difficult than in the theatre or literature, for the tradition was not there. Just a few good films were made on anti-war or anti-Nazi themes – one could cite Helmut Käutner's *The Devil's General*, based on the play by Carl Zuckmayer, and *The Bridge* by the Swiss-born Bernhard Wicki – but the near-totality of the output consisted of banal down-market comedies and thrillers, or equally escapist *Heimatfilme* that gave droolingly sentimental portraits of rural life. In those days before the impact of television, the German cinema was prosperous commercially: but it included virtually no counterpart of the kind of personal film of quality then being made in France or Italy, or even sometimes in Britain. Unlike the theatre, cinema in Germany was not taken seriously by intellectuals as a cultural medium; audiences of all social classes simply wanted to be entertained.

By the early 1960s, however, new talent was impatiently looking for outlets. The event that is often regarded as marking the origin of the new German Cinema was the signing of the 'Oberhausen Manifesto' in 1962: at the festival of short films held annually in the Ruhr town of Oberhausen, twenty-six directors working in short films and documentaries came together and drew up a document proclaiming 'the old cinema is dead' and demanding 'new freedoms' for 'the creation of the new German feature film'. These young radicals were inspired by the recent successes of the *nouvelle vague* in France, and they even took over a number of its ideas and slogans. Only two of them, Kluge and Reitz, went on to achieve prominence as directors (and Reitz was to wait 20 years for this): but the impact of their manifesto was immediate. It focussed attention on the mediocrity of the film industry, and within a very few years it had prompted the Federal Government to start granting regular subsidies for film-making. This funding has not been ideally organised, as we shall see; but it did prepare the ground for the major directors who soon appeared. Without the backing they gained from the state, and later on from co-productions with television, they could never have found the money for their unusual and 'difficult' films.

The breakthrough began in 1966 when Kluge's first feature, *Yesterday's Girl (Abschied von Gestern)*, won the Silver Lion at the Venice Festival and Schlöndorff's *Young Törless* was well received at Cannes. Soon afterwards Fassbinder embarked on his prodigious output of two or three films a year, though it was not until 1974 that he began to attract world-wide attention when *Fear Eats the Soul* won a top prize at Cannes. Within a year or two critics on both sides of the Atlantic were describing this new cinema as 'the liveliest in Europe'. Then in 1979, with the great commercial success of Schlöndorff's *The Tin Drum* and Fassbinder's *The Marriage of Maria Braun*, a film wave that at first had been confined to the art-houses began to achieve wider audiences. The new directors were so diverse in their styles and outlook that they never constituted a 'school': but they nearly all lived in Munich, the German film capital, and many were friends. Like the French *nouvelle vague*, they worked at first on the margins of the main commercial film industry, making low-budget movies with their own little production companies – and again like the French they were true *auteurs*, in the sense that each film bore the personal stamp of its director who often doubled as producer and scriptwriter too. Many of them preferred to work regularly with the same well-tried actors (Herzog with Klaus Kinski, Wenders with Rüdiger Vogler, Fassbinder with Hanna Schygulla and others) who in those early years were not yet stars. And some of the *cinéastes* – notably Schlöndorff, but not Fassbinder – preferred to adapt novels rather than use original screenplays, partly because of the lack of any tradition of good script-writing in Germany. But the vast majority of their films, whether based on some Grass or Böll best-seller or springing from the director's own imagination, were dealing with essentially German themes or looking squarely at German society; or at least, as in the case of Herzog or Syberberg, they were giving expression to the German soul and character. And that is why this New German Cinema is so intensely interesting, and so relevant to a book such as mine. So let us take a look at the work of some of the main film-makers.

Alexander Kluge, born in 1932 near Magdeburg (now in the GDR), is the oldest of them and the most political. Right from the start at Ober-hausen he established himself as the group's chief ideologue and in some ways its spokesman; and just as he himself had been influenced by Brecht, so in turn he influenced some of those who followed in his wake. *Yesterday's Girl*, his first feature and still to date his best, was based on a real-life case: it is the story of a Jewish girl, Anita, who arrives penniless from the GDR and then drifts through a series of casual encounters and disappointments in West Germany, some-times exploited by others, sometimes herself committing petty crime, to end up as an unmarried mother in a penitentiary. The film's original German title, *Abschied von Gestern* (Farewell to Yesterday), was more ironically meaningful than its English one, for Kluge showed how Anita's attempts to make a clean new start in the West were con-stantly thwarted by her own and the collective German past. Himself a lawyer by training, he satirised the clumsy and sententious efforts of the legal and reformatory authorities to help Anita in her predi-cament, as she moved against a backdrop of the glossy greed of the *Wirtschaftwunder*, an isolated drop-out in that pre-1968 era, before such misfits had found any kind of solidarity or identity, as they have today. In the main role Kluge cast his own sister, Alexandra, who had never acted before but gave a mesmeric performance; and this he backed up with a shooting and editing style that was deliberately elliptical and staccato, full of jump-cuts and sudden shifts from

[*289*]

reality to fantasy, leading all the critics to compare him with the early Godard of *Vivre sa Vie* (1962). But, while Godard was the more original lyricist, Kluge was the sharper social analyst. After this promising start, the best-known of his subsequent films, *Artists atop the Big Top: Disorientated* (1967) and *Occasional Work of a Female Slave* (1973), dealt more obliquely with the moral dilemmas of the individual in society; and then, though he stayed in the limelight as an intellectual and polemicist, in his films he seemed to have little more to say. Much of his later work appears pretentious and over-fragmented.

Volker Schlöndorff, like Kluge, is a man of the Left who has made films critical of society: but his approach is far less cerebral and rarified. His work is smooth and entertaining, for he believes in putting across his message to a wide audience and has stated that only as a popular medium can cinema be justified. Born in Wiesbaden in 1939, he trained in France where he worked as assistant to Malle and Resnais. His first feature, *Young Törless* (1966), was based on a novel by Musil set in a boarding-school at the turn of the century. There followed a number of full-length films on contemporary social themes, often feminist, before in 1975 he made his first big public impact with a version of Böll's celebrated novella, *The Lost Honour of Katharina Blum*, published the previous year (see p. 159). This was something close to polemical film journalism, for Schlöndorff took Böll's bitter tale of an innocent hounded by the gutter Press and pointed up the political moral for all it was worth, casting the police in a more pernicious light than the book had done and stridently satirising the *Zeitung* and its owners (a barely-concealed attack on *Bild* and Springer). Some critics felt that the subtlety of the original had been sidestepped: but this vigorous film was a huge popular success, largely deserved.

Four years later Schlöndorff turned to Germany's other great post-war novelist by taking his cameras on location to Danzig for *The Tin Drum*: though it cut short the finale, in other respects his film was remarkably faithful to Grass, physical grotesquery and all, and throughout its assured two-and-a-half hours it packed a terrific punch, helped by a fine performance from the diminutive 12-year-old David Bennent as the child Oskar who refuses to grow bigger. After this Schlöndorff made *Circle of Deceit*, a decent liberal film also drawn from a recent novel, about the dilemmas of journalists in war-torn Lebanon. And then, to the surprise of many of his admirers, he deserted modern political issues for the high-society salons of pre-1914 Paris, by returning to his beloved France to take up a challenge that Visconti, Losey and others had toyed with but declined: the filming of Proust. But, though he sensibly confined himself to just one section of the enormous novel, his *Swann in Love* was little more than a distinguished failure, handsomely mounted, superbly acted by Jeremy Irons and others, but ultimately a hybrid that did not penetrate beneath Proust's wafer-thin skin. Enlisting a galaxy of talent, with British, French and Italian stars, music by Hans Werner Henze, Sven Nykvist of Sweden as cameraman, and script by Peter Brook and Jean-Claude Carrière, it seemed to be just the kind of expensive international prestige production that the New German Cinema had initially set out to oppose; and it left some critics wondering whether Schlöndorff in his search for major commercial success had not somehow lost his way and deserted his German inspiration – especially as his next project, in America, was a version of Arthur Miller's *Death of a Salesman*, with Dustin Hoffman. He is a very fluent and talented director, and his fondness for distinguished literary material is perfectly valid in its way: but his exploitation of trendy subjects has come to seem more than a little glib.

Schlöndorff's former wife, Margarethe von Trotta, collaborated with him on several films, acting as co-director of *Katharina Blum*: and then she went on to make her own features and to become Germany's best-known woman director. As well as being also on the Left, she has decided feminist views (see p. 163) and nearly all her films have been about the struggles of women in German society. Most notably, *The German Sisters* (*Die Bleierne Zeit*: 1980), a study of the terrorist Gudrun Esslin and her relationship with her sister, gave a moving and perceptive account of the pressures that can drive a gentle and educated girl to violent extremism. It deservedly won the Golden Lion at Venice. Then in 1985, with *The Patience of Rosa L.*, von Trotta chose another subject well suited to her: a portrait of the German pre-1919 left-wing leader Rosa Luxemburg. It won the 'best actress' prize at Cannes in 1986 for its star, Barbara Sukowa.

Wim Wenders, for all his recent obsession with America, remains every bit as Germanic at heart as Kluge or von Trotta. His films have a brooding, restless quality: they deal with footloose wanderers searching for home, and they exemplify a certain forlorn German romanticism. Born in Düsseldorf in 1945, Wenders attended film school in Munich and then first attracted attention in 1971 with *The Goalkeeper's Fear of the Penalty*, based on Handke's short existentialist novel, set in Austria: the solitary hero committing the perfect gratuitous murder, in the book a typically cerebral Handke creation, became in the film a typical Wenders romantic. There followed three celebrated 'road movies', all set in Germany, all quests or journeys both emotional and practical, all revealing of modern Germany as Wenders saw it. *Alice in the Cities* (1973), for my money the most attractive of all his films, had a journalist and a girl of nine meeting by chance in New York and travelling back to Wuppertal together in search of the child's family: here Wenders for the first time revealed his love-hate attitude to America and his feeling that Germany, warts and all, might be the more gentle and homely place. *Wrong Movement* (1974), a modernised version, scripted by Handke, of Goethe's *Wilhelm Meister's Apprenticeship*, was altogether more bleak, however: like the novel of 1795, it traced a young man's educational journey across Germany in search of self-realisation, meeting various strange characters on the way. But, whereas Goethe's book was fairly optimistic, Wenders and Handke showed a modern Germany that amidst all its affluence was a melancholy place. The bleakness continued in *Kings of the Road* (*Im Lauf der Zeit* – in the course of time: 1976), about two laconic and wistful young men who travel in a van across a dreary strip of territory beside the GDR border, repairing projectors in small run-down cinemas. The mood of desolation is not as metaphysical or as contrived as, for instance, in Antonioni: in fact, the film has a gentle human warmth about it, as the two men strike up a kind of comradeship. But it hardly paints a very rosy picture of life.

'The Yanks have colonised even our subconscious,' says one of the men in *Kings of the Road*. By now Wenders was not only fascinated by America but also disturbed by what he saw as the damage that it had done to European culture – and this was a theme of *The American Friend* (1977), a thriller set in Hamburg but filmed mainly in English. The 'friend' of the title is shown as a broken, sad drifter, far removed from the confident 'colonisers' of the early post-war period. Then, to explore more closely this tarnishing of the American dream, Wenders moved to the United States itself where he made his next four films. The best-known of them, *Paris, Texas*, won the Grand Prix at Cannes in 1984. Its story of a man with his child on a quest for his estranged wife took up, in a sense, the theme of *Alice in the Cities*, and then developed it much further; again, as in many of Wenders' earlier films, the desolate landscapes and cityscapes enhanced a mood of bleakness redeemed by gentle humanism – but touched this time by sentimentality in its improbable, over-dramatic ending. Some critics saw the film as a marvellous European vision of a certain America: I found it slow and portentous compared with *Alice*, and it seemed that Wenders' search for the American dream might have landed him, like his hero, on a Texan railtrack leading to nowhere. Maybe Wenders sensed this too, for by 1985 he was said to be fed up with Hollywood and with Coppola, his chief sponsor there, and thinking of returning to Europe. But he was soon at work on a film about a voyage round the world. In a very German way, he is a man with the *Wanderlust* spirit, carrying his German obsessions with him across the globe.

The same is true *par excellence* of Werner Herzog, who along with Fassbinder – and now Reitz too – must be reckoned the most important of the post-war directors. He is also much the most eccentric and visionary. He likes to film in extraordinary locations – not only the

Peruvian jungles of *Aguirre, Wrath of God* and *Fitzcarraldo* but, for example, the Sahara where he contracted bilharzia while shooting one of his early films, *Fata Morgana*. And for one sequence of *Heart of Glass* he took his team in open boats through rough seas to the remote and rocky Skellig isles off Ireland. Above all, Herzog's heroes are just as fanatic and visionary as he is – extraordinary, haunted people, operating at the end of their tether or pursuing bizarre dreams. Fitzcarraldo pulling his great ship over a hill in upper Amazonia, and Aguirre on his mad journey into that same jungle, are the best fictional examples: but Herzog will also seek out real-life people just as tormented, as in his documentary about the high-level ski-jumper Walter Steiner, giddily testing himself to the human limits. He will sometimes do astonishing things to his actors, as when he put the whole cast of *Heart of Glass* under hypnosis; or he will seek out un-usual performers for his films, such as the Berlin lavatory attend-ant and former mental home inmate whom he picked to play *Kaspar Hauser*, or the scores of dwarfs who made up the cast of *Even Dwarfs Started Small*.

It follows that Herzog's films are hardly about modern Germany in the manner, say, of Kluge or Fassbinder: most of them are set abroad, or in Germany's past like *Kaspar Hauser*, or in some fantasy realm. Yet he firmly denies that his films are not on German themes – as when I met him at his office in Munich 1984: 'All my work is about what the Germans are feeling inside themselves. They have these poetic images and urges which they suppress, and I help them to bring them out, by showing them Kaspar's dreams. I'm a Bavarian, and my films are in that tradition, they show the crazed Bavarian pursuit of the useless – mad King Ludwig was just like Fitzcarraldo.' I found Herzog a mild, soft-voiced, poetic man, not looking as if he were about to eat his boot or hike from Munich to Paris (two of his better-known exploits). He has often spoken of his belief in the validity of the irrational, of seeking 'planets that do not exist and landscapes that have only been dreamed'. He is a true genius, and his best films are venerated by cinemanes around the globe. But in Germany he is not too popular: most filmgoers find his work outrageous, even dis-gusting, and his box-office takings are low.

Born in Munich in 1942, Herzog grew up on a remote Bavarian farm: his work certainly has the baroque, heavily romantic quality associated with Bavaria. *Aguirre, Wrath of God* (1972), his first film of wide appeal, traced the fortunes of a crazed conquistador in the Amazonian jungle, who in the final mesmeric sequence is alone on a raft with his dead daughter and a swarm of monkeys, the last survi-vor of his lunatic expedition. Much of the film's bizarre effect was due to the presence in the title role of the mad-eyed, skull-faced Klaus Kinski, an actor who has often played with Herzog and whose manic temperament perfectly suits the director's style. Next came *The Enigma of Kaspar Hauser* (*Jeder für sich und Gott gegen alle* – each for himself and God against all: 1974), Herzog's most distinguished film and arguably Germany's post-war best until the arrival of *Heimat*. This was his own version of the true and oft-told story of the young man, brought up apart from all human contact, who was found in the main square of Nuremberg one day in 1828, and was then kindly cared for and taught to speak and behave like a 'normal' person, until five years later he was mysteriously murdered. It was the most warm, humane *and* humorous of Herzog's films, a parable of innocent purity in face of the follies of the world. Then in *Stroszek* (1977) he strayed into Wenders territory with a tale of a trio of German emigrés facing the sour reality of American life. Some other films of this period, such as *Nosferatu* and *Heart of Glass*, were less successful. But two further Kinski vehicles were brilliant: *Woyzeck*, adapted from Büchner's grim story of betrayal, and the astonishing *Fitzcarraldo*, another epic fantasy of mad ambition in the upper Amazon. After this Herzog was off on his travels again, filming in Australia, the Himalayas and Nicaragua. It is impossible to sum him up. He pursues his own luminous vision and has compromised very little with the commercial cinema. Perhaps only a German could make films like his. Sometimes his work topples over into the ludicrous: but it is saved from Germanic gloom or solemnity by his coruscating visual imagination.

Herzog's fellow-Bavarian, the late Rainer Werner Fassbinder, might also be loosely described as 'typically German' or 'typically Bavarian' – he had a sentimental streak tinged with cruelty, a generous but aggressive temperament, and a fondness for excess. Like Herzog he was driven by some inner demon: but his life-style and approach to filming were utterly different. He travelled rarely. Of his prodigious output of 40 or so feature films in the space of 13 years, only one was made abroad. With all the rest, he chose intensely German settings for propagating his own curious brand of provocative yet compassionate pessimism. He had many admirers, who warmed to his patent candour and originality: but there were fierce detractors too, who found his films trite, over-melodramatic and given to maudlin self-pity. I count myself categorically among the admirers.

More than with most artists, the key to his work lies in his life, for his own restless bisexual bohemianism as well as the bitter tears of his films were both of them products of his chronically disturbed psyche – leading to his death at 36. He was born in 1946 in south-west Bavaria, son of a doctor, and his childhood was scarred by his parents' vociferously unhappy marriage. He attended drama school, then in 1968 in Munich he created his famous '*anti-theater*' with some friends, including his star-to-be, Hanna Schygulla. This was a new kind of spontaneous theatre with improvised scripts, performed in derelict cinemas or rooms behind pubs. Next he began shooting low-budget films: one of the first, *Katzelmacher* (1969) – about a Greek *Gastarbeiter* lynched by young Bavarians because his sexuality excited their girls – impressed the critics and won a prize. Throughout his career he always worked very fast, with amazing fluency: he could shoot a film in ten days or write a whole play on a train journey. Both in theatre and cinema, he also liked to use his own little team of regular actors, who tended to idolise him and would tolerate his capriciously alternating bouts of generosity and callousness.

By keeping generally to low budgets, he secured the backing from television and other sources to maintain a steady output. While his films touched upon a wide range of subjects, the more important of them nearly always turned upon the themes – very personal to him – of love rejected or trust betrayed. The archetype, *The Bitter Tears of Petra von Kant* (1972), was drawn from his own stage play about an hysterical fashion designer who has a lesbian affair with a younger woman and is then exploited and deserted by her. This was a deliberately theatrical and hyper-stylised film. But in *The Merchant of Four Seasons* (1971), the study of a middle-class man bullied and rejected by wife and friends and driven to suicide, Fassbinder was able to treat the same theme in a low-keyed naturalistic style; it was a gentle and compassionate film, even though spiced with barbs against bourgeois self-seeking. *Fox* (*Faustrecht der Freiheit* – right fist of freedom: 1975) returned to the motif of homosexuals exploiting one another, this time with Fassbinder himself in the part of the doomed working-class hero. Like much of his work, it was open to the charge of being too fatalistic, with the dice too systematically loaded against its main character.

Unlike Schlöndorff or von Trotta, Fassbinder seldom made films on directly political or topical subjects. But his somewhat simplistic para-Marxist philosophy saw the individual as the victim of 'our phoney society that corrupts all human contact', and this theme constantly recurred – as in the film that first won him international fame, *Fear Eats the Soul* (1973), about a scandalised society's destruction of the love-match between an elderly Munich charlady and a much younger Moroccan *Gastarbeiter*. Generally, as in this case, Fassbinder preferred to write scripts based on his own stories: but, when he found a classic that fitted his *Weltanschauung*, he was able to make a sensitive adaption, as with his version of *Effi Briest* (1974), Fontane's 19th-century story of an innocent woman victimised by family and society – a truly Fassbinderian heroine, finely portrayed by Schygulla. He found an equal affinity with a contemporary writer, none other than his fellow-Bavarian Franz Xaver Kroetz: they worked together on the film of *Wild Game* (1972), one of Kroetz's bitter little studies of peasant ignorance and brutality.

After this spate of small-scale and frequently excellent films in the 1970s, with *The Marriage of Maria Braun* (1978) Fassbinder moved on to a work that had a much bigger budget and broader canvas and dealt far more directly with post-war German society – the story of a woman (Schygulla again) who becomes tough and cynical in her efforts to survive and prosper amid the rapacity of the 'Economic Miracle'. The film was untypical also in the way that the main character this time is not crushed by those around her but outwits them and wins through, though at great cost to her own soul – hardly an upbeat ending. *Maria Braun* was much the most successful commercially of all Fassbinder's work. The previous year he had already forayed into the international field with his first film in English, and with an English star, Dirk Bogarde: this was *Despair*, based on a novel by Vladimir Nabokov set in 1920s Germany. The foreign dialogue clashed uneasily with the German milieu and characters; Fassbinder was clearly not in his element and the film was no great success. After this, he kept again to real German films. In an odd way he had always been fascinated by Hollywood, and he received plenty of offers from it after *Maria Braun*. Wisely, he never let himself be lured. In that ruthless dream-factory, so wayward a rebel would surely have come to the same kind of sticky end as his heroes. But his later work in Germany was very uneven, culminating in a somewhat overblown television series based on *Berlin Alexanderplatz*, Alfred Döblin's picaresque novel of pre-war Berlin.

I interviewed Fassbinder for the *Washington Post* and the *Telegraph Magazine* in 1976. I had heard so much about his turbulent personality that I was surprised to find such a mild, shy-seeming, defensive young man, with an ugly urchin face, smoking nervously and smiling little during our long talk. 'My father was chaotic,' he said, 'and I still bear those scars so deeply that I could never settle in a stable home. The terrible quarrels of my parents have warped me for ever. I'm a behaviourist: I believe that if the parents are playing false roles, then the child copies these mechanisms and is distorted. No authentic relationship is possible. The answer? – abolish marriage and all society based on property and desire for possessions, the root of our ills.' A facile and unoriginal view, maybe, but sincere. Fassbinder did genuinely suffer. This lent him his creativity, but also made him hard to work with. Peter Zadek, for whom he once produced a play in Bochum, told me: 'Rainer's a little shit, but one can't help liking him. He can be so generous, yet feels this need to work in a permanent state of quarrel.' And a film critic added, 'Behind his façade of Hollywood tough-guy, with his black leather jackets and lower-class slang, he's pathetically vulnerable, sensitive, sentimental.' He was always generous towards the spongers who surrounded him: his flat, dirty and disorderly, was full of these parasites making cooking

[296]

smells and sleeping on the floor. He hated smart clothes or nice homes and was frank about his sex life – 'When I was young I preferred older men, substitutes for the father I hardly knew. Then I had a woman phase and now it's both.' Drugs entered into it too. His death in 1982 from a mixture of cocaine and sleeping-pills may or may not have been suicide.

So how lasting will his *oeuvre* prove to be? His films were always a mixture of realism and stylisation, sometimes veering from one to the other within the same sequence, and this disconcerted many critics. But there was remarkable visual elegance and fluency, even in a minor and rather contrived film such as *Veronica Voss*. His plots and treatment were frequently melodramatic – hence his admiration for Hollywood – and this too disturbed the critics. But he claimed that life itself *was* melodrama; and through his genuine compassion he was able to give true emotional force to a trite situation. The sentimentality, the heart-on-sleeve pessimism, were all part of the package. He was not really a political animal. 'In the sense that I hate capitalist society, yes, I'm on the Left,' he told me; 'but I see no remedy and I detest all "isms" and movements.' The German far-left detested him in return. There are plenty of critics who regard him as a crypto-fascist and believe that he would have been quite happy under Hitler. This to my mind is plain nonsense. He was no more than a shallow thinker and his reactions were those of the gut not the head: but he had real strength of feeling, and real pity for the underdog, not just for himself. His life was a minor tragedy, but it produced triumphant art.

These are some but not all of the main directors of the New German Cinema. In their extremely diverse galaxy, a few other names are worth mentioning too. Reinhard Hauff, for example, an associate of Schlöndorff and von Trotta, has made some good political films: his *Stammheim* (1985) was a worthy dramatisation of the Baader-Meinhof trials. Helma Sanders-Brahms, another radical, is Germany's best woman director after von Trotta: her *Germany Pale Mother* (1979) was a highly sensitive portrait of a young woman traumatised by the war and unable to adjust to the world of peacetime. Themes of German guilt and the burden of German history have been evoked also in the weird films of Hans Jürgen Syberberg, most notably in his 'German Trilogy' of biographical studies of Hitler, 'mad' King Ludwig of Bavaria and the popular novelist Karl May. Syberberg, an eccentric outsider in German cinema, has some affinities with Herzog – just as there are echoes of Fassbinder in the films of the engagingly provocative Rosa von Praunheim, whom I met in Berlin in 1985 (see p. 58). He ('Rosa' is a pseudonym) has recently returned to Germany after some years in New York, to continue his vivaciously anarchic studies of his demi-monde of gays and beatniks: *City of Lost Souls* (1982) he described to me as 'a report on the lives of American drag artists living in Berlin. I like to let it all hang out, to show life as it is, dirty, messy and real.'

By 1984 this New German Cinema appeared to be running badly out of steam. Fassbinder was dead; Herzog, Schlöndorff and Wenders had deserted Germany: they and other directors seemed to be repeating themselves and lacking new ideas; very little new talent was emerging; tighter financing was making it harder to find backing for new projects. The situation seemed even graver than in France where the *nouvelle vague* and its successors were similarly jaded and frustrated. And then through the gathering clouds there unexpectedly broke the brightest, most life-giving sun. In the summer of that year, Edgar Reitz's *Heimat* was shown in Munich, then at the Venice Festival and around the world, to an intensity of critical applause that surely has had no equal in European cinema since the early work of Godard, Truffaut and Resnais.

Ironically, this was no 'new talent' but the work of a veteran director in his fifties who had been around for longer than any of them except Kluge. Ironically, too, this 15½-hour masterpiece was conceived and made as an 11-part series for television and only because of its great acclaim was it also shown in cinemas. But, although *Heimat* is most unlike the average small-screen soap-opera, it is the sheer length allowed to a TV series (by cinema standards) that has helped to give this film its special strength, by enabling it to achieve a scale, depth and resonance, and a leisurely sense of detail, that have led many critics to liken it to some classic 19th-century novel. Its story, in a nutshell, is that of three related families between 1919 and 1982, in a farming village on the plateau of the Hunsrück between the Rhine and Moselle rivers, south of Koblenz: and the history of Germany in our time is followed through the lives of these ordinary people, from the poverty and isolation of the 1920s, through the first happy acceptance of Nazism and the weariness and disillusion of the war and its aftermath, to the massive transformation of rural life wrought by the *Wirtschaftswunder*. Though many other German films had dealt with wartime and Nazi themes, this was the first to look quite so honestly at the impact of these events on the 'little people' of Germany; and it was certainly the first to give so detailed and realistic a picture of the too-often-ignored world of rural Germany and its changes (see p. 139). In its mood and human approach too, *Heimat* marked a break with previous German films: here was none of the gloom of Wenders or Fassbinder, nor the rhetoric and symbolism of many of the new directors, but a straightforward and affectionate humanism, critical but ultimately optimistic. Reitz's works appears closer in spirit to Olmi, Satyajit Ray or Renoir than to the German cinema's own tradition. His long and uneven film may have its faults: but it could well be regarded as the most significant single artistic achievement of post-war Germany.

It differs from the usual TV drama series in being an intensely personal work, a true labour of love, with some autobiographical elements. Reitz is a quiet and thoughtful man, with a grizzled beard and gentle eyes, and when I talked with him in his office in Munich in 1985 he seemed quite untouched by the sudden fame that had engulfed him. Son of a watchmaker, he was born in 1932 in the small Hunsrück town of Morbach where his mother and brother, who carries on the family trade, still live. He was the first member of his family to have any academic education, and at the age of 19 he left Morbach for Munich where he took a degree in art, history and theatre. Then he began making documentaries and in 1962 was one of the Oberhausen signatories; along with Kluge, a close friend, he came to be regarded as one of the more intellectual of the new film-makers. His first feature, *Mahlzeiten* (1966), the story of a tragic marriage, won a prize at Venice. But his subsequent films were somehow too unassuming to make any wide impact, though several were of some quality: *Stunde Null* (1976) foreshadowing some of the themes of *Heimat* and most recognisably by the same hand, was a witty and endearing portrait of a group of villagers near Leipzig in July 1945, awaiting their future in a strange limbo between the departing GIs who had just 'liberated' them and the Red Army yet to arrive.

Then came the making of *Heimat* – itself a remarkable saga. 'In 1978,' Reitz told me, 'I made a fairly expensive historical film, *Der Schneider von Ulm*, that was a critical and commercial flop and I was 250,000 DM in debt. I felt I would never film again and I was terribly depressed. I went to stay with friends on the island of Sylt, and there through a long snowbound Christmas I found myself watching the American *Holocaust* series on TV. I was horrified at this cheap sentimental rot being taken seriously by German intellectuals as a treatment of our national guilt, and it made my depression even worse. So I began writing. I wrote pages and pages of notes, trying to explain to myself how I felt about these things, about my childhood memories of the war and the Hunsrück, and then about why I left home at nineteen. I wrote about my mother, my family, my first love, all the idyllic escapades – and gradually I found that fictional elements were entering in, and soon I had part of a kind of film-script. So you could say that *Heimat* grew out of a reaction against *Holocaust*. I took my draft to my friend Joachim von Mengershausen at the WDR TV station in Cologne, and he said: make me a film. I asked the script-writer Peter Steinbach to help, and with him I went back to the Hunsrück where I was upset to see the destruction caused by modernisation and how the place had changed. We visited various villages and in one of them, Woppenroth, we found a hut in someone's back-garden that we could rent cheaply, and there we spent 13 months, writing hard; in the evenings we'd talk to the villagers in pubs, about their memories, so the story filled out and finally we had 2,000 pages of script.'

With a contract from WDR and Sender Freies Berlin, Reitz then took 18 months to shoot his film, in Woppenroth and four nearby villages. It was mostly done chronologically, so the villages were first disguised to look like the 1920s and then gradually brought back to their present neat but ugly state. Reitz used 28 professional players, none of them stars, plus a host of amateurs (the old blacksmith in the film was a real local blacksmith) and some 5,000 extras. 'The Hunsrückers were sceptical at first,' Reitz told me, 'for they felt that as filming is artificial it was bound to be all lies. But steadily they came to trust us. And now this film is more real to them than their own lives, and in their minds its characters still live there with them. It's quite eery.' At the end of the film is a wonderful sequence – one of its rare departures from realism – where all the people who have died during the 63-year story come back to visit the central character, Maria. This was not Reitz's idea: the actors requested it, for they could not bear the story to end without them. A cinema or TV audience too becomes willingly involved in the story and characters, nearly all of them so real and warm. I myself have seen the full 15½ hours three times; and though I grew more aware of the film's flaws I was never for one moment bored and would happily sit through it all three more times.

The story revolves around the Simon family in the fictional village of Schabbach. Young Paul Simon returns from the First War in a restless mood, not too keen on settling back to help his father with his smithy and little farm. He marries Maria Wiegand, daughter of a richer neighbouring farmer and they have two sons. But Paul is still dreaming of faraway places and one day he goes out for a beer – and disappears. Later he writes from America, where in time he becomes a successful factory owner. Meanwhile life in the village goes on, Maria stoically survives, and Paul's sickly brother Eduard goes to Berlin where (somewhat implausibly) he marries a brothel *madame*, the ambitious Lucy, and brings her back to the Hunsrück. Then the Nazi regime arrives and is greeted with a shrug by most of the villagers and quite eagerly by some of them: Maria's younger brother joins the local SS. Schabbach grows patently more prosperous, as cars replace carts in its main street. Maria has a love-affair with a visiting engineer and bears him a son, Hermann. Then comes the war which is patiently endured, as families split up, Maria's lover is killed and her two elder boys go off to fight. In 1945 the gum-chewing GIs turn up on the heels of the Nazis and they too are accepted quite naturally; Paul himself, now rich and self-confident, pays a return visit from Detroit and finds himself welcomed by all the family with a fond passivity as though he had scarcely been away. But they do not need his help, for next comes the Economic Miracle which brings greater transformation to the Hunsrück than all the preceding world events. Anton, the eldest son, builds up a prosperous optics factory in Schabbach and acquires a large yellow Mercedes; Hermann, Maria's love-child, has a love-affair that ends cruelly, then leaves for Munich where he becomes a successful modern composer. Meanwhile the wise and gentle Maria grows old with dignity, puzzled but unruffled by the changes around her, just as Paul's splendid old mother had been before ('Six times in my life there's been a "new era" – they don't stop coming'). Finally, the whole clan gathers at Maria's funeral. With her, a world and a way of life had died.

Reitz passes no moral judgement on these events or characters. Only the SS boy is treated rather too superficially, as something of a stage villain. Despite a few improbable twists in the plot, the supreme quality of the film is its evocative realism: it gives a wonderful sense of place, in this village of stone and timbered cottages amid the copses and rolling cornfields, while the texture of daily life is conveyed in hundreds of little scenes and incidents, some pathetic, some droll, some deliberately humdrum – picnics and birthdays, harvesting and cake-making, bike-rides and family tiffs. Reitz has shot in luminous black-and-white, but with occasional splashes of colour which, he says, 'I used intuitively, to point up an emotion or stress a change of scene, rather than according to any strategy'. This adds to the lyrical quality. But, if the film itself is black and white, the characters are not: apart from the SS boy, there are few stereotypes, and even the saint-like Maria is seen to be capable of acts of meanness, while the most harsh or staid character can show sudden humour or generosity. In particular, in the post-war scenes, Reitz cleverly allows our sympathy to shift from one to the other of the elder Simon sons: Anton, at first an insensitive bigot in the way he stamps out poor Hermann's love-affair, is seen later as an honourable and benevolent employer, while his weak brother Ernst, much kinder towards Hermann, emerges as a drifter and a spoiler of Hunsrück traditional values. And the acting throughout is magnificent – not only from the professionals, led by Marita Breuer, a young actress from Cologne who specially learned the difficult Hunsrück dialect for her role as Maria and who across the 63 years ages miraculously in voice, walk and gesture. The amateurs too are inspired, some of them local farmers, teachers or schoolkids, and one pastor. Glasisch, the village simpleton who acts as a kind of Greek chorus, introducing and linking each episode, is played by a musician and student; and a local amateur theatre group member took the part of Paul's mother, the wise old peasant matriarch who recalls Maxim Gorki's *babuschka* or Ma Joad in *The Grapes of Wrath*.

In this long and imaginative work, Reitz has allowed his material to dictate the form, so that the episodes are of varying lengths and styles and do not slot into each other smoothly as in a studio-made TV soap-opera. This is no matter: but there are some elements of loose editing and even of self-indulgence in this sprawling film, where a few sequences seem irrelevant or drag on too long – the later war scenes, for instance. Also, in his concern maybe to appeal to a wide audience, Reitz in a few instances has sacrificed naturalism to comedy, albeit very good comedy – notably in the case of Lucy, the irrepressible opportunist from Berlin who improbably settles for Hunsrück domesticity. And, as several critics have felt, Reitz does lose his sureness of touch in the one directly (and avowedly) autobiographical episode, the lengthy story of the 15-year-old Hermann's affair with a girl 11 years his senior. One could cavil, too, at the almost total absence of any references to the role of the Churches, in a mixed Catholic/Protestant area where there were certainly conflicts.

A more fundamental criticism is that possibly the film is *too* cosy and generous in its portrait of an enclosed pre-war peasant community that – like any other in Europe in those days – must surely have had its full share of ignorance, prejudice, intolerance and feuding. Such tensions emerge in a few episodes, but mostly they are glossed over or played for their more humorous side. As with Renoir or Truffaut, has Reitz's warm humanism not led him to portray people as just a little nicer than they are? To this, he replied to me: 'I think you are wrong. In those days, the villagers lived so much on top of each other, and needed each other so much, that they were forced into a solidarity that surmounted the tensions. Certainly, a rebel or non-conformist was victimised mercilessly – but he or she then had to accept exile from the community, as happened in the first episode to Apollonia, the girl who has an illegitimate child by a French soldier. Today, all that has changed. An Apollonia would be accepted: but the old warm solidarity has gone.'

This indeed is one of the film's most central themes: the transfer from an old traditional way of life, safe but restricting, to a new more fluid one of greater personal freedom but greater uncertainty, too, and the tensions that this can cause. The old Schabbach that Maria loved was comforting but, for Paul at least, impossibly claustrophobic: is the new wider world, that has opened out for their sons, any improvement? Reitz seems to have his doubts. And linked to this dilemma is the film's recurring *motif* of departure and homecoming, of being at home and feeling for home – all bound up with the great theme enshrined in the film's much analysed and heavily meaningful title, 'HEIMAT'. The word translates as something much more than 'home' or 'homeland'. For Germans, it is also a state of mind. Ernst Bloch described it as 'an abundance of desires and longings, wishes and yearnings, the great storehouse of customs not yet domesticated and desires yet to be fulfilled'; and Reitz himself has said, '*Heimat* means nostalgic memories, and wanting to go back to where you were happy as a child.' This very human desire for belonging has always held a strong appeal for the German imagination. So the Nazis, in their bid for popularity, made concerted propaganda use of the term '*Heimat*' as a sentimental patriotic ideal. Then after the war it was ideologised in a different way, by right-wing exiles from Silesia and other lost territories who formed *Heimatverbände* (homeland associations), demanding the recovery of those areas. Around the same period, the cinema was flooded with the commercial banality of the *Heimatfilme*. So '*Heimat*' was trebly discredited, a word used only sneeringly by German liberals – and it took some courage on Reitz's part to choose it as his title and thus restore it to its proper place.

More than this, one of the reasons for the great success of his film in Germany is that Reitz has helped to bring audiences back in touch with traditional values, not only by portraying the country life of the past – and here his contribution is unique – but also, perhaps better than other post-war artists, by focussing on the Nazi period in a way that has helped to cure the collective blackout caused by that cataclysm. Reitz has said, 'We Germans have a hard time with our stories. Our own history is in the way. The year 1945, the *Stunde Null*, wiped out a lot, creating a gap in people's ability to remember. Our film consists of these suppressed or forgotten little memories. It is an attempt of sorts to revive memories.' And the English film-maker Chris Petit has written perceptively in *Time Out* (February 1985): 'This inability to remember – which is also the impossibility of forgetting – is *the* recurring subject of recent German cinema. It is most often identified as a spiritual homesickness: one sees it in Wenders' restless characters "at home nowhere"; in Herzog's exiled megalomaniacs; and in Fassbinder's pressure-cooked domestic dramas. *Heimat* is a most ambitious attempt to overcome the rupture, to return home in a sense, by trying to restore continuity to those frozen years. As such it is the most patient and painstaking recuperative exercise in German cinema.'

To achieve this, Reitz had to find a way of dealing with the Nazi and wartime periods, which occupy over a third of the film. He shows that these self-absorbed Hunsrückers, people no better or worse than anyone else, easily accepted Nazism for a number of reasons – they had no idea what it was really like, there were no Jews in the village who might trouble their conscience, Hitler specifically gave financial aid to small farmers, and family loyalty was such that Maria's SS brother, though not approved of, was gently tolerated. All this is perfectly convincing. But I do feel that in the later wartime sequences Reitz has failed to illustrate how the villagers really feel about the prospect of defeat – are they resigned, or upset? – have they yet lost faith in the Führer? Nor, after May 1945, does he show properly how they reacted when they finally learned the truth about Nazism. Is he suggesting that so remote was it from their own daily lives that they felt very little? He does seem to have avoided the issue just a little. And so the film leaves the impression, I am sure unintended, of erring more on the side of justifying the ordinary German's acceptance of Nazism than of condemning it. A number of American critics made the same point, and forcibly – 'soft on Nazism, not enough guilt,' wrote the *New Yorker*. But in Germany itself the film ran into a certain hostility for the opposite reason – from older people who did not want to be reminded of their guilt.

These however were only minority voices amid the general enthusiasm. When *Heimat* was first shown on German TV, audience ratings rose from 26 per cent at the start to 36 per cent by the 11th episode, which gives some idea of its impact; since then, cinemas all over the country have held frequent weekend screenings of the film in its entirety. And Reitz himself has suggested that, in this video age, maybe the classic 100-minute cinema feature film has become an outmoded form, whereas the television series with its far greater length can provide the serious *film d'auteur* with a new and vaster scope – this leads us back to the notion of *Heimat* as successor to the classic Balzacian novel. Here again, the film could mark a watershed. Abroad, it has by now been shown in some 30 countries, on the big and small screen. As a result, the dull little village of Woppenroth has become a kind of tourist centre, a mini-Stratford-upon-Avon – and the proud and canny villagers are cashing in on the boom. One local teacher conducts guided tours of the spots where the film was made: the local publican, Rudi Molz, offers a *Schabbacherplatte* of cold meats and sells bottles of *Hermännchen* Schnaps; the mayor has changed the placard at the entry to the village to 'Woppenroth/Schabbach' (echoes of Proust's town, now officially Illiers/Combray). And some of the cohorts of visiting tourists are convinced that the story was real. One Dutch family turned up asking to see 'Maria's grave'. So Molz, saying it was too dark to see anything, put them up for the night, sold them breakfast too, and meanwhile got some pals to mock up a slab in the cemetery. The Dutch went away happy. I had the same feeling myself when Molz showed me the cottage used for the exteriors of the Simon house, with the nailmarks still on the door from one scene where Anton tries to board it up. I caught myself thinking, 'how fascinating, *that* is where it happened' – before I remembered that it was just a bit of filming. When fiction is as powerful as this, we cannot bear it not to be true.

Above all, *Heimat* has proved a marvellous ambassador for modern Germany around the globe. Perhaps it has done more in one stroke than many years of patient work by the Goethe Institut or Inter

Nationes. Its warmly sympathetic and wryly engaging portrait of life on this windy plateau above the Rhine valley has dealt a head-on blow to many foreign clichés about the Germans – above all, that they are stiff and pompous and have no sense of humour. As the *Observer* wrote of Reitz in its profile of him (May 4, 1986), 'he has helped to restore to our consciousness the great tradition of German humanism that was obliterated by the blood and ashes of the 1940s.'

This New German Cinema, as my survey will have shown, has proved an excellent barometer of the shifting moods and preoccupations of post-war Germany – immeasurably more so than the *nouvelle vague* in the case of France, where so many of those lovely poetic movies were pure escapism. A high proportion of the better German films have either sought to look realistically at society (whether in the manner of *Heimat* or of *Katharina Blum* or *Maria Braun*), or else more obliquely they have mirrored certain German dilemmas (*vide* Wenders' loners), or as in the case of Syberberg they have tried to lay the ghosts of a troubled past. Many films by a whole range of directors have dealt with the effects of the war, or with terrorism, or with the position of women or old people in Germany, or with farmers or *Gastarbeiter*. One could mention Werner Schroeter's *Palermo oder Wolfsburg* (1980), an interesting but overblown study of the travails of a young Sicilian working at Volkswagen; or Peter Fleischmann's *Hunting Scenes from Lower Bavaria* (1969), a bitter caricature of the cruelty of a rural society, itself a kind of early anti-*Heimatfilm* albeit in an opposite manner from *Heimat*.[1]

However, German society has seldom reciprocated this interest it by flocking to these various films in any great numbers. The early productions, Kluge's for example, tended to be elitist and 'difficult'. Since then, from Schlöndorff to Reitz, some of the best work while remaining serious has also become much more commercial and accessible: but many other directors have remained too moralistic, didactic and hyper-critical, or too plain fanciful, to attract a general audience.[2] This is a land without a strong film culture where even a

---

[1] Most of the slushy *Heimatfilme* were also set in Bavaria, clearly the place that most often evokes extremes of sentimentality or savagery in portraits of rural life (NB also Kroetz): to find moderation on this subject, one must look north.

[2] Some intellectuals too dislike the new films. Walter Laqueur, an American of German origin, wrote in his *Germany Today* (1984; op. cit., pp. 115–20) that the new directors 'were devoid of compassion and a sense of humour', their treatment was 'heavy-handed', they 'knew only grotesque grimaces of the margins of society', and 'in the last resort these movies tell us very little about Germany in the 1970s'. A view with which I could not agree less.

high proportion of educated people refuse to take cinema seriously in the way they take theatre or music, and so it is little surprise that the new directors have won a far better response abroad than at home: von Trotta told me that her *The German Sisters* had a cinema audience of 2 million in Italy but only 600,000 in Germany despite its topical German subject. It is true that some 120 towns now have subsidised municipal cinemas which give one-off showings of serious films, mostly old ones: but of Germany's 3,500 commercial cinemas only about 150 specialise in the more demanding kind of 'art movie'. Since audiences are predominantly teenage and want easy entertainment, few distributors will take risks. This attitude also effects imported films, which in Germany are virtually always dubbed rather than sub-titled. This may hardly matter for *Star Wars*: but Kurosawa's samurai, Nashville's songsters, and Glaswegian Gregory and his girl, all also talk nothing but German – with ludicrous effect. One reason for this barbarism is that the German dubbing industry is large and powerful enough to exercise a near-veto on sub-titling. It employs top actors and pays them well, and the results are technically superb – John Wayne once said, 'My German voice is better than my own.' But culturally it is a travesty. Non-dubbed versions *are* available, for Switzerland frequently puts German sub-titles on its imports: but these versions do not reach the Federal Republic. And, in this land of cinematic philistines, the popular demand for authentic films is not vocal enough to break the dubbers' grip.

In this disastrous film climate it is remarkable that the New Cinema has been able to get as far as it has. This has been thanks to public financing. Since the late 1960s the German film industry has received subsidies, from federal and *Land* sources, on a more generous scale than in Britain. They were initiated in response to the Oberhausen appeal, with the aim of helping young directors: but matters have since grown more difficult, for the old guard has hit back successfully, with the result that most of the cash is now allocated to routine projects on criteria that are more commercial than artistic. A few grants are also awarded annually on a quality basis for promising new scripts; but the jury that decides them is under the aegis of the Minister of the Interior, of all unsuitable people, and he has the last word – 'This is typical of the way the cinema is regarded in Germany,' said one director. The minister in the Kohl government, Friedrich Zimmermann, has not exactly been a paragon of liberalism, as we have noted earlier, and several times he used his powers to nip in the bud projects that he disliked – including a script by the avant-garde Bavarian director Herbert Achternbusch that was judged 'blasphemous'.

If serious film-makers today can still quite frequently get the backing that they need, it is thanks above all to co-productions with television. A federal law of 1974 obliges the TV stations to spend certain sums each year on sponsoring productions by independent film companies which the networks themselves cannot then screen until two, three or five years later (depending on contract), after the film has exhausted its main cinema potential. This system works fairly well, and Fassbinder was one of those who benefited from it regularly. But as in other countries television is also the main enemy, the prime cause of the decline in cinema attendances which in Germany fell from 16 cinema visits per head in 1956 to 1.9 visits in 1976, the lowest figure in the EEC. And, in today's video age, matters are growing worse. With the exception of Bavaria Film in Munich, which is highly commercial, there are no big production companies in Germany, and most of the serious directors prefer to have their own little independent outfits. This gives them more freedom, but they need to rely on outside backing, and today nearly all of them complain that this is getting harder and harder to find: 'Even the TV networks,' said one, 'now want tame, obvious subjects, not those with any strong critical element.' Some directors have opted for the big commercial subject with international appeal – notably Wolfgang Petersen, who made the massively profitable *The Boat* and *The Never-Ending Story*. Others have gone abroad, and not only because – like Wenders or Herzog – they are genuinely fascinated by foreign subjects: the reason may equally be that the backing is easier to find in America, or that they are dispirited by Germany's lack of good scriptwriters with new ideas. All in all, the kind of heavy commercial/cultural pressures from Hollywood that have long bedevilled the British cinema, and that the French have so cleverly withstood, are today almost as powerfully omnipresent in Germany as in Britain – and this despite the fact that Germany shares with France the *cordon sanitaire* of a language barrier. But *does* she? – many of the biggest German commercial films, such as *The Never-Ending Story*, are now being made in English. As in other areas of modern life, the Germans have only themselves to blame if they let themselves become so Americanised.

After a period of great brilliance, the future of the New German Cinema today looks uncertain. *Heimat* may offer new hope, not only through its own virtues, but because of the prospect it offers of a new kind of television outlet for the personal film of artistic worth that can also tell a good story. But this will depend on the continuing courage and enlightenment of television sponsors such as *Westdeutsche Rundfunk*. And today, as the age of the satellite dawns, the oddly-structured German television system itself faces new challenges. These might usefully invigorate it, but equally they could be harmful to serious feature film-making.

Tame television and barbarous Bild

If the BBC, ITV and Channel 4 constitute 'the least worst television in the world' (in Milton Shulman's phrase), then the West German networks might just about be regarded as the second least worst in Europe. It is no great claim. German television is very competent, very worthy, but generally dull and timid because it is straitjacked by a well-intentioned balance of political interests. This derives from a bid by the Occupying Powers after 1945 to prevent the new German broadcasting from becoming too dependent on a central government and thus again a potential tool of state propaganda, as it was under Hitler. So radio and TV were decentralised and placed under the aegis of the *Länder*, but in such a way that each regional station should enjoy some autonomy and freedom from direct interference – a little like the BBC. This was the theory. In practice it has not worked out well, for television has tended to fall victim to the rivalries of those set to guarantee its balanced objectivity.

The structure is a complex and unusual one. Television in Germany is neither purely private and commercial as in the United States, nor state-controlled as it has been hitherto in France, but something more like a mixture between BBC and ITV. The first network is run by the ARD (very short for *Arbeitsgemeinschaft der öffentlich-rechtlichen Rundfunkanstalten der Bundesrepublik Deutschland*), a federation composed of eight separate regional corporations which roughly follow the *Land* divisions save that Hamburg, Schleswig-Holstein and Lower-Saxony have clubbed together to form *Norddeutscher Rundfunk*, while *Südwestfunk* in Baden-Baden bestrides Baden and Rheinland-Palatinate. These eight bodies each produce some programmes for local consumption and the rest for the network, rather like ITV, so that an evening's viewing can hop, say, from Cologne to Munich to Hamburg. Each station is responsible to a *Rundfunkrat* (broadcasting council) made up of delegates from the local political parties and from trade unions, the Churches and other such 'social groups'. This *Rat* is a watchdog which can conduct postmortems on programmes but is not supposed to interfere in their planning or production: it does however appoint the station's senior executives, notably the *Intendant*, who in theory has editorial freedom together with a statutory duty to be objective and to give a fair voice to all main currents of opinion. The nightly news programme, the *Tageschau*, is run from the NDR's Hamburg studios under the joint aegis of all the corporations – a little like the relationship between ITN and ITV.

ARD operates a radio network as well as television. Its TV rival, the *Zweites Deutsches Fernsehen* (ZDF), is a television-only station based in Mainz and run as a consortium by all the *Länder*, under much the same kind of public supervision as ARD. Today, ARD and ZDF are broadly similar in their programming and appeal: but ARD also operates a Third Channel which is much more regional in its content and a little more cultural and educational. The average audience percentage share-out between the three is ARD 45/ZDF 45/Third 10. The networks derive the major part of their financing from the licence fees (currently some 200 DM a year for a colour set) which they collect directly from viewers and share between them. They are also allowed to show advertising, which yields some 22 per cent of ARD's income and 42 per cent of ZDF's. But this is even more tightly controlled than in Britain. Not only is direct sponsorship of programmes forbidden, but advertisements are limited to 20 minutes a day and can be shown only between 6 and 8 pm, which is the period also reserved for local programmes on ARD. For the rest of the evening, Persil and Pepsi must not disturb the smooth high-mindedness of the German soul at debate with itself on the silver screen.

This broadcasting structure is all very well-meant and rational in its neat German way. And it does lead to a number of very good programmes, especially cultural and documentary, while the sponsoring of feature films and series can sometimes yield superb results, as we have seen. But it has become cramped by politics in ways that were never intended, and this has a harmful effect on the news and current affairs output. Firstly, in each ARD corporation, since the political parties are represented in the *Rundfunkrat* in proportion to their strength in the local *Landtag*, it follows that the majority party can nearly always secure the appointment of an *Intendant* of its own colour. He may have a supposed duty to be impartial, but he is also a political nominee. And, in order to correct bias of this sort, it is the custom that other senior posts in the station should be shared out between the parties also in proportion to their local strength. Thus, if the head of some department is CDU, his deputy will generally be SPD, and this so called *Proporz* system has spread down through the echelons so that technical staff and even programme assistants are paired off. Across the years this has become intensified – 'At this rate, we'll soon be getting *Putzfrauen* with party cards,' jested one frustrated producer. Ironically, while the *Proporzsystem* does indeed help to achieve political balance, it also introduces political tensions at a level where they are hardly relevant. It can lead to stalemates harmful to lively broadcasting, for a programme may be shorn of its controversial content in order to balance the rival views of those making it.

In just a few cases, whole programmes are paired off. On ZDF, for example, of the two main current affairs magazines *Kennzeichen D* is permitted to have a left-of-centre producer giving a radical slant, in order to balance *ZDF Magazin* and its well-known right-wing presenter Gerhardt Löwenthal. This kind of solution at least makes for hard-hitting opinionated programmes, but not exactly for dispassionate seeking-after-the-truth, since each editor strives to counter the other. When there is no such pairing, then balance must be found within the programme and this can lead to worse problems: to cite an example, one producer prepared a report on the Italian Communist Party, only to be told that he must pare it down in order to give equal screen time to the Italian Right and their view of the PCI. This made the item look absurd. In this climate, journalists and pro-ducers who prove too rebellious or outspoken tend to get shunted off the political programmes onto some safe sideline such as science or sport (they cannot be sacked, for once on the staff they have public-service security of tenure). And the ones promoted to executive level are usually the yes-men who will play their roles quietly and cau-tiously. This makes for unexciting television, especially as the job security makes it hard to shift a mediocre man from a top job. What is more, many of the party nominees under the *Proporz* even take pride in their political function and dual loyalty: 'A key part of my job at this *Funk*,' said one head of department in Hamburg, 'is to ensure that CDU views are fairly represented in its programmes.'

The degree to which local politicians exert pressures on television varies very much from *Land* to *Land*. In Bavaria the CSU is so powerful that it dominates the *Rat* and fills most of the *Proporz* posts, so any pretence of balance is lost. So in the *Bayerische Rundfunk* liberal pro-ducers have a hard time of it and controversially radical programmes seldom get accepted. But in the other *Länder* things are easier, especi-ally in Baden-Württemberg where the CDU under the open-minded Lothar Späth deliberately leaves the local station alone and tolerates criticism. At the *Norddeutscher Rundfunk* however the *Rat* is so evenly balanced between the SPD with its fief in Hamburg and the sur-rounding CDU strongholds that there is constant tension and in-fighting: I heard of various cases of TV staff executives, alike CDU and SPD, suppressing items disliked by their own party. Here and elsewhere, though the role of the *Rat* was originally conceived as one of protecting the stations from political interference, in practice it does not always work that way – and one main reason is that German politicians in the past ten or fifteen years have woken up to the huge influence that television can wield electorally, as borne out by all the opinion polls, and so they seek to shape it themselves. And the senior TV executives generally feel the need to be pleasing and subservient to the various delegates on the *Rat*, on whose goodwill they depend for their posts – hence the inordinate amount of air and screen time, on news bulletins or similar programmes, that is devoted to inter-views with spokesmen of the various groups represented on the *Rat*, not only the parties but organisations representing women, sport, culture, farming, the Press, as well as unions, chambers of commerce and the Churches. If, say, a local farmers' union is holding some routine meeting to be addressed by a *Land* minister, it will ring up the *Tageschau* to ask for coverage and probably will get it, whatever the news value. The BBC or ITN would be far more selective. 'It's all very fair and democratic, but it's just not newsy and it makes for dull viewing,' said one jaded producer, weighed down by years of this kind of work; 'my bosses just daren't say no, so the bulletins are filled nightly with these boring pronouncements by official representatives. In Germany, we do not have a genuine public service television but one of multiple interest groups, each wanting its slice of the cake.' Many Germans lament the situation. But it would be hard to change, for the harmony of German society depends on this kind of delicate balancing of rival forces. To weaken it might be to let in just the kind of disorder that the Germans fear most, and with good cause. Might not the tedium of their television be one of the prices they must pay for their stable democracy?

Outside the more sensitive areas of topical subject matter, a fair number of good programmes are nonetheless screened, for there is plenty of talent in German television, and once a programme idea has been accepted a producer is generally left to get ahead with it in some freedom. Excellent documentaries are made quite frequently on historical subjects (including the war and Nazi period) and on foreign countries: alike in its news and general coverage, German television is far less parochial and more international-minded than BBC or ITV. But, when dealing with Germany's own society today, its documentaries tend to be much less bold and probing. Studio discussions and political interviews are formal and wordy in the German manner; interviewers are deferential especially to people of importance, and they will seldom interrupt or question toughly *à la* Robin Day. It is all a bit like the old BBC before it was shaken up by the challenge of ITV. Far less effort is made than in Britain to go out and canvas off-the-cuff *vox pop* views in the street, for it is thought safer to stick to the 'official' reactions of spokesmen invited to the studio. And a news magazine will seldom include off-beat human-interest items, funny or endearing, of the kind so beloved of British TV, for these it considers trivial: it keeps to issues of 'serious public interest', not only political but economic, technical or environmental. In fact, just as in the theatre or the novel, so throughout television a gulf exists between the 'serious' and the 'merely entertaining', and the two genres must not be mixed up. So a studio discussion or magazine item on a basically serious topic is not made lively or amusing; most producers would consider this a betrayal of their duty to the public, and they leave such levity to the variety shows and quizzes (which are usually feeble). It is the opposite extreme from Britain, where jokey casualness and matey frivolity creep into every kind of programme – *ad nauseam*, one sometimes feels. A sitcom satire about the Church, or a cartoon send-up of the Chancellor and his ministers (to allude to two recent British parallels) would be inconceivable. And though there are good programmes on art and music, and some good feature films and series, sophisticated modern TV comedy is rare. So different in fact are the British and German styles, and the French too, that it is not easy to see what an EEC satellite channel of international appeal – the dream of many dedicated 'Europeans' – could possibly be like.

In any event, the arrival of the satellite age will now modify the structure of German television and could have quite an impact on content and attitudes too. For some years, preparations have been going ahead. In 1981 the Federal Constitutional Court ended the monopoly of the public corporations by ruling that private broadcasting was admissible so long as free opinion was assured. Then in 1984 experimental transmission by cable began in a few selected areas, and various major publishing groups – including Springer and Bertelsmann – started to create their consortia for the operation of commercial channels in association with other European concerns. These were due to start when the main satellites were set in place above Europe, possibly in 1987. In 1985 a pioneer channel, SAT-1, 35 per cent of it owned by Springer, began broadcasting by satellite and cable to some 250,000 subscription viewers; its main output was light entertainment and feature films, with some news material.

General public transmission by satellite, however, still requires the authority of the *Länder* – and here the great stumbling-block has been that by mid-1986, after years of bickering, the 11 governments still could not agree whether they wanted it or not. The CDU and CSU are in favour of private commercial television. The SPD and the unions are in the main hostile, for obvious ideological reasons and also because they fear (a) a lowering of cultural standards, and (b) programmes politically biased against them if the stations are controlled by right-wing publishers. So in 1986 the extraordinary spectacle emerged of some *Länder* agreeing to go ahead with satellite TV and others, the SPD-led ones, staying out. Bavaria, Baden-Württemberg and Rhineland-Palatinate signed a contract for joint use of a satellite channel, to be operated by SAT-1, with the proviso that its programmes should be politically balanced. Berlin, Lower Saxony and Schleswig-Holstein signed a similar contract and Hamburg's SPD-led Senate reluctantly joined in, for it did not want the city to lose its role as the German media capital. But the four other *Länder* stayed out, amid comments that the split was 'lunatic' and 'a sin against cooperative federalism'.

The likely effect of these new commercial channels, due to start up in 1987, was in 1986 still far from certain. Many Jeremiahs were predicting a fall in cultural standards, despite all the proposed safe-

guards, for the new networks would put their accent on light entertainment and the existing stations would be forced to compete in
order to keep their audiences. This might make it harder for a culture-
minded corporation such as *Westdeutsche Rundfunk* to keep up its
admirable policy of sponsoring films of quality by directors like Reitz
or Herzog. On the other hand, is it not just possible that commercial
competition might have something of the effect that ITV made 30
years ago on the BBC? – that is, of forcing German television to
become more lively and daring without lowering its level (even
though a fusion of the serious and entertaining comes much less
naturally to Germans). But this in turn will depend on how the satellites affect the *Proporzsystem*, and that is even less certain. Nothing so
far is statutory – save for a general obligation on the new channels to
show balance. So does this mean that the *Proporz* will simply extend
its dread tentacles to these new bodies (with the fantasy prospect of
CDU and SPD hirelings doing battle up in the ether, like US and
Soviet cosmonauts)? Or, on the contrary, if the new programmes are
to be lighter and less topical, might this not diminish the influence of
politicians over television and thus modify the *Proporz*? All the
avenues are open – including the possibility, dreaded by many Germans, that the Springer group might find ways of circumventing
'balance' and extending its dubious ethos? Which brings us to *Bild
Zeitung* and the German Press.

The Press in Germany is strong, free and flourishing. There are no
less than 385 dailies, and they have stood up very well to the rise of
television, actually increasing their total sales from 13 million in 1954
to 21.2 million in 1982. But it is a measure of German decentralisation
that virtually all these papers are regional rather than national. Apart
from the mass-selling *Bild* and its more sedate Springer stablemate
Die Welt, only the *Frankfurter Allgemeine Zeitung*, the businessmen's
favourite, has a truly nationwide readership; the left-of-centre *Frankfurter Rundschau* also sells quite well in other cities and so does the
Süddeutsche Zeitung of Munich, widely regarded as Germany's best
daily, but even this great paper relies on Bavaria for two-thirds of its
340,000 sales. People turn first to their local or regional paper. And
so, in Cologne, Hanover, Stuttgart and many other towns one finds
these immensely solid and respectable dailies, each full of long
serious articles and page upon page of local, national and international
news: their foreign coverage is often excellent, and many have their
own staff correspondent abroad. It is rather as if Britain had nothing
but the *Sun* and the *Financial Times* and then lots of superior *Yorkshire
Posts* all looking like *Le Monde*. Apart from *Bild* none of these dailies
has a sale exceeding 700,000, but many of them are very rich, packed
with advertising (the *Süddeutsche* on a Saturday runs to 150 pages);

and they coped far earlier and more successfully than Fleet Street with the task of persuading the unions to accept the new technology. Their coverage is full and thorough, but not always very newsy: an obvious official declaration may get greater prominence than some more exciting item, buried down page. Nor do they very often indulge in sharp investigative reporting (the *Süddeutsche* and the *Rundschau* can be honourable exceptions) or in the kind of crusading that might inflame local passions: 'We fought the *Rathaus* over its snow-clearance and forced it to act!' I was told proudly at the *Stuttgarter Zeitung* as an example of its radicalism.

Investigative journalism is left mainly to *Der Spiegel*, the weekly news-magazine edited in Hamburg that is the foremost of its kind in Europe and holds a dominant position in the German Press. *Spiegel* was founded under British auspices just after the war by a brilliant young intellectual, Rudolf Augstein, who is still its publisher today; and it was modelled on *Time*. But its style today is far more racy than *Time*'s: for a foreigner it is not easy reading, for its writers make a sport of using the most unusual words possible in the enormous German vocabulary and they create neologisms too (such as *videot*: video-viewing zombie). More important, *Spiegel* is also a far more relentless ferreter-out of unpleasant truths than its American counterparts. Across the years it has proved bolder than the parliamentary opposition in exposing the faults and abuses of government ('*Spiegel* really runs this country,' someone said) and on occasions ministers have hit back. In the famous '*Spiegel* Affair' of 1962, after the magazine had published a well-researched critique of federal defence policy, Franz-Josef Strauss, then Minister of Defence, suddenly lost his head and had the police raid *Spiegel*'s offices and arrest Augstein and some other editors. There was a flaming crisis, as many observers both German and foreign anxiously suggested that such Gestapo-like behaviour by a minister in peacetime did not bode well for the new German democracy, then still on probation. Finally Strauss was pressured into resigning and Augstein had clearly scored a great moral victory. Today *Spiegel* is still prolific with its scoops and exposures: but it always does its homework very carefully and it seldom exaggerates unduly or gets things radically wrong. It is a non-party paper, just as happy to unearth an SPD or trade union scandal (e.g. the *Neue Heimat* affair, see p. 406) as a CDU one. But it is not a moral crusader, working to create a cleaner society: Augstein and his staff are motivated mainly by professional pride in doing a brilliant job, and by the commercial drive to keep up their sales of almost one million copies.

Of the other serious weeklies, by far the most important is *Die Zeit* (circulation, 450,000), a striking contrast to *Spiegel*. This conscience of the German liberal intelligentsia has no news columns but a large number of thoughtful and wordy articles on political, cultural and other topics: it is a little like a much fuller and better *Spectator* or *New Statesman*, plus the *Observer* shorn of its news pages, and it does something to make up for the virtual absence in Germany of serious Sunday papers. The infamous *Stern* magazine used to make efforts to rival *Spiegel* at in-depth reporting: but in 1983 it made a big fool of itself when, like the *Sunday Times*, it published the 'Hitler diaries' believing them to be genuine, and since then it has retreated down-market into sex-and-drug cover-stories and other sensations, though still with a semblance of seriousness. If its circulation has dropped since 1983 from 1.6 to 1.4 million, this could be due not only to the Hitler fraud fiasco but to growing competition from even more trivial and gossipy rivals in the weekly illustrated Press, such as *Quick* and *Bunte*. But there are some good respectable women's periodicals too, such as *Brigitte*, a little bit like *Elle*. All in all, the weekly magazine market is far stronger in Germany than elsewhere in Europe or America. This could be in part a reflection of German affluence: but probably the main reason is that German television is so tame, where-as these papers are able to be far more lively and unhibited.

With one or two glaring exceptions (see below), the German Press today is fair and responsible, and it forms a valued component of the new German democracy; the Constitution specifically protects it against censorship. The principal dailies constitute a reasonable poli-tical balance. On the Right, the *Frankfurter Allgemeine* is conservative but intelligently so and it fairly reflects the attitudes of the business world; Springer's *Die Welt* is far more rabid, but has been losing influ-ence and now sells less than 200,000. These papers are balanced on the left-of-centre by the very honest and liberal *Süddeutsche Zeitung* and the somewhat more radical and *Guardian*-like *Frankfurter Rund-schau* which is sympathetic to the ideas of the Greens. The majority of the better regional dailies such as the *Kölner Stadt-Anzeiger* and the *Stuttgarter Zeitung* are reasonably open-minded and middle-of-the-road: they may not be very zealous at sniffing out injustices them-selves, but once *Der Spiegel* or someone else has done so, then they will decently bring pressure to bear until the guilty politician resigns or makes amends. There may even be some truth – though I wonder how much? – in the point made to me by Christoph Bertram, political editor of *Die Zeit*, that Germany's system of government is so open that the need for investigative journalism is less great than in some countries. There are however some dangers in the present Press situation, and one is the growth of local monopolies due to mergers or ententes made for economic reasons. Many local papers have either come under the control of larger ones or they have grouped and pooled their resources, and this destroys competition and variety: Stuttgart's two dailies for instance, are jointly owned and both editorially very bland, so this *de facto* monopoly means there is no local outlet for radical journalism.

A far worse threat – or so a great many Germans believe – comes from the excessive power wielded nationwide by one stridently right-wing megagroup: Springer. The late Axel Springer himself was the most spectacular of German post-war tycoons, a very rich man who married five times, owned five houses, collected Kokoschkas, and was propelled by an almost mystical Protestant faith and an equal fervent anti-Communism. Like Augstein, he was first given his chance just after the war by the British, who let him start a radio programme guide, *Hör Zu*, and then a Hamburg evening paper. After launching his tabloid *Bild Zeitung* in 1952 he steadily built up a newspaper, periodical and publishing empire that today is the largest in Europe: Springer dailies are read at home by one German in three, and they account for 20 per cent of all newspaper sales.

To be fair, there were some quite attractive things about Springer. He was a generous employer, strong on welfare, and so he was grudgingly liked by the unions. He repaid his debt to the British by remaining warmly anglophile. And he made reconciliations and reparations towards Israel into a personal crusade, pouring money from his own fortune into Jewish causes and obliging his papers to take Israel's side against the Arabs. But his cold-warrior stance, acceptable in the aftermath of the Berlin airlift and the Berlin Wall, made him look increasingly isolated as *détente* developed. In 1959, as a calculated act of defiance, he built his new Springer group headquarters right beside the Wall in Kreuzberg, a 19-storey block with a neon sign beaming out *'Berlin bleibt frei'* from its roof. He fought hard against Ostpolitik, and this led him into a permanent vendetta against Brandt, instructing *Bild* to remind its readers that their Chancellor was born illegitimate and had returned to post-war Germany in Allied uniform. In the 1968 period he campaigned for harsh law-and-order measures against student rioters and terrorists: when *Bild* urged its readers to take the law into their own hands and one of them shot Rudi Dutschke, it was as if Springer had himself pulled the trigger. From then on, he was the number one enemy of the German student Left. He died in 1985, but the group has since continued much as before, in other hands. Springer claimed that his papers, *Bild* especially, spoke for the true feelings of the mass of ordinary Germans and he challenged the right of intellectuals to behave as the nation's conscience. This populism might have been creditable were it not that *Bild* plays so constantly upon the darker side of German popular prejudice – racism, intolerance of non-conformity, and the rest.

Bild Zeitung is a German phenomenon. Published in several cities simultaneously, it is Europe's biggest-selling tabloid (5.4 million circulation), and in Germany it has no rival save for a few small local rags, none of them so strident. As there are no big papers of the *Daily Mail* type to fill the middle ground, it polarises the German Press. Its garish red-black-and-white front page has giant headlines screaming of rape, torture, incest or the intimate vices of the great and famous – and curiously enough it is actually bought and read by a good many such VIPs, and others. They do so not out of voyeurism or a desire for titillation but because, stranger still, *Bild* in its laconic way does include some sharp political reporting. With its massive staff and resources it is able frequently to secure scoops – it was the first, for example, to announce the cancellation of Honecker's visit to Bonn in 1984 – and in its way it is very well informed. So in trains and smart restaurants you will see senior executives quietly reading their *Bild*, though they may not bring it home to their families. The headlines such as 'Sweetheart Beheaded, Cooked and Tinned in 39 Pieces' (front-page lead, December 9, 1985) they glance at with a wry smirk.

Bild is not necessarily more vulgar or sensational than the Murdoch gutter-Press. But it is more ruthless at grabbing or inventing its stories, and at intruding into private grief. When two brothers committed suicide, *Bild* carried a big photograph of the young men swinging on ropes from a tree, next to one of the anguished mother learning the news: photo-reporters were somehow able to follow the police on their way to tell her of the tragedy, and they snapped her at that very moment. On another famous occasion, under a headline 'German Pupil Drank Blood of Girl', *Bild* told how a former butcher's apprentice had brought girls to his flat, taken their blood and drunk it mixed with tea or sherry. The boy was then arrested, and *Bild* ransacked his flat, taking photos and private papers. But at his trial he was fully acquitted: it was found that he had carried out chemical experiments, no more. The *Bild* reporters pleaded guilty of fabrication and were sentenced to eight months' prison, plus a 15,000 DM fine which the paper cheerfully paid. This public verdict at least spotlighted *Bild*'s use of criminal methods. But there have been many other cases that have not come to trial, where a probably innocent victim has had his or her reputation destroyed. *Bild* will sometimes break into people's flats; and if it cannot get the story it wants, then it will invent, for its sales depend on a steady stream of these horror-stories.

That German society tolerates this as much as it does seems to me worrying. Of course there have been protests. After *Bild* had verbally tormented the 'Red terrorist' Heinrich Böll, he retorted with his splendid *The Lost Honour of Katharina Blum* (see above). And in 1977 the famous investigative journalist Günter Walraff had the clever idea of joining *Bild*'s reporting staff for a few months, under a pseudonym, with the aim of writing an exposé of it. He succeeded, and his book *Der Aufmacher* caused a sensation. As in his more recent book about Turkish workers (see p. 243), he may perhaps have done his own share of inventing: but much of what he wrote rang true. Next Walraff founded an anti-*Bild* association, to rally and support its former victims, and soon he had gathered 4,500 names as well as lawyers prepared to help in the fight. This seemed to have some effect for *Bild* did then tone down its excesses a little, and in 1985 a senior Springer executive in Berlin admitted to me that in the past there had been 'irresponsible reporting'. But the problem is that most of *Bild*'s victims are very ordinary people who do not have the initiative or funds for a lawsuit, while the rich Springer group can readily lavish money on brilliant defence lawyers.

Clearly *Bild* hides too easily behind the post-war German insistence on absolute freedom of the Press; and clearly there is a case for tightening the German libel laws, lax as in other Continental countries. But probably more is needed. In 1980 a number of leading radical intellectuals – including Böll, Grass, Habermas, Schlöndorff and Jens – signed a public declaration that they would never write for the Springer group. But when in 1985 I asked senior liberal journalists on *Die Zeit* and the *Frankfurter Rundschau* how they felt about *Bild*, I was startled to find them shrugging it off – 'No one takes it seriously, and it doesn't really do much harm,' said one of them; 'besides, in order to remain free we have to accept a certain misuse of freedom.' He was alluding to the fact that the German newspaper world is still so haunted by the Nazis' murder of Press freedom that it is utterly determined that nothing, repeat nothing, should be done to put limits on its present liberty. This is understandable. But clever German lawyers ought surely to be able to devise some ways of curbing *Bild*'s excesses without harming basic freedoms. That there has not been more effective public action against *Bild* seems to me worryingly symptomatic of the Germans' relative lack of concern for the weaker members of their society, and of the failure of most individuals to take the initiative in tackling public abuses or standing up to established power. *Bild*'s sheer cultural bad taste, its blood and bosoms, is of little consequence: its affront to human rights, in this of all Western democracies, seems to me more serious. So in the final chapter, we shall look at the biggest question of all: how deep and secure is German democracy? Could Nazism ever happen again? But first the 'Other Germany'.

7

DAILY LIFE UNDER GERMAN-STYLE COMMUNISM

Seventeen million Germans live under Moscow-inspired Communist rule in the *Deutsche Demokratische Republik* (DDR – or GDR, to use its English initials). Their lives are in many obvious ways very different from those of the 61 million inhabitants of the Federal Republic: yet they too are Germans, with the same language, culture and history, and many of the same traits and habits. Nearly four million have emigrated from the GDR to the West since the war; many others might still like to do so, if they were free to travel. But the vast majority have now come to terms with their destiny: they find that life under Socialism is perfectly livable and even has some advantages, though they still bitterly resent the travel ban. In this chapter, I avoid making direct comparisons between the two Germanies, and I deal less with power politics than with what it is like to live in the GDR.

Of course I was not nearly as free as in the West to travel and to meet people. I applied to the GDR Embassy in London and was told that they did not at all like the idea of a book about both German States within one cover, as this was contrary to their basic policy. Could I not write two separate books? I explained that in publishing terms this was impossible. Finally Katinka and I were granted permission to visit the GDR, under supervision. We were allotted a pleasant and helpful young guide, who showed us around and was present at interviews. But we also had time free to meet a large number of our own private contacts, unescorted, and we found them very ready to talk frankly, both on this visit and on another which we made informally to East Berlin. We also talked to a great many people in West Germany who knew the GDR well and had once lived there. We were thus able to build up the detailed material for what I hope is a balanced and accurate picture. And I have tried to look objectively at the GDR regime and to give credit where it is due.

Behind the drab façades, an economic mini-miracle

The centre of East Berlin is an odd mixture of ghost town and grandiose modern capital. The old pre-war heart of the city, where imperial palaces, ministries and great cultural monuments stood on either side of the broad Unter den Linden, was nearly all of it here in the east, and only a small part of it (including the Reichstag) lay in what is now the Western sector. The GDR authorities have restored or replaced a number of the main buildings destroyed in the war: but the area closest to the Wall has been left deliberately as a wasteland or semi-derelict jumble. So the first-time visitor arriving from West Berlin, by car at Checkpoint Charlie or by S-Bahn at the Friedrich-strasse station, receives the initial impression of a city more shabby and shattered, indeed sinister, than it really is. The sector round the Friedrichstrasse has now been tidied up a little for the GDR's celebrations of Berlin's 750th anniversary in 1987: but much of it is still a patchwork of vacant lots and gloomy blackened office buildings, some of them still bullet-holed or bomb-scarred.

A few hundred metres to the east however the picture changes radically. Where the Unter den Linden avenue sweeps up to the wide Marx-Engels-Platz, heart of the modern city, several of the old majestic buildings including the State Opera House, the Pergamon Museum and the Protestant Cathedral have been meticulously restored to their original form. And beside them several massive new edifices stand as symbols of the GDR's assertive ambitions as a modern state – notably the towering white rectangle of the Foreign Ministry, and the Palace of the Republic with its gleaming façade of bronze-coloured glass. This part of the city is grandiose to say the least – severe-looking, but tidy. There are plenty of grey uniformed police around, ready to shout at any visitor who jay-walks, and maybe to fine him; and often there are soldiers too. The first time that I saw the steel-helmeted, goose-stepping changing-of-the-guard outside the Memorial to the Victims of Fascism and Militarism, it evoked memories that gave a nasty frisson. How crassly tactlesss to present this sight to tourists on the Under den Linden. The goose-step is still widely used in the GDR's Army, and it serves to symbolise the fact that militarism in this half of Germany did not die with Hitler in the bunker.

At the nearby Alexanderplatz the scene is more gentle. This vast modern piazza, enclosed by new department stores and skyscraper hotels, is now the main shopping and entertainment centre of East Berlin and something of a showpiece too, pleasant and lively in its way, with music playing, a fountain splashing, and a curious 'international clock' used as a meeting-place like Eros at Piccadilly Circus. The crowds seem to be relaxed and good-humoured, and are quite well dressed too in a classless sort of way (some are in jeans, obtained no doubt from Western contacts). Hardly anyone looks *Schick* apart from a few tourists. Close by is the 365-metre Television Tower, the city's most dominant landmark, with its globe-shaped revolving observation tower where East Berliners go to gaze wistfully at the lights of the forbidden Ku'damm. Eastwards from here stretches the long and pompous Karl-Marx-Allee: its giant blocks of workers' flats where built in the 1950s in Stalinist-brutalist style and the street was then the Stalin-Allee. At least the sheer size of these buildings balances the great width of the street, giving it a Champs-Elysées-like scale. It is not exactly ablaze with Parisian glitter: yet, as in other parts of the city, the buildings are often festooned with red bunting, flags and banners, and slogans in the genre of 'Socialism Cares for the Happiness of the People' and 'Actively We Support the Peace Policy of the Beloved Soviet Union' – well, at least they do add a cheerful dash of colour to a town otherwise grey and drab in its façades and bare of commercial advertising. Go further out into the residential and industrial districts, and you find side-streets full of potholes and miles of sad decaying houses, victims not of the bombing but of long neglect. But there are plenty of children's playgrounds, and barrack-like premises that house youth clubs, old people's day-care centres and other manifestations of the all-enveloping welfare state. Everywhere, in this the richest country of the Soviet bloc, patient queues are waiting at the doors of restaurants and outside butchers' and grocers' shops (for a generally dismal selection of meat and fresh vegetables). Inside the routine restaurants at lunchtime, people eat in subdued silence, hardly exchanging a word – yet these are Berliners, famous in the past for being witty, chatty and high-spirited, as in the West they still are. Admittedly, the ambience is somewhat livelier in the evenings.

When we left Berlin to visit the rest of the GDR, we used the motorways where the BMWs and Audis of the West German tourists contrasted with the elderly and hideous little Wartburgs and Trabants of the local citizens. Everyone drives at a vigilant 100 kph maximum, for the police are quick to impose a fine if you go faster; and if you are found to have been drinking alcohol, even a small amount, the penalties are stiff. In the GDR, even more than in West Germany, rules are there to be obeyed. The first provincial city we visited was Dresden. Once this was one of the loveliest cultural capitals of central Europe: today, though largely rebuilt, it still has a stunned, walking wounded feel, as though it had never properly recovered from what are officially described as 'the terror-raids of the barbaric imperialists' (the Soviet Union's allies) in February 1945. The Zwinger and the other great baroque buildings have been patiently reassembled using the original stone: but, while some of this is still its former rich golden colour, other pieces are blackened from the bombing, and the piebald effect is not pretty. Semper's famous Opera House was finally reopened in 1985, after many years of carefully detailed restoration. The effect is lavish and prestigious, and the cost was enormous – but it seems a pity that a few Marks were not spared for giving the rest of this drab city a fresh coat of paint too.

Leipzig, by contrast, wears a more prosperous and self-confident air: not only was it less badly bombed than Dresden, but today with its twice-yearly trade fair, the biggest in Eastern Europe, it is the GDR's commercial window on the world and thus enjoys quite a major international economic role. Its suburbs are stupendously ugly, a mixture of giant graceless utility blocks of flats and semi-derelict older streets; but the spacious central part of the city is pleasing. It has traffic-free piazzas and arcades with well-stocked shops, some of them quite smart, and the people look more cheerful than in East Berlin or Dresden. In the old squares and side-streets around the Thomaskirche, where J. S. Bach was organist, we found cosy little privately-run cafés and tearooms whispering the last enchantments of some pre-war Central European *Gemütlichkeit* and frequented by gentle-looking student couples and civilised elderly music-lovers. Displayed inside the church was an apt quotation from Luther, 'A Christian is a free man in all things and no man's slave'.

Then from Leipzig we drove to Weimar, where Goethe's residence and garden-house and the park where he walked have all been devotedly preserved, as have the houses associated with Schiller, Liszt and Bach. The town gets its fill of tourists but it has not been commercially tarted up in the process as would happen in the West: it remains much as it probably was before the war, a quiet, slightly seedy little place with half-timbered houses, and its melancholy air goes well with its many poetic memories. The surrounding villages of the Thuringian and Saxon countryside also retains the fell of pre-war days: far fewer of their houses have been pulled down or modernised than in the Federal Republic, and one still sees horse-drawn carts, rough-looking peasants and little churches patently in need of repair. Indeed, Westerners with long memories who visit the GDR will often make the observation that in many respects it has preserved the old pre-war flavour of Germany much more than the West has done. The tempo of life is slower and modernism has made a less obvious impact; the little shops and the styles of graphic design are more antiquated, the cars are smaller and less ubiquitous, and many streets are still cobbled. How far these are advantages is open to question. And there are other things that have changed less too – old-style Prussian authoritarianism, for example, is more alive and well under Communism than it is in the *Bundesrepublik*.

* * *

A brief historical survey of the GDR since the war (see also pp. 9–19) could well start with the fact that initially neither Stalin nor the Western Allies intended the division of the country to be permanent: but gradually the logic of the Cold War made this inevitable. Under Russian tutelage, the German Communist leaders began to take some control in the eastern zone from 1945 onwards. Many of them had been in Nazi concentration camps; or they had spent years in exile in Moscow – like Walter Ulbricht, who from 1945 was the Party's effective leader though he did not formally become its First Secretary until 1953. With Russian backing, these men swiftly set about expropriating and punishing the Nazis and their 'bourgeois' accomplices. Full-scale communisation was to take place a little more slowly and initially some multi-party pluralism was permitted. But as early as April 1946 the Communists forced the Socialists to merge with them into the Communist-dominated Socialist Unity Party (SED) that has been the country's ruling force ever since. In 1949, after the Federal Republic had been formally set up in Bonn, the Russians retorted swiftly by taking measures to balance it with a new state of their own; and so, after due elections with a single list of candidates, the people's Council proclaimed the birth of the *Deutsche Demokratische Republik* on October 7, 1949. After this the SED moved steadily to consolidate its power. It set up a National Front organisation to supervise society at local level, and it purged from public positions thousands of people suspected of being pro-Western; in 1951 Soviet-style collective agreements were introduced into factories, and a year later the collectivisation of agriculture was intensified. All these measures, according to the historian Gordon Craig, 'involved the use of ideologically inspired mass terror against whole social groups and sects'. They also provoked a growing exodus to the West of middle-class and professional people as well as of farmers and others – at this time the border was still open and departure was easy.

Even those who had little thought of leaving and might expect to benefit from the regime, notably the workers in factories, were becoming increasingly disgruntled after the first seven or eight years of socialism. The weight of Soviet reparations (see below), and the inefficiencies caused by the massive nationalisation of industry, were putting severe strains on an economy still struggling to recover from the war; and the Government's reaction to this was to ask workers to accept higher production norms and work loads, despite the fact that their living standards were still pitifully low. The building workers in East Berlin could finally stand it no more. On June 17, 1953, they moved spontaneously into revolt, by stopping work and calling for a general strike, and their movement quickly spread to other branches and some other big towns such as Leipzig and Magdeburg. At first the Government responded cautiously: but when some of the demonstrators began to make political demands, for free elections and the restoration of unions, Ulbricht called for Russian help and tanks of the Red Army garrisons were sent into action. The revolt then quickly subsided, but not before 21 people had been killed. Much has been argued and written since – mainly in the West – about this historic 'June 17 Revolt', the first of its kind in post-war Communist Europe. In the eyes of many cold warriors, its suppression was a typical example of Soviet brutality. Others more sympathetic to socialism will point out – not quite unfairly – that Russian fire-power was in fact used sparingly, that the death toll was low in the circumstances, and that anyway the strike was already fizzling out of its own accord for it had no future. It could also be added, more controversially, that some of the strike instigators were rabid anti-Communists such as ex-*Wehrmacht* officers and former pro-Nazi teachers who had been drafted into manual labour after 1945. There may be an element of truth in this. But to go on to claim, as some do, that the strike was wholly orchestrated by 'fascist' agents from the West, is nonsense. It was a largely genuine movement of grievance. And the whole affair and its aftermath of punishment and reprisals led to considerable disillusion among many who had hitherto been sympathetic to the new regime. One of these was Bertolt Brecht, then living in East Berlin. In a poem never published in the GDR, he regretted the official view that the people, by striking, had betrayed the Government's trust, and he added caustically,

> 'Would it not have been simpler
> If the Government had dissolved the people
> And elect another?'

The June revolt did however come just after the death of Stalin and the opening of a new era in the Kremlin, so it was followed in the GDR by a period of modest liberalisation. 'Revisionists' were allowed to criticise some aspects of the regime and to propose changes. But this renewal did not last long or get far: it was cut down by events in Hungary in November 1956. After this, gloom again descended on those who hoped for a less rigid kind of socialism in the GDR, and the exodus to the West increased. It averaged 230,000 a year in 1949–60, rising to 30,000 a month during the first part of 1961. Half of all those who left were under 25, while the older ones included many thousands of engineers, doctors and other specialists who were vital to the GDR. The country was bleeding to death; and it was this brain-drain above all that in August 1961 led Ulbricht, with Moscow's backing, to build the Wall and so block the easy escape route via West Berlin. It was an ignominious confession of failure, and Ulbricht is said to have admitted later, in private, that it was his greatest defeat in the propaganda battle to prove the worth of the GDR. But, he said, he had no alternative. And the Wall did produce the desired results, not only of stopping the haemorrhage but of giving the GDR an entirely new lease of life. East Germans at first reacted with despair and fury at being trapped; but gradually this mood gave way to one of sullen acquiescence, a realisation that after all they had better make the best of it. And Ulbricht was able to build on this, to promote economic reforms and to try to inculcate some sense of national identity and pride into the citizens of this artificial little State. The economy finally started to take off, and the choice of consumer goods in the shops began to extend beyond the most basic necessities.

But, because of the Wall and other East-West tensions, relations with the Federal Republic remained remote and icy. This was the period of the 'Hallstein doctrine' initiated in the late 1950s by Walter Hallstein, than a junior Minister in Bonn – a deliberate West German policy of seeking to boycott and undermine a GDR regime regarded as illegitimate, undemocratic and contrary to the wishes of its own people. Bonn threatened to cut off aid and break diplomatic relations with any State recognising East Germany; it also waged direct economic and propaganda campaigns against the GDR and in some cases it used sabotage. The policy had some effect. But it was smartly dropped when in 1969 Willi Brandt and the SPD came to power and began to develop their *Ostpolitik*. Brandt broke new ground in 1970 by travelling to Erfurt in Thuringia for a meeting with Willi Stoph, the GDR Prime Minister. A year later, Ulbricht was eased out of power by Moscow, for he was judged too rigid and hostile towards a détente that the Russians too now wanted. He was replaced as First Secretary by Erich Honecker, a younger, more flexible and open-minded figure, less tainted by Stalinism and the war years. He and Brandt established relations of a sort between the two Germanies, leading to the exchange of permanent missions and a big increase in trade and in visits to the GDR by West Germans. They also laid the basis for new four-Power guarantees on access to and from West Berlin. During the 1970s Honecker also took some steps towards internal liberalisation. Travel to the west remained virtually impossible, except for the elderly: but the viewing of West German television was sanctioned; a deal was done with the Protestant Church giving it a degree of independence; and with some ups and downs censorship in the arts and literature was relaxed. Honecker has been a success, and today by the standards of East European leadership he is a respected and even popular figure. He still keeps a tight grip, naturally: but he has stabilised his country and made life more tolerable for its citizens. Now in his mid-seventies, he has become a kind of *Landesvater*, national father figure.

One undoubted achievement of the GDR, dating from the 1960s, has been its economic progress. Capitalist West Germany of course is far wealthier: but the more valuable comparisons are to be made with the East. The GDR is economically and industrially much the strongest country in the Soviet bloc, with living standards an estimated 50 per cent higher than in Russia, and by as early as 1970 it had become the world's tenth leading industrial power. This can be attributed above all to the innate German qualities of efficiency, thoroughness, technical flair and so on. And the achievement appears especially remarkable when set in the context of the enormous handicaps that the country had to face at the outset, the heaviest of them being Soviet reparations. In contrast to the very light amount of dismantling carried out by the Allies in the West, and soon outweighed by Marshall Aid, the Soviet Union after 1945 set about exacting revenge on a massive scale. Its dismantling reduced East Germany's industrial capacity by an estimated 40 to 45 per cent, equal to twice the damage done by the war. At first the Russians transported whole plants to their country, for re-assembly there: but when they found this was not very efficient, they chose instead to expropriate the output of East German factories, without compensation, and this pillage amounted to an average of 25 per cent of GNP between 1945 and 1953. But then the Soviet Union changed its policy. Within the context of Comecon, the Eastern bloc's newly-created economic planning system, it decided to oblige each member state to specialise: and the GDR was allotted the role of supplying precision instruments, machine tools and other complex machinery, and some chemical products. Direct reparations were discontinued, but Comecon (i.e. Moscow) set the prices for the GDR's goods. And this remains the position today. If less heavily than before, the GDR is still penalised, for the Soviet Union, its main trading partner, does not always provide a fair deal. The GDR depends on Russia for 80 per cent of its oil and gas supplies, which it has to take at inflated prices; and in return the USSR pays poorly for GDR exports of machinery and other goods.

The GDR has faced other economic handicaps too. It has few mineral resources of its own, apart from some lignite and potash; moreover, in 1945 it inherited the least industrialised part of pre-war Germany, which in 1939 was producing only 7 per cent of its steel and 2 per cent of its hard coal. Much worse, the East Germans have had foisted on them the Soviet system of State centralised planning and bureaucratic management of nationalised concerns, and although they have coped with this a little more sensibly than, say, the Poles, or the Russians themselves, it has not always led to efficiency, to say the least. In early post-war years some 10,000 businesses were nationalised, including all those of any size in industry and commerce. Today some thousands of small private concerns are still permitted (see below), mostly in crafts and the service sector, but they are marginal to the economy as a whole. The main factories have been regrouped into combines (*Kombinate*), each of which has its production levels, its prices and its distribution outlets fixed for it in advance by various State planning bodies within the context of the overall five- and seven-year plans. This kind of coordination and target-setting may bring some advantages (as in France): but the absence of a free market leads to various rigidities, bottle-necks, shortages and sheer irrationalities. In 1963 matters were eased for a while when a much-heralded 'New Economic System' was introduced, giving the combines a little more autonomy of decision-making, and putting more stress on managerial skills as opposed to bureaucratic control. This brought some results, and was certainly a factor behind the rapid economic progress of the mid-1960s. But in 1968 there was a move back towards recentralisation, partly in reaction against the 'dangerous' liberal ideas coming from Dubček's Prague! And so life has continued ever since, following a cyclical pattern common in the Soviet bloc, with moves first towards more autonomy and then back towards the centre. At least the East Germans have shown a little more realism and dynamism than most: hence their better performance. But they are still hamstrung, as one engineer confided to me in East Berlin: 'If only we could manage things our own way, and if so many of our ablest people had not fled to the West, how brilliantly we could do!' Even as it is, the GDR's annual growth rate averaged 5 per cent in the decade after 1963, and in the past 25 years its economic expansions has matched West Germany's – of course from a much lower starting-point.

Collectivised agriculture, like industry, has improved after a difficult start and is now considerably more efficient than in Russia or most other Soviet bloc countries. Directly after the war, all holdings of more than 250 acres were confiscated without compensation from the wealthy land-owning *Junker* class, and most of this land was redistributed to farm workers, peasants and refugees. Massive collectivisation did not follow till a few years later, and at first its results were disastrous, for many farmers naturally opposed to it and the Party bureaucrats installed to run the new co-operatives had little idea of farming realities. Many of the most competent farmers left for the West. Gradually however things have settled down, and today 95 per cent of the land is farmed by cooperatives, numbering 82 per cent of all farmers. This is large-scale industrial farming, well mechanised. It is less productive than on farms of similar size in the West: but in strictly economic terms it compares well with the small-scale family farming so common in the Federal Republic. According to Bonn sources, wheat yields per acre are only about 15 per cent lower in the GDR. Above all, the Party collectivisers were sensible enough to allow members of cooperatives to retain private ownership of enough livestock and farmland (1.2 acres) to meet their own needs, and farmers have thus come grudgingly to accept the new scheme of things. This is a good example of the way the regime tries to balance the requirements of socialism and of individual privacy. So we look next at what it is like to live in this welfare state.

Jobs and security for all: the rewards and restraints of collectivism

'This society may be far from perfect: but at least we have eliminated real poverty, and that is more than you have done in the West.' I was chatting to an idealistic Communist of the old school, a childhood friend of friends of mine in Munich, as we sat in her three-room East Berlin flat for which she pays a mere 60 Mark[1] rent a month. How far was her claim justified? The lives of GDR citizens may in many respects be unpleasantly restricted and supervised: but maybe the regime should also be given credit for a number of positive achievements, social as well as economic. It has at least partly fulfilled its ideal of creating an effective and generous welfare state. It has ironed out major inequalities of class and income, and it provides security and a reasonable standard of living for all those who toe the line and do not dissent too openly.

The eradication of the worst aspects of poverty has been achieved partly by a system of full employment, and partly through a strategy of massive subsidies for many of the basic necessities of life, which are thus very cheap indeed and in many cases have not risen in price for over 20 years. The regime is proud of this policy which in certain obvious respects is admirable. Rents, unchanged since 1960s, account for only 4 to 5 per cent of an average family's income, with fuel bills adding another 1½ to 2 per cent. A tram or S-Bahn ticket in East Berlin costs 20 Pfennig for a journey of any length, the same as in the 1940s. Theatres and concerts too are remarkably cheap, and so are most restaurants: you can get an adequate meal for 6 to 8 Marks. Much basic food, including bread, milk and *Wurst*, is also pegged low in price – but here the government, to save itself money, has been quietly cheating by surreptitiously transferring some categories of food from the cut-price to the non-subsidised ranges. Thus a basic *Wurst* remains very cheap but is none too edible: if you want a good *Wurst*, you must pay maybe four or five times the price and probably

---

[1] A GDR Mark, at the official rate, equals exactly 1 Deutschmark, at a rate that is solidly fixed (on the black market, the DM can fetch up to four GDR Marks).

go to a special quality shop. The artificial gulf between the 'luxury' and 'basic' ranges is enormous: at a bar in a theatre, we paid 4.80 Marks for a glass of *Sekt* and 40 pfg for some horrid GDR Cola, whereas in the West the differential would have been more like two to one.[1] The system is also controversial in economic terms. It is reckoned that some 40 per cent of the State budget goes on these subsidies, which cover some 80 per cent of consumer products and utilities. Certainly this helps to banish poverty, for anyone on a basic income can live tolerably. But many of the GDR's less dogmatic thinkers will suggest in private that the system distorts the economy and impedes its modernisation. Yet politically it would be hard to change.

In line with this assault on poverty, the GDR has also sought to narrow the gulf in incomes and life-styles. Of course senior Party officials and their families enjoy many perks and privileges: but it would seem that they do not form a wealthy elite apart, a new upper class, to nearly the same extent as in the Soviet Union; and, if they live secluded in a special residential zone in East Berlin, this is essentially for security and political reasons. In the ordinary ranks of society, wage differentials are modest. The average worker will earn 800 to 1,000 Marks a month, but an engineer or teacher may well receive no more than 1,100 to 1,500, while a factory manager or senior professional man might rise to 2,000 or so. Apart from a few top Party figures, the most affluent people in society tend to be found among the independent craftsmen, artisans, shopkeepers or successful artists and performers: but even their prosperity is modest by Western standards.

Under the Constitution every citizen has the duty as well as the right to work – in practice the regime does ensure virtually full employment. Again, this is a source of official pride, mixed with scorn for the West. So how is it achieved? Numbers at university and technical colleges are fixed according to the needs of the economy and society, so that a student on entry is more or less assured of a job at the end of his studies, and similarly school leavers know they will be given apprenticeships or other positions. In earlier days there was much forced direction of labour, but today it is generally possible to choose one's career or type of job, at least at the outset: it may be hard to change later. Factories, offices and other bodies each have their quota of staff fixed by the various national plans, and they cannot easily make dismissals: in practice in most firms there is over-manning by about 30 to 40 per cent compared with the West. In addi-

---

[1] Some other goods regarded as luxuries are also made artificially expensive: coffee, chocolate and TV sets all cost three to four times as much as in the West.

tion, many people are obliged to work below their qualifications. So this is how full employment is achieved: by the disguising of under-employment, or by mis-employment. But the government is aware of the problem and changes are now under way (see below).

Meanwhile, somewhat paradoxically, it remains official policy to encourage mothers with young families to take a job as well, in the interests of boosting the economy, and the State helps them through a generous provision of crèches and kindergartens. According to government sources, 87 per cent of women of working age have a job outside the home – and, as wages are not high, most young couples are glad of this second income. Though women are as rare in senior political posts as in West Germany, they account for nearly half the lay judges and well over half the nation's teachers. Yet, at the same time, the regime provides unusually strong incentives for young people to get married and breed several children. Newly-weds under 26 can obtain an interest-free 5,000-Mark loan for furnishing their homes, and its repayment is progressively waived as children are born. What is more, family allowances become very generous for couples with three children or more. A young mother in a job can get six months' maternity leave on full pay for a first child, and then a full year's paid leave at home for each subsequent one. And large families have the highest priority on the long waiting lists for flats. So the regime is simultaneously keeping up a large female work-force and urging its citizens to help increase the population – and this dual policy has achieved some success. The birth-rate was falling gently until 1973, but unlike that of West Germany it has since been rising, and today the annual number of births almost equals the tally of deaths plus emigration, so the population level is more or less static. This is all the more remarkable in that since 1972 both abortion and the pill have been freely available on demand for all women over 16. But a great deal is expected of GDR women and they feel the strain of it: it is not so easy to combine running a full-time job and a young family, in a cramped flat, especially since the shopping requires endless patient queueing, and German husbands under socialism seem to be as reluctant to help with the chores as their capitalist counterparts. All this, and the fact that most couples marry very young, goes a long way to explain the very high divorce rate, which ends two marriages out of three – twice the West German figure.

The health services and hospitals, though sometimes short of modern equipment, are generally efficient and considerate. Yet the GDR's prized welfare state does contain some notable inadequecies. Elderly and retired people are well cared for in a human sense, partly through a network of 'People's solidarity' centres where schoolchildren and others are encouraged to come and help look after the old. But pensions remain quite low: though recently improved, they still account for barely half an average worker's income, a ratio that is better than Britain's but well below that of West Germany. (Is it that old people are judged less useful for the nation's future than working mothers?) Housing too is generally of poor quality. In the 1950s the GDR was so busy trying to strengthen its industrial base that it neglected to create new homes to make good the damage of the war, and its building rate *per capita* in that decade was only one-fifth of West Germany's. In the 1960s, when consumer matters ceased to be such a low priority, the housing programme was speeded up, but more in terms of quantity than quality. In 1971, only 11 per cent of homes had central heating and only 39 per cent had bath or shower; these figures however have since risen to 30 and 70 per cent today. Rents are very low, yes, but the great drawback to this is that the public housing authorities do not have the money for repairs. Hence the shabby, crumbling façades that so forcibly strike any Western visitor to the GDR (see below), as well as another hazard, less visible but worse: leaking roofs. There are many thousands of these: but, if you go to the city housing office to report a leak, you will be met with a helpless shrug or at best be lent a couple of buckets. So tenants try to do the repairs themselves, but it is hard to obtain tiles because most of the GDR's output is exported. Such are the hazards of life.

Today the authorities are at last modernising and redecorating thousands of houses a year: but it will still take them decades to make up for the long period of neglect. This was due not only to shortages of labour, and of paint and other materials, but to an official view that neatness and elegance were decadent bourgeois qualities. And this has affected public buildings of all kinds, as much as housing. Official attitudes today may have changed a little: but for the moment the average street in the GDR still wears a grey, gloomy, tumbledown look, and undoubtedly this must have a psychological impact – as one well-known novelist in East Berlin suggested to me; 'People have grown so used to the drabness that I really doubt they notice it any more. But it's one reason why they are not more cheerful. If only there were a bit more fresh paint in the GDR, and a bit more fun and fantasy too, I'm sure that fewer people would want to emigrate. This is just beginning to dawn on my friends in the Party.'

Housing is still in short supply, too. It is allocated mostly by local councils, and newly-weds have to wait two years on average to get a flat of their own, while a childless couple may have to remain content with one room. The shortage can even make it harder to move to another job. Unlike the Soviet Union, the GDR puts no formal restrictions on changing residence from one town to another. But for a family man the ability to take a new job elsewhere may depend on his being granted a flat – unless he is lucky enough to find someone willing to swap. The regime is now encouraging people to build their own little homes (see below), and in fact nearly a quarter of dwellings are privately owned. But it will still be a long time before citizens are as decently housed as would befit either their level of income or, especially, the GDR's loftly pretensions to be an advanced modern society.

Education, by contrast, has never been stinted to the same degree, for the regime sees this as a crucial investment both for the economy and for political stability; there are more teachers per head than in West Germany, and a larger share of GNP is spent on schooling. The State assumes a kind of para-parental role, as it seeks from their earliest years to win the hearts and minds of its young citizens; and it permits no private schools, Church or other. First, children in their crèches and kindergartens are taught to get used to collective living and are primed in the elements of social obligation, patriotism and 'the anti-fascist struggle'. Then from six to 16 all attend the same kind of ten-year comprehensive 'polytechnic schools', where history and literature are taught the Marxist-Leninist way; everyone learns Russian, while later on English or French are often added. But the main emphasis is on mathematics and science, which in senior class can account for 16 hours a week. The vocational element in schooling is very strong, and it shows itself in the most distinctive feature of the GDR system which is the special link with factory work. Each school is 'adopted' by a nearby factory or farm cooperative, and here from the age of 13 all classes go to spend a full day once a fortnight, where they receive instruction and do some practical work. The aim of the scheme, as one teacher suggested to me, is to 'bring the classroom closer to real life' and to make for an easier transition later from school to working life; also, to reduce some of the bias against manual labour that can still exist even under Socialism. This well-intentioned system has its critics, for some managers complain that the children are a nuisance and some teenagers look on the experience as a waste of time, since they cannot choose their factory. But on the whole it works well; and the GDR philosophy is that all young people, however intellectual their later careers are to be, should acquire some basic technical skill too. Thus I met a young historian who before univerisity had learned to repair tractors, and a TV producer who was also a typesetter. There seems a lot to be said for this.

The majority of pupils leave school at 15 or 16, and then go straight into jobs or into an apprenticeship system that is not so different from West Germany's. Each firm is obliged to take a certain number of recruits, so jobs are assured for all. Some young people to on to helping other students or excelling in Party or youth movement activities. In other words, under their teachers' supervision these young people are set to watch and assess each other, in a manner that certainly militates against non-conformity.

The process begins at a much earlier age, in school, where children are taught 'social responsibility' under a system described to me as 'total education – *Erziehung* as well as *Bildung* (general upbringing as well as academic nurturing)'. One of the more attractive features of the GDR school system is that it provides plenty of scope for hobbies, crafts, sport, culture, debating, and other extra-class activities – in this respect it is closer to the British than to the West German model (pp. 208–10). To a Briton this all seems very admirable – so long as one does not mind the ideological flavouring. Whereas most West German children leave school at 1 p.m. and do not return, GDR ones – seldom left to their own devices – stay on during the afternoon for these supervised pursuits. Mostly they take place within the framework of the Pioneer organisation, which is the junior branch of the ubiquitous *Freie Deutsche Jugend* (FDJ), the 'Free German' youth movement. Membership of the Pioneers is voluntary: but to opt out is not so easy, and in practice some 90 per cent of children belong in the six-to-14 age-group. At 14 they move on to join the FDJ itself, and they also attend preparatory classes for the *Jugendweihe* ('youth consecration'), an initiation ceremony devised to replace Christian confirmation: here they must affirm in public that they have 'grown up in the Socialist faith'. The *Jugendweihe* likewise is not compulsory, but very few youngsters refuse it. In the 14-to-30 age-group some 77 per cent belong to the FDJ, and their smart red-and-navy-blue uniforms are much in evidence at political rallies and other public meetings. The FDJ had delegates in Parliament and branches in villages and factories, and in the upper forms of schools and in universities where its members organise discos and carnivals and hold regular political discussions. In summer Pioneers and FDJ-ists go to holiday camps where they sing Socialist songs lustily. It is rather like Scouts and Guides but more political, and the indoctrination role is manifest. The Pioneers and the FDJ belong to the ruling SED which permits neither the other 'token' parties nor the Churches to have youth organisations of their own.

Many GDR school buildings are still drab: but at Erfurt I was taken to visit one model comprehensive that I found to be neat, airy and spacious, comparing well with similar schools in the West. The atmosphere seemed humane and caring, not too regimented. There was some propaganda on the classroom walls, of the anti-NATO and anti-Reagan type: but it was not too strident, and one room displayed a portrait of Luther. Some senior pupils in their FDJ uniforms were presented for me to interview. One very bright 15-year-old daughter of a policeman declared proudly that her aim in life was 'to identify with the State and serve its interests' and she planned to study law: when I asked her what she thought of the Western multi-party system with its alternating governments, she seemed not to understand what I meant. Others denounced the 'class struggle' in the West and told me

[333]

how they spent part of their spare time caring for elderly and sick people. Clearly the FDJ and the Pioneers do provide an outlet for the idealism and sense of social service of many young people. Or, as one veteran West German reporter in East Berlin suggested to me, 'The Party survives in power not only with the help of Russian guns, but because it still gets enough genuine support from a young idealistic minority in each new generation that emerges.'

Sport, that crucial GDR speciality, is also exploited as a focus for national idealism, and alike in schools and universities it is compulsory. What is more, the GDR's 180,000 sports instructors are systemically on the look-out for young children with athletic promise, who from the age of 13, and sometimes from as early as seven or eight, will be transferred from ordinary classes to one of 20 special sport schools, to be trained as future champions. It was Ulbricht who initiated this policy of using sport as an instrument for winning international recognition and for boosting domestic morale and patriotism. Hence the huge effort deployed: the State spends an estimated 2 per cent of GNP on athletics. And this had paid off: around the globe, the GDR is better known for its sporting achievements than for anything else. As the table below shows, it first fully established its supremacy at the Montreal Olympics in 1976 where it won more gold medals than any other country except the Soviet Union. It did well again at the Moscow Olympics in 1980 (where the USA and West Germany were not competing) and its athletes and others were profoundly disappointed when in 1984 the USSR obliged the GDR to follow its lead in pulling out from the Games at Los Angeles.

	USSR	USA	GDR	W.Germany
1968 Mexico				
Bronze	30	34	7	10
Silver	32	27	9	11
Gold	29	45	9	5
1972 Munich				
Bronze	22	30	23	16
Silver	27	31	23	11
Gold	50	33	20	13
1976 Montreal				
Bronze	35	25	25	17
Silver	43	35	25	12
Gold	47	34	40	40
1980 Moscow				
Bronze	46	—	32	—
Silver	69	—	37	—
Gold	80	—	47	—

At the Lake Placid Winter Olympics of 1980, the GDR also came second, with nine gold medals against the USSR's ten and the USA's nine: its prowess at skiing is especially remarkable for a country with no alpine slopes or tradition of winter sports. As for swimming, in the 1983 European championships its women competitors won every single title. The nation's star athletes receive many special privileges, including large apartments, Trabant cars without having to wait the usual eight years for them, and free seaside holidays in Cuba. This cosseting tends to reinforce Western criticisms that the GDR's sports policy seems to be geared more towards producing champions than providing recreational facilities for a wider public. There may be some truth in this: but mass activity is certainly encouraged too. Some four million citizens hold the GDR Sport Badge, an award for sporting skills and physical fitness whose motto is, 'Ready for Work and the Defence of our Homeland'. Popular attention focusses also on the Spartakliad youth games and sports festival held every other year at Leipzig, a mammoth event with over 70,000 participants. In general, the regime does seem to have succeeded in imbuing its people with a widespread enthusiasm for sport and a veneration for its top athletes. After all, in this enclosed little country, they do not have so many other outlets for their passions.

Not only when they are pupils and students, but on throughout the rest of their lives too, the regime strives to inculcate into its citizens a *sozialistisches Staatsbewusstsein*, or sense of identification with the Socialist State, and it does this through a whole range of collectivist activities. Its motives are undoubtedly mixed. Some of the more idealistic Communists, mainly older ones, are still genuinely committed to developing a warm and brotherly community where everyone can feel secure and wanted: on the other hand, many zealots and functionaries are much more concerned with channelling people's energies and trying to assure their loyalty, so that the Party can retain a firmer grip on power. And some leaders, no doubt including Honecker himself, are to some degree guided by both objectives at once.

Witness above all the way that factories and other work-places are given a far wider and more assertive role in people's daily lives than in the West, extending to welfare services, group social activity and political matters. The SED, as well as the FDJ and other Party-run bodies, are very much present in the work-places where they hold propagandist rallies and meetings for the staff – 'and if you are in a position of any responsibility,' I was told by a doctor who had just emigrated illegally to the West, 'it is not so easy to avoid having to stand up and make public declarations, praising the gallant struggle of the workers, vowing friendship with our Soviet brothers, extolling Party resolutions, or other such Marxist crap. In the hospital where I worked, some people did this sincerely and most others followed suit out of sheer opportunitism. I couldn't bear the shamming any longer – one reason why I left.' All citizens must belong to a 'brigade' or 'collective' attached to the place where they live or work, and since the mid-1960s 'collectives of socialist labour' have been encouraged to develop in factories and offices: these are little groups who show their fervour for the cause by doing extra voluntary work such as putting on cultural events, or helping to run the firm's summer camp, or undergoing further training. Some individuals too, if they are zealous at their work, will be rewarded with a cash prize and a title such as 'Activist of Socialist Labour'; manual workers often win this distinction after 30 or 40 years' service.

Worker delegates in factories sit on 'production councils' whose job is to advise management in its decisions. But the plant's director, and the State bureaucrats above him, always have the last word; and this GDR version of *Mitbestimmung* would seem in practice to have even less influence on policy than the West German kind. So workers tend to feel apathetic about the factory and alienated from the remote men of power at the top – as even some official GDR studies will admit: according to one report made secretly for the Party leadership but then leaked, three-quarters of young workers at the Robotron plant in Dresden felt that they had no say in its affairs, and over 60 per cent said they were afraid to voice any criticism. However, the social and welfare roles of factories and offices brings them much more popularity with their staff. This is far more pronounced than in the West: workers will expect their factories to help them find a flat, to run holiday camps for them and to provide kindergartens. The trade unions too play a big part here. They are denied the right to strike, nor do they conduct wage bargaining; instead, they are in charge of all social security funds, they administer the firm's holiday centres and hospitals, and they spend money on kindergartens, sport and leisure. They are the management's welfare agency, not its adversary.

Another curious example of the 'all-embracing' role of the workplace concerns the handling of minor acts of delinquency and petty offences. These are not referred to outside courts but are dealt with inside the factory by 'conflict commissions' made up of elected employees. 'Here again,' the British journalist Jonathan Steele has written, 'the GDR prefers to handle within the work context issues which Western societies leave exclusively to local civic institutions like magistrates' courts. The idea is that a person's work collective can produce the best form of discipline, control, help and re-education.'[1]

---

[1] P. 139 of his mainly favourable study of the GDR, *Socialism with a German Face; the State that Came in from the Cold* (Jonathan Cape, London, 1977).

To quote an instance I myself was given at one plant, a lorry-driver might be hauled up before his colleagues for stealing vodka from the canteen for a private party. Generally, if found guilty, the offender has to apologise in public, repair the damage done, and maybe pay a small fine. Some 40 per cent of penal cases are handled in this way; other more serious ones, that might involve a prison sentence, are sent to a regular court. As far as I could tell, these conflict commissions work quite well in their way, though some people do treat them somewhat cynically. They are just one example of the earnest school-like moralistic atmosphere that pervades so much of public and working life in the GDR, alike in factories and offices, hospitals and farm cooperatives, State shops and colleges, even newspapers and TV studios. All are run in much the same way. And, except amid the privacy of his family and trusted circle of friends, the individual cannot easily escape the State's nanny-like determination to keep him on the straight and narrow path.

So this in brief outline is the GDR's social system and how it works. Popular attitudes to the regime are of course impossible to quantify: but it is usually estimated that about 15 to 20 per cent of people are sincere supporters (that is, about the same number as the 2 million or so members of the SED). They include, first, a sizeable section of the older working class, the ones who have perhaps benefited most from socialism. Next come the battalions of small Party officials, local bureaucrats and apparatchiks, some of them sincere, more of them opportunists who enjoy their perks and petty power – 'Because I'm a Party member,' said a civic employee in Rostock with ingenuous candour, 'I was able to get special construction materials, normally so scarce, for building myself this nice little house. This is a lovely society, and I live well.' Third come the idealists, not so numerous – some of them young, like my policeman's daughter, but more of them found among the old guard who fought for their faith during the hard Nazi years and then helped to create the regime. Like, for example, the elderly middle-class Jewish lady I know in East Berlin, who after the war returned to the city from her London exile: 'Maybe we're going too slowly, but at least we're on the right lines,' she told me, 'and there's more true social justice than in the West. In London, when I went back this year, people were saying of the good times, "not any more"; here they say, "not yet".' But she went on to reflect with a touch of sadness that her East Berlin friends and neighbours seemed to have lost much of the caring community spirit of the old hard days – 'They've grown too selfish and consumerist, they think it a disaster if they can't get their deep-freeze quickly.'

So much for the supporters. Of the other 80 per cent or so, just a few are true dissidents who hate the regime and try to find ways of emigrating (many have done so). The rest, the vast majority, simply acquiesce and try as best they can to enjoy their own private lives – as we shall now see.

Privacy and a quiet life in the 'niche society'

'The initials "DDR" stand for "Der doofe Rest"' (the dopey dregs) runs an old and familiar joke. Certainly it was the more bright and resourceful people who tended to leave for the West, in the days when they still could, and the less ambitious who stayed, at least in the middle classes. So, far more than Poland or even Hungary, the GDR has been bereft of its enterprising elites – and this makes it a duller place though maybe also, from the regime's point of view, a more easily controllable one. Those left behind after the building of the Wall, at first despondent, have since developed a certain resignation: they have come to terms with a situation they cannot change and have learned to make the most of it. They have found, too, that life has become more tolerable in the past 20 years or so. Living standards have risen and consumer goods become more plentiful, while surveillance by the secret police has lightened: Honecker in effect has reached an unspoken agreement with his people, whereby he allows them some privacy and a decent living, so long as they do not cause him trouble. 'So why should we rock the boat?' is a familiar reaction; 'let's keep our heads down and settle for a quiet and modestly comfortable life.' Or as I was told by Günter Kunert, the well-known dissident poet from the GDR now living near Hamburg, 'The regime treats people exactly like domestic pets – protected, but not free. But you can't be miserable *all* the time: human happiness keeps breaking through.'

People have come to identify with the GDR and to see it as their home, and especially this is so now that a whole new generation has grown up that never knew the days before the Wall. Many people have even come to be vaguely proud of the GDR, and they resent being patronised by affluent visitors from West Germany who tell them how unfortunate they are. Such people are proud of their country's sporting successes, of its economic progress in face of such odds, and of some cultural achievements such as the restoration of old towns. Some of them, without necessarily liking the regime, will even take some pride in the GDR as a society less violent, permissive and over-competitive than the West and one that has better preserved some of the old German values.

These values are essentially private ones: and if they have been retained, it is less by virtue of the regime than in defence against it. To compensate as best they can for the irksome official pressures, the boring collectivism and the generally grey surface of life, most GDR inhabitants retreat into private pleasures and the gentlenesss and trust of their circle of family and close friends. Almost everyone I met who knew both Germanies well remarked to me that, wherever this trust exists, human relations tend to be closer, warmer and more genuinely caring in the GDR than in the Federal Republic where families are more geographically dispersed and so many people are in part corrupted by careerism, consumerism, insecurity and so on. In the GDR, because officialdom is not to be trusted and you never know whether your neighbour might not be an informer, so people who are close to each other depend on each other emotionally much more; because daily life with its queues and shortages is not so easy, so they rely much more on close friends and relatives for practical help; and because the pace of life is less hectic, so they have more time for each other and are readier to look after sick or elderly dependents – one emigrant I met in Hamburg said, 'Now that she's retired, my widowed mother would be able to come and live with me here, but I've dissuaded her. She'd never adapt to the solitude here – and I have a full-time job.' In the GDR people may be bored, but they are less often lonely. However, if a mildy oppressive Communist State has served for the wrong reasons to make people nicer, this hardly serves to justify that regime. The supreme irony is that the warm human community advocated by Socialism is now being created *against* Socialism, within the cell-like private circles.

The people I met privately within the GDR, or recently emigrated from it, struck me as noticeably less worldly and sophisticated than West Germans, more gentle and natural, but more subdued too, with a curiously tentative manner. People do not chat very readily in public, and they queue silently. In one crowded East Berlin cafeteria where I lunched, you could have heard a pin drop, whereas in the West those same clerks and typists would have been laughing and gossiping. And when couples meet for the first time in the home of mutual friends, initially they seem wary of talking to each other. This appears to be more than simply an instilled fear of possible informers or other enemies, in a society where anything you say might be held against you years later. It may also be a deeper kind of cowed spiritlessness after so many years of being told what not to say. (One joke that circulates is about a GDR dog meeting a Polish dog on the frontier, each on his way to the other's country. 'But why on earth are you going to the GDR?' 'Well, I simply must eat. And you, why go to Poland?' 'I simply must bark.')

Most people try to live inconspicuously. Günter Gaus, the distinguished Hamburg-based liberal journalist who knows the GDR well, having served in 1974–81 as first head of the West German mission in East Berlin, has written a book describing it as a *'Nischengesellschaft'*, or society of little niches. 'It's a police state, yes, but not an arbitrary one,' he told me, 'and that's an important distinction. The rules are clear, and so long as you stick to them, nothing awful will happen to you. So, apart from the tragedy of the dissidents, anyone can live quite privately in his little niche without being disturbed. The State has a tacit arrangement to that effect with the citizens.' Another well-known West German journalist, Robert Röntgen, till recently correspondent in East Berlin of the ARD network, described it to me as 'not only a niche society but a group society. Many people form themselves into exclusive little groups of some 20 to 30, where they stick together for discussion and friendship, and above all for mutual help in coping with officialdom, material shortages and so on. The groups therefore tend to be multi-professional, so as to maximise skills and contacts: I know one that includes an actress, a doctor and a factory technician. People depend on such friends much more than they would in the West. The groups are non-political and not actively dissident: but the regime does not like them much, since they tend to shift the focus of loyalty away from State collectivism. There is quite a lot of petty corruption in the GDR, and officials often need to be bribed before they will help you. But, within a group, people *never* cheat each other.' Röntgen, who comes originally from the Rostock area, went on: 'As private individuals, East Germans are full of human virtues, they're so *nice* – it is in reaction to the regime, though I agree with you that this is hardly a justification for it! In the United States, where I lived and worked for 15 years, people are far more spoilt and much less nice.'

It is noticeable too that professional people tend to be much less career-minded than in the West. The State may try to woo workers to greater efforts: but, as it also offers job security, most employees feel little incentive to work hard and will prefer to conserve their energies for their leisure or for moonlighting, which is widespread. As wage differentials are small, it is often thought hardly worthwhile to strive to get a better job that will involve more work and responsibility for little extra pay: apart from a number of SED loyalists, the only people who work really hard in the GDR are the few thousands in the private sector – and a free-lance window-cleaner can earn more money than many an engineer. To climb a hierarchy inside a firm, you must show yourself to be a devotee of the regime or at least pay lip-service: plenty are prepared to do this, but they tend to be looked on as opportunists and they may lose their real friends. So, in this non-competitive, non-risk-taking society, a great many people prefer to settle for a junior position and a quiet life. On the other hand, to opt out completely and live on your wits, as some younger ones might be tempted to do, is not at all easy. As basic necessities are so cheap, it would in theory be quite possible to get by on a very low income as an independent artisan, for example making pottery or even writing stories: but for this you need a permit and a tax number, which are not always given. If you are unable to show them, you can be arrested and prosecuted.

One notable feature of the 'niche society' is that more and more people are building their own little villas or bungalow homes, on plots of land on the edge of towns. This may be a bid to circumvent the housing shortage, or to escape the semi-collective life of blocks of flats, or to pursue the hobby of gardening, or all of these at once. What is especially significant is that the State since 1971 has encouraged this trend, and increasingly so. It leases the land without charge, and it provides access to building materials and loans for families prepared to follow one of the various types of house-design laid down by the Construction Ministry. Those who take advantage of the scheme usually build these simple little homes themselves, with the help of friends: any weekend in the suburbs you can see these amateurs busily hammering and mortaring. Some 20 per cent of new dwellings fall into this category.

Why does the State encourage this kind of private ownership? Firstly, of course, to help it to deal with the housing shortage. But there is another and more important reason that lies right at the heart of the astonishing contradiction today in the regime's collectivist-versus-privacy attitudes. It still pursues its collectivist policies, through the youth movements, the factory brigades and so on: but it has come to accept that these cannot alone satisfy people or make them happy, and that it must find other ways of answering their consumerist urges and desires for a private life. This trend, barely noticeable under Ulbricht, has become much more pronounced under Honecker in the past decade or so. And so the regime – not unlike Tory Governments in Britain – promotes owner-occupation of homes as a means of securing a more stable and contented society, one with a stake in the status quo and thus not so likely to be tempted into Polish-style unrest. This point was put to me forcibly by a number of GDR citizens, including one prominent Communist writer, critical of the regime but not hostile to it: 'Though it will never dare to say so, this deeply conservative government wants the population to be conservative too. And so it is in the process of creating just the kind of selfish consumerist petit-bourgeois society that decent Socialists are supposed to hate. Party leaders I meet are quite aware of these dangers, but it's impossible to discuss them in public.' The dilemma is not new. In 1975 the 'reformist' Marxist, Robert Havemann, wrote an article published in Hamburg, in which he complained that the GDR was entering into artificial competition with the West for all the wrong materialistic things: instead of liberalising towards more true democracy and political freedom under Socialism, it was simply selling out to consumerism. For uttering this and other home truths, Havemann was put under house arrest.

Dilemmas for the church, wooed but wary

The policy of relaxing the reins in private matters (while keeping tight overall political control) has been applied especially to religion and to watching West German television – two vitally important areas of life in the GDR. Until the early 1970s, to view Western TV was not allowed: many people surreptitiously did so, but they risked being punished and sometimes were. In those days, FDJ activists would climb on rooftops to remove westward-turned aerials, and the authorities would try to keep a check on the guilty ones. One trick they used was for teachers to get school classes of young children to 'draw a sketch of the TV logo': so the innocent tots drew the one they knew best, and their poor parents were maybe hauled up for questioning. But since 1973 all this has changed and the crime is now sanctioned. This was fruit of the détente with West Germany after *Ostpolitik*, and of the new milder Honecker line. Also it was never technically possible to jam Western TV; and, as many Party leaders themselves watched it, the hypocrisy of the situation could not last for ever. Today, in the territory reached by West German transmitters, some 95 per cent of GDR citizens view it regularly, including Honecker and the Politburo. People sometimes tune in to films, sport and entertainment, but not so very often because GDR television itself provides quite good programmes here: mainly they watch the news and current affairs documentaries, where the GDR's own coverage is predictably biased, limited and boring. Hence East Germans tend to be very well informed about the world, even though Western newspapers and magazines remain banned. Television is their link with outside reality. Nor is the regime really so displeased with this mass viewing, for so many Western programmes nowadays are filled with news of unemployment, crime, *Angst*, youth demonstrations and so on that it feels that this TV fare may well make its own people more content with their own lot and less keen to emigrate. Also it knows well that the ability to watch Western TV assuages the claustrophobia created by the travel restrictions: they can at least enjoy the West vicariously. It has in fact been noted that applications to emigrate have been consistently much the highest in the Dresden area, which for reasons of terrain is the main part of the GDR unable to pick up West German stations – either this made the people there feel more trapped, isolated and dissatisfied, or else they alone were not sharing the nightly spectacle of the West's miseries, or maybe a bit of both. Anyway, in 1985 the GDR government actually began installing special cables to relay the West German networks to Dresden. This indeed is détente.

The State has also greatly improved its relations with the Protestant Church, which today enjoys a more privileged position than any other church in Communist Europe, including the Catholic in Poland: 'Workers of the world, for God's sake unite!' was the satiric comment of one East Berlin cabaret sketch. Honecker's regime has come to accept that it needs the cooperation of this influential Church, which still has some 7.7 million registered members, almost half the population. Its attendance figures have been declining, as in the West, and today only 7 per cent of East Berliners are regular churchgoers: but this is no true measure of its real support, in a country where the Churches offer the only organised public alternative to the official value-system, and thus attract many people who might not otherwise be very religious. The Catholic Church, in this part of Germany with its firm Lutheran tradition, has always been much weaker than Protestantism and has 1.2 million members. It keeps a low profile and has been more wary than the Protestants of reaching an active accommodation with the State.

After the war, the anti-Nazi resistance record of many Protestant leaders, as well as their social and egalitarian ideals, won them a certain respect from the new Communist rulers, some of whom had even shared prison cells and concentration camps with them. This may explain why the Church was not victimised as severely as in some East European countries at that time. Even so, throughout the 1950s and '60s there was a good deal of harassment, as the State fought to restrict a rival ideology and reduce its hold on youth. A few priests were jailed; church literature was burned; student Christian groups were outlawed from universities and young churchgoers were seldom permitted to take the *Abitur*. During this time when the GDR was struggling to establish its separate identity, the regime was above all angered by the fact that the Evangelical Churches of East and West Germany remained closely united within a single body, the EKD (see p. 233), and it thus tended to see the GDR churches as agents of the West. These tensions even increased after the building of the Wall. Finally in 1969, under severe State pressure, the GDR branches of the EKD decided that it would be best to split off from the rest and form their own federation. They did so, and this has greatly eased the situation. But the Churches in the GDR still retain close spiritual and personal links with their partners in West Germany, and with tacit State approval they rely on them heavily for financial aid, so as to top up the meagre revenue they draw from voluntary taxes on their own faithful.

After the split in 1969, and especially after Honecker succeeded Ulbricht in 1971, the regime steadily modified its hostility. In 1976 the

SED pronounced formal guarantees of freedom of religion and belief. And in March 1978 Honecker held talks with Bishop Schönherr, head of the Lutheran Church in the GDR – the first such meeting between leaders of State and Church for 30 years – at which a *modus vivendi* was established, with the regime offering various concessions and privileges to the Church, and promising to allow Christians the same respect and rights as other citizens, in return for a Church commitment not to meddle in politics. Honecker probably had various motives in making the deal. He wanted to improve the GDR's image abroad; he saw that the Church could be of practical value to the State through its welfare work with the sick and handicapped; and above all, at a time of restiveness and disillusion among young people, he hoped that the Church might be prepared to act as a moderating force by helping to channel and tame the dissidence and promote stability. And the Church, with some misgivings, has tacitly accepted this role.

The situation today, as both Church and Party leaders will admit in private, is one 'not of friendship, but of pragmatism and reasonableness on both sides'. Apart from its practical benefits from the deal, the Church's major moral and political gain is that the State has now largely stopped making atheistic propaganda against it: in the words of one senior priest I met, 'The regime accepts that not only do we have our own spiritual role (which of course it does not believe in), but that we have also an ethical and social part to play, in seeking to improve people's lives.' The *quid pro quo* is that the Church accepts the State and does not fight against it: this still causes heartache among some priests, but most of the more virulently anti-Communist have by now left for the West. Each side today knows and respects its limits. As one open-minded pastor in East Berlin put it to me, 'I don't think old Honecker is entirely atheistic, he considers it normal and right that each village should have its little church. He admires our anti-Nazi record too. And, for our part, Lutherans in Germany have a long tradition of acceptance of the established political order – for good or ill.' (A tradition, you would have thought, that the wiser of them would have learned to forget since the Nazi period.)

As a result of the 1978 agreement, the Protestant Church has found it easier to secure sites for building new churches, financed from the West; and it has won increased time for programmes of its own on State radio and television, including a religious service broadcast each Sunday. Six State universities have departments of theology, where at any time some 600 students are training to become priests. And the GDR is one of the few Warsaw Pact countries to tolerate conscientious objection, at least to the extent that Christian and other objectors – though their careers may suffer for it later – are permitted to do their military service in army construction units that do not carry weapons. These and other concessions to the Church add up to a range of privileges greater than in most Communist countries. The Church is still forbidden to have its own schools or youth movement, but it carries out a great deal of social and welfare work. Backed by State subsidies, the Protestant and Catholic Churches between them run 82 hospitals with some 12,200 beds, and they do most of the work for the mentally handicapped in the GDR. The State is glad of this practical help – just as it seems to be appreciative, even envious, of the Church's disciplining hand over young people. Unruly behaviour tends to be less noticeable at Church rallies than at those run by the Party.

The most extraordinary episode in the regime's bid to move closer to the Church came in 1983, the year of the 500th anniversary of the birth of Martin Luther in the little town of Eisleben, west of Leipzig. It so happens that nearly all the main events in the life of the great reformer took place on what is now GDR territory. He was born and died at Eisleben, he studied and was a monk at Erfurt, he translated the New Testament into German in Wartburg castle and he is believed to have nailed his 95 famous theses to the door of Wittenberg church. But in the first decades after the war the GDR officially regarded Luther as 'an enemy of the people and traitor to the peasants', and as late as the mid-1970s school history-books were still teaching this version. Then all began to change. Luther now became 'a precursor of Marx, as John the Baptist was of Christ' and 'the man who mobilised the progressive forces in Germany against the Papal exploiters'. So the history books were finally rewritten, to the confusion of many loyal Marxist teachers. It soon became clear that the turnabout was partly by way of preparation for the anniversary, when the State staged giant celebrations that matched those of the Church itself and led some foreign critics to pour scorn on this 'ungainly effort to appropriate Luther as an ideological forebear of German communism'.[1] Honecker himself chaired the organising committee, State television gave live coverage of the opening ceremony at Wartburg, and the Opera House in East Berlin was lent to the Church for a festival where Honecker and the Archbishop of Canterbury were among the guests of honour while Protestants poured into the GDR from all over the globe, including several million from West Germany. Once again, the State's motivation was manifestly mixed. Certainly it was not averse to earning extra hard currency from so much tourism: but the rehabilitation of Luther was also clearly a part of the new policy (see below) of seeking to strengthen GDR citizens' sense of national identity by reinstating great figures from the German past. Honecker

[1] Neal Ascherson in the *Observer* of November 6, 1983.

[345]

may equally have wanted to upstage or embarrass the Church, or at least to manoeuvre it into a further *de facto* acknowledgement of the regime's moral respectability. So Church leaders, while glad of this new token of support and recognition, were also a little wary.

They have reason to be so, for even today, despite the entente, the State still pursues subtle or not-so-subtle discrimination against many individuals lay Christians. If not as much as in former days, their children may still find it harder than others to be accepted for university study; and conscientious objectors are still harassed and penalised in their later careers. Practising Christians are barred from almost all teaching jobs ('But would they anyway be happy teaching Marxism-Leninism?' said one SED man) and from posts of a political nature such as mayor or senior ministry official. So Christians can still have difficulty in winning promotion. The only exceptions are the members of the Christian Democratic Union (CDU), which bears *no* relation to its West German homonym but is one of four small satellite parties under the hegemony of the SED: claiming a membership of 120,000, it is made up of 'socialist citizens of the Christian faith', and the regime uses it as a means of pressing talented Christians into State service if it really needs them, for by means of the CDU the formal ban on them can be sidestepped. For example, if some brilliant individual who happens to be a Christian is required to fill some key post as surgeon, professor or engineer, then he will be invited to join the CDU first. Some agree to do so. But Church leaders themselves keep their distance from this party, regarding it with scorn as a creature of the SED – 'it's a farce,' said one priest. So, all in all, Christians in the GDR still face problems: but like other citizens they have learned that the best defence is to stand up for their rights – 'If you have the courage to fight for tolerance, then usually you'll get it,' said one Churchman, adding: 'You also do best if you are open about your Christian faith: this at least earns respect. The State is hardest on those who try to protect their careers by hiding their beliefs.'

The issue of what should be the role of Christians in an atheistic State – how far should they collaborate? – is one that constantly exercises priests and their congregations, and not all see alike. The regime, for its part, keeps up its steady wooing: 'Surely we have a common struggle,' Party members will tell Christians; 'like you, we desire peace, social justice and brotherly love. Was Marx's teaching so different from the Sermon on the Mount? Join us, in building a better society!' And a number of priests react positively: they believe that this Communist regime is here to stay and they even admire its social achievements, so they are prepared to take part in some of its activities and to join in seeking to liberalise it further. Others are more reticent: but even they believe that it is perfectly possible to lead the Christian life in the GDR and that the Church needs the strength of all its supporters. So they continually urge their faithful not to try to emigrate. When the State sanctioned a large-scale exodus in 1984 and six pastors and their families left the Berlin-Brandenburg district, the Church grew worried and appealed to parishioners who had lodged exit applications: 'We know of your distress and hopelessness . . . but remember that the protection of our Lord Jesus Christ guards us in this land too.'

At the same time, because it is one of the rare institutions not directly controlled by the State, the Church inevitably becomes a magnet for all kinds of outsiders, many of them not Christians at all, who are drawn to it for protection or want to use its premises for meetings. They include homosexuals, punks, Oriental sects, unofficial peace groups and others frowned on as 'unsocialist' – and they place the Church in a dilemma. Of course it wants to help those in trouble with the regime: but it sees its first duty as helping its own members, nor does it want to provoke the State in a manner that might prejudice its own privileges.

Latent Church/State tensions of this kind have come to the force recently over the Peace Movement, which manages to struggle along spasmodically in the Soviet bloc despite official measures against it. The anti-missile campaign of 1982–3 in West Germany produced a modest counterpart in the GDR, where in Dresden young people wearing CND badges held a candlelight vigil in the ruins of the Frauenkirche, singing Lennon's 'Give peace a chance'. The badges soon appeared in thousands all over the GDR, whereupon the authorities' patience snapped. Many people were arrested, or had the emblem ripped off their clothes. Peace marches in East Berlin were banned, and leaders of a big rally in Jena were put in prison – to the dismay of some milder Party members, one of whom suggested to me, 'The GDR and the Soviet Union are so peace-loving that we do not require a peace movement here: nonetheless, young people do need protest outlets of some sort and they should have been allowed them.' No doubt Moscow leaned heavily on Honecker: but the official reason for the clamp-down, given by one SED leader, was: 'Dissident elements were moving in to the rallies, and we were worried that counter-revolutionary ideas not confined to the peace movement might take over.'

This conflict put the Church in a difficult position. In the West, the Churches are split on the peace issue, for while many Christians back CND, others believe that NATO including West Germany needs its nuclear defences: but in the GDR virtually all Christians are in favour of the peace movement, for *none* of them wants to be defended by Soviet missiles. So the Church in all sincerity could not disown the demonstrators. It is prudent enough not to campaign too openly on the nuclear issue and devotes its main peace efforts to the more immediate practical aim of trying to prevent the growth of military training in schools (see below). But it does hold discussions on peace in church premises, for its parishioners are passionately interested and it knows that police informers are often present. Recently the regime has begun to mutter veiled warnings that the Church might be in danger of breaching the guidelines of the entente by meddling in politics. And this underlines the central dilemma of the Christian Churches in the GDR today, as in any Communist country. They need the State's support, yet there are moral limits to their room for compromise with it. Dean Günther Krusche of East Berlin told the BBC (quoted in the *Listener* of March 17, 1983): 'There are people in the Church who feel we shouldn't talk too loudly, for fear that we might lose what freedom of action we have achieved. I think we should remain in critical partnership with the State, but we must refuse to stay silent on the peace issue. As Martin Luther King put it, we are a voice for the voiceless. We cannot pay that price.'

The watchful grip of the one-party state

The curbs on freedom of expression – over disarmament and a whole range of other issues – certainly infuriate an important minority of people, the kind who in Western societies would be opinion-makers, social critics or demonstrators. But they are seldom what the average citizen finds most irking about life in the GDR. He has grown used to the system and in most cases has had no direct experience of democracy in the Western sense: so he does not miss it so much. His concerns are more practical and material. If he were asked what annoys him most, he would probably put first the ban on travel to the West, and he might then add the distortions, omissions and tedious repetitiveness of the State newspapers and media, which he can compare nightly with Western TV. But more likely he would cite in second place the unpredictable shortages in the shops and the difficulties in getting the simplest repairs done. 'If Communism were less plain inefficient, people would accept it much more easily,' said one housewife. The shortages are not exactly an advertisement for the centralised planning system, and they contrast oddly with the decent overall level of prosperity where in some respects the picture is quite positive. Some 99 per cent of homes have refrigerators, 87 per cent television sets, 91 per cent washing machines (but only 22 per cent have telephones); and the proportion of homes with private cars has risen since 1970 from 16 to 42 per cent, which compares very well with Russia's 13 per cent. But, unless they have special Party contacts, people still have to wait between six and ten years for a new car, and then all they are likely to get is an ungainly little two-cylinder Trabant or Wartburg, made in the GDR and sold at an artificially high price. In the 1950s and '60s, the private ownership of cars was deliberately restricted on ideological grounds, for it was regarded as a sign of a bourgeois life-style. That no longer happens today; it is essentially the lack of parts and materials, lack of hard currency, and the absolute priority given to exports, that make cars in such short supply.

These same factors are also in part responsible for the recurrent capricious shortages of smaller everyday items: but so is the clumsy centralised distribution system, and the inflexibility of an industrial planning process that will fix a factory's targets with scant regard to consumer needs. Suddenly nails will completely disappear from the shops, or wallpaper, or underpants – or they will re-emerge in bulk but all the same colour. A supermarket may be out of orange juice but have piles of rhubarb juice. And even in summer the selection of fresh fruit and vegetables is appalling. Hence the queues, and the frustrations of daily shopping that takes up far more time than in the West. Much of the best of the GDR's output – of fresh flowers, clothing, furnishing, even things like bathroom tiles – is sold to the West for hard currency so that only the second-rate remains, or maybe nothing. If some key item is suddenly unobtainable, it may well be that it has been used to exploit some unexpected export opportunity, as happened recently when Volkswagen placed a mass order for East German car tyres. But these perfectly sensible commercial deals are not reported in the media, which will never explain *why* some shortage is occurring, and officials when asked refuse to comment. Many of the older Party loyalists I met cited this privately as one of their own main criticisms of the regime. And the ordinary citizen, frustrated and kept in the dark, feels treated like a child. He has money, but not much choice to spend it on – unless via friends or contacts in the West he has access to Deutschmarks, with which he can buy luxury imported goods at the special 'Inter' shops that take hard currency only.

In the ordinary shops, people keep on the alert for something unusual and attractive to appear – say, good linen or Meissen porcelain – and then they seize their chance and buy up a large stock, so as to be able to give most of it to friends in return for other items bought in the same way. 'So life has reverted to barter as in pre-money days,' said one man; 'when I wanted to build a *dacha*, I couldn't find concrete anywhere. Finally I swapped some for a lorryload of sand.' Or else people resort to subterfuge. I heard of a man who was trying to join the Party, so he needed to be very discreet about his Western contacts, especially as he had a brother in West Berlin. His washing-machine kept breaking down, and spare parts for it were unobtainable in the GDR: so the brother was telephoned and came over with the spares, tactfully parking his car two blocks away.

People regard such deviousness as normal routine. Similarly, as services and repairs have been much neglected by the official planners, the State sector includes extremely few plumbers, cobblers, garages or the like. So the gap is left to be filled by private initiative. Demand still greatly exceeds supply: but the State has become aware of the problem and has begun to give loans to encourage small entrepreneurs of this kind.

As in other Communist countries, private business on a modest scale is permitted: as well as the service and repair firms, a good many craftsmen, artisans, smaller shops and restaurants fall into this category. They tend to be family-run, but are allowed up to ten employees each. Most of the better bakeries, boutiques and bistrots in the GDR are privately owned, and they help to make life more pleasant for they have a more personal touch, and a better sense of quality and service, than the bureaucratic State concerns. Usually they work hard and successfully, and such families are often among the more properous in the GDR – for example, the boutique-owner I met in Dresden who had his own pleasure-boat in the Elbe. But they are careful not to flaunt their modest wealth as they might in the West, for this is still ideologically *mal vu* and it could invite closer tax scrutiny or other reprisals. So the status-symbol society is here turned on its head. Most little restaurants, though inside they may be quite cosy and elegant, look deliberately decrepit and down-at-heel from the outside, as if they were actually trying to deter custom. It is another reason for the GDR's general air of drabness.

Although commercial ventures are sometimes arbitrarily refused licences, it seems that on the whole the regime accepts and even discreetly encourages the private sector, for it knows how needed it is. So one might have expected these little firms to be increasing in number, seeing that they do so well and offer some scope for independence and initiative amid the collectivist wasteland. But curiously enough the total of full-time private businesses is actually declining from 250,000 in 1955 to 80,000 today, according to one estimate. And this is not entirely due to State pressure: rather it is that in this passive niche-society few people are prepared to accept the risk and hard work involved. Often they find it difficult to raise the initial capital or a restauranteur in particular will be scared of having to depend on the vagaries of state food supplies; or despite official pledges entrepreneurs may be afraid that the regime might one day change its policy and squeeze them out. For Party dogma, as opposed to practice, is still hostile to private enterprise and ideologues sometimes denounce it. In this general climate, some bakeries for example have been closing down; the older men find no successors as their sons prefer to work in factories where they have easier hours and less responsibility. On the other hand, there has been a marked increase in part-time private enterprise in the form of moonlighting by people with full-time official jobs: for here much less risk and commitment is involved. When his factory work is over, a man in the evenings or at weekends may turn his hand to car-repairing, house-building and suchlike: here he can get away with charging three or four times the official rate for these jobs, and will always find clients. This takes hard work, yes, but it is far more flexible and less worrying than running a proper business.

The failure to report or explain the consumer shortages is just one aspect of a general suppression of information and ultra-selectivity of news coverage in the State-controlled newspapers, radio and television. Any event at home or abroad that embarrasses the regime or goes against its policy is passed over in silence or relegated to one or two inside paragraphs. Thus in 1980 the major crisis over Solidarity in neighbouring Poland was barely mentioned, even though people knew about it from watching West German TV; and when in the 1960s a senior GDR minister committed suicide under political pressure and a storm broke out in the Party, it was not reported at all, and the news only spread later by word of mouth. As in other Soviet bloc countries, news priorities are entirely different from those in the West, and this is not just a matter of expected political bias but of a different philosophy of the role of the media. As Lenin laid down, the task of newspapers is not merely to report events but to 'join in building socialism' by stimulating morale and defining objectives: therefore they must systematically be optimistic about developments in the GDR and the Soviet Union, and must produce daily evidence of the decline of capitalism in the West. But, because the distortions are so obvious, this educative campaign tends to defeat its own ends when directed at an intelligent readership with its own television window on the West. 'Why does the regime not treat us as adults and tell us the truth?' was a complaint I heard widely even from Party sympathisers; 'it asks for our trust, but its lies and suppressions simply serve to destroy it.'

Much the most important daily paper is *Neues Deutschland*, the GDR's equivalent of *Pravda*, with a circulation of about one million. This is the organ of the SED and like the Party's numerous other publications is controlled by its Department of Agitation and Propaganda. It is often described as 'good for use as toilet paper, and for its small ads if you want to buy a second-hand car – but not for much else'. Its main headlines and news stories are often planned weeks in advance, for they tend to relate to anniversaries, Party congresses or economic progress reports, and they are repetitive, pompous and predictable, in the genre of 'Delegates Unanimously Praise Workers' Collectives' or 'Honecker Thanks Soviet Union for Latest Peace Initiatives'. Foreign events are given little coverage for their own sake: the *Greenpeace* scandal in France in 1985, for example, though you might have thought this counted as evidence of Western decay, got no more than an occasional inside paragraph. Probably this was because the GDR then had a policy of friendship with the Mitterand Government, and because the regime anyway treats espionage as a non-subject (on the dwellers-in-glass-houses-shouldn't-throw-stones principle).

The small 'token' parties have their own newspapers too, indirectly controlled by the SED. All papers give extensive space to sport and culture, but very little to crime or gossip; local weeklies are sometimes able to touch on real local problems, such as pollution, vandalism or breakdowns in supplies, but these publications are not seen outside their own areas. The Churches are allowed their own weeklies and magazines, which are distributed privately among their own members and must be careful not to touch on politics or other controversial matters. As for the State-run radio and TV networks, they quite often produce cultural and entertainment programmes of some quality (I saw an excellent one about D. H. Lawrence): but their documentaries and home-grown serials tend to be of the earnest socialism-building kind (the life of a GDR policeman, or how a young divorcee makes a new life thanks to the support of her factory comrades), while the news and current affairs programmes are run in much the same way as *Neues Deutschland*. So citizens turn for their information to the West German networks, with which the GDR ones will not even try to compete: news editors privately will tend to take the defeatist line, 'We know the West will cover this story better than we can, so let's not mention it.' The only retort that GDR TV does make to the Western competition is to run a programme called *Schwarze Kanal* (black channel) that seeks to show up the 'lies' and 'distortions' on West German TV the previous week. Its editors will claim that the Western networks deliberately beam propaganda to the GDR, just as the CIA-backed Radio Free Europe does from Munich: but this is not so. West German stations keep staff correspondents in East Berlin and they cover GDR events as fully as they can: but essentially this is because their own audiences are interested. No programmes are made specifically for GDR viewers.

I found that East Germans are more indignant about the shortcomings of the media than about any other aspect of life in the GDR except the consumer shortages and the travel restrictions – and the grumblers include many of the Party's own members and supporters. 'The failure to mention events like the Prague embassy sit-in,' (see below) said one elderly Communist, 'makes the media a laughing-stock and destroys its credibility, so that people ask: "If

they lie about this, what else might they be hiding?"' And one leading writer, basically in favour of the regime, said to me: 'Censorship
in literature has eased up – that's just fiction, so it's not taken so seriously. But in the media there's been no improvement. For example, a
new stretch of *Autobahn* was opened recently, then suddenly kept
closed for three months: but there was no word of explanation in the
Press, even though everyone was talking about it. When I asked a
Neues Deutschland editor, he merely said, "We're not obliged to report
everything." And why this policy? Well, I do not think it is purely a
rigorous line coming from the top of the Party. Editors could get away
with much more open and critical reporting if they tried. But they
have grown timid and lazy over the years, they can't be bothered to
cope with controversy, so they practise self-censorship more than
they need. It's appalling.'

It would be wrong however to conclude that in the GDR there is no
public opinion, nor any debate on public issues. Debate does take
place, but not in public. It goes on within the two-million-strong
ranks of the SED, where even village and factory cells can express
their views: these are then filtered up to the Party hierarchy, where at
least they are listened to, if not acted upon. This is about as far as
'public opinion' enjoys any organised forum. The party rulers will
also listen to the views of what has been described as 'the institu-
tionalised counter-elite', made up of scientists, academics, industrial
managers and senior officials in economic ministries who must
dutifully execute the Politburo's policies but can also express their
opinions, at least on specialist non-political matters. So the rulers do
consult the ruled. But of course they retain the last word, and there is
no democratic means of ousting them through elections.

As elsewhere in the Soviet bloc, the Party and the State apparatus
operate in parallel, down through a double hierarchy from the
summit to the local level. At the very top, controlling both of these
hierarchical channels, is the all-powerful Politburo, a non-elected
self-perpetuating body made up of some 25 senior SED officials,
ministers, and military men. It alone decides all policy. Below it, on
the Party side of the dual power structure, comes the policy-
executing Secretariat whose general secretary (today Honecker) is
also the Politburo's leader; and below this is the Central Committee,
whose members are elected every five years by the Party Congress.
Seldom does either of these bodies defy the wishes of the leadership.
Then further down the SED hierarchy are the regional bodies and
local cells.

On the State side of the structure, immediately below the Politburo
come the Council of Ministers (a Cabinet) and junior ministers. They
in practice take their orders from the Politburo: but constitutionally
they are also responsible to the *Volkskammer* (People's Chamber), a

parliament made up of the SED and eight other parties and mass organisations, all nine together forming a coalition known as the National Front. In this 500-member chamber, the SED itself has only 127 seats, while each of the other four parties has 52 and the trade union federation 68: three other bodies representing culture, women and youth (the FDJ) are also present. But this semblance of pluralism is little more than a façade. Though the other parties do in theory speak for distinct interest groups – one, for instance, is the Democratic Farmers' Party – it is the SED that effectively controls the National Front, and its dominant role is even written into the GDR's Constitution which declares the State to be 'led by the working-class and its Marxist-Leninist Party'. And the *Volkskammer* is little more than a rubber-stamp assembly. It meets for only four or five days each year, its votes are generally unanimous, and it is elected from a single list of official candidates selected by the National Front. Much the same applies to the regional and municipal councils, where the SED tactfully allows the CDU and other little parties to have their share of mayors.

Even foreign observers generally sympathetic to the GDR's other achievements have few illusions about the nature of its democracy. The distinguished British left-wing journalist Jonathan Steele, of the *Guardian*, published a book in 1977 that gave a good deal of credit to this 'disciplined and orderly society'. But of the SED's broadly-based mass-membership he had this to say: 'It certainly does not ensure genuine influence from the bottom upwards. On the contrary the Politburo still follows the tight-lipped conspiratorial traditions of its days in opposition and the underground. All decisions are taken at the top and there is minimal public or press discussion of them. Under the principle of democratic centralism decisions are passed down the line to the central committee and local party organisations for implementation. Top party politicians still live in suburban seclusion in a guarded residential area at Wandlitz outside Berlin. They probably have less contact with ordinary people than most West European politicians do . . . There is no chance of voters exerting any influence against SED policy.'[1]

How far the average citizen feels irked by the lack of freedom of expression is not so easy to assess. One West German diplomat in East Berlin suggested to me that it is not felt as the worst of deprivations: 'Remember that there has been no democracy here since before 1933, so even the older generation has no clear idea of what it is like. Sometimes people ask me, "Why on earth do you permit those Leftist demos at Frankfurt airport, or the neo-Fascist meetings? It's

[1] op. cit., p. 143.

shocking!" – and I try to explain that democracy must mean giving freedom of speech to those you disapprove of, or else you are on a slippery slope. They do not always get the point.' Others, more sophisticated or better attuned to Western ideas, certainly do feel cramped by the curbs on free speech and political choice. However, they have recently grown a little more relaxed about talking freely in public or to strangers, now that officialdom has become a shade more tolerant. But they still set limits on what they say. They know that nowadays you can get away with airing grievances about the inconveniences of daily living that affect everyone, or about bureaucratic slip-ups in some office or factory: but, if you voice basic dissent about Socialism, or Honecker, or the Soviet ally, or defence policy, you may well be in serious trouble if a security agent overhears you or if someone informs on you – as still happens. 'Twenty years ago they'd send you to prison,' said a student I met; 'today you merely lose your job, or get banished to some remote place or forced to emigrate. An improvement, I suppose.'

While criticism is still taboo in the mass media, it is sanctioned within limits in satiric cabaret, where it reaches smaller audiences and is thus less 'dangerous'. Cabaret of this kind has a potent tradition in Germany, especially in Berlin. Today it is on the wane in West Germany (see p. 273) where there are so many other forums for attacking the follies of government: but in the GDR it provides a rare if modest outlet for national self-mockery and the release of pent-up frustrations, and so it flourishes – and is accepted by the regime as licensed court jesters might be. East Berlin's best-known satiric cabaret, the State-run *Distel* (*Thistle*), opposite the Friedrichstrasse station, is a venerable institution: much frequented by tourists from the West, and even by local FDJ groups and GDR soldiers in uniform, it is very much an establishment affair, but it does have sparkle. In its ugly, cramped theatre, brilliant performers go through the nightly ritual of lampooning GDR life as best they dare, with scripts vetted in advance. The show I attended gave me some idea of how far their satire can go. A sales-girl looks at the dead flies in a State shop-window and says, 'I'd like to clear them away but it's not my job to do so and I daren't,' so she lets them lie there. A boss trying to sack an incompetent worker tells him, 'Don't worry, however much of a dud you are you'll get another job. In the West, no one would hire an idiot like you.' In a factory about to receive a visit from a top Party man, the workers tell their union leader, 'Let's explain to him our real problem.' 'No, that's impossible,' he says, 'you must talk to the comrade optimistically, like on television.' So they play the visitor a banal recorded TV discussion and silently mouth the words. In another factory sketch, called 'Erich is coming', the normally lazy but now panic-stricken workers are frenziedly preparing to work hard because

Honecker is about to pay a visit. Rich West German tourists in the GDR are satirised in a number about an arrogant couple in a white Mercedes, visiting relatives: 'What a bore, having to bring them all these presents. But we don't want re-unification, do we? The Turks are quite enough, we don't need Saxons too.' Lastly, and most pointedly, workers are shown erecting a huge poster in a GDR football stadium, to advertise an Italian fruit juice, Grannini, for a match that will be televised to the West: 'That'll net the GDR 10,000 DM,' says one of them; 'that's how we sell our principles to earn hard currency.'

Other sketches poked fun at the clumsiness of bureaucracy, the consumer shortages (inevitably) and the general apathy. So it is possible for cabarets to satirise people's behaviour under Socialism and their failure to live up to its demanding challenges, or even (more daringly) to chide the regime for compromising its own ideals. But these are not so much attacks on Socialism itself as on the shortfall in achieving it. No cabaret can safely question the system itself or the leadership, or make jokes about foreign policy or the Russians, or indulge in the kind of personal gossip about politicians that is the common coinage of satire in the West. Much the same applies in the provinces, save that some of the small intellectual cabarets there can afford to be a little more outspoken, since they are less in the limelight than *Die Distel*. In Leipzig, at the *Akademixer*, I sat in a lively, crowded studenty atmosphere and listened to a talented young cast making clever word-play about Party hypocrisies and the gulf between reality and the official version of things. The audience was tense and expectant, as at a sporting contest, which in a sense it was: in the GDR, people go to a satiric cabaret for the thrill of finding out just how far the actors will dare to go. Even in these little places, scripts must be authorised, and sometimes they get censored. But there is also some improvisation – and this, if the secret police should happen to be sitting in the hall, can be quite a game of Russian roulette for producer and cast.

The GDR's secret police has admittedly become less oppressive than it was in Ulbricht's day: but behind the smooth façade it still keeps a close and watchful grip, and people do their best to keep clear of it. In the town of Schwerin, in 1985, a drunken policeman had an argument with three men in the street and fired shots at them: none of the onlookers would lift a finger to help, for they felt the men must have done something terribly wrong and it was best not to get involved. They were left lying in the road and two of them later died. This is the kind of story one hears. The uniformed police are far more prevalent than in the West, and though generally polite they will quickly turn to rough-handling any citizen who answers back or fails to obey an order smartly. There may perhaps be another side to this:

'Our kindly police force,' one Communist told me, 'have a secondary *de facto* role as social workers. They keep a close watch on local families, and if, say, they notice that a father is drinking too much or hitting his children, they will report him.' This may well help to reduce the spread of cruelty or child neglect: but such prying certainly has another and less laudable function too. Any citizen however blameless has a police dossier, where reports from his school and workplace are included, and where any little unorthodox things that he may have said or done at any time will be entered too, and might be quoted against him years later. This may all sound rather sinister and *1984*-ish. But except in a very few cases the police system is no longer used arbitrarily. So long as he sticks to the rules and does nothing wrong 'politically' (not always so easy), a citizen can expect to be treated fairly by the law, in a police state that is highly legalistic in the true German manner and anxious to be seen to be behaving legally. Ordinary people are frequently too ignorant or submissive to make proper use of their legal rights: but, if they do so, they will generally get justice. I heard of a young man who had a motorbike accident that was largely his own fault. The police confiscated his licence, and there followed weeks of silence. A lawyer friend advised him to telephone the police's legal department. He did so, and quickly got a response and a fair trial.

The army, like the police, is much in evidence. The 380,000 Soviet troops stationed in East Germany keep a low profile, and though you see their convoys on the main roads, the soldiers seldom wander around the towns or mix with the local population. But the GDR's own army is displayed as much as possible, and is closely meshed in to the life of a nation that today is decidedly more militaristic than the Federal Republic. The National People's Army, with 115,000 men, plus 50,000 border guards and 52,000 in the navy and air force, is not especially large by Warsaw Pact standards, but it is highly modern and efficiently armed. Some 55 per cent of its strength is made up of conscripts who do 18 months' service. When they enlist they are first taken to Buchenwald concentration camp to swear their oath, and are then carefully indoctrinated in the 'anti-imperialist struggle', for one day they might have to fight against fellow-Germans. Controversially, their pre-military training will have started some years earlier, at a very young age. Children as young as 11 to 14 are encouraged to ttend 'defence education' classes in school where they are taught about the role of the army and the wartime heroism of Communists. Then para-military training, including marksmanship, is compulsory for boys of 15 and 16; and apprentices and schoolchildren of 17 and 18 are obliged to attend summer camps where they take part in field manoeuvres and shooting exercises. At a Defence Spartakiad in Halle in 1985, girls as well as boys were seen stripping machine-guns and hurling themselves into trenches. The aim of this early training is two-fold: first, to prepare conscripts for their national service, thus adding to their later usefulness as fighting men; and secondly to imbue them with national and military feeling at an age when they are still malleable As Roger Boyes of *The Times* (July 30, 1985) has commented sardonically, 'The ideologists have to get in quickly before *Dallas* poisons combat morale', now that West German TV is viewed so widely. But the martial indoctrination of the very young has annoyed a great many parents, and in recent years the Protestant Church has protested vehemently and repeatedly to the authorities against the growth of military education in schools – but so far to little effect.

As well as the regular armed forces, the GDR also keeps a large part-time militia of some 400,000 men. Each factory and office of any size has its own militia unit, comprised of some 20 per cent of its male workforce: these men are volunteers, led by SED activists, and at weekends you see them out in the countryside in their grey uniforms, doing field training. This militia was set up after the strikes of June 1953, with the aim of providing cadres to forestall any future workers' uprisings – and this internal security role, as a back-up to the police, is still its main purpose today. 'If only the Poles in 1980 had possessed a militia like ours,' one SED man told me unblinkingly, 'they might well have spared themselves all that trouble with the Solidarity counter-revolutionaries.' I gulped. Few other features of the GDR system struck me as more unpleasant.

Brecht to Biermann: dealing with the intellectual dissidents

Party watchdogs are also on the alert against rumbles of dissidence in the cultural field. Here in the past 30 or so years quite a number of writers, artists and other intellectuals have been harassed, censored, denied publication, expelled from the country, or in a few cases put in prison. But the regime's policy has been strangely erratic, even capricious: at some times quite a degree of open criticism or non-conformism has been allowed, at others the clamp-down has been heavy, for example in the later 1970s when several well-known writers were exiled including the poet and singer Wolf Biermann. The GDR's overall record is about average for Eastern Europe – more oppressive than Poland or Hungary, less so than the Soviet Union, Romania or post-1968 Czechoslovakia. While some writers have been expelled, others have left of their own accord: and they tend to accept exile much more readily than Hungarians, Poles or other Slavs, for the obvious reason that in West Germany they are still in their own culture and can find a responsive readership in their own language.

This puts the regime in a dilemma. Some writers it is glad to be rid of; but for prestige reasons it is sorry to lose too many, for it is proud of the country's literary record. Indeed, a remarkably high proportion of the best post-war German writing has originated in the GDR. As in the case, let us say, of South Africa or the Latin American dictatorships, the challenge of harsh regime will often bring out the best in a writer – but may also drive him out.

In the initial post-war years the movement was in the other direction. A number of committed left-wing writers, many of them Jewish, chose to settle in East rather than West Germany when they returned from their exile in the United States and elsewhere, for they were eager to join in creating the Socialist society of their ideals. They included the novelists Anna Seghers and Stefan Heym, the poet Stephan Hermlin, the philosopher Ernst Bloch, and most notably the playwright Bertolt Brecht. But many of them soon began to be disillusioned. By 1951 the new regime was actively imposing the cultural doctrine of Andrey Zhdanov, Stalin's son-in-law, which laid down that style, formalism and aesthetics were to be rejected since the role of art and literature was to express Socialist Realism and to educate the workers in the spirit of Socialism. Many writers, few of them among the best, agreed to toe this line, and so they dutifully churned out their tales of the gallant struggles for higher production norms in farm and factory – and were well rewarded. Others took refuge in novels about the horrors of the Nazi period, where it was much easier to write sincerely without displeasing the Party. But the more individualistic spirits began to chafe, or even to dare a few criticisms of this cherished new deal that they felt to be turning sour – and before long they were paying the penalty. Brecht, the GDR's leading cultural star, soon fell into some disfavour (see below). The Marxist philosopher Wolfgang Harich was in 1957 sentenced to ten years' hard labour for advocating intellectual liberty and a more flexible Yugoslav-type democracy. His fellow Marxist thinker, the great Ernst Bloch, began to attack the SED's 'petrified dogmatism' in his lectures at Leipzig University: then with the Soviet intervention in Hungary in 1956 his faith in the regime finally snapped, and soon after this he left to settle in West Germany. Around the same time the novelist Uwe Johnson also emigrated.

The Party was by now becoming worried by this disaffection of so many of the best writers, and so at a conference at Bitterfeld in 1959 it launched a new initiative to try to regain their loyalty. Under the slogan, '*Greif zur Feder, Kumpel!*' (Seize your pen, mate), it urged writers to move closer to the workers, decreeing that each of them should spend some time working in factories or on farms, not as manual labourers but for example running the works' library or editing its news journal. This was in many ways an excellent idea, and along with the inevitable stream of hack novels it did produce a few good ones: Christa Wolf's *Der geteilte Himmel* (*The Divided Heaven*, 1963) was partly inspired by her time spent at the railway works at Halle. Wolf was the most talented of a number of new authors emerging in the GDR in the 1960s, who managed to write with some honesty and realism without falling too deeply in disgrace. This was a period of reduced Party pressures, and it continued for a while after Honecker took over in 1971. At first, in line with his more liberal stance in other matters too, he declared that so long as the works were rooted in socialism there could be 'no taboos' in art and literature – and at this many writers took heart. In some respects he fulfilled his promise. Most notably, in 1972 the provocative play *Die Neuen Leiden des Jungen W.* (*The New Sorrows of Young W.*), by Ulrich Plenzdorf, was allowed to be publicly staged and then published as a novel. It is the story of an outspoken young drop-out, long-haired, bejeaned, crazy about rock music, who escapes from the harsh atmosphere of his factory to go and live in a shack outside Berlin. Plenzdorf seemed to be making a plea for a more tolerant official attitude towards youth, and his play was a huge success and caused a great stir. Probably the authorities accepted it because it showed the hero's gesture as finally pointless and self-destructive and implied that the energies of youth could be harnessed to Socialism if only more understanding were shown them.

Soon after this however the climate worsened again. Hardliners in the Party stepped up their policy of infiltrating the Writers' Union, and were thus able to use it as a base for vendettas against non-conformists. Their most celebrated victim was Wolf Biermann, the satrical poet, songwriter and singer. He had been brought up in Hamburg but was drawn by his Communist sympathies to emigrate to the GDR in 1953, where he worked for a while with Brecht's Berliner Ensemble. His immensely popular poems and songs were always pro-Socialist, but they included gibes against bureaucracy, the Wall, the secret police and so on, and as early as 1962 he had begun to be in trouble with the regime, which banned his works from being printed and for a while would not let him perform in public. But he was published in the West, where his witty, passionate lyricism as well as his bold anger won him an immense reputation; and the regime, in a way perversely proud of its rebellious genius, even allowed him to make concert tours abroad. It was after a concert in Hamburg in 1976 that the Politburo finally broke with him, depriving him of his citizenship for 'publicly slandering our socialist State'. So Biermann regretfully settled back in his native city where he still lives today, but he has never since been very creative.

His expulsion caused a furore both at home and abroad. It was denounced by such left-wing luminaries as Jean-Paul Sartre, Joan

Baez and Rudi Dutschke, while within the GDR twelve top writers signed an open letter to the Party begging it to reconsider the move. They included Stefan Heym, Christa Wolf and the normally loyalist poet Stephan Hermlin. But, despite the appalling publicity it was getting, the regime refused to budge and even exacted reprisals. Wolf was expelled from the SED and the Berlin committee of the Writers' Union; Heym was charged with breaches of currency rules. And there followed a much wider tightening-up. The scientist and philosopher Robert Havemann was placed under house arrest for criticising leadership; the eminent economist Rudolf Bahro, who had produced a reasoned Marxist critique of the regime's shortcomings, was arrested on fake charges of espionage and later imprisoned; and several well-known writers were either expelled or else harassed so much that they opted for exile. They included the poets Günter Kunert and Reiner Kunze. After the mild cultural thaw of the first Honecker years, this period of repression in the later 1970s appeared somewhat paradoxical, for Honecker was simulateously liberalising in some other fields – in his relations with the Church, in encouraging private property, and so on. But clearly the Politburo held the view that disaffected intellectuals were especially dangerous: given an inch, they might take a mile, and their influence could easily spread. As Jonathan Steele wrote in 1977, 'The party leadership made it clear that it liked criticism least when it comes from disappointed loyalists, from the Left rather than the Right, from those whose solidarity has become too critical. Other forms of "privatisation" are now acceptable. The "privatisation" of independent criticism is the most antisocial activity of all.'

Günter Kunert left of his own choice in 1979, and he and his wife now live in the Holstein countryside, where I went to see them. He is a frail-looking, sensitive man in his mid-fifties, and besides writing poetry and criticism he produces vividly-coloured expressionist paintings: 'I am Jewish from my mother's side and have always been on the Left, so at first I welcomed the East German regime and was delighted to live there. But gradually things began to get difficult. My poems are on very private themes, and I just could not turn out the kind of ideological "public" poetry they wanted; also, one *Leitmotiv* of mine is the dehumanising effect of modern technology, and Marxism does not tolerate this kind of pessimism. The Party harassed me and finally refused to publish me. But I had contacts in West Germany, where my books were being well received, partly *because* people knew that I was in trouble in the GDR. And after the Wall was built the authorities continued to let me go out, for lecture tours and so on – I suppose they did not want to appear too illiberal. So I benefited from the same kind of paradox as Biermann – oppression at home led to notoriety in the West, which then provided an escape from the oppression! My break with GDR-style socialism was a slow and painful process, since I'd believed in it so much – and I still think the regime has many virtues, but not for an artist. Finally we decided to move here, and it was no culture shock at all. I'm still a GDR citizen, I have an exit visa and can pay return visits when I wish.' Another emigré poet, Reiner Kunze, said that a young engineer he knew was sentenced to six years in prison for supplying him with information which he used in his book about the plight of youth in the GDR, *Die Wunderbaren Jahre* (*The Lovely Years*), published in the West. This in fact is one of the worst sins in the eyes of the regime: to use West German media outlets for 'insulting' the GDR.

Today the situation has quietened down, for the most hostile writers have now left and those remaining are more discreet – but not all of them. The most striking exception is the veteran Stefan Heym, now in his mid-seventies, who is tolerated as a kind of licensed dissident, too old and venerable to be openly victimised or thrown out. Heym, who is Jewish, was born in Chemnitz, and when Hitler came to power he moved to the United States where he became an American citizen and served in the US Army. As a Communist he was persecuted in the McCarthy era, and in 1952 he returned to his native East Germany, but was soon following the all-too-familiar path of disillusion. He wrote a number of critical novels, notably *The King David Report* (1972), an anti-Stalinist allegory, and *Five Days in June* (1975), a dramatised account of the June 1953 uprising that stood somewhere between the Western and official GDR versions of events. Soon he was being refused publication in his own country, and in 1976 was fined 9,000 Marks for publishing his novel *Collin* in the West without asking permission. After this a law was passed that laid down a five-year prison penalty for such 'currency offences'. But Heym, unperturbed, again went ahead. In 1985 I visited him in East Berlin, in his villa on the pleasantly-named Rabindranath-Tagore-Strasse, in the verdant suburb of Grünau – a large, humorous man with a mischievous puckish grin and a mock-arrogance that made a charming contrast to the usual GDR solemnity. 'I am the greatest and the only Social Realist, for I alone describe the truth and know that true socialism will one day come to pass on this earth. Yes, I continue to publish in Frankfurt and Munich, and they don't touch me under their stupid law – they daren't, they know the stink it would cause in the West. People smuggle in copies, so I am read here quite widely. And other writers have benefited from my courage, for they too defy the law and get away with it. So, you see, this is a very mild, scared little dictatorship. Their image took such a punishing internationally over the Biermann affair that never again will they expel or imprison a writer, I'm sure. But they keep close tabs on me. They'll know that you've come to see me here.'

Christa Wolf on the other hand is one of a small number of writers officially permitted to publish in West Germany. She is a very modest, withdrawn person, more concerned with personal than public themes, and she tends to couch her criticisms somewhat obliquely, as in her most famous novel *The Quest for Christa T*, (1968); even so, this book was denounced at the time for its failure to laud collectivism. Today, other such non-conformist books still appear from time to time, one recent example being Volker Braun's *Hinz und Kunz* (*Every Tim, Dick and Harry*, 1985), a satire on East German hierarchies. But critical books of this kind are generally given very limited print runs, so they sell out rapidly in the shops and then circulate from hand to hand like rare editions: it is the opposite of the Western best-seller system. There is an acute paper shortage in the GDR, and the Ministry officials who decide these things see no reason to squander the precious supplies on such renegade novelists. On the other hand, those who write the kind of books officially in favour are assured of large sales and in some cases are given State salaries and other special privileges. But in some other respects there has been an easing up recently, at least as regards the publication of certain classic authors previously taboo under Marxism-Leninism. Freud, once the great enemy, is now permitted; so are Kafka, Joyce and Proust. And in 1985 I found the regime girding itself up to publish Nietzsche, of all people, formerly considered a forerunner of Nazism, as well as *The Tin Drum* by Günter Grass, an author whose outspoken anti-Communism had till now led him to be banned (unlike the works of Böll which have long been much more acceptable). But under comradely pressure from Moscow the Party still draws the line at Solzhenitsyn – 'And quite right too,' one SED lady told me. 'Why should we waste our paper on that CIA-inspired rubbish? No one here would want to read him, anyway.'

In the other arts, life for painters and musicians is generally easier than for writers, since they deal less directly in ideas and facts. A few good artists, such as Roger Loewig, have been harassed and driven into exile: but it is certainly more possible than 20 years ago to produce and exhibit the kinds of modern art that lie outside the canons of Socialist realism. In music, the GDR is proud of its record and has opera, ballet and concerts of a good standard, in the German tradition; its leading singers and musicians are allowed abroad to and fro on the usual international circuits. The East German cinema has produced a number of worthy films on social themes, but unlike the Polish and Hungarian cinemas, or that of Czechoslovakia in the 1960s, its work has seldom been of the quality or originality to make an impact abroad. It is under the same kind of State control as television: unorthodox scripts are rarely accepted and a director dependent on a State budget has even less freedom in the GDR than a writer. As

[*363*]

far as hard currency permits, some films from the West are shown in East German cinemas, mostly of the kind that spotlight the injustices or decadence of capitalist society – e.g. Fassbinder, or *Lady Chatterley's Lover*.

Theatres, like opera houses and concert halls, are nearly always full, for thanks to lavish subsidies the tickets are extremely cheap; also, people have fewer other outlets for their leisure than in the West. But interesting new East German plays on contemporary themes are few: theatre fare consists mainly of the classics, from Shakespeare and Schiller to Brecht, plus routine 'Socialist realist' offerings and a number of approved foreign imports, many of them from Russia. Plenzdorf's remarkable play was quite an exception, for unorthodox writers usually find it as hard as in publishing to secure an outlet for their work. The GDR's best-known playwright since Brecht, Heiner Müller, who is a loyal if critical Communist, sticks mainly to safe historical themes such as Frederick the Great: one of his few forays into the contemporary scene, *Der Bau* (*The Construction*), a frank study of cynical wheeler-dealing by Party bureaucrats in the building industry, won him some odium in the 1960s and was never staged. In this climate, it is hardly surprising that many of the best actors and directors have emigrated to the West, where they can gain more money as well as more freedom. Recently, the authorities have become more flexible by allowing these stars, just like the conductors and opera singers to move to and fro between the two Germanies without losing their GDR citizenship or domicile.

The most widely performed of the classics is Bertolt Brecht, whose Berliner Ensemble theatre still operates as a kind of memorial to him, even though his relationship with the GDR regime was highly equivocal in the years before his death in 1956. Born in Augsburg in 1898, he was much the best-known of the left-wing writers who took refuge in America during the Nazi period and then opted for the GDR. There he founded his famous theatre in 1949, with the aim that it should become the principal focus for acting and play-writing talent throughout the German-speaking world: but the continuing division of Germany made this impossible. Brecht tried to remain loyal to the GDR: but his epic style and his concept of alienation soon brought him into trouble with the prevailing Zhdanovite orthodoxy and his work was variously attacked as defeatist and lacking in realism or respect for German culture. The initial version of his *The Trial of Lucillus* was withdrawn after its first night in 1951, while his play about the 1871 Paris uprising, *Days of the Commune*, suffered similarly. As his biographer Martin Esslin has written, 'Brecht's whole theory is based on his conception that the theatre of Stanislavsky [at the Moscow Art Theatre], by making the audience identify themselves with the characters, prevents them from seeing the world in a detached, critical spirit and is therefore un-Marxist and reactionary. But the party did not want the audience to be put into a critical frame of mind. It *wanted* them to be hypnotized and made uncritical by having their emotions fully engaged in favour of the positive characters and against the negative ones. Brecht wanted them to draw their own conclusions from a critical reflexion of the play'.[1] To his credit, in his own work he never seriously betrayed his artistic principles in the face of official pressures, even though publicly he made obeisance to the regime. In response to the June 1953 uprising, he privately wrote the satiric poem than I quoted earlier; but outwardly, maybe to save his theatre from suppression, he issued a declaration of loyalty. And, since his death too, his position has remained ambiguous. Officially he is still venerated by the GDR as its major postwar writer and greatest cultural status-symbol: yet his work also remains an inspiration to free-thinking writers who are critical of the regime.

After his death, control of his theatre company was taken over by his widow, Helene Weigel, and when she died in 1971 it passed to their daughter Barbara and her husband, Ekkehard Schall, who is the GDR's leading actor. The Schalls are still closely associated with it today. And so highly does the party rate its Brechtian heritage that the family is granted a distinctly privileged status. They are permitted to live in grand upper-bourgeois style in their big flat on the Friedrichstrasse where they have servants to wait on them, and they can travel freely to the West (Frau Schall has many connections in New York where her brother lives and works). As for the Berliner Ensemble itself, just round the corner, it continues fathfully to present a repertoire of the master's works to local audiences and bevies of Western tourists: but the productions, as most Western critics would agree, have tended to become jaded and mechanical, and little attempt is made to polish them up. For example, the *Dreigroschenoper* that I saw in 1985 was quite awful, with sets, cotumes and routines that seemed to have come out of 1950s mothballs. Is this decline due to lack of funds, or of talent, or a fear of controversy, or excess of fidelity to the dead playwright? It is hard to say. In West Germany, as we have seen, directors like Zadek and Palitsch present Brecht with far more sizzle and style. And so, like the GDR's culture as a whole, the rebel genius from Augsburg has become a victim of the division of two Germanies – a theme to be explored next.

---

[1] Martin Esslin: *Brecht: a Choice of Evils* (London, 1959).

Travel to the West: harshest of the curbs on freedom

The notorious division of the German nation is marked physically on the GDR side by a fortification of great depth and complexity that winds for 870 miles from the Baltic to Czechoslovakia. In the first years after the war this remained an open border between the Soviet and Western occupation zones, easily crossed and lightly patrolled, for initially it was never intended to split Germany permanently. But by 1952 the GDR Government had grown so alarmed by the refugee exodus that it installed what it called a 'protective strip', with armed guards and barbed wire, backed by a 5-kilometre-deep 'forbidden zone' where only those with a spcial pass could go. The building of the 'Iron Curtain' – a term made famous by Churchill – had begun. Then, after the Berlin Wall was put up in 1961, the GDR massively strengthened its defences along the whole of its western border too – certainly the first time in world history that so gigantic a fortification had been erected not so much to hold up invaders as to prevent escape, as from a prison. And there it is today with its minefields and barbed wire, shrapnel-scattering trap guns, parallel steel fences, lethal guard dogs and hideous watchtowers on stilts.

Today there are nine regular access routes by road across the border and four by rail. The division of Germany has severed about 160 other roads and 25 railway lines, and it has separated communities that had lived together for centuries; in at least four cases, the barrier goes through the heart of a village or between adjacent villages so that former neighbours can see each other only by making a long detour and meeting somewhere inside East Germany. By a special GDR dispensation, West Germans living within about 50 kilometres of the border are allowed to make up to 36 day-trips a year to visit friends or relatives on the other side. But, as the crossings are few, this can be a laborious process; and often their loved ones are simply not there any more, since the GDR Government for security reasons has evicted nearly all the inhabitants from a zone within five kilometres of the border. Whole villages have been erased and farming goes on under tight military supervision.

On the Western side, the sealing of the frontier was greeted at first with sheer disbelief, followed by fury and fear. But gradually people have grown used to it and in today's climate of détente there are few feelings of tension any more: 'The border's there, it's like living beside a cliff or deep river, we hardly notice it and we've stopped wondering about life on the other side,' said one peasant woman. At Lübeck, the only big West German town very close to the border, in the past ten years or so some middle-class suburban villas have been built within 200 metres of it and – amazingly – the land and house prices here are little lower than anywhere else. At Lübeck and in some other spots – in the Harz mountains, or in Bavaria – the border has even become a tourist attraction for busloads of sightseers and for parties of schoolchildren who are dutifully taken to inspect what has happened to the *Vaterland*. They gaze across at the ever-silent GDR sentinels, and they look at the signs put up on the Western side: 'AUCH DRÜBEN IST DEUTSCHLAND' (over there it's also Germany), or 'DEUTSCHLAND IST UNTEILBAR' (Germany is indivisible). The Federal border police have also erected placards that give full illustrated details – as in any well-run tourist venue – of the deadly arsenal of the GDR defences and how they exterminate escapers. But, if most of the border zone today is serene and prosperous, there are some poorer upland areas or salients half-enclosed by GDR territory that still suffer badly from the loss of their natural hinterland; and, though farms and other businesses in rural districts within a belt some 40 kilometres deep from the border are granted Federal subsidies to compensate for their difficulties, these are not always adequate. In one particularly isolated pocket of northern Bavaria (see pp. 132–4), I found Ludwigstadt the most sad and derelict-looking little town that I have ever come across in West Germany; it has lost all its links with adjacent Thuringia, its industries are moribund, its unemployment high.

The entire border is patrolled by the green-uniformed *Bundesgrenzschutz*, the Federal frontier police. They have a varied security role in West Germany, but their major task is to deal with the GDR, where they keep an eye on its border activity and cope with any incidents. One senior BGS officer took me for a tour near Lübeck, showing me the border itself marked by white posts and beyond it the 50-metre strip of empty ground inside East Germany that runs beside the first steel fence. 'Some local kids like to play cat-and-mouse with the GDR guards by hopping into the strip, but they know what they're doing and there aren't any mishaps. Tourists however tend to be more unwary, especially in wooded areas where they don't notice the white posts – and then there are warning shots and they may get arrested. At a senior level, there is a joint border commission for serious incidents, which works quite well. And locally, if someone gets lost or some other emergency occurs, I have a hot line to the control post on the other side: they register my request, and act on it, but are not allowed to say one word.' Some 3,000 East German guards have defected across the boarder since the war, so now they patrol in pairs or groups and are carefully screened for their political reliability. 'It's a rum business,' my guide went on; 'they peer at us through their field-glasses and hide in the bushes, but they're forbidden to smile or even respond to a wave, let alone utter a word. If they do, they are heavily punished. Here we all are, fellow-Germans in uniform, playing deaf-mute with each other across the years – crazy! Their security is rigorous. Last year, when they were levelling some ground between the two fences, there were two workers watched over by eight soldiers with guns.'

Along the 103-mile Wall around Berlin, the system of controls and barricades is much the same. But how do the GDR leaders explain away this monstrosity? It is not easy. Everyone knows why the Wall was built, and as most Party men tend to be embarrassed about it (just as Ulbricht himself was), they talk about it as little as possible. But sometimes they feel obliged to try to justify what is still known officially as 'the Anti-Fascist Protection Wall'. One recent GDR publication states that it was put up 'to preserve peace in Europe', while as recently as 1985 one East Berlin newspaper wrote that the building of it has been 'vital to head off Western invasion plans and attempts to drain the economy. The soldiers on guard watch that no one from the West comes here to hinder the building of our Socialist state.' But, as thousands of Westerners daily enter the GDR quite freely, this argument is patently nonsense. A more sophisticated justification that I heard was, 'Socialism takes time to be perfected, and in the meantime we must protect ourselves against disruptive influences,' or, much nearer the truth, 'We have expensively trained many key people who are wooed by the West with higher salaries, and until we are stronger, we just cannot afford to let them leave.'

Throughout the difficult 1960s after the building of the Wall, it was not only impossible to get out of the GDR but also hard to get into it, for only those West German with close relatives there could obtain visas. West Berliners too faced tight restrictions (see p. 51). But after *Ostpolitik* had led to the East/West agreements of 1971–2, matters were greatly eased and since then almost any West German has been free to enter the GDR for up to 30 days a year. The number of annual visits rose sharply after 1972, and they now average about 3.7 million a year from the Federal Republic and another 3 million from West Berlin. It is estimated that as many as 90 per cent of these travellers have relatives or close friends in the GDR, and in very many cases they stay with them in their homes: after 40 years of division, roughly one West German in three still possesses a contact of this kind in the East, though inevitably the kinship ties are weakening as close relatives die and the links become more frequently between cousins than brothers or sisters.

Some other people travel to the GDR on business or purely for tourism, while just a few go with the feeling that they have a moral duty to keep in touch with fellow-Germans deprived of their freedom and needing their support. One middle-aged civil servant in Hamburg told me that he goes at least once a year in this spirit and now most of his best friends live in the GDR. He is doing something of value, for GDR citizens will frequently stress to their Western friends, 'Please do not leave us isolated, come and see us as often as you can, we're so grateful for it.' Usually they will talk quite freely to those they trust. Before my own visits, friends of mine in West Germany gave me introductions to families they knew, mostly non-Communist, and they received us warmly into their homes and talked frankly, but urged us not to make contact via their office. People known to have too many Western contacts may still face difficulties with their children's higher education, or be denied the chance to travel abroad themselves on official delegations.

The major restriction on this kind of contact is that anyone in any kind of official position is formally classified as a *'Geheimnisträger'* (bearer of secrets) and is forbidden to have dealings with the West, or he may lose his job. This applies even to teachers, municipal employees, and the junior staff of scientific institutes. One senior West German journalist in Hamburg, originally from East Berlin, told me that his aged mother is still living there and so is his brother, an executive in a State firm: 'He of course is a *Geheimnisträger* and mustn't see me: in fact, his promotion has been blocked because of my very existence. When I go to stay with my mother, he parks his car two blocks away and meets me there. He is sure that the secret police are tailing him, but they do not seem to mind so long as he's discreet. That's the GDR for you.'

Restrictions on talking to foreigners have even been tightened up in recent years, under a 1979 law that makes it illegal for anyone to pass information 'judged to be damaging to the Socialist state'. This hardly affects conversations in private, so long as they are not overheard: but it does greatly limit the scope of Western journalists and television teams. And the reason for the new law is simple. Until 1979, West German TV and radio reporters would regularly do *vox pop* interviews in the streets, and they found that a great many people were prepared to take the risk of talking freely and critically. So GDR screens tuned to the West were nightly full of citizens airing their grievances and thus making nonsense of the official line; moreover, people could see that their own complaints were widely shared across the country. It is hardly surprising that the regime eventually felt obliged to crack down on this. So life is now harder not only for visiting journalists but for the permanent correspondents – and many leading West German papers and networks, with the exception of the right-wing Springer group, keep a staff reporter in East Berlin. Officially they must apply in advance to the Foreign Ministry to do any interview on any subject, however non-political or off-the-record – and this red-tape infuriates them. But the more canny or experienced ones dodge the rules by holding off-the-record talks discreetly in private with their own trusted contacts, and this is generally fruitful.

Another well-known hazard of travel in the GDR – the border controls at the entry and departure – has become much less burdensome than it used to be. The first time you enter the country at one of the *Autobahn* checkpoints, it all looks pretty sinister – the guards with their sub-machine-guns, the successive barriers to be negotiated, the notices not to exceed 20 kph, the long queues of cars, the steely-faced *Beamte* scrutinising every passport. But after a second or third visit it begins to seem quite normal. The officials today have orders to be courteous and will sometimes even smile; just occasionally they will inexplicably search through your wallet, or scour the car from boot to bonnet, or ask probing questions about your trip and whom you plan to see – but this has become rare. Except at peak holiday times, the border crossing seldom takes more than 30 minutes (in the 1970s, it was often several hours) and the list of forbidden imports, headed by West German books and magazines, has become more predictable. There can still however be bureaucratic traps for visas, as Katinka and I discovered on more than one occasion: since my passport was British and hers West German, we faced different sets of rules. When we wanted to extend our visas by one night, our East Berlin hotel fixed this for me on the spot, but Katinka was told at 10.30 p.m. that she would have to leave for West Berlin by midnight and then re-enter. So I drove her to the Friedrichstrasse Bahnhof and then waited for what seemed like an eternity, suddenly loathing this police state with all my guts, while she went through the ludicrous process of checking out through one set of controls, walking across to the incoming platform, and then checking in through the other set where she managed to explain the situation, show her hotel booking, and get a new visa. This she achieved just in time, before midnight struck, when the frontier closed for the night. The operation would have been far more hazardous, indeed impossible, a few years back: today GDR officialdom has at least become more reasonable in helping visitors to find a way through the maze of its bizarre rules. Nonetheless, the little incident did give both of us, however irrationally, a Kafkaesque frisson of hatred and terror – the authentic Berlin experience.

One last frustration concerns hotels. Except for the militarised zones, the visitor nowadays can travel where he likes in the GDR: but he will not get a visa unless he has booked all hotel accommodation in advance or given other written proof of where he intends to stay. Touring impromptu is impossible. And almost all the old country inns, or other small hotels of character, that are so easy to find and delightful to use in West Germany, have long since disappeared from the GDR: this is because after the war the State turned them into private dwellings, to ease the housing shortage. In order to cope with the new tourist trade, it has now built a number of large modern luxury palaces; and it is in these, or in middle-rank business hotels, that the visitors must stay. They are relatively cheap by Western standards and quite well run, but not exactly full of charm. And, as most of the grander ones take only hard currency, they become ghettos for Western tourists which GDR citizens cannot use. The prime reason for this Apartheid may be economic: but it does also serve to cut down on unwanted social contacts. So the sight of these bustling hotel foyers, full of Western visitors and their East German guides, vividly underlines the reality of there being not only two Germanies but two species of German. I found these spacious and comfortable compounds rather depressing. It was a little like staying at a Hilton in some miserable African country – yet here one was among fellow Europeans.

Travel possibilities in the other direction, from east to west, were not improved at all for the average citizen under the 1971–2 agreements: and today people yearn more keenly for this freedom of movement than for any other of the rights denied them. The original 1949 Constitution guaranteed the right to leave the GDR: but this was removed from the 1968 Constitution, still in force today, and it is now graciously allowed only to certain categories. Of these the most important is retired people (women over 60, men over 65), who are allowed to leave for up to 60 days a year – and over 1.5 million such visits are made annually. So the GDR, as the joke goes, is the only country in the world where you look forward to growing old. Few of these travellers elect to remain in the West: but, if they do, the regime hardly cares, for it is thus spared paying their pension and anyway they have ceased to be productively useful. Every night at the Friedrichstrasse you can see them returning by the late trains from their day trips, clutching their bags full of prized goodies given by friends and relatives in West Berlin.

Those under 60 or 65 can get permission to visit close relatives in the West for weddings, funerals, special anniversaries and some other 'urgent family reasons' including death-bed sickness. Some 70,000 such trips are made a year. But a married couple cannot both go at the same time, and single men under 26 are generally barred, while other applications too are often arbitrarily refused. The other category allowed out is the trusted ones who go on official delegations – senior Party members, privileged businessmen and unionists, some youth groups, as well as sports teams and artists, singers and other star performers who earn the GDR prestige and hard currency. They are generally screened for their reliability. Party leaders' wives can go too – for shopping. In West Berlin, you sometimes see chauffeur-driven Volga limousines with GDR number-plates parked near the famous Kaufhaus des Westens (KaDeWe for short), the largest department store on the Continent. Here the lucky ladies make a bee-line for the gigantic and super-opulent food section which rivals Harrods'. Ordinary GDR pensioners visit it too – and the sight of its long counters piled high with scores of varieties of cheeses, *Wurst*, succulent cuts of meat, foie gras, *Torte*, tropical fruits and rare vegetables, must cause acute culture-shock to any East German making a first trip to the West.

Those debarred from such delights can at least go on holiday to other Soviet bloc countries – to the Black Sea, or to Hungary or Czechoslovakia (Poland has been virtually out of bounds since the rise of Solidarity). In these countries they can meet West Germans on holiday, and will sometimes make friends that way; but more often they feel humiliated at being patronised by the rich Westerners or badly served by waiters who prefer clients who tip in Deutschmarks. And they find that even in the East there is no free movement: only Czechoslovakia can be visited without a visa, while between all these brotherly socialist paradises there are strict border formalities. Most people take their annual holiday within the confines of their own little country and, while some may share a rural *dacha* with friends or relatives, the majority go to a hotel, camp or hostel organised by their factory, on the Baltic or in the Harz or Saxon hills. As the facilities are limited often they have no choice but must go where they are sent.

Poles, Hungarians and even Czechs are all much freer than East Germans to visit the West. If the GDR is here so repressive, the reasons are obvious: this is the only Soviet bloc country with a sister nation along its western border, sharing the same language, culture and history, and where some 30 per cent of GDR citizens still have relatives. And, in the eyes of the GDR rulers, West Germany exploits this kinship to exert 'intolerable pressures'. For domestic political reasons (see below) as well as for sincerely-felt moral ones, successive governments in Bonn have not only refused to recognise the legitimacy of the East's regime but have claimed themselves to be the only rightful rulers of all Germany – to the extent that any GDR citizen will automatically be treated as a West German citizen if he or she wishes. Any GDR emigré arriving in the Federal Republic can obtain a passport within minutes of entering a police station, and will straightaway be granted the full rights *and* duties of citizenship, including social security benefits and the obligation of military service for young men. What is more, there are absolutely no border controls on the Western side: you just drive straight through.

The GDR leaders remain furious at this 'suborning' by a richer power. And they seem to believe seriously that if the travel ban were lifted it would lead to a new mass exodus. But would this be so, today? It cannot be proved either way: but it is worth noting that only 2 per cent of pensioners visiting the West decide to stay there. And Western journalists and others who talk to large numbers of GDR citizens get the impression that only about one in ten would leave permanently for the West if they could: many have been influenced by the Western TV programmes about high unemployment. In this smallish country with few touristic splendours of its own, most people simply want to go to take a look, say, at Paris or the Alps and then come back, in the normal way. But the regime doubts this. It appears to believe that this yearning for travel will wane as the family ties with the West loosen, so that all it needs do is wait. But this is certainly mistaken. It is not because he has an aunt in Mannheim that a young East German wants to visit the West, but because he wants to see for himself the fabulous places that appear on his TV screen.

Meanwhile, everyone moans and complains, including a great many SED loyalists. 'The leaders should trust the people more,' I was told by one senior novelist, a Party member; 'the claustrophobia leads to a general national psychosis, affecting even workers and others who would never seek to travel abroad. But, because they can't, they resent it.' And with a new generation now grown up that never knew the pre-Wall days, so the GDR's population has been growing steadily more isolated and provincial, more cut off from direct experience of the world outside. Even educated people will often seem oddly naïve, unable to make comparisons; and, whenever I met someone who was fortunate enough to have travelled to the West, his sophistication and liveliness of mind came usually as a striking contrast. The others are merely wistful. I dined with one academic who said that his requests to attend conferences in the West had always been turned down because he had a sister in Frankfurt. He and his wife gazed down with me at the East Berlin lights below our rooftop restaurant, and he asked sadly, 'Does Frankfurt look like that, or brighter?' 'Not much brighter,' I said tactfully. But, when later I happened to mention that I had been in Kreuzberg the day before, I felt that I had made a gaffe. It was two kilometres from where we were sitting, but might have been on another planet.

Some people take the desperate step of trying to escape physically across the border, but they are few nowadays, for the risk of failure and death is high. In 1970 about 1,000 succeeded, but by 1985 the number was down to 160, only six of whom got away over the Berlin Wall. Estimates of the failures vary, but it is believed that since 1961 some 70 people have been shot dead while trying to climb over the Wall, and some other 3,000 others have been arrested in Berlin while preparing to escape; people found moving towards the 'forbidden zone' along the West German border are generally seized by the police and imprisoned. Escapes across this border have been made by swimming the Elbe, by hiding in barges, by boat on the Baltic, and in many others ways; most spectacularly, in 1979 two families each with two children made their getaway by travelling 25 miles in a home-made hot-air balloon. In Berlin, among the various escape routes through the Wall (see p. 368) one favoured method has been to seek the help of friendly diplomats and hide in their cars, which are not supposed to be searched. In 1979, the East German chauffeur of the American ambassador to the GDR took his family out one at a time in this way.

Much less hazardous than a bolt across the border is the practice of escaping via a third country, when one is either on holiday or on some visiting delegation. Some 3,000 a year successfully try this method. In Cologne I met a couple in their early forties, both doctors, who had gone on holiday to Hungary with their young son. There they found a West German lorry-driver prepared to stow them away with his goods, and he took them into Yugoslavia, where the lorry was searched and they were arrested. Such incidents occur very often and the Yugoslav authorities are basically helpful; that is, they will send the refugees on to West Germany rather than back home to face imprisonment. But it can take time. The family I met spent three weeks in separate cells while their case was being sorted out, and then they were allowed to travel to Cologne where they had friends and eventually found suitable jobs. They had left the GDR, they said, 'because as non-SED members and known churchgoers our careers in our hospitals were blocked and so was our son's education. The older post-war generation of doctors were people with ideals and integrity, and we respected them. But the younger ones now coming to the top, of our own age, are more opportunistic and politicised, and there is now a sharper polarisation between those who back the regime and those who do not. As junior doctors we could escape this: but, if we wanted more senior hospital jobs, we had to join the Party and make the right noises – and this we just could not stomach. So we decided to leave.'

On another occasion, in Karlsruhe, I heard an extraordinary saga from a young teacher: 'As a schoolboy in Leipzig I was already very critical of the system. I asked awkward questions in class, I even proclaimed my sympathy for Dubček, and so I fell into disgrace. I wasn't allowed to be an engineer as I'd wanted, and instead they sent me to a teacher training college where they hoped they could stamp the nonsense out of me. By now I was toying with the idea of escaping to the West. So I kept quiet politically for a couple of years – and they thought they *had* converted me! I was musical, so I joined a folk-song group as a guitarist, for I knew that in this way I might be able to travel abroad one day. My chance came when the group was sent to sing political songs at a big left-wing rally in Milan. Of the ten of us, two were security police and they wouldn't let us out of their sight for an instant. But when we went shopping I dodged them by going to the loo, and then crawled through the back window and made my way to the West German consulate which paid for me to join my sister in Karlsruhe. Finally I got a job here as a teacher, for I had my study diplomas hidden in my guitar. The GDR authorities were furious, of course. They cross-questioned my father and at first tried to get him to pay back the 21,000 Marks they'd invested in my education: but, as my father wasn't responsible, they had to drop this ploy. Instead, they removed him from his job as manager of a factory and set him to be its night-watchman. It was humiliating. But he doesn't blame me. He thinks I did right and he admires my courage.'

In 1984–5 there was a sudden vogue for another attempted means of exit via third countries: sit-ins at West German embassies. The demonstrators hoped that, by entering these premises and refusing to budge, they could cajole the Federal Government into granting them asylum and thus citizenship. It is in fact against international law for embassies to facilitate this kind of venture: but, as under West German law these refugees were its own citizens, Bonn felt obliged to do something to help them, even at the risk of upsetting its new improved relations with Honecker. To the acute embarrassment of both sides, one of the first East Germans to try it on was none other than the niece of Willi Stoph, the GDR Prime Minister, who in February 1984 took refuge with her husband and two children in the West German embassy in Prague. After frantic behind-the-scenes negotiations, the family finally went back to East Berlin with a promise that they would be allowed exit visas; this was honoured, and soon afterwards they left for Hamburg. This success then encouraged a flood of other attempts. During the next year over 200 East Germans 'occupied' Bonn's embassies in Prague, Warsaw, Budapest and Bucharest, and other groups did likewise at the American embassy and the West German mission in East Berlin. Again there was much secret bargaining, and finally most of the asylum-seekers went back home with promises of visas for the West, granted by the GDR in return for large credits from Bonn – a typical example of the familiar German/German barter in human freedom against hard currency (see below). However, after a spectacular three-month squat by over 150 East Germans in the embassy in Prague in the autumn of 1984, the Federal Government warned the GDR population via radio and television that it would no longer tolerate these sit-ins. And since then they have ceased. Kohl was under some domestic right-wing pressure to help the protesters: but at the same time, on top of the diplomatic considerations, he realised that to condone illegal sit-ins of this kind would simply harm his chances of persuading Honecker to increase the flow of legal immigrants.

Today, authorised emigration by those who simply apply for an exit visa and finally get one is much the commonest form of departure: five to ten times more people leave the GDR this way than by escaping illegally. The regime still refuses to release those whom it considers especially valuable, such as scientists or key technicians: but, as we have seen in the case of certain writers, it has become a little readier to say goodbye to restive critics and other malcontents whose presence disturbs morale. But it does not want to encourage too great a flood of visa applications, so it harasses and even penalises those who dare to show ingratitude to the Socialist fatherland by asking to leave it. In many cases, the applicant will rapidly lose his job and possibly also be restricted to one part of the country, while his children will be discriminated against at school. Especially this happens if another member of the family has already left illegally for the West. Applicants may have to wait around for years in this state of disgrace, without knowing whether their visas will ever be granted: so, if you want to leave the GDR, you have to be pretty determined about it. Even so, by 1985 the lists of those who had formally lodged demands were believed to total some 500,000. In a normal year, about 10,000 to 12,000 are let out: so, if the visas were granted in turn, the average delay could be nearly 50 years and it would be more sensible to wait to become a pensioner and then go freely! But the system is more capricious than this. Many applications are simply shelved indefinitely, with no reasons given and no means of finding out what the prospects are: others may get a favourable response within a year or two.

During the first four months of 1984 the gates were suddenly opened more widely: some 22,000 people left in that period, leading to a total for the year of nearly 35,000. There was much speculation as to the reasons. Had Honecker suddenly been smitten with the spirit of generosity? Probably not, for the flow later returned to not much above its normal level. Was he trying to get rid of more trouble-makers than usual? Unlikely. Soon however the most probable explanation emerged. The GDR in 1983 had successfully negotiated a 1-billion-DM bank credit from the Kohl Government, and the unwritten *quid pro quo* was this 'special delivery' of emigrants. It was the largest of a number of secret deals of this kind in recent years, whereby the GDR trades these humanitarian concessions for the hard currency loans that it so badly needs. Bonn will never admit publicly to these transactions: but the news has leaked out, and the average 'ransom' is believed to be around 10,000 DM per head, with the tacit understanding that the GDR will continue to release at least 12,000 a year so long as the economic aid is kept up. This puts the Bonn Government in something of a dilemma. It feels obliged to try to help oppressed Germans and is under some public pressure to do so: on the other hand, it is under pressure from the unions not to be *too* generous, for this would simply add to unemployment. In today's climate, by no means all the emigrants find it easy to get jobs.

When they first arrive in West Germany, they are usually

delighted. They are happy to be free, and amazed at a society where the shops are so full and the buildings so well cared for, and where people can say what they like without fear. Many of them, the more resourceful or those with good qualifications or friends or relatives to help them, succeed in adapting fairly easily. But others do not. Either they fail to find a job, or in other ways they steadily become disillusioned. Used to being cocooned, spoon-fed and herded together, they just cannot cope with having to fend for themselves, with the competitiveness and the faster pace of life, with the difficulty in making friends and the sheer indifference of other people. A woman from Leipzig who had settled in Munich said to me, 'Here, if you paint yourself red, blue or green all over, no one will care or even notice. In the GDR, you must first think carefully how red, blue or green would be interpreted.' And in Hamburg an aristocratic lady running a charitable office for emigrés commented: 'Some of them have been spoilt by Western TV and they come with false ideas of our society. They expect to be supplied with a high standard of living, a big flat and a regular job, and they have no idea how to freelance or fight for themselves to obtain these things. So they end up disappointed and maybe want to go back.' One common cause of disillusion is that they find they are not always greeted with open arms by their fellow Germans, who in this time of longer dole queues have come to treat the newcomers warily – if not with the same resentful hostility that they reserve for Turks. An Allensbach poll in 1984 found 48 per cent of West Germans saying, 'They are also Germans and we should welcome them', but as many as 38 per cent thinking that they would add to the country's difficulties. So the West is no paradise. Of course, some of the misfits are the kind of people who would be unhappy anywhere. A few turn to drugs or petty crime, especially in West Berlin. And each year about 1,500 go back to the GDR. They are taking some risk in so doing, for they are likely to be put in some menial job and may face other penalties too: far from welcoming the prodigals, or exploiting their return as a propaganda victory, the regime prefers to punish them for their betrayal, so as to discourage others from applying to leave.

If the GDR rulers are today resigned to a certain exodus of their citizens at least they strike as hard a bargain over it as possible – and this is true especially of the notorious traffic in political prisoners, whose freedom is bought individually for hard cash, as with slaves in ancient days. It was in 1963 that the GDR first suggested to the Federal Government that it was prepared to sell its convicts: Bonn accepted, and ever since then it has pursued this trade that it discreetly calls its 'special humanitarian activites'. According to Amnesty International, there are about 5,000 'political prisoners' in the GDR, of whom some 70 per cent have been arrested while trying to escape. Since 1963 they have been released to West Germany at the rate of about 1,000 a year, sometimes more, and Bonn is believed to have paid well over 3 billion DM for them. The price for each release is fixed individually, and the money has to be paid over two weeks in advance into an East German account in Frankfurt. Then the ransomed prisoners come out in coachloads, most of them from a prison at Karl-Marxstadt in Saxony, and are taken to a camp at Giessen in Hessen, to be de-briefed. Though the fees are kept secret, it is believed that an artisan will cost about 30,000 DM, a junior teacher 50,000 DM and a doctor or professor 200,000 or more, while 2.5 million DM is said to have been demanded for one senior academic. And so keen is the regime on securing these funds that, as Bonn officials will suggest privately, it seems to be ensuring that its prisons are kept well stocked; at least, the number of political prisoners has been rising recently. On the GDR side, the barter is conducted by the infamous Wolfgang Vogel, an urbane and cosmopolitan private lawyer in East Berlin who comes and goes through the Wall as he pleases and whose big Mercedes can sometimes be seen parked outside the Federal Government office in West Berlin. It is he who has also negotiated many of the high-level Soviet/American 'spy swaps', beginning with the release in 1962 of the U-2 pilot Francis Gary Powers. When asked to justify the selling of prisoners, he will advance the official GDR view that the money is needed, firstly to compensate the State for the 'damage' done to socialism by their political actions, and secondly (the excuse given for the trade in ordinary emigrants too) to repay the money invested in their education. Meanwhile, the Federal Government too has sometimes come in for criticism in the West for taking part in this traffic. Is it morally justified, some people ask, in lending itself as an accomplice to the GDR's breach of human rights? And should it be encouraging the export of the very people whose critical pressure might help to liberalise the GDR if they stayed? There may be some validity in these arguments. But almost any Bonn politician will reply – correctly, in my own view – that the cause of helping victimised fellow-Germans must come first.

Inter-German relations: the reality of détente, the mirage of reunification

Despite these and other fundamental differences between the two regimes, the links between them have grown steadily closer since the early 1970s, leading to the present highly equivocal situation. These two halves of one nation, divided by a barrier of steel, do not formally recognise each other diplomatically, yet they negotiate constantly and they trade intensively in all kinds of commerce; they are sworn ideological foes, yet despite the closed frontier their human contacts and exchanges are closer, warmer and more numerous than between almost any other neighbouring states in Europe. How have they learned to live with these paradoxes?

West Germany, for its part, has long abandoned the Hallstein doctrine of the 1960s and has tacitly accepted that the GDR is probably here to stay and a *modus vivendi* must therefore be reached. The East German regime, on its side, has now greatly modified the policy of *Abgrenzung*, or distancing itself from Bonn, which in response to Hallstein is pursued for so many years. After the arrival of *Ostpolitik*, it found that *Abgrenzung* no longer really worked, nor was it so necessary: so it decided to take the risk of rapprochement and to exploit this for its benefits, which are above all economic. The reconciliation between the two states still has its strict limits: but each side now accepts that it needs the other, and at official level the contacts have multiplied enormously. Since Bonn still refuses to recognise the GDR's sovereignty, there can be no exchange of embassies: but since 1974 each state has maintained a *Vertretung* (permanent mission) in the other's capital, staffed in much the same way as an embassy. And the diplomats and other officials have fairly affable relations, including discreet little lunches where they tease each other about the protocol absurdities that divide them. In Bonn, Chancellor Kohl has a grey telephone in one corner of his office that provides a direct line to Honecker. And, though GDR leaders seldom visit West Germany (see below), the traffic in the other direction has grown remarkably. Franz-Josef Strauss paid two private visits to Honecker in 1983–4, and from these was able to claim the political kudos for having helped to negotiate the loans that led to an increase in emigration. In March 1984, at the twice-yearly Leipzig Trade Fair, Strauss was followed by Count Otto Lambsdorff, then Kohl's economics minister, and by at least one SPD leader – and Honecker and his colleagues were visibly preening themselves at this evidence of their growing respectability in West German eyes. This was a time when Honecker was seeking to win new influence and authority on the world stage too, through his official trips to Austria, Japan and even the Vatican, and by the formal visits paid to the GDR by French, Italian and Greek prime ministers and by Sir Geoffrey Howe, the British foreign secretary, amongst many others. The regime regarded this activity as a means of asserting its claim to be an important and independent nation, loyal to Moscow but not its puppet – and thus of spotlighting West Germany's isolation as the only major country withholding recognition.

The growth of economic links between the two Germanies is illustrated by the fact that the level of trade between them more than doubled between 1974 and 1985, to reach a total of 16.5 billion DM a year. West Germany supplies large quantities of half-finished goods and production materials, and through a special credit system the GDR is able to avoid having to pay for these in hard currency. In turn it sells its neighbour a wide range of consumer good such as clothing, shoes, toys, porcelain and electric motors. What is more, it gains special free access to EEC markets, for since Bonn refuses to treat the border as a true frontier, it has persuaded its eleven partners to affix a protocol to the Treaty of Rome whereby its imports from the GDR escape the normal Common Market tariffs. East Germany has also begun to seek industrial investment and expertise from the West, and has found several major firms ready to cooperate including Siemens and Krupp. Above all, Volkswagen in 1984 signed a 600 million DM contract for setting up a plant at Karl-Marxstadt where it will manufacture for the GDR's Wartburg and Trabant cars the same engines that it uses in its Golfs and Polos. As the GDR's own little two-cylinder engines have hitherto been noisy, pollutant and generally inefficient, this should make a nice change. The Soviet Union exerted pressure to prevent the deal, for it disliked the idea of the GDR becoming too dependent on West German technology. But this was one of those infrequent occasions where Honecker successfully defied Moscow.

Inter-German commerce represents only about 1.8 per cent of West Germany's overall foreign trade, but 9 per cent of that of the GDR, making the Federal Republic its most important trading partner after the Soviet Union. And there are many reasons why the East German leaders have come to set immense store by these commercial exchanges and other economic links, not forgetting the generous loans and credits. They help to shore up the GDR's large external debt and to modify its dependence on Comecon; and above all they make it much easier for Honecker to maintain a decent living standard for his people and thus prevent an increase in restiveness. This is of crucial political importance for him. The Federal Republic, on the other hand, gains little from the exchanges in strictly economic terms. It sees them rather as a key weapon in its moral and humanitarian strategy – a means of exerting leverage over the GDR and persuading it to ease up internally. Trading cash for human concessions has long been the name of the game: in 1983–4, the secret *quid pro quo* for the loans included not only the release of more emigrants but an easing of travel formalities for pensioners and a promise to dismantle some thousands of the deadly scatter-guns along the border.

So there is a fundamental gulf between the two sides' motives in seeking rapprochement, and this may well prevent the links from getting much closer. As one official in Bonn put it to me succinctly: 'Each side propagates its separate fictions – the one, that Germany is really still a single country, the other, that it is two distinct sovereign states, unconnected save that they happen to be neighbours. The GDR's central aim in rapprochement is to have this status quo recognised and confirmed; the Federal Republic's aim is to encourage a more fluid situation that might lead eventually, if not to reunification, at least to a kind of federalism based on a more liberal regime in the GDR. At heart, the two paths are utterly irreconcilable.'

The GDR's strategy is to manoeuvre Bonn into a *de facto* diplomatic recognition through this inter-governmental dealing, and to make it be seen publicly to be treating it as an equal partner. The strategy seems to have made some progress. On the other side, the Federal Republic's attitude is highly equivocal, a kind of double act. For, whereas it still holds to the moral principle that 'the East Germans are part of us' (as one official put it to me bluntly), it is also pragmatic enough to realise that the best way of reducing tensions, strengthening ties, and generally helping the people of the GDR, is by negotiating tactfully with the hated non-State across the border, buttering it up, and wheedling concessions out of it. 'A more self-confident East German Government, stronger both politically and economically, is in our interests,' said the same Bonn official I have just quoted, 'for it will feel more secure and be readier to give its citizens more liberty' – a remarkable *volte face* from the Hallstein doctrine days. This was roughly the Brandt and Schmidt approach, and it has been followed by Kohl who in his own way has made quite a contribution to *Ostpolitik*. And yet, there are plenty of right-wingers who still think it is immoral even to parley in a friendly way with a totalitarian regime that has been imposed on Germans against their will, without free elections, by the force of Soviet arms. And the majority of the West German people, while not going as far as this, nonetheless still believe that it would be wrong to extend full recognition to a government of this kind. It is indeed worth noting that all Allensbach polls of recent years have consistently shown between 70 and 76 per cent of the sample agreeing that the following clause should be retained in the Constitution: 'The entire German people are called upon to achieve in free self-determination the unity and freedom of Germany.' So these are the political realities of domestic opinion that guide Bonn in its difficult balancing-act. It infuriates the GDR and is one cause of its tough stance on travel. And in West Germany there are some on the Left who would like to see the policy modified. When in 1981 Günter Gaus of the SPD returned from his seven years as head of the mission in East Berlin, he caused a stir by proposing in a *Die Zeit* interview that the GDR should be formally recognised as a separate state. For a number of reasons, this is not official SPD policy. But an SPD government might be prepared to be more flexible – or so the GDR leaders are hoping.

In the meantime, both sides play absurd verbal games with each other, in the battle over protocol and status. While the GDR uses its Foreign Ministry for dealing with West Germany, the latter conducts affairs through its special *Bundesministerium für Innerdeutsche Beziehungen*, i.e. the ministry for 'internal' (*not* 'inter') German relations – and this nuance maddens East Berlin. Maps and atlases printed in West Germany, whether for schools or for tourists, show the country as one with the inter-German border hardly visible; weather reports on TV give the same details about rain or shine in Dresden as in Stuttgart; and signposts in Hessen will give the distances to Eisenach or Leipzig. And the GDR hits back in its own way. Its maps of East Berlin show the western zone as a blank space, while bedside telephone directories in its smart hotels will tell you how to dial Oslo or Belgrade but not Frankfurt or Hamburg! West Germany charges domestic rates for letters and telephone calls to the GDR, while the other way the rates are international ones. And so on. The sharpest wrangle is over Berlin: the Allies with legal right on their side still refuse to recognise East Berlin as the capital of the GDR, so the GDR retorts by downgrading West Berlin as much as it can. On the transit *Autobahnen* from the West to the big city, large signs announce the distance to 'Berlin, Hauptstadt der DDR', with just a small side-mention of 'Westberlin' (all one word). It would all seem terribly childish, were it not also so terribly significant.

In recent years, the GDR has been making even more of the running than Bonn in trying to secure closer links between these separate states. In 1983 and again in 1984 Honecker laid plans with the Kohl government for paying his first ever official visit. He was born in Saarland, and no doubt he was filled with an old man's nostalgic desire to see again the places of his childhood; more to the point, he was also keen to win the diplomatic victory of being greeted as a State guest in Bonn. But it was partly over this protocol issue that both projected visits were cancelled, for neither side could agree just exactly how Honecker should be received. However, it was mainly under pressure from Moscow that the second and more determined of the two attempts was abandoned, in the autumn of 1984. It happened soon after Bonn had agreed to the stationing of US Cruise and Pershing II missiles in West Germany, and in this tenser East/West climate the Russians did not want inter-German relations to grow chummier. Honecker fought to preserve his plans, but failed, for on this kind of basic strategic issue Moscow always has the last word. Observers pointed to the irony of the fact that originally in 1971 it was the Soviet Union that had pushed a reluctant GDR into détente with its neighbour, and had ousted Ulbricht in favour of Honecker for that purpose; now the boot was on the other foot. However, despite this particular setback in 1984, inter-German rapprochement in recent years has generally managed to survive quite well the various ups-and-downs of Soviet/American tensions.

So what are the prospects for the future? Relations may continue to improve a little further, especially if the SPD should return to power: but there is unlikely to be any basic change in the status quo. In the years before the building of the Wall, there was endless speculation in the West about reunification; and even today the goal of a reunited Germany remains a kind of official myth in the Federal Republic, helping to explain why as a capital city Bonn still retains such a provisional air. But, short of a basic change in Soviet policy and in Soviet/American relations, reunification has now come to seem increasingly improbable. And it is not certain if anyone outside Germany really wants it – even among the Western Allies. The price exacted by the Russians for a united Germany would certainly be its withdrawal from all military alliances; and this, because of the greater size and power of West Germany, would involve a much greater sacrifice by NATO than by the Warsaw Pact. This big neutral Germany in the heart of Europe would not only be unpredictable and hard to control, but it would become an industrial super-power of 78 million people, towering over all its neighbours and upsetting the present delicate balance of power between East and West. François Mauriac's often-quoted remark made in the 1950s, 'I love Germany so much that I am glad there are two of them', still remains the tacit attitude of many friends of Germany in the West – and not always so tacit, for in 1984 the Italian foreign minister, Giulio Andreotti, said more or less the same thing, in public, to Bonn's indignation.

If Westerners feel like this, Russians, Poles, Czechs and others do so even more, with their memories of wartime suffering under a powerful and aggressive Germany. Much more to the point, while the Soviet Union would gain some strategic advantage from a neutralised Germany, this would be far outweighed by the colossal political and moral defeat of the GDR and its system being merged with West Germany. Any reunification would be bound to include some kind of free elections in the whole country, and though the resulting structure might retain some of the present aspects of the GDR, and could even be 'socialist' in the Western sense (i.e. SPD-ruled), it would certainly be very different from the present regime. For the first time in history, a people would have been given the chance freely to rid themselves of Communism – and the result would be highly contagious throughout the Soviet empire. The Russian leaders, and indeed the GDR ones too, would never for one moment take this risk.

It is not certain how even in West Germany people really want reunification. Certainly they have ceased to expect it to happen. 'They don't believe in it, and nor do I,' Günter Gaus told me in 1985, 'we all realise that the two Germanies have become too different. No compromise between the two systems would realistically be feasible.' The Allensbach institute backs up this view with a number of interesting opinion surveys conducted over the years. In 1981, the number of people saying they would like reunification was still as high as 62 per cent, but the proportion thinking it might one day be possible was down to 13 per cent, as against 28 per cent in 1966. Asked, 'What do you think is the most important problem facing West Germany today?', in 1959 far more people (45 per cent) quoted reunification than any other topic, with East/West détente scoring 16 per cent and economic questions 15 per cent. By 1980 those figures had changed dramatically: the economy came first with 86 per cent, peace and détente second with 33 per cent, while *less than one per cent* cited reunification.

Today this solution to 'the German question' is reduced in most people's minds to a vague cultural longing – a long-term objective that officially is never queried (hence the anger against Andreotti), though privately nearly every politician has shelved it *sine die*. One does meet a few people who believe that reunification may happen slowly by osmosis: but rather more expect that it will steadily become less likely, as the ties of kinship loosen and each state goes its separate way. Today, it tends to be older rather than younger people who go to visit friends or relatives in the East; younger generations have grown up for whom the Berlin Wall is just part of history, and who feel less personal concern for East Germany than their parents. And though the GDR and the division of the nation is still a lively and much-discussed issue in West Germany, this is markedly more so in intellectual and political circles than among a wider public.

So the anomaly of this divided nation will remain. Among the former Allies who fought against Hitler, a great many people see a justice in this division – and so do a certain number of Germans too. Theo Sommer, editor of *Die Zeit*, remarked to me, 'It's our due punishment for Nazism and the war, isn't it? But it's tough luck that some Germans are being punished much more heavily than others.'

Meanwhile, what will happen within the GDR itself? There, the rulers will continue their policy of trying to build up a real national identity, with the dual aim of impressing world opinion and of creating a focus of loyalty for their own people. They utilise sporting achievements to this end, also culture and history. The expensive restoration of historic buildings, including the estimated 300 million Marks spent on the Semper Opera in Dresden, has in part the purpose of encouraging East Germans to feel proud of belonging to a nation with such a heritage. In schools and universities, Goethe and Schiller, Bach, Schumann, and other great writers and composers are shown to be part of that heritage too – and legitimately so, for East German towns such as Leipzig and Weimar lie in the heartland of classic German culture quite as much as any city in the West.

German history is enlisted in the same cause. For some years now, Party leaders and ideologists have been at pains to stress that the GDR emanates from the age-old peasant and worker traditions of the German nation, whereas the Federal Republic represents merely its capitalist and imperialist elements; Honecker has said that the GDR is 'the work of many past generations', with its roots in the peasant revolts of the Middle Ages, the democratic uprisings of 1848 and, of course, the teachings of Marx and Engels. Today, more surprisingly, the Party has even been rehabilitating aspects of the old Prussian past that have no such Leftish credentials. In the heart of the old Prussian capital, the statue of Frederick the Great has been restored to its old place on the Unter den Linden, after having been removed by Ulbricht and hidden for 30 years in a park in Potsdam; the 19th-century military reformer Scharnhorst has been the subject of an appreciative TV series; and Luther too is back in favour, as we have seen. Most curiously, whereas after the war Frederick the Great and Bismarck were both officially denounced as 'forerunners of Hitler'[1] and then for many years treated as taboo subjects, in 1985 the GDR published a detailed and intelligent biography of the Iron Chancellor, written by a Marxist historian, Professor Ernst Engelberg. He chose as his theme a remark of Lenin's, 'Bismarck in his Junker way played a progressive historical role', and went on to stress his reformist work in, for example, founding Germany's social welfare services (see p. 197). For many a loyal history teacher in schools, the turnabouts were bewildering.

How far the regime's policy of instilling a sense of national identity has been successful with its own citizens is not easy to assess. They remain very aware of their Germanness, and they carefully keep up many of the old German habits and traditions – for example, the custom of providing a child on his first day in school with the comforting gift of a *Schultüte*, a gaily-decorated conical bag filled with sweets and toys. They live in a land where, despite the political revolution, life-styles in some ways remain closer to the old, quaint, leisurely Germany of the 1920s than they do in the Federal Republic, much more touched by modernism; and today their isolation tends to reinforce this provincial, old-fashioned quality of life. But whether this leads them to take pride in the GDR as such is not so certain. Through nightly television, and through their own yearnings and curiosity about a world forbidden to them, they tend to feel more

---

[1] For GDR attitudes to Nazism and to war guilt, see page 392.

awareness of West Germany, and more consciousness of the national affinity with their brothers and sisters across the border, than the latter feel with regard to them.

What the future holds for the GDR will depend more than anything on what happens inside the Soviet Union; and, though Gorbachov may in some ways be trying to modernise his own country, he is unlikely to permit any major measures of relaxation in the most strategically sensitive of his satellites. Honecker may be able to defy Moscow on a few particular matters such as the Volkswagen deal: but on basic policy and doctrine, both in domestic and foreign affairs, he must follow the line. Even the degree of liberalisation that Moscow seems prepared to tolerate in Hungary is not quite permissible for the GDR, because of its special vulnerability to its big Western neighbour. Nor would Honecker be likely to want it. Like the other SED leaders of his generation, he is a committed Communist who believes in the system that he has helped to create. Like any ruler in a dictatorship, he is above all concerned that the Party should keep its firm grip on power – and the same is true of the younger generation of SED leaders now coming to the fore. These new men may be more modern-minded on economic matters than the old guard they are due to replace: but they are also more hard-nosed and opportunistic, and they never knew the idealistic period of the anti-Nazi struggle.

The GDR leaders both old and new see the strengthening of the economy as the most crucial element in their strategy. As we have seen, it is important not only for East Germany's world position but for keeping up living standards and thus reducing the risk of unrest. Over the past 25 years the economy has done extremely well by East European standards: but there may be some difficulties ahead. One disturbing problem is that it has not had either the hard currency or the foresight to invest adequately in the new technologies, and it now risks losing its world markets to those who have: for example, it has been successful hitherto in exporting its washing-machines, but is now beginning to lose ground in face of the more sophisticated electronic equipment made in capitalist countries. But to make the transfer to a high-technology-orientated industry is not simply a matter of money, planning and technical expertise: it requires also a change in attitudes. And here, as one expert observer suggested to me, 'The trouble with the GDR is that the structure of management is just not geared to the kind of risk-taking and incentive motivation that these new innovative industries need, in the East as in the West. The top jobs in firms and economic departments are held down by mediocre appartchiks who fear that they would be shown up as inadequate, and maybe replaced, if the system were changed to one of greater competition and risk. So they favour the status quo – and they are numerous and influential enough to be able to ensure that it is preserved. It is a leaden situation.'

The Hungarian experiments with moves towards a semi-market economy have been widely criticised in the GDR, where officials point out complacently that these have led to high inflation and a rising foreign debt. So in East Germany there is still no sign of any plans to shift away from the old Moscow-imposed system of centralised state planning. But the heaviness and inflexibility of this make it very hard to modernise the economy effectively, especially as the policy of huge subsidies for basic goods distorts the whole structure of pricing and producing. The authorities are aware of this dilemma. So in 1984–5 they began to impose on state firms a new employment tax, equal to 70 per cent of an average wage bill. The aim was to induce companies to shed excessive manpower and thus increase their productivity and general efficiency. But it was not at all clear how this could be reconciled with the GDR's ideologically-based policy of full employment.

So what is to be our ultimate verdict on this socialist society? First, that it is a great deal less harsh than it could be – or than it once was. Despite the Wall and all that, life has in many ways become more livable in the GDR over the past 20 years; it remains a police state, but except for a tiny minority of dissenters it is not a savage or unjust one. Most inhabitants accept the situation and even see some virtues in Socialism; or, at least, very few of them have any desire to go back to the old-style capitalism of the Junkers and the big bankers. But they would like a *better* Socialism – and many of them have given up hope that they will ever see it. My own basic feeling is that, while the regime could certainly be much worse than it is, it has rather few constructive qualities of its own from which Western societies could learn. It may have removed unemployment and the darker side of poverty, but at some cost to individual liberty. It vaunts its welfare services, which indeed are good: but those of the capitalist West are better. And above all, as its critics constantly point out, Socialism in the GDR has lost most of its earlier genuine idealism and become a grey, regimented affair, concerned primarily with preserving its own power. If it has achieved a remarkable social stability and on the whole works smoothly, is that not at least partly because it is run by Germans – nay, Prussians – who by nature are so orderly and efficient? And if the citizens outwardly accept the regime and do not demonstrate and rock the boat like Poles, might that not also be because they are Germans, temperamentally inclined to obedience? These may seem like cliché judgements: but I am sure there is a lot of substance in them. And what opportunities the regime has missed! Let me end by quoting an anonymous 'renowned novelist' (Stefan Heym, I strongly suspect) who recently told Stuart Simon of the BBC (as reported in the *Listener* of March 17, 1983): 'The State is out on a limb. It was supposed to offer a spiritual ideal, and it hasn't. I believe socialism is a much better idea than capitalism, but it's never had a chance to prove it here. We're stifled by bureaucracy and the lack of freedom to criticise. If this were a real socialist state, we'd have the whole of Germany by now. But it's not, and the Wall is there to prove it.'

8

CONCLUSION: HOW STABLE A DEMOCRACY?

The citizens of West Germany may have adjusted quite well to the continuing division of their country: but what is their own future to be? In this last chapter, I shall try to draw together some of the threads that have run through this book, and to examine four major questions. What is the influence today of the Nazi period and what scars has it left? How stable is German democracy and how deep does it go? What is the true impact of the values of a new generation (as symbolised by the Greens and others), and how far do their ideas mark a real change? And, lastly, how do the West Germans today perceive their position in the world, and in the defence of the West, and are they at last coming to terms with the old problem of their national identity?

Digesting the legacies of Nazism

What does the average German feel today about Hitler's regime? – about how and why it was able to take hold in a free society, and whether the nation should continue to bear collective guilt for events that only those now well into their sixties experienced as adults. In coming to terms with their Nazi legacy, the Germans have had to face moral problems of horrendous proportions, and it is hard to arrive at any balanced assessment of how they have coped. On the positive side, it is clear that what is loosely known as 'neo-Nazism' is today a marginal phenomenon of little influence. What is more, the media in the past ten or 15 years have done an excellent job in dragging the whole subject of Nazism and German guilt into the open forum of public discussion, through a steady spate of books, articles and programmes; and this, together with the simple passage of time, has served to break the uneasy taboo of silence that had cloaked these issues in the earlier post-war decades. Leading politicians too, CDU as well as SPD, have often set an outspoken example: one could cite Chancellor Brandt's public act of contrition at the Warsaw ghetto in 1970, and President von Weizsäcker's formidable speech to the Bundestag on the 1985 anniversary of May 8, when he told all Germans that only by continuing to remember the shame and horror of their past could they come to terms with it.

But how widely are his attitudes shared? One aspect of the ending of the long silence is that many elderly people who lived under Nazism are now much readier to try to justify themselves in public and to speak out their resentment at the stigma that has been branded onto their generation ('I was only doing my patriotic duty as a soldier', 'how could we have known what was going on in the concentration camps?', or even, 'the Nazis did some good things, as well as bad', are remarks one hears widely). And many younger people, however appalled they are by Nazism, resent being expected to go on feeling guilty for the sins of their grandparents. All in all, it is not easy for an observer to pick his way through the tangle of paradoxes and contradictions.

In the first years after the war, the Western occupying forces tried to carry through a programme of 'denazification' that included the removal of Nazis from public posts as well as the trial of the more actively guilty. This programme was ineptly executed, and it was far from consistent: in many firms and in some professions, there were found to be just not enough non-Nazis with the right ability and experience for the machine of German economic and public life to be set in motion again, and so a good many former party members or supporters were allowed to keep their posts. The most notorious case was that of Alfred Krupp, who at Nuremberg was sentenced to 12 years' prison for using slave labour, but three years later was set free and permitted to take over his steel-works again. Then after 1949 the Adenauer regime pursued the same erratic course as the Allies had done. And today, with hindsight, it seems very clear that first the occupiers and then the German authorities were indeed too lenient towards a number of run-of-the-mill Nazis. True, the issue has been exaggerated by the Left, for there was never any widespread rehabilitation: but there were mistakes. In 1970 about half of the 15,000 magistrates and judges in West Germany had held legal positions in the Hitler era: probably few of them had been active Nazis, but even so the figure seems disturbingly high. Adenauer himself from 1953 to 1963 employed as his state secretary in the Chancellory a certain Dr Hans Globke, who had been a senior official in the pre-war Interior Ministry and was alleged by the Press to have drafted parts of Hitler's anti-Jewish laws. There was controversy over this at the time – as there was over the CDU's choice as Chancellor in 1966 of Kurt Georg

Kiesinger. He was a modest and honourable man who had never been more than a minor time-serving Nazi: nonetheless, he had been in the party for 12 years and a great many Germans felt that this in itself should have disqualified him from high political office. As Professor Eberhardt Jäckel, a leading German historian of the Nazi period, commented to me in 1985, 'Whether these and other men were personally guilty is not the point. It was bad for German democracy, and it set a bad example to the younger generation, that people with *any* kind of Nazi record should have been given such posts. Adenauer and the other CDU leaders should have been more scrupulous.'

There was another and brighter side of this picture, for the Germans after the war also did a great deal to make amends for the Nazi crimes and to punish the guilty. By 1970, German courts had prosecuted 12,900 persons suspected of offences: 5,200 were imprisoned and 76 of these were given the maximum life sentence. Under a German-Israeli agreement of 1962, reparations worth more than 2.5 billion DM were made to Israel during the following years, while 15 billion DM were paid directly to individual Jewish victims or their families under Germany's Restitution Law. This was penance on a vast scale – even though money alone could never atone for the evils done. In addition, various private German bodies carried out their own reparations or publicly confessed their share of guilt – above all, the Protestant Churches. In the 1960s a Lutheran pastor in Berlin set up a 'penance corps' of young German volunteers (architects, carpenters and others) who built Jewish centres in Europe and Israel and restored buildings wrecked by the Nazis.

The 1950s and '60s were an especially difficult time for the German conscience. A new generation grew up with the realisation that its own parents were the guilty ones, and this caused bitter rifts within families: fathers and sons were frequently not on speaking terms. Or, as one writer now in his fifties put it to me, 'You never knew who you were dealing with. If I went to a doctor, or met someone a bit older than me, I kept thinking, "I wonder if *he* was one of *them*."' Small wonder that the vast majority of Germans preferred to brush the troubling questions of the past under the carpet and to channel their thoughts and energies into the happier task of building up the *Wirtschaftswunder* – itself a kind of atonement. One aspect of this situation was the very inadequate schoolroom teaching about Nazism, during that post-war period. Even though the convinced Nazis had been removed from the schools, many passive time-servers were still there, and they were far too involved with the problem of guilt to be able to teach about Nazism properly; there was also a lack of suitable textbooks, for it took some time to prepare new ones to replace those used under Hitler. My wife, who was at a *Gymnasium* in Munich in the mid-60s, says, 'We had new history books with a final chapter on the Nazi period, very dead-pan: but our teachers always left it out, saying that they didn't have time and anyway it wouldn't be needed for the *Abitur*. I think they were just embarrassed. They had no idea how to explain the subject and wanted to avoid controversy. I discovered about the Final Solution through talking to a Jewish schoolfriend.'

Over in the GDR, it was, and still is, all much easier. There, the regime to its credit did winkle out former Nazis far more thoroughly than in the West. But it also dodged the issue of guilt. Right from the start it had taken the simple line, 'Nazism was the product of mono-poly capitalism, and there is no reason why East Germans should feel responsible, for we are all good socialists here. The "bad" Germans are all over in the West.' This is the version fed to schoolchildren, who are not asked to feel any collective guilt for their elders' sins. And the GDR has paid no reparations to Israel, for it claims that it is not the successor to the Third Reich and so has no moral obligation. To this day, the May 8 anniversary is celebrated in the GDR as a day of 'liberation' by the gallant Red Army, and not one of humiliation and defeat. The Nazis are portrayed as an alien people, battled against by noble German communists – and this led Leslie Collitt to comment in the *Financial Times* of April 25, 1985, 'At times it appears to younger East Germans as if East Germany itself had fought beside the wartime Allies to crush the Nazis.'

In West Germany, there has been a most striking change in attitudes since around the early 1970s – as I have noticed on my own visits. When I was first in Stuttgart in 1969–70, researching *A Tale of Five Cities*, I found that very few people would talk to me about their feel-ings towards the Nazi period; and I, not wishing to alienate my useful new contacts, cravenly refrained from pressing them. But, during my long months in Germany in 1984–5, I had no such problems. People of all ages raised the subject spontaneously all the time; they talked openly and excitedly, even made jokes about it. Everyone notices this contrast. Of the many reasons for it, the most important is the obvious one of the sheer passing of time and the change of generations. Today's young people need no longer feel angrily ashamed of their parents, who themselves were too young to have been Nazis; and the grandparents are fast dying out. So families are no longer riven: guilt has become less personalised, more a general national legacy, and therefore easier to talk about. There have been other factors, too. The 1968 upheavals blew away the taboos on many subjects, this one included, and ushered in an era of much more open public discussion of all kinds of questions. Then in 1969 the

Chancellorship passed from Kiesinger to Willi Brandt, the former Free Norwegian officer, whose approach was very different – witness his State visit to Warsaw in 1970, when he dropped on his knees and bowed his head in silent reverence at the memorial to half a million Polish Jews killed by the Nazis in the ghetto. Around the same time, teaching in schools was improving radically, and the media embarked on a far more frank and detailed scrutiny of the Hitler period. In 1979 Hollywood's *Holocaust* series was shown on German TV: vulgar soap it may have been (I agree with Reitz), but it did at least open German eyes far more widely than before to the truth about the Final Solution. It won very high audience ratings of about 40 per cent, and it prompted thousands of schools and colleges to organise discussions on the subject.

Many town councils too have followed the new trend: some have invited exiled former Jewish inhabitants to pay their first return visits since the 1930s, and have entertained them generously. Rather more daringly, by the early 1980s a number of big cities such as Munich had mounted elaborate exhibitions of local life under the Nazis. In 1984 I visited one of these at a museum in Stuttgart, initiated by Rommel himself, and it was mind-blowing – it included a big photo of the 1937 city council all in Nazi uniform giving the Nazi salute and others of happy gentle Swabian teenagers in their Hitler Youth garb. Such an exhibition would have been inconceivable only 15 years ago. Sadly, it was not visited by more than 70,000 people, half of them made up of compulsory school groups. But it passed off with no more than a few isolated protests from older people, some of them saying that it was wrong to rake up the past, or that the evils of Nazism had been exaggerated.

Now that this over-sixty generation has at last become readier to discuss the subject, out very often will come a jumble of mixed feelings of guilt and self-justification, suppressed for so many years. I had a vivid experience of this when Professor Jäckel, who teaches at Stuttgart University, arranged for me to talk to some of his history students. He assembled about 30 of them: half were in their early twenties, doing a normal degree course; the others were 'mature' students attending his extra-mural class, most of them aged 65 or more (the men had all fought in the war). And the sparks flew! First I asked the older group whether they felt any guilt about the war and Nazism. 'No!' was the near-unanimous answer. 'It wasn't Hitler who started the war,' said one former *Panzer* lieutenant, 'it was you British, *you* declared it on us – Hitler wanted peace with Britain.' Other views followed from the others: 'Germany has suffered so terribly from the war, first bombed to bits and now split in two, that she has fully paid the price, and I for one have no more guilt;' 'we never knew about the killing of the Jews, how could we? – it wasn't our fault;' 'yes, I *did* know that Jews were being shot and deported, but I could do nothing, I was just not prepared to be a martyr;' 'I was in the Wehrmacht, merely doing my duty – it's very unfair that we soldiers should be asked to bear guilt for obeying orders.' Some of the group were patently nettled by a Briton asking them smug questions, and they hit back: 'What about Dresden? – that was just as bad – Winston must have drunk too much whisky;' 'what about the Versailles Treaty? – you created Nazism too.' And so on – a predictable mish-mash of classic reactions, all a bit depressing. And yet these sturdy veterans had been taking the trouble to attend the regular classes of a famous liberal historian known for his firmly anti-Nazi line – so there must have been some uneasy consciences lurking behind the gropings after extenuating circumstances. Then some of the more radical of the young students began to attack the old ones. 'You dreadful old fogeys, why do you try to justify yourselves?' said one Green girl; 'why did you fail to speak out against Hitler's war, while we now *are* speaking out against the threat of Reagan's war? If Germany were dragged into a conflict now, *we* would refuse to fight – why did *you* not do so?' Tempers rose. 'You young people have no idea what it was like to live under a dictatorship,' said one veteran; 'no protest was possible. It's only because Germany today is free that *you* can enjoy the luxury of a Peace Movement. And besides, your dangerous pacifism is leading us straight into the Russians' arms.' So here was a horrifying phoney debate: one generation that had failed to stop a fascist Germany from aggressing, at odds with another that would refuse to defend a democratic Germany if aggressed. I was aghast.

At least, with the taboos now lifted, such arguments are today out in the open. And many respectable older citizens will cheerfully explain why at first they found Nazism attractive – 'Yes, of course I was a Nazi, it was the thing to be,' said a charming banker I met in Frankfurt. A great many men of his age, it must be stressed, experienced the better side of Nazism, more than its horrors: in the 1930s they witnessed a go-ahead new regime that restored national pride and confidence, and then during the dark war years they were away from Germany, fighting patriotically. Today, just like many British veterans, it is the camaraderie of those soldier years that they remember most vividly. In Hamburg, I went to dinner in the home of a retired naval officer, courteous, dignified, warmly anglophile: 'Admiral Dönitz was a fine man, I knew him well. We Germans should be proud of our fighting record, it's time we stopped this absurd guilt about the armed forces. Long live the international solidarity of soldiers. Come, drink to it, my friend!' His family and guests roared approval, as we all drank a toast – to Dönitz, so it seemed.

The late 1970s produced a wave of popular cult-like interest in

Hitler, much of it commercialised in the form of films, records and photo-articles. To some older people it may have brought an element of nostalgia. Hitler, it is true, was generally portrayed as a lunatic megalomaniac: but, as one young German suggested to me, 'There's something dangerous in this obsession with Hitler and his cronies as a bunch of mad freaks who led the good German people astray. It tends to absolve that generation of their own share of responsibility. It's a comforting alibi.' In fact, an Allensbach survey in 1977 that put the question, 'Did the German population have any practical means of influencing Nazi policy, for instance over the concentration camps?', found only 4 per cent of the over-60s answering 'yes' and 86 per cent 'no' (among the under-45s, the replies were 16 per cent 'yes', 53 per cent 'no'). Another poll in the same year revealed that 41 per cent of those questioned felt that 'the positive aspects of Hilter's action' should not be forgotten, even though he had 'made numerous errors'. And a few people go much further. 'The Nazis had good ideas, it's a pity they got out of hand,' one sometimes hears; or, 'Hitler would have known how to deal with all those terrorists, punks and drop-outs;' or, 'at least *we* had an ideology that we cared about. The young today believe in nothing.'

Such views, still quite common among the old guard, surely represent little more than a muddled emotional reaction against the permissiveness of modern society, and a vague nostalgia for older and firmer values. They hardly constitute 'neo-Nazism', and it is doubtful whether many of these people would vote for a new Nazi party – as elections have shown. One small neo-Nazi party that survived the war was outlawed in 1952 as unconstitutional. Then in the mid-1960s, with the first breath of recession after the 'miracle' years, the newly-formed National Democratic Party (NPD) suddenly emerged in some strength. Its platform was extreme right-wing and 12 of the 18 members of its executive had been active Nazis: but it managed to remain just outside the orbit of the Constitution's formal ban on parties 'aiming to overthrow democratic society'. It won some seats in *Land* elections and began to cause alarm among democrats both in Germany and abroad. But in the federal elections of 1969 it fell well short of the minimum 5 per cent vote needed to secure seats in the *Bundestag*; and after this, as the economy improved, so it steadily declined. In many ways more Poujadist than genuinely Nazi, the NPD today has no elected representatives anywhere and is seldom in the news.

Neo-Nazism however still possesses a very vocal mouthpiece in the form of the *National Zeitung*, a weekly published in Munich with a claimed circulation of 100,000. This pursues a stridently nationalistic and xenophobic line; it glorifies military leaders such as Dönitz; and, though it stops short of glorifying Hitler, it tries hard to minimise the

Nazis' misdoings – 'They may have killed some Jews, but not six million, that's a wicked exaggeration put about by Germany's enemies,' is its common refrain. This paper, like *Bild*, is protected under the German code of Press freedom – and probably rightly so, for, if such views exist, it is best for them to be out in the open where they can be contested. They do however trouble the German conscience, and they have caused protests from Jews. This led the SPD in 1982 to table its much-contested Bill against the *Auschwitzlüge* (lies about Auschwitz), aiming to make it illegal to spread lies about Nazi crimes that insulted the memory of the Jewish dead. It was well intentioned. But a great many Germans, including some of the most liberal, felt that this legalistic approach was misguided and could prove counterproductive: it could provide a platform in the court for neo-Nazis and enable them to parade in public as martyrs deprived of free speech. After three years of debate, the law was finally passed in an amended form, its scope extended to protect victims of Soviet 'tyranny' (e.g. Silesian exiles, etc.) from similar slander. It was far from certain that this was the best solution.

Neo-Nazi activity today, insofar as it does exist, seems to be confined largely to the elderly and to the young – to those nostalgic for the past, and to young hotheads who never knew that past and are more often motivated by anti-Turk racism. The two elements are very different. On the one hand are the *NZ* readers and other ex-Nazis, including the associations of former SS: since they are war veterans like others, they are permitted to hold their regular reunions, and so they get together in beer-cellars or holiday resorts, where they sing the 'Horst Wessel' song and other Nazi favourites and talk over old times. Young Left-wingers come to demonstrate angrily outside the doors, demanding that the rallies be banned. But these old SS comrades today have no influence and will die out before long; many were forced to join the SS in their teens and were never really Nazi. It seems to me right that in a democracy they should be tolerated.

Far more malign are the small extreme-right groups composed mainly of men under 30, who in recent years have assaulted Turks and other foreigners and have even raided army garrisons – either to seize weapons, or because their xenophobia extends to a hatred of NATO. These groups are fairly similar to the extreme wings of the National Front in Britain or France: but because of the Nazi heritage they are less tolerated in Germany. They are illegal, and their cells are often raided by the police: one of their leaders, who had been training armed gangs of young Bavarians to fight Turks and Leftists, was recently imprisoned. Such groups are recruited mainly from the working class, and sometimes they will stir up soccer hooliganism, just as in Britain. Being of low mental calibre, they have made no impact in student circles. They remain a potential threat: but at present they are far too small and isolated to have any real influence.

The younger generation as a whole seems today to be fairly level-headed and well-informed about the Nazi period – far more than a generation ago. Since the mid-1960s the *Land* authorities have made concerted efforts to improve teaching in schools, and with some success. A number of good history textbooks and audio-visual series are available which present the facts in a clear and truthful if some-what unemotive manner, including details of the Final Solution. Much then depends on the interpretation given by the individual teacher and while of course this varies, the majority of them today do not shrink from depicting Nazism in its true colours. Some schools possibly err too much on the side of stressing the extenuating circum-stances: 'We try to explain the facts that led to Nazism,' I was told at one *Gymnasium* near Stuttgart, 'such as the harshness of the Ver-sailles Treaty, the faulty Weimar constitution and the impact of the Depression.' On the other hand, a number of schools have made excellent efforts to encourage pupils to do their own first-hand research into the period, by interviewing their own grandparents or writing to Jews in exile for details of what happened to the Jewish community in their town. This has yielded some remarkable results – and also reawakened some family tensions! Many schools also take senior pupils on compulsory visits to the concentration camps, nota-bly Dachau and Belsen: Dachau receives some 6,000 school groups each year.

The reaction of a German child when he first learns about these horrors, and compares them with the decent, peaceful Germany that he sees around him, is quite often one of sheer disbelief. 'It *can't* have happened – someone is lying to us,' he may say. Some sensitive children will shut their ears, or else have depressions or nightmares – 'Please can you stop telling my daughter about the Holocaust, it's making her ill,' one mother in Munich told her headmaster. How much children retain of what they are taught about Nazism in school is hard to assess. In 1976 a Kiel educationalist, Dieter Bossmann, organised a survey in 110 schools over Germany that was later published in a book and made the subject of a lengthy *Spiegel* article – and it caused a sensation. Of the 3,042 essays he received on the theme, 'What I have heard about Hilter', some pupils thought that he was an Italian, or a Communist, or had fought in the Thirty Years' War, or had made the first moon landing, or had survived the war to become a CDU deputy in the Bundestag; one contribution affirmed that he had called his opponents 'Nazis' and sent them all to the gas chambers. No one doubted that these answers were genuine. But were they *so* alarming? – the wiser experts soon pointed out that there is always a minority of youngsters who refuse to assimilate information not connected with their own lives, and that a similar survey in France or Britain would produce a handful of similar freak replies about de Gaulle or Churchill (recently I met an educated French girl of 20 who had never heard of Picasso, or *Carmen*, or the scandal over *Greenpeace* that so much involved her country). Other German surveys have in fact given a more reassuring picture; and my own impression, from talking to young people, is that nearly all of them know perfectly well what Nazism was like and what it did. The result is that, even today, a large number of them are not happy to be German (see p. 456). But of course there are others who try to put the whole subject out of their minds – 'Why should we be made to feel guilty for what happened all those years ago?' is a common attitude. Some of them even react against the surfeit of serious well-intended programmes and articles about Nazism in the media – 'Oh God, not bloody Hitler and the Jews *again*! – switch it off!'

For the Germans as a whole, the problem of coming to terms with the awful past is now quite largely a matter of time. It will all have fallen into place in another ten or 20 years, when the last of the guilty generation have died away. Yet the central dilemma will still remain: how to sublimate any personal guilt complex for events long past, without either whitewashing that past or evading a more general sense of collective historical responsibility. How far *is* a nation morally responsible for its history? – no one knows, not even the British when confronted with colonial Africa. At least in the past two decades the Germans seem to have to come some way towards digesting the legacy of Nazism without rejecting it – and they have done this with a much better grace than the Austrians, who even though Hitler came from their country have always tried to pretend that they were not to blame. Witness their election of Kurt Waldheim as their president in 1986, despite the strong evidence against him.

In Germany, reactions to the past are mixed. There are some who believe in sedulously keeping the memories alive, such as the ones who go on visits of penance to the concentration camps, now preserved as memorial parks: Dachau is the fourth most visited site in Germany, with one million visitors a year, and by no means all of them are foreign tourists or school groups. But there are many other Germans who feel that the past should not be raked up any more and that any survivors among the guilty should be left to die in peace. Take the case of Dr Aquilin Ullrich, an elderly gynaecologist living in Stuttgart, who in 1967 together with two colleagues was committed to trial on a charge of 'complicity in mass murder' for his part in the Nazis' euthanasia programme. The three doctors pleaded that they were just obeying orders, and thus got themselves acquitted. Then, much later, new evidence emerged (Ullrich was alleged to have carried out painful sterilisation experiments on Jewish women, without anaesthetics) and back they went on trial in 1986. But in Stuttgart the average reaction even among younger people was, in sum, 'The old boy has been such a kind and respected doctor in this town ever since: maybe he has had a change of heart, and he should not be prosecuted now, not at his age.' Ullrich was even able to produce letters in court from Stuttgart mothers who wrote that he dealt with their maternities so wonderfully and they just could not believe the charges against him. (This seems to me an example of the strange hiatus in Germany between public and private morality: if a man is your friend, or has done you a kind service, then you turn a blind eye to what he may have done to others – see p. 415). On the other hand, if it is a politician whose guilty past comes to light, then at least he can be pressured into resigning. This happened also in Stuttgart, in 1978, when Hans Filbinger, the prestigious prime minister of Baden-Württemberg, was revealed to have signed death sentences on teenage deserters in the last days of the war, when he was a naval judge under Dönitz. At first he denied it, but then he was proved to be lying: so under pressure from the media the CDU had no choice but to force him out. But he went on living in his official residence and was still respected by the local establishment.

However, there are some German leaders who have set the most honourable example to the nation in urging it to accept its collective guilt and never to forget. Foremost among them, along with Willi Brandt, is Filbinger's CDU colleague Richard von Weizsäcker, born in 1920, who just before the war studied law and history at Oxford, Grenoble and Göttingen and then spent six years in the Wehrmacht. Elected Federal President in 1984, he made an inspiring and courageous speech to the Bundestag on the 40th anniversary of the German surrender of May 8, 1945. It was, he said, 'a day that liberated all of us from the inhumanity and tyranny of the National-Socialist regime – the end of an aberration in German history.' He spoke of 'Germany's responsibility for the outbreak of the Second World War', and, after urging the nation to commemorate the six million murdered Jews, he added: 'The perpetration of this crime was in the hands of a few people . . . But every German was able to experience what his Jewish compatriots had to suffer . . . Who could remain unsuspecting after the burning of the synagogues . . . ? Whoever opened his eyes and ears and sought information could not fail to notice that Jews were being deported . . . There was, apart from the crime itself, the attempt by too many people including those of my generation, who were young and were not involved in planning the events and carrying them out, not to take note of what was happening . . . All of us, whether guilty or not, old or young, must accept the past. We are all affected by its consequences and liable for it . . . Anyone who closes his eyes to the past is blind to the present.

Whoever refuses to remember the inhumanity is prone to new risks of infection . . .'

Meanwhile, Chancellor Kohl was having rather more trouble with *his* May 8 anniversary. It is true that in 1984 he had gone honourably to Israel to deliver a *nostra culpa*: and at Belsen on April 21, 1985 he made a good speech, referring to Germany's 'never-ending shame' at the Nazi crimes. But then, typically, he bungled Bitburg. When he first invited Reagan to accompany him on a memorial visit on May 5 to the military cemetery at Bitburg, south of Bonn, he and his advisers did not know or at least, it is still not clear whether they knew – that some of the graves were of young SS men. And, when this became public and caused an outcry on both sides of the Atlantic, Kohl refused to cancel the visit or change the venue. Kohl was not born until 1930, and his entire attitude since taking office had been distinctly different from that of the older von Weizsäcker: he claimed that he represented a new generation of German leaders, no longer tainted by guilt, and that this made the time ripe for reconciliation and normalcy. In this spirit he went to Bitburg. But it was a serious political misjudgement. He had reckoned without the wrath of America's Jews, very many of them exiles from Germany.

Compared with the 550,000 Jews in pre-1933 Germany, today West Germany has only 28,000, and generally speaking they are well accepted and assimilated. Just after the war there was still widespread anti-semitism, for the Nazis had done their indoctrination thoroughly; and it took some years for this to wane, as the full truth about the Holocaust became more widely known. Meanwhile the German authorities had made some attempts at atonement: in addition to the reparations, 15 new synagogues were built with public money for the tiny new communities of Jews who had the courage to settle again in this land of horror. Today they are left in peace – even though, in Germany as elsewhere, so many of the new young radicals have become strongly anti-Israel and pro-Arab. But this is not the same as anti-semitic racism (which in Germany is punishable by law). The Jews today are so few in number that most Germans have probably never met one, and they are so well assimilated that it is not easy to identify them – as a Jewish woman teacher in Karlsruhe told me: 'My friends and colleagues are vaguely aware that I'm Jewish, but it doesn't seem to interest them at all. They are neither pro- nor anti-semitic.' A healthy development, it seems to me.

Dig deeper, and of course one finds that the German conscience is still troubled. Older people in particular do not like to be brought up against reminders of Jewishness. Once at a dinner-party in Bonn I sat next to a sophisticated baroness who talked to me eagerly and flirtatiously. I then happened to mention to the company at large that my mother had been Viennese Jewish. My neighbour froze, and would hardly speak to me again. I have often reflected on this incident. I doubt that she was being anti-semitic as such: more probably she felt, 'This chap will make me feel guilty, or will ask me what I think about the Jews, and that I don't want.' Sometimes, among the war-time generation, old resentments will suddenly flare to the surface, fuelled maybe by the feeling that many Jews have done too nicely out of the restitution benefits and are now again too rich. There was a strange incident in 1986 in a small town near Düsseldorf where the CDU mayor, Graf von Spee (a descendant of the Kaiser's admiral), was reported to have jested to a council meeting that 'a few rich Jews' should be killed off to balance the town's budget. He was then pressured into resigning, and he made a public apology for 'the damage done to German/Jewish reconciliation'. This shows how sensitive the subject still is. But feelings ran higher 20 years ago: in 1970, after Brandt's visit to Warsaw, *Der Spiegel* sponsored an opinion poll which gave 48 per cent of people thinking that his gesture of atonement at the ghetto had been 'overdone', while only 41 per cent thought it 'suitable'.

The confusions and contradictions that are still latent in German thinking about the Jews were vividly illustrated recently by the furore in Frankfurt over Fassbinder's allegedly 'anti-semitic' play, *Garbage, the City and Death*. Frankfurt before the war had a very powerful Jewish community, especially in banking (Rothschild, etc.). Just a few of these Jews have since returned, one of them being Ignaz Bubis, who moved into property speculation and was responsible for many of the new skyscrapers: his brash redevelopment of the city was much disliked, but publicly the criticisms were muted by reason of his being Jewish and thus in a sense immune. Fassbinder in 1975 then made this the theme of his play, which daringly broke the German post-1945 taboo on speaking ill of Jews (*The Merchant of Venice* had remained unperformed for many years). He portrayed a property tycoon who was cruel, sex-crazed, power-hungry and Jewish. And he portrayed too the private local reactions to this character: one ex-Nazi says, 'I could sleep better if this bloodsucker had been sent to the gas-chambers.' When the text of this typical Fassbinder provocation was made available, the outraged Frankfurt press called him a 'Left-wing Fascist', and the hue and cry was such that plans for staging the play were dropped. But Fassbinder said to me in 1976, 'I'm *not* anti-semitic – how could I be? I simply wanted to show a reality that exists in Frankfurt, where developers make use of Jews to do their dirty work for them, because they're above criticism. The play is anti-hypocrite. And isn't it high time in Germany, after all these years, that we should be able to admit that even a Jew can be bad? – just as in Britain it ought to be possible, though it seldom is, to portray Blacks as bad as well as good, without being accused of racism.' This seemed to me a fair argument. But Frankfurt's Jewish community did not see it that way. When in 1985, after Fassbinder's death, the civic Kammerspieltheater made another attempt to produce the play, local Jews stormed the stage at the first night. The director claimed that in its heightened way the work was trying to show that Nazi views were still alive in Frankfurt, and his supporters made its production an issue of free speech. But its opponents alleged that some passages could be exploited by anti-semites and in any case they were intolerable for Jews to hear on a German stage. Most Frankfurt politicians sided with this view. The play was taken off, and a year later this modern Shylock was still off stage.

This was no more than an isolated incident. Mostly, German/Jewish relations have settled down very well, and for some years at least 25 major cities – including Frankfurt – have been inviting former Jewish residents to pay return visits of one or two weeks as the guests of the council. This has been a success. So let me end my survey of the Nazi legacy on an upbeat note, by quoting from an article in the *Guardian* of June 26, 1985 by Joel de Haas, a former German Jew now living in England, who was one of a group of 70 invited back to their home town of Oldenburg, near Bremen. The visit, he wrote, was well organised by the town's Association for Christian/Jewish Cooperation which has no active Jewish members but has worked for years to keep the memory of the Jewish residents alive and to maintain the Jewish cemetery in prime condition. 'More than £100,000 was collected from the citizens to make our visit possible. Every effort was made to make us personally welcome, and we were privately entertained by individual Oldenburgers. All of us were invited to visit our former school. I addressed about 300 students at the Alte Gymnasium, and my theme song was that it is the duty of survivors to tell the tale of the Holocaust. One girl asked, "Do you hate us?" I told them, "No." It was a wonderful and heartwarming experience to meet democratic young Germans.

'Quite different was my meeting and address at the Rotary Club. There for the first time I met my contemporaries. I told them straight of our past experience and our abhorrence of recent German history. I added that in their case we are hardly able to forgive, never mind forget. The leaders of the community were rather distant, if perhaps slightly hostile. It did not help that I reminded them that Rotary in Germany, before it even became legally necessary under Hitler, asked its Jewish members to resign.' But later, at a Jewish cemetery, 'the school children were waiting to give each of us a white rose, the original sign of resistance to Hitler. We were told that they had organised this of their own accord.' Finally there was a Sabbath interdenominational service in a large and packed church: 'The Catholic and Protestant ministers gave sermons. Pastor Dierken said, "We have sinned, we have deserted our brethren in their hour of need. We stood apart in silence when you were persecuted, and mostly for having forgotten the teaching of the Jew, Jesus Christ, 'Love thy Neighbour'."'

Political strengths and community weaknesses

Have the Germans changed since those Nazi days? This artless but crucial question has been posed countless times since the war, and it would seem to me that the answer is clear. Democracy has taken root so firmly, and is so well safeguarded by the Constitution, that any return to a totalitarian regime would be hard to imagine. This at least is the most widely held view – and it is an optimism that I tend to share, though with a few reservations that relate more to the Germans' community sense than to politics in particular.

The success of democracy since 1945 appears especially remarkable when set in the context not only of the Nazi period but of Germany's entire past. As every history book points out, feudal domination persisted far longer than in most neighbouring countries, and even in the 19th-century parliamentary forms of government were still only embryonic. The regime created by Bismarck in the 1860s had institutionally some democratic features including a parliament. But in practice it was highly authoritarian, allowing little scope for popular self-government; and ordinary citizens, so long used to rule by princes, generals and bureaucrats, lacked the tradition or the experience for exerting their influence. Then Weimar in 1919 marked the first proper attempt to set up a fully democratic system in the Western sense. But this young republic had everything stacked against it. It had to deal with a terrible economic situation, caused in part by the harshness of the Versailles Treaty; its leaders were inexperienced; and it was hamstrung by certain weaknesses in its constitution. One of these was the kind of proportional representation used, which led to a pullulation of parties, more than 15 in all; and as economic unrest grew it was the extremist groups, Communist and National Socialist, that came to dominate. In 1932 the Nazis polled 37 per cent of the votes and emerged as the largest party. Hitler was then able to exploit a clause in the Weimar Constitution that permitted him to take emergency measures, and thus he seized power.

After 1945, as I noted at the start of this book, several factors enabled the new regime in Bonn to avoid repeating the errors of Weimar. One was the much more constructive policy of the Western Allies, another the sheer totality of the defeat which gave a stronger impetus for a complete new start. In addition, the new Republic's Constitution, the *Grundgesetz*, has proved far more effective than Weimar's.

[*403*]

It is a very liberal and well-balanced document that protects basic freedoms while allowing curbs to be placed on extremist parties, if necessary. One clause states that no amendments to the *Grundgesetz* can be made that would limit its guarantees of human rights or alter the country's democratic basis – and most experts believe that this would make it virtually impossible for an anti-democratic party to come to power legally, as the Nazis did. Backed by this security, and bolstered too by economic prosperity, German politics since the war have been able to show a high degree of stability. They have been helped by an intelligent system of semi-proportional representation, whereby half of the 496 seats for the Bundestag are decided on a single-member first-past-the-post basis as in Britain, while the other half (plus a few extra ones) are shared between the parties according to their overall voting strength in each *Land*. This system enables smaller parties to be much more fairly represented than in Britain (in the 1983 elections, for instance, the FDP with 7 per cent of the vote won 34 seats, whereas in Britain that same year the SPD/Liberal Alliance won 23 seats with 26 per cent of the vote): but, as any party needs to poll more than 5 per cent nationwide to gain any seats at all, there is some check on the kind of proliferation that was the ruin of Weimar. If one or more parties with extremist views did ever succeed in surmounting this barrier and then formed a bloc in the *Bundestag*, there could be dangers. Mercifully, this has not yet happened. The Rightist NPD in 1969 won only 4.3 per cent. The Greens (whom some might consider 'extreme' in their economic views) won 5.6 per cent of the votes and 28 seats in 1983: but this was not enough to prevent the Centre-Right coalition from securing an overall majority. In general, the PR system allied to the German voters' distaste for extremism has produced a succession of moderate centre-inclined governments, with the FDP sitting in the middle and somewhat opportunistically switching its allegiance so as to make coalitions possible. As a result the alterations of power between SPD-led and CDU/CSU-led governments have always passed off smoothly and democratically, alike on the federal level in 1969 and 1983 and in the *Länder* on various occasions. In 1966–9 in Bonn there was even a 'grand coalition' of all the major parties and it was quite successful.

The bitter lessons of the past have driven the great majority of Germans since the war to look for consensus in public affairs: this is reflected in the relative harmony of labour relations, and also in politics. Of course it is true that this outward avoidance of conflict does mask some very real differences of interest and of ideology; and in the past 20 years, with the rise of a more radical generation, the tensions have become all too apparent, in street demonstrations and in sectors such as the universities – but not nearly so much in parliamentary politics. Here, both at *Land* and federal level, the spirit of consensus has been much more marked than in France, or indeed than in Britain today, and this corresponds to a wide public desire for reason, prudence and the status quo. The SPD since 1959 has turned its back on Marxism and embraced the mixed market economy; the CDU and CSU, though they do contain some Thatcher-like elements, have generally lent their support to generous social welfare policies. Not only in the handling of the economy, but in foreign policy and at least till recently in defence, there has been a broad measure of agreement: as one example, Kohl actively continued the SPD's *Ostpolitik*, despite the initial CDU misgivings about it.

Journalists and politicians are continually analysing the merits and possible weaknesses of their democratic system and asking anxiously, 'Are we democratic enough?' To a foreigner it all seems a little self-conscious, but the reasons are understandable. The voting turn-out at federal elections runs consistently at between 87 and 91 per cent, one of the highest levels in the West; and the ever-useful Allensbach institute has produced some remarkable findings on popular attitudes to politics. According to these surveys, the numbers thinking that 'we need a parliament and deputies in Bonn and cannot manage without' rose from 69 to 83 per cent between 1956 and 1978 (even among the under-30s, the figures went up from 63 to 81 per cent in that period, despite the rise of an allegedly more sceptical generation). The percentage of people preferring a multi-party to a one-party system rose from 53 to 68 per cent between 1950 and 1978, while devotees of a one-party state dropped from 24 to 5 per cent. In 1978, the proportion thinking that the present German democracy is 'the best form of government' stood at 71 per cent, while only 11 per cent thought 'there is another that is better'. And, most curiously of all, the numbers thinking that the deputies in Bonn 'serve foremost the interests of the people' increased from 25 to 55 per cent between 1951 and 1978, while the answer 'they serve mainly personal, private interests' fell from 32 to 15 per cent, and 'mainly party interests' from 14 to 3 per cent. If these figures are to be taken literally, they show that, after the initial post-war period of pessimism, faith in democracy grew steadily.

But, since 1978, has this bright picture been sullied by a few Flicks of the corrupter's pen across his cheque-books (see below)? Possibly so. While the Constitution and the institutions of democracy are still respected, there is some evidence that the public has been losing confidence in those who animate them – the politicians. Another Allensbach survey of 1978, somewhat at variance with those quoted above, found that only 9 per cent of respondents felt that the country's 'most capable people' went into politics, whereas 55 per cent thought they tended to be in business or the universities. Certainly one hears plenty of laments today that the average calibre of politicians has been deteriorating – not so much in the *Länder* as in Bonn, where they tend to live out of touch with the real life of the nation. This is not only due to the well-known artificiality of Germany's little capital. Another harmful factor is that most federal politicians nowadays tend to be recruited from within the ranks of the parties' permanent staffs, which they will probably have joined at a young age. They are thus little more than apparatchiks, with scant experience of ordinary life.

There also appears to have been a disturbing decline recently in the public morality of politicians. In the Adenauer/Erhard era, and in that of Brandt and Schmidt, seldom did any whiff of corruption emanate from the higher ranks of the leadership: but this is no longer so, as the Flick affair has shown. Maybe one reason is that German democracy after 40 years is now so tried and solid that the leaders have become more prepared to take risks with it and less conscientious. However, let me emphasize that corruption is still largely confined to politicians and senior executives and it exists very little at the lower level of petty bureaucracy: this is not Italy, where so often an official expects his palm to be greased before he will sign a permit or grant other favours. And this probity is one of the great strengths of the traditional discipline and strict obedience in Germany's otherwise rather too overpowering civil service. But politics are a different matter. In Munich, there have been cases of property developers bribing local councillors to secure contracts; in one instance, Siemens managed to get one of its directors chosen as candidate for the city council, where once elected he was able to swing a big contract his firm's way, against competition from EMI. In Berlin and Frankfurt, too, there has been trouble. And even the SPD has not been immune. In 1982 Neue Heimat, the huge and prestigious property company owned by the DGB trade union federation, became the subject of a major scandal: it was revealed that some of its highest executives, SPD members, had been lining their own pockets with large sums channelled via 'phantom' holding companies, while some union leaders had used the same means to secure taxfree shelters. Albert Vietor, the firm's managing director, had to pay back 15 million DM. (Add odd epilogue to the affair came in 1986 when the DGB sold *Neue Heimat* to a big Berlin bakery firm).

The CDU and FDP were chortling to see the 'virtuous' Socialists so discomforted. But the laugh was soon on them, when in 1984 the long-simmering Flick crisis came to a head. This revolved around the issue of the funding of political parties. These in Germany receive some public subsidies for running their campaigns: but, in order to avoid the dangers of a 'bought' democracy, strict legal limits are set on the level of donations that they can receive from industry or similar sources. With party costs rising, it had become tempting to find ways of circumventing this rule. And reports began to filter out, via well-researched articles in *Der Spiegel* and elsewhere, that the Flick conglomerate, one of Europe's most powerful financial groups, had been secretly 'laundering' contributions to the parties via dubious charity foundations and other 'front' bodies, in return for tax concessions and other favours from ministers. Count Otto Lambsdorff of the FDP, at the time finance minister under Kohl, resisted these Press accusations for some months: but in June 1984 he resigned and in 1985 he went on trial, charged with having accepted some 140,000 DM for party coffers (not for his own pocket) in return for signing tax waivers of about 800 million DM on certain of Flick's investments. It was the first time since the war that an ex-minister had stood trial for corruption. And in October 1984 the president (speaker) of the Bundestag, the respected Rainer Barzel, also resigned, following allegations that in the 1970s he had received some 1.7 million DM from Flick as a reward for standing down as CDU chairman in favour of Kohl (Flick preferred Kohl to be the next CDU chancellor). The scandal spread, implicating Kohl himself who admitted to having taken cash from Flick in plain envelopes. The reports then began to incriminate the SPD too, leaving only the Greens in the clear – and at one point Franz-Josef Strauss blithely admitted that, yes, it was quite usual to receive funds for one's party in this under-the-counter way.

The Kohl Government soldiered on, refusing to resign despite these blows to its reputation. However, the much graver aspect of the Flick affair was the question of what effect it might have on the Germans' faith in parliamentary democracy – and this has been not so easy to estimate. Some commentators began to liken Germany to some 'banana republic' where politicians are in pawn to powerful business interests. This aspect has possibly been exaggerated, for there is little evidence that the Flick money had gone into private pockets. Even so, public morality has come under scrutiny as never before since the war. After all these scandals, Neue Heimat included, the public now seems to accept cynically that a degree of corruption in high places is part of the normal way of life – in this affluent society where money values count for so much. Ironically, maybe the rule of law itself is partly to blame. In Germany the laws and regulations are so heavy and complex that well-to-do people and businesses are continually searching for legal or semi-legal ways of bending them to their advantages, via tax-free shelters, front organisations and the like. And, if nepotism or other forms of influence are not formally illegal, then they tend to be accepted just a little too readily by a German conscience that reasons in legalistic rather than moral terms. And this leads us to a central dilemma of Germany today. Blind obedience led the Germans down a disastrous path, under Hitler. But if the opposite trend is now gaining ground – a questioning of authority, or a pragmatic bending of the rules – might not this also carry dangers, in a society that has little experience of this common-sense way of conducting its affairs?

*   *   *

'In Germany', so the old saying goes, 'everything is forbidden except what is specifically allowed. In Britain, everything is allowed except what is specifically forbidden. In France, everything is allowed, even what is forbidden. In the Soviet Union, everything is forbidden, even what is allowed.' Today, the Germans have been trying to shift away from their own model, towards the British one. But the move is not proving easy. And it carries some hazards.

The rule of law has a stronger tradition in Germany than in most Continental countries. And so does the rule of the judges who apply the law, and of the bureaucrats who have so long administered the whole system of state with impartial but coldly abstract authority. Even more than in France, laws and regulations have been seen as the best way of holding society together; and, much more than in France, submission to the law and to superiors has been seen as the citizen's most essential duty. The philosopher Immanuel Kant (1724–1804) wrote: 'The characteristics of a child must include, above all, obedience. This obedience may be obtained by force – then it is absolute; or by confidence – then it is voluntary. The latter is important, but the former is an absolute necessity because it prepares the child for adherence to the laws he will have to obey as a future citizen, whether he likes them or not.'

After 1945 it was seen that Hitler's lawyers had managed to exploit and distort the system, and so the rule of law was clarified and in many ways strengthened, in order to prevent a recurrence of such abuses. Hence the massive role given to the Constitutional Court in Karlsruhe, which interprets the *Grundgesetz* – usually very fairly and liberally – and adjudicates on all kinds of grievances and disputes, inter-governmental or between state and citizen. This works quite well. As democracy was still on probation after the war, the instinctive German reaction was to provide it with an explicit legal basis and to give the citizen directives on how to be democratic: so all kinds of laws were devised to guide and nurture the new society, like the wires that bind a growing sapling to its stake. It was all very well meant, and it reflected the old German utopian belief that a wisely regulated society can create universal happiness. Today, nearly all these German laws and rules are individually well intentioned: they aim to protect the citizens' rights from abuse by others, and it could be argued that in some cases they make for better justice than the laxer British system.[1] But, cumulatively, they can be very irksome.

---

[1] For example, a Hamburg lawyer once justified to me the German requirement that any change of domicile must at once be registered with the police: 'In Britain and America, the police do not keep a record of who lives where. This makes it harder for them to find adolescents who have run away from home, or to catch people charged with petty crimes who have failed to answer summonses, or ex-husbands who fail to pay child maintenance. If a German girl has a child by a GI, so long as he's here the US Army will see that he pays his maintenance. But once he's back home the police have no means of tracing him. Our system is more fair, and it makes crime harder'.

Rigidly applied, they can force the individual to choose between mindless obedience or a sly evasion of the regulations that leaves him feeling uneasy: between these extremes, ordinary common sense finds too little outlet. As Professor Nikolaus Lobkowicz, former president of Munich University, suggested to me: 'The excess of law leads to opposition or to apathy and frustration. It tends to make people disillusioned with the process of democracy, which could be dangerous; or it drives them into a French-style *Système D* attitude where they try to find ways of dodging the rules without being caught. And the Germans are psychologically unsuited to this. They are not Latins.'

There are by-laws and regulations in Germany for a thousand and one matters that in Britain would be left to the community common sense or individual goodwill. Some exist to answer the German craving for security. One of the best-known obliges a house-owner to keep the snow, ice and fallen leaves swept clear on the stretch of pavement in front of his property: if he fails to do so, and a passer-by slips and breaks a leg, he is responsible. Other laws are devised to fulfil the German passion for orderliness. The city of Hamburg recently had the good idea that street-numbers outside houses should be illuminated: so an elaborate by-law was passed, stipulating in the minutest detail how large each sign should be, how bright or dim, how high or low above the ground, and of what materials it could be made – German thoroughness run riot. Or a new law will aim to regulate the dissensions between different interest groups – for example in education, where the *Land* ministry decides in detail how each school should operate.

A torrent of ever more complex legislation keeps pouring from the ministries and parliaments in Bonn and in the *Länder*. One of its many victims, Mayor Rommel of Stuttgart, gave me his explanation: 'The trouble is that the bureaucrats and deputies have little else to do all day but prepare new laws. Many of them have a legal background, so it's their idea of fun. But it makes life hell for a city council. If I want to fight some red-tape decisions by a ministry, I can take it to court, but that will involve up to five year's delay, so it's usually simpler to give in. Politicians talk about the need to simplify the administration, but all they do is make it worse.' Nearly everyone today agrees that the nation's laws have become too cumbersome and omnipresent, but no one quite knows how to solve the problem. The CDU blames the SPD and its massive welfare legislation in 1970s. Both the CDU and FDP are pledged to reducing the number of laws, and they claim that in 1983–6 they did abolish or simplify more than 150 of them. They even introduced a Bill to reduce bureaucracy, the *Entbürokratisierungsgesetz* – a law against laws. What its impact will be is not yet clear.

The effect of these long centuries of legalism upon the national character has been, firstly, to make the Germans extremely litigious –

more so than any other people in Europe. And with post-war affluence this has increased, for they now have more money to spend on lawyers' fees. I have already quoted the case of a Berliner who sued a tennis-club next door – of which he himself was a member – because the ping of ball on racquet disturbed his repose. This is typical. If a neighbour is noisy or otherwise tiresome, he is more likely to receive a formal solicitor's letter than be remonstrated with informally. Plenty of matters do get settled before they actually reach court: but they still tend to be dealt with by lawyers rather than be argued out privately, as happens much more often in Britain. This may be something to do with the German trust in law; or, more probably, with the Germans' dislike of direct confrontation that one notices also in the formality of so much social contact.

Secondly, the legal instinct is so deeply ingrained that families, friends and neighbours will sometimes draw up their own private rules for their mutual conduct, for a written code of this kind makes them feel more secure. This can be seen in marriage. As in Britain, many couples ask their solicitor to help them devise a formal agreement on property and other rights, which can help to avoid wrangles in the event of their splitting up. But some couples, wed and unwed, go further: they draft and sign their own private treaty, which has no legal force but lays down clearly the day-to-day rights and duties of each partner. An architect aged 40, living with a girl of 22, told *Quick* magazine (September 26, 1985): 'Before we signed our document, we would constantly quarrel in the evening when the washing-up was still undone. Now it's clearly set out who does it when – and we have no more tiffs. It is also written down that we each have the right to go out on our own two evenings a week, with no questions asked.' Some couples sign treaties on the amount of sexual freedom they allow each other. It works like a charm.

A third effect of legalism is to make the Germans more inclined to follow the set rules than to do what is obviously most sensible, when confronted with some little problem. The cry is always, '*Sie müssen . . .*' In a sauna frequented by my wife in Stuttgart, there was a notice up, 'No bathing costumes', and if a newcomer put one on, the other women would say angrily, 'Can't you read? It's *verboten!*', whereas in Britain the appeal would probably be to reason: 'I think you'd find it nicer and healthier, dear, if you didn't wear it.' Similarly, in the most often-cited example, children at pedestrian crossings are taught to wait for a green light *because* that is the rule, rather than to use their common sense and look out for traffic. ('If reasons are given, how can you call it obedience?' said the well-known 19th-century pedagogue Lorenz Kellner.)

It follows that the Germans still tend to mind your own business for you, if they see you breaking the rules in however minor a way, for

[*410*]

this gives them a sense of unease. If you walk down the street with your shoelaces undone, in France or Britain no one will notice: in Germany, you will soon have it pointed out to you, and not just for your own safety's sake. *Ordnung muss sein*, in all ways. A German may perhaps break the law gently when no one can see him (e.g. tax evasion), but not if others are watching (e.g. at traffic lights), nor does he like to see others doing so. In Hamburg in 1976, early one Sunday morning, I stopped my car for three minutes opposite 'no parking' signs to read my map. There was little traffic about, on a six-lane urban ringway, and I was not causing the slightest obstruction. But the cars that passed hooted at me testily, and one of them stopped right behind me and blared its horn until I moved on.

This at least has been the traditional pattern of German attitudes. But over the past ten to 15 years it has begun to change under the impact of a new generation: please note that my Hamburg traffic incident was back in 1976, whereas in 1984–5 during ten months' driving around the country I encountered no other quite so irritating case of private officiousness, though I had been expecting some. The Germans are changing, I do believe, and so do others. The proportion of pedestrians who wait patiently for a green light at a crossing, when there is no oncoming traffic and no policeman in sight, is still much greater than in Britain or France, but it has been declining noticeably, especially among younger people: those who still obey the rule will often do so primarily to set a good example to children, rather than for the rule's own sake. In other words, the generations of 1968 and after are now beginning to use their common sense and to obey the spirit of the law rather than its every letter – and this seems positive. However, the general decline in law-abidingness does have its more negative side, as is seen in the spread of moonlighting and tax evasion (let alone petty crime), and this can be damaging to the moral fabric of society. So this is a central dilemma for the Germans today: how to become *less* legalistic but *more* morally responsible for each other.

Paradoxically, while bureaucratic legislation has increased, society as a whole has become much more permissive and just a little more tolerant – even in the rules that private citizens set for each other. This can be seen in flat leases. During the housing shortage of the postwar decades, landlords (never the most tolerant of breeds) would exploit their command of the situation by imposing draconian rules on tenants or sub-tenants. When my wife was a child in Munich in the early 1960s, living in rented rooms with her impoverished widowed mother, a refugee from Silesia, they were not allowed to flush the toilet at night, nor to smoke, nor play a musical instrument, nor open the window in cold weather. In those days even in self-contained flats it was commonly forbidden to have guests to stay overnight, to hold a party more than once a month or continuing later than 11 p.m., or to have children whose noise could be heard, and couples frequently had to give proof of being married before a lease would be granted. Even today, the rules against making a noise after 10 p.m., or against hanging up washing or other outward untidiness, are a good deal stricter than in Britain, and in some *Länder* they have the sanction of law. But in general the situation has become much more liberal – partly because housing is now so plentiful that a tyrannical or puritan landlord would not find tenants, and partly because social attitudes have changed.

There has also been an easing of relations between the authorities and the public: the average *Beamte* (petty official) or police officer (see p. 427) may still be at pains to enforce the rules, but unless provoked he is now much less likely to shout at people officiously in the way he used to do. His instructions are to be courteous. Politeness has even crept into some official notices. Outside the main hospital in Stuttgart I saw a picture of a dog with the words, *'Ich muss leider draussen bleiben'* (alas I must stay outside), whereas 20 years ago it would certainly have been simply *'Hunde verboten'*. Along with this goes a generally more relaxed public attitude to authority, less scared or servile than in the old days: this is no longer the Germany of heel-clicking or love of uniforms (see p. 447). The change is even reflected within official hierarchies. At a big public hospital in Munich, a senior doctor told me: 'I have worked a lot in America, and I would say that behind their façade of chummy first-names the Americans are much *more* authoritarian and hierarchy-conscious than we Germans now are. Staff relations used to be very rigid in this hospital, but they have changed. Yes, we still prefer to stick to surnames: but there is now a great deal of easy-going democracy among the staff, and some pressure from the middle ranks for group decision-taking, which can create difficulties.'

Many of these changes derive from the new ideas of the 1968 period, which in various ways have been taken up by a younger generation including the Greens. And this is now affecting school education. Many younger teachers bred of 1968 no longer try to inculcate the virtues of formal obedience (as Kant recommended), but instead they encourage their pupils to examine the meaning of the rules and to question the authorities – officials, professors, and their future employers. Some of them even cast doubt on all authority, including the police and the courts: this can provoke a backlash from parents, and much will then depend on the headmaster's attitude. In a broader sense, too, the new trends are leaning to a number of problems. In some schools, there are conflicts between young teachers and older ones, who want to stick to the old ethos. More important, because of the Germans' past and their psychology it is not proving so easy to instil a new kind of social responsibility that does not depend merely on keeping the law. In Britain, France or the United States, there exists a generalised patriotism that spills over into a moral feeling for community, so that a teacher can tell his pupils that it is 'British' or 'good for Britain' to behave in this or that way. In Germany, for obvious reasons, it is much harder to appeal to this kind of idealism; some teachers will refer to Christian values, but these too are now in some confusion owing to the conflicts within the Churches. So pedagogues have to look for an ethic that is based neither on patriotism, nor on obedience/legalism, nor merely on enlightened self-interest, but somehow on a warm sense of human responsibility to the community, and this does not come easily in Germany (especially with an education system that pays so little attention to practical civic training). Furthermore, the new approach to authority causes problems for the authorities themselves. When a young policeman sees pedestrians crossing on a red light (for which he could impose fines), he does not want to be unpleasantly officious: but his whole value-system is threatened if people no longer obey the rules, and he feels bewildered. Nearly all German authorities face this dilemma, in one form or another. How far can they safely permit the letter of the law to be flouted? Can they learn to be flexible?

The new questioning of authority has notably taken the form of trying to protect the citizen from the encroachments of computerised data-collecting. This is an issue in many countries today – and especially in Germany where memories of the Gestapo police files have made people wary of allowing the State or any other organisation to amass data banks that could be used against the individual. In 1983 the federal authorities prepared a new census: but in the ultra-thorough German manner they overloaded the forms with searching questions about sources of income, life-styles, and so on. There was a widespread outcry that this was an invasion of privacy, and some 300 'boycott' groups were formed. Fears were expressed that the data might be given to the police, or to local authorities hunting for tax dodgers or other social offenders, or that it might be made available for commercial purposes such as market surveys. Finally two bold women lawyers took the matter before the Consitutional Court which duly pronounced that, yes, the questions *were* excessive. So the census was postponed, and by 1986 no new questionnaire had yet been drawn up.

A few years previously, Parliament had passed the famous *Datenschutzgesetz* (law on protection of data) which aims to guarantee the secrecy of personal dossiers collected by public or private bodies, and to prevent their misuse. Not only police bureaux but also tax offices, insurance companies, hospitals and doctors' surgeries, all build up files of this kind, and so indeed do newspaper cutting liberaries. I have good relations with *Der Spiegel,* and I asked if I could consult their library for my research for this book (as I have done on many similar occasions in London and Paris). I was told politely that under the law only staff members had access to it. Luckily I knew a reporter there who was able to get photostats for me of the cuttings I needed. It was explained to me that such libraries are among the very few places that keep massive biographical files on all kinds of people; if an outsider was able to gain entry to them, the material could easily be misused for defamation or blackmail. The precaution seems eminently sensible. But it is characteristic that the Germans should feel the need to pass a law about it.

Authoritarianism may be on the wane: but I am not sure how far there has been any increase in citizen participation, that is, in the individual's continuing feeling of shared responsibility for the daily doings of government, local or federal. He is punctilious about going to the polls to choose his representatives (even local elections have an amazingly high 80 per cent turn-out): but, rather as in France, once he has chosen them he feels it is *their* business to get on with the job of government and he does not intervene. Only in rare cases does public pressure exert the same kind of regular constructive influence as in Britain. The *Beamte* is less aloof and feared than he used to be: but he is still one of 'them', while the citizen is 'us', as in the days when it used to be said that the average German believed that 'the state equals the officials'. In fact, the Allensbach multiple survey of 1978, quoted above, found only 29 per cent of people considering that they were able to influence the decisions of the federal government, while 48 per cent felt they were powerless. This pattern may have changed a little since the arrival of the Greens with their local citizen initiatives: but even Greens very often tire of trying to alter official policy and retreat into their own circles.

It is often the simplest incidents of daily life that are the most revealing of the lack of communal responsibility or even of neighbourly help. My wife reports: 'At my sauna/fitness-centre in Stuttgart if an elderly woman needed assistance or a mother wanted her child minded for a few moments, the other guests would expect the staff to do it all and would not lift one finger. At a similar centre near our home in Kensington, where I now go daily, everyone helps spontaneously without bothering the staff. This is typical of all areas of life, and it is one of the most striking differences I have noticed between the British and the Germans. In Germany, if you ask a person you do not know for a small favour, she is likely to reply indignantly, 'that's not my business – the officials are paid for that'. But this is not so much nastiness as a kind of timidity, a fear of improvising or stepping outside one's role.' And, if this is true of guests at a fitness-centre, what is it like at a much higher level of civic or political responsibility?

This trait may in part derive from the newness of the democratic tradition in Germany, or even from the Germans' problems with their national identity (see p. 456). It is certainly also a by-product of the education system which, as we have seen, concentrates on the child's mind and not on training his character or giving practical lessons in civics and leadership: but this is a chicken-and-egg situation, for a different society would presumably have devised another kind of education. Another related and highly relevant factor, also noted earlier in this book, is the contrast between the warmth of German private life and the stiffness and coolness of public life, and the curious hiatus between the public and private morality. An individual will feel affection, loyalty and moral obligation to his family and friends and others whom he knows and trusts: towards other fellow-citizens he feels little sense of concern, even if they are in trouble, and to the state and local authorities his sense of duty tends to be cold and rational, a matter of self-interest and of wanting to help preserve order. To schematise, this means that those he cares for personally he will defend, whether innocent or not; those he does not know he will leave to their fate. I can give two illustrations from instances previously referred to. One was that of the Stuttgart gynaecologist and alleged former Nazi, warmly supported by his doting female patients who did not seem to care about his black past. And the other, very different, was that of Böll's poor Katharina Blum – a fictional case but one that rings true. This innocent girl, cruelly victimised by the *Zeitung* and arraigned by the police, was most lovingly and loyally supported by her own small circle of friends, and at great cost to themselves, for they became victimised too. But her neighbours and the general public, most of them also decent people, simply accepted the *Zeitung's* line and joined in the persecution – *because they did not know her*. Böll's underlying message was that these good citizens were every bit as guilty as the gutter tabloid itself. It was a trenchant condemnation of an abiding flaw on the German social character.

Similar traits can be observed in German attitudes to the weak, the handicapped or the unsuccessful, in this competitive, success-geared society where failure carries a stigma and the frail or inadequate are sometimes shunned as though infectious. I quote again from my conversation with Hans Magnus Enzensberger: 'I think that the Germans have certainly become far more tolerant in accepting deviants such as homosexuals, punks or other rebels, who are considered a bit shocking but amusing and colourful and fairly innocuous: but once there is a price to be paid in terms of social responsibility for the weak, then the Germans as individuals remain much less tolerant and caring. I know of lots of little towns where people today will accept a gay bar, a porn-shop, maybe a mixed sauna or even a political cabaret making fun of the mayor and the bishop. But once it is proposed to open, say, a home for the handicapped, or for ex-drug-addicts, or for rehabilitating ex-prisoners, then they make a great fuss and say, "Oh no, we don't want that *here*." And this I find very unpleasant. Or let me give you another example. German popular comedy, unlike say Italian or Jewish, has no tradition of sympathising with the under-dog. In Italy, the most popular comedians are losers – there's this little man who's always getting hit on the head, he tries very hard but he can't get the girl or the job that he wants, he's a bit of a fool, a bit innocent, and the audience laugh at him but they also identify with him. In Germany, to identify with a loser is still very, very rare. Peo-ple don't want to know about the loser, or to admit to being a loser. And that's a problem today with unemployment – look at these men who lose their jobs and then go on pretending to leave for work each day because they don't want their friends and neighbours to learn the awful truth.'

It is not that officialdom itself neglects the weak: very far from it. Local authorities and the Churches lavish their funds and their kindly care upon excellent homes for the handicapped, among the best in Europe. But, just because the institutions do so much, the individual does not feel concerned; or, conversely, because individuals are so uncaring, the authorities must bear the full burden – it is the same old divide between public and private morality. Until quite recently, in the more pious rural areas, for parents to give birth, say, to a mongol or spastic was looked on as a kind of divine retribution for some sin they must have committed, and the hapless couple would try to avoid displaying their shameful progeny in public; these attitudes have now been modified, but even today, much more often than in Britain, a handicapped child tends to be put into an institution where he is kindly cared for, rather than live in society with his family, if it is possible. Rather as with Turkish immigrants (see p. 246), people seem to take the view, 'Now, the mongol who lives next door, *he's* awfully sweet, we know him well – but handicapped people as a whole, oh no!' And even today a blind or crippled person will not find it easy to get lodgings, unless he applies via the welfare authorities, who will then put him somewhere suitable. This national trait is more than a dislike of weakness, it is a real fear of weakness as something abnormal, offending against the German desire for order and perfec-tion. It reached its worst excesses under the Nazis' euthenasia policy, and it has still not entirely disappeared. In 1980 an elderly lady in Munich booked a package tour to a hotel in Greece, which she found to contain a big group of Swedish spastics. She was so angry at having her holiday 'ruined' that she sued the German travel firm: the court pronounced in her favour, and she got a big refund. Liberal papers such as *Die Zeit* and *Der Spiegel* were scandalised. All in all, it is hardly a happy picture. However, it must be stressed very strongly that attitudes are different among a younger generation that is less success-oriented and more caring. Young Greens and others will sometimes run day-nurseries where handicapped and normal children mix together; conscientious objectors frequently choose work in homes for the handicapped as their alternative to military service. This seems to me one of the most sympathetic features of the new wave of Greenish idealism; as this generation grows older possibly Germany may become a kindlier community.

Meanwhile, the curious blind spot in public moral attitudes can sometimes extend to political figures, when they fall foul of the law. Consider, for example, the shocking affair of Otto Wiesheu, who in 1983 was secretary-general of the CSU and one of Bavaria's most respected politicians. One October night of that year he was driving his Mercedes blind drunk down an *Autobahn* near Munich when he rammed a small, slow car driven by a Jew from Poland, and killed him. The police took blood tests and questioned witnesses, and charged Wiesheu with drunken driving. Instead of resigning on the spot, he clung to his job, claiming that he was not really so very drunk and that it was partly the Pole's fault. What is more, the CSU stood by him solidly: Strauss said publicly, 'He's a very good man, one of our best,' and, on Wiesheu's next visit to the *Landtag*, he was loudly cheered from the CSU benches. The general view in the party was, 'This is a matter for the courts to decide. Meanwhile, we stick by him in his hour of need.' Some months later in face of a mounting Press campaign against him, Wiesheu did resign: but then the party found another good job for him, as head of a research foundation. A year after the accident, the lumbering legal system produced a trial, where Wiesheu was found guilty. He appealed, and the following year was given a suspended 11-month sentence, while also settling the civil claim by giving 30,000 DM to the Pole's next-of-kin. I am not suggesting, and nor has anyone, that the courts and the police were other than fair, or in any way corrupt. But what an Englishman may find disturbing is, firstly, that Wiesheu did not resign at once, as I think he would have done in Britain: instead of accepting his clear moral guilt, he stuck to his legal rights of being innocent until proved guilty and behaved as if nothing had happened. Secondly, I was shocked by the way that the CSU backed him and that public opinion (with the honourable exception of some local papers) failed to get indignant. In this *macho* society, many CSU stalwarts privately took the view, 'Well, we all drink too much beer sometimes, don't we? That's inevitable. It was just bad luck on old Otto. Such a good chap, such a pity.' Some of them in their cups even murmured that the Polish Jew should not have been driving so slowly down the motorway in such an old car. And, when in 1985 I met Wiesheu's successor in the CSU post, he spoke of 'this terrible thing that happened to our dear colleague'. But what about what 'happened' to the Pole?

Wiesheu's reactions were not so different from those of Count Lambsdorff in the Flick affair, who also refused to resign when the scandal broke, and did so only after the media campaign had made his position impossible. This is the practice in German political life: when accused you try to sit it out and to avoid admitting responsibility. And this seems to me to touch on the weak point of society that depends more on law than on individual conscience. The system of law in Germany may be as fair, and as fairly applied, as anywhere: but it takes too much precedence, and in public life people tend to act by what is legally permitted rather than by what is morally right. Maybe at this point, having quoted Enzensberger of the moderate Left, I could now usefully cite Professor Wilhelm Hennis, of Freiburg, a leading political scientist of the moderate Right, who gave me this critique: 'Not only are the Germans too obsessed with demanding their legal and social rights, but there is a lack of moral idealism in German society. It may have something to do with the lack of patriotic feeling. Leaders of other countries are always making moral appeals to a national ethic. It is hard to imagine this in Germany, where a Kohl or a Schmidt will base their appeals on much more practical arguments, on mutual self-interest or sound financial management. Brandt was the last idealist. But he was too much of a romantic, so he failed.'

I seem to have painted rather a severe picture of some of the weaker points in the German public character. So are we to conclude that democracy in the new Germany is still a fragile plant? There are some observers who believe so. They ask whether economic success is not perhaps the only cohesive force holding society together, and they point to recent signs of a decline in consensus – in labour relations and bipartisan defence policy, and through the emergence of the Greens with their challenge in the whole industrial system. The Germans tend to worry about such matters. Being still an insecure people, they do not find it easy to live with democratic conflict, and by temperament they grow uneasy when things become at all unstable. Hence the over-reactions against left-wing terrorism in the 1970s (see p. 425) and the fears sometimes expressed that it might take only a medium-sized crisis for latent anti-democratic forces to be mobilised, as in the 1930s.

It may very well be that these anxieties are excessive. Despite the reservations I have voiced, there is plenty of evidence that the democratic process has now become firmly established in Germany, where political consensus still remains a good deal stronger than in Britain, France or Italy. And total consensus anyway is inconceivable and undesirable – how boring it would be! Over the past two decades, society has become more open and informal, more tolerant of diversity, and this may have been due partly to the ferment of 1968 – as Enzensberger, amongst others, suggested to me: 'For me, 1968 was the watershed. Before that, we were still in the old Germany – not Nazi Germany, but a far older tradition, very rigid, authoritarian and hierarchical, especially in education or in the relation of bosses to employees and seniors to juniors. This had become more and more anachronistic and disfunctional, sometimes to the point of black-and-white – as when Strauss tried to crack down on *Der Spiegel*. Then in 1968 we intellectuals took a leading role in trying to modify this structure, and we did have some influence. For us on the Left, it was both a victory and a defeat: we did not succeed at all in doing away with capitalism, but we did help to modernise society, towards more openness and participation. So Germany is a much easier place to live in than 20 years ago. But it's a porridge-like situation, very fluid and disparate, where the issues are no longer so clear-cut. And federalism, one surviving German tradition, suits the porridge very well.'

In this new and more flexible world, freedom of expression has increased, so the various tensions are now less suppressed and more out in the open – a healthy trend. In politics, the growth of tolerance is reflected in the way that marches and demonstrations, once considered so threatening, are now accepted as part of normal life; and the police (see p. 426) are finally learning how to deal with them sensibly without over-reacting. Of course the problem of extremist minorities still haunts and troubles the Germans, and Article 21 of the Constitution declares that 'parties which, by reason of their aims or the behaviour of their adherents, seek to impair or abolish the free democratic basic order' shall be unconstitutional if the court in Karlsruhe so decides. This is a right and proper safeguard, in view of Germany's past. But in practice it has rarely been felt necessary to invoke this clause. It was used to ban the German Communist Party in 1956. But in 1968 a new Party was founded, the DKP, that tactfully jettisoned its predecessor's formal objective of revolutionary overthrow of society; and this with its 40,000 members is today allowed to exist normally as in other Western countries. It has little influence, and no more than a handful of seats on local councils.

Popular support for extremist parties seems to have declined: according to Allensbach, backing for Communism is at 2 per cent, while the numbers of those saying they would 'welcome and support' a new Nazi party fell from 5 to 2 per cent between 1953 and 1972. It is true that there remains a strong ground-swell of popular feeling that parties of this kind ought to be banned: quoting

Allensbach again, in 1973 the numbers thinking that the DKP should be prohibited (39 per cent) were almost as great as those (43 per cent) who felt it should be allowed. Or, as one sceptic said to me, 'There are still plenty of diehards around who find the Constitution too liberal and cannot see the point of a democracy that is so permissive.' Fortunately however, governments and the Constitutional Court in recent decades have all wisely tended towards tolerating extremist parties and avoiding too indiscriminate a crackdown on terrorism that would impinge on the rights of oridinary people. As Bernard Levin wrote in an excellent article on Germany in *The Times* of October 4, 1985, 'It has come to be thought better, in a soundly-based democratic state, for anti-democratic organisations to be allowed to do their work in daylight rather than in the dark, where they may prove to be ultimately more dangerous . . . The Constitutional Court had shown itself to be very firm in its interpretation of the provisions under which a party may be banned; the upshot has been that even some of the vilest organisations have been left alone, provided they stay within the law.'

There is however one important exception to this pattern of watchful tolerance: the regulation that prevents extremists whose loyalty to the state is in doubt from being employed in the civil service or in other public posts such as teachers or railwaymen. This notorious and much-criticised *Radikalenerlass* (decree against extremism) was drawn up in 1972 by Chancellor Brandt and the *Land* prime ministers, with the aim of controlling the influence of the rebel student generation; and it has been widely applied, against Communists, the far Left and the far Right. Of course it is normal to expect loyalty from a civil servant, and indeed most democratic countries have ways of excluding undesirable elements from sensitive posts, notably those involving security; but they do so quite informally, with no reasons given. In Germany, characteristically, the problem has been tackled by legalistic decree – and this has caused difficulties, especially as the bureaucratic rules have not been suited to distinguishing between anti-democratic subversives and mere radical critics. So the measure has provoked rumbling allegations of 'McCarthyism'. Many teachers and scientists have been excluded. Recently a driver with the state railways, though not dismissed, was refused promotion and the status of *Beamte* because he was a known Communist; he appealed to the courts, but lost. However, the *Länder* in SPD hands have recently become more lax about applying the decree, and in 1985 Saarland became the first to abolish it formally (as it had the legal right to do): its interior minister declared that the measure had created an atmosphere of fear and intimidation and had damaged West Germany's reputation abroad. Some other *Länder* were expected to follow suit. In fact, today the view is spreading that

[420]

German democracy is secure enough to be able to relax a formal control that is not totally democratic.

So this brings us back to the initial question. Is an anti-democratic regime, whether fascist or extreme-left, conceivable today? – could a new Hitler ever come to power in Germany? Of course no categorical answer is possible. But Article 21 of the Constitution does provide stronger safeguards than Weimar enjoyed; and, more important, the Germans today are far more alert to any possible dangers. As I have tried to suggest, there may still be some traits in the German public personality and in legal and civic attitudes, that do not provide the firmest of bases for democracy: on the other hand, the institutions and the machinery of government have been working quite smoothly and are well accepted. It is true that the implications of the Flick affair are worrying, for if such practices were to become endemic, public faith in the democratic system could be undermined. It is true also that no really major crisis, economic or international, has yet arisen to test the solidity of the system. But some omens are favourable. After all, it was high unemployment above all else that fuelled the rise of Nazism, and in the 1960s many sceptics were predicting similar ugly tensions if the jobless total ever rose above a million or so: today the figure has been above 2 million for several years, and on the labour front there has been scarcely a murmur (fringe Leftist terrorism has quite other causes). It remains true that if the Western economy went into serious recession, or if some East/West crisis threatened peace in Europe, then the insecure and anxiety-prone Germans might react more violently and unpredictably than other NATO nations. This is hard to foresee.

In any event, much will depend on the new generations, those that have emerged since 1968. They appear to be more socially caring, more generous and informal than their elders: but they are also far more sceptical of Western industrial society and of its military defence. So are they to be regarded as a liability for the new German democracy, or as its brightest hope for the future?

The Greens and their values: fundamental social change, or just another youth protest?

The past 20 years have been marked by a number of successive waves of youth protest and revolt against the established order. First came the student uprisings of the late 1960s, exploited by revolutionary leaders and sometimes marked by violence. Amid sporadic disorders on the campuses this movement lurched on into the 1970s, when a fraction of it moved underground to fuel the extreme-left terrorism of the Baader-Meinhof gang. Then in the late 1970s a very different trend emerged, far wider in its appeal, less directly political though still anti-capitalist, and much more peaceful though sometimes infiltrated by fringe violence. It was oriented towards ecology, pacifism, social informality, new life-styles and new anti-materialist values, and it found its sharpest identification in the setting up of the Green party, as well as through 'alternative' ventures such as communes, squats and workshops, extending also to punks, hippies, oriental sects and much else in this motley scene.

All the movements have been essentially middle rather than working-class. And they have had simultaneous counterparts in other countries – for example, the Sorbonne riots of 1968, the Red Brigade terrorists in Italy, and the various environmental and alternative groups in Britain and America. But the German youth protests, the Greens especially, have on the whole been more determined, more widespread and more enduring than elsewhere, and above all more strident in their condemnation of the older generation and its values. Indeed there is plenty of evidence to suggest that the gap between the generations, alike in the late 1960s and today, has been wider in Germany then in other countries. One international survey in 1981 that put to under-25s the question, 'Do you have the same set of moral values as your parents?' found only 38 per cent of Germans answering 'yes', compared with 50 per cent of other Europeans and 77 per cent of young Americans.

What are the reasons for this sharper generational conflict? It has sometimes been put down to the Germans' utopianism, to their dislike of compromise and tendency towards excess – but this view runs somewhat counter to the general post-war pattern of a search for political compromise. A more likely explanation could be that younger people, especially in 1968 and also still today, have been reacting against the exceptional degree of conformism, formality and hierarchy in German society, and against the materialist ethos of parents who had rebuilt Germany after the war while rejecting all ideologies as 'dangerous'. The younger generation today can enjoy the fruits of their hard work: but they never shared in the triumphs and travails of the reconstruction, and they now prefer to concentrate on criticising its harmful effects on the environment and on human relations. They also feel themselves to be living in a society lacking in spiritual values. So the old German idealism, long buried since Nazism, has been coming back – for better or for worse. And thus, as the bourgeoisie in turn show a high degree of intolerance towards the new rebels, the contrast in Germany between two distinct sets of values and life-styles is much sharper than in most Western countries. It is far harder than in Britain to be somewhere in the middle, an easy-going and vaguely messy liberal but certainly not an *Alternativ*. You have to choose. If you hold the balance, each side will denounce you as belonging to the other.

[422]

There are other crucial questions to be explored. Do the new trends extend to the whole of the younger generation, or just parts of it? – and *which* generation? Among the very young, the under-22s, there are clear signs today of a return to more conservative values – how significant is this? Is the broad movement of the past ten years, epitomised by the Greens, just one more youth protest which its protagonists will slough off as they grow older and more settled? – or does it herald a more lasting and fundamental change in values and in society? As an American general said recently in Frankfurt (admittedly, in a different and more military context), 'The question is not so much, "how many Greens are there in Germany?" but "how Green are the Germans?"'

During the initial post-war decades, German youth behaved with its habitual obedience and docility. Then the student revolt came as a bolt from the blue, and it was the first of its kind in Europe. Like the French uprising which followed a few months later, it began as a movement against an outmoded university system and the heavy authoritarianism of senior teachers – and some parents too. It started fairly moderately with some sensible proposals for reform: but it was soon taken over by the political extremists. Some were the children of ex-Nazis and this lent a special moral ferocity to their rejection of society. West Berlin was the powder-keg, as one might expect: when the Shah of Iran paid a visit there in June, students demonstrated against him and the riot police then attacked them, injuring 47 and killing one with a revolver. This provoked a wider uprising, as students besieged the Axel Springer offices and staged campus sit-ins all over Germany. In April 1968 Rudi Dutschke, the best-known student leader though not the most extreme, was shot in the head by one right-wing fanatic (the resulting brain damage crippled him for life, and he died in 1979 aged only 39).

During 1968, rather as in France, the ideas of the reform movement spread outside the university world itself to embrace schools, hospitals, firms, public offices and other institutions, where pupils, nurses, clerks and other juniors began to demand 'participation' and a relaxation of the old rigid hierarchies. And to quite an extent they succeeded. The revolt did not prompt the same drastic official overhaul of the university system as in France: but it did reduce the tyrannical hold of professors, hospital directors and others, and generally throughout working life (as Enzensberger told me, see above) it ushered in a more democratic and informal climate – often amid a certain confusion. But it did *not* break capitalist society as the extremists had intended, and so it left them highly disillusioned. After the wider upheaval had subsided, they formed into little Leftist groups and continued their physical agitation in the universities (see p. 213).

Some of them created the so-called 'Red Cells', Communist-inspired, which in some places were still active in the mid-1980s, violent in nature but led by serious and dedicated intellectuals, now mostly in their forties. This was the unpleasant face of what has been dubbed 'German Left Fascism': these embittered activists were verbally as well as physically violent, and rather than try to convince people they would interrupt lectures and meetings with ferocious heckling and breathe hellfire on anyone who tried to debate with them reasonably. Their influence has never been great, and today it is minimal.

One small group, disavowed by most of the other new Leftists, resorted to brutal terrorism after 1968 – and they gave Germany a nasty fright. Their leaders, many of them women, were highly intelligent, educated and sensitive. Gudrun Esslin, the daughter of a Swabian pastor, was consumed with hate against a Church that she saw as the accomplice of capitalism. Ulrike Meinhof, a brilliant journalist and mother of two, was an uncompromising utopian crusader for equality and pacifism. Her lover, Andreas Baader, though a rougher personality, was nonetheless the son of a professor. So what was it that drove these young people, so disgusted with society, into a kind of romantic idealisation of violence as what they felt to be the only outlet left to them? It has never been clearly explained, though studies with such titles as *Hitler's Children*[1] have looked for clues in some atavistic irrational streak of visionary cruelty in the German psyche. In 1972, after a number of bomb attacks and bank robberies, the three main Baader-Meinhof leaders were arrested and later sentenced to life imprisonment. But this was by no means the end of the terrorism. In their wake a larger, more deadly and much more professional gang emerged, the *Rote Armee Fraktion*, and they stepped up the attacks. In all, between 1970 and 1978, the RAF, Baader-Meinhof and other groups between them killed 28 people, wounded 93, took 162 hostages, and seized 5.4 million DM in 35 bank robberies. In April 1977, after Meinhof's suicide in prison, terrorists took revenge by killing Siegfried Buback, the chief federal prosecutor. Two months later they murdered Jurgen Ponto, chairman of the huge Dresdner Bank: the chief accomplice, Susanne Albrecht, was the 19-year-old daughter of close friends of Ponto, and she coolly explained her motive – 'I'm tired of all this caviare guzzling.'

As the terrorist campaign developed, the public and politicans reacted with varying degrees of panic to what was seen as a threat to the very fabric of society. Armoured cars, sharpshooters and helicopters patrolled the centre of Bonn, where the *Bundestag* was encir-

[1] A book about Baader-Meinhof by an English author, Julia Becker (Michael Joseph, 1977).

cled with barbed-wire. Many wealthy and prominent families took similar precautions against the wave of shootings and kidnappings – as Heinrich Böll described with a touch of satire in his novel *The Safety Net* (*Fürsorgliche Belagerung*, Solicitous Siege, 1977), about a tycoon and his family who become the virtual prisoners of their own police guards, scarcely able to move out of their house. Böll was one of a number of liberals who felt that the Germans were reacting hysterically to a real but strictly limited crisis. But he was shouted down by the cohorts on the Right who began to demand sweeping measures against the terrorists and other known Leftists, of a kind that would have curtailed human rights and led to a *de facto* martial law. This was precisely the kind of breakdown of democracy that the rebels themselves were aiming to provoke. But, fortunately, the Schmidt Government wisely kept cool. Then in October 1977 came the ultra-sensational climax. The RAF had kidnapped the president of the employers' association, Hans-Martin Schleyer of Daimler-Benz, a tough campaigner who seemed to represent all that they most disliked about capitalism. It was a great coup. But when they offered to exchange Schleyer for the release of 20 of their own imprisoned members, including Baader and Esslin, Schmidt refused point blank. Then the RAF hijacked a Lufthansa jet on a holiday flight from Majorca, and forced it to fly via Rome and other places to Mogadishu, in Somalia, where they threatened to kill all on board if their demands were rejected. But a crack German anti-terrorist squad stormed the plane at night, killing three of four hijackers and saving the hostages. A few hours later, it was found that Baader, Esslin and a third ringleader had committed suicide in their prison at Stammheim, outside Stuttgart (whether they did this genuinely in despair at the RAF's failure, or whether they were somehow 'helped' by their guards, was never made clear). The RAF at once retaliated by murdering Schleyer and leaving his body in the boot of a car.

This melodrama was to mark a decisive turning-point in German radical protest. The terrorists' methods had by now disgusted all but a handful of their original sympathisers and from now on youthful campaigners turned away from ideological violence towards more peaceful causes, mostly environmental. By 1980 most of the leading RAF outlaws had been caught and imprisoned. But the gang's violence still continued spasmodically, sometimes taking the form of bank robberies to obtain funds, and sometimes that of kidnapping or even killing – as when, near Munich in 1985, they murdered another senior industrialist, Dr Ernst Zimmermann. The RAF and other German terror cells had by now linked up with a new Europe-wide network whose main targets were NATO installations and military chiefs. Today, this has so far had only limited success and the RAF seem to be a waning force. But posted up in police stations and other offices one continues to see crude snapshots of the most-wanted killers still at large – ghoulish young faces like some nightmare from the German past. Hitler's children, indeed.

It is worth looking briefly at the role of the German police. They have had very great difficulty in learning how to deal with student and other demonstrations, let alone with terrorism. And the many stormy scenes of the past 20 ears have inevitably cast a harsh public spotlight on their methods and behaviour – in a land where since Bismarck's day they have held a certain reputation for brutal authoritarianism. Today, their dilemma has been that of how to adapt to the gentler role required of them in a liberal democracy, while also facing up to modern violence. How have they managed?

At first they just did not know how to cope with the new phenomenon of student riots and they over-reacted, as was seen clearly when the Shah visited Berlin. These clumsy excesses played into the extremists' hands, morally speaking: they were able to claim, 'Look, this fascist society is after all as evil as we've always said!' Even when the less violent demos and sit-ins of the 1970s began (anti-nuclear, anti-motorway or pro-squat), the police still reacted uncertainly, and they were badly trained for this kind of work. Various battles took place, with assorted crowds of young protesters pitched against the lines of grim-faced riot police with their shields and visors. The most notorious sieges were those of the Brockdorf nuclear plant in the later 1970s (see p. 119) and of the Berlin squats (see below) and the Frankfurt airport extension, both in the early 1980s.

When it was decided to build a new runway for Germany's largest international airport, militant opposition came swiftly from various quarters – ecologists, claiming that forests would be pulled down and housing threatened; peacenicks (often the same people), furious that the enlargement would create added facilities for the US Air Force; and Leftists and anarchists of all kinds who eagerly jumped on the bandwagon thrilled at the prospect of a new crusade. Petitions and lawsuits caused several years' delay: but these ultimately failed in the courts, and in 1981 construction work began. So the protesters then took the law into their own hands: they set up a big camp on the site (a larger-scale Greenham Common), and they began massive daily demonstrations. Much of this activity was peaceful and legitimate (apart from a certain amount of arson, bombings, and tearing down of airport fences): but the ecologists were heavily infiltrated by veteran agitators from other German and foreign cities, who proceeded to provoke the police and to try to stir up fighting. Heavily outnumbered, and even hit by stones, the police on several occasions lost their tempers and charged the demonstrators, truncheons flailing. They were totally incapable of distinguishing between the peaceful and the violent elements, and thus a great many innocents were hurt. I met one young Green who was badly hit herself and also saw policemen beating up a girl of five and her parents. All this caused a great emotional outcry which filled the Frankfurt headlines for weeks – and it sharply polarised opinion, completely blurring the original issues of the runway itself. 'It was just not possible to take a fair dispassionate stance,' said a journalist I met on the liberal *Frankfurter Rundschau*; 'it was out of the question, for instance, to say that you were for the runway yet felt that the police had behaved disgracefully; or, conversely, that you were opposed to the runway but thought that the police had done their best under provocation. Tenable positions like that were treated with angry derision by both Left and Right. And, because they hated the Greens, the entire establishment here including the SPD swung their weight behind the police, so that its undoubted excesses were never examined publicly. It was shocking, shocking.' In 1985 Frankfurt conservatives I met, while admitting privately that the police had behaved badly, said they felt that even the most peaceful demonstrations of this kind should always be banned, for they were bound to be exploited cynically by the *provocateurs* and the police could not be expected to tell who was who.

In recent years there have been some other cases of the police rough-handling suspects or pulling their triggers at them a little too readily and then claiming it was self-defence. In Stuttgart in 1976, when searching for a terrorist, they burst into the flat of an innocent British consular employee, fired at him and killed him; in Munich on another occasion, a policeman saw a schoolboy climbing through the window of a youth-club at night and shot him, thinking he was a criminal on the run. Maybe such mistakes are inevitable from time to time, in a climate where the police are made nervous by so much terrorism. But, when a public inquiry is held, the courts seem to be too prepared to uphold the police claim to have been acting in 'putative self-defence'; and the police will never admit any responsibility or give details as to whether an individual officer has later been disciplined. However, such incidents have today grown rarer, now that terrorism has declined; and in the past five or ten years the police have also been making concerted efforts to improve their image with the public and to behave more discreetly. Though they can still over-react in face of violence, they have finally learned how to deal sensibly with the more peaceful kind of demonstration – 'In the Kaiser's day,' Manfred Rommel told me, 'the police were used like an army and would shoot people in the streets. Now they have become more tactful, and ordinary citizens are no longer nearly so afraid of them.' This is true. The police still carry arms, as is general on the Continent: but they now keep a much lower profile. Back in 1974, when three teenagers on the spree began to parade naked in a Stuttgart public swimming-pool, the police were summoned and 20 men arrived bristling with submachine guns to arrest the trio; ten years later, when a rather similar incident occurred, two officers came along with their revolvers well hidden and no arrests were made. This is a measure of the change. As a result, though the climate of mutual trust between police and public is still not as strong as in Britain, it has much improved and is certainly better than in France. The police are becoming more accepted – even by the Greens.

The 'Green' movement that began to emerge in the late 1970s has been widespread in its popularity and also extremely diversified both in its policy aims and in the nature of its support which includes quite a ragbag of differing elements. Though of course the Greens appeal more to younger than to older people, their hard core of strength has resided less in the very young than among an educated middle-class generation in its late twenties and thirties – many of them the former students of 1968 now trying to apply those ideals in other ways. They include those who founded the Green party in 1980: but the Green movement is far wider than this party, which is just the tip of the iceberg of a whole new wave of ideas, aspirations and life-styles.

The basic tenet of their ideology, common to all Greens, is ecological – a desire to conserve resources and protect the environment, a mistrust of modernism and especially of nuclear power, and a liking for a simpler and less materialistic way of life. With many Greens, all this takes a moderate and reasonable form. But some carry it much further, into a passionate hatred of all technology and a romantic yearning to return to some kind of agrarian society, coupled with vague pantheistic feelings about the purity of nature. Another dominant current is anti-militarist; and here again there is a difference between the reasoned anti-nuclear stance of the peace movement (see p. 449) and the minority of extreme pacifists who reject all forms of defence and want the Sermon on the Mount applied literally. In addition, the Greens have attracted a motley assortment of malcontents and single-issue devotees who have happily jumped onto the bandwagon to espouse their own particular cause; they include natural-food freaks, gay and lesbian liberationists, militant feminists, ex-Marxist deviants, doctrinaire anarchists and other political cranks, and even – to the embarrassment of real Greens – a few dotty racists who want to preserve 'aryan ecological purity'.

So why has the whole Green movement in Germany been stronger than its counterparts in most other Western countries? There are several clearly identifiable explanations. First, the peace campaign has been lent a special force by Germany's exposed front-line position in NATO and more especially by the residue of German war guilt and the revulsion against militarism. As for the strength of ecological feeling in Germany, one reason for it is that this is a thickly populated country, not only bursting with industry but so tidily decked out, with forests planted in neat rows and hardly a blade of grass out of place; and this has created a certain claustrophobia, a desire for a more natural kind of nature, of the sort so much commoner in France (and if the Greens are so much weaker in France, maybe it is because there is so much more wild greenery, and far more tradition too, and rural warmth, all providing outlets that the frustrated young German cannot find so easily – and so he turns to dreams of forging a very different utopia). Another factor is that the Green party at its birth was fuelled by a growing disillusion with the older political parties, especially as the SPD after ten years in power had seemed to many radicals to be siding too cosily with the capitalist establishment. But more important than this, as I noted earlier, was the reaction against what appeared as the excessive materialism and bourgeois con-formism of society – one Green activist, Carl Amery, has spoken of the need to 'recapture the German warmth' of pre-Nazi days; 'peo-ple,' he says, 'are so afraid of the cold rigidity of German society.' And this swing of the pendulum carries more than a hint, too, of old-style German romanticism. Very many commentators have noted this, drawing parallels with the famous *Jugendbewegung* of the 1980s, an idealistic youth movement that, though less politically influential than the Greens today, was also anti-industrial and inspired by romantic notions about nature and the simple life.

The Greens have been pursuing their objectives along three main channels – through practical 'alternative' activities such as communes, farms and workshops; through rallies, sit-ins, citizens' initiative groups and other local actions; and, with some misgivings, through parliamentary politics. Their first direct political break-through came in the Bremen elections of 1979, where for the first time their candidates overcame the 5 per cent barrier and entered a *Land-tag*. This was soon followed by similar successes in Baden-Württemberg, Hesse, Lower Saxony, Hamburg and Berlin, where in each case the Greens polled between 5 and 8 per cent, enough to make their presence felt; and in 1984 they entered the European Parliament, replacing the FDP as the third German party there. But their main sights were set on the *Bundestag*. Here they scored a disap-pointing 1.5 per cent in the 1980 elections, just after their party had been formed federally: but in March 1983 the figure rose to 5.6 per cent, and this brought them 28 deputies. Most were youngish and highly educated (several were professors) and more than a third were women. This assertive band set about shaking up the solemn world of the Bonn Parliament. They broke its unofficial dress code by enter-ing the chamber in an assorted garb of jeans and gym-shoes, T-shirts and woolly jerseys, and they plonked pot-plants on their desks. 'We are the anti-party party,' declared their best-known leader Petra Kelly. Though it raised a good many eyebrows, this behaviour appeared sympathetic to many millions of Germans, and so did some other of the Greens' more unusual practices: for example, both in Bonn and the *Länder* their deputies still regularly keep for themselves only about a third of their large state-paid salaries and expenses, and the rest they put into a special party fund, to be spend on Green causes. 'It's ideological,' explained a *Land* MP I met in Berlin; 'of my 5,000 DM monthly salary, I retain 2,000 DM which is roughly the wage of a skilled worker. It is all that I really need if I live simply.'

However, the Greens in politics soon began to fall victim to their own innate weaknesses and divergences. Their essential philosophy is libertarian, anti-authority, anti-discipline; and so it was inevitable that such an untidy coalition of people from different political back-grounds and with varying ideas should soon fall to bickering. Meetings became disorderly, mighty quarrels erupted in public. When I met a somewhat distraught Petra Kelly at the *Bundestag* in May 1985, she confessed her dismay: 'Yes, we are a very diverse party, very chaotic and amateurish. Everything is so disorganised, and we keep wasting our energy on things that should have been settled ages ago. I don't want to create a party like the SPD, God forbid – but some degree of discipline *is* essential.' Kelly was perturbed in particular by the way the Greens were applying one of their cardinal principles, enshrined in their policy manifesto: that of the 'rotation' of deputies and other elected officials. Under this system, every elected person is required to give up his or her post after a stated period time, usually two years, and make way for an understudy. The idea, well-intended in its way, is to allow as many people as possible to gain political experience, and to prevent the growth of elitism or authoritarian leadership. But of course there are drawbacks. It takes time to learn any political job, and to throw away that experience once it has been acquired is wasteful and inefficient – or so many Greens themselves have argued, including Kelly: 'Rotation has killed the dynamism of our parliamentary group,' she told me; 'I'm in favour of some rotation, but not every two years, which is far too quick.' Some other Green leaders, such as Otto Schily, have come to feel that all rotation should be abandoned. But that is not how the purists see it. And in March 1984 they staged a kind of *Putsch* against the six well-known leaders of the parliamentary group, including Kelly and Schily, ousting them as front-benchers and replacing them with six fairly obscure newcomers, all women and militantly feminist to boot.

Born in Bavaria in 1947 of a German mother and an ex-Polish father, Petra moved to America at the age of 13 when her divorced mother remarried an Irish-American army officer called Kelly. She became active in the American human rights movement, idolising Martin Luther King and Joan Baez, and then worked in Brussels with the EEC Commission which nurtured her loathing of bureaucracy. Back in Germany, the Green party provided the perfect outlet for her passionate, crusading nature. Small and frail-looking but vivacious and highly-strung, she sleeps only four hours a night and the zealous intensity of her working life has taken its toll, bringing her several times close to breakdown. She talks very fast nonstop in a manic sort of way, yet has a wonderful sweetness and naturalness of manner that has not been spoilt by fame; and she inspired warm affection even in those who most disagree with her views – in her office, I noticed a letter from the US Ambassador, 'My dear Petra, . . . Do take care of your health. Regards to Gert. Your good friend, Arthur Burns.' How I would love to have been a fly on the wall at their dinner-parties together. 'Gert' is Petra's intimate friend General Gert Bastian, a former *Bundeswehr* officer who joined the the Greens but then resigned from the party in 1984, disillusioned by their inefficiency and internal feuding, and by what he saw as too anti-American a bias in their peace campaigning. His departure was a bitter blow for Kelly. But she, like him, was angered by some Green excesses, as when, for example, one activist threw blood into the face of a US general.

The overriding policy divergence within the party has always been that between the so-called realists ('Realos') and the so-called fundamentalists ('Fundis'). The Realos, led by Otto Schily, believe that the Greens in order to pusue their objectives have no choice but to enter into the fray of parliamentary politics and to aim for a share of power, even if this means making compromises with a democratic system that they dislike. The Fundis, of whom Kelly is one, are afraid that such compromises might alienate the Greens from their principles and weaken their credibility. They have always been wary of forming a political party, and they reject the strategy of trying to reform society via what Rudi Dutschke called 'the long march through the institutions': they want to remain a pressure-group outside formal politics, working at the grassroots and gradually changing society at that level until the hated institutions of democracy somehow wither away. Perhaps it is not so surprising – especially as Green leaders now get used to being in politics and even acquire a taste for it! – that the Realos have steadily been gaining the upper hand over the Fundis. Even so, there are still heated debates as to whether or not the party should enter a ruling coalition with the SPD when it has the opportunity. This has been recently in Hesse, where in 1984 an SPD government with no working majority finally persuaded the hesitant Greens to give it their backing. This agreement broke down after a few months because the Greens refused to tolerate SPD plans to go ahead with a new nuclear power station. But then in December 1985 a desparate SPD made concessions on this issue, and the Greens for the first time formally joined a *Land* coalition, with Joschka Fischer, a prominent Realo, as minister for energy and the environment. The Fundis voiced their disapproval. But it seemed that it might be quite a watershed for the party as a whole, and in some minds it raised the possibility of a 'Red-Green coalition' in Bonn, should the SPD win the 1987 federal elections with no clear majority.

However, by the autumn of 1986 it was appearing uncertain whether the Greens would again muster the 5 per cent vote needed for them to remain in the *Bundestag* after those elections. Although the party did very well in the Bavarian elections of October 1986, raising its vote from 4.6 to 7.5 per cent and thus entering the *Landtag* for the first time, in four previous *Land* elections in 1985–6 it had fared disappointingly; there were some signs that it might have passed its peak politically, and some observers spoke of 'the greying of the Greens'. Probably the adverse publicity over its quarrels and uncertainties had alienated many voters; more important, the big established parties had been appropriating so many of its better ideas that it seemed to be losing some of its *raison d'être*. In fact, today this appears very clearly as the Greens' major contribution to Germany so far: they have greatly influenced the other parties and have forced them to take stock of several important issues hitherto neglected, notably ecological ones. As we have seen (p. 120), the Kohl Government and most *Land* governments have themselves turned a pale green by embarking on expensive environmental policies, under the pressure of public opinion led by the Greens. The SPD, especially since Chernobyl, has moved much closer to the Greens' position on nuclear power, while its left wing under Oscar Lafontaine is tending to side with them on missiles and disarmament (see p. 449). And other Green-sponsored causes such as data protection and local democracy have also been finding more favour with the older parties. The Greens' less realistic utopian ideas are still rejected by the mass of German politicians and public: but their saner ones are becoming common coinage. For Fundis and Realos alike, this is something of a moral victory: but, ironically, as a political force they may be losing out in the process.

On the more local level too, in towns and rural areas, the Greens' main political effect has been to act as a catalyst upon the older parties. They now have their representatives on many local councils, often in alliances with 'Alternative Lists' of other non-aligned anti-establishment radicals; and in some places they form part of the ruling majority. Their principal successes have tended to be conservationist. In Tübingen, for example, they torpedoed a project for an urban ringway; and in one north Bavarian town they persuaded the CSU-led council to drop a plan for tearing down some half-derelict

16th-century timbered houses and to renovate them instead. This is valuable, as far as it goes: but, when it comes to more innovative or constructive schemes, the Greens seem to be either short of valid ideas or else rather too fanciful and unrealistic – in a manner that irritates, rather than influences, the other parties. An SPD politician in Munich gave me a typical reaction: 'The Green councillors here produce a stream of verbose documents which they expect us to read; or they protract the council meetings with long discussions about matters they don't understand, like city administration. They waste our time fearfully. And they have useless romantic ideas about bringing back more streetcars to replace the Metro and car traffic. Some of them even want to abolish Munich airport, so that we'd all have to use Frankfurt. They're crazy.' That is one point of view: on the other hand, it could be argued that in some towns they have broken the cosy ententes between the older parties and forced a new appraisal of local needs. But the Greens' forte in local affairs lies not so much within the political arena as in extra-council activity – notably through their *Bürgerinitiativen* which proliferate everywhere. These are ad hoc citizen associations, again mainly environmentalist, which lobby local councils into improving waste disposal, building cycle paths, desisting from new road-building, sparing trees, and so on. A bearded art teacher in northern Bavaria gave me a picturesque example: 'A local property firm wanted to cut down a 150-year-old oak tree to make way for a new superstore. Twenty of us kept vigil by the tree for a fortnight, in a rota, day and night, and this so impressed opinion that the firm was persuaded to put the store elsewhere.'

It might be unfair to suggest, as some critics do, that the Greens are more concerned about trees than about people. Nonetheless, there do seem to be a number of curious lacunae and confusions in their policies. While their environmental blueprint is so clear, on social and welfare matters their official programme is remarkably vague; and at a local level, whereas they will campaign vociferously for purer air or recycled milk-bottles, they have relatively few ventures aimed at helping the weak and lonely, or promoting a warmer sense of community, and so on. As individuals, Greens and other 'alternatives' are certainly more caring and spontaneous than the other generation (as I noted earlier): but even they seem still to suffer a little from the German inhibition against transferring private warmth into public responsibility, as far as social relations are concerned. One explanation given to me by several Greens was, in effect, 'Officialdom does this kind of welfare action so well that we are hardly needed.' But this is no valid argument – and the real difficulty lies elsewhere. It is simply that the Green movement is still profoundly split, ideologically, between an active Marxist or ex-Marxist minority that wants more state involvement, i.e. more socialism, and a liberal majority that certainly favous social justice but is deeply suspicious of *étatisme* and prefers grass-roots democracy. The debate goes on, and is unresolved. So there is no clear social policy, and this seems to inhibit even the Greens' more informal local ventures.

Environmentalism however poses no such problems, and with many Greens it has become an obsession – perhaps a little too much so. Concern about asbestos walls, toxic fluids or over-use of water supplies is of course legitimate and valuable: but some crusaders seem to have become fixated on such matters to the neglect of other even more important aspects of life. Take for example the tree issue. Of course the sickness of Germany's own forests is extremely serious: but there are other less populated and polluted areas of the world, such as Canada or Scandinavia, where vast forests can easily be replanted, and in this respect an ordinary tree for use as paper or furniture is simply a replenishable practical commodity like wheat or flowers or livestock. It is not a sacred being to be preserved for its own sake (as might be true of some much-loved old oak or elm in a village square). And it could be argued that the recycling of paper, so much in favour with the Greens, uses up more resources (in terms of energy) than it saves. Yet in German schools the teachers tell their pupils to be as economical as possible with paper – 'Daddy,' one ten-year-old rebuked her journalist father, 'you shouldn't waste all that paper on your articles. One big sheet of it kills a tree, we're taught that in class.' Schoolteachers tend to be among the most assiduous of Greens, and they have been imbuing a whole new generation with their ideas – especially in the cities, for this nature-loving movement is essentially an urban phenomenon and few of its activists have real knowledge of the countryside. Some of the more ardent of them raise farmers' hackles (see p. 143) when they arrive with their missionary zeal to lecture them on how to sow organic crops or to return to the sublime purity of pre-industrial agriculture. And, though their anxiety for the forests is admirable, they sometimes have odd ways of showing it: tree-trunks in the Black Forest have even had notices pinned into them with rusty copper nails, 'The Trees are Dying!' Quite so.

The Greens have also been much criticised for their views on the economy and on industry. They believe that each individual should receive a basic income, whether or not he or she works. And their policy manifesto says, 'Large corporations should be split up into manageable units and administered democratically by the people who actually work there.' The more moderate Greens prefer that this should happen gradually and without revolution: 'To go back to an agrarian economy would be impossible,' Otto Schily told me; 'we cannot change industrial society completely, nor would we want to. We are not against modern technology: we simply want it humanised

[434]

and prevented from damaging the environment. Yes indeed, we favour the spread of small-scale "alternative" firms, but we don't say that the whole economy should be changed to this system.' However, there are plenty of romantics that would like Germany to go back to some semi-rural utopia full of little communes and workshops, with scarcely a tractor, car or aeroplane. How they must regret that Roosevelt spurned Morgenthau! And they trumpet their ideals so loudly, claiming to speak for all Greens, that they give this serious movement a greater reputation for silliness than it deserves.

In other ways, too, the Greens are often the prisoners of their own ethos of total democracy and freedom of speech for all minorities. Their doors are wide open to all sorts – not only the food freaks, bra-burners, machine-haters and other relatively harmless fanatics, but others more sinister whose vocal presence damages the party's cause. At one *Land* election campaign meeting in Düsseldorf in 1985, an ultra-libertarian Green group was able to propose the legalisation of all non-violent sexual relations between adults and children: this filled the headlines ('Greens Favour Child Sex!') and was certainly a factor behind the party's poor showing in the North-Rhine-Westphalia poll. Some extreme-right and anti-Turk elements have also infiltrated the party, claiming that racial purity is 'ecological' and that 'the Nazis were really the first Greens'; not only because of their racism but because they too preached the virtues of the simple rural life and opposed technology. Such maniacs are few, but enough to cause embarrassment.

Even mainstream Greens will very often overstate their case – especially the Fundis – by dogmatically denouncing all aspects of bourgeois society and arrogantly shouting down anyone who disagrees with them. This provokes a polarising chain-reaction, for the more the older bourgeoisie intolerantly opposes the Greens, the more their own dogmatism increases. Even many pleasant and decent citizens see the Greens as a threat – or they criticise them for their hypocrisy. 'They reject industrial civilisation while enjoying its benefits,' is a common complaint, and quite well justified, for indeed it is easy to find young people from well-to-do families who drive to anti-nuclear demos in smart cars and extol their anti-capitalist ideals while playing with their expensive hi-fi and videos. But not all Greens are like that. Many sincerely try to practise the 'alternative' life.

A great many Green sympathisers with ordinary jobs – as teachers or civil servants, or even in banks or factories – will pursue an 'ecological' life-style as far as they can. I have friends in Munich who travel right across the city to buy organically-grown vegetables at a cooperative, and who together with eight other families have formed a rota whereby they take it in turns to drive deep into the country to get their milk from a farmer whose cows receive only pure feed – 'not that dreadful imported American stuff'. Many families also making a point of buying only recycled paper, 'bio' cleaning materials, and milk in bottles not cartons; they bicycle everywhere, using their car rarely or maybe giving it up; and some of them fix solar heating panels on their roofs or wear hand-knitted clothes and home-made shoes.

Some others choose to opt out of a regular job within 'the system' and to join the so-called 'alternative economy'. This extremely diverse and haphazard phenomenon spreads far wider than the Green movement itself; it embraces many people who are not necessarily Green, just as only a small percentage of Green voters are actively part of it. In strictly economic terms its impact has been minimal, for it has impinged hardly at all on capitalist and official structures: but in other respects it is one of the most interesting developments in modern Germany.

Like so much else, it was born of 1968 – or rather, of a reaction against the failure of 1968. Just as in France, many of the rebels of those days have now made their peace with society and have settled down as respectable bourgeois parents with secure jobs. But others are continuing the struggle in a new form. Not only were they disgusted by the way that 1968's bright idealism degenerated into violence and terrorism, but they soon became aware of the futility of Dutschke's proposed 'long march', that is, of the plan to reform society by infiltrating the institutions of government and bodies such as the universities, the Churches and the media. This proved impossible. Not only did a strong and entrenched society resist very skilfully (through the *Radikalenerlass* and other means), but the rebels themselves were too weak and divided to make much headway. So a number of them gradually decided instead – and this was the crucial change – to turn their backs on the hated system and to build up their own little counter-society, through a range of small-scale practical ventures. This is the essence of the 'alternative economy'. Compared with the big dreams and endless theoretical discussions of 1968, it is all very concrete, modest, and private. At first it led to the communes (*Wohngemeinschaften*) of the 1970s: but, as in other countries, these experiments in group living rarely proved successful, for they led to too much bickering over personal property, sleeping-partners, washing-up rotas, and the like. Today a few communes do still exist: but most *Alternative* now live more individually, maybe on a house-sharing or flat-sharing basis. They include a number of 1968 veterans now in their late thirties or forties, as well as many younger drop-outs from middle-class society who had failed at their exams, or wanted to avoid the career rat-race, or were impelled by some kind of anti-bourgeois idealism. Their ranks have been swelled recently by rising unemployment.

Numerical estimates vary widely. Brigitte Sauzay in her rather starry-eyed portrait of the new German trends, *Le vertige allemand* (Orban, Paris, 1985), says that some 500,000 people work directly in the 90,000 projects of the alternative economy, while another six million sympathise with it or support it with their custom. These figures may well be excessive. Even so, the movement is said to be growing slowly. What these ventures have in common is that they are all very small, they are non-profit-geared, they are run as cooperatives whose members share out the revenue equally between them, they follow ecological principles, and as far as possible they all service and trade with each other in one vast closed-circuit relying on the outside world only for certain raw materials and for essential services such as telephone and electricity. A joint organisation called *Netzwerk*, based in Berlin, provides a certain coordination and helps to fund new projects. The scene includes publishing and printing houses, a daily newspaper (the *Tageszeitung* of Berlin), pubs and cafés, theatres and arts centres, shops and workshops of all kinds, organic farms, cooperatives of lawyers, architects, engineers, doctors, social workers and taxi-drivers, as well as infant schools run by mothers, and the *Frauenhäuser* for women in distress (see p. 166). So complete in fact is this network that in a big city it is possible to depend on it more or less completely, for all work and leisure needs, without dealing with the German mainstream except for paying taxes and utility bills. Of course the scene also includes a substantial fringe of zero-work freaks, drug addicts, psychopathic cases, and other less enviable dropouts. But largely it is a serious and even high-minded movement.

I myself am rather attracted to the concept of this kind of pioneering social enterprise – and therefore I only wish that I could report more enthusiastically on its results, at least as I observed them in a number of places and notably in Berlin, which is very much the central focus of Germany's alternative world. The city has traditionally been a magnet for every kind of outsider (see p. 59) and today its various free-lance activities include bakeries, potteries, weavers, an electrical workshop, and a farm for children with pigs, rabbits and horses in a former railway yard. The *Tageszeitung*, selling about 40,000 copies a day throughout Germany, is run as a cooperative, with all decisions taken collectively and all its staff drawing the same very modest salary. But if it possesses a headquarters it is Mehringhof, in Kreuzberg, known as 'the Alternative Rathaus'. This disused graphics factory was bought by a few pioneers for 2 million DM in 1979 and now it houses not only the offices of *Netzwerk* but some 30 cooperatives where about 200 people work. You enter through a gateway into one of those typical Berlin inner courtyards, enclosed by tall gloomy buildings. All has deliberately been kept shabby and derelict-looking, for that is part of the alternative ideology. Tattered posters, from this year or last year, advertise punk street-breakfasts, Turkish folklore fêtes, and the like. A few black-jacketed coxcombs sourly ask for a coin or a cigarette. Amongst much else, the buildings house a sort of cabaret, a bike shop, an adult education centre, an incredibly messy-looking kindergarten, a Turkish group, a shop run by feminists selling goods from Nicaragua, a big café where a rock band was practising lustily, and a publishing firm that produces the *Stattbuch*, a fat guide to the Berlin alternative scene. I was shown round by one of its editors, Ulf Mailänder, a Berlin philosophy graduate aged 30: 'I came here basically because I wanted to create my own work structure and not join an organisation. In our little firm we share equally all that we earn; and, as in many of the ventures here, we take it in turns to go 'unemployed' so that some of us can collect dole money and thus add to our funds. We are anti-marriage and against private property, but not too much so: I even own an old car which I share with others. Above all, we feel that we are doing something useful and practical, whereas 1968 was merely destructive. And our movement is growing steadily – over 100,000 now live and work 'alternatively' in Berlin. Even the local CDU rulers grudgingly approve of us – they admire our spirit of self-help which accords with their own ideals, and they see that we are helping to keep unemployment down.' (Shades of Norman Tebbit's 'let the jobless start their own firms'!)

For all my host's enthusiasm, I must confess that I found the ambience of Mehringhof somewhat dreary and apathetic – and the same was true of my visit to the UFA Fabrik, largest and best-known of Germany's still-surviving communes. This occupies the former UFA studios in Berlin's Tempelhof district, where *Metropolis, The Blue Angel* and other great movies were made, and then Goebbels' wartime propaganda films. The commune, previously existing in Kreuzberg, began squatting at UFA in 1979 and was then granted a contract by the city and allowed to stay. Sixty hippy characters now live there – 'we're a sort of kibbutz but less organised,' said one of them. In the barrack-like sheds, families have their own rooms but children aged over 3 sleep in dormitories. No one has an outside job; chores are shared; and the commune earns the money it needs by running a saddlery, a health-bread bakery, a cinema and a circus – 'So we're offering Berliners *panem et circenses*,' said one cultured inmate, 'plus a touch, too, of *pane, amore e fantasia*.' The circus itself is certainly full of *fantasia*: with its clever performing dogs it has become very well known and successful, and it travels all over Germany. 35 of the inmates make up the troupe, as jugglers, acrobats and musicians: and the performance I saw was lively and talented. But the commune as a whole gave off vibrations that I found oddly depressing. In true hippy style it was quite astoundingly filthy, untidy and run-down-looking – and this appeared to be more a matter of attitudes than lack of funds, for to clean and tidy costs almost nothing. The inhabitants, once out of their circus-ring, seemed listless and passive. I was given a conducted tour by their spokesman, Yupi, a gentle young man with long ginger hair who called me *du*: 'We have no particular ideology here,' he said, 'save a feeling that society needs more leisure and quiet. We have a very loose collective structure with no real leader-ship. But this does lead to a certain amount of chaos, so now we're evolving towards more discipline.' I did indeed come away with the feeling that a community of this kind, to be successful, needs either a charismatic leader or else an ideology or some spiritual base. Com-pared with the various religious communes I have visited, such as Findhorn in Scotland, or the wonderful l'Arche in Languedoc, the UFA venture struck me as lacking in some crucial ingredient. On the other hand, its members are freely being what they want to be, and they have chosen it that way.

UFA also runs a school, for five-to-13-year olds who come both from the commune itself and from outside. This is a prolongation of the *'Kinderläden'* (child-shop) movement of the late 1960s, when in various German cities a number of young radicals decided to take education into their own hands by opening small junior schools in former retail shops (hence the name) where they did much of the teaching themselves. It was an anti-authoritarian initiative, influ-enced by the ideas of A. S. Neill in Britain. In the 1970s the movement began to gather momentum in Berlin, where it was actually encou-raged by the very liberal-minded education ministry of the SPD-led city government, which officially recognised a number of the schools. But then things went badly – as I was told in 1985 by one kindly min-istry official: 'At first we were sympathetic. But when our inspectors visited the schools, they began to find that very little class work was being done. The parents and teachers were sitting around chatting and smoking, or they had gone off to a café, and the kids were play-ing on their own. Academically they learned very little, so when later they went into the State system they could not cope. Today almost all these schools have been closed. UFA's still provisionally recognised by us, but we are not too happy about it.'

There has been a happier ending, however, to another and far more notorious saga of alternative Berlin – that of the squatters. By the late 1970s some 30,000 flats in the city were lying empty, most of them in large older tenement buildings owned by private landlords or by property firms such as *Neue Heimat*. Rather than pay the cost of repairs, these owners frequently preferred to let the properties run right down to the point where they could obtain state subsidies for pulling them down and then replace them with far more profitable middle-class housing: and the SPD-led *Land* government cynically connived at this, for its policy of low fixed rents was such that no landlords could be expected to pay for proper repairs. In some cases, demolition was also made difficult by the presence of sitting tenants in one or two flats. But many of the students and *Alternative* flocking into Berlin had nowhere to live, or they were in bourgeois flats paying more rent than suited them. So a mass squat became an obvious temptation, alike materially and politically. By the time it had reached its peak in 1981, some 170 partly or wholly abandoned buildings were occupied, most of them big tenement blocks with scores of flats in each. The squatters were of various kinds. Some were middle-class youngsters wanting a cost-free escape from the parental nest. Some – to an extent the same ones – were eagerly seizing this opportunity for spectacular political protest against capitalism and its iniquitous accomplices. And a smaller minority, as in the case of the Frankfurt airport drama, were *provocateurs* from extreme-left or anarchist groups, who came in from West Germany and further afield (and even from the GDR too, under orders), all too ready to stir up violence.

The squatters claimed that they were not really acting illegally, for Berlin's constitution laid down that all housing, if not pulled down, should be kept in repair and made available for use – and thus it was the owners who were breaking the law. The city authorities at first wavered in face of this challenge. Then the CDU came to power in 1981 and under pressure from the landlords it ordered the police to start evictions. There followed a drama lasting several months that filled all the German headlines and many foreign ones too, as the Leftists seized their chance and led street demonstrations against police 'brutalities'. Repeated pitched battles took place in Kreuzberg and in the Ku'damm area, and one rioter was killed. As at Frankfurt airport, undoubtedly the police committed excesses and just as undoubtedly they were provoked. However, the city had meanwhile persuaded some owners to negotiate with the squatters for a legislation of their stay. This was quite a success, and finally about half of the intruders signed contracts, while the rest were evicted and the houses gradually pulled down. The squatters legally committed themselves to paying a nominal rent and to carrying out ad hoc improvements, which many of them did gladly – they set about repainting, re-wiring, re-plumbing, mending doors and windows, even re-roofing, and quite often the city helped to train them and to provide materials and expertise. It was an inspired and useful campaign of urban renewal. In 1985 I visited one big block in Kreuzberg whose young occupants had decorated the entire façade with a really lovely multi-coloured mural – 'It's a symbolic picture of liberation,' they said – 'look at the arrow pointing skywards.' Here in one renovated flat a group of students were living cheerfully and messily: it struck me as not especially 'alternative', more like a bohemian version of the kind of flat-sharing that is common in London even among Sloane Rangers. One gentle philosophy student, rather unpolitical, said, 'It's been a great moral victory; we've got the cheap housing that we need and we've proved that use *can* be made of these old buildings.' His flat-mate, much more militant, added, 'Yes, but it's no real victory. We failed to boot the CDU out of power as we'd hoped.' Probably the great majority of the original squatters were nearer to the first than the second of those two views: elsewhere in Berlin I met another Left-ist, an older man, who told me, 'During the battles against the police evictions, I tried hard to organise those young people to join the poli-tical cause and fight for their rights. But they were all so passive and apathetic, they seemed to have no ideas at all. I just could not communicate.'

In some other cities too, there have been squats and a few small ventures of the Mehringhof type. In rural areas, alternative activity more often takes the form of organic farming: the produce is sold to health-food stores, or direct to consumers' cooperatives formed by Greens and others. Some 1,500 farms are involved, 2 per cent of the German total and mostly very small ones. Their numbers have been growing recently, but the movement remains less widely developed than in some other countries such as Switzerland, Holland and Britain. This may seem strange, in view of the special strength of the Greens in Germany. Perhaps the problem is that, as one organic grower lamented to me, 'the Greens are so intellectual and dogmatic that the real farmers don't trust their ideas. And when they drop out from the cities and try to run their own little farms, it's usually a dis-aster.' Near Stuttgart I did however visit one professional operated and old-established enterprise, run on 'bio-dynamic' principles: this was the main farm of the Demeter movement, created in the 1920s by none other than Rudolf Steiner who was almost as interested in bio-dynamic agriculture as in education (see p. 210) and saw it as a key element in his antroposophical programme. Cereals and vegetables are sown and planted in relation to minerals in the ground and the positions of the moon and the stars. The results are claimed to be tastier and more nutritious than ordinary produce and to stay fresh longer: but as so much of the work has to be done by hand, and only at specific times, retail prices are up to 60 per cent higher. Perhaps this is why so many Demeter farms have failed since the war – though they have recently been given a new lease of life by the Greens' interest in them. I do not wish to scoff at scientific ideas that may be very sound: but it did seem to me that, in this domain, the great Steiner has been somewhat let down by his later apostles. In striking contrast to the splendid *Waldorfschulen*, the Demeter venture that I visited was most unimpressive – a draggle of dreamy cranks and apathetic hirelings, sitting around in unkempt greenhouses amid disorderly piles of mangy-looking carrots. More bio than dynamic, I felt.

Clearly it is not easy to pass any fair objective judgement on Germany's alternative scene and its economy. What future can it have? Why in practical terms has it not made more impact, when so many young people subscribe to its values? Has it anything to teach conventional society, and might the two ever move closer together? Ulf Mailänder of Mehringhof himself raised the pertinent question, 'Are we a safety-valve for established society, or a destabilising factor?' And I heard an unexpected answer to this from the president of the Berlin police, Klaus Hübner, the very man who had directed the squatter evictions: 'The alternative scene here is very peaceful now, and it's creating new structures which prevent the special crimes of our affluent society. This is because of its different attitude to property: no one wants to feather his nest at others' expense. So we have no police problems in Kreuzberg today. We all have to learn from this kind of social structure, made up of rich chaps who want to become poor. It cannot be the society of the future, but it can give impulses.'

There may well be truth in this. In all kinds of ways, the alternative world acts as a testing-ground for new ideas and thus influences society; and it provides valuable outlets for those who do not want to conform to the career rat-race. But it hardly constitutes any serious 'threat' to society (as some people believe), for even though it has been slowly expanding, in its present form it seems unlikely to grow so very much larger – as many of its more clear-eyed sympathisers (such as Schily) will frankly admit. Above all, so it seems to me, this is because it is the prisoner of its own ethos, which is *anti-success* in the world's terms, even while claiming to be practical and concrete. Being anti-profit, anti-hard work, and even anti-organisation, most of these little economic ventures find it hard to compete with bourgeois enterprises if they try to do so; and there are limits to which they can flourish and develop within the closed circuit. Equally, they reject on principle the kind of discipline that they probably need if they are to survive, and this applies also to the communes and other social or cultural projects. One young non-Green spoke to me of a youth centre he had joined near Stuttgart: 'It was splendid when it first started ten years ago, but it's now developed into a messy and worthless shambles. This is because it's been taken over by a lot of Green types who refuse any leadership or organisation and believe that all members should be free to do what they want. So I and my friends have left.' Examples of this kind can be found everywhere. Just as they reject bourgeois tidiness and swing to an opposite very un-German extreme, so on moral grounds the *Alternative* reject the usual German pattern of authority, self-discipline and methodical organisation. Without any of it at all, they can hardly succeed – but do they *want* to 'succeed'? Maybe, in their terms, their shambles *is* success, an ethical victory over other values. It is a dilemma that is still not resolved.

They are of course of many different kinds, these *Aussteiger*.[1] Some, probably the majority at the grassroots level, are very passive, gentle, umambitious, lacking in willpower, not so dogmatically ideological. Another far more energetic minority, attracting much publicity recently, are the so-called *'Spontis'*: these little groups are more existentialist or anarchist, and they believe in acting spontaneously, in going where the action is and having adventures. If there is a demo or strike or squat, or any other crusade, they will join in: but they reject all 'isms' and politics and are seldom violent. Thirdly, an important hardcore of Greens and other alternatives, few in number but influential, are very ideological, doctrinaire, intolerant and moralistic. Not only are they dogmatically anti-planning, anti-property, anti-American, anti-intellectual and pro-emotions, leisure and spontaneity, but they often have a Teutonic pessimism about the world, an apocalyptic doomsday philosophy – and this may help to explain their streak of wild and self-indulgent hedonism.

These are extreme examples of new currents in Germany today. But how far are they widespread or typical of a whole generation? More important than the Green party itself, or the alternative scene, seems to me the much broader emergence of new values and social attitudes among the post-1968 generation as a whole, in all classes. It is important to stress that many of these changes are quite moderate and non-revolutionary and they do not necessarily involve being an *Aussteiger*, or prophesying doom, or even voting Green or living the Green way. These changes have been noted repeatedly throughout this book, in different areas of life; and though they may contain some negative or disturbing aspects, they seem to me generally encouraging for the future of Germany – among them, the rejection by younger people of stiff social formality, the declining use of pompous titles, the greater individual concern for the weak and handicapped, the waning of hostility to children, the replacement of workaholism by a stronger emphasis on leisure and enjoyment (dangerous for Germany, if carried too far), the easier, more informal spirit in education (ditto), the questioning of authority (ditto) and the trend away from blind obedience towards more individual responsi-

[1] The term is less negative than the English 'drop-out' and applies to anyone who has taken some conscious decision to 'get out' (*aussteigen*) of conventional society. A worker at Mehringhof is an *Aussteiger* but not really a drop-out.

bility, the return to tradition and to *Heimat*, the fringe cultural scene, the street-festivals and other new informal community activities . . . Nearly everyone under about 40 is involved in these changes to some extent or another. And younger ones especially, in their late teens or twenties, appear as in other Western countries to be returning to private personal values and to be disregarding politics (again, possibly dangerous). This is the generation of what has been called 'the new tenderness' – gentle and caring, with each other and towards animals. And their search for private individual fulfilment can very often take the form not only of hedonism but of a quest for spiritual satisfaction. Hence the revival of interest in Christianity among young people, as well as the popularity in Germany of the various 'oriental' cults that have arrived via the United States. To the inevitable alarm of many parents and teachers, Hare Krishna, Scientology, the Moonies and other sects have all held a certain appeal for young Germans wanting warmth and certainty and finding a spiritual emptiness in modern society.

The Baghwan Rajneesh movement was proportionately stronger in Germany than anywhere else, even in the United States and India, in the period before September 1985 when the bearded guru was finally expelled from his Oregon headquarters and his ashrams around the globe were disbanded. In those days, in Cologne, Hamburg, Berlin and other cities, smiling sanyassin in their pink, red and purple clothes ran shops, cafés and discothèques open to the public – all exceedingly clean, bright and business-like, in striking contrast to most of the rest of the alternative scene. Why the special appeal of the Baghwan to young Germans? Some critics felt that it reflected a typically German love of a charismatic leader and father-figure whose word should be obeyed implicitly. But more probably these young middle-class people were involved in an equally Germanic search for the absolute, and in this very international movement they felt able to escape from soured German nationalism and find a new identity – at the Cologne ashram in 1984 I met a brilliant sanyassin aged 43 who told me, 'My father had been a Nazi, and I was haunted by guilt about the German past and a longing for a way out. So as a young man I went to Cambridge and became a don at St John's College. But this attempt to turn myself into an Englishman did not really work. Then I came across Rajnesshism, and ever since then I have this beautiful love-affair with Baghwan and my problem is solved.' Unfortunately, I have not re-met Nirvano since the Oregon débâcle, to ask him what he now feels. Even so, I remain less blatantly scornful of this particular cult than most people, for I have a special interest which I should declare: my own son by my first marriage was with Baghwan for four years in Oregon and Poona, and through him I observed the good side of the movement and how it helped him to a far greater spiritual maturity and self-confidence.

In my own view, there have been other far more negative aspects to the youth revolt and the quest for new values or forms of escape. Like other Western countries, Germany has its share of punks and skinheads, and of young drug-addicts. The drug scene is worst in Frankfurt and Berlin, where it has thrown up a number of sensational case-histories, most notably that of one young girl, *Christiane F.*, as told in a best-selling book and film of the 1970s. She recounted how her loveless home background and her search for tenderness led her to enter a clique where she took marijuana, and then heroin, and then to pay for it she turned to prostitution and by the age of 15 was earning up to 4,000 DM a month. Much publicity has also been given to the problem of youth suicides: though the rate for the Federal Republic is not much above the Western average, in Berlin it is said to be the highest in the world. In 1985, four 16-year-olds in Aachen formed a suicide pact and tried to kill themselves with car exhaust: three of them succeeded and the fourth, who survived, said he would soon try again. Their motive was that they were all without jobs and they saw no future in life.

Incidents of this kind have lent some support to the view, much canvassed in the media, that the younger generation as a whole is riddled with *Angst*, insecurity and nihilism. Probably this has been much exaggerated. It is true that in the early 1980s there did appear to be a sudden new wave of pessimism: it was fuelled by rising unemployment and fears of the impending installation of missiles, and it was nourished as well by older anxieties about the difficulty of being German and by the feeling of being trapped both by geography and by the past. All of this was much analysed by the Press and in radio and TV debates. But it was also pointed out that for centuries the Germans have been more prone to *Angst* than most peoples. It is nothing new. It informs much of their literature, even the Grimms' fairy tales, and amongst artists and intellectuals it has long been a kind of fashion, even a token of respectability. Not to worry and be gloomy is not to be taken seriously as a thinker. But how far is German youth really coloured by this today? My own impression, and that of many others, is that German fears tend to go in mysterious cycles of obsession, and that in 1984 the wave of *Angst* subsided quite considerably, after the missiles debate had been and gone and people had come to terms with the situation. During my own months in Germany in 1984–5, even amongst young people I found much less talk of *Angst* and 'No future' than I had expected. And one father with children aged 18 and 20 suggested to me: 'Even today, it may still be a fashion among young people to display a certain pessimism and dislike of society, when talking with each other. But if you speak with them privately and individually, they are often much more positive and serene. It's just that they daren't show this side to their peer group, for if they seem to betray the youth cult of rejection, then they lose face.'

There are signs today that this new trend back towards acceptance of society goes much further still. Nearly all the observers of the youth scene – parents, educators, social scientists and others – seem to agree that the new rising generation now in its late teens or early twenties is much more conservative and less anti-materialistic than its immediate predecessors. So the pendulum may be swinging back. Some outward signs are that very young people are manifesting more concern for private possessions, they are again dressing more elegantly and they show an aesthetic feeling for nice clothes; instead of straggly long hair they have neat hair-cuts; and they prefer smart, bright cafés to bohemian dives. More important, they are again becoming more career-minded, more keen on making money and a little readier to work hard for it, and they admire achievement and individual performance – their emulated prototype, you could say, is the very young Boris Becker, just as Petra Kelly was that of an earlier generation. 'We too, as in 1968, are in revolt against our teachers,' said one 17-year-old *Gymnasium* pupil, 'but the other way round, for *they* are now the Leftist ones. They come to school in beards, sandals and woolly jerseys, so *we* turn up in smart clothes and we reject their propaganda.' Or as an American diplomat told me how he saw the situation, from *his* particular slant: 'The worst of the Green wave may be over, so I'm fairly optimistic. The young are again healthily con-sumerist and less anti-American. They even seem to admire JR in *Dallas*.'

It is far too soon to tell the real significance of this new trend. Many of these young people, especially the ones from richer homes, are clearly being self-centred, opportunistic, even snobbish. They know about the failure of earlier protest movements to refashion society – and so they are readier to accept the established order and get what they can out of it. But others, the more altruistic, are seeking to apply the lessons of Green and radical excesses by pursuing the path of change in a more moderate and realistic way: instead of totally oppos-ing modernism, they try to give it a more human dimension. In any case, there has been no complete return to the old values by the new generation. Neat clothes and careerism may again be 'in': but the new informality, the new gentleness, the new questioning of hierarchy and authority, these remain. And so it is hard to answer what is perhaps the most important question: has the entire Green and alter-native movement been just one more youth protest that will later fade away, or does it symptomise fundamental and permanent change in German society and values? Probably a bit of both. The least attractive aspect of the more militant Greens and other rebels is that too often they have spoilt their own cause through dogmatism, absolutism, refusal to compromise, intolerance of opposition, and other forms of Germanic excess, and this has prompted the question: the Greens may talk of radical change, but are they not simply perpetuating certain less pleasant German traits in a new guise? But these activists are not typical of German youth as a whole, which for the most part is more gentle and reasonable and has quietly been pursuing its own 'long march' through social values. The Greens and the 'alternative' minority have made an interesting contribution. But much wider than this is the tentative groping of young Germany towards a more tolerant, caring and informal society – and about this I am cautiously optimistic for the long term, even if Germans have not yet fully resolved the problem of their national identity and of Germany's place in the world.

Germany and the world: how crucial is national identity?

The Germans' view of their role in the world is bound up inevitably with the issue of defence. Few people doubt that historically and culturally Germany belongs to the West: but should she also be part of NATO? Is it right for a country with such a warmongering record to be a member of any military alliance? Should she not become neutral, like Austria or Sweden? Such views are today voiced quite widely, more often by the Germans themselves than by their allies.

A neutralist trend, even a pacifist one, certainly exists in Germany today: but it was much stronger 30 years ago. When Adenauer in 1954–5 brought Germany into NATO and agreed with his Western allies to create a new German army, the *Bundeswehr*, he was greeted by a great wave of anti-militarism. It came not only from the SPD, the trade unions and a large part of the Protestant Church, but from sections of his own party and from much of German youth. These feelings were understandable, and morally speaking they were laudable – though in practical terms it might have been disastrous if they had proved strong enough to force Adenauer to change his plans. As it was, the *Bundeswehr* was gradually built up and today it is the largest European army in NATO: the German armed forces comprise some 500,000 men.

Anti-militarist thinking has left its impact however upon the style and the spirit of these forces. From the outset the Government agreed that the *Bundeswehr* should be a 'citizens' army', shorn of all goose-stepping and even of heel-clicking, based on persuasion and discussion rather than unthinking obedience, and closely integrated into society. Conscription was retained, partly because it is an old German tradition but also for more important reasons – it was feared that a purely professional army would never attract enough recruits, and that if it grew powerful it might become politically dangerous. Conscripts today serve 15 months (about to be increased to 18) and at any one time there are 220,000 of them, nearly half the total under arms. This is much less than the full strength of the age-group: many young men are granted exemption for health, study or family reasons, while each year some 60,000 conscientious objectors are allowed to do an *Ersatzdienst*, usually in the form of heavy physical work in hospital or homes for the handicapped.

As far as is possible, conscripts do their service near to their own homeland, rather than be sent to some far corner of Germany. The aim of this policy is to give them the sense that they are defending their own homes and families – an important factor in a country where local feeling is often much stronger than national patriotism. In one battalion that I visited near the Czech frontier, most of the recruits were from northern Bavaria. It follows that nearly all of them go back to their families at weekends, and quite a number even commute daily from their homes: so, apart from the much longer hours, in some ways it is not so different from doing an office or factory job. This in fact is a rather sedentary modern army without much sense of adventure: as Germany has no overseas commitments and only just a few troops stationed in other NATO countries, for conscripts and regular soldiers alike there are not the outlets for service abroad, that the Americans or French can find, and this makes for a certain dullness. The conscripts I talked to were not hating their months under the colours, but they did not seem to be getting much real satisfaction from them. In many ways their life is made easy. If a soldier of any rank has a complaint of any kind, he can take it to a senior officer; and if that does not satisfy him, he can appeal to a kind of federal Ombudsman that deals with such cases. If a soldier commits a crime, he is tried by a civil court, for there are no more courts martial. This is all very decent and democratic, and it works well: but there are no legal provisions for any change in this system in time of war, to deal for example with mutineers or deserters, and several officers told me they were worried about what effect this might have on battle discipline – especially as so many young Germans today claim that they would not be prepared to fight for their country.

Relations between officers and NCOs, or between NCOs and other ranks, are today noticeably more informal and free-and-easy than in the British army, and salutes are just casual little gestures – so unlike the old *Wehrmacht* days. Some senior officers told me that, while they felt the change was necessary, they wondered if it had not gone too far. I spent two days on field exercises with a division in Bavaria, and was more impressed by the conviviality than the efficiency. When I checked in with military punctuality at its HQ in Regensburg, the officer due to receive me was not there and no one knew where he was, and I was kept hanging around for an hour while amiable corporals joked and smoked cigarettes in the corridors. The next day, the general gave me an appointment for 4.0 p.m. which I was later told was cancelled. At 4.30 he rang up the major I was with to ask where the hell I was – there had never been any cancellation. 'Sorry, old chap,' said the major in a Yankee drawl, 'we seem to have fouled this up along the line somewhere.' In a sense it came as a relief, in this relentlessly efficient Germany to find at last a little corner of inefficiency – though not in the most suspicious or likely area. Perhaps these were untypical incidents, for the *Bundeswehr* as a whole has the reputation of being not only the best-equipped NATO force in Europe but one of the most effective. Despite the influence of the peace movement and other such trends, it is generally popular with Germans; and there were remarkably few murmurs of objection when in 1985 the Government decided to increase military service from 15 to 18 months, as from 1989, in order to make up for the impending lack of recruits caused by the decline in the birthrate.

Organised opposition to the *Bundeswehr* comes mainly from the peace movement, and it was inflamed in 1983 by the decision to allow the installation of American Cruise and Pershing II missiles on German soil, for the peace crusaders see the German army as the accomplices of American aggressive interests in Europe. The writer Günter Grass gave vent to this feeling in a speech in November 1983, at the height of the missiles debate: 'With the decision to station these missiles in Germany, the *Bundeswehr* has become an offensive instrument, instead of a defensive one as laid down in the Constitution. Therefore it is the duty of every young citizen who believes in the Constitution to refuse military service.' Allensbach then conducted an opinion survey, which found 22 per cent saying that they agreed with Grass and 58 per cent disagreeing, while the rest had no opinion. Among the 16 to 29-year-olds, 47 per cent disagreed while an important minority of 35 per cent felt that he was right.

This gives some idea of the influence of the peace movement, which is stronger in Germany than in most Western countries and is backed not only by the Greens but a great many Socialists, trade unionists and Church leaders. One of their main arguments is that Germany, being in the front line, is in danger of becoming a Russian–American nuclear battlefield in the case of war: and that, as both Germanies are forbidden under the Potsdam agreements to possess nuclear weapons of their own, then they should not provide bases for others. These feelings led to mass demonstrations during the 'hot autumn' that preceeded the *Bundestag* debate on the US missiles in November 1983. On one occasion, 300,000 protesters paraded in Bonn; on another, a 'human chain' with hands joined was formed along the whole of the 55-mile route from Stuttgart to the American base at Ulm. The protests died down after the *Bundestag* voted in favour of the missiles, but they were renewed the next year when the dreaded weapons began to arrive: left-wing activists including the writer Walter Jens were arrested and fined for blocking the road to the US nuclear base at Mutlangen, near Stuttgart. In the spring of 1987, when Gorbachev made his 'double zero option' proposal for the removal of all short and medium-range missiles in Europe, opinion polls showed some 92 per cent of Germans favouring the acceptance of this offer by the West. Foreign Minister Genscher was also sympathetic: but Kohl and his CDU colleagues were much more reserved, for they feared that the removal of the missiles would serve to emphasis the Warsaw Pact superiority in conventional weapons and thus make West Germany more vulnerable to this kind of attack.

A small but militant minority within the peace movement also wants Germany to leave NATO and become neutral. Quite often from young people one hears a view that goes something like this: 'Reagan is a greater threat to world peace than the Soviets, he is almost as bad as the Nazis. So we must campaign to prevent his war, just as our grandparents failed to prevent Hitler's war' – the view that I heard from Professor Jäckel's younger students (see p. 394). These young people never experienced the Nazi tyranny and they have probably never been in the United States, so they fail to realize the gravity of their misjudgement in equating the two. They are filled with generous idealism about the Third World, so they dislike what they know of American policies in Central America; they are also strongly anti-capitalist, and some of them believe that Regan is a pawn in the hands of the powerful American arms industry lobby that would like to provoke a new war, for economic reasons. These dangerously naive feelings are not shared by many people: but they have been cunningly exploited by the German communists, who with the backing of Moscow have been infiltrating the peace movement with the aim of weakening NATO. They have even manoeuvred the movement into launching appeals condemning the US missiles but making no mention of Soviet ones, and this has angered the more balanced peace campaigners such as Petra Kelly and Gert Bastian. In Germany as a whole, the minority anti-NATO view is quite distinct from the far more widely shared anti-missile view, and it is unfortunate that the two are sometimes confused. Opinion surveys in 1983–4 showed that the great majority of Germans – as many as 86 per cent, according to one poll – were opposed to the deployment of Cruise and Pershing in Germany, but 75 per cent wanted the Federal Republic to remain in NATO and closely allied to the United States. Not to welcome foreign missiles on one's own soil is one thing, but to want neutrality is quite another; and the wave of anxiety in recent years about growing German neutralism, voiced in recent years by Germany's allies and especially the French, seems to have been very much exaggerated. The neutralist current was much stronger soon after the war. In 1956, a poll showed that 56 per cent of Germans would like American troops to leave Europe: this figure fell to 11 per cent in 1979, then rose to 25 per cent in 1983 and has since levelled off at about 20 per cent – a proportion that NATO can probably live with. In line with other recent youth trends, anti-military and anti-NATO feeling is stronger among those in their late twenties than in the new generation now emerging from its teens.

Much has also been said and written recently about the alleged rise of anti-Americanism in Germany: but this needs to be examined. Of all the people of Europe, only the British and Irish have a more 'special' relationship with America than the Germans, and today emotions towards the United States are as powerful and equivocal in Germany as anywhere. Some 5.5 million Germans emigrated to America between 1820 and 1920, followed later by the waves of Jewish and other refugees from Hitler; and today, if we exclude the Irish, Welsh and Scots, more Americans are German than of English origin. Small surprise that so many prominent Americans have German names. Maybe this helps also to explain why the two people are in some ways so similar: they may differ greatly in their degree of social formality, but they share something of the same business ethos, and the same liking for thoroughness, efficiency and modernism.

After 1945, the Germans developed a sometimes quite obsequious admiration for the powerful nation that had both defeated and liberated them; and their bid to create a new and prosperous democracy was modelled much more consciously on the United States than on Britain. The British may have bequeathed the structures for broadcasting and the trade unions: but much of the inspiration for Germany's Constitution came from America, which also provided Marshall Aid and thus the impetus for the economic miracle. During those post-war years the Germans defined themselves in relation to America, which was also responsible for their defence, especially in Berlin. For better or worse, they copied and upheld many American values – freedom of speech, consumerism, the success ethic – and many of them saw America as the promised land. But then in the 1960s all began to change. The Vietnam war, the assassinations of Martin Luther King and the Kennedys, the growing student unrest – all this and much else produced a new image of America, and it was young Americans themselves on their campuses who led the national self-criticism of a dream that seemed to be turning sour. The virus spread to Europe where anti-Americanism became rife; and it was the Germans, hitherto the greatest admirers, who inevitably now suffered the keenest disillusion. Typically, the swing of the pendulum was more sharply expressed in Germany than elsewhere, though in part it was merely an aspect of Germany's own youth revolt of the late 1960s. A new generation took up arms against consumerist values – and all too readily they identified these with America, forgetting maybe that young America was waging the same battle and sharing many of their ideals. America became the universal Aunt Sally for a lot of confused thinking. This new German generation, and the Green one that came after it, had never known the post-war era, the Berlin Airlift and Marshall Aid, and so they had less reason than their elders to feel grateful. This new mood of disenchantment found expression in some of the films of Wenders, and in Herzog's *Stroszek* (see pp. 291–4); and, though it died down a little during the Carter era, it was refuelled by Reaganism and the missiles crisis.

As elsewhere in Europe today, a good deal of the hostile feeling is really a matter of the dislike of Reagan and of what is perceived by many young Germans as his aggressive overseas policy, both in the military and the economic field – and this hardly constitutes anti-Americanism as such, any more than to abhor Thatcher is to be anti-British. It is true that some young Germans go further than this and express a general distaste for all that they think America stands for: but, if they actually visit the United States, they usually like it far more than they expected. They meet lots of young Americans who share their own critical view of society, and they find themselves admiring American informality and easy friendliness – 'One good thing about American influence,' said one student I met, 'is that it makes us uptight Germans less German.' Even so, a current of anti-American sentiment certainly exists in Germany, on the Right as well as the Left and in all age-groups; and I have noticed it especially among people now in their thirties and forties, the first generation that did not have direct experience of America's post-1945 help. I could give one or two examples. In Munich I know a liberal publisher aged about 40, with many friends in New York, who told me: 'When I am in the depths of the English or French provinces, I can talk to the local peasants or workers and immediately sense common values. But in Oregon or Alabama I feel myself to be in an alien world with other values – and these are the people who elected that dreadful Reagan.' As has often been pointed out, until a few years ago it was French intellectuals who were the most stridently anti-American in Europe, but that has changed with the decline of the Marxist Left and the rise of the *nouveaux philosophes*, and instead it is German thinkers who are now the more critical – as exemplified by Günter Grass, who is staunchly anti-Communist but told *Newsweek* in an interview in 1983: 'I see no difference between the Soviet Union's insolent, arrogant occupation of Afghanistan and the power-wielding of the United States in Central America . . . America has been betraying its own ideals.' Nor are such feelings confined to the Left. I met an industrialist also aged about 40, who breathed fire against the SPD and the unions and then added, 'America's NATO forces in Germany were foisted on us before we got back our sovereignty and we had no say in it. So, in a way, we're a colonised country. If an SPD government ever acted like de Gaulle and asked the American troops to leave, I bet they would refuse. That's because the Pentagon sees West Germany as far more strategically important than France.'

These currents of thought certainly cause some anxiety to senior US Army officers in Germany – such as the general I quoted earlier; 'The question is not so much "how many Greens are there in Germany?" but, "How Green are the Germans?"' When the demonstrators parade outside the nuclear bases, American officers sometimes tell them, 'Remember that we are here to protect your right to protest like this. Under Communism, you'd have no such right.' This message may not always be appreciated: but it is worth stressing that confrontations between American servicemen and the peace protesters are nearly always free of any personal animosity – 'We like you and we have nothing against you as people,' the more responsible peaceniks will say, 'it's just your government's policy that we don't like.' And, at the VII Corps headquarters in Stuttgart, I heard a fairly sanguine view of the situation from a US colonel married to a German, who had been stationed in Germany for 15 years: 'As compared with thirty years ago, the Germans today are far less dependent on us, and they've grown cannier at dealing with us and exerting pressures. America is no longer the wonderland, the shine has worn off, so now they have a more realistic assessment of us. This is healthy. We now have a better basis for working together'.

That was a little glib, maybe: but it would be entirely wrong to give the impression that the 170,000 American troops in Germany, many of them accompanied by their families, are harassed outcasts amid a hostile population. About half of them today live 'on the German economy'; that is, in ordinary German rented housing and not within their own barracks: so opportunities for contact are numerous, and fraternisation is even discreetly encouraged. Of course there are some problems. Black GIs, as one might expect, are not always easily accepted by the Germans. And when GIs make certain pubs, restaurants and discos into their favourites, and crowd there together, the owners sometimes take fright that this will loose them their German clientele, and so they stick up 'Off Limits' signs – as legally they should not do. This has sometimes led to trouble. Generally the US commanders and the German local authorities collaborate in trying to persuade the publicans to remove the signs (some have even been taken to court) and generally this has met with success. Meanwhile, at officer and NCO level, an organisation called Kontakt arranges regular social gatherings and other activities between the German civilians and the Americans and their wives, and this works quite cordially – even extending to Christmas invitations to meals in German homes. I was told that 180 such visits had been made one Yuletide to families in one small Swabian town. All in all, human contacts of this kind are warmer and closer in the US zone of south Germany than in the British zone to the north, where the British Army of the Rhine though perfectly friendly is a little more reticent about fraternisation.

Anti-Americanism must therefore be seen in perspective. Like other German obsessions it seems to come and go in waves, and it is strongly tinged with emotionalism, irrationality, even petulance – almost the feeling of a spoilt child for its parent. If it were to grow much more intense and widespread, this could be disturbing for the Western alliance. At its present level, it can be lived with – and it must be viewed against the background of the very strong links of friendship and sympathy between many Germans and Americans, as the contacts with the US army show. Allensbach surveys between 1965 and 1980, in response to the question 'Which country in the world do you consider to be Germany's best friend?', have consistently put the United States far ahead of all others, with between 49 and 54 per cent; France in 1980 lagged a poor second with 17 per cent, while Britain trailed fourth-equal at 2 per cent.

It would be wrong however to infer from these figures that the Germans are uninterested in Europe. They see no incompatibility – and why should they? – between support for the European Community and friendship with the United States within the NATO alliance. In the years of creation of the EEC in 1957, the surge of European idealism was stronger in Germany than anywhere else, for obvious reasons: the Germans were hoping to find a new identity within a United Europe, and an escape from their own past and their problems of nationalism. They have succeeded to some extent, though of course not completely. Their positive feeling for Europe may have waned in the past ten or fifteen years, but in my view this is not because they have grown more chauvinistic and anti-European: it is simply that they have become frustrated by the slowness of the pace towards European integration, disillusioned by the tedious bureaucracy of Brussels and the petty wrangling of the politicians, and irritated by the way that wealthy Germany is expected by her partners to shoulder so large a part of the EEC's budgetary burden. One interesting set of Allensbach surveys has shown that the proportion of people wanting progress towards a United Europe to move faster, rather than slower, rose from 38 per cent in 1978 to 62 per cent in 1984, while the numbers wanting it to go slower dropped from 7 to 4 per cent. This does not sound like a nation that is turning its back on the European ideal, and it is very different from the mood in Britain.

Another Allensbach poll, in 1979, found 61 per cent favouring either a supranational or a superordinate European government, while only 7 per cent wanted no such government. Thirdly, a survey in 1984 about the decision then just taken to reduce Franco–German frontier controls found 57 per cent in favour and 27 per cent against it: of those aged over 60 only 40 per cent were in favour, but the figure rose to 67 per cent among the 16 to 29-year-olds – an indication that young people are the keenest on European integration and the gradual abolition of frontiers.

The burying of the Franco–German hatchet, after three major wars in the space of 80 years, has been one of the greatest of Europe's post-war success stories; and personal relations today are quite cordial, despite the differences of temperament between the two peoples. There are some 600 active twinnings between French and German towns and regions: Franconia, for example, has formed a successful one with Limousin where the village of Oradour-sur-Glane was in 1944 the scene of the worst of the SS massacres in France (642 inhabitants were murdered, most of them women and children who were shut up in the church and killed by smoke-bombs). The initiative for the various exchanges has tended to come more from the German than the French side, and many older Frenchmen were at first reticent or even hostile: but this feeling has diminished as war memories fade and the older generation die, and today the younger Germans and French get on perfectly easily, without complexes. This is seen especially in the very numerous school and youth exchanges, which have been fostered by the Franco–German Youth Office, set up in 1963 under the de Gaulle/Adenauer friendship treaty. More than four million young people have travelled on group visits to each others' countries under this scheme, which today continues at a slightly lower rate of 130,000 individuals a year (the budget has been reduced: but many other visits are privately arranged). A French Jew once said to me, 'You can't expect me to like the Germans, but rationally I'm in favour of the *rapprochement*. Germany and France are today like man and wife. Germany raped her in 1940, but then did the honest thing and married her. It's an uneasy marriage, but it works.'

Of a *mariage à trois* to include Britain there is not much sign. The Allensbach surveys quoted above showed that between 1965 and 1980 the percentage of Germans seeing France as 'Germany's best friend' rose from 9 to 17, while in the case of Britain the figure fell from 6 to 2 per cent. It is not that the Germans dislike the British, more that they sense that the British are not very interested in *them* – as the school exchanges show. A great many *Gymnasien* have active partnerships with *lycées*, where big groups of pupils go for two-week visits in term-time and are readily housed and entertained by French parents: exchanges with schools in Britain are far fewer, and many have collapsed, partly because the British show less interest in learn-ing German, but above all because not enough British families are prepared to welcome the young visitors to their homes. The Germans today quite admire the British for their easy-going tolerance and so on, while scorning them for their industrial failures and archaic trade unions. But there is very little of the passionate love-hate relationship that exists with the United States.

Yet in general the Germans today continue to be very inter-nationally-minded – again, the desire to escape from their past plays a big role. One sign is their readiness to learn and talk foreign lan-guages, especially English (admittedly, one reason for this is the diffi-culty in getting foreigners to speak their own extraordinarily difficult tongue). Allensbach shows that the numbers able to speak English 'fairly well' rose from 22 to 41 per cent between 1961 and 1979, at which date the figure stood at 67 per cent for the 16 to 29-year-olds, against 19 per cent for the over-60s: only 13 per cent said they could talk French. That Schmidt and Giscard could not speak each other's language but conversed fluently in English, at their summit meetings, was entirely symptomatic. It should also be noted that the Germans show a lively interest in the Third World and give more in develop-ment aid than most richer countries: aid from public funds reached 8,700 million DM for 1985, which represented 0.47 per cent of GDP against an average for the industrialised West of 0.35 per cent.

So we come to the famous question of the German national identity. In a stream of books, articles, lectures, and debates in the media, the Germans talk and worry about this endlessly – 'What does it mean to be German?' 'Are we a real nation or not?' – and it often occurs to me that nothing identifies a German so much as this search for his identity. But we have to differentiate between national identity and patriotic feeling, for the two are not quite the same. The Germans in my experience are intensely aware of being German (or how could they talk about it so much?): but what distinguishes them from many other peoples, such as the British or French, is that they take little joy in being what they are. Some of the causes may lie deep in German history or even geography, or in the lack today of a proper national capital to provide a focus for nationhood: but the principal one is obviously the Nazi legacy. So it is hardly surprising that the Germans have less patriotic pride than others. A Gallup international survey in 1982 put them firmly at the bottom of the table in this respect: asked, 'Do you feel very proud to be . . . (American, British, etc.)?', 80 per cent of Americans said 'yes', 55 per cent of Britons, 41 per cent of Italians, 33 per cent of French (an unexpectedly low figure), 30 per cent of Japanese, and 21 per cent of Germans.

Anyone who travels around Germany as I did is likely to gain impressions that tend to the same conclusion. The people he meets may feel vaguely proud of German culture and local tradition, the German way of life, German economic or sporting achievements – but not of 'being German' in a patriotic sense; the national anthem[1] is seldom played, the black-red-and-gold flag rarely waved, and there is little equivalent of the kind of jokey jingoism so common in Britain, where people wear Union Jack T-shirts or drink tea from Union Jack mugs – that would be considered in appalling taste. The younger generation will very often admit that being German means little to them; and those like my wife who marry a foreigner are usually happy to exchange their nationality for another, such as British. Far more readily than the British or French they then adapt to the ways and attitudes of their spouse's country rather than expect the reverse. When young Germans visit London, they will sometimes envy the British their easy patriotism – but they have little desire to emulate it. And they possess few national heroes of their own, as the opinion polls show.[2] This whole situation inspired a recent article in *Stern* to suggest: 'The German attitude to patriotism is like the Victorian attitude to sex.'

But, when the Victorians individually and privately got around to sex, they often rather enjoyed it. Could this yet be true of German nationalism? It is fashionable among observers of Germany today to detect signs of a revival of this. They point to the recent wave of neutralist feeling, the pan-German ideals of some of the anti-NATO campaigners, the adulation that has surrounded Boris Becker as a new blond young German hero, and even the increasingly assertive stance of the Bonn Government in EEC matters and its new insistence that the German language should not be eclipsed by English and French at EEC and other international meetings. But these trends seem to me quite unpronounced. The neutralist and anti-missile campaign contains little element of real nationalist feeling; reunification with the GDR, an essential goal of German neo-nationalism, is generally accepted to be farther off than ever; and the tougher German bargaining in the EEC has been caused mainly by the need to placate

---

[1] The German TV networks have recently returned to playing *Deutschland über Alles* at the end of each evening. This is not however for nationalistic reasons but to identify themselves to viewers in this age of transmission by satellite. It is worth pointing out to those with poor German that 'Alles' does not mean 'everyone' (as they might think) but 'everything'. The phrase means 'Germany my first priority' and not 'Germany supreme over other nations'.

[2] An Allensbach survey in 1985 that asked people which famous figures they admired most, German or foreign, living or dead, found that head of the list was Albert Schweitzer (an Alsatian, born German, who later became French). Then came Mother Teresa, and Lech Walesa. German politicians did poorly – Adenauer was fourth, Schmidt eighth, von Weizsäcker ninth and Willy Brandt eighteenth. Luther, Bismarck and Frederick the Great were not mentioned.

local pressure-groups such as the Bavarian farmers. If there does exist any new nationalist trend, it is not aggressive or political, but peaceful and largely cultural in character. The Germans are certainly very conscious of their culture, which they see as being bound up with a certain musical tradition and with their language and literature; and as such it is to them not solely German but something that they share with the Austrians and German Swiss – and this pan-Germanic culture they eagerly promote, as we have seen in the case of theatre. They have been returning also to their folk and other traditions, but much more on a local and regional level. Whereas July 4 and July 14 are national fêtes in America and France, Germany has never had a national day, and *Karneval* and *Fasching* are local celebrations. 'The *Heimat* tradition may be reviving quite strongly,' one sociologist told me, 'but not in any national sense. There is a *Heimat Bayern*. But there was never a *Heimat Deutschland* – only a *Vaterland*, and that concept is still quite out of fashion.'

Is this relative absence of patriotism to be regarded as an asset or a handicap for the Germans? Those old enough to remember the havoc of the Nazi period very often see it as the former: Marion von Dönhoff, for example, the co-editor of *Die Zeit*, said to me, 'I myself am glad about this lack of patriotic feeling, and I see it as a progress. We have quite enough to be legitimately proud of in Germany today, and we don't want nationalism too.' But there are others who argue that patriotism is not a quality that a people can lightly dispense with – that it provides an inspiration for all kinds of positive community feelings and that individuals with low national pride are generally the ones most lacking in other kinds of loyalty and positive motivation, towards democratic institutions or even towards work, friends and family. According to this view, some of the German sense of insecurity and rootlessness can be explained in this way. The problem is less acute for intellectual or richer people, who have wider horizons and more opportunities for travel abroad, and thus have less need of a national context; but, for the more ordinary citizens, the lack of a strong sense of nationhood, and of easy flag-waving outlets for expressing it, can build up frustrations and may help to account for the Germans' relatively weak sense of community responsibility and for the radical rejection of society by so many of the young.

There may be elements of truth in such a view. But, if the continuing shame about Nazism is the main cause of wariness over national pride, this will surely ease as the years go by. It could then lead to a revival of the less pleasant aspects of German nationalism. But as yet there is little sign of this: and it is important to stress that nationalism today is diluted and even transmuted by the new feeling for Europe, as it was not in the Nazi time. The young are not only less guilt-ridden about Nazism than their elders, but despite everything they have a stronger sense of European identity; and, like young Italians, French and others, they set less store by national frontiers. So I do not consider that the quest for national identity is the most serious of Germany's problems today, even if it does interrelate with some of the others. The unusually low birth-rate, though it has other causes too, seems to symptomise a nation that is not fully at ease with itself and lacks confidence in the future. The division of Germany, however much now an accepted fact, will continue to cause tensions and trouble the German mind. And some of those old rooted German traits – mistrust of neighbours, polarisation of attitudes, legalism, inability to live with imperfection – may continue to make it harder than in some Western countries to achieve an ideally stable and moderate democracy. And yet – at the risk of sounding patronising, as in this context an Englishman can so easily be – one must affirm that democracy has made enormous strides in this land that had little tradition of it, and that the younger German generation for all its follies and excesses is full of positive qualities that offer hope for the future. But the Germans, like all of us, cannot manage on their own and should not be allowed to do so. The best guarantee for this new Germany is that we all continue to strive towards the ideal of a united Europe. In that promised land – so long as the West as a whole survives – I am confident that the troubled Germans will finally find their escape from Nietzsche's 'hidden paths to chaos'.

ACKNOWLEDGEMENTS

Many hundreds of people, of all kinds, gave up their time to help me with my field research and in many cases were generously hospitable. Alas, they are too numerous for me to mention all by name. But first I wish to thank a few who were especially kind and helpful. In Bonn: Brigitte Lohmeyer; Horst Schirmer, former director of Inter Nationes, and his staff, notably Maria Theres Holubek and Ellen Langen. In Munich, Anna Maria Schmitz, my mother-in-law. In Stuttgart, Heinz Krämer and Sigrid Stellwag. In Allensbach, Prof. Elisabeth Noelle-Neumann and her colleagues at the Institut für Demoskopie. In Frankfurt, Albert and Elisabeth von Metzler. In Hamburg: Marion and Hans Heibey, Charlotte and Henry Glass. In London, Günter Coenen, director of the Goethe Institute, and his staff; Bernd von Waldow, Press Counsellor at the West German Embassy, and his colleagues.

Amongst many others, my special thanks go also to:

In Munich: Christina Hederer of Inter Nationes; Herbert Winkler, Linda Baumgärtner and Gertrud Schaller of the city tourist office; Günter Wolfbauer and his colleagues at the Rathaus; Georg Welsch of the Greens; Tom Byrant and his staff at the British Consulate-General; Daniel Contenay, French Consul-General; George Bailey. Franz Münsterer; Richard Gaul of BMW; Peter Olfs and others of Siemens; Randolf Rodenstock. Prof. Nikolaus Lobkowicz, Prof. Wulf Steinmann, Eberhard Dünninger, Georg Knauss, Elizabeth Magana; Rupert Graf Strachwitz; Dr. Jost Martinius; Ludwig Kippes, Carla Baran; Kirchenrat Paul Rieger, Pfarrer Turner. Hans Magnus Enzensberger, Lothar Menne; Wolfgang Ebert; Werner Herzog, Alexander Kluge, Margarethe von Trotta, Edgar Reitz, the late Rainer Werner Fassbinder; Jürgen Kolbe and his staff in the city's cultural department; Michael Wachsmann; Dieter Schröder and others at the *Süddeutsche Zeitung*; Richard Dill, Renée Goddard, Hano Frei. David and Birgit Kehoe, Gert and Ulla Pegler, Andrea and Jürgen Kölble (Dutton), Reinhardt and Utta Riemerschmid, Sue and Peter Kafka, Hella Schwerla, Jürgen Claus, Francis Jurgsaitis.

Acknowledgements

Rest of Bavaria; Major-General Wolfgang Odendahl and his Bundeswehr colleagues at Regensburg; at Ansbach, Rolf and Renata Fütterer; at Augsburg, Gerda Rutsche of the tourist office; Rolf Mantler and his staff and pupils at Landschulheim Schondorf; Klaus-Dieter Hartmann of the the Studienkreis für Tourismus, Starnberg.

In Stuttgart: Lothar Späth; Manfred Rommel and his colleagues at the Rathaus; Frau Weber of Inter Nationes; Anneliese Schuhholz of the Baden-Württemberg tourist board; Brian Rose, former British Consul-General, and his staff; Bob Larson, Rob Michael; General Galvin of the US Army. Prof. Johann Lohn; Hans Georg Kloos and his colleagues at Daimler Benz; Wolfgang Knellessen, Rüdiger Stephan, and their colleagues at Robert Bosch; Peter Schutz of Porsche; Alfred Krone. Prince and Princess Mainrad von Hohenzollern; Prof. Eberhard Jäckel, Prof. Georg Turner, Prof. Ewald Bockenhoff, Fritz and Pauline Hejl, Magda Meier and her colleagues at the Waldorfschule. Thomas Löffelholz, Erich Peter, Johann Kannicht and their colleagues at the *Stuttgarter Zeitung;* Jürgen and Susanne Offenbach; Roderich Klett, Hans Heiner Bolte and their colleagues at Süddeutsche Rundfunk; Klaus Hübner, Michael Maegraith; Peter Palitsch; Marcia Haydee and her colleagues at the ballet. Anthony Gibbs; Liselotte Hoover; Frau von Egloffstein; Dr Heino and Ursula Flemming, Erwin and Ingrid Wartenburg, Graf and Gräfin zu Knyphausen.

Rest of Baden-Württemberg: in Tübingen, Prof. Walter Jens, Axel Markert, Heinrich Lang of the tourist office. In Horb, Prof. Rainer Nagel and his wife; in Dornstetten, Erhard Eppler; in Konstanz, Hans Willauer; in Freiburg, Prof. Wilhelm Hennis, Ernst Philip, Richard Farnsworth; in Baden-Baden, Sigrun Lang, Richard Schmitz; in Karlsruhe, Renate Stiehl, the Niemann family. Friedrich Karl Fürst zu Hohenlohe-Waldenburg and his wife.

In Frankfurt: Barbara Schander of Inter Nationes, Jost Enseling; Klaus Mehrens of IG Metall; Florian Schilling and other INSEAD alumni. Carmen Lakashus, Burkhard Schwarz; Prof. Iring Fetscher; Stephen Castles, Rosi Wolf-Almanasreh. Prof. Hilmar Hoffmann and his colleagues in the city cultural department; Brian Michaels; Karlheinz Braun; Werner Hölzer, Peter Iden and others of the *Frankfurter Rundschau;* Prof. Günther Gillessen and others of the *Frankfurter Allgemeine Zeitung.* Prof. Klaus and Ellinor Lüderssen, Prof. Kurt and Ingrid Shell, Kate and Steve Murray-Sykes.

Rest of Hesse, also Rhineland-Palatinate: Reinhard Gross and his colleagues at the Hesse *Landtag;* Rudi Molz and his friends at Woppenroth, Hunsrück.

In Bonn: Immo Stabreit in the Chancellor's office; Karl-Günther von Hase; Carl-Dieter Spranger, Gerhard Heuer and others of the Interior Ministry; Hans Schauer and others of the Foreign Ministry; Lothar Ruhl and others of the Ministry of Defence; Marlies Jansen of the Ministry for Intra-German Relations; Petra Kelly, Otto Schily and other Greens; Ernst-Günter Pätzold of the federal Press office; Julian Bullard, the Ambassador, and Catherine Pestell, Alistair Hunter, Alan Hatfull, George Chantrey, Tom Macan, all of the British Embassy. Dinnies von der Osten of BP. Prof. Hans Peter Schwarz, Karl Roeloffs, Gerhard Müller; Dr Martin Friedrichs. Michael Binyon, Rupert Cornwell, David Smeeton, Michel Meyer. Armgard Rostowski, Elisabeth Gräfin von Werthern.

In Cologne: Marianne Esch and others of the city tourist office; Robert Arbuthnot of the British Council; Werner Ende of the German Industries Association; Joachim von Mengershausen; Helga Ihlau; Carnival Prince Karl-Josef Kappes; Klaus and Lizzi Barisch.

In Düsseldorf: Prof. Reimut Jochimsen; Kurt Birrenbach of Tyssen; Ulrich Borsdorf and others of the DGB; Prof. Herbert Reuter, Fritz Conzen, Dame Lilo Milchsack.

Rest of North-Rhine-Westphalia: in Dortmund, Prof. Kurt Kosyk; in Bochum, Udo von Hagen and his wife; in Essen, Alfred Plitzko, Andreas Schlieper; in Mönchengladbach, Col. Kay Coates of BAOR; in Buir, the Brecher family.

In Hamburg: Klaus von Dohnanyi and his colleagues in the *Land* Government; Freimut Duve; Michael Platte of the tourist office. Arend Oetker, Karl Freiherr von Hahn; Hartmut Mehdorn of MBB. Jil Sander; Eva Rühmkorf; Angelika Jahr, Mario Scheuermann, Karl Theodor Walterspiel, Wolfgang Schüler; Bishop Krusche, Siegfried von Kortzfleisch; Prof. Peter Fischer-Appelt, Alexis Lober. Rolf Liebermann, Peter Zadek, Hanna Hurtzig, Eberhard Möbius; Marion Gräfin von Dönhoff, Theo Sommer, Christoph Bertram, Rudolf Walter Leonhardt, all of *Die Zeit*; Günter Gaus; Peter Scholl-Latour, Peter Gatter, Bernd Leptihn. Borries and Irmgard de Grahl, Hans Meckel and his family, Karl-Heinz Piepenbrink and his family, Albrecht and Regine Eggert, Sabine Skoruppa and her husband, Prof. Werner Selberg, Hans Eppendorf, Dennis Clark.

In Bremen: Hans Koschnik, Manfred von Scheven, Dieter Opper.

In Schleswig-Holstein: Günter Kunert; Beate Uhse; Hans Hermann Petersen and his family, Peter Rabe and his family, Dierk Boie and his family, Franz Hollmann; Senator Lund of Lübeck.

In Lower Saxony: in Göttingen, Prof. Rudolf von Thadden and his wife, Artur Levi, Gerd Pistohlkors. In Wolfsburg, Karl-Heinz Schüling of Volkswagen. The Abeln family of Dörpen, Emsland.

In West Berlin: Günter Rexrodt, Jörg Henschel, Klaus Wittwer and his wife; all of the city government; Klaus Hübner; Horst Winkelmann, Lothar Nass; Alex Bidder of the tourist office; David Wyatt of the British Military Government; Nelson Ledsky of the American Military Government; Major Michael Hoover, Daniel Hamilton. Barbara John, Cemalettin, Çetin, Emine Altiok of the

Kreuzberg Turkish centre. Prof. Werner Knopp; Prof. Peter Wapnewski, Rosa von Praunheim; Dirk Sager, Joachim Braun, Wolfgang Hauptmann, Donald Armour; Marlies Menge. Peter and Isabella von Jena, Gisela Wille, Jan Schäfer.

In the German Democratic Republic: Georg Menzel and Karl Steiner of the Foreign Ministry; Ekkehard Fahldieck and Gert Mangelsdorf of the Internationales Pressezentrum; Stefan Heym, Stephan Hermlin, Hermann Kant, Ekkehard and Barbara Schall, Klaus Dieter Flor; Reiner Oschmann and his wife; Manfred Ackermann; Robert Röntgen; and a great many others who for obvious reasons must remain anonymous.

In Paris: Charles Hargrove, Bernard Brigouleix, Brigitte Sauzay, Roger Keyes.

In London: Günter Nischwitz and his colleagues at the German National Tourist Office; Günter Bruhn of Berolina Travel; Brian Stone, Alex Hamilton, Victor Price, Barbara Beck; Richard and Jocelyn Mayne, Peter Fabian, Edith Rudinger, Erich Fried, Leonie Cohn, Alexander Wathenphul, Irene Hawkins, Angelika Sahla; Ian and Ruth Bell, Michael Balfour.

And last but very far from least, my thanks go to my publishers in London, Christopher Sinclair-Stevenson and Clare Alexander of Hamish Hamilton, who have been unfailingly helpful and encouraging.

BIBLIOGRAPHY

(In the case of German books translated into English, only the English version is given)

General and political:

George Bailey, *Germans*, Avons Books, New York, 1972.

Luigi Barzini, *The Impossible Europeans*, Weidenfeld and Nicolson, 1983.

Bernard Brigouleix, *Les Allemands*, Balland, Paris, 1984.

Jonathan Carr, *Helmut Schmidt, Helmsman of Germany*, Weidenfeld and Nicolson, 1985.

Gordon Craig, *The Germans*, Putnam's, New York, 1982 and Penguin Books, London, 1984.

Marion von Dönhoff, *Foe into Friend*, Weidenfeld and Nicolson, London, 1982.

Alfred Grosser, *Germany in Our Time*, Pall Mall Press, London, 1971.

Wilhelm Hennis, *Die missverstandene Demokratie*, Freiburg, 1973.

Walter Laqueur, *Germany Today*, Weidenfeld and Nicolson, 1985.

Rudolf Walter Leonhardt, *This Germany*, Penguin Books, 1966.

Richard Löwenthal and Hans Peter Schwarz, *25 Jahre Bundesrepublik Deutschland*, Seewald, Stuttgart.

Richard Mayne, *Postwar*, Thames and Hudson, 1983.

Ray Mellor, *The Two Germanies, A Modern Geography*, Harper & Row, 1978.

Michel Meyer, *L'Allemagne inachevée*, Denoel, Paris, 1976.

Joseph Rovan, *L'Allemagne du Changement*, Calmann-Levy, Paris, 1983.

Anthony Sampson, *The New Europeans*, Hodder and Stoughton, 1968.

Brigitte Sauzay, *Le vertige allemand*, Orban, Paris, 1985.

Adolph Schalk, *The Germans*, J. M. Dent, 1972.

Werner Weidenfeld (editor), *Die Identität der Deutschen*, Hanser, Munich, 1983.

Allensbach Institute, annual collections of opinion polls; also *Eine Generation später, Bundesrepublik Deutschland 1953–1979*, Saur, Munich, 1983.

Facts about Germany, Bertelsmann Lexikothek, Gütersloh, 1984.

Society, including youth, Greens and immigrants:

Jillian Becker, *Hitler's Children*, Michael Joseph, 1977.

Fritjof Capra and Charlene Spretnak, *Green Politics*, Hutchinson, 1984.

Stephen Castles, *Here for Good: Western Europe's Ethnic Minorities*, Pluto Press, 1984.

Ralf Dahrendorf, *Society and Democracy in Germany*, Weidenfeld and Nicolson, 1968.

Hans Magnus Enzensberger, *Politische Brosamen*, Suhrkamp, Frankfurt, 1982.

Angelika Gardiner-Sirtl, *Gleichberechtigt?*, Brigitte, Hamburg, 1982.

Elim Papadakis, *The Green Movement in West Germany*, Croom Helm, 1984.

Günter Walraff, *Ganz unten*, Kiepenheuer & Witsch, Cologne, 1985.

Regions and cities:

John Ardagh, *A Tale of Five Cities*, Secker & Warburg, 1979.

George Bailey, *Munich*, Time-Life Books, Amsterdam, 1980.

Hans Eppendorfer, *St. Pauli*, Hoffmann und Campe, Hamburg, 1982.

Bob Larson, *Your Swabian Neighbours*, Schaben International Verlag, Stuttgart, 1980.

Rudolf Walter Leonhardt, *Hamburg*, Süddeutscher Verlag, Munich, 1985.

John Mander, *Berlin, Hostage for the West*, Greenwood Press, London, 1962.

Thaddäus Troll, *Stuttgart*, Belser, Stuttgart, 1969.

Culture and media:

Peter Iden, *Theater als Widerspruch*, Kindler, Munich, 1985.

Brian Keith-Smith (ed.), *Essays on Contemporary German Literature*, Oswald Wolff, London, 1966.

John Sandford, *The New German Cinema*, Oswald Wolff, London, 1980.

Günter Wallraff, *Der Aufmacher*, Kiepenheuer & Witsch, Cologne, 1977.

Cultural Life in the Federal Republic of Germany (various hands), Inter Nationes, Bonn, 1981.

German Democratic Republic:

Anthony Bailey, *Along the Edge of the Forest*, Faber & Faber, 1983.

David Childs, *The GDR: Moscow's German Ally*, Allen & Unwin, 1983.

Timothy Garton Ash, *Die DDR heute*, Rowohlt, Hamburg, 1983.

Günter Gaus, *Wo Deutschland liegt*, Hoffmann und Campe, Hamburg, 1983.

Jonathan Steele, *Socialism with a German Face*, Jonathan Cape, 1977.

The German Democratic Republic, Panorama DDR, East Berlin, 1984.

INDEX

Principal page references are in **bold type**. With the exception of Edgar Reitz' *Heimat* which occurs so frequently, book, play and film titles are not indexed: see under name of author or director. Some general themes are indexed, e.g. 'unemployment' – but not where the contents of the subject is evident from the Contents list (e.g. industry, women). Almost all German proper names are indexed: foreign ones are listed only when they are specially relevant.

Aachen university, 219
Abendzeitung, 156
Abitur, 207, 211, 214, 216, 217, 392
abortion, **170–1**
Abs, Hermann, 97
Achternbusch, Herbert, 306
acid rain, **see** forests
Adenauer, Konrad, 10, 11, 13, **16–17**, 28, 390–1, 447
Adorno, Theodor, 259, 263–4
AEG, 54, 85, 95
agriculture, **127–39**, 142–3, 434, 441; in the GDR, 327–8
Airbus, 45, 93
aircraft industry, **93–4**
Albrecht, Susanne, 424
Allensbach opinion polls, 69, 85, 114, 115–16, 143, 159, 164, 165, 166, 167, 168, 173, 198, 236, 254, 255, 265, 377, 381, 384, 395, 405, 414, 419–20, 449, 453, 454, 455
Allied occupation forces, 8–10, 12, 19, **51–3**, 64, 70, 94, 272, 308, 390

Alternative, 432, 436, 442–3; *see also* Greens and Berlin
Altiok, Emine, 246
Altun, Kamal, 254
America, 2, 188; armed forces in West Germany, 452–3; attitude towards, 291–2, **450–4**; influence of, 70; relations with, 52
Amnesty International, 377
Andersch, Alfred, 259
Andreotti, Giulio, 383
Angst, 227, 235, 445
apprenticeships, **112–14**
aristocracy, **150–3**
Ascherson, Neal, 345
Audi cars, 92
Augstein, Rudolf, 314
Austria, 153, 398
Autobahnen, 3, 5, 89, 126–7
automobile industry, **89–93**; catalytic convertors, **124–7**

Baader-Meinhof group, 234, 259,

Baader-Meinhof group (contd)
297, 421, **424–5**; Baader,
Andreas, 424–5
Baden-Baden, 201, 203–4
Badenweiler, 203
Baden-Württemberg, 26, 66, 67,
74–7, 103, 104, 109, 119, 124, 155,
253, 286, 310, 399; education in,
207, 208, 224, 225
Bad Godesberg, 38
Bach, J. S., 322
Bahro, Rudolf, 361
ballet, *see* dance
banking, 36, 86, **96–7**
Baran, Carla, 248
Barzini, Luigi, 6
Basic Law, *see* Constitution
Bastian, Gert, 431
Bausch, Pina, 258, **283–4**
BASF, 94
Bavaria, 14, 24, 26, 27, 30–4, 66, 67,
142, 150–1, 156, 162, 168, 181,
193, 194, 231, 233, 243, 253, 293,
305, 310, 367, 417; education in,
204, 207, 230; farming in, 128,
129, 132–4, 136, 138; industry in,
74–7, 11, 119; Duke of, 30, 150
Bayer (firm), 94
BBC, 273, 277, 308, 348, 387
Beckenbauer, Franz, 193
Becker, Boris, 192, 193, 446, 457
Becker, Julia, 424
Belsen camp, 397, 400
Benneet, David, 290
Benz, Karl, 90
Berlin, 24, 27, 185, 205; East Berlin,
53, 63, **320–1**, 370, 373–4, 382,
385; West Berlin, 12, 19, 26, 29,
49–64, 67, 77, 368, 371, 382, 423;
airlift, 12; *Alternative*, 52, **58–60**,
437–41, 442; cultural life, 267,
276, 278, 279, 284; immigrants
in, 245–6, 252; Kreuzberg, 59,
245, 440, 442; Mehringhof, 59,
437–8; *S-Bahn*, 64; squatters,
439–441; *UFA-Fabrik*, 57, 438–9;
universities, 212, 213, 225; Wall,
49, **61–3**, 316, 320, 324–5, 366,
368, 373

Berliner Ensemble, 364–5
Bernhard, Thomas, 273
Bertelsmann (firm), 265, 312
Bertram, Christoph, 315
Beuys, Joseph, 4, 211, 257, 258, 270,
279, 284, **285**, 286
Bhagwan Rajneesh, 444
Biermann, Wolf, 260, 358, **360**
BIG (Berlin), 55, 98
Bild Zeitung, 65, 114, 256, 260, 290,
313, **316–18**
birth-rate, decline of, 7, 55, 109–10,
171–2, 458
Bismarck, Otto von, 25, 76, 102, 130,
197, 232, 385, 403, 426
Bitburg, 400
Black Forest, 123, 134, 191, 201, 434
Bloch, Ernst, 263–4, 302, 359
Blohm und Voss, 44, 105
BMW, 30, 33, 89, 91, 92, 93, 109, 125,
134, 286
Bochum, 29, 79, 80, 267, 269, 273,
277, 281; university, 219
Bocuse, Paul, 184
Böhringer (firm), 121
Böll, Heinrich, 257, **258–60**, 264,
318, 363, 425; *Lost Honour of
Katharina Blum*, 159, 290, 317,
415
Bohne, Horst, 113
Bonhoeffer, Dietrich, 228
Bonn, **27–8**, **38–9**, 65–6, 406, 424
Bormann, Martin, 9
Bosch (firm), 34, 73, 93, 96, 101, 107,
109, **113**, 244; Robert, 35
Bossmann, Dieter, 397
Boulez, Pierre, 281
Boyes, Roger, 358
Brandt, Willy, 18–19, 54, 80, 170,
220, 234, 316, 325, 390, 393, 420;
Brandt Government, 205, 219
Braun, Volker, 363
Brecht, Bertolt, 271, 272, 273, 275,
278, 289, 324, 359, 364–5
Bremen, 24, 26, 29, **47–50**, 67, 75, 76,
77, 90, 93, 175, 180, 268, 429; uni-
versity, **214**
Bremer Vulkan, 48
Breuer, Marita, 301

Brigitte, 166, 315
Britain, *see* Great Britain
Brockdorf nuclear plant, 119, 426
Buback, Siegfried, 424
Bubis, Ignaz, 401
Buchenwald camp, 357
Bundestag, 13, 69, 163, 404, 424, 429–30, 432, 449
Bundesrat, 68
Bundeswehr, 17, 234, **447–9**
Bunte Illustrierte, 157
Burns, Arthur, 431
Buschhaus plant, 122
business schools, 100–1

cabaret, satiric, 273; in the GDR, 355–6
Castles, Steven, 247, 252
catalytic convertors, *see* automobile industry
Catholic Church, 170–1, 193, **227–36**, 241, 260, 274; in the GDR, 343, 345
chemical industry, 94
Chéreau, Patrice, 282
Chernobyl disaster, 2, 116, 118–19, 432
Christiane F., **445**
Christian names, use of, **159–60**
Christlich Demokratische Union (CDU), 110, 228, 312; in power federally, 2, 17, 19, 86, 108, 200, 390–1, 404–5, 407, 409; in *Land* and city government, 37, 54, 60, 65, 72, 119, 122, 245, 250–1, 278, 310, 440
Christlich-Soziale Union (CSU), 17, 19, 33, 138, 166, 200, 227, 228, 286, 310, 312, 404, 405, 417
Churchill, Winston, 9, 10, 273, 366
class divisions, **146–50**
Club Méditerrannée, 190
Club Robinson, 190
coal mining, **78–9**, 105, 116–17, 118, 121
Cohn-Bendit, Danny, 38
Collitt, Leslie, 392
Cologne, 24, 29, 39–41, 73, 110, 121, 186, 444; carnival, **195–7**; cultural life, 267, 281; university, 219

Commerzbank, 96
Common Market, *see* European Community
communes, 72
Communist Party, 18, 419–20
computer industry, 95
Constitution, 13, 66, 67, 69, 163, 214, 228, 252, 315, 381, 395, 403–4, 405, 419, 420, 421, 449; Constitutional Court, 28, 53, 312, 408, 413, 420
consumer spending, 177–8; in the GDR, 348
Craig, Gordon, 16, 57, 232, 275–6
Cranko, John, 36, 268, **283**
Czechoslovakia, 372

Dachau camp, 397, 398
Daimler-Benz, 34, 36, 73, 87, **89–90**, 91, 101, 109, 125, 206
Daimler, Gottlieb, 36, 88, 90, 105
dance, 268, **283–4**
Darmstadt, 281
defence, 447–50
Demeter farms, 441
democracy, 4, 10, 16, **403–7**, **418–21**
demography, *see* birth-rate
Deutsche Bank, 36–7, 90, **96–7**
Deutsche Demokratische Republik (DDR), *see* GDR
Deutscher Gewerkschaftsbund (DGB), **102–4**, 106, 108, 243, 406
Diepgen, Eberhard, 54
Distel cabaret, 355–6
Döblin, Alfred, 296
Dönhoff, Marion Gräfin von, 151, 164, 458
Dönitz, Admiral, 394, 395, 399
Dörpen, 72
Dohnanyi, Klaus von, 43, 45
Dornier (firm), 94
Dorst, Tankred, 272, 273
Dortmund, 29, 187, 217, 267
Dresden, 321–2, 336, 342–3, 347, 384, 394
Dresdner Bank, 96, 424
drink, **186–7**
Dubček, Alexander, 327

Düsseldorf, 29, **39–41**, 103, 227, 235, 246, 273, 435; art in, 267, 284–5, 286
Dürrenmatt, Friedrich, 273
Duisburg, 29, 79
Dutschke, Rudi, 316, 423, 431, 436

ecology, *see* environment
education, 147–8, **204–6**, 229, 242–3, 391–2, 397–8, 412, 439; in the GDR, **332–4**
Eickmayer, Dr, 71
energy resources, **116–19**
Engel, Johann Friedrich, 190
Engelberg, Ernst, 385
Ensslin, Gudrun, 165, 271, 291, 424–5
environment, **120–2**, 428–9, 433, **434–6**
Enzensberger, Hans Magnus, 258, 259, 260, **261**, 415–16, 419, 423
Eppler, Erhard, 234, 236
Erfurt, 325, 333, 345
Erhard, Ludwig, 11–12, 17, 178, 263
Ertl, Josef, 137
Essen, 29, 78, 81, 286
Esslin, Martin, 364
Eureka, 96
Europe, attitudes towards, 8, 16
European Coal and Steel Community, 17
European Community (EEC), 17, 44, 79, 84, 108, 117, 125–6, 129, 177, 200, 241, 247, 380, 431, **454**, 457; Common Agricultural Policy, 130, 133, **135–8**
European Parliament, 429
Evangelische Kirche in Deutschland (EKD), *see* Protestant Churches

Fasching, 195, 197
Fassbinder, Rainer Werner, 239, 258, 288, 289, **294–7**, 303, 307, 364, **401–2**
federal system, 23, **25–28**, 65–70, 204, 218, 312
feminism, **165–6**
festivals, **193–7**
Fiedler, Hans, 98

Filbinger, Hans, 399
Financial Times, 74, 392
Fischer, Joschka, 433
Fleischmann, Peter, 142, 305
Flensburg, 169
Flick, Karl, 405; Flick affair, **406–7**, 418, 421
Fontane, Theodor, 141, 162, 259, 295
Ford Motors, 91
foreign workers, *see* Gastarbeiter
forests, sickness of, 116, **122–4**, 127, 434
France, 2, 3, 129, 135; comparisons with, 141, 142, 149, 153, 159, 182, 250, 262–3, 289, 408, 423, 429; relations with, 454–5
Frankfurt, 27, 28, **36–8**, 97, 185, 401–2; airport extension crisis, 426–7; Book Fair, 37, 265; cultural life, 263, 267, **279–80**, 282–3, 286; immigrants in, 245, 248, 251, 256
Frankfurter Allgemeine Zeitung, 37, 263, 313, 315
Frankfurther Rundschau, 37, 280, 313, 315, 318, 427
Frederick the Great, 385
Frei, Peter, 157
Freiburg university, 217
Freie Demokratische Partei (FDP), 18, 404, 407, 409, 429
Freie Deutsche Jugend (FDJ) in the GDR, 333–4, 335
Frisch, Max, 237, 273

Gallup poll, 456
gas imports, 117, 118
Gastarbeiter, 38, 183, 184, 190, **237–56**, 280
Gaulle, Charles de, 5, 17, 263
Gaus, Günter, 339, 381, 383
Genscher, Hans-Dietrich, 95, 220
German Democratic Republic (GDR), 13, 18, 64, 121, 124, 195, 229, 230, 234, 252, 289, **319–88**, 440; armed forces, 357–8; economy, 326–7, 328–9, 348–51, 379–80, 386–7; June 1953 revolt,

German Democratic Republic (GDR) (contd) 323–4, 362, 365; labour relations, 335–7; literature in, **260–1**, **358–63**; relations with West Germany, 325, **377–84**; travel to the West, **371–8**

Gesamtschulen, 205–6

Gielen, Michael, 267, 282–3

Giscard d'Estaing, Valéry, 455

Globke, Hans, 390

Godard, Jean-Luc, 290

Göring, Hermann, 9, 156

Goethe, Johann Wolfgang von, 5, 37, 201, 275, 276, 292, 322

Goethe Institut, 29

Göttingen, 71

Gordon-Lennox, General, 52

Grass, Günter, 257, **258–60**, 264, 273, 290, 318, 363, 449, 452

Great Britain, 2; armed forces in West Germany, 453; comparisons with, 142, 149, 168, 175, 205; influences of, 46, 70; relations with, 52, 116, 124, 125, 136, 155, 455

Greek immigrants, 113, 184, 240–1, 294

Greens, 4, 96, 111, 158, 173, 177, 261, 417, 422, **428–36**, 443, 446–7; and the environment, 118–20, 143, 428, **434–5**, 441; in local government, 65, 72, 414, 429, **431–3**; political party, 20, 163–4, 180, 404, **429–32**

Grimm brothers, 172, 258

Grundig (firm), 95

Grundgesetz, *see* Constitution

Gruppe 47, **259**, 261, 263

Guardian, The, 285, 402

Güney, Yilmar, 241, 244, 246

Guillaume, Günter, 19

Gymnasien, 147–8, 205, 207–10, 455

Haas, Joel de, 402

Habermas, Jürgen, 263–4, 318

Hahn, Kurt, 212

Hallstein doctrine, 325, 379, 381

Hamburg, 26, 27, 29, 41–7, 67, 68, 76, 119, 166, 184, 185, 360, 409, 411; cultural life, 266, 267, 269, 277, 279, 282, 283, 310; industry in, 93, 105, 121; St Pauli, **46–7**; university, 225

Hammer, Julius, 122

Handke, Peter, 273, 291, 292

Hanover, 29, 73, 175

Harich, Wolfgang, 359

Harris, Air Marshall, 42

Havemann, Robert, 341–2, 361

Hauff, Reinhard, 297

Haydee, Marcia, 283

health service, **197–9**

Hegel, G. W. F., 221

Heidegger, Martin, 263

Heidelberg university, 212, 219, 225

Heimat (film by Reitz), 24, 128, 134, **139–40**, 176, 258, 287, **298–305**, 307

Hennis, Wilhelm, 418

Henze, Hans Werner, 282, 291

Hermlin, Stephan, 359, 361

Herzog, Werner, 4, 258, 261, 289, **292–4**, 303, 451

Hessen, 26, 65, 67, 109, 118, 204, 431–2

Heym, Stefan, 359, 361, **362**, 387

Heyme, Hans Günter, 276

Heyworth, Peter, 282

high technology, **94–6**

Hirschbrunn, Hans Wolfgang, 101

Hitler, Adolf, 32, 33, 91, 150, 162, 212, 228, 281, 297, 308, 315, 320, 394, 395, 397, 403

Hochhuth, Rolf, 258, 260, 272, 273

Höchst (firm), 94

Höfer, Werner, 163

Hölderlin, Friedrich, 221

Hoffmann, Hilmar, 286

Hohenzollern, Mainrad Prinz von, 152

Hohenlohe-Waldenburg, Friedrich Fürst zu, 152–3

holidays, 187–92

Holocaust, (film), **299**, 393

homosexuality, 167

Honecker, Erich, 317, 325, 338, 341, 342, 343, 344, 345, 353, 356, 360, 361, 376, 379, 380, 382, 385, 386
Horkheimer, Max, 263
hospitals, 68, 198, 229, 412; in the GDR, 374
housing, 59–61, **174–7**, 411–12; in the GDR, 331–2, 341
Hübner, Klaus (Berlin), 442
Hübner, Klaus (Stuttgart), 269
Humboldt, Wilhelm von, 212
Hungary, 324, 359, 374, 386, 387
Hunsrück, 139–40, **298–305**

IBM, 77
Iden, Peter, 280
IG Farben, 94
IG Metall, 103, 104, 107, **108–9**, 110
immigrants, *see Gastarbeiter*
Inbucon (firm), 147
inflation, 85
INSEAD, 100, 101
Italian immigrants, 240, 244, 255, 280, 305

Jäckel, Eberhard, 391, 393, 450
Januszczak, Waldemar, 285
Japan, competition with, 41, 89, 93, 94–5
Jaspers, Karl, 263–4
Jens, Walter, 221, 261, 318, 450
Jews, 36, 97, 220, 228, 254, 257, 277, 391, 393, 396, 397, 399, **400–3**, 455
Johnson, Uwe, 259, 260, 359

Käutner, Helmut, 288
Kagel, Mauricio, 281
Kant, Immanuel, 408
Kappes, Karl-Josef, 195
Karajan, Herbert von, 58, 267, 281
Karlsruhe, 28, 73, 113, 243
Kellner, Lorenz, 410
Kelly, Petra, 430–1, 446
Kennedy, John F., 51
Keynes, Maynard, 11
Khrushchev, Nikita, 51
Kiechle, Ignaz, 138
Kiesinger, Kurt Georg, 17, 100, 391, 393

Kiessling, General, 167
Kinski, Klaus, 289, 293–4
Kirchentag, 227, **235–6**
Kirchner, Alfred, 276
Kluge, Alexander, 288, **289–90**, 299
Koblenz, 101, 120
Kölner Stadtanzeiger, 315
Kopke, Karl-Heinz, 163
Kohl, Helmut, 149, 211; as Chancellor, 19, 85, 87, 96, 108, 110, 119, 122, 137, 165, 172, 200, 263, 375, 379, 381, 400, 405, 407
Kohl Government, 69, 86, 87, 95, 112, 119, 124, 127, 165, 172, 180, 200, 247, 250, 376, 382, 407, 432
Kolle, Oswald, 168
Konstanz, 71
Koschnik, Hans, 48–9
Kossak, Egbert, 43
Kroetz, Franz Xaver, 142, 258, **274**, 295
Krupp (firm), 11, 76, 78, 79, 80, 380; Krupp, Alfred, 80–1, 390
Krusche, bishop, 234
Krusche, Günter, 348
Küng, Hans, 219, 221, 232
Kunert, Günter, 338, 361
Kunze, Hugo, 88
Kunze, Reiner, 361, 362
Kuwait, 90

Lafontaine, Oscar, 432
Lakashus, Carmen, 5, 148, 157, 168
Lambsdorff, Otto Graf von, 379, 407, 418
Laqueur, Walter, 306
Le Carré, John, 39
legalism, 6, **408–14**, 418
Leipzig, 37, 265, 322, 335, 356; Book Fair, 379
Lenin, Vladimir Ilyich, 351, 385
Levin, Bernard, 420
Liebermann, Rolf, 43, 282
Lobkowitz, Nikolaus, 409
Löwenthal, Gerhard, 309
Loewig, Roger, 363
Lower Saxony, 26, 43, 67, 116, 122, 153
Lübeck, 366–7

Lufthansa, 53, 87, 425
Luther, Martin, 227, 228, 322, 333, **345**, 385
Luxemburg, Rosa, 291

Mailänder, Ulf, 438, 442
Mainz, 29
Mann, Heinrich, 259
Mann, Thomas, 31, 260
Mannesmann (firm), 41, 81
Marshall Aid, 11, 84, 326
Mauriac, François, 383
May 8 anniversary, 390, 392, 399–400
Mayne, Richard, 273
MBB, 30, 45, 87, 93
Meier, Richard, 286
Meinhof, Ulrike, 165, 424
Mengershausen, Joachim von, 299
Mercedes, *see* Daimler-Benz
Messerschmidt, Willy, 88
Michaels, Brian, 280
Michelin, 184
Milz, Peter, 11
missiles (Cruise and Pershing-2), 123, 382, 445, 449–50
Mitbestimmung, 105–6
Mönchengladbach, 286
Mogadishu, 425
Molz, Rudi, 304
Moore, Henry, 271
Morgenthau, Henry, 10, 435
motoring, 5, 126–7
motorways, *see Autobahnen*
Müller, Heiner, 275, 364
München Leuchtet, 31, 273
Munich, 27, 28, 29, **30–4**, 35, 72, 93, 126, 150, 175, 176, 184, 186, 187, 192, 194, 197, 199, 232, 233, 406, 412, 427, 433; cultural life, 265, 266, 267, 268, 273, 279, 286–7, 288, 294; immigrants, 243, 248, 250; smart society, **156–7**; universities, 218, 220, 225
museums, 266, **285–7**
music, **281–3**

National Demokratische Partei Deutschlands (NPD), 18, 142, 395, 404

national identity, 7, **456–8**
nationalism, 7
National Zeitung, 395
NATO, *see* North Atlantic Treaty Organisation
Nazis and nazism, 6, 9, 25, 33, 43, 58, 130, 142, 150, 162, 171, 193, 197, 206, 210, 220, 227–8, 284, 286, 287, 298, 300, 324, 344, 384, 403, 416, 421, 423; legacy of Nazism today, 4, 8, 11, 16, 87, 102, 114, 146, 231, 252, 257, 258–9, 272, 303–4, 318, 389–403, 444, 456, 458; legacy in the GDR, 392; denazification, 10, 390; neo-Nazism, 18, 254, **395–6**, 419, 435
Nebel, Gerhard, 189
Neue Heimat, 103, 406, 439
Neue Rundschau, 263
Neues Deutschland, 351, 353
Neumeier, John, 266, 283
newspapers, **313–18**; in the GDR, 351–2
Newsweek, 452
New Yorker, 304
Niemöller, Martin, 228, 234
Nietzsche, Friedrich, 5, 363, 458
1968 uprisings, influence of, 160, 209, 213, 261, 393, 411, 412, 419, 421, **423–4**, 436
Nixdorf (firm), 55, 95, 96
Nobel prizes, 220, 260
Noelle-Neumann, Elisabeth, 164
Nordhoff, Heinz, 92
North Atlantic Treaty Organisation, 2, 17, 234, 347, 383, 396, 425, 428, 447, 450
North-Rhine-Westphalia, 26, 67, 69, 77, 82, 435
nuclear energy, 2, **118–19**, 432
nuclear weapons, 234
Nuremberg, 12, 28, 29; Nuremberg trials, 9, 390

Oberhausen manifesto, 288, 289, 299, 306
Observer, The, 276, 282, 305
oil imports, 116, 118
Oktoberfest, 31, 33, 194, 287

Oldenburg, 402
Olympic Games, 192, 334–5
Opel (firm), 79, 89, 91
opera, 266, 267, 269, **282–3**
Oradour-sur-Glane, 454
Orff, Carl, 279
Organisation for Economic Cooperation and Development (OECD), 87, 94
Ostpolitik, 18–19, 51, 234, 316, 325, 368, 379, 381, 405

Palitzsch, Peter, 271, 365
peace movement, 234, 235, 394, 428, 449–50; in the GDR, **347–8**
Petersen, Wolfgang, 307
Petit, Chris, 303
Peymann, Claus, 271, 275
Philips (firm), 95, 96
philosophy, 263–4
Pietists, 233, 234, 236, 271
Plenzdorf, Ulrich, 360, 364
Poland, 9, 18, 234, 358, 372, 393
police, 367, 426–8; in the GDR, 356–7
Ponto, Jürgen, 424
Pope, John Paul II, 151, 231
Porsche (firm), 89, **90–1**; Porsche, Ferdinand, 90
Potsdam conference, 9, 12, 13
Prague, 374
Praunheim, Rosa von, 58, 297
privatisation, 87
Protestant churches, 34, 164, **227–36**, 241, 391; in the GDR, 325, **343–8**, 352, 358
Proust, Marcel, 290–1
Prussia, 128, 151, 152
publishing industry, 265

Quick, 410

Rabe, Peter, 138–9
Ratcliff, Michael, 276
Rau, Johannes, 2, 235
Reagan, Ronald, 394, 400, 451
refugees from the eastern territories, **13–16**, 25; from the GDR, 14, 55, 324; from the Third World, **252–4**

Regensburg, 448
regional planning, 82
Reich-Ranicki, Marcel, 263
Reitz, Edgar, 128, 134, 139–40, 143, 176, 258, 287, 288, **298–305**
reunification of Germany, 383–4, 457
Rexrodt, Günter, 54
Rheinbraun (firm), 121
Rhineland-Palatinate, 26
Richter, Hans Werner, 259
Rieger, Paul, 231
road accidents, 127
Röntgen, Robert, 340
Rommel, Manfred, 34, 36, 72, 73, 179, 194, 200, 270–1, 393, 409, 427
Roosevelt, Franklin, 9, 10
Rote Armee Fraktion (RAF), 424–5
Rotel-Tours, 190
Rothschild bankers, 36, 97
Rückert, Friedrich, 158
Rühmkorf, Eva, 170
Ruhr, 75, 76, **77–82**, 121, 131, 146, 183, 219, 220, 283–4, 286; Ruhrkohle, 79
Rumford, Count, 32

Saarland, 26, 67, 75, 420
Sagerer, Alexis, 279
Salem school, 211
Salzgitter (steel firm), 87
Sampson, Anthony, 176, 191
Sander, Jil, 161, 164
Sanders-Brahms, Helma, 297
Sauzay, Brigitte, 437
Schäfer, Walter Erich, 266, 268, 271, 282, 283
Schall, Barbara and Ekkehard, 365
Scharnhorst, 385
Schell, Maximilian, 276
Schelling, Friedrich Wilhelm von, 221
Schiller, Friedrich von, 272, 275, 276, 280, 322
Schiller, Karl, 18
Schily, Otto, 430, 431, 434
Schleswig-Holstein, 14, 26, 43, 67, 119, 138–9, 142

Schleyer, Hans-Martin, 425
Schlöndorff, Volker, 288, 289, 290–1, 318
Schmetzer, Uli, 172
Schmidt, Helmut, 19, 23, 43, 220, 228, 455; Schmidt Government, 122, 178, 201, 219, 425
Schönherr, Bishop, 344
Schondorf school, 211
Schretzmaier, Werner, 271
Schumacher, Kurt, 18
Schutz, Peter, 91
Schwerin, 356
Schygulla, Hanna, 289, 294, 295–6
scientific research, 97–8
Seghers, Anna, 359
Shah of Iran, 423
shops, **178–80**; in the GDR, 349–50
Shulman, Milton, 308
Siemens, 30, 54–5, 76, 87, 96, 100–1, 118, 244, 380, 406
Silesia, 13–15, 25, 231, 303
Simon, Stuart, 387
Sirtl-Gardiner, Angelika, 166
social security, 197, 204; in the GDR 330
Solzhenitsyn, Alexander, 363
Sommer, Theo, 384
Soviet Union, relations with, 9, 12–13, 18–19, 51, 64, 117, 135; influence on the GDR, 323–4, 326, 357, 380, 382–3, 386
Sozialdemokratische Partei Deutschlands (SPD), 2, 17, 118, 119, 147, 160, 164, 180, 205, 312, 381, 396, 405, 406, 407; in power federally (1969–82), **18–19**, 86, 108, 215, 404, 409, 429; in *Land* and city governments, 32, 37, 43, 48, 54, 65, 72, 76, 151, 214, 278, 310, 420, 431–2, 439; Bad Godesberg manifesto (1959), 18
Sozialistische Einheitspartei Deutschland (SED) in the GDR, 323, 333, 335, 337, 344, 346, 351, 353–4, 358, 373, 385, 386
Späth, Lothar, 24, 65, 68, 69, 77, 98, 119, 122, 149, 253, 271, 310

Spiegel, Der, 75, 256, **314**, 315, 397, 401, 406, 414
sport, **192–3**; in the GDR, **334–5**
Springer group, 42, 62, 290, 312, 313, **316**, 318, 369, 423; Springer, Axel, 230, **316**
Stalin, Josef, 9, 12, 323, 324
Stammheim prison, 425
steel industry, **79**, 105
Steele, Jonathan, 336, 354, 361
Steen, Edward, 123
Stein, Peter, 58, 275, **276–7**, 278
Steinbach, Peter, 299
Steiner, Rudolf, 210–11, 441
Steinkühler, Franz, 109
Stirling, James, 36, 271, 286
Stern, 315
Stimson, Henry, 10
Stockhausen, Karl-Heinz, 282
Stölzl, Christoph, 286–7
Stoph, Willy, 325, 375
Strachwitz, Rupert Graf von, 152
Strauss, Botho, 261, 274–5, 278
Strauss, Franz Josef, 4, 23, 24, 30, 65, 76, 87, 138, 149, 150–1, 168, 314, 379, 407, 417
strikes, 104, 109
Stuttgart, 2, 25, 29, **34–6**, 149, 154, 157–8, 175, 179, 185, 187, 194, 210–11, 236, 316, 392, 393, 398–9, 410, 412, 414, 427–8; cultural life, 266, 267, **270–1**, 276, 281, 283, 286; farming in, 131, 135; immigrants, 241, 244–5, 252, 255; industry, **88–91**, 101, 107, 111, 113; local government, 70, 73, 200; university, 77, 211, 393
Stuttgarter Zeitung, 314, 315
Süddeutsche Zeitung, 263, 313, 315
Sukowa, Barbara, 291
Sunday Telegraph, 123
Swabia, 34–6, **87–8**, 90, 131, 175, 185, 234; Swabians, 24, 113, 149, 158, 183, 194, 270–1
Switzerland, 306
Sylt, 191
Syberberg, Hans-Jürgen, 289, 297, 305

Tageszeitung, 437
Tamil refugees, 252–3
television, 167, 299, 304, 307, **308–13**; 456; in the GDR, **342**, 352, 369
Tetley, Glen, 283
textile industry, 94
theatre, 266, 267, 269, 271, **272–81**; in the GDR, 364–5
Third World, aid to, 229, 456
Thurn und Taxis, Fürst von, 151
Thust, Peter, 100
Thyssen (steel firm), 11, 41, 79
Time Life, 182
Time Out, 303
Times, The, 248, 358, 420; *Literary Supplement*, 264
titles, **153–5**
tradition, 7, 139–40, 175–6
trade unions, 84, **101–11**, 178, 180; in the GDR, 336
Trotta, Margarethe von, 163, 291, 306
Trumpf (firm), 252
Tübingen, 253, 432; university, 214, 218, 219, **221–2**, 224, 225–6, 232
Turkish immigrants, 56, 59, 113, **237–56**, 396, 438
Tynan, Kenneth, 273

Uhse, Beate, **169–70**
Ulbricht, Walter, 323, 324–5, 334, 341, 356, 368, 382, 385
Ullrich, Aquilin, 398–9
unemployment, 79, 85, 108, **109–10**, 112, 114, 165, 216, 242, 246–7
United States, *see* America
universities, **212–26**

Veba (firm), 87
Versailles Treaty, 11
Vietor, Albert, 406
Vitali, Christof-Johannes, 278
Vogel, Wolfgang, 378
Vogler, Rüdiger, 289
Volkswagen, 87, 89, **91–3**, 106, 109, 305, 349, 380

Wagner, Richard, 281, 282

Waldheim, Kurt, 398
Waldorfschulen, **210–11**
Wallmann, Walter, 37, 270, 280, 283
Wallraff, Günter, 243, 317–18
Walser, Martin, 258, 260
Washington Post, 296
Wayne, John, 306
Weigel, Helene, 365
Weimar, 322; Weimar Republic, 6, 16, 25, 130, 162, 403
Weiss, Peter, 258, 260, 272, 273
Weizsäcker, Richard von, 54–5, 150, 235, 245, 390, **399**
Welt, Die, 313, 315
Wenders, Wim, 261, 289, **291–2**, 303, 305, 451
Weyer, Hermann, 155–6
Whyl nuclear plant, 119
Wicki, Bernhard, 288
Wiehl, Reiner, 264
Wild, Wolfgang, 220
Wiesbaden, 65
Wiesheu, Otto, 417–18
Wilhelm, Kaiser, 76
Wittelsbach family, 30, 150–1, 152, 232
Wörner, Manfred, 167
Württemberg, Duke of, 151
Wuppertal, 283–4
Wolf, Christa, 261, 360, 361, 363
Wolfsburg, 91–2
work ethic, 84; decline of, **114–16**
World Cup (football), 193
Wulf-Mathiesen, Monika, 164

Yugoslav immigrants, 240, 255, 374

Zadek, Peter, 258, 269, 275, 276, **277**, 296, 365
Zeit, Die, 43, 151, 160, 193, 220, 256, 263, 314, 315, 318, 381, 458
Zerning, Heidi, 273
Zhadnov, Andrey, 359
Zille, Heinrich, 61
Zimmermann, Ernst, 425
Zimmermann, Friedrich, 120, 243, 254, 306
Zuckmayer, Carl, 288